Mystic Cults in Magna Graecia

Mystic Cults in Magna Graecia

EDITED BY GIOVANNI CASADIO AND
PATRICIA A. JOHNSTON

University of Texas Press Austin

This book has been supported by an endowment dedicated to classics and the ancient world and funded by the Areté Foundation; the Gladys Krieble Delmas Foundation; the Dougherty Foundation; the James R. Dougherty, Jr. Foundation; the Rachael and Ben Vaughan Foundation; and the National Endowment for the Humanities.

Copyright © 2009 by the University of Texas Press
All rights reserved
Printed in
First edition, 2009

Requests for permission to reproduce material from this work should be sent to:
   Permissions
   University of Texas Press
   P.O. Box 7819
   Austin, TX 78713-7819
   www.utexas.edu/utpress/about/bpermission.html

♾ The paper used in this book meets the minimum requirements of ANSI/NISO Z39.48-1992 (R1997) (Permanence of Paper).

Library of Congress Cataloging-in-Publication Data
Mystic cults in Magna Graecia / edited by Giovanni Casadio and Patricia A. Johnston. — 1st ed.
    p.   cm.
  Includes bibliographical references and index.
  ISBN 978-0-292-72354-2
  1. Magna Graecia (Italy)—Religion. 2. Mysteries, Religious—Italy—Magna Graecia. I. Casadio, Giovanni, 1950- II. Johnston, Patricia A.
  BL793.M34M97 2010
  292.070937′7—dc22   2009019434

Contents

Illustrations   vii
Abbreviations   xi

1. Introduction   1
   GIOVANNI CASADIO AND PATRICIA A. JOHNSTON

I. Dionysus and Orpheus

2. Dionysus in Campania: Cumae   33
   GIOVANNI CASADIO

3. The Meaning of βάκχος and βακχεύειν in Orphism   46
   ANA JIMÉNEZ SAN CRISTÓBAL

4. New Contributions of Dionysiac Iconography to the History of Religions in Greece and Italy   61
   CORNELIA ISLER-KERÉNYI

5. Who Are You? Mythic Narrative and Identity in the "Orphic" Gold Tablets   73
   RADCLIFFE G. EDMONDS

6. *Imago Inferorum Orphica*   95
   ALBERTO BERNABÉ

7. Putting Your Mouth Where Your Money Is: Eumolpus' Will, *Pasta e Fagioli*, and the Fate of the Soul in South Italian Thought from Pythagoras to Ennius   131
   R. DREW GRIFFITH

II. Demeter and Isis

8. Aspects of the Cult of Demeter in Magna Graecia: The "Case" of San Nicola di Albanella   139
   GIULIA SFAMENI GASPARRO

9. Landscape Synchesis: A Demeter Temple in Latium   161
   KATHRYN M. LUCCHESE

10. The Eleusinian Mysteries and Vergil's "Appearance-of-a-Terrifying-Female-Apparition-in-the-Underworld" Motif in *Aeneid* 6   190
    RAYMOND J. CLARK

11. Women and Nymphs at the Grotta Caruso   204
    BONNIE MACLACHLAN

12. "Great Royal Spouse Who Protects Her Brother Osiris": Isis in the Isaeum at Pompeii   217
    FREDERICK BRENK

13. Aegyptiaca from Cumae: New Evidence for Isis Cult in Campania: Site and Materials   235
    PAOLO CAPUTO

14. The Mystery Cults and Vergil's *Georgics*   251
    PATRICIA A. JOHNSTON

III. Mithras

15. The Amor and Psyche Relief in the Mithraeum of Capua Vetere: An Exceptional Case of Graeco-Roman Syncretism or an Ordinary Instance of Human Cognition?   277
    LUTHER H. MARTIN

16. The Mithraic Body: The Example of the Capua Mithraeum   290
    RICHARD GORDON

17. Why the Shoulder? A Study of the Placement of the Wound in the Mithraic Tauroctony   314
    GLENN PALMER

Bibliography   325
General Index   359
Index Locorum   367
Index of Authors   371
About the Contributors   373

Illustrations

4.1. Attic black-figured amphora by the Amasis Painter. **65**

4.2. Cup by the Kallis Painter, Napoli Stg. 172, Side A. **67**

4.3. Cup by the Kallis Painter, Napoli Stg. 172, Side B. **67**

4.4. Attic red-figured *stamnos* by the Villa Giulia Painter. **69**

4.5. Attic red-figured volute crater from Spina, Ferrara. **70**

6.1. Fragment of Apulian pottery from Ruvo, c. 350 BCE. **99**

6.2. Apulian crater, Ruvo 1094. **110**

6.3. Locrian pinax, Reggio Calabria 58729. **114**

6.4. Locrian pinax, Reggio Calabria 21016. **115**

6.5. Apulian crater, Toledo, Ohio. **116**

6.6. Apulian crater from Canosa, Munich Museum 3297. **117**

6.7. Apulian crater from Armento, Naples Museum SA 709. **118**

6.8. Apulian amphora from Basel, Antikenmuseum 540. **119**

6.9. Olbia bone tablet. **119**

6.10. Apulian crater, British Museum F270. **120**

8.1. The enclosure with the area of the hearths, the sacrifices by fire. **143**

8.2. The enclosure after excavation seen from the east. **144**

8.3. The hearths b, e, g. **144**

8.4. Statuette of female offerer with piglet: Type A I. **146**

8.5. Statuette of female offerer with piglet and cist placed upon the shoulder: Type B I. **147**

8.6. Statuette of female offerer with piglet and cist placed upon the shoulder: Type B IIA. **148**

8.7. Statuette of female offerer with piglet and cist placed upon the shoulder: Type D IIA. 149

8.8. Statuette of female deity seated on throne, low *polos* on her head. 150

8.9. Statuette of male offerer with piglet held to chest: Type F IA. 152

8.10. Statuette of male offerer with piglet held to chest: Type F IB. 152

8.11. Statuette of male offerer with piglet in his right hand and arm held to his side: Type G I. 153

8.12. Statuette of male offerer with piglet in his right hand and arm held to his side: Type H IA. 154

8.13. Statuette of male offerer with piglet in his right hand and arm held to his side: Type H Ib. 155

9.1. Map of the Caffarella/*Pagus Triopius* in suburban Rome. 162

9.2. La Caffarella from the north side of the valley. 164

9.3. Portrait bust of the emperor Augustus's wife, Livia, as Ceres. 165

9.4. A *Kanephoros* or *Kistophoros*, carved from Hymettan marble. 167

9.5. Inscription 1 from Visconti 1794. 170

9.6. Inscription 2 from Visconti 1794, "Of Marcellus." 171

9.7. The exterior of S. Urbano, taken from the southeast. 173

9.8. Canina's reconstruction of the interior of S. Urbano, in section crosswise and lengthwise. 174

9.9. An altar to Dionysus. 174

9.10. Stucco representations of weaponry. 175

9.11. Stucco boss in the center of the vault of S. Urbano. 175

9.12. Photos taken inside the *megaron*: (a) The hatch as viewed from directly below; (b) The view from east to west of the *megaron*. 176

9.13. Rough plan of the *megaron* and tunnels and chambers. 177

9.14. Photograph of the Bosco Sacro. 178

9.15. Canina's rendering of the *Fons Egeria*. 180

11.1. Feminine *daimōn* from the Locrian Persephoneion. 205

11.2. Grotta Caruso showing altar and (quadrated) rock. 208

11.3. Grotta Caruso showing staircase. 208

11.4. Terracotta votives from the Grotta Caruso: Kneeling females with truncated limbs and throne. 209

11.5. Terracotta votives from the Grotta Caruso: Kneeling females. **210**

11.6. Terracotta plaque from the Grotta Caruso: Three female heads with Pan. **211**

11.7. Terracotta from the Grotta Caruso: Three female heads with altar and tauromorph hero. **213**

11.8. Detail of terracotta from Grotta Caruso (Fig. 11.7), showing outline of altar and inscription *Euthymos*. **214**

12.1. Ekklesiasterion: Io, Hermes, and Argos. **221**

12.2. Ekklesiasterion: Nile, Io, Isis, Hermanubis, Nephthys, and Harpokrates. **221**

12.3. Portico: Priest with sacred asp. **223**

12.4. Isis with the Body of Osiris, Sacrarium. **224**

12.5. Sacrarium: Drawing, "Isis and Osiris Enthroned." **225**

12.6. Sacrarium: Osiris, "Isis and Osiris Enthroned." **226**

12.7. Ekklesiasterion: "Adoration of the Mummy." **227**

13.1. Cumae (Campaniae). The harbor area. **236**

13.2. Cumae (Campaniae). Plan of the Isaeum. **238**

13.3. Cumae (Campaniae). Section of the Isaeum. **240**

13.4. Cumae (Campaniae). Section of the Isaeum. **242**

13.5. Cumae (Campaniae). *Porticus* of the Isaeum. **243**

13.6. Cumae (Campaniae). Isaeum: *Inaros* statue. **244**

13.7. Cumae (Campaniae). Isaeum: Isis statue. **245**

13.8. Cumae (Campaniae). Isaeum: Sphinx statue. **245**

13.9. Cumae (Campaniae). Isaeum: Statue of Harpokrates-Horus like a child. **246**

13.10. Cumae (Campaniae). Isaeum: Statue of a standing Harpokrates. **247**

15.1. Amor and Psyche. **278**

16.1. Capua general. **292**

16.2. Capua plan 1. **293**

16.3. Schematics of scenes on the podium frescoes. **296**

16.4–16.10. Images of initiation from the mithraem of S. Maria Vetere Capua. **299–303**

17.1. Tauroctony. **315**

17.2. Bovine skeleton. **316**

17.3. (a) The Egyptian constellation of the Foreleg, shown as a portion of the constellation Ursa Major; (b) the Foreleg (Big Dipper); (c) the Foreleg depicted as an adze. **319**

17.4. Procession of the Spirits of the North toward the Foreleg of Seth. **320**

17.5. Ritual of the Opening of the Mouth. **322**

Abbreviations

Journal titles throughout are abbreviated according to *L'Année philologique*, unless listed below.

Aesch. = Aeschylus
   Ag. = *Agamemnon*
   Cho. = *Choephoroe*
   Eum. = *Eumenides*
   PV = *Prometheus Vinctus*
   Sept. = *Seven against Thebes*
   Supp. = *Suppliants*
Anec. Graeca = *Anecdota Graeca*
ANRW = *Aufsteig und Niedergang der römischen Welt*
AP = *Palatine Anthology*
Ap. Rhod. *Argon.* = Apollonius Rhodius *Argonautica*
Apul. *Met.* = Apuleius *Metamorphoses*
Aristoph. = Aristophanes
   Ach. = *Acharnians*
   Av. = *Birds*
   Eq. = *Equites*
   Nu. = *Nubes*
   Th. = *Thesmophoriazusae*
Aratus *Phaen.* = *Phaenomena*
Arist. = Aristotle
   Phys. = *Physics*
   Prob. = *Problemata*
   Rhet. = *Rhetoric*
Aristid. = Aelius Aristides
   Or. = *Orations*

Ath. = Athenaeus
Bacch. = Bacchylides
Beazley, *ABV* = J. D. Beazley, *Attic Black-Figure Vase Painters* (1956)
Callim. = Callimachus
CCCA = *Corpus Cultus Cybelae Attidisque*
Cic. = Cicero
  Amic. = *De amicitia*
  N.D. = *De natura deorum*
  Tusc. = *Tusculanae disputationes*
  Verr. = *In Verrem*
CIG = *Corpus inscriptionum Graecorum*
CIL = *Corpus inscriptionum Latinarum*
CIMRM = M. J. Vermaseren, *Corpus Inscriptionum et Monumentorum Religionis Mithriacae*, 2 vols. (The Hague, 1956–1960)
Clem. Alex. = Clement of Alexandria
  Paed. = *Paedagogus*
  Protr. = *Protrepticus*
  Strom. = *Stromateis*
CVA = *Corpus Vasorum Antiquorum*
Dio Cass. = Dio Cassius
Diod. Sic. = Diodorus Siculus
Diog. Laert. = Diogenes Laertius
Dion. Hal. = Dionysius Halicarnassus
  Ant. Rom. = *Roman Antiquities*
Eleuth. = Eleutherna (Orph. frr. 478–480 Bernabé = 32b I–III Kern and 482–483 Bernabé)
Ent. = Entella (Orph. fr. 475 Bernabé)
Epigr. Gr. = G. Kaibel, *Epigrammata Graeca ex lapidibus conlecta* (1878)
Eur. = Euripides
  Ba. = *Bacchae*
  Cret. = *Cretans*
  Cyc. = *Cyclops*
  El. = *Electra*
  Hel. = *Helen*
  HF = *Hercules furens*
  Hipp. = *Hippolytus*
  IA = *Iphigenia at Aulis*
  IT = *Iphigenia among the Taurians*
  Or. = *Orestes*
  Phoen. = *Phoenissae*
  Tr. = *Trojan Women*

FGrH = *Fragmente der griechischen Historiker*
Firm. Mat. *De err. prof. rel.* = Firmicus Maternus *De errore profanarum religionum*
Hdt. = Herodotus
Hes. = Hesiod
   Theog. = *Theogony*
   WD = *Works and Days*
Hesych. = Hesychius
Hipp. = Hipponion (Orph. fr. 474 Bernabé)
Homer *Il.* = *Iliad*
   Od. = *Odyssey*
Hor. *Sat.* = Horace *Satires*
Hymn Dem. = Homeric *Hymn to Demeter*
IG = *Inscriptiones Graecae*
IGBulg. = *Inscriptiones Graecae in Bulgaria repertae*
IGDOlb. = L. Dubois, *Inscriptions grecques dialectales d'Olbia du Pont* (Geneva, 1996)
Iulian. *Or.* = Julian *Orations*
LIMC = *Lexicon Iconographicum Mythologiae Classicae*
Lucian
   Cat. = *Cataplus*
   DD = *Dialogi deorum*
   Dial. Mort. = *Dialogi mortuorum*
   Peregr. = *De morte peregrini*
Lycophr. = Lycophron
Macrobius *Sat.* = *Saturnalia*
Malib. = Malibu (Orph. fr. 484 Bernabé)
Mart. *Epigr.* = Martial *Epigrams*
OF = Orphic fragments
Orph. fr. B = A. Bernabé, *Poetae Epici Graeci Testimonia et fragmenta*, pars. II, fasc. 1, *Orphicorum et Orphicis similium testimonia et fragmenta* (Monachii and Lipsiae, 2004).
Orph. *Hymn.* = Orphic Hymn
Ovid *Met.* = *Metamorphoses*
Parm. = Parmenides
PCG = R. Kassel and C. Austin, eds., *Poetae Comici Graeci* (Berlin and New York, 1984)
PBonon. = Bononiae Papyrus
PDerveni = Derveni Papyrus
Pel. = Pelinna (Orph. frr. 485–486 Bernabé)
Pet. = Petelia (Orph. fr. 476 Bernabé = 32a Kern)

Petronius *Sat.* = Petronius *Satyricon*
PGM = K. Preisendanz, *Papyri graecae magicae: Die griechischen zauberpapyri*, 2 vols. (Leipzig, 1928-31)
PGurob = Gurob Papyrus
Phars. = Pharsalus (Orph. fr. 477 Bernabé)
Pher. = Pherai (Orph. fr. 493 Bernabé)
Philostr. = Philostratus
   Imag. = *Imagines*
   VS = *Vitae sophistarum*
Pind. = Pindar
   Nem. = *Nemean Odes*
   O. = *Olympian Odes*
   Pyth. = *Pythian Odes*
Pl. = Plato
   Crat. = *Cratylus*
   Gorg. = *Gorgias*
   Leg. = *Laws*
   Phdr. = *Phaedrus*
   Phd. = *Phaedo*
   Rep. = *Republic*
   Tim. = *Timaeus*
Pliny *NH* = *Natural History*
Plot. = Plotinus
Plut. = Plutarch
   Alex. = *Alexander*
   Amat. = *Amatorius*
   Def. orac. = *De defectu oraculorum*
   Is. Os. = *De Iside et Osiride*
   Lyc. = *Lycurgus*
   Mor. = *Moralia*
   Mul. Virt. = *De mulierum virtutibus*
   Quaest. conv. = *Quaestiones convivales*
   Sup. = *De superstitione*
   Thes. = *Theseus*
PMG = D. L. Page, *Poetae Melici Graeci* (1962)
Porph. = Porphyry
   Antr. = *De antro nympharum*
   De abst. = *De abstinentia*
Procl. = Proclus
   H. = *Hypotyposis*

PSI = *Papiri Greci e Latini, Pubblicazioni della Società italiana per la ricerca dei papyri greci e latini in Egitto*
RE = A. Pauly, G. Wissowa, and W. Kroll, *Real-Encyclopädie d. klassischen Altertumswissenschaft* (1893-)
RGVV = A. Dieterich, R. Wünsch, L. Malten, O. Weinreich, and L. Deubner, *Religionsgeschichtliche Versuche und Vorarbeiten* (1903-)
Rom. = Roma (Orph. fr. 491 Bernabé = 32g Kern)
Sen. = Seneca
   Ep. mor. = *Epistulae morales*
   De benef. = *De beneficiis*
Sext. Emp. *Math.* = Sextus Empiricus *Adversus mathematicos*
Simplic. *in Cael.* = Simplicius *In Aristotelis de Caelo Commentarii*
Soph. = Sophocles
   Ant. = *Antigone*
   El. = *Elektra*
   OC = *Oedipus at Colonus*
   OT = *Oedipus Rex*
   Tr. = *Trachiniae*
Stat. *Silv.* = Statius *Silvae*
Suet. *Aug.* = Suetonius *Augustus*
Symm. *Ep.* = Symmachus *Epistles*
Tertullian *De cor.* = *De corona militis*
Themist. *Or.* = Themistius *Orationes*
Theophr. *Char.* = Theophrastus *Characters*
ThesCRA = *Thesaurus cultus et rituum antiquorum*
Thuc. = Thucydides
Thur. = Thurii (Orph. frr. 487–490 and 492 Bernabé = 32f–cd and 47 Kern, quoted with the number of the fragment of Bernabé)
TrGF = *Tragicorum Graecorum Fragmenta*, ed. Snell (vol. 1) and Radt (vol. 4) (Göttingen, 1977)
Tzetz. *Chil.* = Tzetzes *Historiarum variorum Chiliades*
Verg. = Vergil
   Aen. = *Aeneid*
   Ecl. = *Eclogues*
   G. = *Georgics*
Vitr. = Vitruvius
Xen. = Xenophon
   Hell. = *Hellenica*
Xenoph. = Xenophanes

Mystic Cults in Magna Graecia

CHAPTER I

Introduction

GIOVANNI CASADIO AND PATRICIA A. JOHNSTON

The definition of "Magna Graecia" has varied from the time the Greeks first settled the coastal regions of Italy—sometimes including the area from Campania to Sicily, at other times excluding significant portions of this territory.[1] But this area has always been home to the mystic cults and traditions that preceded and accompanied Christianity, including the Sibyl of Cumae, the worship of Demeter and Persephone (her abduction took place in Sicily), Dionysian and Orphic cults, and other cults such as those of Cybele, Isis, and Mithras. In June 2002 and 2004 symposia were held by the Vergilian Society and Brandeis University at the Villa Vergiliana in Cuma, Italy, on the topic, "The Cults of Magna Graecia." The purpose of these symposia was to examine the evidence in the material remains and surviving literature related to cults of Greek, Oriental, and Egyptian origin in southern Italy and the religious perceptions of these practices in Rome. It was believed, as Vergil implies, that those who have been initiated into the mystery cults enjoy a blessed (*fortunatus*) situation both in life and after death—a basic belief in the mystery cults that was later adopted by Christianity.[2]

Why "Mystic" Cults? Historical and Critical Perspectives

In introducing the papers collected in this volume, one must inevitably consider the degree to which these cults, particularly the so-called mystery cults, often referred to as "mysteries," can properly be viewed as religio-historical phenomena. We must also recognize the existence of a certain tension between the evidence pertaining to these cults as practiced at the "local" level, and their practice in the more "central" metropolises (such as mainland Greece, especially Attica, Anatolia, and Egypt), for example, by taking into consideration the links between the cults and the geographical and ecological realities.

Mysteries and the Orient are inherently intriguing. They have always held a remarkable appeal even for the most traditional students of the ancient world. Before World War II, two interpretive approaches dominated the arena. One was historical, propagated by Richard Reitzenstein (1861–1931),[3] who envisaged an Iranian origin of all the saving gods, including the Judaeo-Christian messiah, and Franz Cumont (1868–1947),[4] who interpreted Mithraism as the mystical offspring of Persian religion. The alternative model was phenomenological, based on the pattern of the "dying-and-rising gods" (gods prevalently of oriental origins), formulated by James G. Frazer (1854–1941) and developed by British and Scandinavian adepts of the Myth-and-Ritual School. "'Mystery' was taken to be the essence of oriental religiosity."[5] In spite of its painstaking erudition, broad comparative perspective (including Christians and Australian aborigines), and characteristic awareness of historical dynamisms, even the groundbreaking work of Raffaele Pettazzoni (1883–1959) paid homage to these clichés. Now, however, Pettazzoni's historical reconstructions are seriously impaired by progress in philological research.[6] As in other domains of the history of ancient religions, Arthur Darby Nock (1902–63) was perhaps the most brilliant and constructive actor in reassessing the evidence and theories about the mysteries. A useful synthesis of the work done in the period after Cumont is provided by Vermaseren (1981) in a collection of monographs on the individual cults by eminent specialists, completed by Carsten Colpe's invaluable introduction.

More recently, Ugo Bianchi (1922–95) gave a tremendous impetus to the research on mystery cults (and related phenomena) in ancient Mediterranean cultures and the Roman Empire. His primary merit was that of gathering specialists of various disciplines (philologists, archaeologists, epigraphists, orientalists, historians of religions) who were not previously accustomed to converse together, and of convincing them—despite a certain reluctance—to share their data and interpretations on a common terrain. Four scholars who participated in Bianchi's historic conference on Mithraism in Rome in 1978, and also in his conference on the soteriology of oriental cults in the Roman Empire in 1979—Beck, Gordon, Sfameni Gasparro, and Casadio—also participated in the Cumae 2002 symposium, and thus were in a position to reflect on changes and/or persistence in the focus of the research. One of these witnesses aptly recalls:

> The most useful recent typology of Greco-Roman mysteries as forms of personal religious choice is that of Bianchi and others. Three modes

are distinguished: "mystery" proper, an entire initiatory structure of some duration and complexity, of which the type (and in many cases the actual model . . .) is Eleusis; "mystic" cult, involving not initiation but rather a relation of intense communion, typically ecstatic or enthusiastic, with the divinity (e.g., Bacchic frenzy, or the *kybeboi* of Cybele); and "mysteriosophic" cult, offering an anthropology, an eschatology, and a practical means of individual reunion with divinity—the primitive and original form is Orphism, . . . Hermeticism and Gnosis, though these are late Egyptian and Judaeo-Christian forms of religiosity. Bianchi himself has sought to provide an element of thematic unity by adapting Frazer's "dying-rising god" typology: these cults are all focused upon a "god subject to some vicissitude." This tack has rightly been criticized, but the scheme has heuristic value without it.[7]

It is perhaps helpful to report Bianchi's definitions in his own terms, because there every single word is the result of a long-lasting, careful analysis of historical data. For the term *mystic* he understands

> the concept and the experience of a lively participated interference between the divine, the cosmic and the human realms, and this both in the sense of a participation of some divinities to *vicissitudes* and fates, "human" in character (disappearance and return, death and life, etc.), and in the sense of a participation of human beings in a destiny and a vicissitude relating to the "divine" (attainment or restoration of divine or celestial conditions of immortality, happiness and totality). (Bianchi 1979: 5)

The category of mystic cults and deities (as opposed to the Olympic cults and gods, untouched by any vicissitude in their Olympic serenity and immortality) can be further specified in two more restricted types: cults to be properly called *mystery religions,* which are centered on a sanctuary and a precise form of gradual initiation and esotericism (the prototype is the cult of Demeter and Kore at Eleusis, on which are based the mysteric forms of the cults of Isis or Cybele), and cults conventionally denominated *mysteriosophical,* in which "the initiatic element consists mostly of a *sophia* and a *gnosis* (initiation through 'reading,' doctrine, 'knowledge,' illumination—from Orphism down to Hermeticism and gnosticism)" (Bianchi 1979: 7).

Another clear distinction between "mystic" in the broad sense of the word (including the fertility cults of the ancient oriental religions in which the female element is stable, albeit sympathetic with the crisis of the male god, as in the couples Isis-Osiris and Cybele-Attis) and the more specific categories of "mysteries" and "mysteriosophies" may be found in the consideration that mystic cults in general "concern the country with whatever lies in it (fields, animals, and human collectivity represented by its king), while the mystery and mysteriosophic cults also concern (or only concern, in the case of mysteriosophy) human individuals" (Bianchi 1979: 9).

Certainly, as Bianchi himself acknowledged at the end of his 1979 conference, dedicated to the oriental cults (see his "Epilegomena" in Bianchi and Vermaseren 1982: 917–929, which is pervaded by a sense of disillusion), the "historical typology" for which he had always pleaded is a kind of chimera. Robert Turcan, one of the most prestigious scholars present at the 1979 meeting, had already recommended in the "final document" of the proceedings the avoidance of any generalizations. He pointed out, for example, that the god Mithras does not seem so mystic, in the sense that he does not suffer any *pathē* or crisis, and, in any case, in its drama no goddess plays any role; and in Mithraism, afterlife salvation is connected with salvation in this life, "dans une continuité et une solidarité biocosmiques" (Bianchi and Vermaseren 1982: xvii). A certain vein of skepticism vis-à-vis the rigidity of certain typologies can also be seen in a survey of the literature on the mysteries as a historical category.[8] How extremely precarious it is to fix boundaries between mystic-orgiastic practices, mystery cult, and mysteriosophic (or "Orphic") religiosity is evident from subsequent research carried out by Casadio and others in the field of the Dionysus cult.

Bianchi's two conferences resulted in a fervid stream of initiatives, reinterpretations, and criticisms, the repercussions of which have been wide and long-lasting. One of the first fruits was a synthesis article written by Kurt Rudolph for *The Encyclopedia of Religion* (1987), from which the assessment of some basic topics concerning the typology of the mysteries and their historical developments will here be drawn.

Mysteries in general entail special initiation ceremonies that are esoteric in character and often connected with the yearly agricultural cycle. Usually they involve the destiny of the divine powers being venerated and the communication of religious wisdom that enables the initiates to conquer death. They were part of the general religious life, but they were separate from the public cult that was accessible to all; for this reason, they were also called "secret cults" (*aporrhēta*). Because of the obligation of strict secrecy, we now know little more about the mysteries than what was occasionally passed on as "reliable" information by the ancient sources, including ancient Roman literature. Our historical knowledge is limited because of the polemical and/or apologetic interpretations that color the accounts given by Christian writers such as Clement of Alexandria and Firmicus Maternus.

We do have relatively sound information about the general structure of some of the ceremonies, such as those of Eleusis, Samothrace, Isis, and Mithras. We know that processions and public functions (sacrifices, dances, music) framed the actual celebration, which was held in closed rooms (*telestērion, spelunca*, temple) and usually comprised two or three acts, consisting of the dramatic action (*drōmenon*), including the "producing and showing" of certain symbols (*deiknumena*), and the interpretation (*exēgēsis*), consisting of communication of the myth (*legomena*) and its attendant formulas. The sacred action (*drōmenon*) and the sacred narrative (*legomenon, mythos, hieros logos*) were closely connected. We know relatively little about the central ceremony, that is, the initiation proper. Consequently we can only interpret it hypothetically. It would appear that the heart of the celebration was intended to link the initiate (*mystēs*), through word and performance, with the destiny of the divinity or divinities and thereby to bestow the basis for some kind of better hope (*agathē elpis*) after death. This interpretation is also suggested by burial gifts for the deceased (e.g., the "Orphic" gold plates from southern Italy, discussed in this volume by Edmonds and Bernabé). The ancient human problems of suffering, death, and guilt undoubtedly played an important part in the efficacy of the mysteries. The idea of rebirth can be documented only in later Hellenism. There is no evidence, however, of a unitary theology of the mysteries common to all the mysteries, since the discrepancies in their origins and historical developments, including even later philosophical explanation of their *logos*, were too great to allow that.

The historical and phenomenological problem of the origin of the mysteries remains unresolved. Repeated attempts have been made to move beyond the apparently outdated nature-myth theory. Ethnologists in particular have repeatedly focused on the mysteries and interpreted them as survivals of ancient "rites of passage," a theory maintained especially by Mircea Eliade and Angelo Brelich. Both interpretations merge in the traditional idea that the origin of the mysteries is to be sought in some stage of primitive agricultural development. The Hellenistic mysteries of Isis have been influenced by the Eleusinian mysteries of Demeter and Persephone (Kore). In any case, all our ancient informants confirm the view that the so-called oriental mysteries in general took their character primarily from the Eleusinian mysteries and became widespread only as a result of Hellenization. Within the confines of this overview, therefore, we must begin with the ancient Greek mysteric (in the narrower sense of the term, as opposed to the more inclusive term, "mystic," as defined above by Gordon and Bianchi) cults, particularly those of Eleusis and Dionysus/Orpheus, and move on to related oriental cults, namely of Cybele and Mithras.

The Greek mysteries were from the outset cults of clan or tribe. They can in many cases be traced back to the pre-Greek Mycenaean period and were probably ancient rituals of initiation into a clan or an "association." The most important were the mysteries of Eleusis, which in fact provided the pattern for the idea of mysteries. The independent town of Eleusis became an Athenian dependency in the seventh century BCE and thereby acquired, especially from the sixth century on, a pan-Hellenic role that in the Roman imperial age attracted the attention of Rome. Augustus, Hadrian, Marcus Aurelius, Commodus, and Gallienus chose to be initiated into the Eleusinian mysteries. The mythological background for the Eleusinian mysteries was provided by the story of the goddesses Demeter and Kore, preserved in the Homeric *Hymn to Demeter*. The pair was presented as mother and daughter. Their relationship developed in a gripping manner the theme of loss (death), grief, search, and (re)discovery (i.e., life). The interpretation of the story as purely a nature myth and specifically a vegetation myth is actually an old one and can appeal to ancient witnesses for support (see below); nonetheless, it is oversimplified precisely because it loses sight of the human and social content of the myth.

The public ceremonies of the annual Eleusinian ritual are well known to us and are confirmed by archaeological findings. The director was the hierophant, who from time immemorial had been a member of the Eumolpides, a noble family that had held the kingship of old. The Kerykes family filled the other offices. All classes, including slaves, were admitted to the cult. According to degree of participation, a distinction was made between the *mystēs* ("initiate") and the *epoptēs* ("contemplator"); only the latter was regarded as fully initiated. But this distinction was not original; it came in when the Eleusinian mysteries were combined with the mysteries of Agrai on the Ilissos (near Athens) in the seventh century BCE. The Lesser Mysteries at Agrai took place annually in February (the month Anthesterion) and were regarded as a preliminary stage leading to the Greater Mysteries held at Eleusis in September (16–20 Boedromion). Sacrifices, libations, baths, ablutions, fasts, processions (especially bringing the "holy things," the cult symbols, to Eleusis), and torches all played an important role in both feasts. The center of all activity was the ceremony, which was not open to the public. It was held in the "place of consecration" known as the *telestērion*, which is not to be confused with the temple of Demeter at the same location.

Perhaps more important for our purposes were the Dionysian mysteries, about whose character and date of formation there is no agreement among the specialists. As is well known, Dionysus was an unusual god who represented a side of Greek life long regarded as un-Greek—a view that has caused interpreters many difficulties. His *thiasos* ("company") was probably originally an association of women that spread throughout Greece, especially the islands, and carried on a proselytizing activity by means of itinerant priestesses. There was no one central sanctuary, but there were centers in southern Italy (Cumae), Asia Minor, and Egypt. Ecstatic and orgiastic activity remained characteristic of this cult as late as the fourth century CE and only after the Classical age assumed more strictly regulated, at times esoteric, forms, as can be seen from the laws of the *Iobacchoi* community at Athens, where the cult of Dionysus (Bacchus) had become a kind of club. The myth of Dionysus had for its focus the divine forces hidden in nature and human beings; these forces were enacted in ecstatic nocturnal celebrations that showed traits of promiscuity (compare the companionship of maenads and satyrs in the myth, and of course pejorative accounts in later sources) and took place in the open air.

As Jiménez shows in her chapter here, the myth of Dionysus was at an early stage combined with Orphic mysticism. The hope of another world that was promised and confirmed in the rites is well attested by burial gifts (gold plates) from Greece and southern Italy. Even after death, the initiate remained under the protection of the god. Orphic mysticism is a difficult phenomenon with which to deal. Often it is not easily distinguished from the Dionysian mysteries. It is certain that at an early date, Orpheus was credited with being the founder of the Eleusinian, Dionysian, and Samothracian mysteries. Orphism therefore had no central sanctuary. It seems to have been more of a missionary religion that, unlike the official cults, devoted itself to the theme of the immortal soul (*psychē*) and its deliverance from the present world. It had an ethical view of the relation between initiation and behavior. A way of life that was shaped by certain rules served to liberate the soul or the divine in human beings. The anthropogonic and cosmogonic myth that provided an explanation of the hybrid human condition also showed the way to redemption; thus cosmology and soteriology were already closely connected. As a result, Orphism broke away from the religion of the *polis*, not only because it possessed holy books that contained its teachings, but also because the idea of the immortality of the soul made the official cult superfluous. Greek philosophy, beginning with Pythagoras (see Drew Griffith's contribution here) and Plato, gave a theoretical justification for all this.

Mysteries of Cybele, the great mother-goddess (*Magna Mater*) of Anatolia, are attested on the Greek mainland and islands from the third century BCE. Oddly, little mention is made of Cybele's companion Attis in the early period, although some inscriptions and depictions place Attis with Cybele as early as the fourth century BCE in the Piraeus and Thrace[9] (where an even more common male companion is Hermes, along with Hekate/Persephone). The mythological relation is attested by Catullus in his Poem 63 (first century BCE),[10] and by Pausanias in the second century CE, the earliest written witnesses to the connection. We know nothing about the structure and content of these mysteries; perhaps they were an imitation of the Eleusinian mysteries. In any case, the Roman cult of Cybele, who was worshiped on the Palatine from 204 BCE on, was not a mystery religion. Beginning in the second century CE and down to the fifth century, the literature speaks of the mysteries of *Magna Mater* or *Mētēr Megalē* but tells us no more about them. On the supposition that we are not dealing simply with a misleading terminology, these mysteries may have focused on the ritual castration of novices (*galli*) and the deeper meaning of this practice. With regard to Attis, inscriptions from Pessinous in Asia Minor dating from the first century CE speak of the "initiates of Attis" (*Attabokaoi*). The initiation involved an anointing of the initiates (see Firm. Mat. *De err. prof. rel.* 22, 1); there is also reference to a kind of sacred meal (eating from a tambourine, drinking from a cymbal). The meaning of an accompanying formula is uncertain in the version given by Clement of Alexandria (*Protr.* 15): "I have entered the *adyton* [bridal chamber?]." Firmicus Maternus has a simpler version: "I have become an initiate of Attis" (*De err. prof. rel.* 18.1). At the end of the fourth century CE, the cult of Cybele and Attis also included baptism in bull's blood (*taurobolium*). This ceremony had developed out of an older sacrifice of a bull performed, in most cases, *pro salute imperatoris*, which is attested from the middle of the second century (as in a recently discovered Beneventum *taurobolium* inscription) onward.[11] It was supposed to bring renewal to the initiates; only a few inscriptions interpret the renewal as a "new birth." The baptism was, in these cases, a one-time rite and perhaps was intended to compete with Christian baptism. Cybele was in all respects responsible for her people's well-being in peace and in war, as goddess of fertility and as goddess of the mountains and mistress of wild nature, symbolized by her attendant lions.

The Hellenistic cult of Isis in late antiquity undoubtedly involved secret initiatory celebrations. We learn something about them from Apuleius's famous novel, *Metamorphoses*, or *The Golden Ass* (second century CE). Greek influence is especially clear here: it was only through the identification of Isis with Demeter (attested in Herodotus 2.59) and the Hellenization of the cult of Isis that the latter came to include mysteries (first attested

c. 220 BCE on Delos). In this form it spread, despite occasional opposition, throughout the whole civilized world of the time, reaching Rome in the first century BCE. It became one of the most widely disseminated oriental cults of late antiquity, especially from the second century BCE on. Isis became the great thousand-named, universal goddess (*panthea*) who had conquered destiny and was invoked in numerous hymns and aretalogies that display a remarkable Greco-Egyptian atmosphere and tone (see the chapters by Brenk, Caputo, and Johnston below).

This successful Hellenization was probably due to the introduction of the cult of Sarapis under Ptolemy I, son of Lagus (305–283 BCE), when this novel Greco-Egyptian cult (*Sarapis* combines *Osiris* and *Apis*) was celebrated with both an Eleusinian priest (Timotheos, a Eumolpid) and an Egyptian priest (Manetho) participating. Isis, Thoth, and Anubis were naturally linked with Sarapis (Osiris). The well-known story of Isis, Osiris, and Horus (Harpocrates) acquired its complete form only in Greek and in this version was probably a product of Hellenism (Osiris being assimilated to Adonis). The ancient Egyptian cult of Osiris was originally connected with the monarchy and displayed the character of a mystery religion only to the extent that the dead pharaoh was looked upon as Osiris and brought to Abydos not simply to be buried but also to be greeted by the people as one restored to life in the form of a new statue in the temple. The hope of survival *as* or *with* or *like* Osiris was the predominant form that the hope of another world took in ancient Egypt, and it continued uninterrupted in the Greco-Roman period; it provided a point of attachment for the mysteries of Isis.

The cult of Isis had its official place in the Roman festal calendar (beginning in the second century CE) and comprised two principal feasts: the Iseia, which was celebrated from 26 October to 3 November and included the *drōmenon* of the myth, with the "finding" (*heurēsis, inventio*) of Osiris as its climax; and the sea-journey feast (*Navigium Isidis, Ploiaphesia*) on 5 March, the beginning of the season for seafaring, of which Isis had become the patron deity. According to Apuleius (*Metamorphoses* 11), the actual mysteries began with preliminary rites such as baptism (sprinkling), a ten-day fast, and being clothed in a linen robe. At sunset the initiates entered the *adyton* for further ceremonies to which only allusions are made: the initiate made a journey through the lower world and the upper world (the twelve houses of the zodiac, which represented the power of destiny) and was vested as the sun god (*instar solis*); the initiate was *renatus* ("reborn") and became *sol* ("the sun") — in other words, experienced a deification (*theomorphosis*). He thereby became a "servant" of Isis and "triumphed over his destiny (*fortuna*)." In addition to a consecration to Isis, there was evidently also a consecration to Osiris, but we know even less about this ceremony. In the Roman period, Isis and Demeter sometimes merge but still retain their powers, as P. A. Johnston and R. J. Clark demonstrate in their examinations of Vergil's *Georgics* and *Aeneid*.

The cult of Mithras in the Roman imperial age, like that of Isis, was not originally oriental but was a creation of Hellenistic syncretism. It is true that the name of the god Mithras is Indo-Iranian in origin and initially meant "contract" (*mithra, mitra*) and that some Iranian-Zoroastrian elements are recognizable in the iconographic and epigraphic sources; these facts, however, do not point to a Persian origin of the cult. No testimonies to the existence of Mithraea in Iran have as yet been discovered. On the other hand, the vast majority of these sanctuaries have been found in the Roman military provinces of central and eastern Europe, especially in Dalmatia and the Danube Valley. The Mithraeum at Dura-Europos on the Euphrates is the most eastern. It was built by Roman soldiers from Syria in 168 CE, rebuilt in 209 CE, and expanded in 240 CE. It was thus not the creation of a native community. The "Parthian" style is simply a matter of adaptation to local tradition and no proof of an Iranian origin of the mysteries.

According to Plutarch (*Life of Pompey* 24), Mithraea were introduced into the West by Syrian pirates in the first century BCE. This report may have a historical basis because the veneration of Mithras in Syria, Pontus, and Commagene is well attested, though no reference is made to any mysteries of Mithras. It is likely that soldiers from this area, where Greeks and Orientals came in contact, brought the cult of Mithras to the West in the first century CE. In the second century CE, however, the cult was transformed into mysteries in the proper sense and widely disseminated, until finally Mithras was elevated to the position of Sol Invictus, the god of the empire, under Diocletian (r. 284–305 CE). As in the case of the cult of Isis, the Hellenistic worshipers of Mithras transformed the foreign god and his cult along lines inspired by the awakening individualism of the time, with its rejection of the traditional official cult and its longing for liberation from death and fate.

We are poorly informed about the myth and rites of the Mithraic mysteries. We have mainly a large mass of archaeological documents that are not always easy to interpret. The Mithraic mysteries took place in small cave-like rooms that were usually decorated with the characteristic relief or cult statue of Mithras *Tauroctonus* ("bull-slayer"). In form, this representation and its accompanying astrological symbols are Greco-Roman; its content has some relation to cosmology and soteriology, that is, the sacrifice of a bull is thought of as life-giving. Other iconographic evidence indicates that the god was a model for the faithful and wanted them to share his destiny: birth from a rock, combats like those of Herakles, ascent to the sun, dominion over time and the cosmos. Acceptance into the community of initiates (*consecranei*) or brothers (*fratres*) was achieved through consecratory rites in which baptisms or ablutions, purifications (with honey), meals (bread, water, wine, meat), crownings with garlands, costumes, tests of valor, and blessings played a part. There were seven degrees of initiation (Corax, Nymphus, Miles, Leo, Perses, Heliodromus, Pater), which were connected with the planetary deities and certain symbols or insignia. Surviving inscriptions attest the profound seriousness of the mysteries. Also worth noting is the close link between Mithras and Saturn (Kronos) as god of the universe and of time (Aion, Saeculum, Aevum); Saturn is the father of Mithras and the one who commissions him, whereas Mithras is in turn connected with the sun god (Sol, Apollo).

Mystic cults of Greek, Egyptian, Persian or Phrygian genealogy all have in common certain family resemblances that converge in a definite typology. This typology is based on two categories, one pertaining to the deities involved in the mythic-ritual pattern, that of the Mediterranean "dying and rising gods," the other pertaining to the human actors, that of "initiation" (in Greek, *myēsis* or *teletē*). Both categories have been seriously challenged, the first one since the pioneering researches of Pierre (Pieter) Lambrechts (1910–74) in the 1950s, so that it has now become commonplace to assume that it is a product of modern imagination.[12] The attempts to deconstruct the second category are more recent but no less surreptitious. In a recent collection, *Initiation in Ancient Greek Rituals and Narrative* (Dodd and Faraone 2003), one of the two editors maintains that current perspectives in "critical theory" (namely American rumination on French postmodernist and deconstructionist ideas) have ultimately rendered the usage of the category irrelevant, "since it reveals it to be merely a tool for the production of false consciousness."[13] This view is largely based on the "genealogy of scholarship" (on the topic "initiation") devised by Bruce Lincoln in the concluding chapter of the above-mentioned book.[14] Lincoln's argument is clearly dictated by an ideological agenda: if an interpretive paradigm sounds unsympathetic with "correct" political views, its banishment from the academic discourse is surely welcome. From a scholarly point of view, on the contrary, a paradigm should be disposed of if it sounds unsatisfactory in comparison with the historical data. So, if, for historically based arguments, the usefulness of the concept of initiation as an explanatory paradigm for a range of religious and nonreligious phenomena of antiquity is questionable,[15] its suitability cannot be objected to when it is used in relation to cults (like the ancient mysteries) that contain rites that in classical antiquity were recognized as *teletai* or *initiationes*.

Similar considerations can be developed to show the hermeneutical suitability of the type of the "deity subject to change or vicissitude" (to use Bianchi's terminology, which is more adherent to historical realities than the Frazerian ill-reputed model of the dying/rising god that is, in any case, its recognizable ancestor). The facets of this suffering, quasi-human demon (not necessarily a male: its characters are present even in such female acolytes as Kore, Leukothea, or Ariadne) are easily recognizable in the divine actors of the mystery cults examined above (see further examples in Johnston's contribution to this volume). More important, this notion is of an emic type; that is, it involves an analysis of cultural phenomena from the perspective of the participants in the culture being studied (as opposed to the etic type, which reflects the perspective of the outsider). This notion of *daimōn* (to use the corresponding Greek term) has manifested itself since the beginning of Greek theological and historical reflection. First, the Ionian poet and philosopher Xenophanes of Colophon (c. 570–480) declared the affinity between the cult of the Greek Leukothea, who was worshiped with funeral dirges (*thrēnoi*) but was considered a deity (and therefore, for the Greeks, immortal), and the cult of the Egyptian Osiris, who was ritually mourned by his worshipers (as befitted a dead god) but was at the same time honored as a very high-ranking god.[16] This ability to perceive religious phenomena cross-culturally, which earned Xenophanes the mantle of "precursor of comparative ethnology,"[17] is certainly connected with his experience as an Ionian citizen who since birth had been familiar with the beliefs and customs of the other peoples of Anatolia: the Lydians, the Carians, and the Median-Persian dominators. One century later, Herodotus (*fl.* 450 BCE) does not hesitate to call *mystēria* the rites of Osiris enacted by the Egyptians on a lake to commemorate the god's sufferings (*pathē*). He notices the analogy (actually the *homology*, inasmuch as he envisaged a common origin, namely a transmission of the rite from Egypt to Greece) between Osiris' mourning ritual and the *teletē* of Demeter "that the Greeks call Thesmophoria" (*Hist.* 2.171). In fact, he is first induced to call the Osirian ritual *mystēria* because of the similarity between the mourning for Osiris in the Khoiak festival and the dirge for Persephone in the Eleusinian mysteries. Then, for an association of ideas, he mentions the Thesmophoria, another Demetriac ritual, which, though not *mystēria* in the strict sense of the word, were shrouded in the atmosphere of secrecy and taboo particularly associated with such cults.[18] (See Gasparro's contribution in this volume for more details.)

It thus becomes clear that the experience of *pathē* (or *pathēmata*) is the characteristic trait shared by these Greek and Egyptian divine pairs in the myth and in the liturgical enactment.[19] *Pathos* at the same time means "change" (affecting the ontological level) and "suffering" (affecting the ethical level of the divinity) and can be aptly rendered with a polysemic term like "vicissitude." This characteristic of experiencing a *pathos*, or rather a sequence of *pathē*, is shared by other ancient deities who bear family resemblances to Osiris and Persephone. Apparently this category of gods "subject to vicissitudes" (a vicissitude embodies the tension inherent in the seasonal drama, as stressed by Johnston in the introduction to her contribution) was not invented by modern scholars (either Frazer or Bianchi), but was individuated much earlier by the Greek writer Plutarch (c. 46–120 CE), a historian and theologian with a keen comprehension of religious dynamisms.[20] Starting from his (middle-Platonic) speculations on the *daimones*, he individuates a class of gods intermediate between the Olympian, unaffected attitude of the celestial deities like Zeus, and the quasi-human precariousness of the heroes. In *De defectu oraculorum* (10.415A), his spokesman Cleombrotus of Sparta assesses clearly this category of *daimones* or demigods "midway between gods and men" and, in a style that would be fitting to modern supporters of the theory of the Eastern origins of basic traits of Greek culture (such as M. L. West and W. Burkert), draws a genealogy of the doctrine of the common fellowship of gods and men (mediated by the "race of *daimones*"),

> whether this doctrine comes from the magi of Zoroaster, or whether it is Thracian and harks back to Orpheus, or is Egyptian, or Phrygian, as we may infer from observing that many things connected with death and mourning in the rites (*teletai*) of those lands are combined in the ceremonies celebrated there as *orgia* and *drōmena* [technical terms for ritual components of the mystic cults]. (Plut. *Def. orac.* 10.415A)

Phrygian and Egyptian *logoi* recur again in connection with the poems of Orpheus in a passage of the *Daedala* (fr. 157, 1 Sandbach). Further, Attis is probably the Phrygian god alluded to in *De Iside et Osiride* 69.378D-F, where the set of resemblances between the Greek and oriental suffering gods is clearly established:

> Among the Greeks also many things are done that are similar to the Egyptian ceremonies in the shrines of Isis, and they do them at about the same time. At Athens the women fast at the Thesmophoria sitting upon the ground, and the Boeotians move the halls of the Goddess of Sorrow

(*Achaia*) and name that festival the Festival of Sorrow, since Demeter is in sorrow (*achos*) because of Kore's descent to the underworld.... The Phrygians, on the other hand, believing that the god is asleep in the winter and awake in the summer, sing lullabies for him in the winter and in the summer sound the reveille, after the manner of Bacchants.[21] (Plut. *Is. Os.* 69.378D-F)

The role of the seasonal drama (a role that is nonetheless obstinately denied by a number of influential contemporary historians) in the *imaginaire* of the mysteries is explicitly stressed by Plutarch in the subsequent chapter of the treatise:

The season of the year also gives us a suspicion that this gloominess is brought about because of the disappearance from our sight of the crops and fruits that people in days of old did not regard as gods, but as necessary and important gifts of the gods contributing to the avoidance of a savage and bestial life. At the time of year when they saw some of the fruits vanishing and disappearing completely from the trees, while they themselves were sowing others in a mean and poor fashion still, scraping away the earth with their hands and again replacing it, committing the seeds to the ground with uncertain expectation of their ever growing up again and giving a fruit, they accomplished many things similar to the ceremonies enacted by those who bury and bewail their dead. (Plut. *Is. Os.* 70.378F-379A)

The synergism between vegetal and human life could not be established in a clearer or more suggestive way.

In 1987, Walter Burkert produced a work (*Ancient Mystery Cults*) that has since become one of the more frequently read books on the ancient mystery cults. Notwithstanding some flaws, which have been highlighted by critics,[22] the book presented for the first time a kind of "comparative phenomenology of ancient mysteries" (Burkert 1987: 4) rather than a collection of monographs on the single cults, as his predecessors had done.

Robert Turcan's 1989 manual (*Les cultes orientaux dans le monde romain*) comes closer to Cumont's approach. Consequently, instead of declaring his distance from Cumont and other scholars (from Ernest Renan to Maarten Vermaseren) who had the model of the "oriental religions" as their frame of reference, he simply states that it is more exact to refer to "religions of oriental origin or Graeco-oriental religions." Turcan has no preference vis-à-vis any methodology in vogue; he simply pleads for the avoidance of generalizations based on the oriental mirage or an idealized mysticism in favor of empirical research (his motto is "comparing for distinguishing, distinguishing for understanding"). He does not refrain from typologies as such, only from applications to historical phenomena that—in his view—do not fit the type involved. He recognizes, for example, the legitimacy of the category of the "suffering gods" (including Dionysus, Attis, Osiris, and Adonis), but he excludes from it a god such as Mithras, who is only "operating in this world" (Turcan 1989: 336).

John North's short but insightful 1992 essay, "The Development of Religious Pluralism," is important because, in the best British polemical vein, it challenges current general views about the mysteries that Burkert (1987: 3 and 51–52) has upheld in a most determined way. North claims that Burkert's statement that mysteries were from beginning to end Greek in their attitudes and never offered their adherents any alternative to the civic religion of their contemporaries or any space for subversion of the normal ancient way of life (as Christians did, undeniably) is simply untrue. Like many contemporary ancient historians in the Oxbridge lineage who are familiar with a strong social-scientific tradition, North holds that the most solid criteria for establishing the potential for change of a religious movement are to be found "in terms of the social/religious behavior of groups and their members rather than in the nature of the beliefs or aspirations they held" (North 1992: 184). Having fixed these criteria (autonomy, commitment, separateness with regard to values, rituals, dietary rules), he proceeds to demonstrate that religious groups like the "Bacchists" and the "Mithraists" broke the rules of the established paganism and roused a conflict with the authority of family and state. Thus these groups were in a position, at least potentially, to start a revolution in religious life in the same way the Christians did. Notwithstanding both a certain overstatement in his handling of historical data and a kind of sociological rigidity, North raises an issue that is well founded and of relevance also for the methodology of comparison in the history of ancient religions. In this volume, Richard Gordon pursues similar concerns, with further innovations.

In the proceedings of the international conference of Montpellier (Moreau 1992—which provided, *inter alia,* a useful bibliography on initiation in general and initiation in Greece in particular), only a few contributions deal with initiation in Greek mystery cults, and all of these have to do with Dionysus. There Casadio seeks to date the initiation ritual attested in the Lernaean cult back to the Classical age. Turcan instead denies that full-fledged mysteries of Dionysus existed in Greece before the

Hellenistic-Roman age and (rightly) refuses to assign this characteristic to the orgiastic-ecstatic procedures of the bacchants in archaic and classical Greece.[23]

The old evidence and the new theories have been aptly summarized by Zeller, Gordon, and Turcan in three entries in encyclopedias that appeared almost contemporaneously in subsequent years. The first one is the work of a New Testament scholar, Dieter Zeller,[24] who has a remarkable insight into issues of comparison within the field of the religions produced by Hellenistic syncretism (including, historically, Christianity). His contribution distinguishes itself for the thorough analysis of the evidence focused on the individuation of traits related to a doctrine of salvation (he recognizes his debt to Bianchi's school and adopts his terminology of the *dio in vicenda*, "god subject to vicissitude"), a synopsis of the general characteristics common to all (or some) mysteries with emphasis on mythic and ritual structures, and a balanced assessment of the thorny issue of the relationship with early Christian sacraments (Baptism and the Eucharist).

Whereas Zeller's article has appeared in a theological encyclopedia that, because of its subject matter, tends to be unfamiliar to ancient historians, Richard L. Gordon, an expert in Mithraism and an extremely astute interpreter of ancient world religious phenomena in general, contributed a pithy article on the same subject for the *Oxford Classical Dictionary*,[25] the standard reference work for all classical scholars. Gordon firmly refused the (Christiano-centric) model of the *Religionsgeschichtliche Schule* and adopted without reservation the three-pronged typology devised by Bianchi. Consequently, he characterized the hopes of the mystery cults in general, and the Eleusinian cult in particular, as decidedly mundane, in contrast with the world-rejecting, dualistic attitudes of the Orphics or other mysteriosophic circles.

The third of these publications[26] is important both because it is signed by Robert Turcan, an unparalleled authority in the field, and because it appeared in a prestigious lexicon that, as indicated by its own title—*Reallexikon für Antike und Christentum*, referring to the interrelationship of antiquity and Christianity—is a reference tool to be used by students of both classical antiquity and ancient religions.[27] In this article, all the sources are analyzed in detail and the relevant bibliography is discussed with customary shrewdness. What is more important, the discussion is focused on the core and meaning of the various initiation rituals, with attention to similarities and differences. For example, in the Eleusinian initiation, by which all subsequent mystery cults were apparently influenced, the mother goddess Demeter guarantees prosperity in this world, and the daughter Persephone provides a better hope for the other world. In other words, one helps the initiates during their lives, the other in their afterlives. In a similar way, the Bacchic rituals (*teletai*) — at least in certain cases — promised bliss after death, but also bestowed in this life escape and oblivion from everyday anxieties. By contrast, the oriental mystery cults — Isis/Osiris, Cybele, and Mithras — integrated the single devotees into a cosmic order, warranted by divine grace and providence, within a perspective that can appropriately be defined as "cosmotheandric."[28] In a final synthesis, Turcan outlines the six elements that were shared by all the mystery cults (secret, preliminary purification, symbolic formulary, simulation of death, visual revelation, sacramental meal) and the four functions inherent to initiation: a feeling of belonging to a privileged group; protection in this and the other world; an explanation of the world and one's individual fate; and the initiate's identification with the god and participation in his destiny (Turcan 1998: 121).

Giulia Gasparro, an eminent expert in ancient mystery cults from the viewpoint of the history of religions, agrees with Burkert on basic issues such as the definition of the mysteries[29] (Gasparro 2003: 22) and the typological differences from Christianity[30] (Gasparro 2003: 15 and 43), but sympathizes with the cutting-edge research on Mithraism recently carried out by R. Beck[31] and R. Gordon with regard to the speculative dimension and the ritual and social dimension of the Mithraic mysteries, respectively. She is more cautious about the most sophisticated reconstruction of the origin of the mysteries they have recently elaborated, in a delicate balance of the Iranian and Anatolian matrix and the Roman innovation (Gasparro 2003: 37–42). The vindication of the oriental side of Mithras (shared by these scholars) is consistent with Gasparro's resolute opposition to recent attempts to "deconstruct" the oriental (Phrygian in the case at issue) identity of two *oriental* deities such as Meter[32] and her *paredros* Attis,[33] in order to overemphasize the role played by Hellenization in the mythopoeic process of these figures (Gasparro 2003: 18–21). Theoretical preconceptions (of blatantly postmodern genealogy) whose historical reliability is quite dubious — if not utterly inconsistent — lie hidden behind these apparently innocuous scholarly constructs.

Burkert's comprehensive article, "Initiation," in the second (2004) volume of the *Thesaurus cultus et rituum antiquorum* (*ThesCRA*), presents a collection of sources (mainly in German translation) related to initiation as a social and religious phenomenon in Greece and Rome, with preliminary discussion. Unfortunately, the Greek or Latin original wording is given only sporadically (this is understandable, since the *Thesaurus* is a reference work designed primarily for archaeologists), and very few pictures are included (this is also explainable, given the fact that the *ThesCRA* has been conceived as a continuation of the *Lexicon Iconographicum Mythologiae Classicae* [*LIMC*], which offers a much broader corpus of illustrations). In his concise but engaging compendium of extensive, multifarious materials (including useful sections on pubertal initiations, initiations to priesthood, and various secret and non-secret associations), the author reaffirms the views he has developed over more than forty years of untiring research, and in great part already made known in his epoch-making 1977 handbook on ancient Greek religion[34] and in his 1987 treatise. In this article's section "*Bakchika*,"[35] however (a subject to which he has contributed first-hand and ground-breaking inquiries), Burkert's deliberate merging of Dionysiac ritualism and Orphic mysticism is open to debate. If it is sometimes hard to distinguish between these two entities (especially in Magna Graecia: see contributions in this volume by Bernabé and Edmonds, whose views often diverge), the distinction between the rather mundane Bacchic mysteries[36] and the eminently transmundane Orphic initiations (variously connected with esoteric Pythagorean lore: see Drew Griffith in this volume) is (as stated above) an important one and, in specific historico-geographical contexts, did operate in actuality.[37]

The chapters related to aspects of Eleusinian, Dionysiac, and Orphic mysteries in a recent volume on the Greek mysteries edited by archaeologist M. B. Cosmopoulos[38] are of special relevance here. Christiane Sourvinou-Inwood brilliantly argues[39] that the Eleusinian cult "had a double nature: it was an integral part of Athenian *polis* religion and at the same time a restricted cult accessible through initiation by individual choice" (p. 26). She further argues that the nature of the cult changed in the early sixth century, when it became mysteric and eschatological, promising a happy afterlife. The focus of the Eleusis festival was on the "divine advent"[40] (of Demeter, of Kore, of the sacred implements), an element existing in the premysteric phase and then reshaped in the mysteric scenario to encompass the initiatory-eschatological dimension. The main concern of Kevin Clinton[41] in the same volume is typological. He examines the Eleusinian terminology in the literary and inscriptional evidence with the intention of determining the precise meaning of *myēsis* and *teletē*. The important inference of his investigation is that *teletai*, which originally denominated rituals with emphasis on performance (including, for example, the Thesmophoria and some Bacchic rites), in the post–Classical period was narrowed to indicate only initiation. The meaning of *mystēria*, on the other hand—previously rather technical and restricted to the preliminary grade of initiation in the Eleusinian mystery cult—was subsequently broadened, so that thereafter it simply hinted at a kind of esotericism.[42] Susan Guettel Cole[43] examines the evidence about Dionysian afterlife in connection with the role of the gods (primarily Dionysus and Persephone) in the Eleusinian and Orphic literature. (She refrains, in fact, from using the latter category, referring simply to "independent groups supervised by inspired leaders" [in Cosmopoulos 2003: 207].) Her prospectus—which provides a list and description of all the gold tablets from northern Greece, western Crete, and southern Italy organized according to location, date, type of burial, gender of the dead, shape, placement, literary type and imagery, password, mystic terminology, divinities mentioned, and names of the initiates—will render a great service to any future research. In "Orphic Mysteries and Dionysiac Ritual,"[44] Noel Robertson attacks the current approach, which envisions as a background to the Greek mysteries a prehistory of initiation rites, and renews the older view that mysteries go back to standard ceremonies of public worship and are in fact rather more indebted to ancestral fertility rites involving a kind of magic sympathy between man and natural life than to any initiatory rituals of private or collective character.

In 2005, an important exhibition dedicated to the imagery of the mysteries in Greece and Rome took place in Rome. The catalogue (Bottini 2005) has an intriguing title (*Il rito segreto: Misteri in Grecia e a Roma*), but in fact the great majority of the illustrations have a very loose (if any) connection with the mystery cults. The introduction by Fritz Graf is concise but provides a fine survey of topics and critical issues.[45] Graf's approach is characterized by a critical awareness of typological distinctions (the rituals of Dionysus or Cybele have the character of a mystery cult only under certain conditions; eschatological hopes and ecstatic experiences can only be attested factually in a few cases), but he perhaps overemphasizes the role played by tribal initiations and male secret societies in the prehistory of the mysteries. Monographic chapters signed by qualified specialists (Sfameni Gasparro, Isler-Kerényi, and Coarelli) deal with individual cults (from Eleusis to Mithras) in compendious style, whereas two specialized contributions investigate in depth the same topics that are addressed in the present collection, although from a different point of view. In "I pinakes di Locri: Immagini di feste e culti misterici dionisiaci nel santuario di Persefone" (in Bottini 2005: 49–57), Madeleine Mertens Horn provides a new comprehensive exegesis[46] of the famous Locrian *pinakes,* unearthed more than a century ago from the most celebrated sanctuary of Persephone in Italy. Her interpretation focuses on the special relationship between Persephone, queen of the underworld, and Dionysus (as a child and as a male adult), thus supplying the most appropriate background for the Orphic scenario outlined by Bernabé in this volume. From both contributions it ensues that the religious perception of these two deities in Magna Graecia differed significantly from that which was current in the Greek metropolis. Mertens Horn provides also an explanation of the characteristic interplay between funeral and nuptial imagery present in the *pinakes* that supplements the interpretation envisaged by MacLachlan in this collection. Fausto Zevi, in "Demetra e Kore nel santuario di Valle Ariccia" (in Bottini 2005: 59–67), analyzes the evidence of the Thesmophoria in an extramural sanctuary of Demeter and Persephone situated in the countryside of Ariccia, a town in the surroundings of Rome. The presence of this Thesmophoriac sanctuary (active from the fourth century until the beginning of the second century BCE) in the center of Latium supplies an apt chronological link between the fifth-century Thesmophoriac sanctuary in the *chora* of Poseidonia-Paestum (studied by Sfameni Gasparro in this volume)[47] and the much later (dating at the second century CE) temple of Ceres and Faustina, where the presence of a Thesmophoriac ritual has been advocated by Lucchese in another contribution to this volume.

This, then, is the current status of research in the field of mystic cults with particular reference to Magna Graecia, to which we hope this volume will contribute new insights.

The Contributions to This Collection

The first contribution in this book deals with the cult of Dionysus and related Orphic religiosity in the vicinity of Cumae. In "Dionysus in Campania: Cumae," Giovanni Casadio examines the sources and secondary literature concerning the Dionysiac cults in Cumae, within Campania: "The place where the most pagan of all the gods of Mediterranean paganism—Dionysus-Bacchus—might have liked to spend his third age, without renouncing his most deeply ingrained habits, can ideally be identified with Campania: a land of intrinsically orgiastic nature." He presents evidence and arguments to demonstrate the connection between the famous archaic inscription from Cumae and the circumstances of Dionysiac worship there under the tyrant Aristodemus Malakos. Ana Jiménez San Cristóbal interprets the meaning of βάκχος and βακχεύειν in Orphism as different from their meaning in other religious contexts. The traditional meaning of *bakcheuein* is "to go into ecstasy" or "to celebrate Bacchic rites," which in most cases implies a violent attitude that, in principle, is incompatible with the rules of the Orphic life. The Orphics avoided bloody practices. Instead, they considered the ecstatic experience implied in *bakcheuein* as the means of access to an *Orphikos bios* through the observation of certain rules that affect the initiates' personal existence as well as through the performance of certain rites that convert them into *bakchoi*. For the Orphic initiate, the ecstasy consists of putting oneself at the level of the worshiped divinity, not as a transitory ecstasy but as a lasting condition. This leads to the rebirth of the initiates into a new existence, free from bodily ties.

In "New Contributions of Dionysiac Iconography to the History of Religions in Greece and Italy," Cornelia Isler-Kerényi examines the question of how painters and users of Greek vases in the seventh and sixth centuries BCE viewed Dionysus. During this period, Greek ceramics can be dated with sufficient precision, and hence it is possible to establish a connection between the history of the images and the history of the cult. The Dionysus theme, moreover, is numerically the most important of the vase inventory. Kerényi pays particular attention to the iconographic themes that refer to ritual: the meeting of Dionysus with a matronal figure, the dance of grotesque characters and of satyrs with or without Dionysus, and the ride of the mule. Every one of these subjects constitutes its own iconographic line whose sequence can illuminate the history of the cult of Dionysus.

Radcliffe G. Edmonds and Alberto Bernabé then pursue close examinations of Orphic cult, with the one focusing on the narrative, the other on the imagery. Edmonds, in "Who Are You? Mythic Narrative and Identity in the Orphic Gold Tablets," focuses on the narrative itself rather than, as earlier scholars have done, on the texts behind the variants, such as on an Orphic *katabasis* poem or a Pythagorean *Book of the Dead*. Edmonds examines the narrative created by verses in the Orphic tablets, and concludes that the nature of the afterlife and its contrast to the world of the living is less important than the contrast between the nature and identity of the deceased as compared with the nature of other people. In *"Imago Inferorum Orphica,"* Bernabé is concerned with the Orphic imagery of the netherworld, as based on the testimony found in both the Orphic texts (the gold leaves and other literary texts) and the images of southern Italian pottery. In both these sources, Hades is seen to be an underground place containing buildings, presided over by Persephone and Pluto. The underworld is a dual space, with one way leading to a *locus amoenus* (a "pleasant place") and the other, for the uninitiated, leading to mud, physical punishment, and terror. Initiation provides the *mystēs* (initiate) with the knowledge necessary for taking the correct path, aided by the goddess Mnemosyne (Memory). The initiates are protected by Orpheus, while Dionysus and Orpheus act as mediators, so that, for the initiate, the underworld may be a pleasant rather than terrible place. Then, on a lighter note, R. Drew Griffith examines the codicil to Eumolpus' will in Petronius' *Satyricon* in "Putting Your Mouth Where Your Money Is: Eumolpus' Will, *pasta e Fagioli,* and the Fate of the Soul in South Italian Thought from Pythagoras to Ennius." Griffith examines the passage (*Satyricon* 141) where Eumolpus asks that his heirs make him a "living tomb" by eating his mortal remains, as a basis for considering the Pythagorean doctrines of reincarnation, the body-tomb image, and such dietary laws as the ban on beans in view of their influence on Vergil (*Aen*. 6.734). He argues that the Pythagoreans acquired these ideas from Croton and Metapontum, and not the reverse.

The cult of Demeter in Italy is reflected in the articles by Giulia Sfameni Gasparro, Kathryn M. Lucchese, and Raymond J. Clark. Gasparro, in "Aspects of the Cult of Demeter in Magna Graecia: The 'Case' of S. Nicola di Albanella," provides a general overview of Thesmophoria in Greece, then presents the relevant materials found in a characteristically rural sanctuary located near Paestum. These findings (especially the terracottas) permit acknowledgment of the Demetriac (and in particular the Thesmophoriac) pertinence of this shrine. At the same time, the presence of male donors highlights the peculiarity of this local cult. As a result, it is possible to assume in this site the confluence of male and female worship, even if at different times and on different occasions.

In "Landscape Synchesis: A Demeter Temple in Latium," Lucchese examines the late fall pre-planting rites of the Thesmophoria, which, in addition to the Eleusinian mysteries, were characteristic festivals of Demeter. The *thesmophoria* themselves were offerings flung into a natural crevice or man-made chamber in the rock known as a *megaron*, left to decay, and then retrieved and ploughed into a nearby ritual field, thus securing the region's fertility for the season to come. By metaphoric extension, the Thesmophoria became associated with the civilization that developed in the wake of sedentary agriculture, the "things laid down" (*thesmophoria*) being understood as a code of civil laws, and the goddess' title being translated into Latin as *legifera*, "law-giver." A small temple just outside Rome, built by Herodes Atticus, can now be firmly identified as dedicated to Demeter/Ceres, due in part to the recent discovery of a well-preserved *megaron* there. Herodes used the construction of this sanctuary as a gesture of *synchesis*, linking himself to the goddess of laws in order both to exonerate himself of his wife's bloodguilt and to increase his own social standing. Raymond J. Clark, in "The Eleusinian Mysteries and Vergil's 'Appearance-of-a-Terrifying-Female-Apparition-in-the-Underworld' Motif," focuses on the single incident in *Aeneid* 6 where Aeneas raises his sword in terror against the phantoms of the Gorgons and other monsters who appear before him in Pluto's house (*Aen*. 6.285–294). He compares a number of Greek passages that Eduard Norden believed were influenced by a now-lost epic version of the descent into the underworld by the Eleusinian Herakles, and concludes that Vergil's account cannot be associated with the Eleusinian mysteries.[48]

Bonnie MacLachlan raises probing questions about the ritual activities of women at the Grotta Caruso outside the ancient city of Locri, in "Women and Nymphs at the Grotta Caruso." Although Persephone stands at this intersection, the significance of these details undergoes a striking transformation at the Grotta between the Classical and the Hellenistic periods. Other questions raised are what the significance was of the eroticized dead in Greek ritual practice, and how the divinization of the dead in hero cults intersected with Orphism in Magna Graecia, and finally, what role was played by Dionysus in women's ritual activities at a cave of the nymphs, including the mystical wedding of this god and Ariadne celebrated in Athens at the Anthesteria, or on the iconography of the frescoes in the Villa of the Mysteries.[49]

The cult of the Egyptian goddess Isis arrives in Italy somewhat later, but is also of great importance in the Roman Empire. Isis' temple at Pompeii was one of the first to be restored in that city after the 62 CE earthquake preceding the eruption of Mt. Vesuvius in 79. Frederick Brenk examines the Temple of Isis at Pompeii in the light of recent publications, beginning with the partial recreation of the temple in 1992 and in 2000. Since a detailed analysis of the Egyptian and other artifacts discovered there is still lacking, Brenk, in "'Great Royal Spouse Who Protects Her Brother Osiris': Isis in the Isaeum at Pompeii," examines these materials. Piecing together the evidence of the relative worship of Isis and Osiris in the temple, he shows that the temple, in a Hellenistic zone of Pompeii, seems to represent primarily the Augustan complex of Isis worship,[50] which appears to be quite different from that later found in the Isaeum Campense in Rome, as rebuilt by Domitian and as portrayed in Apuleius. At Pompeii, Isis is dominant, with limited representations of Osiris, but there are a number of indications of the presence of Osiris in the shrine. This was probably the situation at Rome by the time of Domitian, offering a strong contrast to Osiris' role at Pompeii.

Paolo Caputo, director of excavations at Cumae, Italy, then presents a report on the status of the Temple of Isis found at Cumae in 1992, in "Aegyptiaca from Cumae: New Evidence for Isis Cult in Campania: Site and Materials." This is the first evidence for the presence in Cumae of a place for the cult of Egyptian deities, apart from the uncovering of an Anubis statue (in 1836) and a fragmentary Harpocrates statue (in 1837), both now lost. The extensive remains and the findings provide new evidence for a re-evaluation of the question whether Cumae also had an Isaeum.[51]

The appearance of all of these cults in Vergil's *Georgics,* which were composed in Campania, is then discussed by Patricia A. Johnston in "The Mystery Cults and Vergil's *Georgics.*" The cult of Cybele appears only in the fourth *Georgic,* in reference to her followers noisily masking the cries of the infant Zeus and feeding him honey, but the references to the more properly "mystic" cults—Eleusis, Isis, and Dionysus—are, as one might expect in a poem on agriculture, much more prominent throughout the poem than is usually acknowledged.

The final group of chapters here is concerned with the Mithraic mysteries. Luther Martin focuses on initiation, drawing on cognitive theory, an approach to Mithraic studies that he developed in a series of papers and that has since then been adopted by Roger Beck. In "The Amor and Psyche Relief in the Mithraeum of Capua Vetere: An Exceptional Case of Graeco-Roman Syncretism or an Ordinary Instance of Human Cognition?" Martin considers the degree of syncretism operative in this cult, as exemplified by the Amor-Psyche relief at Capua. He is particularly interested in the variations in these rituals, which differ considerably from one location to another. Richard Gordon then discusses the rite of Mithraic initiation in order to establish whether that rite led to a specifically Mithraic type of knowledge. He focuses on the figures painted on the walls of the Capua Mithraeum, which appear to reveal the stages of initiation at that site. In "The 'Ritualized Body' in the Mithraeum at Capua," he points out the fairly consistent pattern of the nudity of the initiate, as opposed to the clothed, supervising figure, and finds a parallel between the sufferings of these figures and of Christian martyrs. He interprets these sufferings in a Foucauldian perspective. Glenn Palmer, in "Why the Shoulder? A Study of the Placement of the Wound in the Mithraic Tauroctony," then contrasts the placement of the sword into the shoulder, which is common to all Mithraic representations of the killing of the bull, with the more usual placement of the knife in actual bull sacrifices, and concludes that stabbing the bull in the shoulder would never be adequate anatomically to kill a bull. He then explores other possible reasons for the placement of the sword in the shoulder, and argues for a connection between the tauroctony and Egyptian mythology, astrology, and funerary ritual.

Notes

1. In current historical usage, Magna Graecia (*Megale Hellas* in original Greek sources) is virtually equivalent to (hellenized) southern Italy. In addition to classical *loci* of Cicero (*Amic.* 4.13), Strabo (6.1.2), and Pliny (*NH* 3.95: *a Locris Italiae frons incipit Magna Graecia appellata*), an apt definition is that by the fifth-century

scholiast pseudo-Acron (ad Hor. *Sat.* 1.10.27–35): *per ipsius regionis tractum* [*Apulia*, etc.] *Graeca lingua in usu fuit: unde ea pars Italiae Graecia Magna dicta est.* A prominent specialist in the area of ancient Italian linguistics, Paolo Poccetti, has demonstrated that the linguistic *Graecitas* lasted until the Byzantine period, and in fact Greek is spoken even in the present day in certain villages of Sicily and Calabria. Moreover, in the south of Italy there is a "Università della Magna Grecia" and a Società di studi sulla Magna Grecia that since 1960 has organized 47 annual meetings whose proceedings are found in most libraries of classical studies. (Any discussion about Magna Graecia requires at least a perusal of the 45 volumes of its proceedings.) For an authoritative presentation of the sources and discussion of problems, see now D. Musti, *Magna Grecia: Il quadro storico* (Rome and Bari, 2005), which, however, does not replace the classic *Storia della Magna Grecia,* by E. Ciaceri, 3 vols., 2d ed. (Milan, Genoa, Rome, and Naples, 1928–40).

2. *Gens fortunata* (Verg. *G.* 4.287) refers to the fabulous blissful Egyptian race; *O fortunatos nimium agricolas* (*G.* 2.458) connects the farmer with initiates of Eleusis (= Greek ὄλβιοι); *fortunatus et ille deos qui novit agrestis* (*G.* 2.493); *O fortunatae gentes, Saturnia regna* (*Aen.* 11.252—the "golden race" of Saturn = the Latin people); *locos laetos et amoena virecta / fortunatorum nemorum sedesque beatas* (*Aen.* 6.638–639) refers to the *locus amoenus* where Anchises dwells in the underworld, explicitly described by the ghost of the father to Aeneas as *amoena piorum / concilia Elysiumque colo* (*Aen.* 5.734–735). The *pii* (= Greek εὐσεβεῖς) are the initiates (including privileged heroes of mythical times); Elysium is the paradise reserved to them. Initiation is connected with the sphere of *fortuna* also in that an ultimate purpose of the mystery ritual was to overcome the vicissitudes of Fortuna, a blind, cruel goddess. See Martin 1987: 58–59: "Broadly speaking, these Mysteries involved an initiation in which the problematic nature of an existence ruled by Tyche/Fortuna was not denied, escaped, or controlled, but rather transformed into an existence ruled by a goddess in her guise of True Fortune"; cf. Bøgh 2007: 330.

3. On this key figure, see Prümm 1985, and Fauth 1989. The basic shortcoming of Reitzenstein's approach is lucidly highlighted by Prümm (1985: 206): "D'une part, il recourt à la terminologie du Nouveau Testament et en particulier de Paul pour une meilleure compréhension de la terminologie des mystères. Mais, d'autre part, il cherche dans cette 'langue des mystères' une clé qui résoudrait les énigmes du vocabulaire et des concepts utilisés par Paul.

4. For some issues neglected by C. Bonnet, "Franz Cumont," in Jones et al. 2005, see Casadio 1999b.

5. R. Gordon 1996a: 1017.

6. In the foreword to the second edition (1997) of Pettazzoni 1924, D. Sabbatucci (1923–2002) criticizes his insistence on an agrarian frame of reference but ignores more serious blemishes (e.g., the recurrence of nonexistent resurrected gods or of dubious Persian mysteries). In a reappraisal of "recent researches and new problems," which appeared originally in French in 1955 as "Les mystères grecs et les religions à mystères de l'antiquité" and was reprinted in the second edition, Pettazzoni takes issue with the new interpretative tendencies (Nilsson, Nock, Festugière). He corroborates the oriental connection by extending the comparative frame of reference to the entire world and, with far-sighted perspicacity (cf. North 1992: 176), reacts to the widespread and somewhat overstated tendency to down-

play the similarities between Christianity and the mysteries by emphasizing their solidarity with the ethnic religions in which they are imbedded. His final statement that "le religioni di mistero sono strutturalmente più vicine al Cristianesimo che alla religione civica, alla religione pubblica e ufficiale dello Stato" (Pettazzoni [1924] 1997: 231) is based on an acute intuition of the mysteries' religious structure and cannot be easily disposed of.

7. R. Gordon 1996a: 1017.
8. Casadio 1982.
9. Vermaseren 1977–89, 2: no. 308. Cf. Johnston 1996.
10. See, most recently, Bremmer 2005.
11. The traditional reconstruction has been recently challenged by Borgeaud (1998: 185).
12. The most determined supporter of this view is J. Z. Smith (1987; 1990: 100-101). His arguments are extremely sophisticated but not utterly convincing. For a reassessment of the category from a different viewpoint, see G. Casadio 2003.
13. D. B. Dodd, "Preface," in Dodd and Faraone 2003: xiii–xiv.
14. B. Lincoln, "The Initiatory Paradigm in Anthropology, Folklore, and History of Religions," in Dodd and Faraone 2003: 241–254.
15. As has been asserted for a long time by, among others, N. Robertson and G. Casadio (see Casadio 1990a: 171–174: a critique of the arbitrary adoption of the initiatory model by several scholars in the wake of A. Brelich) and is recently stressed with convincing arguments but also with some sweeping generalizations by F. Graf, "Initiation: A Concept with a Troubled History," in Dodd and Faraone 2003: 3–24.
16. Xenoph. 21A13 D-K (Testimonia): Arist. *Rhet.* B26, 1400b5: "The citizens of Elea asked Xenophanes if they should sacrifice to Leucothea and mourn for her, or not; he advised them not to mourn if they took her to be a goddess, and not to sacrifice to her if they took her to be human"; Plut. *Amat.* 18.12.763d: "Xenophanes urged the Egyptians, if they considered Osiris a mortal, not to honor him insofar as he was a mortal, but if they considered him a god, not to mourn for him"; Plut. *Is. Os.* 70.379b-c: "Quite rightly Xenophanes insisted that the Egyptians not mourn if they considered them gods, and if they mourned, not to consider them gods"; Plut. *Sup.* 13.171e: "Xenophanes, observing the Egyptians singing dirges and conducting mourning rituals, properly suggested: 'If these are gods,' he said, 'do not mourn for them; and if they are human, do not sacrifice to them.'" Cf. also (not in Diels-Kranz) Clem. Alex. *Protr.* 2.24.3, p. 34 Marcovich (with further testimonia in the apparatus). This reproach became topical in Christian apologetic polemic in their confrontation with the pagan Platonic philosophers: cf. Turcan 2003: 49–51.
17. G. Casadio, s.v. "Xenophanes," in Jones 2005, 14: 9854-9856 (with the pertinent bibliography).
18. Cf. Lloyd 1988: 209–210.
19. Cf. Turcan 2003: 49–50.
20. F. Brenk's article, "Plutarchos," in Jones 2005, 11: 7199-7202, is essential reading in this respect.
21. For more examples and the relevant discussion, see Casadio 1996b: 222–227. Cf. also Bernabé 2001b: 9–10; Turcan 2003: 35: "Les allusions aux mystères

orphico-dionysiaques, isiaques ou métroaques ne laissent ici aucune place au doute," and 42: for Plutarch, "les démons . . . ont souvent partie liée avec les mystéres en tant que dieux sauveurs."

22. See esp. F. Brenk, *Gnomon* 61 (1989): 289–292; R. Turcan, *RHR* 206, 3 (1989): 291–295; and G. Casadio, *QUCC* 40, 1 (1992): 155–160. U. Bianchi, in *Gnomon* 67 (1995): 1–5, provides a reassessment of his own views more than a review. Some criticisms of Burkert's book are of more general concern: e.g., a certain terminological fuzziness, a constant attempt to downplay the spiritual and otherworldly concerns, and a kind of nonchalance in dealing with the archaeological evidence.

23. Burkert (2004: 97) dates the emergence of Dionysiac mysteries "vom Ende des 5. Jh. V. Chr.," but this is because of his disregard of typological distinctions. See instead Clinton (in Cosmopoulos 2003: 54–55), who denies the character of a mystery cult to the initiation undergone by the Scythian king Scyles. M. Slavova (2002) offers an interesting new assessment of the epigraphical evidence from Thrace, a region traditionally connected with early propagation of Dionysiac mystery practices. In the Hellenistic period, the *mystai* (the term is first attested for Dionysopolis in 48 BCE, but a *bakcheion* with apparently mystic connotations dates back to the third century BCE and is therefore coeval with the edict of Ptolemy Philopator that regulates the Dionysiac mystery clubs in Egypt) are often organized "either around the priest of an official cult or around a private charismatic practitioner of the mysterial [sic] cult" (Slavova 2002: 138). In total, there are 17 inscriptions geographically and chronologically ordered, which increase significantly the dossier collected by A. F. Jaccottet (2003: 73–143 [including Moesia]).

24. Zeller 1994.
25. R. Gordon 1996a.
26. Turcan 1998 [offprint dated 1996].
27. On the difficult dialogue between classical scholars and scholars of religion, see Burkert 1996 (Italian augmented edition, 2000).
28. This formula has been introduced by the intercultural theologian Raimon Panikkar (b. 1918) in his book *The Cosmotheandric Experience: God, Man, World* (1993).
29. "Mysteries are initiation ceremonies, cults in which admission and participation depend upon some personal ritual to be performed on the initiand" (Burkert 1987: 8).
30. This is a leitmotif of Burkert's research: see esp. Burkert 1987: 3 (general statement: *contra* North 1992, as mentioned above), 46 (absence of a credo), 76 (absence of a suffering god in Mithraism), 101 (baptism and rebirth).
31. The "final" work on Mithraism by this scholar has appeared as *The Religion of the Mithras Cult in the Roman Empire* (Beck 2006).
32. See Borgeaud 1996.
33. See Roller 1999: "The Attis of Greek cult and Greek myth was largely a Greek construction," based on the stereotype "of the Phrygian as effeminate Oriental barbarian" (pp. 177 and 182). Apart from the disputability of this specific view, which clashes with an overwhelming amount of historical data, the mere theoretical premises of this reasoning look fallacious. The charge of "Orientalism" ("Orientalism," when capitalized, notoriously does not define the discipline of oriental studies but an—alleged—inbred tendency of Western scholars from

antiquity to present times to downgrade Eastern cultures in the interest of a hidden political agenda) is a facile stereotype that is basically groundless when it is not substantiated by historical proofs. In the specific case, scholars as distant as Franz Cumont, H. Graillot, G. Thomas, and H. S. Versnel are indiscriminately and gratuitously charged with accusations of "racist attitudes" (p. 21) and even with the taint of anti-Semitism (p. 23 n. 59), simply because they represent historical realities without paying homage to the jargon of political correctness.

34. Burkert 1977; English translation, 1985.

35. Burkert 2004, section II.B: 96–101.

36. In the very selective list of literary testimonies, a reference that apparently provides the most explicit attestation of Bacchic initiation on a ritual basis is missing: ἵσταται δὲ ὁ φαλλὸς τῷ Διονύσῳ κατά τι μυστήριον (Schol. ad Aristoph. *Ach.* 243a), to be related to Clem. Alex. *Protr.* 2.34.4. Cf. Casadio 1994: 75 and 303–312 (Lernaean mysteries).

37. For a recent delimitation of the borders between the Orphic and Dionysiac cults, see Bernabé 2004c: 283: "El orfismo es una filosofía vivida de la liberación personal. El dionisíaco no órfico entra en éxtasis con el sacrificio sangrante. El órfico alcanza su estado por una ascesis, un sacrificio personal. La gran novedad del orfismo es la interiorización del rito."

38. Cosmopoulos 2003.

39. Sourvinou-Inwood, "Aspects of the Eleusinian Cult" (in Cosmopoulos 2003: 25–49).

40. Most recently, the same author has applied the same model to wide-ranging research on myth, ritual, and ethnicity in Greek religion: *Hylas, the Nymphs, Dionysos and Others* (Sourvinou-Inwood 2005).

41. Clinton, "Stages of Initiation in the Eleusinian and Samothracian Mysteries" (in Cosmopoulos 2003: 50–78).

42. It is to be regretted that the extensive bibliography (spanning the period since an obsolete 1934 monograph) ignores the work on mystery terminology done recently by Bianchi and his school: for a discussion of primary and secondary literature, see Casadio 1982, and especially the more specialized article by the same author, "Per un' indagine storico-religiosa sui culti di Dioniso in relazione alla fenomenologia dei misteri" (1983: 127), where a similar conclusion was drawn on the basis of a broader evidence.

43. Guettel Cole, "Landscapes of Dionysos and Elysian Fields" (in Cosmopoulos 2003: 193–217).

44. In Cosmopoulos 2003: 218–240.

45. Graf 2005.

46. Based for the first time on the complete monumental publication edited by E. Lissi Caronna, C. Sabbione, and L. Vlad Borrelli for the "Società Magna Grecia" (Taranto, 1996–2006).

47. The cult of Demeter Thesmophoros had been officially introduced in Rome, on the Aventine hill, at the beginning of the fifth century. An Etruscan *thesmophorion* is attested for Veii (Campetti) since the sixth century BCE: see the recent investigation by Simona Carosi (2002, with full bibliography).

48. See now Parvulescu 2005.

49. See the archaeological investigation by C. Sabbione and R. Schenal, "Il santuario di Grotta Caruso" (1996).

50. Cf. Blanc, Eristov, and Fincker 2000: 227–309, dating the temple at the Augustan age. The first foundation of the Isaeum is usually dated to the second century BCE (cf. most recently Varone and Iorio 2005: 392). See now the section "Case Studies: Aegyptiaca in and around Pompeii and Rome," in *Nile into Tiber: Egypt in the Roman World, Proceedings of the Third International Conference of Isis Studies, Leiden 2005* (Leiden and Boston, 2007), 111–239, in particular the contributions by M. Swetnam-Burland and E. M. Moormann focusing on aspects of the Isaeum at Pompeii.

51. Caputo's contribution here supplies the first report in English of this discovery, which attests to the wide-ranging diffusion of the Isis cult in the context of Campania: see Bricault 2001: 158.

PART I

DIONYSUS AND ORPHEUS

CHAPTER 2

Dionysus in Campania: Cumae

GIOVANNI CASADIO

Gods rise and die—and rise again, despite the contrary opinion of an eminent Chicago professor of history of religions.[1] Gods, at least the gods of paganism,[2] have a body. They drink, eat, copulate, and with advancing years they waste away, stricken with the infirmities of old age. The place where the most pagan of all the gods of Mediterranean paganism— Dionysus-Bacchus—might have liked to spend his third age, without renouncing his most deeply ingrained habits,[3] can ideally be identified with Campania: a land of intrinsically orgiastic nature given the effervescence of its soil (the Vesuvius, the Flegrean Fields) and the ebullience of its inhabitants (the whirling tarantella dance, the Satyric and Phlyacic figure of Pulchinello).[4] It is a fact that in Campania, the worship of Dionysus is recorded over a period of a thousand years, from the mid-sixth century BCE (Cumae) to the mid-fifth century CE (Nola). During this time span, of a length seldom reached in the other regions of Magna Graecia or of the eastern periphery or of the motherland itself, the cult of Dionysus presents itself in the various, seemingly contradictory forms that characterize the god's ethos.

In previous research (Casadio 1995), I dealt with the conditions under which the worship of this god spread across the other areas of Magna Graecia (Bruttium, Lucania, Apulia-Calabria), and I concentrated my attention on the literary and archaeological evidence relative to Tarentum, Metapontum, Siris-Heraclea, Sybaris-Thurii, Croton, Rhegium, and Locri. Finally, in the wake of important contributions by eminent specialists of Greek religion (and sometimes in disagreement with them), I wondered if the forms—undoubtedly peculiar—of Bacchic worship in ancient Italy were so varied as to suggest the effects of an acculturation determined by the meeting of the Greek invaders with the natives. My response was cautiously positive,[5] for it is presumable that in Campania, too, the meeting of the Greek settlers with the native Oscans and with other immigrated peoples of complex civilization, such as the Etruscans and the Romans (who themselves, as we know, experienced cultural colonization by the more refined Greeks), produced significant results in terms of cultural morphogenesis.[6]

Campania evidently derives its name from the people (Campani) who originally inhabited the *Ager Campanus,* that is, the territory surrounding Capua, the town most representative of Campania's original civilization and the capital of the Etruscan settlement in the area.[7] In ancient times, the region was famous for exceptional fertility (*felix Campania:* Pliny 3.5.60; *terra pulla,* loose, black, volcanic earth, Cato *De agricultura* 34), certainly due to the predominantly volcanic nature of its soil. It is therefore little wonder that this region, most notably the area between Cumae and Pompeii (around Neapolis and the Vesuvius), has always been one of the most densely populated in the world. Very populous it certainly was in the first century CE, one of the most brilliant periods in its history, when Campania (after being merged with Latium to form the first Augustan *regio*) not only enjoyed great economical prosperity thanks to its manufacturing activities and an agricultural production among the best in the whole Roman Empire (grain, wine, oil), but also had become the favorite holiday destination for Rome's aristocrats (especially Baiae, Bauli, Surrentum, and Capreae).[8] One of those aristocrats was Petronius Arbiter, the author of the *Satyricon,* who chose one of those places as the backdrop for his novel. The sentence that Petronius puts in the mouth of Quartilla, a priestess of Priapus, is extremely eloquent if regarded from an ecology-of-religion perspective:[9] "Utique nostra regio tam praesentibus plena est numinibus, ut facilius possis deum quam hominem invenire" (*Satyricon* 17.5). The mentioned *regio* is without doubt the area around Neapolis, regardless of what town is identifiable with the *Graeca urbs* that provides the background to a large part of the novel.[10] This land, so abundant in human beings (as the flippant Roman writer puts it), is even more abundant in divine beings, all of them available, helpful, and efficient (just as helpful and efficient as today's numberless saints and madonnas). Among those deities, one of the closest (*praesens*)[11] to the hearts of the Campanian people—even though his role is less official than that played by Apollo (the tutelary god of the *apoichiai*) or by the other *dii patrii* (Artemis, Hera, Demeter) whom the Greek settlers had brought along from their native island of Euboea—is undoubtedly Dionysus, alias Bacchus, or, in the *interpretatio latina, Liber Pater.*

Petronius' contemporary Pliny the Elder, a man of immense learning who spent the last part of his life on the Campanian coast, did not fail to notice (*NH* 3.60) the harmonious relationship that typically linked the Campanian environment with the Dionysian *numen* embodied by the god. The undulating *vitiferi colles* that enliven the coastal area from the Gulf of Gaeta to the Gulf of Naples—through Ischia, the Vesuvius, and the peninsula of Sorrento—and the ensuing *temulentia nobilis* (a state of drunkenness elevated to an almost spiritual level, as in the celebrated Horatian example) are emblems of the Campanian landscape. But contrasted with those hills are the fields of wheat that extend as far as the eye can see over the flat area called Terra di Lavoro, anciently known as *campi Leborini* (probably from *lepus,* "hare," turned into *terra laboris* through a process of popular etymology). So here we have the ideal place for a meeting—a contest, even—between Dionysus and Demeter, between grapes and grain, between wine and bread. As the ancients noticed (*ut veteres dixere,* undoubtedly the Greeks of southern Italy), Campania provides the setting for a *summum Liberi Patris cum Cerere certamen.* And the names of two gods are no mere metonyms; as we shall see, the antagonism between the two and ultimately their dialectical coexistence will be transferred to a cultic level. This conflict, unlike the Athenian one between Athena and Poseidon, comes to an end at last without a winner, but remains confined to a state of tension between two divine worlds—a tension that reflects also a gender tension between the two sexes.

In order now to have a first piece of evidence relative to the cult of Dionysus in Campania, it will be useful to proceed in a north-south geographical direction that (not by accident) roughly corresponds to the chronological path followed by the cult in its propagation. It was from north southward and from the coastal area inward that the region was first settled by the Greeks and was later conquered by the Romans. We find in fact the oldest traces of the Dionysiac cult in Cumae, the most northern of the Greek colonies.

The founders of Kyme (Cumae) were natives of the towns of Chalcis and Eretria (on the island of Euboea) who had previously colonized the island of Ischia (Pithekussai) off the Campanian coast. Judging from the archaeological evidence, and contrary to the widespread tradition, which regarded Cumae as the oldest Greek town in Italy and Sicily, the settlement took place in the mid-eighth century BCE.[12] In the early 1900s, an inscription was unearthed in the town's necropolis that proved to be a real brainteaser for its interpreters ever since it was published in 1905. The writing was inscribed on a tuff slab used as roofing material for a rectangular tomb of large dimensions. The date of the inscription, easily determinable from the shape of the letters and accepted unanimously, can be placed in the mid-fifth century BCE, certainly before the Samnite invasion that in

420 BCE stripped Cumae almost entirely of its Greek features. After Comparetti's brilliant intervention (1906), there is no longer any doubt about the correct interpretation of the inscription: Οὐ θέμις ἐν-τοῦθα κεῖσθ-αι ἰ (= εἰ) μὲ (= μὴ) τὸν βε-βαχχευμέ-νον ("Lying buried in this place is illicit unless one has become *bakchos* [i.e., has lived like a *bakchos*]").[13] Still open to question, instead, is the meaning of *bakcheuesthai*, that is, the action of behaving ritually like a *bakchos*.[14]

The facts that can be inferred from this inscription are in my view so indisputable as to be hardly susceptible to any complicated interpretation. In fifth-century Cumae, as elsewhere in the Greek world in different epochs, individuals of both sexes were customarily allowed to join the family of *bakchoi*, or *sectatores Liberi Patris*, by a procedure unknown in its ritual details but intimately familiar to us in its essence through the literary evidence (Herodotus and Euripides in the first place). This community (*koinon*), sometimes specifically called *thiasos*[15] or *bakcheion*, used to reserve for itself a communal burying place (communion in death as well as in life), from which, though, was excluded everyone who was not affiliated to the cult.[16]

In a masterly article, which is really an interpretative essay on the controversial issue of the relationship between *orphica* and *bakchica*, R. Turcan collected all the details that supported an Orphic interpretation of the Cumaean laws: "La défense d'ordre religieux (Οὐ θέμις) et l'exclusive (ἰ μέ) qu'elle exprime en termes de prohibition absolue; 2) l'application funéraire (κεῖσθ-/αι) de cette interdiction catégorique liée à des interdits qu'ignore le dionysisme; 3) l'exigence d'une mutation volontaire, personnelle, intérieure, totale et définitive que postule . . . le parfait médio-passif βεβαχχευμέ-/νον."[17] A reply to this preeminent Dionysus scholar came from his younger fellow countryman, J. M. Pailler, arguably the leading expert on the dossier concerning the Dionysus of southern Italy. Pailler reexamined the whole dossier thoroughly, took a stand on Turcan's and J.-P. Vernant's divergent views, and came to a fivefold conclusion ("passivité," "vêtement," "dionysisme," "au-delà," "continuité") that I find absolutely convincing (except for the passive-form issue).[18] Of his reasoning, nearly always supported by a strong awareness of the role of historical realities and by a strict philological method, it is worth underlining the central statement: "Il faut renoncer à la chimère d'une césure radicale entre dionysisme et orphisme." In other words, if there is—and it is beyond question—a boundary that marks the limits between Dionysism (a concrete reality) and Orphism (a much more nebulous reality), we are unable to determine where that boundary lies exactly. In the specific case of the Cumaean inscription (but the same is true of the Orphic tablets from Hipponium, Thurii, and Petelia, as well as of vase iconography), too much contextual evidence is still missing for us to be able to make a clear-cut distinction (the steadfastness of an ascetic life devoted to spiritual training versus the ephemeral exaltation of an orgiastic ritualism performed as a sacramental tool) based on a semantic-grammatical reasoning supported by *argumenta e silentio*.

One fact of sociological nature remains incontrovertible: "La ségregation des morts procède sans doute d'une dissidence des vivants,"[19] as Turcan cogently puts it. But such dissidence can be defined only insofar as it proceeds from a *ritual* practice or exercise, where "ritual" (in the sense that historians of religions give to this word) denotes a complex of stereotyped actions (the -εύο denominative indicates the practice of an activity) that are ends in themselves (as shown by the use of the middle form) and have a strong symbolic connotation (characterized in this case by the prohibition).[20]

Very little knowledge can be gained from the remaining traces—few and controversial—that Dionysus left at Cumae.[21] More fruitful is a piece of information (not usually associated with the worship of Dionysus) that, if interpreted correctly, may help to increase the scanty evidence of *bakchika* in Campania's Chalcidian settlements and may also provide a background to the practice referred to in the Cumaean inscription. Among the few facts ascertained about the Euboean colony in the first three centuries of its existence, pride of place is taken by the deeds of Aristodemus (also called Malakos), a character well known to Roman historians because he gave hospitality to Tarquinius Superbus after his expulsion in 495 BCE.[22] That the tyrant of Cumae was nicknamed "effeminate" by his fellow citizens (and by the barbarians as well) not in the sense of "cowardly wimp" is evident—and was evident to ancient historians as well—from the following circumstance: in the battle of Cumae (524 BCE), against the overwhelming forces of the Etruscans, who had joined forces with other Italic peoples, Aristodemus as a horse-soldier had killed—unaided—the enemy's general and many of his guard. Twenty years later, he repeated his exploits in the still more decisive and uneven battle of Aricia (504 BCE). Soon afterward, capitalizing on the glory earned on the battlefield and profiting from the dissatisfaction of the demos, he overturned the aristocratic government and made himself tyrant of his town. His style is that of a Peisistratus or of any of the chieftains who in those times were active in the Greek motherland, in Ionia, and in Sicily. A few years later, the exiled sons of the aristocrats came back for revenge: they slew the tyrant together with his family and comrades (taking advantage of their delirious state following a wine-based banquet, undoubtedly a bacchanal) and re-established the oligarchic government (490 BCE). In the light of further details available from the sources, it is arguable that in this case, the term *malakos* (which Dionysius finds in the sources: μαλακὸς εἰς ὀργήν) denotes one affected by Dionysian *mania*, that is, one who compulsively indulges in the ritual frenzy typical of Bacchic religiousness.[23] Likewise, exactly in the same period of the Cumaean inscription (around the mid-fifth century), the philhellenic Scythian king Skyles used to revel in a Bacchic fashion (*bakcheuein*) as he walked—delirious under the god's influence—in a *thiasus* along the streets of the Greek town of Olbia.[24] Evidently, in the easternmost and westernmost Greek colonies, the rulers themselves were keen to be initiated (*telesthai* is the exact term used by Herodotus) into Dionysian rituals, and they did not hesitate to exhibit *in public* the emblem of their membership in an esoteric group.

Let us now revert to Aristodemus. Besides his uncontrolled—but ritual—wine-drinking habit, which proved his undoing in the end, another indication of his membership in the *bakchoi* brotherhood comes from an explicit insinuation made by those same local historians from whom Dionysius of Halicarnassus derived his information: as a boy he once acted as *femminiello* (a Neapolitan word sounding like "drag queen" and corresponding exactly to the Greek *thēlydria*) καὶ τὰ γυναιξίν ἁρμόττοντα ἔπασχεν, which is an explicit exegesis of the particular initiation to which the god himself had been subjected in the mythical-ritual complex of Lerna[25] and to which were also subjected (with varying degrees of enjoyment) the Roman youths involved in the so-called Bacchanalia affair. The affair in question, which in 186 BCE (in the aftermath of the Punic War) greatly alarmed the Senate and offended the sense of decency of Rome's high society,[26] had its origins precisely in Campania. In fact (as the squealer Ispala revealed to the consul), it was a Campanian woman—Annia Paculla—who raised the scandal by introducing a "reform" that legalized nocturnal clandestinity and promiscuity. And it was in Magna Graecia, especially in Bruttium and Apulia, that bacchanals enjoyed—until 181 BCE—a short-lived revival that was ruthlessly suppressed by the praetors, whom the consuls had sent *in situ* and invested with full powers to implement the sanctions (*vincula* or death penalty) imposed by a *senatus consultum* dated 7 October 186. (A bronze replica of the decree was lodged *in agro Teurano*—the modern Tiriolo, near Catanzaro—where it was found in 1640.)[27]

Three centuries before that event—which disrupted the Bacchic life of the southern Italian peoples and brought to an end that state of exhilaration determined by an unsteady balance between genuine mystical enthusiasm, transgression, ritualism, and deliberate abuse—the tyrant Aristodemus had tried to give a Dionysian impetus to the life of the surviving young aristocrats of his town (obviously also with a view to foiling any possible opposition to his policy of democratic levelling)[28] by realizing a project that predates by a few centuries the political-religious experiments of the Hellenistic monarchs or of a Marcus Antonius (and prefigures certain trends of the *jeunesse dorée* of all times). With the aim of emasculating the boys, Aristodemus ordered them to wear their hair long, gathered up and adorned with flowers. And he ordered them to wear long garments and supple cloaks and to live as retiringly as the girls of the aristocracy. He consequently closed down the schools and gymnasiums where the young men used to train their minds and tone their bodies and ordered instead the opening of special schools where the young would be taught orgiastic music and dances and the other arts cherished by the Muses. At the head of those schools he placed fashionable ladies, who—armed with parasols and fans, and carrying combs, mirrors, and ointment containing *alabastra*—were in charge of accompanying the young men to the baths. All this continued until the youths reached the age of twenty, when they were allowed to play roles more congenial to manhood (though it is easy to imagine what a wealth of experience they had acquired). The foregoing is what Dionysius of Halicarnassus reports (*Ant. Rom.* 7.9.3–5). Another source speaks of similar regulations applicable to girls: while the boys were forced to wear long hair and gold ornaments, the girls had to cut their hair very short and wear men's garments.[29] We are in the presence of nothing less than the ritual realization—by typical Dionysian procedures well known to us through other textual and figurative sources—of an "inverted world" within the sphere of gender roles.[30]

At a figurative level, the best-known example is offered by a series of representations on the so-called Anacreontic vases (S. Karouzou, J. Beazley), mostly red-figure vases of Attic provenance produced between 510 and 460, ergo contemporary with the exploits of Aristodemus. Depicted on the vases are male and female characters who wear masks and thereby reverse their respective sex roles. Most of the women are represented as players of instruments, notably strings (*kithara, barbiton*) and, more often, winds (the Dionysian *aulos*); and it is clear from their postures that it is they who actually direct the musical performance and the dance: "Il semble bien que le point focal de l'image soit la flûtiste et que la circulation des danseurs s'organise autour d'elle, comme s'ils tournaient et se déplaçaient par rapport à elle."[31] As the present writer once pointed out,

> La pratique du komos anacréontique est exclusivement masculine. La femme y figure seulement comme instrumente accessoire. Les hommes profitent de cette occasion pour se faire "autres," un peu femmes, ou

mieux des êtres bisexués, dépassant la distinction du sexe, un peu orientaux ou barbares, sans jamais toutefois outrepasser les barrières de la décence et de la mesure. Le dieu qui préside à cette pratique, travesti par excellence, c'est Dionysos.[32]

This ritual procedure, of which there is evidence in the late-sixth-century Attic environment, must surely have been familiar as well to the neighboring Chalcidians, who presumably exported it to their Cumaean colony. There the ritual circulated surreptitiously (as usually happens with Dionysian practices) and re-emerged only when historical circumstances allowed it to circulate again in a political key and with almost grotesque overtones, without ever losing, though, its original mystical and liberating character. After the overthrow of the tyrant Malakos, who was undoubtedly an object of sharp criticism by Hellenistic historians (who had great familiarity with other models of *Neoi Dionysoi* advocating *tryphē* and *abrosynē* but were nonetheless reluctant to rewrite history on the basis of stereotyped models), a certain type of ritual transgression incurred political condemnation and consequently either went underground again (only to re-emerge in 186 BCE) or was remodelled into milder forms on a higher mythological and eschatological level.

In fact, one or two centuries after the glories of Aristodemus' tyranny, the various mirrors, parasols, fans, and bottles of perfume revert into the hands of their rightful female owners, in the luxuriant iconography of vases from Apulia (but also from Lucania, Campania, and Paestum). Although the pictorial language of late-fourth-century Italiot iconography has not been fully deciphered yet—mainly for the lack of a comprehensive and systematic study drawing on such different disciplines as epigraphy, classical philology, history of religions, and, obviously, archaeology[33]—there is no doubt that the dominant divine figure in this *imagerie* imbued with "eschatogamy"[34] is that of Dionysus-Bacchus "in his triple capacity of god of wine, drama and the mysteries."[35] This dream world—a sort of ideal archetype of the paradise described by Muhammad in the Koran—is alive with seductive, daintily attired girls in amorous pursuit of young men who are dressed only in a heroic nudity, who are inclined to assume erotically passive attitudes,[36] and who are not averse to handling cosmetic stuff now and then.[37] This process of feminization, which involves at first the activities of the male sex and then progressively also the forms of the male body, is reserved exclusively for winged Eros figures, which are omnipresent and are of course indispensable in a world dominated by women.[38] This is presumably the last phase in a process of successive rearrangements and functional re-adaptations of an ethos that regards inversion and androgyny as *coincidentia oppositorum,* an ethos whose origin can be traced back to the tragicomic parades that Aristodemus Malakos in his devotion to Dionysus imposed on the boys and girls of the Cumaean aristocracy. To quote Plutarch about the rules laid down by the tyrant (*Mul. Virt.* 26.261f–262a), "It was the will of the god that adolescent boys should wear their hair long, adorned with gold jewels; and he forced the girls to cut their hair short and to wear boys' garments and scanty petticoats."

Notes

* I thank my learned friend Paola Ceccarelli (Università di L'Aquila and University of Durham), who generously supplied me with precious information concerning bibliography. The current state of affairs of scholarship makes it impossible for the generalist historian of religions to carry out a research work without ad hoc advice from a specialist.

1. Jonathan Zittel Smith in various interventions, of which the most assertive is Smith 1987. A further contribution to the discussion—well thought-out (though not entirely convincing) and up-to-date (though neglecting D. Zeller's and G. Casadio's works)—is by another Smith (M. S. Smith 2001: 104–131). My views on this issue converge with Mettinger 2001.

2. This term, though it was and is still used with manifestly polemical overtones by supporters of monotheist religions, deserves to be preserved in scientific debate. The analogous form "polytheism" is a late scholarly creation (introduced by Jean Bodin in 1580, it seems) and for this reason an anemic word lacking the vitality of everyday language: we would hardly call anyone a "polytheist" to indicate his or her materialism, hedonism, and so on. In addition, the very notion of polytheism has been so harshly criticized recently that using it has become extremely problematic.

3. The attribution of human characteristics to a fictitious entity such as a Greek deity may certainly seem a decadent mannerism but has in fact a hermeneutical justification if one bears in mind the approach taken by the most ingenious interpreter of Greek religion of the twentieth century, Walter Friedrich Otto. As Veyne observes (1998: 114), "Si l'on veut bien voir la religion grecque telle qu'elle était (*et que Walter Otto la voyait*), les présents considérations sur la personnalité d'un dieu paraîtront peut-être moins hypothétiques qu'il ne semble" (emphasis mine). It is symptomatic that the most deconstructionist of all French historians should have endorsed W. F. Otto's divine ontology, which had been so intensely disliked by the leading comparative historical methodologists of the first half of the twentieth century (a veritable *damnatio memoriae* was enacted against him by two such dissimilar exegetes as M. P. Nilsson and H. Jeanmaire). Veyne (1998: 299 n. 287) suitably underlines the tendency (in his view, developed in the first place by the "School of Leiden": Versnel, Pleket, Van Straten) to center the history of religions "sur la relation métaphorique entre hommes et dieux."

4. A. Dieterich (1897) demonstrates that the ambivalent, melancholy, scurrilous ethos of this character derives from the *fabulae satyricae* of Greek-Oscan origin. Bacchus, especially the Italiot Bacchus, is more appealing than any other

gods. "Il jouit d'une véritable popularité, c'est une star parmi les stars; alors qu'on ne disait pas, des autres dieux, qu'ils sont 'populaires.' Il est brillant, il est séduisant, d'où cette popularité que n'ont pas d'autres dieux qui sont respectés pour leur sérieux ou leur puissance" (Veyne 1998: 114).

5. Casadio 1996a. Cf. Casadio 1995: 81. This particularist, anti-unitarian view of the development of Greek religion (dissenting from that of A. Brelich and G. Pugliese Carratelli) does not require that we appreciate the pretentious title—in point of fact a mere label not supported by pertinent arguments—of a recent summary of the religion of the ancient Greeks written by a specialist of the religions of the Roman empire (Price 1999). That it is mere labelling is proved by the fact that the author fails to give his own views—exactly where he is expected to—on the polymorphism of Greek religion, in time as well as in space. Cf. F. Mora's review in the journal *Polifemo* (vol. 1 [2001]: 21-24; http://homepage.mac.com/polifemo/), complaining—among other things—about the lack of "ein Vergleich zwischen der griechischen Religion in dem Mutterland und in den kolonialen Gebieten (mit nicht-griechischer Unterschicht)" (p. 24).

6. A point of view confirmed by the results obtained independently (and by a completely different methodology) by Luraghi (1994: 111): "La complessità di questi rapporti acculturativi, che oggi è possibile cogliere solo in modo estremamente limitato, è tale da suggerire già di per sé che non si sia trattato di un processo 'a senso unico,' in cui l'elemento greco svolgesse solo un ruolo attivo, e del resto la documentazione stessa, ancora una volta nel campo delle pratiche funerarie, sembra confermarlo." ("The complexity of these acculturative relationships, which today can be explained only to a very small extent, is such as to suggest—already in itself—that this was not a one-way process in which the Greek component played only an active role; in any case, the evidence itself—once again in the field of funerary customs—seems to confirm this.") Metalwork (in particular, fibulae used by women) acknowledged to be of native origin and found as grave goods at Greek sites (Pithekoussai and Syracuse) seems to suggest a direct correlation between the origin of the objects and their owners, and consequently it would support the case for intermarriage between native women and the Greek settlers. (See the accurate and prudent analysis in Shepherd 1999). For a further argument based on an analysis of the socio-political and military customs of the Greeks in Campania, cf. Luraghi 1994: 118.

7. *Campanus* from *kapv-ano* through the form *kappano* appearing on some Oscan coins. In addition to Livius 22.15 and Polybius 3.91.2, cf. G. Radke, s.v. "Campania," in *Der kleine Pauly* (Munich, 1975), 1031-1032 (with bibliography); C. Marcato, s.v. "Campania," in *Dizionario di toponomastica* (Turin, 1990), 123.

8. For a detailed picture of the economic activities, see Levi 1967-68: 155-159. For tourism, cf. Peterson 1919: 84-85, 303, 315.

9. "Ecology of religion is the investigation of the relationship between religion and nature conducted through the disciplines of religious studies, history of religion, and anthropology of religion" (Å. Hultkrantz, "Ecology," in M. Eliade, ed., *The Encyclopedia of Religion* [New York and London, 1987], 4: 581-585, 581). While geography of religion studies the impact of religion on the environment, ecology of religion studies more specifically the relationship between environmental factors and religious morphogenesis.

10. Probably Neapolis itself: Peterson 1919: 36 n. 3 (with bibliography); or Pu-

teoli: Salanitro 1992: 202 (Puteoli in concurrence with the Etruscan-Oscan Capua as site of the *Cena Trimalchionis*) and 190 n. 11 (with annotated bibliography); M. von Albrecht, *Storia della letteratura latina*, trans. Aldo Setaioli (Turin, 1995), 3:1214 (with bibliography). No specific identification is suggested by A. La Penna, "Aspetti e momenti della cultura letteraria in Magna Grecia nell'età romana," in *La Magna Grecia nell'età romana*, Atti Taranto 15 (Naples, 1976), 387-438, esp. 431.

11. One should bear in mind either Horace's hierophany evoked in three Bacchic odes or Ovid's *Met.* 3.658-659: "nec enim praesentior illo / est deus" ("*Praesens deus* ist der Gott, der mit seiner Macht als gegenwärtig offenbart, was in den allgemeineren Begriff wirksamer Macht übergeht": M. Haupt, *ad locum*, in P. Ovidius Naso, *Metamorphosen*, 10. Aufl. [Zürich and Dublin, 1966], 189, postulating parallel uses in Ovid himself and in Cicero). Cf. Veyne 1998: 116.

12. Cf. Ciaceri 1928: 66-81 (discussion of the problem) and 317-319 (sources); W. Johannowski, s.v. "Cuma," in *Enciclopedia dell'arte antica* (Rome, 1959), 970; H. Comfort, s.v. "Cumae," in *Princeton Encyclopedia of Classical Sites* (1976), 250. The latest excavations confirm the dating: A. Gallina, in *Enciclopedia dell'arte antica*, suppl. 1970 (but actually appearing in 1973), 274.

13. Contrary to what I suggested many years ago (Casadio 1983: 137) in the wake of Liddell and Scott, s.v., I find it impossible here to attribute a passive value to the verb *bakcheuein*, in agreement with Turcan (1986: 232), *contra* Pailler 1995: 113. Cf. notably the German translation by Burkert 2004: 99: "Wer nicht Bacchos geworden ist," and the English one by Seaford (2006: 51): "'Made bacchic' in some sense."

14. Of the huge bibliography on this subject, I only mention: Sogliano 1905 (wrong reading but correct dating); Comparetti 1906 (fundamental); Peterson 1919: 70-71 (Orphism); Pettazzoni [1921] 1954: 122; Cumont [1906] 1929: 197 and 306 n. 17 (he does not give his view); Macchioro 1930: 277 (Orphism); Bruhl 1953: 63; Nilsson 1957: 12 and 120; Sokolowski 1962: 202-203 (drawing important epigraphic parallels and reporting the evidence of burials reserved for members of a religious association); Bianchi 1976b: 89-90 (rejecting the Bacchic-Dionysian nature of the *bakchoi*); Cole 1980: 231; Henrichs 1984: 85 n. 63 (distinguishing, without solid arguments, *bakcheuein* from *mainesthai*); Turcan 1986 (thorough and accurate, but not acceptable *in toto*); Casadio 1989: 301; Bottini 1992: 58-61 (on the basis of E. Gabrici's publication, he corrects Comparetti's hypothesis that the inscription was supported by a stela); Pailler 1995: 111-124 (well-founded criticism of Turcan's Orphism); Frisone 1999: 45-55 (an exhaustive examination of the historical, epigraphical, and archaeological evidence).

15. E.g., in inscription no. 126, Sokolowski 1962: 210-212, which requires adherents to take part in the funerals of the members of the association (*thiasotai*).

16. Cf. Comparetti 1906: 16-17, an illuminating report on the historical context; Frisone 1999: 51, offering a rich documentation of parallel cases in which burial rights were reserved exclusively for members of politico-religious associations.

17. Turcan 1986: 243.

18. Pailler 1995: 119. But cf. Casadio 1989: 301, which implicitly anticipated the same point of view.

19. Turcan 1986: 228. Similar reflections are made by Bottini (1992: 60-61),

although his reasoning is flawed by the typical mechanicalness of the Italian socio-archaeological approach. Frisone (1999: 55) points out that in this case—differently from the case, analogous in some other respects, of Hipponium—the "volontà di distinzione" seems to border on "autoisolamento."

20. Possible Eleusinian connections of this cultic milieu have recently been suggested by I. Leventi 2007: 107-141, esp. 135-137.

21. Cf. Peterson 1919: 71; Turcan 1986: 243.

22. Dionys. Halic. 7.2.4-12.2. For further sources (Livius, Diodorus, Plutarch), see Ciaceri 1928: 322-323; Ciaceri 1940: 53-54, 276-281; and esp. Caccamo Caltabiano 1984.

23. So argues Caccamo Caltabiano 1984: 277-278, with insight and the support of suitable linguistic evidence. *Contra* Luraghi (1994: 98-99), who, in a legitimate attempt to refute the hypercritical attitude of G. de Sanctis and his followers, opts for a rather convoluted alternative interpretation (*malakos* as *antipais*: "One who looks like—but is no more—a boy"). As concerns the debate between historians of the hypercritical tradition (which goes back to Niebuhr) and hyperconservative historians—represented in Italy by, e.g., Pareti (in his later orientations)—there is a methodological point to clarify: ancient sources (Dionysius, in this particular instance) must certainly be taken into account when supplying *data,* but must be regarded with skepticism when offering *interpretations* (especially in the domain of etymology).

24. Hdt. 4.79. Cf. Casadio 1999a: 107 n. 54; and A. Corcella in his commentary on Herodotus: *Le storie,* vol. 4 (Rome and Milan, 1993), 297-298. Obviously, in this case nobody speaks of Orphism, despite the presence in Olbia of the famous—but enigmatic—bone tablets (for an up-to-date bibliography, see Bottini 1992: 151-157 and 178; but shamanic interpretations à la C. Ginzburg must be regarded with suspicion).

25. Clem. Alex. *Protr.* 2.34.4: "In fulfillment of the vow to his lover Dionysus hastens to the tomb and feels lust to be penetrated." (Note the interesting use of the desiderative-intensive form πασχητιάω. Cf. Casadio 1994: 295-312.)

26. Cf. Casadio 1992: 210-211 (with bibliography).

27. Livy 39.13. Cf. Peterson 1919: 30; Bruhl 1953: 92-93; Casadio 1995: 81-82, with further sources and bibliography.

28. The connection between Dionysian propaganda and the people-oriented policy of tyrants (Cleisthenes of Sicyon, Cypselus of Corinth, Peisistratus of Athens, and maybe Gelon of Syracuse, whose pro-Demeter sentiments are well known) was highlighted several times by, among others, Dabdab Trabulsi 1990: 59-102 (with insightful arguments, despite a certain Marxist stiffness); cf. Casadio 1992. The best summary of Aristodemus tyrant of Cumae is, without comparison (despite an excess of rationalization), the one offered by Luraghi (1994: 79-118), who is always in complete control of the bibliography (both primary and secondary).

29. Plut. *Mul. Virt.* 26.261ff. Cf. Caccamo Caltabiano (1984: 274-277), who takes credit for valorizing this source (previously neglected or misinterpreted) and rightly speaks of a "process of feminization of men" enhanced by the project of attributing an outstanding role to the female element. Less fruitful is the articulate—not to say convoluted—interpretation offered by Luraghi (1994: 100-105), who assumes that a "thick stratification of literary motives, cultural influences and

fashions" (the *tryphē* of Ionicized aristocracies that tyrants supposedly try to make their own) was devised in Timaeus of Tauromenium's historiographical workshop and interprets Aristodemus' tactics as an "anti-ephebic" operation. The supposed result of this practice is the adoption of the "orientalizing lifestyle of the archaic aristocracy" cherished by the regime that he himself had overthrown. Such lifestyle would subsequently "assume a negative connotation" in the eyes of that same social class by which it had been invented and imposed, and would be ultimately associated with tyranny. But even if we take for granted that life and history are so extremely complicated, such complication must be substantiated by solid arguments (absent in this case).

30. Cf. Casadio 1999a: 113-123, indicating the sources and the relevant bibliography and suggesting an interpretation.

31. Frontisi-Ducroux and Lissarrague 1983: 25. The description, although seemingly a faithful replica of the report by Dionysius of Halicarnassus (the women as teachers of dancing and music), is in fact absolutely independent of that text, unknown to the two specialists of iconography.

32. G. Casadio, in *Mentor: Guide bibliographique de la religion grecque* (Liège, 1992), 381-382, where I follow up the conclusions reached by Frontisi-Ducroux and Lissarrague 1983 in an article that partly incorporates — but is also a brilliant improvement on — the "oriental" interpretation offered by J. Boardman in an essay issued in 1986 but already known to the mentioned authors before its publication (cf. Frontisi-Ducroux and Lissarrague 1983: 12 n. 3 and 17).

33. Besides the well-known works by K. Schauenburg, G. Schneider-Hermann, A. D. Trendall, A. Cambitoglou (and the exhaustive summaries by Trendall 1989, where one can find the relevant bibliography), still indispensable is a study by H.R.W. Smith (1972), who, despite the improbability of most of his interpretations and the obscurity of his style, remains the only author to have attempted a classification of "chattel symbolism."

34. A term suitably coined by H.R.W. Smith (cf. Keuls 1976: 444).

35. Trendall 1989: 256. In the words of the great Australian iconologist: "He is probably to be identified with the youthful male figure, holding thyrsus, phiale or bunch of grapes, who is to be found on so many South Italian vases; here we should see him in his role as god of the mysteries, offering his initiates a better life in the hereafter, where he will be in mystic communion with them."

36. Cf. Veyne 1998: 111: "La femme n'est pas seule et c'est elle qui prend l'initiative amoureuse."

37. For example, in the bell-shaped crater — reproduced by Smith 1972: pl. 29b — at the Museo Provinciale in Lecce, the handsome young man dressed in a tight bodice and wearing a curious sugarloaf headdress holds a bronze mirror, usually reserved for women.

38. Cf. Keuls 1976: 444-446, pointing out the androgynization process undergone by Eros figures in late-fourth-century Apulian pottery.

CHAPTER 3

The Meaning of βάκχος and βακχεύειν in Orphism

ANA JIMÉNEZ SAN CRISTÓBAL

The meanings of the denomination βάκχος and the verb βακχεύειν in Orphic context differ from their value in other religious circles. Generally speaking, the adjective βάκχος denominates those who have experienced rituals of purification or ritual ecstasies.[1] Βάκχος and the verb βακχεύειν describe states of mystical and cathartic exaltation peculiar to the enthusiastic devotees[2] of Dionysus Bacchus. In fact, in spite of some opposition[3] to including it in the Dionysiac field before the fourth century BCE, the name βάκχος is always applied—when it refers to mortals—to the followers of Dionysus and not of other gods.[4] Therefore, it is not a theonym[5] but an attribute that manifests a particular condition of men or gods. Obviously, βάκχος is connected with the worshipers of Dionysus, who is called Βάκχος[6] and Βάκχιος[7] in numerous testimonies. Still, Βάκχος is not identical with Dionysus, for an initiate can receive the name "Bacchus" but never "Dionysus."[8]

With regard to the verb βακχεύειν, in the oldest testimonies[9] it denotes the condition reached when one is inspired or possessed[10] by a god. Among the early writers, the Bacchic language is used to describe the Dionysiac poetry and ritual;[11] but only with Euripides does the Bacchic terminology get the peculiar sense that traditional criticism gives to it, on the basis of Dionysiac worship. In this context, the verb βακχεύειν can refer both to the feeling and to the performance of the Bacchic rites that caused such enthusiasm. In fact, the verb is a denominative that denotes the exercise, the practice of an activity. It is derived from βακχεύς,[12] an agent name received by Dionysus when he acts as bacchus, as well as his followers when they imitate him and behave as bacchi.[13] Worshiper and god are described by the ritual activity. In general terms, βακχεύειν can be translated as "to experience bacchic deliria or raptures,"[14] attained by performing several rites,[15] such as bearing the thyrsus,[16] ornamenting oneself with ivy[17] or with the nebris,[18] shouting *evoe*[19] *saboi*,[20] dancing,[21] or drinking, mainly wine.[22] But there are as well instances, some of them early, of a figurative use of βακχεύειν to describe the delirium and ecstasy of the lyrists[23] or the state of perfection of the human soul.[24]

After this short introduction, we shall try to find the peculiarities displayed by βάκχος and βακχεύειν in the testimonies connected with Orphism. Above all, we must note that it consists of a very limited number of texts, which include passages of Heraclitus,[25] Herodotus,[26] Euripides,[27] Plato,[28] and Clement of Alexandria,[29] the lamella of Hipponion[30] (fifth century BCE), and inscriptions in Cumae[31] (about mid-fifth century BCE) and Torre Nova[32] (second century CE). Therefore, if we exclude the Clement text and the Torre Nova inscription, the bulk of the texts belong to a limited period, between the sixth and fourth centuries BCE. Likewise, the context in which the terms appear is very precise, for they are limited almost always to the rituals and funerals.

Let us begin with the term βάκχος. If we intend to make a comparison with the βάκχοι of other mysteries, the first question we have to answer is with what kind of rites the Orphic βάκχοι are connected in the sources. Heraclitus criticizes the initiates and bacchi and the μάγοι and νυκτιπόλοι who perform rites.[33] In Orphic environments, the *magoi* are mentioned in the Derveni Papyrus[34] in connection with an ἐπῳδή (an enchantment) and with offerings and libations. Concerning the adjective νυκτιπόλος, "night-wanderer," it may refer to private and secret rites.[35] In this passage, Heraclitus mentions as well fire, which is sometimes identified with Dionysus.[36] In a fragment of the *Cretans*, Euripides mentions a rite consisting in bearing torches.[37] To these rites are added others like drinking[38]—perhaps water[39] or wine[40]—mentioned in the lamella of Hipponion. Another common activity in the celebrations was the bearing of thyrsi.[41] As is well known, the thyrsus is common in the performances of the maenads in Dionysiac worships;[42] but among the Orphics, such an instrument acquires special connotations due to the existence of a story recounting how the Titans attracted Dionysus with the thyrsus and finally dismembered him. The Titans are considered the ancestors of men, who are, correspondingly, the heirs of the Titanic guilt. Therefore, it is advisable to keep in mind this myth when we try to discover the use of the thyrsus among the Orphics. Clement of Alexandria mentions the thyrsi with which the bacchi—in this case, the worshipers who celebrate the mysteries of Sabazios—are crowned, and a passage from the Platonic *Phaedo*[43] passes on a well-known Orphic line:

ναρθηκοφόροι μὲν πολλοί, βάκχοι δέ τε παῦροι.

Many bear the thyrsus, few are the bacchi.

According to the context in which we find the sentence, it is very likely that the expression was uttered (φασιν) by those who took part in the ritual (οἱ περὶ τὰς τελετάς). This would probably happen during the execution of a rite in which thyrsi were borne[44] and the tragic fate of Dionysus might be played. This hypothesis seems to be endorsed in a few lines by Proclus according to which those who celebrate Dionysus bear the thyrsus.[45] As we said above, the Orphic myth of the dismemberment could give a context to the origin of the expression passed on by Plato. Not in vain do two passages of Damascius insist that the Titans are thyrsus-bearers (ναρθηκοφόροι) and that, by extension, those who live like the Titans are called ναρθηκοφόροι.[46] Anyway, since it is a line long and often discussed, there is no harm in going over the different exegeses of the expression.[47] Plato himself noticed the double meanings it offered and interpreted the bacchi as the ones who had philosophized correctly. Most of Plato's commentators just glossed this philosophical interpretation of the line.[48] I will not use these sources, as my purpose is to fix the meaning of the sentence in mystery circles.

Some modern critics hold that the expression reflects the dichotomy between the profane and initiates, so that "thyrsus-bearers" (ναρθηκοφόροι) is equivalent to the profane, and "bacchi" (βάκχοι) to initiates. If so, "thyrsus-bearers" would refer to the bulk of humanity dragging behind itself the sad heritage of the Titans. On the other hand, the bacchi could be the ones who have been able to free themselves from that guilt. This reading seems to fit perfectly with the opposition expressed by Plato in previous lines between the profane and the initiates, as well as with the destiny that awaits the former and the latter. However, I disagree with this explanation, first on philological grounds. The expression is not stated in terms of exclusive opposition of the kind οἱ μὲν ... οἱ δὲ ("Some ... , but others"), but it marks an inclusive opposition—πολλοὶ μὲν ... δέ τε παῦροι ("Many ... , but a few")—that may mean that, among the many thyrsus-bearers, only a few are or will become bacchi. In the same way, the Titanic heritage is carried by the whole of humanity, which includes not only the profane, but also the initiates who try to free themselves from it in this life. Second, according to the adage cited in Plato, the initiated believers would play the role of the Titans, the embodiment of the profane. However, it is not impossible that the believers identified themselves with Dionysus himself, to whom the Titans gave the thyrsus. In fact, in an Orphic hymn,[49] Dionysus is called "thyrsus-bearer," and the Rhodians worshiped a Dionysos Narthakaphoros.

A second line of interpretation defends the argument that both the thyrsus-bearers and the bacchi are initiates, but with differences between them. This position allows different readings. First, it could be held that the expression was used by the Orphic followers to distinguish themselves from the Dionysiacs, so that the "thyrsus-bearers" would be the Dionysiac followers in general, whereas the term "bacchi" would be restricted to the Orphics alone. Although this interpretation looks initially correct, it does not fit well with the ritual context in which Plato places the expression. Why would the Orphics want to utter in a ritual a sentence with which to manifest their difference from the rest of the Dionysiac initiates? Besides, we do not find suggested any intention of the Orphic followers to distinguish themselves from the Dionysiacs. Rather, the divergences between both of them have been unravelled by modern criticism. Other scholars have held that the sentence refers to different degrees of initiation depending on the authenticity of the ecstatic experience,[50] so that the βάκχοι would be initiates of a higher level, whereas the ναρθηκοφόροι would belong to a lower one. This interpretation would be acceptable in a mystery environment like that of Eleusis, where the differences of level in the initiation are extensively evidenced, but not in Orphic worship, whose ritual does not show such specialization.

The explanation I find most persuasive for this polemic Orphic hexameter, anticipating some of the features of βάκχος we shall expound in this study, is that the expression shows that many may take part in the mystery ceremonies, but few can reach the condition of βάκχος, that is, of those who reach the real union with the deity.[51] This interpretation differs from the previous one on several points, but it agrees in the fundamental one: there is a difference between the thyrsus-bearers and the bacchi; but what changes is not the rite itself but the involvement of the followers in it and in the Orphic doctrines. This way, ναρθηκοφόροι, "thyrsus-bearers," denotes by synecdoche those who perform rites, initiates who still need to travel a long journey to deliver themselves from the Titanic heritage that they shared with the rest of humanity. To attain the final conversion into βάκχος and the resulting union with the god in the other life, it is necessary to commit oneself to respect the Orphic precepts. Only a few out of all the ναρθηκοφόροι will reach it. According to this reading, the sentence uttered in the ritual might be a kind of remembering warning: the initiates were ναρθηκοφόροι, heirs of the Titanic guilt, and will keep being ναρθηκοφόροι, as long as they do not respect the Orphic precepts. The occasional performance of a rite like bearing the thyrsus is not enough.

Orphism implies a philosophy of life that goes beyond the limits of the cultic practice. Plato also suggests this idea by his use of the perfect participles κεκαθαρμένος and τετελεσμένος—we shall go again over their meaning—in a previous context in which the disparity of the fates of the profane and the initiates is established.[52] As Bianchi says, "L'anima non si divinizza nel breve arco della estasi orgiastica ma stabilmente nella purificazione e—infine—nella reintegrazione, dopo la morte, nel mondo degli dèi."[53]

This reading, moreover, seems to be more acceptable from a philological point of view, for it expresses an exclusive opposition of the kind πολλοὶ μὲν . . . δέ τε παῦροι, "many . . . few." In fact, the interpretation by Christian writers[54] of the expression "many are the called, few are the chosen" also goes in this direction. And in his peculiar philosophical reading of the line, Olympiodoros[55] identifies the bearers of the thyrsus with the political philosophers and the thyrsus-bearing bacchi with the purified ones.

But let us follow with the concepts of βάκχος and βακχεύειν. In all the analyzed passages, the bacchi perform rituals that are similar to the ones we find in other mystery cults, those around Dionysus in particular. In fact, the ecstatic experience described by Euripides in the *Cretans* coincides with the one described in the *Bacchae* (120-167). While the experience of the bacchantes seems to have its goal within its own sphere, however, the ritual of the *Cretans* confers a permanent mark: it includes the initiate in the category of bacchi and makes him ὅσιος.[56] Other texts emphasize the differences between the Orphic and the Dionysiac bacchi. For instance, Euripides' reference in the *Hippolytus*[57] seems to show that there is a close connection[58] between βακχεύειν and the practice of the Ὀρφικὸς βίος, the specific *modus vivendi* of this cult, which includes an ascetic life and the performance of rites. For the Orphics, βακχεύειν consists in following the precepts of the Orphic life, among which are vegetarianism, refusal to shed blood, and participation in rites during which certain doctrines are proclaimed. In this way, the value of the Orphic βακχεύειν becomes different from two of its traditional traits: violent activity[59] and the transience of ecstasy. Orphics do not renounce the use of this verb, but have changed its meaning, rejecting its violent senses. Besides, the non-Orphic Dionysiac goes into ecstasy with the bloody sacrifice. The Orphic, on the other hand, understands the ecstasy as a final condition of blessedness that is attained through a personal exercise of asceticism (*askēsis*). This *askēsis* is in practice equivalent to accepting the Ὀρφικὸς βίος. The perseverance implicit in βακχεύειν can be seen in the use of the perfect participle βεβαχχευμένον, found in an inscription of Cumae.[60] The verbal form has been translated in different ways, "initiated" being the most usual,[61] although this translation does not cover all of its shades. The use of the perfect tense allows us to specify that it is not a single or isolated fact, but a condition resulting from a regular practice: one has strived to become a bacchus, has lived in and of that effort. In the same way, in the passage of the Platonic *Phaedo*, the perfect participles κεκαθαρμένος and τετελεσμένος express the lasting condition reached by the initiates who have performed the rites and have purified themselves; the bacchi identify themselves only with them. Being βεβαχχευμένος is the result of the action of the individual who aspires to attain the condition of βάκχος through βακχεύειν.

Orphism, then, is different from other manifestations of Dionysism in that, for Orphics, βακχεύειν is not a transient action, a passing delirium, but a continuous exercise through which one can attain a permanent state of holiness. The initiate does not look for the transient ecstasy that ends with the collective celebrations, but a lasting condition only attainable through the internalization of the rite.[62] This is the great innovation of Orphism. Βακχεύειν goes beyond the limits of a simple ritual or initiation act and becomes a referent for the constant activity of the followers of that way of life. Nevertheless, a passage of Herodotus shows the possibility that the performance of certain rites could cause states of cathartic agitation.[63] By the verb βακχεύειν, the historian describes the crisis of agitation and the state of religious trance similar to madness[64] reached by the Scythian king Skyles, which overpowers his ego and alienates him from the deity. The slight difference between the passage of Euripides and that of Herodotus consists in that, in Euripides, βακχεύειν refers to the whole and manifests a way of life and of behaving, while in Herodotus the verb refers only to the particular rite included in that way of life.

The connection of the Orphic βάκχοι with a specific *modus vivendi* is confirmed at the formal level by its frequent association with the term μύστης, "initiate." In most of the testimonies, βάκχος appears together with μύστης, which reveals that the follower belonged to a select group, access into which was gained through an initiation. Heraclitus is the first of our sources that shows a connection between μύσται and βάκχοι,[65] and he mentions explicitly the connection of both terms with the mysteries. The fragment of Euripides' *Cretans*[66] and the lamella of Hipponion show that this kind of devotee lives a particular experience, probably of ecstatic character, that changes him from an initiate into a "bacchus."[67] In the Orphic expression cited in the *Phaedo*, the bacchi, unlike the noninitiated, identify themselves with the ones who have been purified and have performed certain rites. In Herodotus, initiation precedes and conditions the act of βακχεύειν:[68] one can become bacchus only through a personal initiation.⁶⁹ Skyles had to be initiated before he could participate in the τελετή and behave like a bacchus. The verb λαμβάνω used by Herodotus may show the symbolic adoption by the god,⁷⁰ who receives him among his initiates in return for the personal *askēsis* expressed in βακχεύειν.

The values proposed for βάκχος and βακχεύειν allow us to solve the old question about the differences between μύσται and βάκχοι.⁷¹ Initiates and bacchi share rites and beliefs, but the terms do not express two consecutive initiation degrees; rather, they show that the βάκχοι are a special group that stands out among the μύσται.⁷² The expression μύσται καὶ βάκχοι⁷³ is a hendiadys in which βάκχος refers to the μύστης that has been able to behave by the precepts of the Ὀρφικὸς βίος. According to the fragment of the *Cretans,* the initiate (μύστης) who agrees to follow an ascetic life, renouncing sex and flesh-eating, and avoiding contact with the dead, is called βάκχος. The term βάκχοι specifies μύσται:⁷⁴ only those who have striven to βακχεύειν in a continuous and constant way will advance in the sacred path that—in the lamella of Hipponion—leads to the paradise of the blissful ones.

The real privilege of the βάκχοι is that they are put on a level, even in their name, with the deity to which are devoted: Dionysus Bacchus. The believer in Bacchus is himself βάκχος, while the god is, equally, βάκχιος⁷⁵ like his devotee.⁷⁶ Damascius himself tells us that the devotee can bear the name of the god⁷⁷ once he has been possessed and purified by him. The identification between the initiate and the god is common in the orgiastic cults.⁷⁸ This is not new in Orphism, where the search for the divine union by the believers and the officiants seems to be constant. In two lamellae from Thurii, there is a greeting to the devotee who has acquired the condition of θεός⁷⁹ after dying. In the earthly rite, moreover, the priests are frequently described with qualifiers peculiar to the main deity. Two instances of this are the term νυκτιπόλος, "night-wanderer," which refers to the officiants in Heraclitus and to Dionysus Zagreus in the fragment of the *Cretans* of Euripides; and the occasional use for Orphic officiates of the term βουκόλοι,⁸⁰ a denomination characteristic of Dionysus with bull's horns.⁸¹ On the other hand, it is possible that in the formal level, the identification with Bacchus is proved by the use of the masculine epithet βάκχος. In fact, it is significant that the feminine βάκχη is hardly found in the Orphic testimonies, although these cults allowed women to participate and βάκχαι is a common term in other mystery circles⁸² for describing the male and female followers of Bacchus. The absence of the feminine seems to show that βάκχος is not simply one of the names of the devotees but describes as well a specific quality of them—the identification with the deity—that the Greek language cannot express with the feminine βάκχη. It is perhaps for this reason that the feminine does not appear in an Orphic context, except in the Torre Nova inscription, a late text (second century CE), in which the masculine βάκχος, also present in this inscription, has already lost the shades of meaning under discussion and both masculine and feminine simply refer to the members of a Bacchic college. It is possible as well that in Orphic circles the feminine βάκχαι is not used due to its possible association with the violent nature of the maenads.[83]

Another interesting aspect is the relationship of the βάκχοι with the other world. In the aforementioned testimonies, the bacchi belong to a group of initiates for whom both the performance of rites and the asceticism correspond to an eschatological need. All of the precepts they observe aim to overcome death and its consequences. In this sense, the text of the Platonic *Phaedo* connects the ritual practice mentioned by Heraclitus and Euripides with the funeral environment of the lamella of Hipponion. The text from Heraclitus emphasizes the post mortem threat that comes over the profane and mentions fire, a destructive power closely connected with death.[84] That threat cannot be other than the sad fate that awaits the profane after death, equivalent to the Platonic image of laying in the mud. By being included among the μύσται καὶ βάκχοι, the dead woman of Hipponion has fulfilled her aspirations: only the initiates and bacchi go along the sacred road that leads to the sacred prairies and groves of Persephone[85]—or, in the words of Plato, the happy fate where she will dwell in the company of the gods.

This link of the Orphic bacchi with the other world confirms that the true union with the deity only happens after the death of the body. Βάκχος is the status kept by the initiates in their earthly life through βακχεύειν. Only those who persevere in it and successfully carry out their passage through Hades gain the right to identify themselves with Bacchus.[86] In the light of this conception, the aspiration of the followers at Cumae to be buried in a separate place begins to make sense. The peculiarity of the inscription lies in that the differences between those who have become bacchi and those who remain profane are manifested not only in the respective fates of bliss and misery that await them as a result of their behavior in the earthly life, but also, and in a much more material way, in the places in which they will be buried after death.[87]

If the true identification with the deity happens only at the death of the body, we have still to explain why the followers of the earthly rite are called βάκχοι. This apparent paradox can be understood on the basis of the Orphic conception of the *teletē*, the ritual, as an anticipation of what will happen to the soul in the other world.[88] The rite is a preparatory rehearsal that anticipates the identification of the initiate with Bacchus; but the final union will only take place after the death of the body, at which moment real life begins for the Orphic.

Notes

Research for this chapter was financed by the Spanish Public Program for the Development of Knowledge (PB98-0763). I am grateful to Professors A. Bernabé, G. Casadio, and P. A. Johnston for their helpful review and their useful suggestions. For the citations of the Orphic Fragments (*OF*), I follow Bernabé's new edition; the correspondences with those of Kern or Pugliese (see in bibliography Bernabé 2004a, 2005; Kern 1922; Pugliese 2003) are offered in brackets.

1. West 1975: 234; Guettel Cole 1980: 226.
2. Pugliese Carratelli 1988a: 161; cf. also Graf 1985: 286.
3. West 1975: 234-235; Bianchi 1976b: 89-90.
4. Guettel Cole 1980: 230. In the Orphic Hymns it is one of the names by which Apollo is invoked: Orph. *Hymn*. 34.7: Βάκχιε καὶ Διδυμεῦ; cf. Ricciardelli 2000a: 369-370.
5. See Jeanmaire 1951: 57-58; Festugière 1935a: 373 (= 1972: 39); Zuntz 1976: 147; Pugliese Carratelli 1976; Casadio 1994: 80 n. 46.
6. The name Βάκχος applies both to Dionysus (Eur. *Ba*. 623, 1020; *Hipp*. 560-561; *IT* 164; *IA* 1061; Soph. *OT* 211) and to the initiate (the texts will be presented along this work).
7. The name with the form Βάκχιος is attested in the lamellae of Pelinna, *OF* 485-486 (II.B.3-4 Pugliese); Soph. *Ant*. 154; Eur. *Ba*. 67, 195, 225, 366, 528, 605, 632, 998, 1124, 1145, 1153, 1189; *Cyc*. 519, 521; *Ion* 716; *IT* 953; Antiphanes 234 K-A; Aristoph. *Ach*. 263; *Th*. 988. The variant Βακχεῖος is found in Soph. *OT* 1105 and Hdt. 4.79; Sophocles (*Ant*. 1121) calls it also Βακχεύς. For the epigraphic testimonies, see the important discussion of Dionysos Baccheus/Baccheios/Bacchios/Bacchos in Graf 1985: 285-291, and Jaccottet 2003, with index.
8. Cf. Burkert 1975: 90; Graf 1985: 287; Henrichs 1994: 47-51; Jaccottet 1998.
9. Aesch. fr. 58*.1 Radt.
10. According to Jeanmaire (1951: 58), the verb describes a state of religious trance extremely difficult to translate into modern languages.
11. *AP* 13.28 describes a dithyrambic contest as Bacchic. This terminology is found as well in a traditional song sung in the Dionysiac *phallophoria* (851b Page). Herodotus (4.108) associates βακχεύειν with the Dionysiac festival held every two years in Gelonus by the Budini. Aeschylus (*Sept*. 498; *Cho*. 698) employs the Bacchic terminology as a metaphor, but always connected with a Dionysiac source (*Eum*. 25). Sophocles describes the Bacchic dance (*Tr*. 219), calls the grape Bacchic wine (*Tr*. 704), and uses the Bacchic language metaphorically to describe the frenzy with which Polynices attacks Thebes (*Ant*. 136).
12. Cf. Chantraine 1970, s.v. Βάκχος; Perpillou 1973: 315-316.
13. Cf. Turcan 1986: 231-232.
14. Eur. *HF* 899, 1085, 1122, 1142; *Tr*. 341, 367; *Or*. 411; *Ba*. 40, 251, 298,

313, 317, 343; Plut. *Def. orac.* 432E; Hesych. s.v. βακχεύει, s.v. βακχευθεῖσα, s.v. βακχεύοντες, s.v. βακχία· μανία; Schol. in Aesch. *PV* 836.1 οἰστρήσασα ὑπὸ οἴστρου βακχευθεῖσα; Suda s.v. Βακχεύων.

15. Eur. *Ba.* 76-82; *Hel.* 1364-1365; *Io* 218; *AP* 6.172.3 βάκχευεν; Diod. Sic. 4.3.3; Plut. *Is. Os.* 364E; Clem. Alex. *Protr.* 12.118.5.3, 12.120.2.2; *Paed.* 2.8.73.1, 3.

16. Xenophanes defines βάκχοι as "branches," so βακχεύειν can be interpreted as the act of bearing the branch, manifesting by dances the inspiration and the madness of the god: Xenoph. fr. 21.F.17 D-K; Schol. in Aristoph. *Eq.* 408: βάκχους (. . .) τοὺς κλάδους, οὓς οἱ μύσται φέρουσι. μέμνηται δὲ Ξ. ἐν Σίλλοις· ἑστᾶσιν δ᾽ ἐλάτης βάκχοιν πυκινὸν περὶ δῶμα ("Bacchi [. . .] the branches, borne by the initiates, as Xenophanes remembers in the *silloi:* 'The branches of the fir tree rise up around the solid mansion'"). Cf. Hesych. s.v. βάκχος: ὁ ἱερεὺς τοῦ Διονύσου. καὶ κλάδος ὁ ἐν ταῖς τελεταῖς, οἱ δὲ φανὸν λέγουσιν· οἱ δὲ ἰχθύν ("The priest of Dionysus. The branch as well in the rituals. Some say it is gleaming, others it is a fish"). Cf. Guettel Cole 1980: 229. See also Schol. in Eur. *Or.* 1492.3.

17. Hesych. s.v. βακχᾶν: ἐστεφανῶσθαι κισσῶι, "To be crowned with ivy."

18. Schol. in Eur. *Phoen.* 792.12: νεβρίς ἐστι δέρμα ἐλάφου κατάστικτον ὃ φοροῦσιν οἱ βακχευταί, "*Nebris* is the mottled deer-skin worn by those who experience Bacchic deliria."

19. Hesych. s.v. εὔσαμα: ἀναφώνημα εὐαστικόν, καὶ βακχικὸν ἐπίφθεγμα. καὶ γὰρ τὸ βακχεύειν εὐάζειν, καὶ σαβαῖοι βακχεύοντες ("Bacchic cry, Bacchic acclaim, for to experience Bacchic deliria is to shout the *evoe*").

20. Hesych. s.v. σαβάξειν: εὐάξειν βακχεύειν. Cf. also the explanation that Plutarch tries to offer (*Quaest. conv.* 671F), comparing the Jewish rites with the Greek ones, of the name of Sabus and the cry that appears in Demosthenes (18.260) and Menander (fr. 610 K-A).

21. Hesych. s.v. ὀρχεῖται: διασείεται. βακχεύει ("To dance: to jump, to act the bacchus"); s.v. χορεύει: μελωιδεῖ. βακχεύει. ὀρχεῖται ("to dance in a ring; to sing, to act the bacchus, to dance"); Suda s.v. βακχευούσας σὺν τῶι μέλει τῶι βακχείωι τε καὶ ἐνθέωι ("Maidens who celebrate with the Bacchic singing inspired by the god").

22. Schol. in Aristoph. *Nu.* 606.1: κωμαστής·Ὅτι καὶ μεθύοντες βακχεύονται καὶ ὥσπερ ἐκμαίνονται ("Who participates in a festival: because those who are drunk experience deliria as if they were beside themselves"); Hesych. s.v. ληνεύουσι: βακχεύουσιν. The term ληνός means "barrel, wine-vat," and therefore it is possible that ληνεύουσι refers to drinking wine, an act not foreign to ritual; cf. Bernabé and Jiménez San Cristóbal 2001: 118-122.

23. Pl. *Ion* 534a; *Leg.* 700d.

24. Like this in the Neoplatonists: Procl. *H.* 3.11. See Van den Berg 2001: 197-198, 207-208.

25. Heraclitus fr. 87 Marc. (B14 D-K). It is passed on by Clement of Alexandria (*Protr.* 2.22.2), and there has been much discussion on its authenticity. See Marcovich 1995: ad loc.; Bremmer 1999: 3 and n. 20 for the discussion; Burkert 1999: 71, 94 and n. 19. The rites performed are probably like those we find in Olbia.

26. Hdt. 4.79; cf. Jeanmaire 1951: 58, 89; Festugière 1935b: 83-85 (= 1972: 77-78); Casadio 1983: 137; Versnel 1990: 140-141; Henrichs 1994: 47-51; Jaccottet 1998: 11-12.

27. Eur. *Hipp.* 952-954; cf. Burkert 1982: 11-12; Wilamowitz 1891 and Barrett 1964: ad loc.; Linforth 1941: 50-60; Guthrie 1935 (1967 ed.): 11-12, 16, 197; Lucas 1946: 65-68; Montégu 1959: 89; Des Places 1969: 200-201; Sfameni Gasparro 1984: 142; Freyburger-Galland, Freyburger, and Tautil 1986: 124-125; Turcan 1986: 235-237; Sorel 1995: 10-12; Casadesús 1997: 167-168; Eur. *Cret.* fr. 472.15 Kannicht; cf. Casadio 1990b; Cozzoli 1993; Bernabé 2004b: 281-283; Taylor 2004: 85-88.

28. Pl. *Phd.* 69c; cf. Rohde 1899, 2:279 n. 1; Dieterich [1893] 1913: 73; Tannery 1901: 316-317; Rohde 1925, 2:279 n. 1; Kern 1920: 45; Nilsson 1935: 203-205; Guthrie 1935 (1967 ed.): 194, 243; Colli 1948: 197; Montégu 1959: 86; Hackforth ad *Phd.* 55; Graf 1974: 100 n. 30; Bianchi 1975: 230 n. 1; Bernabé 1998a: 48, 76, 82.

29. Clem. Alex. *Protr.* 2.16.3.

30. *OF* 474.15-16 (I.A.1 Pugliese). Primary edition: Pugliese Carratelli 1974; cf. Bernabé and Jiménez San Cristóbal 2001: 25-86.

31. Cf. Sokolowski 1962: 202 n. 120 (*OF* 652). An excellent article by Turcan (1986: 227-246) collects the previous literature; Freyburger-Galland, Freyburger, and Tautil 1986: 71; Turcan 1992: 217-218; Pailler 1995: 111-126; Parker 1995: 485; Dubois 1995: 52 n. 19.

32. *OF* 585, col. B.; cf. Vogliano 1933: 215-231; Cumont 1933: 232-263, republished in Moretti 1968: 138, no. 160; Bruhl 1953: 274-276; Freyburger-Galland, Freyburger, and Tautil 1986: 65-69; Ricciardelli 2000b; Jaccottet 2003: no. 188.

33. Graf (1994: 34) highlights the irony of Heraclitus when he threatens these fortune-tellers and sorcerers with the same punishments with which they try to scare their clients. According to Burkert (1999: 71), Heraclitus criticizes them for being initiated in human mysteries, conventional ones, far away from the sacred.

34. *PDerveni* col. VI.2 (*OF* 471); cf. Tsantsanoglou 1997: 110-114; Burkert 1999: 104-111; Casadesús 2002: 77-82; Janko 2002: 12; Jourdan 2003: 37-39; Betegh 2004: 79-82. For the bibliography of the papyrus, cf. Bernabé 1992: 33-35, 2001a: 352-353; Casadesús 1995; Funghi 1995: 565-585; Laks and Most 1997; Betegh 2004.

35. Cf. Graf 1994: 32-33. Subsequently Lucian (*Peregr.* 29.8) will use it as an epithet of the hero Proteus, in a passage ascribed to the Sibyl that is very critical of priests and night initiations. See also Aesch. fr. 273a.

36. For instance, in a lamella from Thurii (*OF* 492.8 [fr. 47 Kern]: ΩΤΑΚΤΗΡ ἱερά ΜΑΡ Δημῆτερ, πῦρ, Ζεῦ, Κόρη Χθονία ΤΡΑΒΔΑΗΤΡΟΣΗΝΙΣΤΗΟΙΣΤΝ, "Sacrifices, Demeter, fire, Zeus, the Subterranean Maiden") that can be interpreted as a mention of the four god-elements: Demeter (earth), Fire (Sun-Dionysus), Zeus (air), and the subterranean maiden, evidently Persephone, as personification of water, cf. Bernabé and Jiménez San Cristóbal 2001: 189-197.

37. Eur. *Cret.* fr. 472.13 Kannicht.

38. *OF* 474.15-16 (I.A.1 Pugliese): καὶ δὴ καὶ σὺ πιὼν ὁδὸν ἔρχεα⟨ι⟩ ν ἄν τε καὶ ἄλλοι / μύσται καὶ βάκχοι ἱερὰν στείχουσι κλε⟨ε⟩ινοί, So once you have drunk, you will also take the sacred path / along which the other initiates and bacchi advance, glorious." Cf. also *PGurob* 25 (*OF* 578, fr. 31 Kern): ο]ἶ[ν[ο̣]ν ἔπιον ὄνος βουκόλος, "I have drunk wine, ass, shepherd"; see also Demosthenes 18.259, 19.199; Clem. Alex. *Protr.* 2.15.3, 2.21.2.

39. *PDerveni* col. VI.6-7 (*OF* 471): ἱεροι[ς] ἐπισπένδουσιν ὕ[δω]ρ καὶ γάλα, ἐξ ὧνπερ καὶ τὰς χοὰς ποιοῦσι, "They pour on the offerings water and milk, with which they do the libations, too." The libation expressed by σπένδω is followed in many instances by the ingestion of a part of the liquid that has been offered. In a Homeric expression, σπένδω means the offering to the gods made before drinking: *Il.* 9.177; *Od.* 3.342, 395; 7.184, 228; 18.427; 21.273 (αὐτὰρ ἐπεὶ σπεῖσάν τ' ἔπιόν θ' ὅσον ἤθελε θυμός, "And after imbibing and drinking as much as they felt like"); cf. *Il.* 6.258-260; 16.225-227; cf. also Casabona 1966: 232-233; Rudhardt 1958: 243-244.

40. Among the proposals about the term that precedes ἔπιον in the quoted line from the Gurob Papyrus (*PGurob* 25), Hordern (2000: 139) has suggested ο[ἶν[\ο]ν, "wine," due to the role of this drink in the rite, as is shown, for instance, in the lamellae of Pelinna: *OF* 485.6 (II.B.3 Pugliese); *OF* 486.5 (II.B.4 Pugliese): οἶνον ἔχεις εὐδ⟨α⟩ίμονα τιμη[ν], "You have wine, happy privilege"; cf. Bernabé and Jiménez San Cristóbal 2001: 117-125. Wine is undoubtedly the drink related above all with the Dionysiac mysteries. Its presence in worship, literature, and art has been recently studied by Casadio (1999a: 9-43) and Bremmer (2002: 121-122).

41. Pl. *Phd.* 69c; Plut. *Alex.* 2.9; Clem. Alex. *Protr.* 2.16.3; Procl. *In Hes. Op.* 52 (33.20 Pertusi). Moreover, a priest of Roman times has the title ναρθηκοφόρος, "thyrsus-bearer," in an inscription from Cila of the second century CE (*IGBulg.* 3.1517, p. 251ff). Cf. Bremmer 2006: 38.

42. Cf. Eur. *Ba.* 113; *Suda* s.v. νάρθηξ (3.437.2 Adler). See note 16 above.

43. Pl. *Phd.* 69c. Cf. Bernabé 2002.

44. Tannery 1901: 316-317. In an amphora discovered in Vulci, perhaps of the fourth/third century BCE, unfortunately lost but known to us thanks to a description from the 1920s (cf. Albizzatti 1921: 260; Bernabé and Jiménez San Cristóbal 2001: 59), there appeared two naked youths, crowned with ivy and each bearing a thyrsus, in an infernal context similar to the one described in the Orphic gold lamellae. The thyrsus appears as well in the iconography of some Apulian funeral vases, like the crater of the Museum of Art of Toledo (Ohio); cf. Johnston and McNiven 1996: 25-36.

45. Procl. *In Hes. Op.* 52 (33.20 Pertusi): ὡς καὶ οἱ τελούμενοι τῶι Διονύσωι δηλοῦσι ναρθηκοφοροῦντες, "As those show who, bearing the thyrsus, celebrate Dionysus."

46. Damascius *In Phd.* 1.170 (103 Westerink): καὶ γὰρ τῶι Διονύσωι προτείνουσιν αὐτὸν (*sc.* νάρθηκα) ἀντὶ τοῦ πατρικοῦ σκήπτρου, καὶ ταύτηι προκαλοῦνται αὐτὸν εἰς τὸ μερισμόν. καὶ μέντοι καὶ ναρθηκοφοροῦσιν οἱ Τιτᾶνες, "For they offer [the thyrsus] to Dionysus instead of the paternal scepter and this way they attract him toward the divided existence. And certainly the Titans also bear the thyrsus." Damascius *In Phd.* 1.170 (103 Westerink): ὁ Σωκράτης τοὺς πολλοὺς καλεῖ 'ναρθηκοφόρους' Ὀρφικῶς, ὡς ζῶντας Τιτανικῶς, "And Socrates calls the many 'thyrsus-bearers' in the Orphic way, as if they lived like the Titans." Cf. Westerink 1977: ad loc.; Bernabé 1998a: 82 and n. 164.

47. For the bibliography, see above, note 28.

48. Clement of Alexandria, for example, interprets the quotation from Plato in the light of a passage of the Gospel (*Mark* 13:20), conferring on it in this way a proverbial meaning that later enjoyed great prestige: Clem. Alex. *Strom.* 1.19.92.3,

πολλοὺς μὲν τοὺς κλητούς, ὀλίγους δὲ τοὺς ἐκλεκτοὺς αἰνιττόμενος, "Saying enigmatically that many are the called, few are the chosen"; see also Clem. Alex. *Strom.* 5.3.17.4-6; cf. also Hermias Alexandrinos *In Phdr.* 172.7-10 Couvreur; Theodoret *Graecarum Affectionum Curatio* 12.35 (430.6 Canivet).

49. Orph. *Hymn.* 42.1; cf. Ricciardelli 2000a: 400; cf. Themist. *Or.* 21.254b3 Harduin: ἀλλὰ τῶι οὐ κατὰ νόμον μεμυημένωι τὸν ναρθηκοφόρον Βάκχον ἡγεῖσθαι συγχωρεῖ τὰ μυστήρια, "But, for the not initiated, according to the rule it is possible that the thyrsus-bearing Bacchus conducts the mysteries." See also *I Peraea* 4 *Inscr. griech. st. aus Kleinasien* 38: *Die Inschriften der rhodischen Peraia*, ed. Wolfgang von Blümel, Nr. 4; cf. Bremmer 2006: 38.

50. West 1983: 159 and n. 68 (= 1993: 170). See also Henrichs 1978: 147 n. 84; Bremmer 2006: 38.

51. See Rohde 1899, 2:128 n. 6; Guthrie 1935 (1967 ed.): 194; Dodds 1944: 79 (v. 115); Bernabé 1998a: 82 and n. 164; Jiménez San Cristóbal 2005: 53-63.

52. See also Pl. *Rep.* 366a; cf. Dieterich [1893] 1913: 73; Rohde 1899, 2:279 and n. 1; Montégu 1959: 86; Graf 1974: 100 and n. 30.

53. Bianchi 1975: 230.

54. See above, note 48.

55. Olympiodorius *In Phd.* 7.10 (115 Westerink): καὶ ναρθηκοφόροι μέν, οὐ μὴν Βάκχοι, οἱ πολιτικοὶ φιλόσοφοι, ναρθηκοφόροι δὲ Βάκχοι οἱ καθαρτικοί, "The thyrsus-bearers that are not bacchi are the political philosophers, while the thyrsus-bearing bacchi are the purified ones"; Olympiodorius *In Phd.* 8.7 (123 Westerink): ναρθηκοφόρους οὐ μὴν Βάκχους τοὺς πολιτικοὺς καλῶν, ναρθηκοφόρους δὲ καὶ Βάκχους τοὺς καθαρτικούς, "Calling the politicians non-bacchus thyrsus-bearers, and the purified ones, thyrsus-bearing bacchi."

56. Casadio 1990b; Bernabé 2004b. According to Festugière (1935b: 84 [= 1972: 78]), βακχεύειν in the *parodos* of the *Bacchae* (vv. 72-77), with the addition of ὁσίοις καθαρμοῖσιν, implies an idea of divine sanction (ὁσίοις), of purity (καθαρμοῖσιν), and of spirituality (ψυχάν). The need to be pure for approaching the god, pure in his own essence, is an immemorial rule in most religions.

57. Linforth 1941: 53-60; Burkert 1982: 11-12. Cf. the annotation to the passage, Schol. in Eur. *Hipp.* 954.1: βάκχευε· μεγαλαύχει τὰς μωρίας πολλῶν γραμμάτων ἐπιστάμενος. τὸ γὰρ ληφθῆναί σε σκαιὰν ἐποίησέ σου τὴν ἄσκησιν; τιμῶν καπνούς: προσποιοῦ ἔνθεος εἶναι, "Doing the bacchus: he boasts of knowing the foolishness of many books. For having been caught makes it become a terrible practice; 'honoring the smoke': this adds he is possessed by the deity."

58. Turcan 1986: 235-236.

59. Cf. Eur. *HF* 899, 1085; Palaephatus 33 (50.7 Festa; cf. Linforth 1941: 208-209; Molina 1998: 284-285, 521); Diod. Sic. 4.3.3; *AP* 6.74.6.

60. See above, note 31.

61. Cumont [1906] 1929: 197; Festugière 1935a: 392 (= 1972: 58); Jeanmaire 1951: 396; Nilsson 1957: 12.

62. In the words of Turcan (1986: 237): "Le bacchant des thiases n'est *bacchos* que pour un temps, le temps même de l'*ekstasis* qui le dépersonnalise provisoirement dans l'ivresse du vin et de la danse. Il doit sortir de soi pour devenir *bacchos*. À l'inverse, le *bacchos* orphique se réalise en réintégrant et libérant définitivement, semble-t-il, le soi divin et profond de l'âme incarnée. Il est, il se fait βεβαχχευμένος grâce à la constance d'une vie ascétique, et non pas simplement

bacchos dans l'exaltation éphémère de l'orgie. Le dionysisme n'est qu'une drogue, une technique d'évasion collective. L'orphisme est une philosophie vécue de la libération personnelle." Cf. also Turcan 1992: 224. Contra: Pailler 1995: 111-126; and Casadio in Chapter 2 here.

63. Hdt. 4.79 (*OF* 563). For the relationship between ecstasies and intoxication, cf. García Sanz 1994: 169-173.

64. Jeanmaire (1951: 58, 89) attributes the state of μανία to the possession by the god. The association of θίασος and βακχεύειν evokes, according to Festugière (1935b: 83-84 = 1972: 77-78), a state of delirium. See also Henrichs 1994: 47-51; Jaccottet 1998: 14-15.

65. Burkert 1980: 37-38.

66. Cf. Casadio 1990b: 293-294.

67. Cf. Bernabé and Jiménez San Cristóbal 2001: 222.

68. The use of the singular of τελετή and the context (for instance, the incident of the punishment with the lightning) seem to show this; cf. Turcan 1986: 229.

69. Graf 1991: 89.

70. According to Graf (1991: 89), this passage offers an example of Διόνυσος Βακχεῖος as the epiklesis of the god of the βάκχοι, the ecstatic worshipers; cf. Graf 1993: 243.

71. Μύστης is the generic term for an initiate without any reference to a particular cult, whereas the term βάκχος is more restricted to the Dionysiac environment. It is just because of the βάκχοι of the gold leaf from Hipponion that the question about the Orphic character of the lamellae has been decided; cf. Bernabé and Jiménez San Cristóbal 2001: 231-242, esp. 233.

72. Burkert 1987: 46-47.

73. The ritual sense of the sentence μύσται καὶ βάκχοι has been emphasized by Bernabé (1991: 229) in the light of a similar testimony in the *Hymn to Demeter*: *Hymn Dem.* 481-482: ὃς δ' ἀτελὴς ἱερῶν, ὅς τ' ἄμμορος, οὔ πόθ' ὁμοίων αἶσαν ἔχειν φθίμενός περ ὑπὸ ζόφωι εὐρώεντι, "But the noninitiate in the rites, the one who has not participated in them, will never have such a fate after dying under the gloomy darkness."

74. For Burkert (1975: 90-91), the μύσται καὶ βάκχοι are the initiates, and especially the ones who have really gone into ecstasy. In this sense, καί would be used in the function of adding an expression that restricts or specifies; cf. *LSJ*, s.v. καί.

75. As we read, among other passages (see above, note 7), in the lamella of Pelinna, where Dionysus is called Βάκχιος.

76. Ricciardelli 1992: 30; Bernabé and Jiménez San Cristóbal 2001: 100.

77. Damascius *In Phd.* 1.171 (105 Westerink): Ὅτι μὲν πρῶτος Βάκχος ὁ Διόνυσός ἐστιν, ἐνθουσιῶν βάσει τε καὶ ἰαχῆι, ὅ ἐστι πάσηι κινήσει, ἧς δὴ καὶ αἴτιος, ὡς ἐν Νόμοις (II.672a5-d4) ὁ δὲ τῶι Διονύσωι καθιερωθεὶς ἅτε ὁμοιωθεὶς αὐτῶι μετέχει καὶ τοῦ ὀνόματος, "Because the first Bacchus is Dionysus, possessed by the dance and the shout, i.e., by all movements of which he is the cause, according to the *Laws* (II.672a5-d4): but one who has consecrated himself to Dionysus, being similar to the god, takes part in his name as well."

78. Harrison 1903: 474; Dodds 1944: 79 (ad 115).

79. *OF* 487 (fr. 32f Kern): θεὸς ἐγένου ἐξ ἀνθρώπου, "God have you been born, from man that you were"; *OF* 488 (fr. 32c Kern): ὄλβιε καὶ μακαριστέ, θεὸς δ' ἔσηι ἀντὶ βροτοῖο, "Happy and fortunate, god you will be, from man that you were."

80. *PGurob* 25 (*OF* 578, fr. 31 Kern): ο]ἶν[ο]ν ἔπιον ὄνος βουκόλος, "I have drunk wine, ass, shepherd"; cf. Hordern 2000: 139.

81. Soph. fr. 959 Radt. Such a depiction appears as well in a crater from Thurii, cf. Kerényi 1976: fig. 114; Bérard 1976: 61-73; see also Plut. *Aetia Romana et Graeca* 299B; Ath. 35E, 38E.

82. See, for example, Alcman 7.14; Aesch. *Eum.* 25; Aristoph. *Nu.* 605; Pl. *Ion* 534a.

83. See, for example, Eur. *Ba.* 135-140, 734-758, 847-849, 977-981, 1093-1136, 1160-1164; see also the appendix of Dodds 1951: 270-282: "Maenadism in the *Bacchae*." The maenadic behavior is, indeed, specifically feminine; cf. Bremmer 1984, 1992; Dabdab Trabulsi 1990: 227; Jaccottet 1998: 14-15.

84. In a lamella from Thurii we read (*OF* 492.2, fr. 47 Kern): ΤΑΤΑΙΤΤΑΤΑΠΤΑ Ζεῦ ΙΑΤΗΤΥ ἀέρ ΣΑΠΤΑ Ἥλιε, πῦρ δὴ πάντα ΣΤΗΙΝΤΑΣΤΗΝΙΣΑΤΟΠΕ νικᾷι Μ, "Zeus, Air, Sun. Fire conquers everything." For the initiates, the cosmic power of fire is manifest in the destruction of the Titans by the purifying lightning of Zeus. Besides, in other lamellae from Thurii (*OF* 488, 489, 490, frr. 32c, d, e Kern), it is the initiate himself who is transformed by the purifying lightning of Zeus; cf. Bernabé and Jiménez San Cristóbal 2001: 148-155.

85. Cf. a lamella from Thurii, fr. 487B, 5-6 (fr. 32f Kern): χαῖρ⟨ε⟩ χαῖρε· δεξιὰν ὁδοπόρ⟨ει⟩ λειμῶνάς θ' ε} ἱεροὺς καὶ ἄλσεα Φερσεφονείας, "Hail, hail, when you take the path of the right / to the sacred prairies and groves of Persephone." Plato *Phd.* 69c.

86. According to Pugliese Carratelli (1988a: 166), those initiates (μύσται) who attain the state of perfection that allows distancing themselves permanently from the "bodily remains" are the ones who succeed in becoming βάκχοι.

87. According to Dubois (1995: 54): "Notre inscription délimitait donc l'endroit où était ensevelie l'élite des sectateurs cumains de l'orphisme."

88. Jiménez San Cristóbal 2002.

CHAPTER 4

New Contributions of Dionysiac Iconography to the History of Religions in Greece and Italy

CORNELIA ISLER-KERÉNYI

How did painters—and users—of Greek vases in the seventh and sixth centuries BCE view Dionysus? It was this question to which I intended to respond in a new history of the images of Dionysus and his followers up to the years before 500 BCE.[1] This history had to be reconstructed in the most objective and systematic way possible, by searching in the meanwhile to overcome the preconceptions of Dionysus that we all have inherited from the nineteenth and twentieth centuries.[2] Given that in the period under investigation, Greek ceramics can be dated with sufficient precision, it would not seem too hazardous to establish a connection between the history of the images and the history of religions.

It is necessary to say forthwith that the Dionysus theme is, numerically, the most important of the vase inventory. This is not surprising if it is considered that the Greek figured pottery is functionally linked to the symposium—certainly not a daily event but relatively widespread and frequent in the ancient world. In this mass of representations, the evidence of mythological deeds involving the participation of Dionysus, such as the wedding of Thetis and Peleus, the return of Hephaestus, the Gigantomachia, and the birth of Athena, are relatively few. Much more consistent are iconographic themes that cannot be attributed in an unambiguous way to the mythical sphere, but that would seem rather to refer to that of ritual: the meeting of Dionysus with a matron figure, the dance of grotesque characters and of satyrs with or without Dionysus, and the rider of the mule. Every one of these subjects constitutes its own iconographic line whose sequence can illuminate the history of the cult of Dionysus.

The Beginnings of Dionysiac Iconography

In the seventh century, the decorative inventory of pottery is dominated in all of Greece by the animal frieze. The few mythological images are found on vases of defined categories, as, for example, on the monumental Cycladic craters (the so-called Melian amphorae) or on Protoattic pottery. But already in this phase—an important observation also for the history of religion—we meet the first images of Dionysus and of the Dionysiac world: the god facing a bride,[3] the figure of a savage satyr attacking a female figure,[4] and above all—not only in Attica—the grotesque dancers whose only attribute, when it exists, is the drinking horn, and whose dance is displayed around a crater.[5]

In the first quarter of the sixth century, the general panorama of ceramic representations changes conspicuously with the introduction of new shapes, often in lesser dimension, and with an increase in the quantity of production. This innovation can be put in the context—at least at Athens, where ceramic production is particularly conspicuous—of the new political order attributed to Solon. A notable increase in the citizenry, and thus in the custom of symposia, appears to be related to this new order.[6] In this phase, again dominated by animal friezes, the Dionysiac theme remains preeminently that of the grotesque dancer found especially on Corinthian perfume vases, Attic symposium cups, and ritual vessels used in Boeotia.[7] There are also examples of satyrs attacking nymphs[8] and of the mule-rider, possibly identifiable with Hephaestus.[9]

Dionysus, Guarantor of Stability

Near or shortly after 580 BCE, we have the first reliable representation of Dionysus on some luxurious *dinoi,* of which the most complete comes most likely from an Etruscan grave.[10] (Some fragments with the same theme, however, were found at the Acropolis of Athens.) The god is depicted in an image signed by the great artist Sophilos, one of the few that also represents mythological scenes. It is not possible here to address interpretations, influenced by nineteenth-century preconceptions, of the Dionysus in this image as a marginal or minor deity.[11] I will limit myself to observations more relevant to the history of religions. The very elaborate composition of this scene relates to the fact, well attested in Homer, Aeschylus, and Pindar, that the marriage of Peleus and Thetis was intended by Zeus to avoid a cosmic revolution. A revolution would in fact have come to pass if Thetis, whose son was destined to be stronger than his father, had been impregnated by Zeus himself or his brother Poseidon. With Peleus as father, this son remained a mortal, and so no danger to the order of the cosmos. To the extent that he was the protagonist of the Trojan War, necessary because of the overpopulation of the earth, Achilles would then instead have contributed to the stability of the rule of Zeus.

In the procession of the gods who celebrate the marriage of Peleus and Thetis, Dionysus, god of the vine, appears in a central position and with a more active role than that of the other actors. Of the many deities present, he is in fact the only one represented in the act of speaking—and he is turned toward Peleus. Sophilos—and after him also the great vase painter Kleitias—therefore attributes to Dionysus a crucial role in the wedding of Thetis and Peleus: that of the guarantor of the stability of the cosmos.

Sophilos' and Kleitias' images can be dated between c. 580 and 565 BCE. Thus we find them in the years in which the reforms of Solon were put into effect. The purpose of these reforms was, as is well known, to avoid internal revolution and to guarantee the continuity and stability of the *polis*. Hence the choice of the theme of the marriage of Peleus, which also represents the benefit of making clear the centrality of a proper marriage, that is, of the *oikos*, as the basic foundation of the *polis*-system of Solon.[12]

In the second quarter of the sixth century, the panorama of Dionysiac iconography becomes more complex. The subject of the dancers remains on cups, but explicitly associated with the symposium setting. Dionysus is represented jointly with a matron figure—as on the Cycladic crater of the seventh century—on tondos of a series of these cups:[13] the allusion to matrimony is still evident here.

The crater, and then the *dinos*, remains another type of important vase of this phase, also in regard to support of the now more frequent mythological imagery. Here the figure of the satyr returns, but in two versions, one savage and one domesticated and associated with wine. I will not dwell on this theme, which is important for the history of religion but too complex for this discussion.[14] The figure of Dionysus is present in the first representations of the Gigantomachia, on the side not of the Giants but, significantly, of the Olympians. We then find him in two contexts on the famous François Vase, dated around or shortly after 570 BCE.

In the procession of the gods depicted by Kleitias, Dionysus has substantially the same role as on the *dinos* of Sophilos.[15] It is an analogous role, here also of the peace-maker of the Olympic family and thus of the guarantor of cosmic stability, which becomes attributed to the return of Hephaestus (not by chance, another tale of marriage).[16] The figure of Hephaestus, a son repudiated and then reintegrated, as well as the god of fire, with doubtful Eastern or Lemnian origins, is perfectly explained, from the point of view of the history of religion, as a mythological reflection of the system of Solon, which made possible, as is well known, the return of the exiled Athenians and promoted the development of the crafts.[17]

The Dionysiac *Thiasos*

Already on the François Vase we have a first version of the Dionysiac *thiasos*. This subject henceforth becomes increasingly more important. We fit it in monumental versions, on the famous crater of Lydos in New York,[18] and then in variations on many amphorae. The fact that the latter dramatically increase in number around 560 BCE, and that these mythological images then definitively supplant the animal frieze, is related to the demand of the Etruscan market.[19] The problem of the relationship between Athens and its western market, hitherto unduly neglected by archaeologists, is important also for the history of religions, as will be seen at the conclusion of this chapter.[20]

In the *thiasos*, the anonymous matron figure often returns with Dionysus, as we noted earlier.[21] The grotesque dancers are replaced increasingly by satyrs accompanied by their partners (who would be called not "maenads" but "nymphs," as they are explicitly identified on the François Vase[22]). Inside the *thiasos*, we often meet the mule-rider, normally anonymous but sometimes identifiable with Hephaestus. For the history of religions, it is important to note that the images of the mule-rider seem to refer rather to a ritual than to the myth of the return of Hephaestus to Olympus managed by Dionysus; it must, then, deal with a ritual of reintegration. In any case, the *thiasos*, with or without Dionysus, with or without the mule-rider, does not appear to develop only at the mythological level, but also at the human level; that is, it reflects a ritual situation.

Ritual Signs in Dionysiac Iconography

It is in the third quarter of the sixth century that Dionysiac iconography marks the most dramatic changes, plausibly related to innovations in Athenian cult practice. The most important two types of support are now the amphora and the cup. Among amphorae, the most innovative productions from the iconographic point of view are those by the Amasis Painter, an

Figure 4.1. Attic black-figured amphora by the Amasis Painter, Munich 8763. Panteon 35.4, 1977, 290 fig. 2. Courtesy Staatliche Antikensammlungen und Glyptothek.

excellent vase painter who was particularly interested in Dionysus. Here there are two innovations to keep in mind. The first pertains to the series in which Dionysus is seen in the center of a group of ephebes with the attributes of hunters or with equipment associated with the transportation of wine (Fig. 4.1). Here also, one would have to dwell on their particular iconography.[23] Obviously the representations, all anonymous, allude to an event that is not mythological but ritual, which concludes a period of time spent by the ephebes outside the city. A mythological model of their encounter with Dionysus, patron of the *polis,* could be that of Oinopion with his father, as the great contemporary of the Amasis Painter, Exekias, represents it.[24] The written information that survives is too fragmentary to know what kind of ritual and what kind of festival of the Athenian cult calendar are involved. The representations on vases, moreover, would not be descriptions of but allusions to them. In any case, we can deduce from these images that wine had an important role.[25]

The second innovation that interests us here is contained in the images of the *thiasos* by the Amasis Painter, in which not only is a role of leadership attributed to the partners of the male dancers, but ritual symbols, such as wreaths and shoots of ivy, are added. The representations say clearly that women are to introduce the dancers (and the satyrs) into the sphere of

Dionysus.²⁶ Here, too, we are in the dark as to the corresponding rituals, but we will find elements capable of clarifying the sense of these figures in contemporary productions of cups.

The *kylikes* were and remain the most important supports of the Dionysiac images. Cups with scenes of men's lives, including symposia and grotesque dances, are followed by particularly refined vases, such as Little-Master cups. The choice of figures here is greatly reduced, but one of the most frequent motifs is that of the female bust, evidently of a *hetaera*. We therefore remain in the ambience of symposia. Little-Master production continues to about 540 BCE. At this point, a type of cup entirely new in shape and decoration comes into fashion, apparently invented by Exekias: the eye-cup, the first and most celebrated of which is the one at Munich, from Vulci, with Dionysus reclining on a ship in the shade of a vine, encircled by dolphins.²⁷

Indications of Bacchic Ceremonies in Greece and Italy

Instead of dwelling on the cup of Exekias, I shall look, if only for a moment, at a contemporary *kylix* from Capua of the same shape but without eyes on the outside, the work of a great anonymous vase-painter labeled by Beazley the Kallis Painter. The decoration is absolutely unique, which has made its interpretation difficult.²⁸ On side A and side B we see only busts of Dionysus, explicitly named, and of *hetaerae,* similar to those of the Little-Master cups (Figs. 4.2–4.3). The fact that Dionysus is the protagonist of both sides indicates that we are dealing not with a singular scene but with two separate episodes, connected by a path. The attributes confirm this. On side A are branches of ivy and a drinking-horn (signs of a moment still very close to wilderness); on side B, vine-shoots and a cantharus (symbols of a civilized life).

On side B, in front of Dionysus, is a single female character explicitly called Semele, identifying her as the mother of Dionysus. Curiously, she is presented not as a matron but as a maiden. The gesture of Semele is also most unusual, without parallel in all of ancient art. It represents the goal of a Dionysiac journey and can be interpreted as gestural equivalence of the maxim, "I have seen but I do not speak." The Dionysiac journey is thus a journey of initiation. We have two pieces of evidence for this reading. First is the fact, well attested even in Homer, that Semele died before the birth of Dionysus; she has therefore retained the status and the image of a maiden. She became a mother and her status changed, in death, just as happens to the initiate. The second confirmation lies in the fact that

Figure 4.2. Cup by the Kallis Painter, Napoli Stg. 172, Side A: photograph of the museum. Courtesy Ministero per i Beni e le Attività Culturali.

Figure 4.3. Cup by the Kallis Painter, Napoli Stg. 172, Side B: CVA Napoli I pl. 22.1. Courtesy Ministero per i Beni e le Attività Culturali.

Semele was killed by lightning, as some of the famous Bacchic Mystery Leaves also say about initiates.[29] If this interpretation is plausible, we must consider the Capua cup as evidence of Bacchic mysteries with Semele as *protomystēs*.

We have, then, a piece of evidence for placing the institution of Bacchic ceremonies at Athens around or shortly after 540 BCE. In this light, the *thiasoi* by the Amasis Painter, which assign to women the role of intermediaries in the encounter between men—dancers and satyrs—and Dionysus, would be explained. The motif of the pair of eyes, standard decoration of Attic cups of these same years and lasting for two generations, would also be explained: the eye-cups signify seeing, even understanding by way of seeing, and are easily understood as a playful allusion to the mysteries. All this happens between 540 and 530 BCE, in the age of Peisistratus. We know of important innovations in the cult of Dionysus created by Peisistratus, like the procession in honor of Dionysus Eleuthereus, and like the performance of tragedies (in which the problem of seeing, which can fail to coincide with knowing, is one of the recurring themes, i.e., in the case of Euripides' Pentheus and Auge, and of Lycurgus and Oedipus).[30] To Onomacritus, active at Athens in these same years, Pausanias attributes the establishment of the Bacchic *orgia*.[31] The iconographic situation cannot but confirm the introduction of Bacchic ceremonies at Athens and, shortly after, their adoption at Capua.

There can be no doubt that the *kylix* with Semele was created at Athens, but it is well established that it comes from S. Maria Capua Vetere—the perfect state of preservation shows this—from a noble tomb of ancient Capua. The evidence here, even if from two or three generations later, comes from the so-called Lenaea *stamnoi*, some of which were found at Capua (Fig. 4.4). This, too, is a topic that would deserve a separate presentation. In this case, I limit myself to assuming the relevant dates for the history of religion, which can be deduced from research of the past thirty years.[32]

What dates are secure, or at least highly likely, for these famous *stamnoi*? It is a question of an Athenian production destined generally for export to the West, especially to Vulci and to the zones of Campania culturally bound to Vulci, namely Capua and the surrounding area.[33] The figures allude to orgiastic rites performed by women—not formal but rather domestic rites—concentrating on a temporary effigy of Dionysus and including the consumption of wine by women. An entire series of *lekythoi* in late black figure (i.e., in the fifth century), the majority found in tombs of Greece, alludes to rituals similar to those on the *stamnoi*. The archaeological evidence thus confirms the existence in the years around 500 BCE, in

Figure 4.4. Attic red-figured *stamnos* by the Villa Giulia-Painter, Rome, Villa Giulia 93: Frontisi-Ducroux 1991: 73, figs. 7–8. Courtesy Françoise Frontisi-Ducrouz.

Figure 4.5. Attic Red-figured Volute Crater from Spina, Ferrara 2897: From S. Aurigemma, Scavi di Spina I (Rome, 1960), pl. 22a. Courtesy Museo Nazionale Archeologico de Spina.

Greece as well as at Vulci and in Magna Graecia, of Dionysiac rites performed by women (even if the sporadic presence of satyrs confirms that men, too, were permitted to participate).[34] The provenance from tombs of both *stamnoi* and *lekythoi* makes it plausible that these rites would have had—or would have been able to assume—a funerary orientation.

With this I come to the final vase that contributes to the history of religions in Greece and Italy, the famous Attic volute crater of the Parthenon period, found in one of the richest tombs of Spina (the famous Etruscan harbor on the Adriatic), whose owner was an aristocrat of Vulci descent (Fig. 4.5).[35] We have here, too, the representation of an orgiastic Dionysiac dance, in which not only women but also men and children participate. A procession with a covered *liknon,* clearly an allusion to secret rites, is seen in addition to the dance. The object of the celebration is a divine couple on a throne, the iconography of which associates it more with Hades than with Dionysus. I will not dwell on earlier interpretations, which propose to identify the divine couple as Sabazius and Cybele (we know the couple's provenance is Asia Minor).[36] It is in fact not only the iconography that renders the identification unlikely, but also the Etruscan provenance of the crater and the well-known, rich tomb equipment of which it was a part. If instead we consider the archaeological dates and compare them to what we know of the reception of the Greek gods, especially Dionysus, by the Etruscans, we would be able to deduce that here we are dealing with a ceremony that is secret, Dionysiac, and funerary, Athenian in origin but adapted to the religious custom of the Etruscans.

Conclusion

What is the contribution of the history of the images of Dionysus and his followers on Greek vases to the history of religions? The first important datum is the confirmation that Dionysus pertains not—or not only—to the exterior but to the center of the *polis:* that he is a peace-maker and guarantor of continuity. This is not intended to deny the importance of Dionysiac escapes such as the symposium, official festal moments of Dionysus, and Bacchic cults. But these escapes, of limited duration and in a controlled space, were the instruments through which the *polis* managed to reconfirm its cohesion and stability.[37]

After 550 BCE, in vase-paintings, the indications of rituals for which explicit *testimonia* are lacking in the surviving ancient texts increase. One of these rituals develops, one could say, around the mule-rider: one could speak of a rite of integration for people who did not enjoy complete citizenship, whose mythological prototype was Hephaestus. Another ritual would appear to have had as protagonists the ephebes of Athens, who were readmitted to the city after staying outside of it. To less official Dionysiac rituals could be referred the many images of *thiasos* beginning around 560 BCE.

Iconography can make important contributions also to the discussion of the Bacchic mysteries. Eminent examples are the *kylix* by the Kallis Painter discovered at Capua from around 540 BCE, the ritual scenes around an effigy of Dionysus that can be dated between 490 and 420 BCE, and the crater discovered at Spina, dated between 440 and 430 BCE. It is not unlikely that precise observations of Dionysiac iconography of the fifth century will, in the future, reveal further information relating to the history of religions in Greece and Italy.

Notes

1. Isler-Kerényi 2001a.
2. Isler-Kerényi 2001b.
3. Isler-Kerényi 2001a: 35, figs. 1–2; disregarded by Carpenter 1986.
4. Isler-Kerényi 2001a: 38, fig. 7.
5. Ibid.: figs. 8–9. The connection of this dancer with the theater, i.e., with the origin of comedy, so often discussed in the past, is not in fact verifiable: see Isler-Kerényi 2007b: 77–95.
6. Ehrenberg 1965: 25; Isler-Kerényi 1993: 3ff.
7. Isler-Kerényi 2001a: 39–80.
8. Ibid.: 107, fig. 34; 108, figs. 35–36; 109, fig. 37.
9. Ibid.: 70, fig. 13.

10. Ibid.: 109ff., figs. 38–40.
11. Carpenter 1986: 126. For a more extensive analysis, see Isler-Kerényi 1997a and then 2001a: 83–87.
12. Vernant 1973; Lacey 1983: 171 and passim.
13. Isler-Kerényi 2001a: 78, fig. 27.
14. It is treated separately in a forthcoming monograph: *Civilizing Violence*.
15. Isler-Kerényi 2001a: 111, fig. 41.
16. Ibid.: fig. 42.
17. Isler-Kerényi 1993: 8–9; Isler-Kerényi 2001a: 96ff. and 225.
18. Metropolitan Museum 31.11.11; Carpenter 1989: 29 (108.5); Shapiro 1989: tab. 74c.
19. Carpenter 1986: 35.
20. But see now Reusser 2002.
21. But neither in the sixth century nor later does she bear the name of Ariadne. On this problem, see Isler-Kerényi 2001a: 122ff.
22. On the problem of the correct denomination, see Hedreen 1994: 47–54.
23. Isler-Kerényi 2001a: 131–133.
24. Ibid.: 134 and 160, fig. 75: the two protagonists are explicitly named.
25. Cf. Scheibler 1987: 68–69, 107; Bérard and Bron 1984: 126–127.
26. Isler-Kerényi 2001a: 127–129.
27. For an interpretation of this cup, see ibid.: 178–188.
28. Ibid.: 175–178.
29. Riedweg 1998: 392–393, A1, A2–3; for a critique of the Orphic interpretation of the lamellae, see now Calame 2002.
30. Isler-Kerényi 2001a: 181.
31. Pausanias 8.37.5 (cf. Isler-Kerényi 2001a: 226–227); Scarpi 2002: 376–377.
32. Isler-Kerényi 1997b: 99–101, with nn. 101–127. See also Peirce 1998.
33. We also know a *stamnos* from Kerch (Panticapaion) in the Crimea: CVA Pushkin State Museum of Fine Arts, Moscow (IV), pls. 12–13.
34. Cf. Guettel Cole 2003: 206: "Any rituals certifying completion of the ceremonies that generated these texts [= the tablets] must have been privately organized, performed in obscurity, and under no official control."
35. For an analysis, see Isler-Kerényi 2003, where I discuss the Etruscan side of the phenomenon.
36. Simon 1953: 80–85.
37. So, with different arguments, see Vernant 1990: 238; Bierl 1991: 49–54, 219–226.

CHAPTER 5

Who Are You? Mythic Narrative and Identity in the "Orphic" Gold Tablets

RADCLIFFE G. EDMONDS

I am parched with thirst and I perish.
But give me to drink from the ever-flowing spring on the right, by the
  cypress.
"Who are you? Where are you from?"
I am the son of Earth and starry Heaven.[1]

"Who are you?" ask the unnamed guardians, as the deceased begs for the water of Memory. "Where are you from?" From the discovery of the first gold lamellae in the nineteenth century to the most recent discoveries, scholars have asked much the same questions about the tablets themselves: Who are the people who chose to have these enigmatic scraps of gold foil buried with them in their graves? Where do these texts come from? How can we reconstruct the religious context of these mysterious texts?

Studies of the tablets have often sought to answer the "Who are you?" question by asking "Where are you from?"—trying to find the source of some of the elements that appear in the tablet texts in other recognizable contexts. Some scholars have concentrated on the deities involved—Mnemosyne, Persephone, or Dionysus—but all these deities appear in a variety of contexts. Since eschatology is one of the favored typologies for historians of religions, others have compared the eschatology revealed in the tablets to label them as Orphic and Bacchic, Egyptian and Pythagorean, or even Eleusinian. The texts, however, are frustratingly vague about the eschatological rewards imagined for the deceased. From Dietrich to West to the most recent study by Merkelbach,[2] scholars have sought to construct a stemma of influence that limits the use of these mythic elements to certain contexts, like errors passed down in a manuscript tradition, rather than accepting them as options within a larger mythic tradition that a poet, religious specialist, philosopher, or any other bricoleur could employ in a wide variety of contexts within Greek culture.

Whereas some editors of the tablets' texts tended to seek the Urtext behind the variants, be it an "Orphic" katabasis poem or a Pythagorean Book of the Dead, other scholars have sought the origins of the texts in ritual, trying to reconstruct a lost ritual context. Graf has examined the tablets from a ritual perspective, concluding that an initiatory context is more likely than a funerary one, and recent studies by Riedweg and Calame have examined the texts of the tablets from a semiotic or narratological perspective, trying to identify the ritual contexts in which the words might have been uttered.[3] All these approaches concentrate on discovering where the tablets' texts are from, seeking the source of the text as the answer to its identity. Rather than trying to place the scene enunciated in the tablets within a hypothetical ritual or to trace the verses back to a lost canonical text, I think it better to focus instead upon the narrative created by the verses, examining how this narrative structure can help us figure out who and what these tablets are.

I argue that analyzing the gold tablets as narratives of a journey to the underworld brings out significant contrasts with other tellings of the journey, contrasts that show what social and religious ideas were most important to the creators of the tablets. A narrative, particularly a mythic narrative that draws on a rich tradition of familiar elements and patterns, can convey more information in compact form about where a text came from and who produced it than a non-narrative text. Not only are the traditional elements evocative of associations beyond their simple meaning, but their deployment and elaboration within the structure of the narrative can also convey meaning to the audience. In contrast to gold tablets that are simply blank or contain only the name of the deceased or a dedication "To Persephone and Plouton," some of these tablets evoke a narrative; they present a piece of the story of the deceased's journey to the underworld and her encounter with the powers there.[4] The verses present a sequence of actions by a character (the deceased) who interacts with other characters in a determined temporal setting. To be sure, the story on the tablets is evocative rather than exhaustive; it presents a brief glimpse of the action rather than an elaborated whole. Nevertheless, the basic narrative sequence is clear and familiar: the deceased leaves the world of the living and journeys to the realm of the dead.

In this chapter, I analyze the relative importance of structural components of the narrative: the obstacle the deceased faces, the solution that allows her to bypass the obstacle, and the result she obtains. I also compare the selection of certain traditional mythic elements for these components to the selections made in other myths of the journey to the underworld. The results of this analysis can provide a better answer to the question "Who are you?" than any hypotheses based on the search for the origins of the text.[5] The tablets articulate the identity of the deceased as someone who stands out from the mainstream of society, marked by her special qualifications of divine lineage and religious purity. Such a concern with religious purity and the rejection of normal means of identification within human society, such as family, city, or occupation, locates the deceased within the countercultural religious currents that provided an alternative to normal *polis* religion.

A narrative "dramatizes values," showing through the course of its tale what, from the perspective of the narrator, is important or good and what is useless or bad. The dramatized values presented by a narrative can help the scholar understand the religious and social context in which the narrative was created. Both the general story patterns and the individual elements or motifs within them may carry resonances and complex associations for the tale's audience, especially a tale that is part of a mythic tradition, like the journey to the underworld. Moreover, both the selection and deployment of particular elements and the emphasis on or elaboration of certain sections of the narrative indicate the creator's ideas in the narrative. This is not to say that the tablets without narratives may not have come from precisely the same religious contexts as the ones that evoke a narrative, merely that those tablets do not provide enough information for us to tell whence they came. Even a partial narrative can convey more meaning to its audience than a label, especially when the narrative pattern is as familiar as a journey to the underworld.

A journey to the underworld is a passage from one location to another, but that does not necessarily make it a rite of passage, much less an initiation ritual. While any tale of a journey could be divided up according to van Gennep's schema of separation, liminality, and re-aggregation, his analytic tool for making sense of rituals of passage is not necessarily the one best suited for understanding a narrative.[6] The traditional elements employed may be the same, but the structure of a narrative is different from that of a ritual. To be sure, a ritual can include the recitation of a narrative, but it is unnecessary to imagine a ritual context in which a narrative is being performed and then to analyze the hypothetical ritual. To glean the information about the context that is embedded within the structure of the narrative (even if that narrative should actually happen to have been recounted during a ritual), a narrative analysis is most useful.

My analysis of these tablets considers three crucial aspects of the narratives in the tablets: the obstacle that the deceased faces in her journey to the underworld, the solution provided by the tablet that enables her to overcome or bypass the obstacle, and the result that the deceased hopes to obtain. While this strategy draws on the analysis of structural elements similar to Propp's morphemes, I suggest that a simpler division of the narrative into a complex of obstacle, solution, and result proves more fruitful than Propp's elaborate schema devised for the specifics of the Russian folktale, which Scalera McClintock has employed to analyze the tablets.[7] It should be stressed that this complex of obstacle-solution-result is not, in itself, a traditional story pattern whose meaning I am attempting to determine. Rather, the obstacle-solution-result complex serves as an analytic tool for breaking the narrative up into manageable pieces, for carving it up at the joints of the narrative action, the better to see how the creator of the narrative has constructed the story.[8] In my analysis, I shall look first at the specific choices of traditional elements the creator of the narrative has selected for each of these structural components, and then at the emphasis within the structure on one component or another. The selection of particular elements shows the specific ideas important to the creator of the tablet, whereas the choice to elaborate on certain sections while abbreviating others reflects their relative importance. As a representative example of this kind of analysis, I shall examine the particular details in the tablets A1, A2, and A3 from Thurii, although I shall make some reference to the other "Orphic" tablets as well.

The selection of a particular traditional motif to fill the slot within a structure that is itself familiar from the mythic tradition determines the focus and meaning of any given telling of a traditional tale. One vital aspect missing from Scalera McClintock's (and indeed from Propp's) morphological approach is the comparison of the particular texts with structurally similar narratives, noting the substitution of morphemes within the structure. The significance of an individual text is to be found precisely in such selection and substitution of morphemes. The choices of the obstacle the deceased must overcome, the solution that permits her to overcome that obstacle successfully, and the result she obtains, all provide information about the religious ideas of those who composed the narrative on the tablets, that is, they help answer the questions of who they were and where they were from.

In these tablets, the obstacle is always a confrontation with the goddess "Phersephoneia," the Queen of the Underworld. The deceased has an audience with the dread queen as a suppliant or petitioner seeking the favor of the ruler; the encounter is not a hostile confrontation, nor even a judgment and trial. The obstacle that challenges this traveler is not some physical barrier that literally obstructs the journey, like the river Ocean that Odysseus must cross, or even the river Styx that blocks the journey of Patroklos.[9] The deceased in these tablets is not at a loss for which path to take or in danger of losing her way in the darkness of Hades, as she is in some of the longer tablets of the B series, nor is she confronted with the crossroads that appears in some of the Platonic myths. Other barriers the traveler could face might be walls or gates that block her progress or the guardians posted at these barriers. In other stories, the guardians that bar the way range from doorkeepers or ferrymen to horrific monsters like Cerberus or Empousa.[10] By contrast, the deceased in the Thurii tablets goes straight to the ruler of the underworld herself, unchecked by any threatening watchdogs or other barriers.

The deceased arrives as a suppliant to a presumably favorable ruler, not as a prisoner coming to judgment, where the past deeds of the deceased are weighed by special judges who lay down sentences of appropriate punishment or reward.[11] Instead, like Orpheus before Persephone or like Odysseus coming as a suppliant to Arete in Phaeacia, the deceased must win the favor of the ruler of the realm in which she finds herself.[12] Thus, the obstacle is Persephone as the queen of the underworld, a goddess who in Magna Graecia appears as the supreme power in the realm of the dead, a figure with kourotrophic aspects as goddess of marriage and children, a deity who is very different from the more familiar Kore of the Eleusinian mysteries.[13]

The type of solution is, obviously, linked to the particular choice of obstacle in the narrative. To overcome the physical barriers of distance or bodies of water, some sort of magical means of crossing otherwise uncrossable distances must be supplied, be it the golden cup of the sun for Herakles or simply Odysseus' normal ship with a divinely aided wind.[14] A monstrous guardian must often be fought and conquered, whereas a doorkeeper or ferryman may be paid off or placated. If, as in the tablets, the obstacle is the need to win the favor of the goddess Persephone, heroically violent solutions appropriate to taming Cerberus will not work, and the deceased in the tablets has no need of an arduous journey to Hades, having come by the swift passage of death.[15] We may note that even Herakles is sometimes depicted as relying not on his famous strength, but on the favor with Persephone that his initiation at Eleusis brings.[16] Likewise, the deceased in the tablets relies on special qualifications to win favor with the queen of the underworld. Her solution to the obstacle is the proclamation of her identity, which fills the majority of the lines on these tablets from Thurii. The declaration of identity is similarly the most prominent feature on the Pelinna tablets and the B tablets, although the longer B tablets do include another obstacle, the choice of paths, which occupies some of the narrative.

The statement of identity, this formula of self-definition so central to the gold tablets, is composed of a number of important elements, each of which provides information for modern scholars seeking to understand the people who created the tablets. Our example of the A tablets contains claims both to ritual purity and to divine lineage, self-identifications that set the deceased in opposition to the ordinary ways of defining identity, such as familial descent and heroic action. The Pelinna tablets, however, claim only special ritual status, whereas the B tablets concentrate wholly on the claim to divine lineage.

"Pure I come from the pure," claims the deceased in tablets A1–3. Not only has the deceased herself attained purity, but she comes from a lineage that is also pure. In tablets A2 and A3, the deceased further claims to have paid the penalty for unjust deeds. This line does not, as some scholars continue to argue, refer to the supposed "original sin" of the Orphics, the murder of Dionysos Zagreus by the Titans, since this idea of "original sin" was, in fact, fabricated by turn-of-the-century scholarship in the wake of the discovery of the Thurii tablets.[17] Rather, as the ancient evidence shows, these unjust deeds could have been committed either by the deceased herself or by some of her ancestors, since the anxiety about bad things happening to good people because of unknown crimes perpetrated by one's ancestors recurs in ancient Greek thought from the tragedies of Aeschylus to the *History* of Herodotus and beyond.[18] Ritual purification could be found from a number of sources to wipe away these stains, and the deceased on the tablets claims to have successfully atoned for any misdeeds.[19]

The claim to have been struck by lightning may also be a claim to a special sacralization by the purifying bolt of Zeus. While the lightning bolt could be a punishment for wrongdoers like the Titans and Typhon, heroes such as Asclepius, Herakles, and even Semele were also punished for the unjust deeds of their mortal life and raised to divine status by the lightning strike.[20] The traditional tales of all of these heroes provide a model for those undergoing the same process of heroization, a purification through the fire of the lightning bolt, which simultaneously strip them of their mortal impurities and translate them to the realm of the immortals. Thus, the claim, on A2 and A3, to have paid the penalty for unjust deeds may be a further explanation of the claim, on all three tablets, to have been mastered by Fate and the lightning bolt.[21]

These claims—to have paid the penalty, to have been struck by lightning, and to come pure from the pure—all show a concern with purity characteristic of the religious movements that arose as a counter-culture to the mainstream *polis* life and religion.[22] The claim, then, to have come from the pure seems most likely to refer not to the actual parentage of the deceased, but to her ritual predecessors. The ritual genealogy thus replaces the *polis*-centered family lines as the efficacy of the purification becomes more important for determining one's place in the cosmos than the ordinary distinctions of gender, family, clan, or *polis*. The claim to superior status by these groups, on the grounds of the purity of their life, served to compensate for their dissatisfaction with their status within the social order.[23]

In the Thurii tablets, the deceased indeed claims genealogical connection with Persephone herself, with the race of the gods: "For I also claim that I am of your blessed race."[24] Such a claim by a mortal when addressing Persephone is unlikely to be a reference to a myth of human descent from the Titans, which indeed would be counterproductive in the situation.[25] Rather, like the claim to be a child of Earth and starry Heaven on the B tablets, it indicates that the deceased considers herself a part of the family of the gods, a member of the divine community. This kind of self-identification stakes a claim that transcends the genealogical claims of her contemporary political world; it employs the familiar mythic element of descent from some divine ancestor, not to support the prestige of an aristocratic family in the competitions within the locative order of the *polis*, but rather to recall a mythical communion of gods and mortals like that of the Hesiodic golden race.[26] The deceased in the tablet does not identify herself as so-and-so, daughter of so-and-so, that is, as a part of one of the lineages that define the places of all the ordinary people in the human world, but rather as part of a divine order that transcends the vicissitudes of mortal life.

The Thurii tablets proclaim that the deceased is pure and of the race of the gods. This concern with genealogy and identity shows the mode of protest adopted by the creators of these A tablets, a rejection to some degree of the socio-political hierarchy of the *polis* centered on the aristocratic families. The composers of the gold tablets employ the language of myth, drawing on a variety of mythical elements familiar from the tradition to communicate the important facets of the deceased's identity.[27] The solution offered to the obstacle of the confrontation with Persephone in these tablets is a self-identification composed of claims that identify the deceased as an extraordinary person, one who not only is ritually pure, but who also stands in a special relation with the gods, a relation that entitles her to status and treatment in the afterlife far beyond that of her position in the mundane world of the living.

The result, the afterlife in the underworld to which the deceased claims to be entitled, is, however, never spelled out in great detail, and the eschatological indications vary even within the Thurii tablets. Tablets A2 and A3 ask Persephone to send the deceased to the seats of the blessed, a locale where those who have been made pure and holy dwell apart from the unpurified.[28] Tablet A1, however, makes no reference to a place, but rather proclaims the apotheosis of the deceased: a god you shall be instead of a mortal. Before this transformation, the deceased claims, she has fled from the circle of wearying heavy grief to reach the desired crown and pass beneath the bosom of Persephone herself. This process could be either an escape from the grievous circle of mortal life or an escape from a cycle of reincarnations, but, in either case, the line represents a rejection of the importance of earthly life in comparison to the afterlife, whether that earthly life is envisaged as occurring once only or multiple times before the individual can escape from it.[29] The end results seem to be the desired crown and the bosom of Persephone, although the significance of the latter has been much debated. Persephone here seems to be imagined in a kourotrophic role, receiving the deceased like a newborn to her bosom, and the mysterious line, "A kid I fell into milk," may signify that the deceased is thought to suckle at the breasts of Persephone as part of her rebirth into divine status, just as Herakles suckled at the breast of Hera.[30] The tablet, in any case, does not make clear whether the deceased's welcome by Persephone into the new status of divinity is a permanent escape from the circle of grief or merely a respite. All of these eschatological motifs appear in a variety of other contexts in the mythic tradition, and the details of the results are insufficient to use the eschatology implied in the tablets to pinpoint any particular religious context, be it Pythagorean (because of the hints of reincarnation) or Eleusinian or "Orphic."

The very uncertainty of the eschatological vision in the tablets is indicative of the emphasis in the tablets on the solution rather than the result of the encounter. This focus on the solution stands in contrast to other tellings of the journey to the underworld. Particularly in a medium, gold leaf, in which every extra word included takes up space that is literally valuable, the choice to expand upon one section rather than another is significant. The structure and elaboration of the narratives themselves can convey information about the context of production, and the focus in all the tablets is not upon the obstacle the deceased faces or the result she obtains, but rather upon the solution by which she overcomes the obstacle.

Some texts elaborate the result, the heavenly pleasures or hellish torments that the traveler to the underworld experiences. While a few myths of the journey to the otherworld describe the delights awaiting the worthy, more often the gruesome tortures in store for all the wicked dominate narratives that describe the life in the afterlife.[31] Often these otherworldly torments or bliss are compensatory for the failure of justice in this world, although Plato, in particular, sometimes has more complex purposes in mind. In any case, such an emphasis on the result signals the cosmological or theological interests of the creator of the text, who wants to illustrate the nature of the cosmos and the powers that rule it by this juxtaposition of a description of the otherworld with the familiar world of the audience of the text.

Other texts focus on the obstacle, how horrific or mighty it is and how great the power or effort needed to overcome it. Description of the obstacle creates suspense in the plot of the story, building the narrative tension to be released by the hero's successful solution. With each gruesome detail about Cerberus, the question arises, will even Herakles be able to handle the beast? And then, when he does wrestle the beast down, his heroic status is even more greatly magnified. Such a telling sets the ground for a solution that involves heroic, clever, or courageous action on the part of the protagonist, an effort or activity commensurate with the magnitude of the obstacle.

By contrast, a tale that puts little emphasis on the obstacle creates no suspense about the outcome of the protagonist's confrontation with the obstacle. The conclusion to the narrative is foregone; the only point of interest is in the precise details of the solution that brought it about. The narrative evoked in the tablets focuses upon the declaration of identity, whether that self-definition is the "pure I come from the pure" of the A tablets or the "I am the child of Earth and starry Heaven" of the B series. The guardians in the B tablets are nameless and featureless, and even Persephone in the A tablets is invoked with a minimum of epithets, in contrast to other hymns and prayers. In the shorter B tablets, the obstacle is indicated only by the questions: "Who are you? Where are you from?" No suspense arises, because the whole point of the narrative is that the deceased will have no trouble overcoming the obstacle. She need do nothing beyond proclaim her identity; she is defined by her own statements, not by her actions within the plot.

Because this definition of identity is a self-definition, it highlights all the more clearly what the deceased considers important in life: not aristocratic lineage but divine lineage, not heroic action but ritual purity. The deceased need not boast of her achievements in the competitive excellences, the *aretai* by which the hero might win *kleos aphthiton*, immortal glory, in overcoming dreadful obstacles.³² She relies instead on the virtues of justice and purity to link her to immortality; these are the qualities that distinguish her from others. Moreover, it is the contrast itself, not the result of that contrast, that occupies her attention. Whereas Plato refers to those who contrast their own afterlife of everlasting drunkenness with those who will lie wretchedly in the filth,³³ the tablets make such an eschatological vision secondary to the essential contrast of identity; what will happen to the deceased in the afterlife is less important than who they are. The qualities of the deceased—ritual purity, divine lineage—are, after all, truly important, more important than the marks of status that might normally be recorded in a grave—family name, profession, etc. Of course, all these ways of defining oneself are meaningful not only after death, but during life as well, so the claim to superiority is just as valid in this life as in the next, even if the exceptional qualities are not given the recognition and reward by mainstream society that they deserve.

The observation that distinguishing herself from others, both in life and after, is of prime importance to the deceased helps us characterize the nature of the religious group that produced the tablets, even if the evidence is insufficient to allow us to specify which of the various religious cults we know about might have produced the tablets. The chorus of initiates in Euripides' *Cretans* proclaim their purity in similar ways,³⁴ and the *bebaccheumenoi* at Cumae, who claim that it is not right that any but they be buried in the cemetery, seem to have a similar emphasis on their difference from others, in contrast, for example, to what we know of ritual maenadic cult (although the fact that the woman at Pelinna was buried with a statuette of a maenad indicates the complexities involved).³⁵ If we think of Theseus' condemnation of Hippolytus in Euripides,³⁶ I think we may see a parallel case of a type who hold themselves apart from the mainstream of society, not necessarily by physical separation, but by a superior attitude and disdain for the ways of the ordinary. Like Hippolytus, they make a claim to special purity and special connections with the gods that have priority over the normal connections of family and society. Theseus associates such folk with Orpheus, and the *orphikos bios* and *orpheotelestai* are linked in our sources with extraordinary purity, out of the ordinary in either a positive or a negative sense.³⁷

An association with Orpheus indicated no specific doctrine or eschatology; rather, I would argue, it was a way for the ancient Greeks to label the extraordinary in the religious tradition, from the prestigious Eleusinian mysteries to innovative cosmologies to the itinerant charlatans who took advantage of the superstitious.³⁸ Whether or not the people who produced the gold tablets claimed any authority from Orpheus, the tablets themselves may have been seen as "Orphic" in such terms.[39] Such a label must be used with caution in modern scholarship, however, since (like the word "magic") the word "Orphic" has suffered much abuse in the past century, being used to evoke a particular set of doctrines of original sin and redemption that have little to do with ancient Greek religion and a great deal to do with the debates over the origins of Christian doctrine among historians of religions.[40] With cautionary quotes, however, the term "Orphic" may be used to indicate the nature of religious cults such as those that produced the gold tablets, groups to whom the difference between themselves and the common herd was of primary importance, who emphasized their ritual purity and special divine connections over other qualifications more valued by the mainstream society. These "Orphics," then, whatever they may have called themselves—*hoi katharoi,* the pure, or *Asterioi,* the children of Earth and starry Heaven—left traces in the narratives evoked by the gold tablets of what their most important religious ideas were.

The specific choices of obstacle, solution, and result in the mythic narrative provide information about the particular nature of the religious group that produced each tablet. The scattered hints of eschatology, however, remain secondary to the importance of self-definition, and the various types of tablet all offer different results that await the deceased. The A tablets and the Pelinna tablets all have confrontation with Persephone as the obstacle, whereas the B tablets have guardians, but the basic type of obstacle is nevertheless the same. Still, the preeminence of Persephone in the Thurii tablets stands in contrast to the important role of Dionysos Bacchios in the Pelinna tablets and to the absence of either in the B tablets. Although the solutions in the tablets are all types of self-definition, the contrast between the Pelinna tablets' focus on the ritual experience (Bacchios has set you free) and the B tablets' emphasis on the divine lineage no doubt reflects differences in the specific religious contexts that produced these different sets of tablets. The differing answers in the tablets to the question "Who are you?" posed by the underworld power can help us, as modern scholars, reconstruct who they were.

Notes

1. Gold Tablet from Crete (B4): δίψαι αὖος ἐγὼ καὶ ἀπόλλυμαι· ἀλλὰ πιέ(μ) μοι κράνας αἰειρόω ἐπι δεξιά, τῆ κυφάριζος. Τίς δ' ἐζί; · πῶ δ' ἐζί; Γᾶς υἱος ἠμι καὶ Ὠρανῶ ἀστερόεντος

2. Dieterich [1893] 1913; West 1983; Merkelbach 1999.

3. Graf 1991, 1993. Cf. Calame 1995 and Riedweg 1998.

4. In addition to the twenty tablets with sizable inscriptions, a number of other tablets have been found, either uninscribed or with a line or two containing the name of the deceased and a salutation to the powers of the underworld. Cf. the Pella tablet inscribed with the lines Φερσεφόνηι Ποσείδιππος μύστης εὐσεβής, and another that simply has the name of the deceased, Φιλοξένα. The discovery of fifteen other graves with tablets in the mouths of the deceased has been announced, but the tablets have not been published. At Aigion, three tablets have been found, inscribed Δεξίλαος μύστας Φίλων μύστας and, simply, μύστης. In Macedonian Methone, a tablet was found in the mouth of the deceased, inscribed with her name, Φυλομάγα. See Dickie 1995. Guarducci 1985b mentions another tablet found in Crete, (Πλού)τωνι καὶ Φ(ερσ)οπόνει χαίρεν. Riedweg 1998 mentions a few other tablets, some of which are silver, rather than gold. The Pherai gold tablet is a more difficult case, since some of the lines could be read as a narrative: Εἴσιθι ἱερὸν λειμῶνα· ἄποινος γὰρ ὁ μύστης, "Enter the sacred meadow; for the initiate is without penalty." The narrative elements these two lines offer, however, yield little information in comparison with the narratives evoked by the other tablets.

5. For an expanded version of this discussion, see ch. 2 of Edmonds 2004, from which I have distilled the bulk of this analysis.

6. Van Gennep 1960.

7. See Scalera McClintock 1991. Such a morphological approach seems useful, but I think that Propp's sequence itself is not necessary. Scalera McClintock's Proppian morphology is, not surprisingly, better suited to Propp's folktales than to the tablet texts. Although function D (the hero is tested or interrogated) could be seen as present in all the texts (explicitly in the B tablets, implicitly in A and P), the acquisition of a magical object (F or Z) only occurs in the B's. Moreover, the transference between kingdoms (G or R) is the final result of the tablets' narrative, instead of an instrumental step along the way. Rather than selecting a few of Propp's wonder-tale elements, one may identify more generally useful categories of elements, basic components of a tale of the journey to the underworld.

8. Cf. Plato's *Phaedrus* 265e. While Dundes' or Greimas' bipartite structures could likewise be considered analytic tools that divide the tale into the problem and the resolution of the problem (cf. the use of Greimas in Riedweg 1998), I find that separating the solution to the problem from the final result provides a more comprehensive understanding of the teller's manipulations of the mythic elements. I use the somewhat awkward term "creator of the narrative" because it is by no means certain, or even likely, that the individual who composed the verses is the same as the one who inscribed the verses on any given tablet. Moreover, in the light of the kind of scribal errors found on many of the tablets, it is quite likely that often the inscriber had no idea of the nature of the text he was inscribing. To further complicate matters, we cannot tell if the person who decided to have the text inscribed was the deceased herself or merely a helpful relative. We are left with the possibility that the deceased had no knowledge of what was put in her grave, but that some relative went to a local craftsman and asked for "one of those Orphic amulets," which the craftsman copied from a perhaps illegible template. Nevertheless, we can draw conclusions about the person who created the narrative that was eventually inscribed; and the variations between tablets, particularly in the A series, suggest that the content was significant enough that the tablets were crafted for individuals (although A3 is probably just a copy of A2).

9. The water barrier takes various forms in the Greek tradition. The river that Odysseus must cross to reach the realm of the dead is the "river" Ocean (*Od.* 10.508, 11.11-19), while in the *Iliad*, Patroklos complains that he cannot cross the river Styx until his body is buried:

θάπτέ με ὅττι τάχιστα πύλας Ἀΐδαο περήσω.
τῆλέ με εἴργουσι ψυχαὶ εἴδωλα καμόντων, οὐδέ μέ πω μίσγεσθαι ὑπὲρ ποταμοῖο
  ἐῶσιν,
ἀλλ' αὔτως ἀλάλημαι ἀν' εὐρυπυλὲς Ἄϊδος δῶ.
καί μοι δὸς τὴν χεῖρ· ὀλοφύρομαι, οὐ γὰρ ετ' αὖτις
νίσσομαι ἐξ Ἀΐδαο, ἐπήν με πυρὸς λελάχητε. *Il.* 23.70-76 (trans. Lattimore)

Bury me as quickly as may be, let me pass through the gates of Hades. The souls, the images of dead men, hold me at a distance, and will not let me cross the river and mingle among them, but I wander as I am by Hades' house of the wide gates. And I call upon you in sorrow, give me your hand; no longer shall I come back from death, once you give me my rite of burning.

In *Iliad* 8.369, Athena mentions how she helped Herakles cross the river Styx to get the hellhound.

10. As early as Hesiod, dangerous guardians appear at the gates of the house of Hades:

... ἀμήχανον, οὔ τι φατειόν
Κέρβερον ὠμηστήν, Ἀίδεω κύνα χαλκεόφωνον,
πεντηκοντακέφαλον, ἀναιδέα τε
κρατερόν τε. ...
... δεινὸς δὲ κύων προπάροιθε φυλάσσει
νηλειής, τέχνην δὲ κακὴν ἔχει· ἐς μὲν ἰόντας
σαίνει ὁμῶς οὐρῇ τε καὶ οὔασιν ἀμφοτέροισιν,
ἐξελθεῖν δ' οὐκ αὖτις ἐᾷ πάλιν, ἀλλὰ δοκεύων
ἐσθίει, ὅν κε λάβῃσι πυλέων ἔκτοσθεν ἰόντα
ἰφθίμου τ' Ἀίδεω καὶ ἐπαινῆς Περσεφονείης. (*Theog.* 310-312, 769-774)

A monster not to be overcome and that may not be described, Cerberus who eats raw flesh, the brazen-voiced hound of Hades, fifty-headed, relentless and strong. ... A fearful hound guards the house in front, pitiless, and he has a cruel trick. On those who go in he fawns with his tail and both his ears, but suffers them not to go back out again, but keeps watch and devours whomever he catches going out of the gates of strong Hades and awful Persephone.

The monstrous figure of Cerberus, three-headed watchdog of Hades, appears regularly in the Apulian vase underworld scenes. Cf. Empousa (whose very name signals her impeding role) in Aristophanes *Frogs* 289-304, or the gorgon that Odysseus fears in Homer's Nekyia, *Od.* 11.633-635.

11. The first references to the actual process of judgment come in Pindar's second *Olympian,* where the "wicked souls straightaway pay the penalty and some judge beneath the earth judges the crimes committed in this realm of Zeus, having

delivered the strict account in accord with the harsh order of things" (αὐτικ' ἀπάλαμνοι φρένες ποινὰς ἔτεισαν, τὰ δ' ἐν τᾷδε Διὸς ἀρχᾷ ἀλιτρὰ κατὰ γᾶς δικάζει τις ἐχθρᾷ λόγον φράσαις ἀνάγκᾳ; Pindar O. 2.57-60). Although the judge is unspecified in Pindar, Aeschylus makes Hades the judge of mortals when they come to his realm: "Hades calls men to reckoning there under the ground" (μέγας γὰρ Ἅιδης ἐστὶν εὔθυνος βροτῶν ἔνερθε χθονός; *Eum.* 273-274). In the *Suppliants*, this judge is referred to as κἀκεῖ δικάζει τ' ἀμπλακήμαθ', ὡς λόγος, Ζεὺς ἄλλος ἐν καμοῦσιν ὑστάτας δίκας, "Another Zeus among the dead [who] works out their final punishment" (*Supp.* 230-231; all translations by Lattimore). Although facing the judges plays a small part of the soul's journey to the underworld in the *Phaedo* (107d-114d) and the *Republic* (614b-621d), Plato elaborates the description of judges in the *Gorgias* myth (523a-527a).

12. Orpheus: Eur. *Alcestis* 357-362; Moschos *Lament for Bion* 3.123-124; Odysseus comes as a suppliant to Arete, *Od.* 7.146-152; cf. 53-77:

Ἀρήτη, θύγατερ Ῥηξήνορος ἀντιθέοιο,
σόν τε πόσιν σά τε γούναθ' ἱκάνω πολλὰ μογήσας
τούσδε τε δαιτυμόνας· τοῖσιν θεοὶ ὄλβια δοῖεν
ζωέμεναι, καὶ παισὶν ἐπιτρέψειεν ἕκαστος
κτήματ' ἐνὶ μεγάροισι γέρας θ', ὅ τι δῆμος ἔδωκεν·
αὐτὰρ ἐμοὶ πομπὴν ὀτρύνετε πατρίδ' ἱκέσθαι
θᾶσσον, ἐπεὶ δὴ δηθὰ φίλων ἄπο πήματα πάσχω.

"Queen Arete," he exclaimed, "daughter of great Rhexenor, in my distress I humbly pray you, as also your husband and these your guests (whom may heaven prosper with long life and happiness, and may they leave their possessions to their children, and all the honors conferred upon them by the state), to help me home to my own country as soon as possible; for I have been long in trouble and away from my friends."

13. As Sourvinou-Inwood notes, "Persephone's personality at Locri includes some of the aspects which characterize her Panhellenic personality, but without the close association with Demeter. Moreover, it contains some other functions not associated with her elsewhere: she presided over the world of women, with special reference to the protection of marriage and the rearing of children, that is of those female activities that were most important for the life of the polis" (Sourvinou-Inwood 1991: 145-188, 180). Cf. T. Price (1978: 172), who sees the *pinakes* with Persephone and an infant in a basket as dedications by mothers for Persephone's protection of their children. Cf. also Musti (1984: 71-72) on the relations between the Panhellenic aspects of Persephone and her personae at Eleusis and in Magna Graecia: "Abbiamo insomma nell' insieme *1) un complesso di credenze sull'oltretomba; 2) aspetti di religiosità agraria; 3) motivi ierogamici*, tutti presenti in questa 'massa' di nozioni e rappresentazione religiose; questa 'massa' assume tuttavia un'assialità diversa nei diversi luoghi, per ciò che attiene al contenuto ed alla funzione stessa dell'espressione religiosa. Ad Eleusi prevalgono in definitiva gli aspetti della religiosità agraria, accanto ad esigenze di purificazione individuale attinenti a speranze ultraterrene (1-2); a Locri prevale Persefone (ce l'ha ribadito, da un lato, ed anche approfondito, dall'altro, Torelli nella sua rela-

zione al convegno 1976 su Locri) e l'aspetto della ierogamia, fortemente simbolico dell'istituto storico e sociale del matrimonio locale (1-3); nei testi orfici prevale la prospettiva dell'oltretomba (1)."

14. Herakles, not being the sailor that Odysseus is, crosses the Ocean to the otherworld of Geryon by commandeering the golden cup of the sun (Stesichorus 185 *PMG;* Pherecydes *FGrH* 1.18; cf. Athenaeus 11.469e, 470c, 781d; Eustathius *Od.* 1632.23).

15. Cf. Elpenor's journey, swifter than Odysseus' ship in *Od.* 11.57-58. In Aristophanes' *Frogs,* Dionysos and Herakles joke about routes to the underworld. Herakles and Dionysos play with the descriptions of methods of self-slaughter, using different metaphors of travel (117-135). Thus, the way of hanging is stifling (πνιγηράν); taking hemlock—ground by mortar and pestle—is a well-beaten shortcut (ἀτραπὸς ξύντομος τετριμμένη), but too cold and numbing (ψυχράν γε καὶ δυσχείμερον); while jumping off a building is a short, quick, downhill path (ταχεῖαν καὶ κατάντη). All these suggested routes are rejected by Dionysos, who wants a path neither too warm nor too cold (μήτε θερμὴν μητ' ἄγαν ψυχράν), but the traditional journey that Herakles took.

16. Herakles' journey is alluded to in many sources, beginning with Homer, but the earliest full telling that survives is not found until Apollodorus 2.5.12; cf. *Il.* 8.367-368; *Od.* 11.623-626; Bacch. 5.56-70; Eur. *HF* 23, 1277; Pindar fr. 249a OS-M; Pausanias 2.31.6, 2.35.10, 3.18.13, 3.25.5, 5.26.7, 9.34.5; Diod. Sic. 4.25.1, 4.26.1. Cerberus is Herakles' objective in his journey to the halls of Hades, and, in many versions, Herakles must fight to get the dog. The *Iliad's* references (5.395ff.) to the fight at the gates of Hades, in which Herakles wounds Hades himself, allude to this episode, as do a number of vase illustrations showing conflict between Herakles and Hades and/or Cerberus (*LIMC,* s.v. Herakles 2553, 2559, 2566, 2567, 2570, 2581-2582, 2584, 2586, 2605, 2608). In some versions, Herakles undergoes initiation in the Eleusinian mysteries before he descends, and Herakles' mention in Euripides' *Herakles* (610ff.) implies that his task was aided by his initiation. (Cf. Plut. *Thes.* 33; Diod. Sic. 4.14.4, 4.25ff.; Schol. on Aristoph. *Plutus* 845; Apollodorus 2.5, 12. According to the pseudo-Platonic *Axiochus* [371e], both Dionysos and Herakles were initiated before their descents.) Boardman (1975: 3-10) suggests that the shift in the mode of telling is due to the introduction of Herakles as the archetypal initiate at Eleusis in the Lesser Mysteries and lists a number of vase illustrations (cf. *LIMC,* s.v Herakles 2554-2558, 2562, 2574, 2592, 2599, 2600, 2602, 2607).

17. See the arguments in Edmonds 1999 and 2008b for a full discussion.

18. Solon assures the wicked that even if they do not pay for their crimes in their lifetime, their descendants will pay (ἀναίτιοι ἔργα τίνουσιν ἢ παῖδες τούτων ἢ γένος ἐξοπίσω, fr. 1.31). While the affliction of an entire family line for such crimes as murder and perjury goes back to Homer and Hesiod, the tales of the punishment of an entire family as retribution for the murder of a family member, incest, or cannibalism become a favorite subject in tragedy: Solon fr. 1.31, cf. esp. 25-35. For hereditary punishment of perjury, see *Il.* 4.160-162, cf. 3.300ff.; Hesiod *WD* 282-285. For affliction of whole families, see *Il.* 6.200-205; *Od.* 20.66-78; cf. *Od.* 11.436. In tragedy, see Aesch. *Sept.* 653-655, 699-701, 720-791; *Ag.* 1090-1097, 1186-1197, 1309, 1338-1342, 1460, 1468-1488, 1497-1512, 1565-1576, 1600-1602; Soph. *El.* 504-515; *Ant.* 583-603; *OC* 367-370, 964-965, 1299; Eur.

El. 699-746, 1306ff.; *IT* 186-202, 987-988; *Or.* 811-818, 985-1012, 1546-1548; *Phoen.* 379-382, 867-888, 1556-1559, 1592-1594, 1611. See further Parker 1983: 191-206. Some of these crimes, such as oathbreaking and wronging a guest-friend or a parent, were depicted in the tradition as bringing forth Erinyes upon the wrongdoer, to torment him in life or after death (cf., e.g., Aesch. *Eum.* 269-275; Homer *Il.* 19.259). Nor is the family curse, as a result of which each member must pay for the misdeed of an ancestor, confined to tragedy; this mythical idea was employed in practical politics as well. The prominent Athenian noble family of the Alcmaeonids, which boasted such members as Cleisthenes and Pericles, contended constantly with their political enemies about the stain that the murder of Cylon had left upon their family (cf. Hdt. 5.70-72; Thuc. 1.126-127).

19. Along with the idea of paying for an ancestor's crimes naturally comes the idea of somehow evading the penalty. Herodotus' myth of the fall of Croesus (Hdt. 1.90-91) is fascinating in this regard: Croesus is doomed to fall, despite his many sacrifices to Apollo, because his ancestor Gyges murdered King Candaules and took his throne and his wife. When Croesus rebukes Apollo for ingratitude, Apollo informs him that his sacrifices were not ignored, but rather procured for him a three-year delay of the inevitable downfall. The Orpheotelests described in Plato's *Republic* seem to have promised more complete results from the sacrifices they advised, and, in the *Phaedrus,* Plato mentions Dionysiac purifications as bringing relief to those suffering under the burdens of the crimes of their ancestors (*Rep.* 364e-365a; *Phaedrus* 254de, 265b). Damascius refers to the role of Dionysos Lusios and his rites in freeing an individual from the penalty of crimes committed by ancestors (*OF* 232). Plato's Orpheotelests and the practices of Theophrastus' Superstitious Man indicate that individuals and whole cities tried to relieve their anxieties about the misdeeds of their forebears (Theophr. *Char.* 16.12).

20. As Rohde states in his appendix, "Consecration of Persons Struck by Lightning" (1925: 581-582), "In many legends death by *lightning* makes the victim holy and raises him to godlike (everlasting) life." Herakles: Diod. Sic. 4.38.4-5. Semele: Pind. *O.* 2.27; Diod. Sic. 5.52.2; Charax ap. Anon. *de Incred.* 16, p. 325.5ff West; Arist. 1.47D ind.; Philostr. *Imag.* 1.14; Nonnus *Dion.* 8.409ff. Asclepius: Hesiod fr. 109 Rz.; Lucian *DD* 13. Cf. also figures such as Erectheus, Kapaneus, and Amphiaraus. The sacralizing effect of lightning may be seen from later testimonies in the reverence for the lightning-struck tombs of Lycurgus and Euripides in Plut. *Lyc.* 31 and Pliny's report that the thunderbolting of the statues of Olympic victor Euthymos indicated his heroic status (*NH* 7.152). Although Kingsley (1995: 257 n. 21) indeed suggests that Herakles was *the* figure to whom the deceased in the Thurii tablets was assimilated, as Seaford (1986) and others have argued with regard to the Titans, I would rather argue that Herakles, Semele, Asclepius, and others served more as analogies for the individual than as a specific model.

21. Cf. Graf (1991: 96) and Zuntz (1971: 336), who see the claim on A2 and A3 to have paid the penalty as representing a different level of incarnation than that of A1, which proclaims the deceased's transformation into a god. This claim is itself sufficient evidence for the idea that the result expected in A1 differs from that expected in A2 and A3, and I'm not sure that the claim to have paid the penalty necessarily supports it.

22. Cf. Redfield 1991: 107b: "Thus is projected on a cosmic scale the Orphic withdrawal from society; religion is not intended to show us our location in the

social order, but rather to rescue us from it. The alternative to mediation is salvation.... A claim to personal immortality is a political act; it is a claim to personal value as against the evaluations of this world, and as such sets one against the powers of this world." Purification rituals that had formerly been performed only in abnormal moments of crisis became a normal practice for those who defined their lives outside the normal order of the society. Cf. Sabbatucci 1979: 68: "La catarsi orfica potrebbe non voler risolvere una crisi occasionale, ma risolvere piuttosto la crisi esistenziale; non purificare da una follia episodica, ma purificare dal vivere profano, inteso come una lunga follia, eccetera eccetera.... Onde la catarsi diventerebbe propriamente una iniziazione alla nuova vita, l'*orphikos bios*." Burkert (1982) has shown the distinction between the craftsmen who were brought in as specialists in time of crisis and the members of the religious sect, who routinized the practices of the specialists in their protests against the normal order. It is of course impossible to tell if those buried with the tablets were themselves members of a group that lived such an *orphikos bios* or merely were buried with an amulet indicative of such a worldview.

23. Such dissatisfaction need not be that of lower-class or disenfranchised members of a society; indeed, it seems more likely, considering the historical parallels, to imagine that the resentful are members of the elite who are losing in competition with their peers. As J. Z. Smith notes in his discussion of magic (Smith 1996: 19), *ressentiment* of any kind triggers the language of alterity, whether it be accusations of witchcraft or claims to arcane power. "Any form of *ressentiment*, for real or imagined reasons . . . , *may* trigger a language of alienating displacement of which the accusation of magic is *just one possibility* in any given culture's rich vocabulary of alterity."

24. As Depew notes of εὔχομαι (1997: 232): "The verb denotes an interactive process of guiding another in assessing one's status and thus one's due. The purpose is not to 'boast' or 'declare' something about one's past, but to make a claim on someone in the present, whether in terms of an actual request or of recognition and acknowledgement of status." Depew, drawing on the researches of Adkins and Muellner, describes the epic uses of the verb. "When Homeric heroes εὔχονται, what they are doing is asserting their identity and their value in the society they inhabit, and by means of this assertion creating a context in which the claim they are making on another member of that society will be appropriate and compelling." Cf. Adkins 1969; Muellner 1976.

25. Cf. the arguments of Zuntz 1971: 321, which have never been refuted. Unfortunately, just as Comparetti immediately associated the line ποινὰν δ' ἀνταπέτεισ' ἔργων ἔνεκ' οὔτι δικαίων in A2 and A3 with the murder of Zagreus by the Titans, so, too, he linked Γῆς παῖς εἰμι καὶ Οὐρανοῦ ἀστερόεντος to his story of the supposed Orphic doctrine of original sin (Comparetti 1882: 116): "The Titanic origin of the soul is here explicitly confirmed; it is well known that the Titans were the sons of Uranos and Gaea." Before Comparetti, the only discovered tablet of the B series, B1 from Petelia, was thought to be associated with the Trophonius oracle, and Mnemosyne, not the deceased, was thought to be the child of Earth and starry Heaven, as indeed she is in Hesiod (*Theog.* 135). Cf. Goettling 1843: 8. Since Comparetti's time, however, the increase in the number of tablets that make no reference to lightning or paying a penalty (twelve new tablets) seems to indicate that the death by lightning is a unique feature of the context that produced

the tablets of Timpone Piccolo, rather than a feature of the doctrine underlying all the tablets but simply abbreviated out of B1, which happened to have an explicit identification of the Titans in the reference to the child of Earth and starry Heaven. A1, A2, and A3 are the only tablets that make any reference to lightning, and only A2 and A3 mention a punishment for unjust deeds.

26. At *WD* 120, Hesiod's golden race live blissful lives, "dear to the blessed gods," before the split with the gods: φίλοι μακάρεσσι θεοῖσιν. The claim to be treated as a member of the divine family recalls as well the ideal of the time before the separation of mortals and immortals: "For there once were common feasts and councils of immortal gods and mortal men together," ξυναὶ γὰρ τότε δαῖτες ἔσαν, ξυνοὶ δὲ θόωκοι ἀθανάτοισι θεοῖσι καταθνητοῖς τ' ἀνθρώποις (*Eoiae* fr. 1.6-7 Merkelbach-West; *Theog.* 535ff.). Cf. also the feasting of Tantalus and Ixion with the gods for other tales of the disruption of primordial unity. The deceased employs this mythic motif in a claim of descent that supplants the ties of the human, mundane, and civic *genos* with those of a divine, otherworldly, and primordial *genos*. Sabbatucci describes the claim to be part of the divine *genos* that descends from Earth and Heaven as a way of rejecting the political hierarchy that depends on the human families (1975: 44-55): "Il fatto che il defunto si proclami 'figlio di Urano e di Gaia,' se non stabilisce la realtà storica contestuale di una identificazione del 'genetico' col 'mondano,' è probativa soltanto della rinuncia da parte del defunto al *genos* determinato dai suoi genitori reali." As Sabbatucci explains the mystic's point of view, the human condition is unreal in comparison with the reality represented by the divine condition, because the life of a human is ephemeral, while that of a god is eternal. The *genos*, however, represents a human reality that transcends the brief mortal lifespan and provides a permanent framework within which the individual can define herself for the entirety of her life. If, however, one rejects this framework and the hierarchies into which it is tied, the divine *genos* and the ideal world of the gods provide a substitute framework within which the individual can define herself.

27. The resonance of each of these elements is lost if they are all read as referring to a single myth of original sin inherited from the Titans, especially since this myth was not created until more than two millennia after the tablets were composed. See Edmonds 1999.

28. It is tempting, given the prominence of lightning in these particular tablets, to speculate that the seats of the blessed here may be the Elysian Field, since some commentators drew the connection between the Elysian Field, Ἠλύσιον πεδίον, and a field that had been struck by lightning, ἐνηλύσιον πεδίον. Cf. Burkert 1961. Hesychius, for example, defines ἠλύσιον: Elysion—a land or plain that has been struck by lightning. Such places are not to be walked upon, and are called ἐνηλύσια. κεκεραυνωμένον χωρίον ἢ πεδίον· τὰ δὲ τοιαῦτά εἰσιν ἄβατα, καλεῖται δὲ καὶ ἐνηλύσια. Puhvel (1969), however, argues that the association with lightning is a late etymologizing upon a word that originally meant "meadowy field." Cf. also Gelinne 1988: 227-229.

29. This circle has most often been interpreted as a cycle of rebirths undergone by the soul in the process of metempsychosis, but it may also be seen as a term for the burdens of a single lifetime. Casadio has no doubts (1991: 135): "Che nella laminetta più lunga e meglio conservata delle tre proveniente dal 'Timpone piccolo' sia fatto espresso accenno al dogma della metempsicosi nessuno l'ha mai du-

bitato." Aristotle uses the phrase κύκλος τὰ ἀνθρώπινα πράγματα to refer to human life rather than to transmigration (*Phys.* 4.14.223b24; *Prob.* 17.3.916a28). Cf. Herodotus 1.107.2, simply meaning the affairs of human life in its cyclical patterns. On this interpretation, the deceased has escaped from the toils and trammels of mortal life and looks forward to a blissful and apparently endless afterlife. However, the Neoplatonists Simplicius and Proclus, in discussing the cycle of births, κύκλος γενέσεως, attribute to Orpheus a prayer in the rites of Dionysus and Kore for relief from the cycle of evils: ἧς καὶ οἱ παρ' Ὀρφεῖ τῷ Διονύσῳ καὶ τῇ Κόρῃ τελούμενοι τυχεῖν εὔχονται· Κύκλου τ' αὖ λῆξαι καὶ ἀναπνεῦσαι κακότητος (Proclus in Pl. *Tim.* 42cd, v. 330 = *OF* 229; cf. *OF* 230 = Simplicius in Arist. *De Caelo* 2.1). The debate over the presence of reincarnation is beyond the scope of this paper, but the fundamental discussions are Long 1948; Zuntz 1971; and Casadio 1991. For further discussion, see Edmonds 2004.

30. Kingsley argues that these images should be taken as referring to the deceased going to suckle at the breasts of Persephone (1995: 267-268): "The individual in question makes straight for the breasts of Persephone, queen of the underworld, just like an infant to the breast of its nurse or mother. Ultimately, only prejudice and preconception can justify failing to see in this and the other statements on the gold plates the use of a consistent, coherent, and starkly simple imagery: a new birth, making straight for the maternal breast, rushing for milk." The prejudice and preconception to which Kingsley refers is, of course, that of Zuntz, who reacted with outrage to the suggestion of Dieterich, "Lepidissime sane dicitur et haedulum nunc domum rediisse ad matris lactea ubera et Dionysi ministrum et mystam, nunc et ipsum deum, qui ὑπὸ κόλπον ἔδυ Φερσεφονείας, adiisse ad beatae vitae prata lactea" (Dieterich 1891: 37). Despite his own suggestion that the imagery is that of an infant and mother, Zuntz rejects Dieterich's suggestion, most probably because Dieterich included the identification of the deceased with Dionysus as a kid, an "Orphic" idea intolerable to Zuntz's interpretation of the tablets as purely Pythagorean: "The speaker is standing before the chthonian Goddess. Is he, the *renatus*, rushing to suck the milk of immortality from her *lactea ubera*? This idea, though quite proper with Egyptian devotees of Isis, makes him shudder who has the slightest notion of Persephone, the goddess of the dead" (Zuntz 1971: 324). Suckled like a newborn infant, the deceased is, in effect, transformed into or adopted as the child of Persephone. This interpretation gains credence with the parallel of the adoption of Herakles by Hera, which is sometimes depicted, especially in Etruscan and South Italian art, as a ritual suckling. Cf. Pausanias 9.25.2; Diod. Sic. 4.9.6-7. Jourdain-Annequin notes that this scene has been "accepté par les historiens comme le symbole de l'adoption d' Héraclès par la déesse . . . le symbole de la 'renaissance' du héros, renaissance à un monde différent: celui des dieux auxquel il accède grâce à cette Mère divine" (Jourdain-Annequin 1989: 400). Not only does the ritual suckling signify Herakles' adoption by his stepmother, Hera, but the adoption into the family of the goddess itself signifies Herakles' apotheosis. Just as with the motif of lightning as a mode of apotheosis, we may have here a motif used in the story of the apotheosis of Herakles used to describe the fate of the deceased in the tablets. As with the lightning, this mythic reference need not imply Herakles as an explicit model, but rather that the traditional mythic motif of being suckled by a goddess signified the process of apotheosis, particularly in southern Italy, and that the story of Herakles was one of the most prominent appearances of

this idea in the mythic tradition. Δεσποίνας δ' ὑπὸ κόλπον ἔδυν χθονίας βασίλειας may signify, in the language of myth, the process by which the deceased, newly born into a different life, is adopted as Persephone's own and transformed from mortal to immortal, θεὸς δ' ἔσηι ἀντὶ βροτοῖο. Ultimately, one must conclude with Guthrie, "Ancient sources provide no parallels which will throw a direct light on this, and the opinions of scholars make rather amusing reading" (Guthrie 1935 [1952 ed.]: 178).

31. In a fragment of a dirge, Pindar describes the blissful afterlife of those in the Isles, including their recreations (Pind. fr. 130; cf. Pind. O. 2.71-77). Plato's *Phaedo* describes the heavenly realm for pure spirits (111b1-c1). A few of the souls headed for realms above go beyond the surface of the earth into indescribable realms of purity and dwell there entirely freed from bodies (114c2-6). This realm, like the realm above the heavens in the *Phaedrus*, is so far beyond mortal experience that "of that place beyond the heavens none of our earthly poets has sung, and none shall sing worthily" (τὸν δὲ ὑπερουράνιον τόπον οὔτε τις ὕμνησέ πω τῶν τῇδε ποιητὴς οὔτε ποτὲ ὑμνήσει κατ' ἀξίαν, *Phaedrus* 247c2-3). By contrast, the impure must suffer in rivers of fire and mud (*Phd*. 111d4-e2, cf. 112e-113c). Plutarch's imagery is even more vivid.

32. Cf. Adkins 1960 on the shift of values from competitive to cooperative excellences. In the mythic tradition, the first people to receive a blissful afterlife were those who had achieved mighty deeds. The heroes of Hesiod's semi-divine fourth race go to the Isles of the Blessed as a result of their valiant deeds in the battles of epic (*WD* 167ff.). While Hesiod speaks in general terms, later authors named specific heroes worthy of an afterlife on the Blessed Isles. Not surprisingly, the two greatest Greek heroes of the *Iliad*, Achilles and Diomedes, are the earliest to be named (cf. Ibycus 291 = Simonides 558), where the scholiast records that, in Ibycus and Simonides, Achilles goes to Elysium and is paired with Medea (of all people). Cf. Pindar (*Nem*. 10.7), who mentions Diomedes, and Hellanikos (4F19), who puts the otherwise unknown Lykos, son of Poseidon, on the Blessed Isles. But heroic deeds worthy of a favorable afterlife need not be deeds of epic; a sixth-century drinking-song places Harmodios in the company of Diomedes and Achilles on the Blessed Isles: "Dear Harmodios, surely you have not perished. No, they say, you live in the blessed islands where Achilles the swift of foot, and Tydeus' son, Diomedes, are said to have gone" (φίλταθ' Ἁρμόδι', οὔ τί που τέθνηκας, νήσοις δ' ἐν μακάρων σέ φασιν εἶναι, ἵνα περ ποδώκης Ἀχιλεὺς Τυδείδην τέ φασιν Διομήδεα, *Carm. Conv.* 894 = Diehl 10 = Lattimore 1 (trans. Lattimore). The assassination of Hipparchus ranked, at least for some, with the epic heroism of Diomedes and Achilles, and such heroic deeds sufficed for admission to a better place after the mortal life was over.

33. In the *Republic*, Adeimantus refers to this symposium of the blessed, συμπόσιον τῶν ὁσίων, as the promise of eternal drunkenness held out by Musaeus and his son, "where, reclined on couches and crowned with wreaths, they entertain the time henceforth with wine, as if the fairest mead of virtue were an everlasting drunk" (εἰς Ἅιδου γὰρ ἀγαγόντες τῷ λόγῳ καὶ κατακλίναντες καὶ συμπόσιον τῶν ὁσίων κατασκευάσαντες ἐστεφανωμένους ποιοῦσιν τὸν ἅπαντα χρόνον ἤδη διάγειν μεθύοντας, ἡγησάμενοι κάλλιστον ἀρετῆς μισθὸν μέθην αἰώνιον, Pl. *Rep*. 363c4-d2).

34. Eur. *Cret*. fr. 472 = Porph. *De abst*. 4.56: Φοινικογενοῦς παῖ τῆς Τυρίας

τέκνον Εὐρώπης καὶ τοῦ μεγάλου / Ζηνός, ἀνάσσων Κρήτης ἑκατομπτολιέθρου· ἥκω ζαθέους ναοὺς προλιπών, οὓς αὐθιγενὴς τμηθεῖσα δοκὸς στεγανοὺς / παρέχει Χαλύβῳ πελέκει καὶ ταυροδέτῳ κόλλῃ κραθεῖσ' ἀτρεκεῖς ἁρμοὺς κυπαρίσσου. ἁγνὸν δὲ βίον τείνων ἐξ οὗ Διὸς / Ἰδαίου μύστης γενόμην, καὶ νυκτιπόλου Ζαγρέως βροντὰς τοὺς ὠμοφάγους δαίτας τελέσας μητρί τ' ὀρείῳ δᾷδας ἀνασχὼν / καὶ κουρήτων βάκχος ἐκλήθην ὁσιωθείς. πάλλευκα δ' ἔχων εἵματα φεύγω γένεσίν τε βροτῶν καὶ νεκροθήκης οὐ / χριμπτόμενος τήν τ' ἐμψύχων βρῶσιν ἐδεστῶν πεφύλαγμαι. ("Son of the Phoenician princess, child of Tyrian Europa and great Zeus, ruler over hundred-fortressed Crete—here am I, come from the sanctity of temples roofed with cut beam of our native wood, its true joints of cypress welded together with Chalybean axe and cement from the bull. Pure has my life been since the day when I became an initiate of Idaean Zeus and performed the (ritual) thunders of night-wandering Zagreus, and having accomplished the raw feasts and held torches aloft to the Mountain Mother, yea torches of the Kuretes, was raised to the holy estate and called Bakchos. Having all-white garments, I flee the birth of mortals and, not nearing the place of corpses, I guard myself against the eating of ensouled flesh.")

35. οὐ θέμις ἐντοῦθα κεῖσθαι ἰ μὲ τὸν βεβαχχευμένον, "It is not right that any be buried here if he has not been bacchic." As Turcan points out, the form of βεβαχχευμένον indicates that the initiate was not merely βάκχος during the limited period of a Dionysiac ritual, but that a permanent status is envisaged (1986: 237): "Il se fait βεβαχχευμένος grâce à la constance d'une vie ascétique, et non pas simplement *bacchos* dans l'exaltation éphémère de l'orgie." A Dionysus cult in the *polis* provides a controlled and temporary disruption of the normal order, but to prolong this disruption throughout one's life in a mystic religious group is to register a protest against the normal, civic order. Cf. Sabbatucci (1979: 51) on the role of Dionysus cult in the *polis* to reaffirm the order by a temporary suspension of it: "Pertanto tutte le manifestazioni cultuali che sotto il segno di Dioniso realizzavano una *temporanea* rottura dell'ordine, vanno correttamente interpretate, almeno fino allo scoperta del contrario (il che può avvenire di volta in volta, caso per caso, e non mediante uin giudizio di carattere generale) come espedienti rituali per rinnovare, reintergrare, rafforzare l'ordine stesso, e non come tentavi di distruggere l'ordine vigente." This function of Dionysus as the bringer of temporary disorder may, of course, be expanded by the mystical movements into a permanent disruption of the normal order.

36. Eur. *Hipp*. 948–957: σὺ δὴ θεοῖσιν ὡς περισσὸς ὢν ἀνὴρ / ξύνει σὺ σώφρων καὶ κακῶν ἀκήρατος / οὐκ ἂν πιθοίμην τοῖσι σοῖς κόμποις ἐγώ / θεοῖσι προσθεὶς ἀμαθίαν φρονεῖν κακῶς. / ἤδη νυν αὔχει καὶ δι' ἀψύχου βορᾶς / σίτοις καπήλευ' Ὀρφέα τ' ἄνακτ' ἔχων / βάκχευε πολλῶν γραμμάτων τιμῶν καπνούς· / ἐπεί γ' ἐλήφθης. τοὺς δὲ τοιούτους ἐγὼ / φεύγειν προφωνῶ πᾶσι· θηρεύουσι γὰρ / σεμνοῖς λόγοισιν, αἰσχρὰ μηχανώμενοι, "Are you, then, the companion of the gods, as a man beyond the common? Are you the chaste one, untouched by evil? I will never be persuaded by your vauntings, never be so unintelligent as to impute folly to the gods. Continue then your confident boasting, take up a diet of greens and play the showman with your food, make Orpheus your lord and engage in mystic rites, holding the vaporings of many books in honor. For you have been found out. To all I give the warning: avoid men like this. For they make you their prey with their high-holy-sounding words while they contrive deeds of shame."

37. Cf. Pl. *Laws* 782c; Theophr. *Char*. 16; Aristoph. *Frogs* 1032. Cf. Redfield

1991b: 106. "We call the eschatological passage in the Second Olympian 'Orphic' (although Pindar does not mention Orpheus) because that is our general—and necessarily vague—term for those aspects of Greek religion marked by concern for personal purity and personal immortality. Probably the Greeks themselves were vague about the category; Theseus assumes that since Hippolytus claims to be chaste (a claim not characteristic of the Orphics) he must also be a vegetarian and read Orphic books. All three would be tokens of a rejection of the world, and therefore mutually convertible."

38. I develop this argument further in Edmonds 2008a: 16–39.

39. Cf., e.g., the initiates in the fragment from Euripides *Cretans* (fr. 472 = Porph. *De abst*. 4.56), who never associate themselves with Orpheus, but who make a similar set of claims about themselves.

40. As I argue in Edmonds 1999 and 2008b; cf. J. Z. Smith 1990.

CHAPTER 6

Imago Inferorum Orphica

ALBERTO BERNABÉ

Materials for an Analysis

One of the features that most differentiates between Olympic religiosity and mystery cults in general (and particularly Orphic religiosity) is the image of the underworld. The religion of the *polis* is public and collective; its rites, its sacrifices, its processions serve as an element of social cohesion, as a way of integrating the individual in the community. This "bent toward this world" of the Olympic religiosity is consistent with the negative appeal offered by its image of the underworld, a dark and sinister place, populated by ἀμενηνὰ κάρηνα (*Od.* 10.521, etc.), ghosts without feelings. The Homeric image of Hades is so negative that a great hero like Achilles (*Od.* 11.489-491) says the following:

> I should choose, so I might live on earth, to serve as the hireling of another,
> of some portionless man whose livelihood was but small,
> rather than to be lord over all the dead that have perished.
> (Trans. G. Murray)

Nobody, not even Achilles himself, is free of this dark and sad fate, common to all. Mystery cults, on the other hand, allow people a religious life, to which they gain access by free choice, through initiation and the celebration of certain rites (τελεταί). They present an underworld in which the believer can reach different states, better or worse, by performing certain acts during his or her lifetime.

We have some data at our disposal that allow us to reconstruct a relatively coherent Orphic image of the underworld. Our information is both textual and iconographic.

The textual information available is of three types: 1) the gold lamellae, which allude to the joyful fate of the initiates after death and present us with some of the characteristics of the underworld;[1] 2) other texts that attribute features of the afterlife, either to Orpheus or to anonymous τελεταί, and that complement the image offered by the golden lamellae, especially regarding the fate of the initiates or of those who fail in the journey of the soul to the meadow of the blessed; and 3) texts that talk about the underworld, without quoting the source of the expressed ideas, but that are fairly coincident with the scheme reconstructed from the texts of the other two types, and therefore seem to be related to the Orphic world or a very similar field.

Iconographic information is problematic, and therefore it has been discussed whether there are parallels between the Orphic scheme of beliefs and the one shown by some pieces of Apulian pottery, specifically those that represent infernal scenes and some *pinakes* from Locri. For instance, Guthrie (1935: 187) denies the existence of such parallels, while Schmidt (1975: 129) considers that the Apulian vases representing Hades must be interpreted within an Orphic context, although she does not believe that they coincide with the world of the gold lamellae (cf. Schmidt 2000). Pensa (1977) dedicated a monograph to this topic with a well-balanced discussion of all relevant literature. Giangiulio (1994), for his part, has studied the relations between the religious and cultural thought of the gold lamellae, Apulian pottery, and the *pinakes*, as well as the Orphic-Pythagorean field.

In this chapter I focus on the analysis of a concrete aspect: the reconstruction of the common features between the Orphic infernal imagery and the imagery presented by the quoted iconography (Apulian and Locrian). However, it is not an iconographic analysis (which would be quite out of my professional expertise), but the attempt to reconstruct what we could call a common conceptual paradigm of the underworld expressed either in texts or in images, which has some points in common with the traditional Homeric one, but which differs from it in some fundamental features. In order to make the comparison easier, I itemize the different aspects.

The Place and Its Characteristics

We find in the text of the gold lamellae some verbs meaning "going down," referring to the access of the soul to Hades, which obviously implies that Hades is situated in its traditional place, that is, beneath the earth.[2] Some passages also allude to its darkness.³ The iconography on its part presents Hekate or Persephone or the Erinyes bearing torches (almost always in the shape of a sail) and includes the infernal image of Cerberus and some mythical damned sinners, which tradition places beneath the earth (ex. gr. Ruvo 1094, Naples SA 11, Munich 3297). To this extent, the image of Hades as an underground and dark place is not different at all from the traditional one (cf. ex. gr. *Il.* 8.477-481, 22.61, 22.482-483; *Od.* 24.203-204).

Both Homer and the gold lamellae refer to Hades as δόμοι or δῶμα.⁴ Homer even repeatedly alludes to the "doors of Hades" (*Il.* 5.646, etc.), but we find a marked difference in assessment between the Homeric description of Hades (*Od.* 20.64-65) as "the dread and dank abode, for which the very gods have loathing," as opposed to its description as the "well-built house" of Hipponion 2.

The image of Hades in Apulian pottery shows buildings with smart columns, dwellings worthy of the divine sovereigns that inhabit them. On the other hand, a characteristic of the infernal geography of the gold lamellae is a white cypress, which is repeatedly alluded to as an enticement of one of the springs⁵ but is absent both in other literary descriptions of the place and in the figurative representations.

Two Roads, Two Fates

In contrast to Homeric Hades, defined as hateful without exception, the underworld described in the gold lamellae presents a totally different feature, since it has two roads, two possibilities, two fates for its inhabitants. First, we are told about two springs; to one of them, that of Memory, go only those who have been warned by the author of the sacred text included in the gold lamellae, while to the other, which has no name—but logically we have to consider it the spring of Oblivion—go the rest of the souls of the dead.⁶

There is also in Hades a privileged space, a *locus amoenus*, defined as a sacred meadow⁷ and separated from a much more unpleasant and gloomy place, often identified with Tartarus. The access to this *locus amoenus* is controlled by guards and by Persephone herself.

In one amphora, maybe from Vulci, today lost, the souls of the initiates were represented, standing before the guards that keep watch on Memory's fountain, according to a description of the piece written by Albizzatti (1921: 260; cf. Pairault-Massa 1975: 199): "In a meadow full of flowers, separated from the region of the condemned by two trees with birds among the branches, two naked young men crowned with ivy and bearing thyrsus are on a grassy elevation, from which a spring rises. Behind each tree an oriental archer is kneeling and shooting an arrow."

The Initiation and the Demand of Purity

Those who have been warned not to drink of Lethe's spring know a certain kind of truth;[8] they have a knowledge of something that they must have acquired before, when they were alive, and that is not shared by everybody. It is, then, an initiatory knowledge that they must retain.[9] It is clear, therefore, that in order to gain access to the privileged space in the underworld, it is necessary to be a μύστης, to have received an initiation. The μύσται know the roads they must follow and some kind of password (σύμβολα, Ent. 19, Pher.) that they have to say before the beings that guard the underworld,[10] who block the way for those who do not have this information. Because of that, the water they have to drink is that of Memory, the goddess-guarantor of memory and initiation, and for this reason it is said that the gold lamellae themselves were Μναμοσύνας ... ἔργον.[11]

The initiates are called μύσται καὶ βάκχοι ... κλε(ε)νινοί, "famed initiates and bacchi" (Hipp. 16). The gold leaf from Pherai tells us that the μύσται are free of punishment, which implies that those who are not μύσται are exposed to punishment. The Thurii lamellae reveal to us that the initiates also pay a penalty;[12] we must therefore suppose that it is a general punishment for the whole of mankind. Our documents define this punishment as a terrible cycle from which the initiates manage to free themselves.[13]

However, apart from being initiated, the candidates to inhabit the *locus amoenus* claim to be in special conditions of purity, as in the famous initial declaration of the purity of the gold lamellae from Thur. (488–490) 1: "Pure I come from the pure."

The demand for the purity of the μύσται is also found in a fragment of the *Rhapsodies* (Orph. fr. 340 B. = 222 K.):

> All who live purely beneath the rays of the sun,
> so soon as they die have a smoother path
> in a fair meadow beside deep-flowing Acheron, (...)
> but those who have done evil (ἄδικα ῥέξαντες)
> beneath the rays of the sun,
> the insolent, are brought down below Kokytos
> to the chilly horrors of Tartaros. (Trans. W.K.C. Guthrie)

Figure 6.1. Fragment of Apulian Pottery from Ruvo. Ancient collection Fenicia, c. 350 BCE.

It is worth mentioning that in this passage, the pure are contrasted with the unjust, which implies that the observance of justice is a feature of the ritual Orphic purity and therefore that acting against Justice supposes impurity.

Apulian iconography would appear to confirm this idea, if indeed the goddess Justice (Dike) is represented in a ceramic fragment from Ruvo (ancient collection Fenicia, c. 350 BCE [Fig. 6.1]). Here the goddess appears next to Victory (Nike), who half-opens a door. Persephone and Hekate are also present with two torches.[14] This door, half-opened by Victory, who seems to be offering a dead follower of Orpheus a way to a better place, is extremely suggestive. Justice is a well-known divinity within Orphism. In an old Orphic theogony, there were undoubtedly some passages referring to her as a goddess partner of Zeus, who watches the injustices of men so that Zeus can punish them. Plato refers to this immediately after alluding to Zeus' hymn:

With him followeth Justice always, as avenger of them that fall short of the divine law. (Pl. *Leg.* 716a; Orph. fr. 32B. = 21K, trans. R. G. Bury)

Burkert has pointed out that the Platonic passage seems to paraphrase a similar verse from the *Rhapsodies*:

And Justice, bringer of retribution, attended him [Zeus], bringing succor to all.[15]

The same topic appears in a passage from a judicial speech in which one of the litigants tries to have an influence on the jury's vote, referring to the way in which Justice watches over the unfair:

You must magnify the Goddess of Order (Εὐνομία) who loves what is right and preserves every city and every land; and before you cast your votes, each juryman must reflect that he is being watched by hallowed and inexorable Justice, who, as Orpheus, that prophet of our most sacred mysteries, tells us, sits beside the throne of Zeus and oversees all the works of men. Each must keep watch and ward lest he shame that goddess.[16]

It is quite significant that in the Derveni Papyrus (col. IV.5-9), the only fragment quoted from Heraclitus (B94 D.-K. = fr. 52 Marcovich) is that according to which the sun will never go above its measures, because the Erinyes, Justice's assistants, will know how to find him. This passage, which refers to a transgression and to a punishment, reminds us of Hesiod's description of Justice and the just state in *Works and Days* 212-224.

Therefore, the knowledge they have and the keeping of a pure way of life, which includes respect for Justice, allows the initiates that persevere with a pure or "correct" way of life to have a special fate in the underworld, in a sacred meadow.[17] Because of that, we find several instances of gold lamellae that only indicate that the bearer is a μύστης (cf. Bernabé and Jiménez San Cristóbal 2008: 161-163, 267-269), thus serving to identify his (or her) status.

Those who gain access to the meadow are described as ὄλβιοι (Pel. 7; Thur. [488] 9) due to the happiness of their fate, and they are even claimed to achieve a special status, defined either as that of a ἥρως,[18] or even as that of a θεός.[19] The knowledge they require is revealed by an authorized anonymous narrator, whom we suppose is Orpheus (cf. Bernabé and Jiménez San Cristóbal 2008: 181-183).

A similar framework appears in other texts in which the τελεταί are mentioned. Pindar (fr. 131a Maehl. = 59 Cannatà) therefore refers to the happiness produced by the "initiations that free from sorrows," and in another fragment (fr. 137 Maehl. = 62 Cannatà) mentions the fortune of the initiates that know "the end of life and the beginning disposed by Zeus." The place where the blessed arrive in the underworld is a sweet-smelling *locus amoenus,* full of flowers, where they devote themselves to activities of the spirit (Pind. fr. 129 Maehl. = 58 Cannatà), whereas those who have lived unholy lives lie in the darkness (Pind. fr. 130 Maehl. = 58b Cannatà). In *Olympian Ode* 2.56, Pindar contrasts the fate of the violent souls, who immediately pay their punishment, to that of the good, who win themselves an existence free of hardship.

Plato for his part talks also about those who established the τελεταί to present us with a dual Hades, with one fate for initiates and those who have been purified, and another for those who have not:

> And I fancy that those men who established the mysteries (τελετάς) were not unenlightened but in reality had a hidden meaning when they said long ago that whoever goes uninitiated and unsanctified to the underworld will lie in the mire, but he who arrives there initiated and purified will dwell with the gods. (Pl. *Phd.* 69c; Orph. fr. 434 III B. = 5 K.; trans. W.R.M. Lamb)[20]

Such an opinion had to be widespread in Athens, judging by the harsh criticism made by Diogenes the Cynic against those who believed that it was possible to win a special fate in the underworld only by being initiated:

> It is absurd of you, my young friend, to think that any tax-gatherer,[21] if only he be initiated (ἕνεκα τῆς τελετῆς), can share in the rewards of the just in the next world, while Agesilaus and Epameinondas are doomed to lie in the mire. (Iulian. *Or.* 7.25 [Diog. V.B332 Giannantoni = Orph. fr. 435 B.; trans. W. C. Wright)[22]

Diodorus transmits an important piece of information, which he probably took from Hekataeus of Abdera (fourth to third century BCE, cf. *FGrH* 264F25):

> Orpheus . . . brought from Egypt most of the mystic ceremonies, the orgiastic rites . . . and his fabulous account of his experiences in Hades . . . the punishments in Hades of the unrighteous, the Fields of the Righteous, and the fantastic conceptions current among the many, which are

figments of the imagination—all these were introduced by Orpheus in imitation of the Egyptian funeral customs. (Diod. Sic. 1.96.2–5; Orph. fr. 55B; trans. C. H. Oldfather)

Leaving aside the question of the supposed Egyptian origin that Diodorus' source ascribes to the τελεταί,[23] we find in this text the same scheme in which the punishments are opposed to the meadow. We can also see that Orpheus is held responsible for this imagery. The τελεταί seem, then, to be accompanied as λεγόμενα by a series of texts, which the old tradition mainly attributed to Orpheus.

The Space for the Noninitiated: The "Terrors of Hades"

The gold lamellae are silent[24] about what happens to those who do not know the passwords or cannot identify themselves as μύσται. It seems that they should have a worse fate, without doubt in the dark and muddy places referred to in the other sources. Let's try to get a more precise idea of this "space for the noninitiated."

First of all, the Derveni Papyrus, clearly belonging to the Orphic framework, mentions the "terrors of Hades," regrettably in a very fragmentary context:

> The terror of Hades . . . ask an oracle . . . they ask an oracle . . . for them, we will enter the prophetic shrine to enquire, with regard to people who seek prophecies, whether it is permissible to disbelieve in the terrors of Hades.[25] Why do they disbelieve [in them]?[26] Since they do not understand dream-visions or any of the other realities, what sort of proofs would induce them to believe? For, since they are overcome by both error and pleasure as well, they do not learn or believe. Disbelief and ignorance are the same thing. For if they do not learn or comprehend, it cannot be that they will believe even if they see dream-visions. . . . (P.Derveni col. V.3ff.; Orph. fr. 473B; trans. R. Janko)

The vague allusion to the "terrors of Hades" ([τὰ] ἐν Ἅιδου δεινά) only informs us about the fact that in the Orphic lore, there was talk of those terrors. And an Orphic priest, as the Derveni's commentator seems to be, considers it absurd that people do not believe in them.[27]

We find also in some close passages of the papyrus the presence of Erinyes that threaten the souls, of demons beneath the earth, of punishments in the underworld or perhaps also of initiates,[28] as well as of certain rites carried out by the *magoi* to avert these dangers.

The fact that the terrors of Hades were also subject of the τελεταί is clear from a pair of texts of Origen:

> And accordingly he [Celsus] likens us [sc. the Christians] to those who in the Bacchic mysteries introduce phantoms and objects of terror. (Origen *Contra Celsum* 4.10; Orph. fr. 596.I.B)

> Celsus ... shows us who have been moved in this way in regard to eternal punishments by the teaching of heathen priests and mystagoges.[29] (Origen *Contra Celsum* 8.48; Orph. fr. 596.II.B)

As a concrete instance of punishment for the noninitiated, Plato mentions, in *Phaedo* 69c (a text to which I have already referred), "to lie in the mire." This detail is recurrent in other texts. In addition to the ones that I will mention later, there are two by Aristophanes in the parody of the journey to the underworld of *Frogs*,[30] and one by Aelius Aristides.[31]

Another text by Diodorus, coming from the same source as the one previously quoted, offers further information:

> Many other things as well, of which mythology tells, are still to be found among the Egyptians, the name being still preserved and the customs actually being practiced. In the city of Acanthi, for instance, ... there is a perforated jar to which three hundred and sixty priests, one each day, bring water from the Nile.[32] (Diod. Sic. 1.97.1; Orph. fr. 62 B.)

Disregarding again the supposed Egyptian origin of the rites, it is clear that Diodorus' source tries to base on an Egyptian custom (probably only a way of measuring time on a big clepsydra[33]) the typical image of the infernal punishment that involves pouring water into a large earthenware jar with holes. The two specific punishments that we have found so far in the texts, the mire and the sentence to carry water to vessels that cannot be filled, can be also found in Plato, in a curious variant: carrying water in a sieve.[34]

> But Musaios and his son [cf. Bernabé 1998a: 46] ... the unrighteous and unjust they plunge into a kind of mud in Hades and make them carry water in a sieve. (Pl. *Rep.* 363c; Orph. fr. 431 B. = 4 K.; trans. W.K.C. Guthrie)

In another text, Plato refers to the same tradition, to which he gives a symbolic interpretation:

> The part of the soul in which we have desires is liable to be overpersuaded and to vacillate to and fro, and so some smart fellow, a Sicilian, I daresay, or Italian, made a fable in which—by a play of words—he named this part, as being so impressionable and persuadable (πιθανόν), a jar (πίθος), and the thoughtless (ἀνόητοι) he called uninitiates (ἀμύητοι); in these uninitiates that part of the soul where the desires are, the licentious and fissured part, he named a leaky jar (πίθος) in his allegory because it is so insatiate. So you see this person, Callicles, takes the opposite view to yours, showing how of all who are in Hades—meaning of course the invisible (ἀιδές)—these uninitiates will be most wretched, and will carry water into their leaky jar with a sieve, as my story-teller said, he means the soul: and the soul of the thoughtless he likened to a sieve, as being perforated, since it is unable to hold anything by reason of his unbelief and forgetfulness. (Pl. *Gorg.* 493a; Orph. frr. 430.II, 434.II.B; trans. W.R.M. Lamb)

Leaving aside the symbolic interpretations (which show that this kind of analysis was quite common in the fourth century BCE), as well as the free Platonic re-elaboration, which served his own philosophical and literary interests, the analyzed text presents the noninitiated in the underworld as being punished by bearing water in a sieve to a vessel with holes.

The pseudo-Platonic dialogue *Axiochus,* after narrating the fate of those inspired by a good spirit when they were alive, who are going to gain access to the place for the righteous, tells about those who directed their lives toward bad deeds (cf. Violante 1981):

> They are led by Erinyes to Erebos and Chaos through Tartarus, where they find the dwelling of the unrighteous, the Danaids' jars without bottom, Tantalus tormented by thirst, Tityos' entrails devoured and always reborn, Sisyphus' stone without end.... There they waste away in everlasting punishments, licked by wild beasts, constantly burnt with Furies' torches and ill-treated by all kind of tortures. (Ps.-Pl. *Axiochus* 371e; Orph. fr. 434.IX B.)

In the burlesque description of the underworld offered by Aristophanes (*Frogs* 144–145), he does not mention the wild beasts, but he alludes to "snakes and vermin of all kinds."

Another passage enlarges our knowledge about the close relation existing between the description of the terrors of Hades and the initiations:

> In this world it [the soul] is without knowledge, except when it is already at the point of death; but when that time comes, it has an experience like that of men who are undergoing initiation into great mysteries: and so the verbs τελευτᾶν [die] and τελεῖσθαι [be initiated], and the actions they denote, have a similarity. In the beginning there is straying and wandering, the weariness of running this way and that, and nervous journeys through darkness that reach no goal (ὕποπτοι πορεῖαι καὶ ἀτέλεστοι), and then immediately before the consummation every possible terror, shivering and trembling and sweating and amazement. But after this a marvelous light meets the wanderer, and open country and meadow lands welcome him; and in that place there are voices and dancing and the solemn majesty of sacred music and holy visions. And amidst these, he walks at large in new freedom, now perfect and fully initiated, celebrating the sacred rites, a garland upon his head, and converses with pure and holy men; he surveys the uninitiated, unpurified mob here on earth, the mob of living men who, herded together in murk and deep mire, trample one another down and in their fear of death cling to their ills, since they disbelieve in the blessing of the Otherworld. (Plut. fr. 178 Sandbach; Orph. fr. 594 B.; trans. F. Sandbach)

This passage was analyzed by Díez de Velasco (1997: 413–416) as an excellent example of the features of a mystic experience: the result of a voluntary itinerary, movement through phases of darkness and suffering, and passing through an ineffable peak experience, which changes the identity of the one who feels it and which is ended with the union with an otherness of a transcendent kind. I consider this frame to be quite correct regarding the analysis of the phenomenon as included within a general typology; however, there are some details that could be added (cf. Bernabé 2001b).

Plutarch specifically states that the experience of death is similar to the one suffered by those who take part in the initiations into great mysteries. The identification of the mysteries to which he is referring has been a matter of discussion among scholars. Thus Foucart (1914: 393) believes that Plutarch refers to the mysteries of Eleusis. Díez de Velasco (1997: 413) seems to agree with this. However, Mylonas (1961: 265) considers that he alludes to an Orphic initiation, on the basis of the mention of the mire. Dunand (1973, 3:248) for his part thinks that Plutarch talks about Isis' mysteries (but cf. Graf 1974: 132–139). The most likely interpretation would be that he refers to mysteries in general, and this is the most widespread opinion nowadays.³⁵

In any case, the experience of the τελετή is considered to be very similar to that of death. This statement is "confirmed" by an etymological argument, quite typical of the philosophical analysis of the time: there is a strong bond between death (τελευτή) and τελετή, which motivates, in a cause-effect relation (διὸ καί), the etymological bond existing between their names. Such a bond, if not made explicit, was suggested by Plato in a famous passage, in which the etymological relation is a kind of wink at the reader:

> And they produce a mass of books of Musaios and Orpheus, ... according to whose recipes they make their sacrifices. In this way they persuade not only individuals but cities that there are means of redemption and purification from sin through sacrifices and pleasant amusements, valid both for the living and for those who are already dead (τελευτήσασιν). They call them *teletai,* these ceremonies which free us from the troubles of the Otherworld.³⁶ (Pl. *Rep.* 364e; trans. W.K.C. Guthrie)

But what are the strong relations between the τελετή and death? Plutarch's description is outstandingly ambiguous, because in some moments of his exposition he expresses contents that are common and similar to initiation and death, but in other cases he talks about realities that are only proper to initiation, and in others, about aspects that are only ascribed to death. We need to analyze the text part by part to see what comes from the *imago inferorum* and what from τελετή, although it seems in advance that the second tries to reproduce in some way the conditions of the first.

The journeys in darkness at the first moment are without doubt the movement of the soul toward Hades, a dark and gloomy place. The effects of terror, which are described, are physical effects, more suitable for initiation, where it is the person, not the soul, who suffers the experience; but it is not ruled out that Plutarch had in mind that the soul, when it arrived at Hades, would see the terrors that are alluded to several times.

It is obvious that the initiate passes through a phase of fear and confusion. But Plutarch subtly plays with the words. In the initiation level, ἀτέλεστοι does not mean "unfinished," but "who are not yet initiated" (later, τέλος will mean "initiation"). By using ὕποπτοι, he can even play with a correlative ἐπόπται, "initiated in the highest grade of the mysteries," and then invoke the meaning, "that they have not yet reached contemplation."

Later, by means of a strong contrast, Plutarch describes what the soul of the dead sees at the end (τέλος) of the journey: it is a meadow and pure places (καθαροί), where there are a series of ὁρώμενα (light, dances, holy visions) and a series of λεγόμενα (sounds, sacred words). We suppose that in the τελετή these pleasant visions would be represented in some way. But now the description tends more to the experience of death than to the one of the mysteries, since what Plutarch describes is more similar to the meadow of the blessed in the underworld than to the entrance to an illuminated *telesterion*.

The description that follows, however, is exclusive to the mysteries. According to the mystery beliefs, the soul that, after death, reaches the meadow of the blessed never comes back. Therefore, the return described by Plutarch is the return of an initiate after initiation, while the following passage, in which is described the mob of living beings that persist in the fear of death in the middle of mire, is absolutely imprecise. It could be said to belong to real death. We have already seen the texts that talk about the mire, where the noninitiated lie, but if Plutarch is referring to them, how can those who are already dead persist in the fear of death? The persistence in the fear of death and the distrust of good things in the afterlife is characteristic of people who are alive and uninitiated. The reference is, then, deliberately ambiguous.

On the other hand, Plutarch informs us about the acquisition of knowledge in the τελετή. He tells us that the soul obtains knowledge at death's door and that this situation is similar to the τελετή, from which can be deduced that knowledge is also acquired in the τελετή. Outside of initiation and death, there is only ignorance. Plutarch tells us about a liberation, which is without doubt opposed to the fear of the noninitiated, and he mentions the sanctity and purity of those who have been initiated, in contrast to the dirtiness and the mire of those who have not been initiated. Finally, he refers to the hope in a fate in the underworld, which the noninitiate cannot enjoy. We suppose *a contrariis* that the initiate would have hope in the underworld.

Thus, it seems that the τελετή was an experience similar to death or, better, a kind of rehearsal, so that the individual experiences the real death in advance and is not afraid of it. So it is possible to explain the constant confusion between the domain of initiation and that of real death, with which the author plays in the whole passage.

In another interesting text, a Bononiae Papyrus (third to fourth century CE, published after several other editions by Lloyd-Jones and Parsons 1978 = Orph. fr. 717B; cf. Bernabé 2003: 281–289), we find part of a poem in which is described the fate of the blessed and the condemned in Hades, whose coincidences with book 6 of the *Aeneid* have been highlighted countless times. In verses 77 and 79 of the anonymous poem, we are told about the circulation of souls into and out of the underworld, and two roads are mentioned. There is probably one that goes down, that of the dead, and another one that goes up, that of those who have to be reincarnated. In verse 78 we are told about other souls that arrive, probably of those who have just died. In 124 there is mention of the "daughter of Justice, the very famous Retribution."

In verse 129, we read θ]νητῶν μελ[έ]ων σκιόεν[τα] χιτῶνα, "the gloomy tunic of the mortal members," an image that expresses the idea of reincarnation. We already know a similar image in other texts—for example, in Empedocles (B126 D-K), σαρκῶν ἀλλογνῶτι περιστέλλουσα χιτῶνι, "clothing in an unfamiliar garment of flesh" (cf. Gigante [1973] 1988). As components of the punishment, we find (*PBonon.* 26ff.):

]Ἐρινύες [ἄλλο]θεν ἄλλαι
]ς δ' ἐκέλευσ[εν] ἑκάστη⟨ι⟩
πληγαῖς φον]ίοισιν ἱμά[σσει]ν.

Erinyes, one from one place, another from another,
and *someone* urged each of them
to whip them with bloody lashes.

And in verse 33, we see γαμψ]ώνυχες εἰλαπινασταί, "guests with crooked talons," which, according to Lloyd-Jones and Parsons, refer to Harpies (cf. Pherecydes fr. 83 Schibli: φυλάσσουσι δ' αὐτὴν . . . Ἅρπυιαι, "The Harpies guard it [sc. Tartarus]"). Both the Erinyes whipping the souls and the Harpies with terrible faces coincide with Vergil's *Aeneid: virginei volucrum* [sc. *Harpyiarum*] *vultus, foedissima ventris / proluvies, uncaeque manus, et pallida semper / ora fame* (3.216-218); *Gorgones Harpyiaeque* (6.289); *hinc exaudiri gemitus et saeva sonare / verbera* (6.557-558); *continuo sontes ultrix accincta flagello / Tisiphone quatit insultans* (6.570-571). The privileged place is described in the Bononiae Papyrus as "splendid shining multicolored dwellings" (v. 126) and as a place where "neither the cloud of black waters nor hail accumulate nor the incessant rain oppresses, but there is prosperity day after day" (vv. 131ff.).

To sum up all that we have seen so far, it seems that the infernal punishments consisted mainly in: 1) a stay in a dark and muddy place, which involves fear, lack of comfort, and anxiety; 2) carrying water in a sieve to a vessel with holes (one of the models of useless effort, which was the worst punishment of which the Greeks could conceive in the underworld); 3) the attack of hostile beings, either wild animals and snakes, or Furies,

Harpies, or similar monsters, which tore the souls into pieces or lacerated them, or burnt them with torches, although that naturally did not involve their destruction; and 4) after a period of punishments, the opportunity to try for salvation again in a new existence.

The most remarkable thing about the punishments imagined in Hades is that they are corporal. It is clear that it was assumed that the ψυχαί would keep in the underworld a kind of corporal configuration; at least, they were supposed to be able to suffer from physical agents. They also drink water, talk, and, in general, behave like people. The Orphic woman buried in Hipponion had a lamp beside her, and she had in her mouth a gold leaf, which gave her instructions for her journey through the underworld. If she hoped to use the lamp and to read the letters of the gold leaf, then she did not imagine this journey without her eyes and hands.

Apulian iconography offers us a similar frame in a series of pieces in which the infernal punishments of archetypical sinners are represented. This is the case of a crater of St. Petersburg (B.1717, 325-310 BCE), where Ixion's punishment is shown. The center is occupied by a magnificent building seat of the infernal rulers, Persephone and Hades. Hades attends Hermes' arrival. Below we see the Danaids carrying jugs of water to fill the vessel that is never filled. In the upper part appears one of the typical punishments—Ixion, tied to the wheel and accompanied by a Fury, a typical character in these representations (cf. Aellen 1994: passim), where the Furies are attendants of the gods responsible for punishing the condemned. In another two vases we find Hades and Persephone, out of their shrine: in one, from St. Petersburg (B.1716, 330-310 BCE), a Fury is at their right and the Danaids are below in the center; in another, from Ruvo (1094, 360-350 BCE [Fig. 6.2]), a Fury punishes a condemned person who seems to be more terrified than mortified. Indeed, literary sources do insist more on the "terrors of Hades" than on the physical punishments.

The Happy Space

The space reserved for the initiates is nicer. It is in Hades, under the earth, imagined as a meadow,[37] called the "meadow of the blessed" (Diod. Sic. 1.96.2-5 = Orph. fr. 55 B.) or "Persephone's meadow,"[38] and it is the place reserved for those who are in a situation of ritual purity.[39] Plutarch presents it as full of light and pleasant music.[40]

A wide description of the happiness of this place can be found in the pseudo-Platonic *Axiochus* 371c, and it includes typical features like the meadow, the limpid waters, the music and dances, the gentle breeze under

Figure 6.2. Apulian Crater. Ruvo 1094.

a warm sun, together with more cultural ones, like conversations for philosophers and a theater for poets. The author points out, too, that "there the initiated have an honored place, and they perform there their sacred rites."

Linked to the mention of a meadow in Orph. fr. 487.6 are Persephone's groves (ἄλσεα).[41] Meadows and groves create an idyllic *locus amoenus*, which evokes rest and happiness, in short as reflection in the underworld of many earthly *loci amoeni* consisting in a little forest on the banks of a river. This will be the place where the initiate will enjoy eternal happiness. Similar descriptions can be found in fragments from Pindar's *Threnoi* (see above).

Apulian pottery does not offer us clear images of the happy place, which we could ascribe to an Orphic environment, although a series of pieces represent a heavenly place related to Dionysus.[42] Other works belonging to the immense Dionysian iconography are not, of course, incompatible with this universe. For example, a Basel amphora (S29; cf. Schmidt, Trendall, and Cambitoglou 1976: 6 and 35ff., tab. 8e, 10a)[43] in which we find an "automatic" wine miracle. This image reminds us of the "wine happy honor" of Pelinna gold leaf, or of a crater from Tarentum (61.602) in which a woman receives a satyr in a *naiskos*, as well as the numerous symposiac scenes, including those that decorate the sarcophagus from the so-called Tomb of the Tuffatore (Diver), that could allude to a banquet in the underworld. However, it is obviously difficult to demonstrate an Orphic presence in these cases. We also find works in which Orpheus appears, where the possible relation to the *locus amoenus* or the netherworld meadow would be indicated by the presence of the mediator or by details such as Nike (Victory) half-opening a door.[44]

A Different Image of the Gods of the Netherworld

The goddess that rules over the netherworld according to the Thurii gold lamellae is Persephone. The souls come, imploring, before her.[45] The goddess may also be mentioned in Ent. 20, καὶ φε (cf. Bernabé 1999b). Persephone is without doubt identified with Brimo, mentioned in Pherecydes, and with the one called "Queen of the Dead" in the Thurii lamellae ([488–490] 1), the Roma lamella (1), and probably in the Hipponion lamella (13).[46] She is not only the queen of the dead, but she is also responsible for the last decision regarding those that arrive at the netherworld.[47] Hades, under the name Eucles, and Dionysus, with the epithet Eubuleus, are also mentioned together with her. In the Pelinna fragments, Dionysus appears again in a more significant way, as Βάκχιος, to whom is attributed the liberation of the soul of the dead. The strange epithet Ἀν⟨δ⟩ρικεπαιδόθυρσον, which serves as σύμβολον in Pher., also refers to him.

The relationship between Bacchus and Persephone is typically southern Italian,[48] and it is probably due to the well-known Orphic myth according to which Dionysus is Persephone's son, the Titans tear him apart, and from the remains men are born (cf. Bernabé 2002).

The same role for Persephone can be found in Pindar (fr. 133 Maehl. = 65 Cannatà; cf. Bernabé 1999a). Persephone and Dionysus also appear, together with Orpheus, in a fragment of the *Rhapsodies*:[49]

The happy life . . . which the initiates in Dionysus and Kore according Orpheus wish to achieve:

"He commends them
to cease from the cycle and have respite from evil."

This role for Dionysus is absolutely alien to the Homeric world, and Persephone's role is totally different from the one represented by the goddess in Homer and Hesiod, where she is repeatedly mentioned as a horrible goddess.[50]

The Mediators

The hypothesis that the text of the gold lamellae was considered a work of Orpheus is very plausible (cf. Bernabé and Jiménez San Cristóbal 2008: 181–183; Riedweg 2002). Orpheus, due to his quest for his dead wife, is supposed to have seen what happened in the underworld and come back to tell about it. It is therefore clear that the Thracian bard was considered by the users of the gold lamellae as a human mediator, who through initiation explains the path that the souls have to follow to achieve their salvation. The numerous texts that ascribe to Orpheus the τελεταί or concepts about the underworld related to them insist on the same idea.[51]

But we have seen that there is also a divine mediator, Dionysus, because it is this god who intercedes with Persephone for the soul of the Pelinna believer, a role he has also in the Gurob Papyrus (18–22; cf. Hordern 2000), in which the participants in the rite invoke Eubuleus (Dionysus), also called Ἰρικεπαῖγε, and they ask the god to save them.

Some features of this view of the netherworld appear in the Locri *pinakes*, from the second quarter of the fifth century BCE (cf. Giangiulio

1994; Olmos 2008: 284-288). In one of them (Mus. Arch. Naz. Reggio Calabria 58729 [Fig. 6.3]), the wine-god offers a *kantharos* of wine and a branch with bunches of grapes to the corn goddess. It is highly probable that they are Dionysus and his mother Persephone. There are other exemplars, one of which was precisely found in Hipponion. In these images, Dionysus is the mediator who symbolically substitutes the faithful supplicant on his arrival at the kingdom of death, when he presents himself before the god's mother. In another model (Reggio Calabria 21016, mid-fifth century BCE; cf. Olmos 2008: 284-288, with discussion of interpretations [Fig. 6.4]), we find Persephone represented as the "goddess of underworld beings," to whom the Thurii gold lamellae allude, enthroned with Hades and accepting the offerings of an invisible supplicant, who is without doubt deceased.

Apulian pottery offers us a series of pieces in which, together with the kings of the underworld and the condemned, appears a mediator who can be either Dionysus or Orpheus. In an Apulian crater conserved in the Museum of Art of Toledo, Ohio (340-330 BCE; cf. Johnston and McNiven 1996; Olmos 2008: 291-293 [Fig. 6.5]), we find the only representation preserved in which Dionysus makes a pact with Hades, shaking hands with him in the presence of Hermes. Next to Dionysus are the members of his retinue, a *paniskos* and a maenad with a thyrsus and a tambourine, who dances with the bare breast. On the other side of the temple are represented the condemned Actaeon and Agave. The message of the pact is clear: the initiates in the mysteries of Dionysus, the *mystai*, will receive special treatment in the netherworld and will find rest from their toils.

Frequently, Orpheus is the mediator. It is obvious that his presence in the netherworld is related not to the search for Eurydice (who never does appear, at least in an unequivocal manner),[52] but rather to his role as a protector of certain souls on their arrival at the underworld. In an Apulian crater from Canosa of the Munich Museum (Fig. 6.6),[53] Orpheus arrives at the palace of Hades and Persephone. He is dressed in the oriental manner, as a Thracian singer, and his long priestly dress flaps to the rhythm of his dancing step, which follows the sounds of the zither. It seems as if he wants to seduce the gods with his chant. A man, a woman, and a child come behind him. Although the role of these characters has been discussed, it seems obvious that they are a family of initiates. In the vessel we find also numerous personifications and heroes: Justice beside Theseus and Peirithoos; the judges of the netherworld, Aeacus, Minos, and Rhadamanthys; the Erinyes; great sinners like Sisyphus or Tantalus; Hermes Psychopompus; Cerberus, tamed by liberator Herakles; and the Danaids; but, as Schmidt (1975: 123) points out, they show little zeal in

Figure 6.3. Locrian Pinax. Reggio Calabria 58729.

their hard work, as though they are going to be absolved soon.[54] The big Apulian crater is a representation of the kingdom of Justice and the cosmic order, which punishes the impious actions of the noninitiated. The queen Persephone and her husband Hades preside over its reestablishment in the underworld space.

We find a similar model in other Apulian craters, like one of Matera (no. 336, 320 BCE), and another at Karlsruhe (B4, 350–340 BCE; cf. Pensa 1977: 24). In another one, at Naples, from Armento (SA 709, 330–310 BCE [Fig. 6.7]; cf. Pensa 1977: 27), the same themes are repeated, but without the characteristic representation of a building. Orpheus arrives in the presence of Hades and Persephone, and he has a woman by the hand. In the light of the other exemplars, it seems clear that we have to interpret the scene as

Orpheus presenting a deceased woman before the gods of the netherworld rather than as a rendering of Orpheus with Eurydice.[55]

An interesting variant is offered to us by the fragments that were in Ruvo (ancient collection Fenicia, c. 350 BCE [see Fig. 6.1]; cf. Pensa 1977: 25), to which I have already referred, in which we see Victory half-opening a door—that of the netherworld—and Justice, Orpheus, Persephone, and Hekate with two torches.

Figure 6.4. Locrian Pinax. Reggio Calabria 21016.

Figure 6.5. Apulian Crater. Toledo, Ohio.

Finally, in another crater at Naples (3222, 350–340 BCE; cf. Pensa 1977: 24), we find beside Orpheus other characters and personifications, like Megara, the Poinai, Ananke, Sisyphus, Hermes, Triptolemus, Aeacus, and Rhadamanthys.

As for Victory, she is not alien to the world of the gold lamellae either: in Thur. (488) 6, the reference to the soul that was liberated from the cycle and "came on quick feet to the desired crown" is that of the winning athlete; although the image of the crown in the gold lamellae is polyvalent, it is at the same time a funerary crown and a mystic, banquet, and triumphal one (cf. Bernabé and Jiménez San Cristóbal 2008: 121–128).

Together with this quite widespread type, in which we find the scene of prizes and punishments, the divine rulers and the mediator, there is a different type that also shows Orpheus as mediator, but without the presence of the damned sinners and of Persephone. We have variants: one is a red-figured Apulian amphora attributed to the Ganymedes painter (Basel, Antikenmuseum 540, 330-320 BCE; cf. Olmos 2008: 280-283 with bibliography [Fig. 6.8]). A man seated within a white shrine or *naiskos*, very similar to Persephone's palace represented in other pieces, receives Orpheus. He is seated on a portable chair. It is curious enough that a chair with these characteristics seems to have been represented in one of the bone tablets from Olbia, also from an Orphic environment (*IGDOlb.* 94c Dubois; cf. West 1982 [Fig. 6.9]). The most interesting feature is that the deceased holds a *volumen* in his hand. There is little doubt that this is a funerary initiation text. The image makes explicit that the knowledge that Orpheus transmits to the initiates is in a text.

Another Sicilian piece, from Leontini (Trendall 1967: 589 n. 28; cf.

Figure 6.6. Apulian Crater from Canosa. Munich Museum 3297.

Figure 6.7. Apulian Crater from Armento. Naples Museum SA 709.

Schmidt 1975: 177-178), is also similar to piece from Olbia in many aspects, but without the presence of a text. We see Orpheus and Hermes in a *naiskos* with a deceased woman.

A different type is found in a crater of the British Museum in London (F270 [Fig. 6.10]; cf. Schmidt 1975: 120-122 and tav. XIV; also Pensa 1977: 30). Orpheus and a young man are at the entrance to Hades, marked by a herm. Orpheus bears Cerberus with a chain because he has tamed him with his music, and thus he assumes the function of a protector that defends the young man, without doubt an initiate, against the terrors of Hades.

Conclusions about the Orphic Origin of the Apulian and Locrian Infernal Imagery

We see that the basic features of the underworld represented in the iconography we have studied make up a conceptual universe in agreement with the one presented in the textual Orphic fragments:

1. The underworld is an underground and dark place, but has buildings.
2. It is ruled over by Persephone and Hades, although the main character is a friendly and affable Persephone.

Figure 6.8. Apulian Amphora from Basel. Antikenmuseum 540.

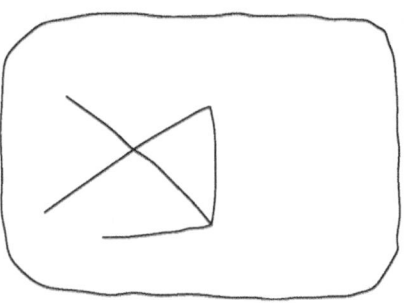

Figure 6.9. Olbia Bone Tablet.

Figure 6.10. Apulian Crater. British Museum F270.

3. It is a dual space, with prizes and punishments.
4. For the punishments, the artists choose as paradigmatic representation the clearest and most recognizable sinners of the mythical tradition, like Sisyphus, Ixion, or the Danaids. The latter appear to be carrying out the typical punishment of filling vessels that cannot be filled. The beings responsible for the punishment are the Erinyes.
5. The prizes are related to the idea of proximity to the divine, and they are symbolized by the presence of the mediators.
6. There is a divine mediator, Dionysus, and a human one, Orpheus (always represented at the frontier between the palace and the rest of the space, sometimes with the clear presence of the believer).
7. We find in one case the representation of text as support of the Orphic revelation.
8. The personifications of Justice and Victory allude to the need of the *mystēs* to respect the dictates of the former and to the triumph they can receive in the underworld if they reach the status of the privileged. They also indicate that Justice presides over the triumph of those who are privileged in contrast to the defeat and punishment of those who are not.

Schmidt (1975: 129), however, states that the universe of the Apulian infernal pottery does not coincide with the one of the gold lamellae:

The original inspiration of the netherworld images in Apulian art perhaps must be searched in an epic of religious coloring, or better in religious poetry belonging to a certain cultural level. This poetic background is not necessarily Orphic.

Yet Orpheus' presence, particularly in the amphora of the Ganymede artist, led this scholar to assert:

> We could suppose that the figurative creation derived from these sources would have been reused also by followers of some Orphic ideas ... in the ... image of the new amphora by Ganymede painter ... we could deal with an "Orphization" of a more generic prototype.

This statement is unfounded and dictated, I think, by two prejudices, which seem to be superseded. The first prejudice is the idea that the gold lamellae reflect the beliefs of people of low cultural level. But it does not seem appropriate to attribute low cultural level to believers who can afford expensive gold lamellae, put in rich tombs, whose beliefs seem to have been shared by the Sicilian tyrants that contract Pindar. The second prejudice is the supposition that the verses of the gold lamellae are a kind of sub-literature. Riedweg (2002) makes a strong case that there is a *hieros logos* behind them. This poem would be without doubt an example of an "epic of religious coloring" or a "religious poetry belonging to a certain cultural level" required by Schmidt. Also wrong is the idea (Schmidt 1975: 133) that the representation of Dionysus' birth from Zeus' thigh is not Orphic because Semele's son is not Orphic. As I have demonstrated in another paper (Bernabé 1998b), and as is reflected in the corresponding fragments of my edition (Bernabé 2004b), this topic was already dealt with in the *Rhapsodies* and probably before.

The only possible doubt is whether we can call "Orphic" this religious continuum that we have reconstructed, which would probably present differences of detail from place to place. But it is obvious that if we do not do so, the explanation is more complicated. What other movement could we reconstruct that joins Persephone and Dionysus with Orpheus as mediator, resorts to sacred texts, and presents a netherworld with the possibility of prizes and punishments? It seems more plausible to think that the texts serving as basis for the artists would be the ones used in the τελεταί, which would include performances of the sacred mystery in the form of κατάβασις in a kind of *imitatio mortis*, preparing the believer for the great experience.

The underworld of Apulian pottery is not always a terrible place. It can be a pleasant place if the faithful resorts to the due mediators, and if he/she is a follower of the Orphic-Dionysian mysteries. These vessels transmit, then, above all, a religious message, a message of hope, which is substantially the same as the one found in the gold lamellae.

The reasons for the few differences between the texts and the representations have to be seen in the nature of both channels: one is discursive, and the other is a visual representation, which forces the artist to represent, condensed, in one scene, what the texts would tell in several episodes, and to visualize some concepts that are difficult to reflect by means of images.

Characteristics of Life after Death

The benefits of the situation obtained by the initiate's soul in the underworld, about which pottery is not very explicit, can be known through the statements of the gold lamellae. First, the initiate is free of punishment (ἄποινος, cf. Pher.), which implies that the noninitiated must suffer punishment.[56] Second, he enjoys the privilege of wine, mentioned in the Pelinna gold leaf as "happy honor" (Pel. 6: οἶνον ἔχεις εὐδ⟨α⟩ίμονα τιμή⟨ν⟩) and present in the Gurob Papyrus, according to a recent rereading (Hordern 2000). Thur. (488) 6 mentions a crown (although the crown is a polyvalent symbol, as we have seen; see above). Both features, characteristic of the symposium, approximate the situation ridiculed by Plato, defined as "everlasting drunkenness," the frame of happy life in the underworld alluded to in the gold lamellae:

> But Musaios and his son grant to the just more exciting blessings from heaven than these. Having brought them, in their writings, to the House of Hades, they make them recline at a drinking-party of the righteous which they have furnished, and describe them as passing all their time drinking, with garlands on their heads, since in their opinion the fairest reward of virtue is everlasting drunkenness. (Pl. *Rep.* 363d (Orph. fr. 431B; trans. W.K.C. Guthrie; cf. Bernabé 1998a: 46)

Other passages coincide in presenting the underworld as a banquet with plenty of wine. Aristophanes (*Frogs* 85) alludes to the "feast of the blessed" in the underworld, and (fr. 504 K-A) puts forward the need to go soon down to Hades to drink, because those who are there are called happy precisely due to their constant drinking of wine. Pherecrates (fr. 113.30-33 K-A) describes how, in the underworld, young maids offer cups full of wine (cf. Aristoph. fr. 12 K-A). In an epigram from Smyrna (*Epigr. Gr.* 312.13ff. Kaibel) is described the present fortune of the deceased: "The gods are seeing me as a friend, while I enjoy the banquet beside the tripods and immortal tables." Passages like this have led Pugliese Carratelli (1993: 64 [= 2001: 118s]) to consider that Orphism, which primitively would have been a mere mystic theology, would have degraded due to a materialist version later spread and spurned by Plato. But the situation can be exactly the opposite.

The third benefit that the soul of the *mystēs* achieves in the underworld is happiness (ὄλβος),[57] a complex concept, which we do not know how to define, whether as a "material wellness" or as a deeper feeling arising from the company of the gods. Finally, the *mystēs* achieves also glory, according to Hipp. 16. These conditions are consistent with the sensation of triumph underlying the mention of the crown, to which I have repeatedly alluded. After the hard proof of having passed through several lives in this world, and after the constant training of the one that keeps an ascetic life, the soul achieves the crown of triumph: after its victory in the final proof, it is glorious and happy and celebrates with an eternal banquet.

The condition acquired by the soul is defined in different ways. Plato's statement (*Phd.* 69c), "It will dwell with the gods,"[58] places the initiates in a clear situation of privilege, although he does not tell us plainly that they also become gods. The gold lamellae offer us an ambiguous testimony. Sometimes the *mystēs* is called "hero" (Ent. 2, Pet. 11), which means a change in the traditional heroic status that belonged to those who had distinguished themselves by their deeds in war. It seems that, in the religious schema of the gold lamellae, it is the memory of the initiation that allows one to reach this status (Ent. 2).[59] It is predicted that the soul will "reign" (Pet. 11), but, since it is a reign shared with a group ("you will reign with the other heroes"), we suppose that the expression only means that the soul has freed itself from any submission. Finally, the new state of the soul is alternatively defined as "becoming a god" in the lamellae from Thurii as well as in the lamella from Rome,[60] but probably we do not have to understand that it is a personal god who receives worship if we take into account that the idea of divinization was exceptional in the Greek religious world.[61] It is more likely that the situation reached by the initiate after his liberation and definitive death, which is defined as a rebirth in the bosom of the chthonic goddess and is symbolized by the image of the divine kid breastfed by her in his new happy life, is a glorious new life, in which the *mystēs* identifies with Dionysus (let us remember that he is βάκχος himself). Although his stay in the underworld does not totally match that of the gods, it involves going beyond the human condition and acquiring a divine (superhuman) status, although probably of a lower grade than that of traditional gods,[62] that is, that which is defined by a synonymous term as the condition of "hero."

Two Models of Access to the *Locus Amoenus*

Above I reviewed a series of conditions that the *mystēs* must fulfill to gain access to the privileged space in the underworld. In short, he must have experienced initiation, which gave him a certain knowledge about the course of the universe and the place of his soul in the whole; and he must have passed through certain rites, which included the ecstatic experience and which involved both the expiation of a blame shared by all human beings and the acquisition of a ritual purity, which had to be retained subsequently within the strict confines of justice. All of this allowed the initiate's soul to triumph in the tests that served as filters for the soul on its way to the underworld.

Nevertheless, the sources describe for us two models of access to the *locus amoenus*. In one of them, the ritual element was the main one, in such a way that it was enough that the initiate know a series of formulas and passwords (on some occasions, it seems that it was enough that he simply bear the identification as *mystēs*) to gain access to the due place. This is the schema we find in the Orphic gold lamellae. Another model existed as well, according to which the soul suffered a trial. (This is the one that we find, for example, in Pind. *O*. 2, or in the Er myth of Plato's *Republic* and later in the Bononiae Papyrus.) In this case, what was fundamental for determining the fate of a deceased in the underworld was his behavior on earth. We do not know whether both models coexisted or if the second was a result of an evolution of the first (in which case it would have been proposed for the first time by Pindar and Plato and assumed later in Orphism).[63] In any case, the image of the Orphic underworld seems to have its roots in very old precedents: an early belief in a Mother Earth that produces a new rebirth; the image, probably Indo-European, of the green meadows of the underworld;[64] possible Egyptian influences in which the soul is questioned and has to pronounce certain passwords to gain access to a more pleasant underworld; and perhaps East Indian influences in a theory of reincarnation—all of this set in an infernal scenario, which is basically the traditional Greek one of Homer and Hesiod, but subverted in its symbolism and its meanings. The result is an original synthesis, and, as such, is deeply Greek. This model had validity for a long time, although it was always limited to more or less isolated groups of followers who never formed a Church.

The naiveté of some aspects of this belief makes it unacceptable for more rationalist minds. That, together with the fact that the punishments probably had from the very beginning a precise symbolic value, favors a reinterpretation and reanalysis of the described schema. The mire is typical of people who have not cleaned themselves of their sins (cf. Plot. 1.6.8), and the sieve is a reminder of the cause for the punishment: the inability to separate from the soul the titanic and evil elements that belong to it while retaining the Dionysian and positive elements (cf. Bernabé 1998a: 76). In Plato, on the one hand, we find traces of symbolic interpretations, which could be his or could reflect those existing in his time. On the other hand, the philosopher adapts the initiation model to philosophy and points out that the initiates are the real philosophers, whereas those who are in the mire and in darkness are the ignorant. The process of symbolization will come to its late consequences with the Neoplatonists, but this is not the right moment to go into this question. Let us leave as more interesting, then, the function that the presentation in the Orphic τελεταί of the terrors of the underworld initially assumed: on the one hand, the scale representation of fate in the underworld led the subject to carry out the rites due and to behave correctly; on the other, it calmed his anxieties by convincing him why he has thus been given a means of attaining happiness in the underworld. The presentation of the terrors of Hades functioned, then, as a kind of psychological vaccine that must have been extraordinarily effective.

Notes

This chapter is one of the results of a Research Project financed by the Spanish Ministry of Education and Science (HUM2006-09403). I am very grateful to Helena Bernabé for the translation of this paper into English, to Sara Olmos for her drawings, and to Patricia Johnston and Giovanni Casadio for their revision of the text and helpful suggestions.

1. In this chapter and only for the sake of convenience (for want of a more explicit term), I talk about "initiates," referring without distinction to those who have received the μύησις and to those who have celebrated the τελεταί, although it is obvious that the τελεταί are not only limited to initiation (cf. Jiménez San Cristóbal 2002). From now on, I will use the following abbreviations for the gold leaves: Eleuth. = Eleutherna (Orph. frr. 478–480 Bernabé [from now B.] = 32b I–III Kern [from now K.] and 482–483 B.); Ent. = Entella (Orph. fr. 475 B.); Hipp.

= Hipponion (Orph. fr. 474 B.); Malib. = Malibu (Orph. fr. 484 B.); Pel. = Pelinna (Orph. frr. 485-486 B.); Pet. = Petelia (Orph. fr. 476 B. = 32a K.); Phars.= Pharsalus (Orph. fr. 477 B.); Pher. = Pherai (fr. 493 B.); Rom. = Roma (Orph. fr. 491 B. = 32g K.); Thur. = Thurii (Orph. fr. 487-490 and 492 B. = 32f-cd and 47 K., quoted with the number of the fragment of B.). The English translation of the gold leaves is generally that of Radcliffe G. Edmonds.

2. Hipp. 4; Ent. 6: ἔνθα κατερχόμεναι ψυχαὶ νεκύων ψύχονται, "There the descending souls of the dead refresh themselves"; Pel. 7: καὶ σὺ μὲν εἰς (Luppe: κἀπ⟨ι⟩μένει ed. pr.) ὑπο γῆν, "And you will go (or 'they await you') beneath the earth."

3. Hipp. 9: Ἄιδος σκότος ὀρφ(ν)ήεντος, "The misty shadow of Hades"; cf. Ent. 11.

4. Hipp. 2: εἰς Ἀίδαο δόμους εὐήρεας, "To the spacious halls of Hades"; cf. Pet. 1: εὑρήσ{σ}εις δ' Ἀίδαο δόμων ἐπ' ἀριστερά, "You will find in the halls of Hades a spring on the left"; Phars. 1: Ἀίδαο δόμοις, "In the halls of Hades"; as well as *Il.* 15.251, δῶμ' Ἀίδαο, and *Od.* 10.491, εἰς Ἀίδαο δόμους.

5. Hipp. 3: πὰρ δ' αὐτὰν ἑστακυῖα λευκὰ κυπάρισ(σ)ος, "And by it stands a glowing white cypress tree"; cf. Ent. 5; Pet. 2; Phars. 2. About its symbology, see Bernabé and Jiménez San Cristóbal 2008: 25-28, with bibliography.

6. Hipp. 2: ἔστ' ἐπὶ δ(ε)ξιὰ κρήνα / . . . / ἔνθα κατερχόμεναι ψυχαὶ νεκύων ψύχονται, "A spring is on the right . . . there the descending souls of the dead refresh themselves"; 5: ταύτας τᾶς κράνας μηδὲ σχεδὸν ἐγγύθεν ἔλθῃς, "Do not go near to this spring at all"; cf. Ent. 4 and 7; Pet. 1 and 3. Cf. also Hipp. 6: πρόσθεν δὲ εὑρήσεις τᾶς Μναμοσύνας ἀπὸ λίμνας . . . ὕδωρ, "Further on you will find, from the lake of Memory, refreshing water"; cf. Pet. 4; Ent. 8; Phars. 4. The idea only reappears in Pausanias 9.39.8, about a place that is not infernal, but that tries to be a reflection of the otherworld, the Trophonius' cave.

7. Thur. (487) 6: λειμῶνάς θ' {ε} ἱεροὺς καὶ ἄλσεα Φερσεφονείας, "Persephone's sacred meadows and groves"; Thur. (489) 7: ὥς με{ι} πρόφ⟨ρ⟩ω⟨ν⟩ πέμψῃ⟨ι⟩ ἕδρας ἐς εὐαγέ{ι}ων, "That, gracious, may send me to the seats of the blessed."

8. Phars. 7: πᾶσαν ἀληθείην καταλέξαι, "You should relate the whole truth." Cf. Tortorelli Ghidini 1990.

9. Thur. (487) 2: πεφυλαγμένον εὖ μάλα πάντα, "Bearing everything in mind"; cf. Ent. 2: μ]εμνημέ(ν)ος ἥρως, and Bernabé's (1999b) interpretation, "Hero that remembers" (i.e., the one who is a hero because he remembers initiation).

10. First before the guards that keep watch on Mnemosyne's water; cf. Hipp. 10: Γῆς παῖ⟨ς⟩ εἰμι καὶ Οὐρανοῦ ἀστερόεντος, "I am the child of Earth and starry Heaven" (cf. Ent. 10; Pet. 6; Phars. 8; the declaration ἐμοὶ γένος οὐράνιον ["My race is heavenly"], Ent. 15; Pet. 7; Malib. 4; and Ἀστέριος ὄνομα ["My name is Asterios"], Phars. 9), and last, before Persephone herself, Thur. (488-490) 1: ἔρχομαι ἐκ καθαρῶν καθαρά, "Pure I come from the pure"; or Thur. (488) 3: ὑμῶν γένος ὄλβιον εὔχομαι εἶμεν, "I also claim that I am of your blessed race."

11. Hipp. 1: Μναμοσύνας τόδε ἔργον, "This is a work of Memory"; cf. Orph. *Hymn.* 77.9-10: μύσταις μνήμην ἐπέγειρε / εὐιέρου τελετῆς, λήθην δ' ἀπὸ τῶν⟨δ'⟩ ἀπόπεμπε, "For the initiates stir the memory of the sacred rite and ward off oblivion from them" (trans. A. N. Athanassakis).

12. Thur. (489) 4: πο⟨ι⟩νὰν δ' ἀνταπαπέ{ι}τε{σε}ι⟨σ⟩' ἔργων ἕνεκα οὔτι δικα⟨ί⟩ων,

"I have paid the penalty on account of deeds that are not just." About ποινή among the Orphics, cf. Santamaría Álvarez 2005.

13. Thur. (488) 5: κύκλο(υ) δ' ἐξέπταν βαρυπενθέος ἀργαλέοιο, "I flew out of the circle of wearying heavy grief."

14. It seems to me much more likely to read ΔJIKH instead of EYPYΔJIKH (too long for the space) in the inscription next to the seated woman, and NIKA instead of AIKA next to the winged woman. The winged Victory is a topic figure. But cf. Pensa 1977: 47.

15. Burkert 1969: 11 n. 25; Orph. fr. 233 B. = 158 K., trans. W.K.C. Guthrie. The passage has echoes in Parm. B1.14 D-K: τῶν δὲ Δίκη πολύποινος ἔχει κληῖδας ἀμοιβούς, "And Justice, bringer of retribution, holds the keys, which allow her to open first one gate then the other"; cf. also Bernabé 2004b: 54-57, 129.

16. Ps.-Demosthenes 25.11 (Orph. fr. 33 B. = 23 K.), trans. J. H. Vince. About Eunomia, cf. Hes. *Theog.* 902; Solon fr. 3.32 Gent.-Prato; Pind. *O.* 13.6, B.13.18, 15.55; Orph. fr. 252, *Hymn.* 43.2, 60.2.

17. We are also told about a sojourn of the pure in Thur. (489-490) 7, and specifically about a meadow, Thur. (487) 5, in addition to Pind. fr. 129.3 Maehl. (in a fragment with probable Orphic influences; cf. Bernabé 1999a); Pherecrates fr. 114 K-A; Aristoph. *Frogs* 449; Synesius *Hymn.* 3.394ff. The image of the meadow is not alien to Platonic eschatology. In a series of passages with a possible Orphic influence, we are told that the judges pronounce the definitive sentence in the meadow, where two roads start—one leads to the Island of the Blessed, and the other to Tartarus (Pl. *Gorg.* 524a)—or that the souls have to stay seven days in a meadow before going to Necessity and the Parcae and finding a new fate (Pl. *Rep.* 616b). But the philosopher seems to have innovated; cf. §11. About the Orphic signification of the presence of Dike in the Apulian pottery, cf. Pensa 1977: 7-8; about δίκη among the Orphics, cf. Jiménez San Cristóbal 2005.

18. Pet. 11: ἄ[λλοισι μεθ'] ἡρώεσσιν ἀνάξει[ς], "You will reign with the other heroes"; cf. Ent. 2: μ]εμνημέ(ν)ος ἥρως; and note 9 above.

19. Thur. (487) 4: θεὸς ἐγένου ἐξ ἀνθρώπου, "You are born god, instead of a mortal"; cf. Thur. (488) 9.

20. Cf. Bernabé 1998a: 46; and Pl. *Rep.* 363c, where there is attributed to Musaios and his son (that is, to Orphic traditions) a doctrine, according to which the fair and the unfair and the impious have different fates in the underworld, as well as Pl. *Gorg.* 493a; Origen *Contra Celsum* 4.10, 8.48.

21. The contrast is outstandingly sarcastic, since this group of people has a very bad reputation, because of the procedures they used to collect.

22. Cf. Graf 1974: 81, 103-107, 141; Bernabé 1998a: 56.

23. The assertion that Orphic rites come from Egypt seems to be a sign of the attempt of the Ptolomean to associate Greek religion with the Egyptian one, and to favor religious syncretism. Cf. Díez de Velasco and Molinero Polo 1994, related to another reference by Diodorus Siculus (1.92.2), about the hypothetic Egyptian origin of Caron and his boat (these conclusions are, however, perfectly applicable to the passage with which we are dealing); cf. also Díez de Velasco 1995: 44 and n. 106; Bernabé 2000; Casadio 1996b: 205 n. 16, with bibliography.

24. Probably because they have only selected the information that is immediately useful for the initiate and also because it could be considered a bad omen to

mention the possibility of failure in the moment of death. Cf. Bernabé and Jiménez San Cristóbal 2008: 232-233.

25. Janko (2001: 20 n. 85) brings up Protagoras' book Περὶ τῶν ἐν Ἅιδου, quoted by Diog. Laert. 9.55 and Sext. Emp. *Math.* 9.66, 74.

26. Tsantsanoglou (1997: 110) understands that the commentator addresses the profane, whose punishments in Hades are evident, trying to convince them of the fact that only by purifying themselves and by initiation will they be able to achieve a happy life in the netherworld. Cf. Pl. *Rep.* 364b-365b, as well as Janko 1997: 68.

27. The reference to dreams probably alludes to nightmares suffered by certain individuals and considered as proofs of the real existence of torments in the netherworld.

28. We can read]υστ[in col. III.11 (maybe μ]υστ[-?).

29. Cf. also Procl. *In Pl. Rep.* 2.108.17 Kroll, in which, nine centuries later, we still find the association of the τελεταί with the terrors of Hades within a scheme, which seems to be the same: there are initiations associated with terrors, which have a cathartic effect, because they produce in the faithful a community with the divine, according to the idea that the divine is indescribable.

30. Aristoph. *Frogs* 145 (where we are told about "much mud and shit of eternal flow"), 273.

31. Aristid. 22.10; cf. also Plot. 1.6.6. About the topic, cf. Graf 1974: 103-107; Kingsley 1995: 118-119; Casadesús 1995: 60-63; Watkins 1995: 289-290; West 1997: 162 and n. 257. Other passages in which we are told about prizes and punishment in connection with Orpheus are Pl. *Rep.* 363c (Orph. fr. 431I, 434I B. = 4 K.); Diod. Sic. 1.96.2 (Orph. fr. 55 B.); cf. also the symbolic interpretation by Pl. *Gorg.* 493a; and Bernabé 1998a.

32. The Munich Attic amphora with black figures (Beazley, *ABV*, p. 316) from the end of the sixth century BCE, in which are shown Sisyphus and some winged beings (the ancestors of the Danaids) that throw water into a big jar (Albinus 2000: pl. 4).

33. Cf. the commentary by Anne Burton 1972: ad loc., p. 279.

34. The instrument for the punishment, the sieve, maybe evokes the cause of suffering: the incapacity to separate the soul from the evil aspects. Cf. Harrison 1903: 604-623; and Bernabé 1998a: 76.

35. Sorel 1995: 107-108; cf. Burkert 1987: 91-92; Brillante 1987: 39; Riedweg 1998: 367 n. 33; Lada-Richards 1999: 90, 98-99, and 103.

36. We can ask ourselves if Plato points out this resemblance or if, rather, he ironically alludes to an etymology, which may be Orphic. The latter possibility will not surprise us, considering the great love of etymological games typical of the Orphic; cf. Bernabé 1999c.

37. Pher.: εἴσιθ⟨ι⟩ ἱερον λειμῶνα. ἄποινος γὰρ ὁ μύστης, "Enter the holy meadow. For the initiate has paid the price."

38. Thur. (487) 5-6: χαῖρ⟨ε⟩, χαῖρε· δεξιὰν ὁδοιπόρ⟨ει⟩ / λειμῶνάς θ' {ε} ἱεροὺς καὶ ἄλσεα Φερσεφονείας, "Hail, hail, by taking the path on the right / toward the sacred meadows and the groves of Persephone." The same meadow appears in a funerary epigram dedicated to someone called Aristodicus of Rhodes (*AP* 7.189.3-4), and in the Orphic hymn dedicated to Persephone, who is reborn in spring and

is kidnapped in autumn (Orph. *Hymn*. 29.12, cf. 18.2). Λειμωνιάδες, a derivative of λειμών, describes the Hours, "partners in games of holy Persephone," in Orph. *Hymn*. 43.3. Cf. also Orph. *Hymn* 51.4, 81.3, and the commentaries by Ricciardelli (2000a) on the quoted passages. A similar epithet, Λειμωνία, is assigned to Persephone in an inscription from Amphipolis (middle of the third century BCE); cf. Feyel 1935: 67. About the meadow in general, cf. Velasco López 2001.

39. Thur. (489-490) 7: ὥς μ{ει} πρόφ⟨ρ⟩ων πέμψη⟨ι⟩ ἕδρας ἐς εὐαγέ{ι}ων, "That she [Persephone], gracious, may send me to the abode of the blessed" (cf. Orph. fr. 340 B. = 322 K.). For this reason, the soul declares its purity in Thur. (489-490) 1.

40. Cf. also the description of the world of the blessed in Aristophanes' *Frogs*.

41. Persephone's sacred grove is already known to Homer and to other authors—for instance, Eur. *HF* 615. The echoes of this image even reach a Latin author as late as Claudianus (fourth century CE), who was much influenced by Orphism and describes in *De raptu Proserpinae* (2.287ff.) the goddess's happy world as a pleasant place with groves and meadows.

42. I am referring to the images studied by Cabrera Bonet (1998).

43. From the same tomb where the Apulian amphora attributed to the Ganymedes painter (Fig. 6.8) appeared.

44. Cf. the quoted fragments of the ancient collection Fenicia (c. 350 BCE).

45. Thur. (489) 6: νῦν δ' ἱκέτι⟨ς⟩ ἥκω παρ⟨ὰ⟩ ἁγνὴ⟨ν⟩ Φε⟨ρ⟩σεφόνε⟨ι⟩αν, "Now I come, a suppliant, to holy Phersephoneia."

46. If we accept the extremely plausible corrections ἐρέουσιν (Lazzarini) and ὑποχθονίωι βασιλείαι (West). Maybe ὑποχθονίωι βασιλείαι was also in Ent. 16.

47. In addition to Hipp. 13, cf. Thur. and Pel.

48. Cf. Casadio 1994, in particular the evidence from Taras, Locris, and Sybaris.

49. Procl. *In Pl. Ti*. 3.297.3 Diehl; Simplic. *in Cael*. 377.12 Heiberg (Orph. fr. 348 B. = 229-230 K.).

50. Cf. *Il*. 9.457: ἐπαινὴ Περσεφόνεια, "awesome Persephone" (in other cases in *Il*. 9.569; *Od*. 10.491 534, 564, 11.47; Hes. *Theog*. 568). Only once (*Od*. 10.509) are the ἄλσεα Περσεφονείη ("groves of Persephone") mentioned in a non-negative form.

51. For example, in the quoted passages Pl. *Rep*. 364e; Ps.-Demosthenes 2.5.11; Diod. Sic. 1.96.2-5; Procl. *in Pl. Ti*. 3.297.3 Diehl; Simplic. *in Cael*. 377.12 Heiberg.

52. Cf. Pensa 1977: 5-7, about the possible presence of Eurydice in some Apulian vases.

53. Munich, Antikensammlungen 3297, IV BCE fin.; cf. Pensa 1977: 23-24; Olmos 2008: 288-291, with bibliography (Fig. 6.6).

54. Pensa (1977: 37-46) offers a very interesting alternative interpretation of the Danaids.

55. According to Pensa (1977: 46), the little Eros between Orpheus and the woman confirms that she is Eurydice, but Eros has many different and important functions in Orphism; cf. Calame 1999: XI; Bernabé 2004a: frr. 64 and 65.

56. They coincide in this with other examined sources; see Pl. *Phd*. 69c, *Gorg*. 493a, *Rep*. 364e; Iulian. *Or*. 7.25; Plut. fr. 178 Sandbach.

57. The *mystēs* is called ὄλβιε in Thur. (488) 9 and τρισόλβιε in Pel. 1.

58. Iulian. *Or.* 7.25 talks also about "dwelling with the divine beings." Cf. the "holy visions" of Plut. fr. 178 Sandbach.

59. If we have to read in line 2 μ]εμνημέ⟨ν⟩ος ἥρως, "Hero that remembers"; cf. Bernabé 1999b.

60. Thur. (487) 4: θεὸς ἐγένου ἐξ ἀνθρώπου, "You are born god, instead of a mortal"; Thur. (488) 9: ὄλβιε καὶ μακαριστέ, θεὸς δ' ἔσηι ἀντὶ βροτοῖο, "Happy and most blessed one, a god you shall be instead of a mortal." Scarpi (1987: 200ff.) has pointed out the difference in the use of tenses: "You will be god" projects deification into the future, in contrast to "You are already god," now, as a consummated fact, maybe the result of the experience never lived before. In Rom. 3 we read: Καικιλία Σεκουνδεῖνα νόμωι ἴθι δῖα γεγῶσα, "Come, Cecilia Secundina, legitimately converted into goddess."

61. Cf. the reference of Hdt. 4.94 to Zalmoxis' followers. In the Hellenistic period only, the deification of the dead is integrated within the frame of official religion, but as a privilege reserved for the sovereigns.

62. Scarpi (1987) compares the situation of the souls of the initiates with that of the Hesiodic men of the golden age (Hes. *WD* 109-126), who, when the Earth hides their bodies, become demons, guardians of justice, and of givers of wealth.

63. García Teijeiro (1985: 141) considers turning the meadow into the place where the judgment of the souls was celebrated to be a Platonic innovation; cf., from a different point of view, Bañuls Oller 1997: 10-12.

64. Cf. Puhvel 1969; Motte 1973: 247; García Teijeiro 1985; Velasco López 2001: 136-144.

CHAPTER 7

Putting Your Mouth Where Your Money Is: Eumolpus' Will, *Pasta e Fagioli*, and the Fate of the Soul in South Italian Thought from Pythagoras to Ennius

R. DREW GRIFFITH

You will recall that near the end of the extant portion of Petronius' *Satyricon*, the anti-hero Encolpius finds himself shipwrecked at Croton with his associates, Eumolpus the poetaster, their boy-toy Giton, and hired man Corax. Here the tireless grifters launch their final sting, Eumolpus posing as a wealthy magnate, conveniently both childless and moribund, with the others masquerading as his slaves. So styled, the foursome dines out on invitations from local *captatores* eager to fawn and wheedle their way into Eumolpus' will (Tracy 1980). Finally, tired of the game and no doubt threatened with imminent exposure as the Felix Krull he is, in a breach of decorum worthy of Trimalchio himself (cf. *Sat.* 71.4), Eumolpus has his will read out to the assembled company of his heirs.

It is an odd will, for it calls on them to eat his corpse in public as a precondition of coming into their inheritance (*Sat.* 141). The idea of cannibalism is not itself surprising, for though most Greeks and Romans may have balked at eating their dead, others as diverse as Diogenes the Cynic and the Stoics Zeno and Chrysippus were more open-minded (Diog. Laert. 6.73, 7.121). What *is* truly shocking is that the cannibalism be mandated in a will, for legal texts are usually *against* cannibalism. The Court of Queen's Bench, London, for example, passed a landmark ruling in 1884 that sailors cannot legally kill cabin-boys for food, though it did not specifically forbid eating any who died of natural causes (Arens 1979; Simpson 1984). Only one Roman other than Eumolpus ordered his heirs to eat his body, and that case is more sensible than this, for the testator, M. Grunnius Corocotta, was quite literally a pig—I'm referring to the fourth-century CE schoolboy spoof in which a porker, summoned to execution by the household chef, arranges for the posthumous disposition of his various cuts of meat (Champlin 1987, with bibl.).

Gareth Schmeling (1991: 376) has demonstrated that each intact section of the *Satyricon* ends with something outrageous, like the deflowering of the prepubescent Pannychis at the close of the Quartilla episode (25-26), or the arrival of the fire brigade that ends the *Cena Trimalchionis* (78). If that pattern obtained for the now-fragmentary sections also, there is a good chance that our passage, shocking as it is—and its last words describe mothers clutching their half-eaten babies to their breasts (Sallmann 1999: 128)—was the original end of the whole novel. If so, we may suppose that it affords "the benefaction of significance in some concordant structure" (Kermode 2000: 148) that draws together thematic threads from disparate parts of the work. Certainly the theatricality motif, whose prominence Costas Panayotakis (1995) has recently shown, is given free reign with the Plautine-cum-Shakespearean shipwreck: Hell is empty and all the devils are here, including the *faux riche* Eumolpus and his *trompe l'oeil* servants. Theatrical, too, is the detail that this new-fangled testament requires the grotesque Eucharist (Bowersock 1994: 134-139) to be performed before a live audience. I would argue that two other recurrent themes that surface and intersect meaningfully at this point are parody of philosophic dialogue (Courtney 1962; Cameron 1969; Bessone 1993; Cucchiarelli 1996) and the play on significant names that Italian scholars have dubbed *la poetica dei nomi* (Schmeling 1969; Priuli 1975; Barchiesi 1984; Labate 1986).

The point of intersection is the one heir *not* repelled by Eumolpus' stipulation, who, citing impressively obscure precedents, mounts an erudite "defense of necessity" argument in favor of carrying it out (*Sat.* 141; Rankin 1969 = 1971: 100-101; Shey 1971). This man, presumably among those glumly chewing in the alfresco banquet that ends Fellini's 1969 film version, is named Gorgias. This cannot fail to recall the "indefatigable stylist" (Dodds 1959: 8; Harrison 1964; McComiskey 2002, with bibl.) from Leontini, Sicily, who enthralled Athenians at the turn of the fourth century with his verbal pyrotechnics developed as "an analog of the culinary art" (Conte 1996: 134-135; cf. Aristoph. *Av.* 1695-1696; Dunbar 1995: 741)—remember that the connection between rhetoric and cuisine is drawn in the very first chapter of the *Satyricon* (1.3, 2.1, 2.8-9; Shey 1971: 81). His encounter with Socrates inspired the Platonic dialogue that bears his name, which hinges on a spirited encomium of the "natural justice" wherein Might is right, citing Pindar's poem, "Custom, king of all . . ." (*Gorg.* 482c-484c, fr. 169a Maehler). This poem has special relevance for us, for Plato was not the first to quote it. Two generations earlier, Herodotus invoked the very same text (3.38; Rankin 1969: 383) to sum up the strange case of the Callatiae, an Indian tribe who refused Darius' inducement to adopt a novel funeral-rite. They begged the Great King never again to mention in their hearing anything so horrible as cremation, and to allow them instead to go on, as their forebears had always done, laying their dear departed to rest by eating their flesh.

The echo of the Callatiae episode is so apt to our passage that it would by itself have justified Petronius' choice of name for the greedy heir, the more so since we have tended to see Encolpius as an impoverished Socrates since, with the curse of Priapus, he was forced to sleep with Giton as chastely as the sage with Alcibiades (*Sat.* 128; Sommariva 1984). Yet there is more. Gorgias was not just a literary *character*, but also an *author* in his own right. One of his most notorious turns of phrase—one copied by Ennius (*Annales* fr. 138 Vahlen = 125 Skutsch) and the atomist Lucretius (5.993; Meurig Davies 1949: 73)—was his γρῖφος or kenning for vultures, ἔμψυχοι τάφοι (82B.5a D-K; Waern 1951 [who does not discuss this example]). The idea of "living" (or, more literally, "ensouled") tombs recalls the doctrine that everyone's body (σῶμα) is the tomb (σῆμα) in which his or her own soul is imprisoned (Philolaus 44B.14 D-K; Pl. *Phd.* 81e; *Crat.* 400c, etc.).

This σῶμα σῆμα notion was popularized by Socrates, and is the sort of thing that might indeed lead a dying man to offer a cock to Asclepius, the god of healing (Pl. *Phd.* 118a, with Damascius apud Schol. ad loc.; Most 1993: 100), but the Athenian philosopher himself associated it with Italy (*Gorg.* 493a), and if it was not first espoused by Pythagoras—most famous citizen of where else but Croton?—he seems most fully to have explored its philosophical implications (Dobrochotov 1992). Though ascetic, the doctrine was not *all* doom and gloom, for it accompanied the belief in transmigration of souls. Pythagoras in turn must have acquired this idea from somewhere (Keith 1909: 605), and Cicero (*Tusc.* 1.38) says that he learned it at the knee of the Samian, Pherecydes. Herbert Long (1948: 14), however, convincingly dismisses this as an instance of the ancients' habit of reading all pupils' teachings back into the work of their masters. In fact, the idea seems totally foreign to Greeks—"a drop of alien blood in [their] veins," as Erwin Rohde put it (Dodds 1951: 139). Sensing this, Herodotus (2.123) claims that Greeks derived it from Egypt; but there is a fly in this ointment as well, for Egyptians never believed any such thing, though their tomb-paintings may have led Herodotus to think they did (Zabkar 1963). It is curious that, if we join Long in doubting that Pherecydes taught it, every Greco-Roman writer to espouse reincarnation prior to the Church father Origen is associated in some way with Magna Graecia. Apart from Pythagoras himself, there is the Theban Pindar—but apparently only when working for Theron of Acragas (*O.* 2.57–80; cf. fr. 133 Maehler); the Acragantine Empedocles (31B.115 D-K = 107 Wright = 11 Inwood); Plato, who spent his formative years in Syracuse (*Epistle* 7, which mentions metempsychosis at 335b-c, *Phdr.* 249a, etc.); and the Calabrian Ennius (*Annales* fr. 15 Vahlen = 11 Skutsch). Even Vergil set his account of reincarnation (*Aen.* 6.724-751) in the underworld, which Aeneas enters via Cumae. The conclusion most economically drawn from these data is that Greeks acquired the doctrine of reincarnation from southern Italy, just as it has been argued (R. D. Griffith 2008, with bibl.) that they borrowed the equally alien, though very different, doctrine of Elysium from Egypt.

If I am right that it is Italian in origin, it will come as no surprise that belief in rebirth affects one's diet, for Italians live to eat. After all, what other people's words for "to be" and "to eat" (Latin *esse* and *ēsse*, Quintilian 11.3.136; Juvenal 15.102) are one and the same? Indeed, Pythagoras believed in rebirth not on theoretical grounds, but from personal experience, recalling his prior incarnation as Euphorbus (Hor. *Odes* 1.28.9-15; cf. Nisbet and Hubbard 1970: 327-328). Euphorbus was the Trojan who in a cameo role in the *Iliad* (16.805-815) changed literary history by wounding Patroclus, making him vulnerable to Hector's death-blow. That Pythagoras should have believed himself a reincarnation of just *this* person, rather than, say, a shrubbery, as Empedocles claimed to have been in an earlier life, or a peacock, as Ennius once was (*Annales* fr. 15 Vahlen = 11 Skutsch), may be no accident. Euphorbus' Homeric credentials give Pythagoras a kind of aristocratic prestige, and the Trojan connection must have played well in his adopted homeland of Italy, since Romans thought themselves offspring of the Trojan Aenêas (Dionys. Halic. 1.49-53, 55-60; Livy 1.1-3; Lucretius 1.1; cf. Ogilvie 1965: 32-35). But above all, as Otto Skutsch (1959) notes, Euphorbus' name means "well-fed." Naturally it is comforting to think one was fed well in a previous life, but Pythagoras would have interpreted good eating in the specific sense of having abstained from improper foods, for he promulgated a number of dietary taboos.

You might think a philosopher's rules for living could be explained logically. After all, lest one offend a transmigrated human soul, one must abstain from harming animals, as Pythagoras scolded a man for whipping a puppy in whose bark he recognized the voice of a dead friend (Xenophanes 21B.7 D-K). This can hardly be done without being vegetarian, so it is not surprising that meat was *verboten* among Pythagoreans, as with Empedocles and the devotees of the Cretan Zeus (31B.128 D-K; Eur. fr. 472.16-19 *TrGF;* cf. Demand 1975: 352-353). (It is true that human souls might also be reborn in plants, but apparently just *inedible* ones, like Empedocles' shrub.)

There is a problem with this logical explanation, however. The problem is beans. Pythagoras decreed them, too, taboo, and not just as food. He barred his followers even from walking in fields where they were growing. This notorious prohibition, merely weird to us, verged on blasphemy in antiquity, for the "Baked Bean Festival" (*Pyanopsia*) was so important in the liturgical calendar that it gave its name to an Athenian month (Harrison 1927: 320). The prohibition has sparked various explanations. Walter Burkert (1972: 184) thinks beans were shunned due to an aesthetic aversion to their intestinal after-effects, disturbing as these must be to sensitive urban shamans. But perhaps, as Pliny thought, the opposite is true, and beans are so irresistible that they can never be sampled without inducing gluttony (*NH* 18.118). Or again, perhaps Pythagoreans had a tragic propensity for the rare, devastating bean-allergy known to medical science as "favism" (Scarborough 1982, with bibl.). For my part, I incline rather to think that Pythagoreans avoided beans for *symbolic* reasons.

Beans are seeds, as Greeks well knew, for they perhaps correctly derived their word for "bean" (κύαμος) from κύω, "conceive," or κυέω, "be pregnant" (Onians 1951: 112 n. 2; Chantraine 1970: 593). Seeds are obvious symbols of rebirth. So, in an argument shared by St. Paul, Rabbi Meïr explained resurrection to Ptolemy V's wife, Cleopatra, as a kind of sowing wherein the seed, buried in the earth, comes to life again in new and different form (Babylonian Talmud *Sanhedrin* 90b; 1 Corinthians 15:35-44; cf. Riesenfeld 1970: 171-186). Reincarnation is not resurrection, to be sure, but the farming analogy works just as well to describe it. That is why pomegranate seeds are the food of the dead in the Proserpina story (*Hymn Dem.* 372, 411-413), which had wide currency in Sicily, given that, as Cicero tells us, the whole island is sacred to Ceres and Liber (*Verr.* 2.4.48 [106]; cf. Diod. Sic. 5.2.3, and the comment by Zuntz 1971: 70-75). It is also why, as the same myth shows, it can be dangerous to eat even a single seed, if one hopes ever to get free of the underworld. Moreover, this might also explain why Aristotle (fr. 195 Rose) darkly says beans resemble the gates of Hades and why Pliny reports them to contain the souls of the dead (*NH* 18.118). As with beans, so with meat: I would argue that Pythagorean vegetarianism is fundamentally symbolic, serving above all as an act of religious faith to proclaim "the kinship of all types of living things and life in general with the ultimate principle of the Universe," (Anton 1992: 32), or, to put it in Petronian terms, the belief that "our region is so full of present divinities that you can easier run across a god than a man" (*Sat.* 17).

The nuances of the Pythagorean diet seem far removed from Eumolpus' will, but Paolo Fedeli (1987: 20-21) has shown that Petronius has them very much in mind. It was when interrupted while shelling beans that Polyaenus (as Encolpius now calls himself) killed Priapus' sacred goose, which Oenothea promptly turned into *paté de foie gras* (*Sat.* 135–137). This breaks so many taboos of Croton's most famous citizen at once that it brings them all forcibly to mind. And then, just four chapters later, we have Eumolpus' will. It is for this reason that I would argue that the will, which on the face of it rides roughshod over all religious norms, whether those of the traditional Olympian faith or of the (I have been arguing) native Italian eschatology of metempsychosis, does not in fact *ignore* the doctrine of rebirth, but rather *deconstructs* it. In one sense, Eumolpus lives up to his billing as philosopher manqué, for he compels his would-be heirs to pursue their materialism beyond mere crassness to its logical conclusion as a guiding ontological and ethical principle, collapsing in the process the space between legal testator and property, owner and owned, body and self. If Gorgias, impervious to any chastising effect of this *reductio ad absurdum*, indeed makes himself a *vivum bustum* by carrying out the terms of the will, as he seems inclined to do, Eumolpus *will* transmigrate into his body, but atom by atom in a way that Lucretius would have approved of and not at all in the spiritual sense intended by Pythagoras. In this process, Eumolpus will have successfully posited himself as coextensive with his own flesh. Like Jeremy Bentham, still sitting in the south cloister of University College 170 years after his death (Marmoy 1958; Richardson and Hurwitz 1987; Collings 2000; Crimmins 2002), or Lenin in his tomb on Red Square, he *is* his body. With him, what you see is what you get, or—if we may express this from Gorgias' point of view—you are whom you eat.

PART II

DEMETER AND ISIS

CHAPTER 8

Aspects of the Cult of Demeter in Magna Graecia: The "Case" of San Nicola di Albanella

GIULIA SFAMENI GASPARRO

Due to the extremely limited number of literary sources, which are often merely scholiastic or hypomnematic documents providing scarce information, our reconstruction of the religious panorama of Magna Graecia, like that of Sicily, remains largely based on archaeological, monumental, and epigraphical evidence. We need not stress the importance of this documentation, insofar as it bears direct witness to the specific local realities, nor do we need to mention the difficulties and risks at times involved in its historico-religious exegesis. Such risks are even greater when we try to deal with monumental complexes that, due to the absence of explicit identifying elements (in a few lucky cases we have dedicatory inscriptions), leave us more or less uncertain regarding their association with one cult or another. The very structure of the religious horizon in Magna Graecia and Sicily, with its peculiar Greek-style polytheistic features, characterized by the departmentalization of divine figures and their respective sphere of influence, but also—at the same time—by the possibility of associations and convergences between them, leads scholars to be extremely cautious in circumscribing and defining the sphere of divine action and of the respective cults in relation to archaeological evidence. There do exist, however, some special cases for which the significant frequency of the emergence of sufficiently homogeneous and peculiar documentary contexts from a monumental point of view, throughout the area of Greek cultural and religious influence, makes it possible with reasonable confidence to identify the divine personality to which they are linked and their underlying ritual *praxis*. This in fact is the situation for the many sacred sites recognizable as dedicated to the Demeter cult and in particular associated with that characteristic ritual *praxis* that literary and epigraphic sources call *Thesmophoria*. Without being able here to dedicate space to a description of a phenomenon that is in any case well known, it is sufficient to mention that in the wide-ranging and varied panorama of Greek religious tradition, in terms of antiquity and pan-Hellenic diffusion, a major role was played by cults to Demeter Thesmophoros, named according to a common use of Greek liturgical language in the form of the neutral plural, τὰ θεσμοφόρια, that is, the "Thesmophoria."[1]

Among the peculiar characteristics of these cults, in addition to being strictly esoteric and reserved for women,[2] there is on one hand the mesh of qualified relationships between the mythical and ritual plane, and on the other the type of sacred space in which the latter is situated.[3] The literary sources, while of varying documentary value in relation to their age and provenance, testify to the existence of a fairly specific connection between the cult actions performed by the *Thesmophoriazousai*, that is, the women who celebrate the rite, and a primordial crisis involving Demeter and her daughter Kore-Persephone, who is ritually evoked in the Thesmophoria context. To use the definition of Clement of Alexandria, the women who celebrated the Thesmophoria performed a sacred festival evoking the divine event, narrated in the myth (τὴν μυθολογίαν . . . ἑορτάζουσι), to which he briefly alludes by mentioning

> Pherephatta's flowerpicking, her *kalathos,* and her rape by Aidoneus, and the cleft in the earth, and the pigs of Eubuleus that were swallowed up together with the Two Goddesses, according to which aetiology the "megarising" women at the Thesmophoria threw in pigs. This myth the women celebrate variously in festivals around the city, Thesmophoria, Skirophoria, Arrhetophoria, acting out the rape of Pherephatta in many ways.[4]

This event substantially corresponds to that described in the pseudo-Homeric Hymn to Demeter, which, however, is specifically Eleusinian, explicitly linked to that peculiar religious structure which were the *mysteria,* namely the esoteric initiation rites celebrated only at the sacred site of Eleusis.[5] The mythical theme in question is reflected in extensive literary documentation, with more or less significant variations often linked to local traditions and cults, including, in fact, some of a Thesmophoria nature. These are Hades-Pluto's abduction of Kore-Persephone, her Mother's grieving and search for her, and the Daughter's return, albeit only periodically, which brings an end to Demeter's grief, with positive consequences for humanity. In particular, they represent the restoration or foundation of the agrarian rhythms of cereal farming and thus of chthonic fertility, a guarantee of continued survival for men and animals.

These mythical events are articulated within a cosmic scenario, implying a series of movements of the protagonists not only in a vertical perspective (descent of Demeter from Olympus, ascent of Hades from the underworld and his katabasis with the abducted maiden, return of her to her Mother on the earth and then together with her to the heavenly dwelling), but also horizontally (Demeter's wandering over the earth looking for her Daughter, and her many *xeniai* at human hosts). This creates a sort of mythical "cartography" involving the three cosmic levels but whose fulcrum is the earth. It is, in fact, here that the vectors of action of the deities come into contact and conflict (Persephone picks flowers on a plain, from which emerges Hades' chariot, only to plunge back down into it; the earth is journeyed over by a mourning Demeter, is made sterile by the angered goddess, then once more blossoms with Persephone's re-emergence from the underworld). The divine event and its "geography" involve the human dimension, which in turn is actively collocated in the "space" and time of myth through ritual practice and the definition of the sacred space in which this unfolds.

De facto, the sacred site, the Thesmophorion, presents some typical structural connotations that—although we should take all the precautions necessary in the exegesis of the individual monumental complexes—often clearly indicate its identity as a center of the Demeter cult. The typical elements that combine to help identify a Demeter Thesmophoros scenario are an extramural location,[6] a site in an elevated position (on high ground or hillsides), proximity to water (seashores or riverbanks), and—less often archaeologically verifiable even if often mentioned by ancient sources—the presence of natural or artificial underground cavities (the *megara*).

There naturally exist many variables in this scenario, as can be seen in the passage quoted above, when Clement of Alexandria stresses that the women celebrate their festive rites connected to the mythical theme of the abduction and search for Persephone ποικίλως κατὰ πόλιν (which can be translated not only as "variously in festival around the city" but also as "in different ways from city to city") and mentions, alongside the Thesmophoria, other ceremonies such as the Skirophoria and Arrhetophoria,[7] which the sources also connect to the sphere of Demeter. In any case, the data evoked recur with significant frequency in the archaeological contexts identifiable with certainty or good approximation as Thesmophoria, or are illustrated as such by the relevant sources. It can be seen from this that the Thesmophoria and the numerous similar cult centers identifiable in the area in which Greek religious history unfolded[8] imply a qualified relationship between the symbolic organization of the ritual space and the specific mythical parameter to which the ceremonies performed there are linked. Much more important, then, is the contribution of archaeological evidence to the historico-religious knowledge of the widespread and articulated mythical-ritual Demeter sphere, relatable to a varying extent to the Thesmophoria, as is illustrated by the literary sources. At the same time, the many "variables" that this evidence displays in the different regions of the Greek and Hellenized world confirm the continuous adaptability of this sphere to local realities, differentiated over time and in their respective historico-cultural referents. More widely, they illuminate the flexibility of the religious model represented by Greek polytheism, in its peculiar dialectic between general structures of a pan-Hellenic dimension and local "inventions," linked to the various communities and relative traditions composing the variegated scenario of the peoples that saw themselves as Hellenes, due to community of language, customs, and religious traditions (cf. Hdt. 8.144.2).

In this background, it is possible correctly to collocate the historico-religious exegesis of the wide-ranging material that has come to light in recent years in the *chora* of Poseidonia-Paestum, in San Nicola di Albanella, and that is now fully accessible to critical study, after preliminary information[9] provided in M. Cipriani's excellent and methodologically exemplary monograph.[10] It is part of an articulated framework of Demeter presences that archaeological investigation is revealing to be increasingly wide and rich, with local peculiarities, not only in the area of Paestum[11] but in Magna Graecia as a whole.[12] This has led us to reappraise that impression of marginality which once seemed to characterize the pan-Hellenic personality of Demeter in this region, compared to the extensive evidence of major cults in the ancient sources associated with important sanctuaries, such as those of Hera in Poseidonia[13] and Crotone[14] or of Persephone in the grandiose complex of Mannella at Locri.[15]

Without offering a detailed description of the site, impossible here as well as being superfluous to my ends, it is sufficient to consider the peculiar geographical situation of the sacred site, situated in a small valley 16 kilometers northeast of Poseidonia, in the northern section of the La Cosa River and dominated by the uplands of San Nicola and the Vetrale. This is thus a country environment abundant in water, perfectly in line with the whole series of Demeter Thesmophoros sites.[16] The sacred area, which dates back to the fifth century BCE, consists of a dry-stone-walled enclosure (Figs. 8.1–8.3), perhaps with a partial or temporary roof, within which are situated fireplaces for sacrificial offers and a number of votive deposits, containing numerous miniature vases (skyphoi, kotyliskoi, one-handed cups, and krateriskoi) found turned over toward the ground, according to a custom reported in various Thesmophoria sanctuaries, and in particular at Gela Bitalemi, which, defined explicitly as such by a dedi-

Aspects of the Cult of Demeter in Magna Graecia 143

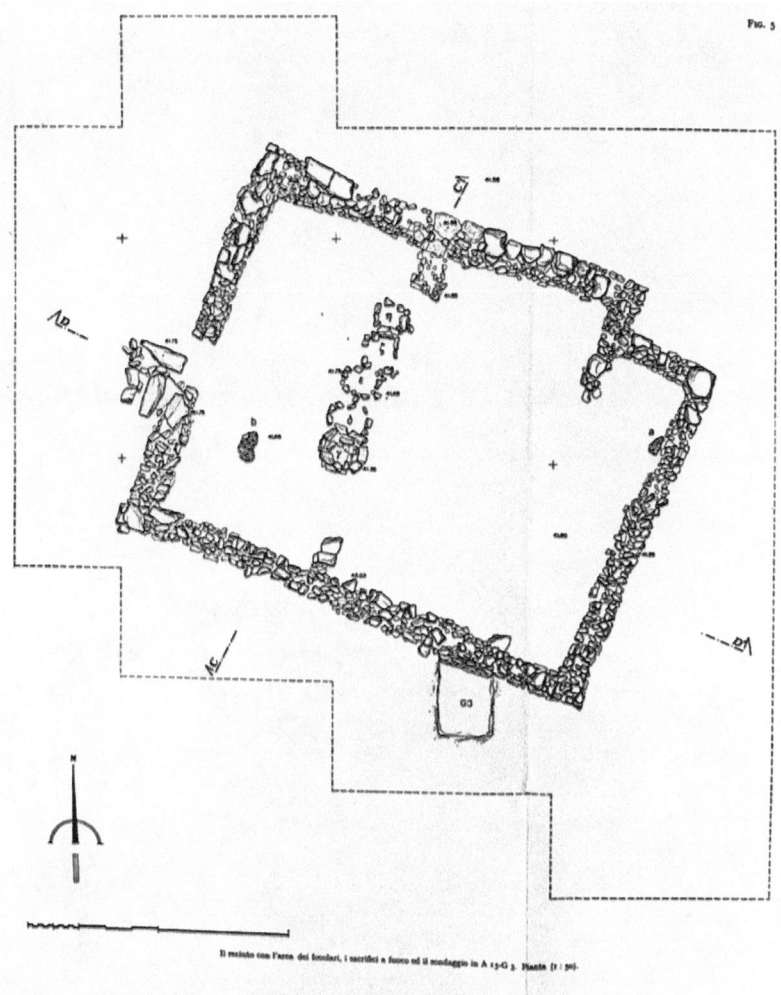

Figure 8.1. The enclosure with the area of the hearths, the sacrifices by fire. Fig. 5 Cipriani.

catory inscription "to Thesmophoros,"[17] is the closest and most specific parameter of comparison for the sacred site in question.[18] In addition to ceramic cooking containers, bearing traces of fire as a witness to their use for communal meals inside the sacred area, the votive deposit in which all the material was sealed at the end of the fifth century BCE, when the religious activity of the small sanctuary seems to have ceased, has provided a rich series of votive terracottas displaying various iconographic typologies. These represent one of the most significant elements of the entire context

Figure 8.2. The enclosure after excavation seen from the east. Tab. 5 Cipriani.

Figure 8.3. The hearths b, e, g. Tab. 8a Cipriani.

Aspects of the Cult of Demeter in Magna Graecia   145

from the historico-religious perspective and confirm a specifically "local" component of the cult practiced there, explicit clues of which were already provided by the many choroplastic items coming from votive offerings of the region of Paestum or other sites in Magna Graecia.[19]

This region has moreover been identified as the origin of the iconographic motif. Alongside a rich group of fictile statuettes of various sizes showing a female character wearing drapes, with a high *polos*, carrying a piglet (Figs. 8.4–8.7), and sometimes a large cista or a patera or plate with objects identified as cakes,[20] according to a popular iconographic pattern that probably originated in ancient Gela, there is a smaller but nevertheless significant number of fictile representations of young men with similar attributes (see Figs. 8.9–8.13 below).[21]

The female figures in question may be interpreted as images of offerers, even if in many cases we may justifiably suspect an alternative or perhaps intentionally ambiguous meaning, such as representations of the titular deity of the cult (Fig. 8.8),[22] or, in the cases of ascertained or probable Thesmophoria identity of the cult context, of Demeter herself carrying the animal and considered as the speaking emblem of the essential ritual act. The entire documentation, from Aristophanes' *Thesmophoriazousai* to a well-known scholion of Lucian's *Dialogues of the Courtesans,* highlights the central role played by the bloody rite in the form of sacrifice of the animal for food[23] and in that entirely peculiar action of the *megarizein,* that is, of throwing the piglets in underground cavities called *megara.* Lucian's scholion,[24] rather late but probably depending on a source of the first century BCE, reveals with great expressiveness a scenario of a secret female rituality from which, sources agree, men were barred. Any indiscreet curiosity on their part put them at the risk of terrible punishments, as recounted in well-known mythical and historical episodes.[25] The passage deserves to be remembered, since, while it confirms that dialectic relationship of the Thesmophoria cult with the mythical horizon of the primordial divine event, already evoked in the text of Clement of Alexandria, it mentions a male figure explicitly linked to the very act of the *megarizein.* The text then reads:[26]

> Thesmophoria: a festival of the Greeks encompassing mysteries, also known as Skirophoria (Θεσμοφορία ἑορτὴ Ἑλλήνων μυστήρια περιέχουσα, τὰ δὲ αὐτὰ καὶ Σκιροφορία καλεῖται). It was [or "they were"] held, according to the more mythological explanation, because [when] Kore, picking flowers, was being carried off by Pluto (ἤγητο δὲ κατὰ τὸν μυθωδέστερον λόγον, ὅτι [ὅτε] ἀνθολογοῦσα ἡρπάζετο ἡ Κόρη ὑπὸ τοῦ Πλούτωνος), one Eubuleus, a swineherd, was at the time grazing his pigs

Figure 8.4. Statuette of female offerer with piglet: Type A I. Tab. 16 Cipriani.

on that spot, and they were swallowed up together in Kore's pit (τότε κατ' ἐκεῖνον τὸν τόπον Εὐβουλεύς τις συβώτης, ἔνεμεν ὗς καὶ συγκατεπόθησαν τῷ χάσματι τῆς Κόρης); wherefore, in honor of Eubuleus piglets are thrown into the pits of Demeter and Kore (εἰς οὖν τιμὴν τοῦ Εὐβουλέως ῥιπτεῖσθαι τοὺς χοίρους εἰς τὰ χάσματα τῆς Δήμητρος καὶ τῆς Κόρης).

The rotten remains of what is thrown into the *megara* below are recovered by women called "dredgers" who have spent three days in ritual purity and descend into the shrines and when they have recovered the remains deposit them on the altars (τὰ δὲ σαπέντα τῶν ἐμβληθέντων εἰς τὰ μέγαρα κάτω ἀναφέρουσιν ἀντλήτριαι καλούμεναι γυναῖκες καθαρεύσασαι τριῶν ἡμερῶν καὶ καταβαίνουσιν εἰς τὰ ἄδυτα καὶ ἀνενέγκασιν ἐπιτιθέασιν ἐπὶ τῶν βωμῶν). They believe that anyone who takes some and sows it with their seed will have a good crop (ὧν νομίζουσι τὸν λαμβάνοντα καὶ τῷ σπορῷ συγκαταβάλλοντα εὐφορίαν ἕξειν).

They say that there are also serpents below about the pits, which eat up the great part of the material thrown in; for which reason they also make a clatter whenever the women dredge and whenever they set those models down again, so that the serpents they believe to be guarding the shrines will withdraw.

The same thing is also known as Arrhetophoria and is held with the same explanation to do with vegetable fertility and human procreation.

Figure 8.5. Statuette of female offerer with piglet and cist placed upon the shoulder: Type B I. Tab. 17b Cipriani.

Figure 8.6. Statuette of female offerer with piglet and cist placed upon the shoulder: Type B IIA. Tab. 18a Cipriani.

On that occasion, too, they bring unnameable holy things fashioned out of wheat-dough: images of snakes and male members. And they take pine branches because of that plant's fertility. There are also thrown into the *megara* (so the shrines are called) those things, and piglets, as mentioned above—the latter because of their fecundity, as a symbol of vegetable and human generation, for a thanksgiving offering to Demeter; because in providing the fruits of Demeter she civilized the race of humans. Thus the

Aspects of the Cult of Demeter in Magna Graecia   149

former reason for the festival is the mythological one, but the present is physical. It is called *Thesmophoria*, because Demeter is given the epithet "Lawgiver" (*Thesmophoros*), for having set down customs, which is to say laws (*thesmoi*), under which men have to acquire and work for their food.[27]

The text of the scholion, subject to numerous exegetic approaches since E. Rohde placed it at the disposal of the scientific community,[28] is certainly

Figure 8.7. Statuette of female offerer with piglet and cist placed upon the shoulder: Type D IIA. Tab. 2Ia Cipriani.

Figure 8.8. Statuette of female deity seated on throne, low *polos* on her head. She wears a chiton and himation; in her right hand she holds a phial and in her left a patera with pomegranates. Tab. 29 Cipriani (from the small votive deposit).

the result of a complex tradition, with the intervention of one or more editors and epitomists. However, it seems to be related substantially to the Thesmophoria, despite the mention of two other festivals, both reserved for women, and one of which, the Skirophoria, was also dedicated to Demeter. We should note, together with the ritual's nature as "fertility cult,"[29] its strong "political" value, insofar as it is aimed at founding and ensuring the continuity and prosperity of the human group through "fair offspring" celebrated on the Athenian day of *Kalligeneia,* which are the prevalent values of Thesmophoria cults. In its intimate links with a dramatic divine event of the time of the origins, it evokes, together with the great figures of the divine realm (Demeter, Kore-Persephone, Hades-Pluton), a figure—the swineherd Eubuleus—who, despite his anthropomorphized guise, also has the traits of a superhuman figure, and in fact was offered the piglets thrown into the underground cavities.

Our documentation often presents the couple of the Mother and Daughter linked, in a triad formula, with a male figure, a Zeus or a Hades, often designated by the euphemistic attribute of Eubuleus,[30] in the context of cults whose identity as Thesmophoria is more or less evident. The literary and epigraphic sources that reflect this religious framework are at times confirmed by the presence of images of a male figure found in sites identifiable as places of Demeter's cult. An example of this situation is found at Iasos,[31] where a bearded figure with a high *polos*, cloaked and bearing a patera, evokes a divine personality of the type of Zeus or Hades, as opposed to the young image of offerer with a piglet, such as is found in the sanctuary of San Nicola d'Albanella. The latter, as has been noted, has more specific parallels in Greek contexts in Asia, such as Halicarnassus,[32] and in Corinth, from whose Thesmophorion come statues of youths bearing on their chests animals, which are not clearly identifiable (Figs. 8.9–8.13).[33] I should add, however, that the style of the statuette from Paestum is extremely similar to that of some images of youths found in the Demeter sanctuaries of Morgantina, which also provided, in the sanctuary in the north of the city, a dedication to a mysterious male figure called Elaielinos.[34]

If, then, the existence of a male figure of a divine nature in the Thesmophoria mythical-ritual context is fairly widespread and may represent a precise religious referent for the iconographic motif under discussion, in my opinion this latter probably reflects a cultic practice, that is, the presence of male offerers. This does not, however, exclude the divine referent, but rather is composed harmoniously with it. De facto, there are some known cases of Demeter cults with a significant male component, such as the sanctuary of Demetra Prostasia and Kore situated in the sacred wood (ἄλσος) at Pyraia, mentioned by Pausanias:

> On the direct road from Sicyon to Phlius, on the left of the road and just about ten stades from it, is a grove called Pyraea, and in it a sanctuary of Demeter Protectress and the Maid. Here the men celebrate a festival by themselves, giving up to the women the temple called Nymphon for the purposes of their festival. In the Nymphon are images of Dionysus, Demeter, and the Maid, with only their faces exposed (τὰ πρόσωπα φαίνοντα).[35]

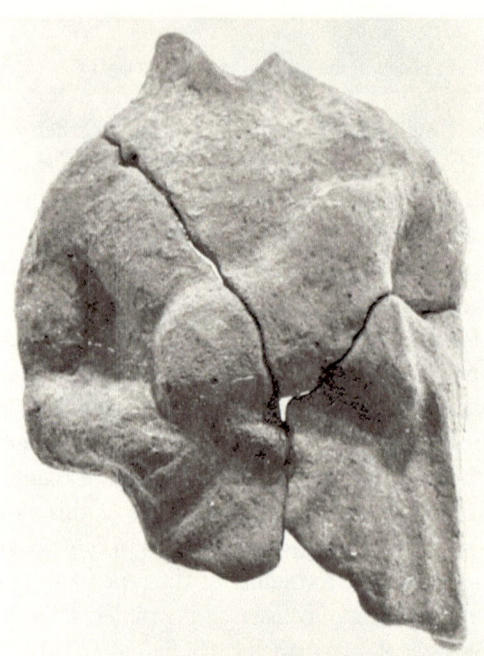

Figure 8.9. Statuette of male offerer with piglet held to chest: Type F IA. Tab. 24b Cipriani.

Figure 8.10. Statuette of male offerer with piglet held to chest: Type F IB. Tab. 24d Cipriani.

Figure 8.11. Statuette of male offerer with piglet in his right hand and arm held to his side: Type G I. Tab. 25a Cipriani.

In other cases, the men play a complementary ritual role, as Pausanias narrates of the sanctuary known as Misaeum, near Pellene:

> It is said that it was founded by Mysius, a man of Argos, who according to Argive tradition gave Demeter a welcome in his home. There is a grove in the Mysaeum, containing trees of every kind, and in it rises a copious

Figure 8.12. Statuette of male offerer with piglet in his right hand and arm held to his side. The left hand held to the chest holds a plate of fruit: Type H IA. Tab. 26b Cipriani.

supply of water from springs. Here they also celebrate a seven days' festival in honor of Demeter. On the third day of the festival the men withdraw from the sanctuary and the women are left to perform on that night the ritual that custom demands (καταλειπόμεναι δὲ αἱ γυναῖκες δρῶσιν ἐν τῇ νυκτὶ ὁπόσα νόμος ἐστὶν αὐταῖς). Not only men are excluded, but even male dogs. On the following day the men come to the sanctuary, and the men and the women laugh and jeer at one another in turn (σκώμμασιν).[36]

The ritual *praxis* described by Pausanias, unlike that of Demetra Prostasia, involves the contemporaneous presence of men and women in an initial phase of the rite, followed by a strict separation of the sexes with the celebration of a nighttime *dromenon,* exclusively for women, which we may justifiably recognize as a Thesmophoria ritual. This seems confirmed by the element of play, with verbal obscenities, peculiar to Thesmophoria contexts. The integration of the two sexes in the first and last phases of the

Figure 8.13. Statuette of male offerer with piglet in his right hand and arm held to his side. The left hand held to the chest holds a plate of fruit: Type H Ib. Tab. 27a Cipriani.

Mysaeum ritual may find a parallel in the Sicilian festivals mentioned by Diodorus Siculus, which also lasted for a long time (ten days), with widespread popular participation and the exchange of *skommata,* although his accounts make no explicit references to separation of the sexes or practices reserved for women.[37]

A confirmation of the presence of men in contexts of an evidently Thesmophorian nature, in circumstances and ways that naturally remain unknown to us, comes also from archaeological finds from many Demeter cult sites, through male images, dedications, or objects connected to the male world. Among the various examples of Demeter sanctuaries that have given wide and qualified evidence of male devotion are Heraclea; the new foundation of the ancient Siris in Magna Graecia, where a sanctuary of Demeter Thesmophoros was found to contain many votive dedications made by men;[38] and Fratte near Salerno. Among the various terracotta statuettes found in a votive deposit, there are many of male offerers with a pig.[39] The case of the sanctuary of San Nicola di Albanella, however, entirely maintains its specificity. The iconographic model in question is to be identified as a local "creation" of the Paestum region. It seems to reflect an extremely peculiar religious horizon, of which it is impossible to measure all the significances, but which in any case vividly expresses an active and qualified male presence on a cultic level in a Demeter scenario with clear connotations of a Thesmophoria ritual. Probably, as in the case of the cult of Demeter Prostasia, this scenario will have involved a parallel, distinct, but complementary ritual activity of the two sexes. This confirms the richness and typical mobility of the Demeter mythical-ritual context, which, while clearly displaying on the one hand fundamental pan-Hellenic tendencies, on the other unfolds in a myriad of local expressions, creating a dense constellation of cults deeply rooted in the territory that were able to adapt to the various socio-cultural and religious situations of the numerous communities in the Greek world.

Notes

1. For a detailed description of the ritual practice and its mythical foundations, cf. Sfameni Gasparro 1986: 223-306. See also Parke 1986: 82-88; Chandor Brumfield 1981: 70-103; Versnel 1993: 229-288; Clinton 1996: 111-125.

2. A fresh look on the variety of religious rules of the women in classical Greece is offered by Dillon 2002. See also my previous contribution (Sfameni Gasparro 1991: 57-121).

3. An analysis of the theme may be found in Sfameni Gasparro 2000: 83-106. Cf. also Guettel Cole 1994: 199-210 (reprint in Buxton 2000: 133-154).

4. Βούλει καὶ τὰ Φερεγάττης ἀνθολόγια διηγήσωμαί σοί καὶ τὸν κάλαθον καὶ τὴν ἁρπαγὴν τὴν ὑπὸ Ἀιδωνέως καὶ τὸ σχίσμα τῆς γῆς καὶ τὰς ὗς τὰς Εὐβουλέως τὰς συγκαταποθείσας ταῖν θεαῖν, δι' ἣν αἰτίαν ἐν τοῖς Θεσμοφορίοις μεγαρίζοντες

χοίρους ἐμβάλλουσιν Ταύτην τὴν μυθολογίαν αἱ γυναῖκες ποικίλως κατὰ πόλιν ἑορτάζουσι, Θεσμοφόρια, Σκιροφόρια, Ἀρρητοφόρια πολυτρόπως τὴν Φερεφάττης ἐκτραγῳδοῦσαι ἁρπαγήν: Clem. Alex. *Protr.* 2.17 (Marcovich 1995: 26).

5. Cf. Sfameni Gasparro 1986: 29-134, with relevant documentation. Among later contributions, cf. Clinton 1987: 1499-1539; 1988: 69-79; 1992; 1993: 110-124.

6. Therefore, this is only one of the three patterns of sanctuary location for Demeter cults, as noted by Guettel Cole (1994: 199-216, reprinted in Buxton 2000: 133-154). The sanctuaries of Demeter, in fact, may also be located between the walls of the city and the country or placed within the walls, even on the acropolis, as in the case of Thebes. The problem of the extramural location of some cult centers and of their probable characteristic as privileged meeting places for Greek colonists with the indigenous populations has been dealt with and variously solved by scholars. Here I would like to mention only, apart from Hermann's rather schematic classification (1965: 47-57), the analyses of Vallet (1968: 67-142), Ghinatti (1976: 601-630), and Pugliese Carratelli (1988b: 149-158). A sociological interpretation of the relations between the Greeks and local people that takes into account the changes in the historical situation is proposed by Torelli (1977a: 45-61). Asheri (1988: 1-15) opportunely proposes the possibility of various motivations, in relation to different times and places, recommending caution in interpreting the phenomenon, not limited to Magna Graecia and Sicily, but widely reported also in the motherland and in the colonies of Asia Minor. A detailed list of the extraurban places of worship in the Archaic age in Magna Graecia can be found in Leone 1998.

7. Cf. Chandor Brumfield 1981: 156-179; Sfameni Gasparro 1986: 259-277; Foxhall 1995: 97-110.

8. Sfameni Gasparro 1986: 285-307.

9. Cf. Ardovino 1986: 97-99; Cipriani 1988: 430-445; Cipriani and Ardovino 1989-90: 339-351.

10. Cipriani 1989.

11. A brief but clear overview of these presences can be found in Ardovino 1986: 91-102.

12. For Taranto and its territory, cf. Lippolis 1981; De Juliis 1982: 295-296: votive offering of Via Regina Elena (cf. Tab. XLVII.3-4: female figure with cross-shaped torch, piglet, and plate with fruit). For Locri, Sanctuary Parapezza, cf. Grottarola 1994; for Santa Maria d'Anglona (Matera), cf. Rüdiger 1967.

13. Cf. de la Genière and Greco 1990: 63-80; Tocco Sciarelli, de la Genière, and Greco 1988: 385-396. See a brief overview on the cults of ancient Bruttium in Sfameni Gasparro 1999: 53-88; 2002: 329-350.

14. For the cult of Hera Lacinia, cf. Giangiulio 1982: 7-69; 1984: 347-351.

15. Cf. *Locri Epizefiri*, ed. Barra Bagnasco 1977; Barra Bagnasco 1984. Among the numerous studies on the terracotta tablets with religious scenes, see Prückner 1968 and Torelli 1977a: 147-184. The complete publication of the *pinakes* is in progress. Cf. Lissi Caronna, Sabbione, and Vlad Borrelli 1999.

16. Cf. Sfameni Gasparro 1986: 223-338, for a detailed discussion of the theme accompanied by ample documentary exemplification. See also Kron 1992: 611-650; Lissi Caronna, Sabbione, and Vlad Borrelli 2003 and 2007.

17. See the various reports of Orlandini 1966: 8-35; 1967: 177-179; 1968: 17-66; 2003: 507-513. A graffito on a fifth-century Attic vase fragment is a dedica-

tion "to the Thesmophoros from the *skanai* of Dikaios." On other fragments of Attic skyphoi there are fragmentary inscriptions: DA . . . and (T)ESMOFOR. . . . The sanctuary of Demeter and Kore was in use from the mid-seventh century to 405 BCE, that is, up to the Carthaginian destruction of Gela.

18. The numerous and peculiar analogies between the two contexts have been highlighted by Ardovino (1999: 169-185), who made an in-depth comparative analysis and identified two correlated religious "systems" in the sites at Gela and Paestum.

19. Cf. Cipriani (1989: 119), who mentions similar types found at Fratte, Eboli, Capua, and Taranto (Winter 1903: 189, 5a-b).

20. Distinctions are made between a number of different types, which, however, are all considered to be based on prototypes from Gela analyzed by Sguaitamatti (1984). Cf. Cipriani 1989: 104-118. The typology identified by the scholar may be schematically summarized as follows: Section I: Plastic of medium size (100-103)—Type A: Female statue with piglet held to her chest; Type B: Idem with piglet in front of her bust, cist, and torch; Type C: Female head with cist. Section II: Small plastic—Type A: Female statue with piglet in front of her bust (see Fig. 8.4); Type B: Female statue with piglet in front of her bust and cist (see Figs. 8.5-6); Type C: Female statue with piglet in front of her bust and patera or plate with sweets; Type D: Female statue with piglet held head-down along the right side of the body and cist (see Fig. 8.7); Type E: Female statue with piglet held head-down along the right side of the body and patera with sweets.

21. Cipriani 1989: 118-128. Three main types have been identified, with minor variants: Group F: Male statuette with piglet held in front of the bust (see Figs. 8.9-10); Group G: Male statuette with piglet held head-down along the right side of the body (see Fig. 8.11); Group H: Male statue with piglet held head-down along the right side of the body and patera with sweets (see Figs. 8.12-13). All the types are dated to the mid-to-late fifth century.

22. This is the case of the female figures sitting on a seat or throne, which are most probably intended to represent the goddess, as in Figure 8.8.

23. The most explicit literary source on this use is an Aristophanes' scholion: Schol. in *Ranas* v. 338: "He said this because in the Thesmophoria meat is eaten and since they sacrifice the piglet to Demeter and Kore . . . he said this since the piglet is sacrificed at the Thesmophoria" (τοῦτο εἶπε διὰ τὸ κρεοφαγεῖν ἐν τοῖς Θεσμοφορίοις καὶ ὅτι Δήμητρι καὶ Κόρῃ δύουσι τὸ ζῷον . . . τοῦτο δὲ εἶπε δὶ τὸ χοιροσπαθεῖν τοῖς Θεσμοφορίοις). The archaeological documentation widely confirms this use. In addition to the site under consideration, it is sufficient to remember the highly significant cases of Bitalemi, with its rich votive deposits including a head of the animal, and Corinth, with its many banqueting halls. See White 1981: 24, with reference to Second report, LA 9 (1977), p. 172 pl. 74b: a stone statuette of a seated figure bearing a plate on which, among fruit or small loaves of bread, is found a piglet's head, in an evident allusion to the sacrifice of the animal and to the consequent communal meal. Cf. White 1993.

24. For a recent discussion of the text, its chronology and authorship, see Lowe 1998: 149-173.

25. See, for example, the story of Battos, the founder of the city of Cyrene, who was said to have tried to profane the secret rites of Demeter and was thus subjected to the terrible punishment of eviration by the *Sphaktriai*, the priestesses in charge

of sacrifices to the goddess. For an exegesis of this tradition, related by Elianus (fr. 44 Hercher) and confirmed in two entries in the Suda s.v. Θεσμοφόρος ("Demeter tesmophoros: Battos, the founder of Cyrene desired to know the mysteries of Demeter and used violence, rejoicing with greedy eyes") and s.v. Σφάκτριαι ("Priestesses in charge of sacrifices: dressed in the sacred stole all the sacrificers, abandoned the sacrifice and raised their drawn swords, with their hands full and faces wet with the blood of their victims, all together on an agreed signal, leapt on Battos to evirate him"), see Detienne 1979: 185-214 (Italian trans. 131-148); Cosi 1983: 123-154.

26. Scholion to Lucian *Dialogues of the Courtesans*, ed. H. Rabe, *Scholia in Lucianum* (Leipzig, 1906), 275-276.

27. Translation by Lowe (1998: 165-166). Cf. also Chandor Brumfield 1981: 73-74.

28. Rohde 1901: 355-369.

29. This traditional definition is to be understood in the sense of a ritual *praxis* finalized to promote and to control the fertility of both the fields and the female citizens. This interpretation is proposed by Nixon (1995), who stresses the antifertility drug or *pharmaka* resulting from the use of some plants (pennyroyal, pomegranate, pine branches, and vitex) linked with the Demeter and Kore cults, both Eleusinian mysteries and Thesmophoria. These cults, therefore, are intended also to control human fertility.

30. Cf. Sfameni Gasparro 1986: 102-110.

31. Cf. Levi 1967-68.

32. These are ephebic images with a piglet, which, according to Cipriani, were wrongly interpreted by Higgins (1954: 130 and tabs. 64, 454-455 and 457) as female and from the early fourth century. See also the terracotta statuettes from a votive deposit in Gortina (Crete) in Platon 1957: 144-145.

33. Cf. Bookidis and Fischer 1972: 317: many fragments of statues. "All appear to depict a young man wrapped in himation, carrying an offering. . . . Best preserved is a statue of a draped youth," which "date[s] to the late fifth or early fourth century B.C. (Pl. 63 a, b)." A terracotta mask depicting a bearded man was found east of the theater. Bookidis identifies the type as Dionysos-Hades (Bookidis and Fischer 1974: 290-291 pl. 59). Cf. the previous preliminary reports by Stroud 1965: 18, pl. 8 (terracotta figurines of small children, and several examples of the type of the "temple-boy") and 1968: 325, pl. 95c, e (a standing, draped archaic kouros), pl. 95d (fragments of male figure). See also the final publication of the Corinth sanctuary by Bookidis and Stroud (1987).

34. Cf. the reports of the excavations by Sjöqvist (1958a, 1958b, 1960, 1962, 1964), Stillwell (1959, 1961, 1963, 1967), and Stillwell and Sjöqvist (1957).

35. Pausanias 2.11.3, ed. and trans. W.H.S. Jones (London and Cambridge, Mass., 1964), 304ff.

36. Pausanias 7.27.9-10, ed. and trans. W.H.S. Jones (London and Cambridge, Mass., 1961), 342ff.

37. Diod. Sic. *Bibl.* 5.3-4.

38. Cf. Neutsch 1968: 187-234, tabs. 1-33; Ghinatti 1980: 137-143; Sartori 1980: 401-415. The sanctuary of Iasos, which with every probability is also a *Thesmophorion*, due to the quality of the archaeological finds, has provided a significant number of fictile statuettes depicting a bearded male figure, with *polos* and

patera, interpretable as a deity (perhaps Hades or Zeus Eubuleus), companion of the Thesmophoros goddesses. They illustrate a triadic formula common in many sites, above all in the Cyclades (cf. Sfameni Gasparro 1986: 91-110, 169-175). At the same time, these votive images could also reflect, with a particular relief of the male component of the divine sphere, a cultic role of the male element on the human level. Cf. the documentation in Levi 1967-68: 569-579.

39. Cf. Sestieri 1952: 126, Stratum XIX-XX.

CHAPTER 9

Landscape Synchesis:
A Demeter Temple in Latium

KATHRYN M. LUCCHESE

Abstract

Besides the Eleusinian mysteries, the late-fall pre-planting rites of the Thesmophoria were the most characteristic of the festivals of Demeter. The *thesmophoria* themselves, usually translated as "the things laid down," were offerings flung into a natural crevice or man-made chamber in the rock known as a *megaron*, left to decay, and then retrieved and plowed into a nearby ritual field, thus securing the region's fertility for the season to come. By metaphoric extension, the Thesmophoria became associated with the civilization that developed in the wake of sedentary agriculture, the "things laid down" being understood as a code of civil laws, the goddess's title being translated into Latin as *legifera*, "law-giver." A small temple just outside Rome, built by Herodes Atticus, can now be firmly identified as dedicated to Demeter/Ceres due in part to the recent discovery of a well-preserved *megaron* there. Herodes used the construction of this sanctuary as a gesture of *synchesis* linking himself to the goddess of laws in order both to exonerate himself of his wife's bloodguilt and to increase his own social standing.

The Notion of *Synchesis*

For those classicists unfamiliar with the field of cultural geography, I should explain that it functions as a sort of theoretical archaeology, specifically accounting for the placement of man-made features within the context of the natural environment—a system of both built and natural features commonly referred to as a "landscape"—by means of studying these features' location, function, and meaning. Geographers often refer

162 Kathryn M. Lucchese

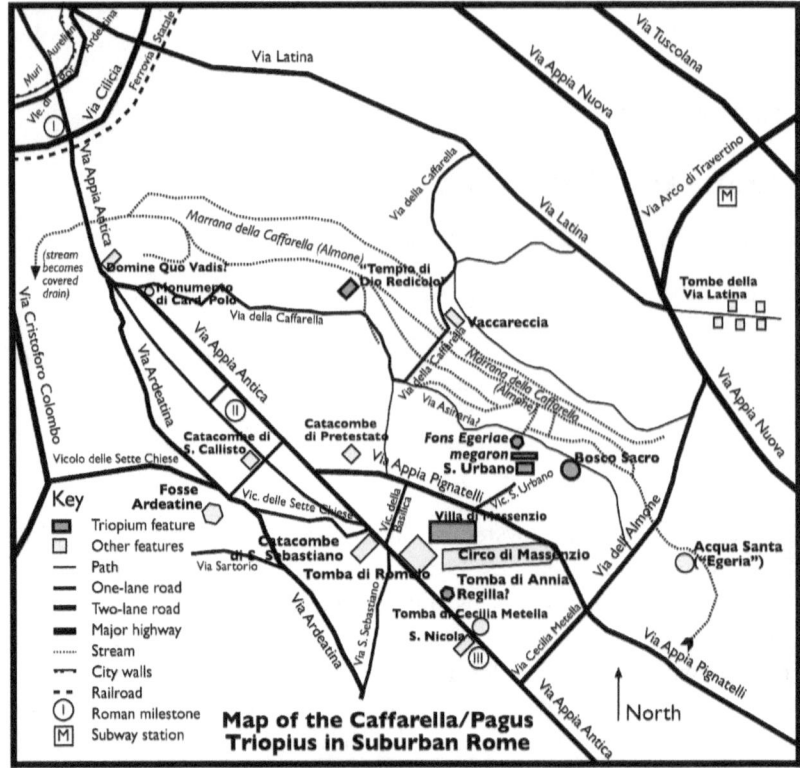

Figure 9.1. Map of the Caffarella/*Pagus Triopius* in suburban Rome. By the author.

to this study as a "reading" of the cultural landscape, and its construction as "writing." The implication is that we communicate cultural values such as wealth, status, and national origin by how we construct or "write" these systems. It struck me that a particularly felicitous subject for such a study might be a sacred landscape system "written" by the famous Greek sophist and antiquarian Herodes Atticus. I knew of such a site through reading Rodolfo Lanciani's narrative of the remains of a sacred grove in the Almo Valley, south of Rome,[1] and, given the opportunity to study it during a sabbatical semester spent in Rome from January to June 1993, determined to learn all I could. I carried out research both at the site in the Caffarella valley just off the Via Appia Pignatelli southeast of Rome's Porta Appia (Fig. 9.1), and in the libraries of the Vatican and the American Academy at Rome. This body of information ultimately became the core of my Master's thesis. With the help of my husband, Robert R. Lucchese, I was able to explore a series of caves and tunnels at the site that I identified,

I believe for the first time, as a perfectly preserved thesmophoric *megaron*. I quickly shared my discovery with local archaeologists at their Via Campitelli office, and it was clear that they were as yet unaware of the existence of the *megaron* at the site. In the summer of 2000, I returned to the site and discovered a vent resembling a man-hole cover over the bailing hatch of the *megaron*. This suggests that some exploratory work has proceeded below, the extent of which I do not know. It is high time, however, that a wider audience of classicists was made aware of this uniquely complete temple complex, and perhaps that excavations begin.

In reading landscapes, geographers often discover that their creators or "authors" have made figurative references, creating some higher symbolism at the site. This is especially the case, I would argue, when the landscape's creator *is* in fact an author—in this case, a sophist, famous for his store of antiquarian references and clever figures of speech.[2] The method by which Herodes Atticus seems to have evoked complex implications from this temple complex struck me as being like the trope of *synchesis*. In *synchesis,* nouns and their modifiers appear in a line of poetry in an interlocked word order, *a-b-a-b,* or, to use Clyde Pharr's example from the back of the "purple Vergil," *saevae memorem Junonis iram* ("fell Juno's unforgetting hate").[3] The effect is for syntactically unrelated words to attract each other's meaning in the reader's eye and ear, so that unconsciously, they are linked: Juno with "hate" and "mindful" in a way that underlines her general state of mind in the *Aeneid*.

Synchesis seems to me to be a particularly fruitful figure for studying the sanctuaries of traditional "animistic" religions like those of Greece and Rome. Evocation of divine presences by a particular setting perceived as numinous is in itself *synchesis,* linking feeling to deity. One thinks of the awe-inspiring Shining Rocks of Delphi and their uncanny focusing of light and sound, their beauty and loftiness, their enclosure of the Kastalia spring, creating a natural focus of the numinous that became Apollo's precinct. In the case of Herodes Atticus' construction of the Demeter temple complex, the setting is natural enough, peaceful and enclosed, the soil fertile as only volcanic tuffs can make it (Fig. 9.2). But many symbolic linkages are also both made and exploited if already extant, linkages intended, as I argue, to improve the sophist's status as well as symbolically to refute the suspicion that he had killed his wife.

In presenting this information, I follow a threefold scheme. First, I present the basic premise of Ceres as an "indigenous deity in Magna Graecia," as the theme of this symposium would require. Then, I detail the ritual of the Thesmophoria and the landscape features it requires for

Figure 9.2. La Caffarella from the north side of the valley, on the bluff near the Vaccareccia farmhouse. Photo by the author, June 1993.

its performance in terms of Herodes Atticus' temple complex, within the context of the surrounding Pagus Triopius area.[4] Finally, I return to the trope of *synchesis* in this sacred pagan landscape.

The Italic/Roman Nature of Ceres

The indigenous Italic cult examined in this chapter is that of the great Italic goddess Ceres. Magna Graecia is here understood as extending northward (by Roman imperial times) to include Rome. Ceres seems to have provided the "increase" or growth function to the grain, the most mysterious and delicate aspect of farming: In *The Roman Goddess Ceres*, Barbette Spaeth traces the stem *Cer-* to the Sanskrit *ker-*, meaning "to create, to be born." Spaeth additionally claims that Ceres has "the oldest written evidence of any Roman divinity." She cites the inscription found at Falerii, dating to about 600 BCE: "Let Ceres give *far*."[5] The "old-time" religious rites of the Arval Brethren, aimed at securing the peace and health of the Roman state, included prayers to Ceres paired with Tellus, goddess of the earth, in their celebration of the Cerealia on 19 April.[6]

The chief Ceres cult spot within the *pomerium* was the *Aedes Cereris* on the Aventine hill, founded after the great famine of 493 BCE. The Sybilline books called for the importation of her cult from Sicily, where the grain shipments also originated, complete with a priestess who continued to conduct all her rituals in Greek.[7] While there was a distinctly Greek character to the pre-existing cult of Ceres in the city of Rome, it had some unusual local and typically Roman political linkages, quite different from those we will see made by Herodes. This temple was associated with the *plebs*: records of the *Tribuni Plebis* were kept here, and here Ceres formed a sort of plebeian triad with Liber and Libera (Italian equivalents of Dionysus/Triptolemos and Kore/Persephone) against the patrician Capitoline (and originally Etruscan) triad of Jupiter-Juno-Minerva.[8] Thus there is a sufficiently early presence for the cult of Ceres in central Italy to call it "indigenous" by the time of Herodes Atticus, the Greek sophist whose importation of a very Greek version of the Ceres cult in about 170 CE is under consideration here.

By imperial times, all these deities had become uniquely entwined with local Roman culture, whatever their places of origin. Augustus, no less than his adoptive father Julius Caesar, placed himself firmly within the popular camp, wooing the impecunious but undeniably numerous *plebs* in part by identifying himself with the grain dole and thereby with the goddess who secured a continuing supply of that grain: Ceres (Fig. 9.3). By means of statues and coinage depicting his wife Livia in the guise of Ceres and himself in the Cereal crown of the Arval Brethren, Augustus implied that his own godlike charisma helped keep the plebeians fed, just as, less symbolically, he did in fact administer the system that provided the dole. From that time forth, Ceres was commonly paired with the emperor and his wife.[9]

Figure 9.3. Portrait bust of the emperor Augustus's wife, Livia, as Ceres. Capitoline Museum. Photo by the author.

The Thesmophoria

Walter Burkert calls the Thesmophoria "the most widespread Greek festival and principal form of the Demeter cult."[10] This is saying a great deal when one considers the modern fascination with the Eleusinian mysteries; it seems logical that the most frequent appeals to Demeter must have been for the yearly harvest and not for individual concerns about afterlife, a function additionally performed by other deities. Thus, the Thesmophoria were to be observed with regularity each fall, for a period of three days just before the fall planting in November (= 11-13 *Pyanopsion*). Whether the Aventine temple carried out these rituals is questionable, as they required the presence of a ritual wheat field, and Burkert does specify that they were common to *suburban* sanctuaries. The point of the ritual is clearly to provide some kind of sympathetic magic to assist the fertility of the whole season's crop. By opening the planting season with the Thesmophoria, the rest of the region's fields could be thought of as being blessed as well.

This ritual was strictly off-limits to men or to unmarried women; we are told that Athenian husbands were required by law to allow their wives to take part, and it would be very interesting to know what Roman laws were on the subject. Given the already greater freedoms enjoyed by Roman matrons over their Athenian sisters, one may assume that their access was not hampered by any special prejudice. How popular the Thesmophoria was among Roman women, however, is not clear, as we have no record of such performances at Rome that I have found, whereas we do read of the famous ritual of the Bona Dea—possibly a Latin equivalent of Ceres, with rituals similarly off-limits to men.[11]

The worshipers spent three days and nights camped out, as it were, at the sanctuary, the nights taken up with stories and songs, mostly lewd and thus bringing good luck, the days concerned with the retrieval of last year's offerings, the proper treatment of these remains, and the production and insertion of new offerings. The hatch leading down into the *megaron* was unsealed, and one woman was sent first to scare away any snakes with noise or song, and perhaps to set up lamps like those found at the Demeter sanctuary at Knossos.[12] Then the "bailers" descended into the chamber to scoop the remains of last year's offering of piglets and cakes, known as *megara* or *magara*, into special baskets called *kistai*, which they put on their heads as they ascended once more into daylight. The *kistophora* figure is a standard representation of this part of the ritual, and several such statues, elegantly rendered in Hymettan marble, were found in the fields near the tomb of Cecilia Metella, off the Via Appia not far from the temple

Figure 9.4. A *Kanephoros* or *Kistophoros*, carved from Hymettan marble and found near the Tomb of Cecilia Metella on the Via Appia in 1784. Now in the Braccio Nuovo of the Vatican Museums. Photo by the author.

site (Fig. 9.4).[13] The remains were then apparently offered to the goddess on the altar (possibly mixed with grain and hopefully accompanied by fragrant incense smoke) before being plowed into the adjacent sacred field. It would seem that this last chore must have been performed by a man, since it is so depicted in iconography representing the first farmer, Triptolemos.[14]

Perhaps the blessed offering waited until the closing of the festival to be plowed, as there was still the new offering to be laid down, the whole point of the Thesmophoria. The "laying-down" was after all originally the application of the magical fertilizer of rotted piglets and cakes, scooped up from the *megaron* into the *kistai*, onto the sacred field, before the planting of the seeds. In preparation for the next Thesmophoria, new female piglets[15] were dropped into the *megaron* along with cakes made into phallic and other appropriate shapes.[16] Once the hatch of the *megaron* was resealed, the contents of the baskets plowed in, and no doubt the tidying of the sanctuary done, the business of the festival was complete.

Metaphorical Extension

Establishing as it does the preeminence of Demeter/Ceres as the bringer of agriculture to human society, the festival of Thesmophoria symbolized for thoughtful Greeks the coming of civilization itself.[17] Once the realization of the full consequences to human society of the discovery and adoption of sedentary agriculture had been made, the thanks due to the great civilizer Ceres could properly be rendered. The very structure of civilization could be attributed to her arrival on the scene, just as civilization could collapse if she withdrew her favor. Sanctuaries recorded the results of her wrath: crop failures so radical that people were reduced once more to eating acorns, as in the troglodytic days, destroying the stratified fabric of society.[18] Thus the "things laid down" of the festival were identified with human laws, laws that came about with the complexity of the urban society that agriculture made possible.

Proper keeping of the festival of Demeter Thesmophoros must have been important, then, not just to the continuation of agriculture in the form of the local wheat crop, but also to the continuation of urban civilization. The whole complex structure of civilization, after all, was based on the foundation of these particular laid-down things. The Latin translation of *thesmophoros* is the much less ambiguous *legifera*—"law-giver."[19] The Roman *plebs* could support Ceres' worship in this sense as much as in that of the matron of the grain-dole; after all, it was protective institutions like the *Tribuni plebis* that began to protect the *plebs* from the arbitrary customs of the patricians. With a sense of her enlarged importance, the city fathers as well as the mothers could support the cult of Ceres as one of those to be honored above local deities, and beside the great sky-gods Jupiter and Juno, who brought not only supreme justice but also the rain and breezes to assist Ceres in the growth of the seed. Civic leaders could use their loyalty to Ceres to reinforce the favor not only of the distant Olympian goddess but also of the very tangible, and numerous, common people.

The Cult Site: The *Pagus Triopius*, or *Triopium*

The lands known as *Pagus Triopius* or the *Triopium* belonged to the family of Annia Appia Regilla, the wife of Herodes Atticus at the time Herodes built the Ceres temple there. Although it well could have been named *Pagus*[20] since time immemorial, it is clear that it is its association with

Ceres that gave it the modifier *Triopius*. Triopas was a mythical Thessalian king who somehow offended Ceres, possibly by misappropriating materials for her temple.[21] He fled to Caria, where he is said to have founded the Ceres sanctuary of Triopium, though traces of this sanctuary have not yet been found. The extent of ancient *Pagus Triopius* seems to have corresponded roughly to the lands between the Via Appia and the Via Latina from the Via della Caffarella to the Via di Cecilia Metella (see Fig. 9.1), or perhaps as far down the Via Appia as the Villa of the Quintilii, who were famous detractors of their neighbor Herodes, as he was of them.[22] The part of this land that borders the little Almo (or Almone) River is now known as La Caffarella, after the Almo's medieval name, Marrana della Caffarella.

In any case, at the death of his wife, Herodes dedicated this rich and extensive region, with any villages and farms upon it, to the exclusive use of the goddess Ceres, to Liber and Libera, the deified Faustina, and to the goddess of fertility and vengeance, Ops/Nemesis. This he declared in verse on two marble tablets, set up within *Pagus Triopius,* which fell into the hands of the Borghese family (see Figs. 9.5 and 9.6, and see the appendix here for the full *CIG* reference and translation). One of these ("of Marcellus") is easily visible in the Greek inscription room of the Louvre Museum in Paris. These inscriptions warn all comers that this land is not to be used for any purpose but to honor the goddesses, or else Nemesis will take her revenge. The first, excerpted below, has no author attribution, but according to Jennifer Tobin[23] may be the only surviving piece of writing by Herodes—the expert in ex tempore speaking, not literature:

3   Come here, both of you, that you may honor this rich place
4   In the neighboring suburbs of hundred-gated Rome,
5   Pagus, host to Triopa of the Grain [Demeter]
6   So that you may call it Triopea's among the immortal gods.[24]

The Assemblage: The Temple Proper, and Its *Megaron*

The assemblage of sacred structures within the *temenos* of the Demeter temple is quite complete. There is, of course, the little temple itself facing due east, the *megaron*, lying along its northern flank and also running due east-west, the sacral field in which the *megaron* lies, the remains of the oak grove on the hill just east of the temple, and the *Fons Egeriae,* just under the lip of the bluff to the northwest—seemingly unconnected, but I rather

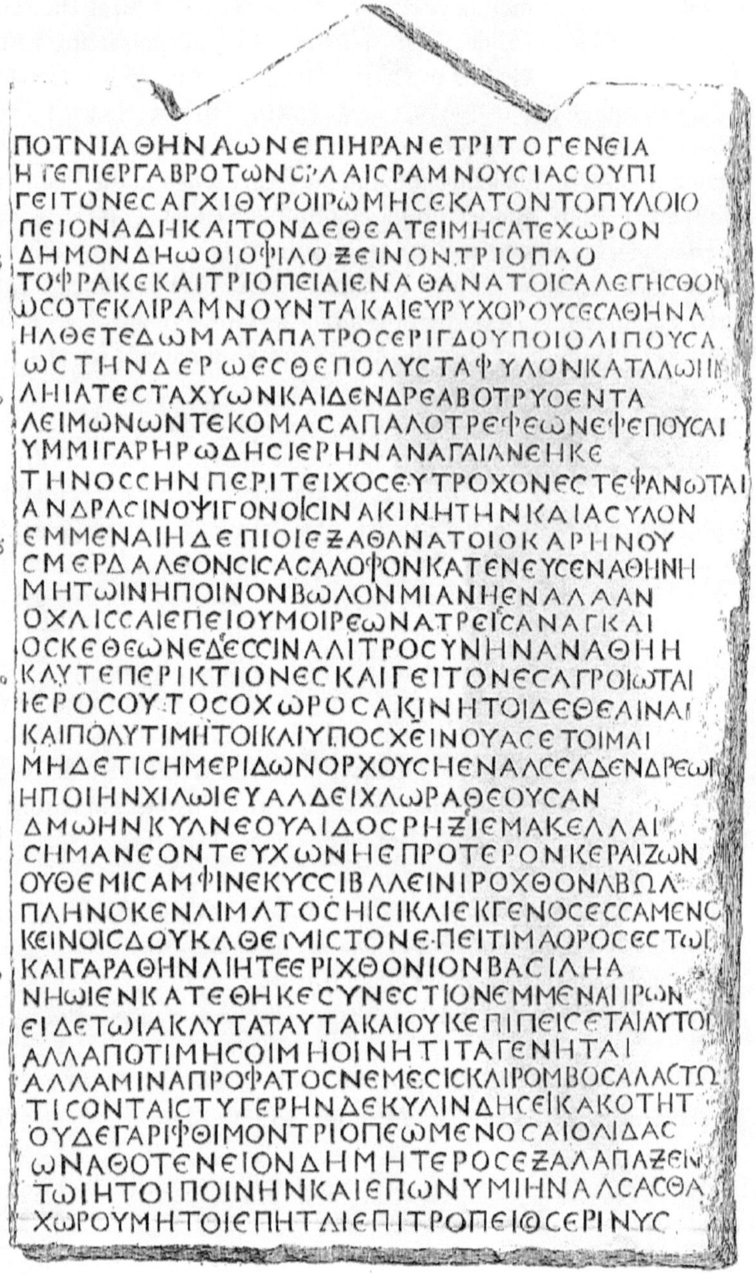

ΠΟΤΝΙΑ ΘΗΝΑωΝ ΕΠΙΗΡΑΝΕ ΤΡΙΤΟΓΕΝΕΙΑ
Η ΓΕΠΙΕΡΓΑ ΒΡΟΤωΝ ΟΛ ΑΙΣ ΡΑΜΝΟΥΣΙΑΣ ΟΥΠΙ
ΓΕΙΤΟΝΕΣ ΑΓΧΙΘΥΡΟΙ ΡωΜΗΣ ΕΚΑΤΟΝ ΤΟΠΥΛΟΙΟ
ΠΕΙΟΝΑ ΔΗΚΑΙΤΟΝ ΔΕΘΕΑΤΕΙ ΜΗΣ ΑΤΕ ΧωΡΟΝ
5 ΔΗΜΟΝ ΔΗωΟΙΟ ΦΙΛΟ ΞΕΙΝΟΝ ΤΡΙΟΠΛΟ
ΤΟ ΦΡΑΚΕΚΑΙ ΤΡΙΟΠΕΙΑΙΕΝ ΑΘΑΝΑΤΟΙΣ ΑΛΕΓΗΣΘΟΝ
ωΣ ΟΤΕ ΚΛΙΡΑΜΝΟΥΝ ΤΑ ΚΑΙ ΕΥΡΥΧΟΡΟΥΣΕΣ ΑΘΗΝΑ
ΗΛΘΕ ΤΕΔωΜ ΑΤΑ ΠΑΤΡΟΣ ΕΡΙΓΔΟΥΠΟΙΟΛΙΠΟΥΣΑ
ωΣ ΤΗΝ ΔΕΡ ωΕΣ ΘΕΠΟΛΥΣ ΤΑΦΥΛΟΝ ΚΑΤΑΛωΗΝ
10 ΛΗΙΑΤΕΣ ΤΑΧΥωΝ ΚΑΙ ΔΕΝΔΡΕΑ ΒΟΤΡΥΟΕΝΤΑ
ΛΕΙΜωΝωΝ ΤΕ ΚΟΜΑΣ ΑΠΑΛΟΤΡΕΦΕωΝ ΕΦΕΠΟΥΣΑΙ
ΥΜΜΙ ΓΑΡ ΗΡωΔΗΣ ΙΕΡΗΝ ΑΝΑ ΓΑΙΑΝ ΕΗΚΕ
ΤΗΝΟΣ ΣΗΝ ΠΕΡΙ ΤΕΙΧΟΣ ΕΥΤΡΟΧΟΝ ΕΣΤΕΦΑΝωΤΑΙ
ΑΝΔΡΑΣΙΝ ΟΥ ΓΟΝΟΙΣΙΝ ΑΚΙΝΗΤΗΝ ΚΑΙ ΑΣΥΛΟΝ
15 ΕΜΜΕΝΑΙ ΗΔΕ ΠΙΟΙ ΕΖΑΘΛΝΑΤΟΙΟΚΑΡΗΝΟΥ
ΣΜΕΡΔΑΛΕΟΝ ΣΙΣΑΛΟΦΟΝ ΚΑΤΕΝΕΥΣΕΝ ΑΘΗΝΗ
ΜΗ ΤωΙΝΗΠΟΙΝΟΝ ΒωΛΟΝ ΜΙΑΝ ΗΕΝΑ ΛΛΑΝ
ΟΧΛΙΣΣΑΙ ΕΠΕΙ ΟΥ ΜΟΙΡΕωΝ ΑΤΡΕΙΣ ΑΝΑΓΚΑΙ
ΟΣΚΕΘωΝΕΔΕΣ ΣΙΝ ΑΛΙΤΡΟΣΥΝΗΝ ΑΝ ΑΘΗΝΗ
20 ΚΛΥΤΕ ΠΕΡΙΚΤΙΟΝΕΣ ΚΑΙ ΓΕΙΤΟΝΕΣ ΑΓΡΟΙωΤΑΙ
ΙΕΡΟΣ ΟΥΤΟΣ ΟΧωΡΟΣ ΑΚΙΝΗΤΟΙ ΔΕΘΕΑΙΝΑΙ
ΚΑΙ ΠΟΛΥΤΙΜΗ ΤΟΙ ΚΑΙ ΥΠΟΣ ΧΕΙΝΟΥΑΣ ΕΤΟΙΜΑΙ
ΜΗΔΕ ΤΙΣ ΗΜΕΡΙΔωΝ ΟΡΧΟΥΣ ΗΕΝΑΛΣΕ ΑΔΕΝΔΡΕωΝ
ΗΠΟΙΗΝ ΧΙΛωΙ ΕΥΑΛΔΕΙ ΧΛωΡΑ ΘΕΟΥΣΑΝ
25 ΔΜωΗΝ ΚΥΛΝΕΟΥΑΙΔΟΣ ΡΗΞΙΕ ΜΑΚΕΛΛΑΙ
ΣΗΜΑΝΕΟΝ ΤΕΥΧωΝ ΗΕ ΠΡΟΤΕΡΟΝ ΚΕΡΑΙΖωΝ
ΟΥΘΕΜΙΣ ΑΜΦΙΝΕ ΚΥΣΣΙ ΒΑΛΕΙΝΙΡΟ ΧΘΟΝΑ ΒωΛ
ΠΛΗΝ ΟΚΕΝΑΙΜΑΤΟΣ ΗΙΣΙΚΛΙΕΚΓΕΝΟΣ ΕΣ ΣΑΜΕΝΟ
ΚΕΙΝΟΙΣ ΔΟΥΚΑΘΕΜΙΣ ΤΟ ΝΕΠΕΙ ΤΙΜΑΟΡΟΣ ΕΣΤω
30 ΚΑΙ ΓΑΡ ΑΘΗΝΑΙΗ ΤΕΕΡΙΧΘΟΝΙΟΝ ΒΑΣΙΛΗΑ
ΝΗωΙ ΕΝΚΑΤΕΘΗΚΕ ΣΥΝΕΣΤΙΟΝ ΕΜΜΕΝΑΙ ΙΡωΝ
ΕΙ ΔΕ ΤωΙ ΑΚΛΥΤΑ ΤΑΥΤΑ ΚΑΙ ΟΥΚΕΠΙΠΕΙΣΕ ΤΑΙ ΑΥΤΟΣ
ΑΛΛΑ ΠΟΤΙΜΗΣ ΟΙΜΗ ΟΙΝΗ ΤΙΤΑ ΓΕΝΗ ΤΑΙ
ΑΛΛΑΜΙΝ ΑΠΡΟΦΑΤΟΣ ΝΕΜΕΣΙΣ ΚΛΙ ΡΟΜΒΟΣ ΑΛΑΣΤω
35 ΤΙΣΟΝ ΤΑΙΣ ΤΥΓΕΡΗΝ ΔΕ ΚΥΛΙΝΔΗΣ ΕΙΚΑΚΟΤΗΤ
ΟΥΔΕ ΓΑΡΙΦΘΙΜΟΝ ΤΡΙΟΠΕω ΜΕΝΟΣ ΑΙΟΛΙΔΑΣ
ωΝΑΘΟΤΕΝΕΙΟΝ ΔΗΜΗΤΕΡΟΣ ΕΖΑΛΑΠΑΞΕΝ
ΤωΙ ΗΤΟΙ ΠΟΙΗΝ ΚΑΙ ΕΠωΝΥΜΙΗΝ ΑΛΣΑΣΘΑ
ΧωΡΟΥ ΜΗ ΤΟΙ ΕΠΗ ΤΑΙ ΕΠΙΤΡΟΠΕΙ ΘΣ ΕΡΙΝΥΣ

Figure 9.5. Inscription I from Visconti 1794.

Figure 9.6. Inscription 2 from Visconti 1794, "Of Marcellus."

ΜΑΡΚΕΛΛΟΥ

ΔΕΥΡΙΤΕΘΥΒΡΙΑΔΕΣΝΗΟΠΠ ΟΤΙΤΟΝΔΕΓΥΝΑΙΚΕΣ
ΡΗΓΙΛΛΗΣΕΔΟΣΑΜΦΙΘΥΟΣ ΚΟΛΙΡΑΤΕΡΟΥΣΑΙ
ΗΔΕΠΟΛΥΚΤΕΛΝΩΝΜΕΝΕΗΝΕΖΑΙΝΕΛΛΔΩΝ
ΑΓΧΙΣΕωΚΛΥΤΟΝΑΙΜΑΚΑΙΛΔΑΙΗΣΑΦΡΟΔΙΤΗΣ
5 ΓΗΜΑΤΟΔΕΣΜΑΡΑΘωΝΑΘΕΛΙΔΕΜΙΝΟΥΡΑΝΙωΝΑ
ΤΙΟΥΣΙΝΔΗωΤΕΝΕΗΔΗωΤΕΠΑΛΛΙΗ
ΤΗΣΙΠΕΡΙΕΡΟΝΕΙΔΟΣΕΥΖωΝΟΙΟΓΥΝΑΙΚΟΣ
ΑΓΚΕΙΤΑΙΑΥΤΗΔΕΜΕΘΗΡωΝΗΣΙΝΕΝΑΣΤΑΙ
ΕΝΜΑΚΑΡωΝΝΗΣΟΙΣΙΝΙΝΑΚΡΟΝΟΣΕΝΒΑΣΙΛΕΥΕΙ
10 ΤΟΥΤΟΓΑΡΑΝΤΑΓΑΘΟΙΟΝΟΟΥΕΙΛΗΧΕΝΑΠΟΙΝΟΝ
ωΣΟΙΖΕΥΣωΚΤΕΙΡΕΝΟΔΥΡΟΜΕΝΟΝΠΑΡΑΚΟΙΤΗΝ
ΓΗΡΑΙΕΝΑΖΑΛΕωΙΧΗΡΗΙΠΕΡΙΚΕΙΜΕΝΟΝΕΥΝΗΙ
ΟΥΝΕΚΑΟΙΠΑΙΔΑΣΜΕΝΑΜΥΜΟΝΟΣΕΚΜΕΓΑΡΟΙΟ
ΑΡΠΥΙΑΙΚΛωΘωΕΣΑΝΗΡΕΙΨΑΝΤΟΜΕΛΑΙΝΑΙ
15 ΗΜΙΣΕΑΣΠ ΛΕΟΝωΝΔΟΙωΔΕΤΙΠΑΙΔΕΛΙΠΕΣΘΗΝ
ΝΗΠΙΑΧωΑΓΝωΤΕΚΑΚωΝΕΤΙΠΑΜΠΑΝΑΠΥΣΤω
ΟΙΗΝΣΦΙΝΗΛΗΣΚΑΤΑΜΗΤΕΡΑΠΟΤΜΟΣΕΜΑΡΨΕ
ΠΡΙΝΠΕΡΓΗΡΑΙΗΣΙΣ   ΜΙΓΗΜΕΝΑΙΗΛΑΚΑΤΗΣΙ
ΤωΙΔΕΖΕΥΣΕΠΙΗΡΟΝΟΔΥΡΟΜΕΝωΙΑΚΟΡΗΤΟΝ
20 ΚΑΙΒΑΣΙΛΕΥΣΑΠΑΤΡΙΦΥΗΝΚΑΙΜΗΤΙΝΕΟΙΚωΣ
ΖΕΥΣΜΕΝΕΣωΚΕΑΝΟΝΘΑΛΕΡΗΝΕΣΤΕΙΛΕΓΥΝΑΙΚ
ΑΥΡΙΙΣΙΖΕΦΥΡΟΙΟΚΟΜΙΖΕΜΕΝΝΗΛΥΣΙΗΣΙΝ
ΑΥΤΑΡΟΑΣΤΕΡΟΕΝΤΑΠΕΡΙΣΦΥΡΑΠΑΙΔΙΠΕΔΙΛΑ
ΔωΚΕΝΕΧΕΙΝΤΑΛΕΓΟΥΣΙΚΑΙΕΡΜΑωΝΑΦΟΡΗΝΑΙ
25 ΗΜΟΣΟΤΑΙΝΕΙΑΝΠΟΛΕΜΟΥΕΖΗΓΕΝΑΧΑΙωΝ
ΝΥΚΤΑΔΙΑΔΝΟΦΕΡΗΝΟΔΕΟΙΠΕΡΙ   ΣΣΙΣΑωΤΗΡ
ΠΑΜΦΑΝΟωΝΕΝΕΚΕΙΤΟΣΕ   ΑΙΥΚΑ
ΤΟΝΔΕΚΑΙΝΕΛΛΑΙΠΟ   ΕΝΕΡΡΑΨΑΝΤΟΠΕΔΙω
                        ΗΓΕΝΕΕΣΣΙΓΕΡΑΛ
30 ΟΥΜΙΝ   ΟΣΣΗΤΑΙΚΑΙΚΕΚΡΟΠΙΔΗΝΠΕΡΕΟΝΤΑ
ΤΥΡΣΗΝωΝΑΡΧΑΙΟΝΕΠΙΣΦΥΡΙΟΝΤΕΡΑΣΑΝΔΡωΝ
ΕΡΣΗΣΕΚΓΕΓΛωΤΑΚΑΙΕΡΜΕωΕΙΕΤΕΟΝΔΗ
ΚΗΡΥΧΗΡωΔΕωΠΡΟΓΟΝΟΣΕΘΗΣΙΛΛΔΟ
ΤΟΥΝΕΚΑΤΕΙΜΗΕΙΣΚΑΙΕΠωΝΥΜΟΣΗΜΕΝΑΝΑΣΣΑΝ
35 ΕΣΒΟΥΛΗΝΑΓΕΡΕΣΘΑΙΙΝΑΠΡωΤΟΘΡΟΝΕΣΕΔΡΑΙ
ΕΛΛΑΔΙΑΟΥΤΕΓΕΝΟΣΒΑΣΙΛΕΥΤΕΡΟΣΟΥΤΕΤΙΦωΝΗΝ
ΗΡωΔΕωΓΛωΣΣΑΝΔΕΤΕΜΙΝΚΑΛΕΟΥΣΙΝΑΘΗΝΕωΝ
ΗΔΕΚΑΙΑΥΤΗΠΕΡΚΑΛΛΙΣΦΥΡΟΣΑΙΝΕΙωΝΗ
ΚΑΙΓΑΝΥΜΗΔΕΙΗΚΑΙΔΑΡΔΑΝΙΟΝΓΕΝΟΣΗΝ
40 ΤΡωΟΣΕΡΙΧΘΟΝΙΔΑΟΣΥΔΦΙΛΟΝΙΕΡΑΡΕΖΑΙ
ΚΑΙΘΥΣΑΙΘΥΕωΝΑΤΑΡΟΥΚΑΕΚΟΝΤΟΣΑΝΑΓΚΗ
ΕΙΔΕΤΟΙΕΥΣΕΒΕΕΣΣΙΚΑΙΗΡωΝΑΛΕΓΙΖΕΙΝ
ΟΥΜΕΓΓΑΡΘΝΗΤΑΡΟΥΔΕΘΕΑΙΝΑΤΕΤΥΚΤΑΙ
ΤΟΥΝΕΚΕΝΟΥΤΕΝΕωΝΙΕΡΟΝΛΑΧΕΝ ΟΥΤΕΤΙΤΥΜΒΟΝ
45 ΟΥΔΕΓΕΡΑΘΝΗΤΟΙΣΑΤΑΡΟΥΔΕΘΕΟΙΣΙΝΟΜΟΙΑ
ΣΗΜΑΜΕΝΟΙΝΗωΙΙΚΕΛΟΝΔΗΜωΙΕΝΑΘΗΝΗΣ
ΨΥΧΗΔΕΣΚΗΠΤΡΟΝΙΛΔΑΜΑΝΘΥΟΣΑΜΦΙΠΟΛΕΥΕΙ
ΤΟΥΤΟΔΕΦΑΥΣΤΕΙΝΗΙΚΕΧΑΡΙΣΜΕΝΟΝΗΣΤΑΙΑΓΑΛΜΑ
ΔΗΜωΙΕΝΙΤΡΙΟΠΕωΙΝΑΟΙΠΑΡΟΣΕΥΡΕΕΑΓΡΟΙ
50 ΚΑΙΧΟΡΟΣΗΜΕΡΙΔωΝΚΑΙΕΛΛΙΗΕΝΤΕΣΑΡΟΥΡΑΙ
ΟΥΜΗΝΑΤΙΜΗΣΕΙΕΘΕΗΒΑΣΙΛΕΙΑΓΥΝΑΙΚωΝ
ΑΜΦΙΠΟΛΟΝΓΕΡΛωΝΕΜΕΝΑΙΚΑΙΟΠΛΟΝΑΝΥΜΦΗΝ
ΟΥΔΕΓΑΡΙΦΙΓΕΝΕΙΑΝΕΥΘΡΟΝΟΣΙΟΧΕΑΙΡΑ
ΟΥΔΕΡΣΗΝΓΟΡΓωΠΙΣΑΠΗΤΙΜΗΣΕΝΑΘΗΝΗ
55 ΟΥΔΕΜΙΝΗΡωΝΗΣΙΠΑΛΑΙΗΣΙΝ ΜΕΔΕΟΥΣΑ
ΚΑΙΣΑΡΟΣΙΦΘΙΜΟΙΟΠΑΡΟΨΕΤΑΙΟΜΠΝΙΑΜΗΤΗΡ
ΕΣΧΟΡΟΝΕΡΧΟΜΕΝΗΝΠΡΟΤΕΡΑωΝΗΘΕΑωΝ
ΗΛΑΧΕΝΗΛΥΣΙΗΣΙΧΟΡΟΣΤΑΣΙΗΣΙΝΑΝΑΣΣΕΙΝ
ΛΥΤΗΙΤΑΛΚΜΗΝΗΤΕΜΑΚΑΙΡΑΤΕΚΑΔΜΕΙωΝΗ

think part of the whole. Finally, there is the tomb or cenotaph of Regilla, once proudly fronting on the Via Appia, but now entirely vanished.

The temple was built of elegant second-century brickwork and once boasted a porch with two marble Corinthian columns *in antis*. Within the last few hundred years, however, this porch has been bricked in to prevent a collapse, as may be observed from the impressive crack that runs up the left face of the entablature (see map and Fig. 9.7). A glance at the plan (Fig. 9.8) shows that the interior is a single, barrel-vaulted room, lit by windows high in the end wall and one over the entry door. Stairs behind the apparently sixteenth-century church altar lead down to a tiny crypt (decorated with a Madonna and Child fresco). A very un-Christian marble altar stands to the right of the door as one enters: circular and wound about with a writhing carven snake (Fig. 9.9), it is inscribed in Greek as being offered to Dionysus by the *hierophant*, the standard appellation for one who has been an initiator at Eleusis.[25]

The statues of Faustina the Elder as Ceres, of Faustina the Younger as Libera, and of Annia Regilla in her function as priestess have all vanished from the temple.[26] Remaining, however, is the original, well-preserved stucco decoration (Fig. 9.10) on the vault and upper walls of the cella, although the wall panels themselves were frescoed in the eleventh century with scenes from the lives of Christ, St. Cecilia, and St. Urbano, to whom the temple was rededicated at some early date. The stuccoes feature two friezes of trophies and a vault decoration of octagonal coffers with a central boss. This boss is decorated with two divine figures: a bearded male figure undraped to the waist and holding a bird in his hand, and a draped female figure, also with a bird (Fig. 9.11). If we can assume Jupiter and Venus as the attributions of these figures, these in addition to the friezes would seem to refer to Annia Regilla's Trojan ancestry, as the *gens Appia*, along with many other patrician families, apparently traced their lineage back to Troy.

On the three oblique sides of the temple is a partial wall, perhaps for shoring up the higher ground behind it. Directly to the north of the temple is a small oblong field, level and currently kept free from briars, which one may assume is the sacral field for the first plowing. In this field, at an unknown distance from the temple,[27] is the hatch to the *megaron*, now exposed to the open air for the first time in perhaps 1,500 years (Fig. 9.12a). The *megaron* beneath the hatch (Fig. 9.12b) also runs due east-west, and is square-cut out of the reddish tufa below. The ceiling is not far above the head, and one suspects the soft dirt of the floor has risen considerably since its time of ancient use. The chamber is perhaps 2 meters wide and 27 meters in length, at least to the point where there is a collapse or an in-

Figure 9.7. The exterior of S. Urbano, taken from the southeast; note the massive crack running from frieze to roof, no doubt necessitating the brick infill. Photo by the author, 1993.

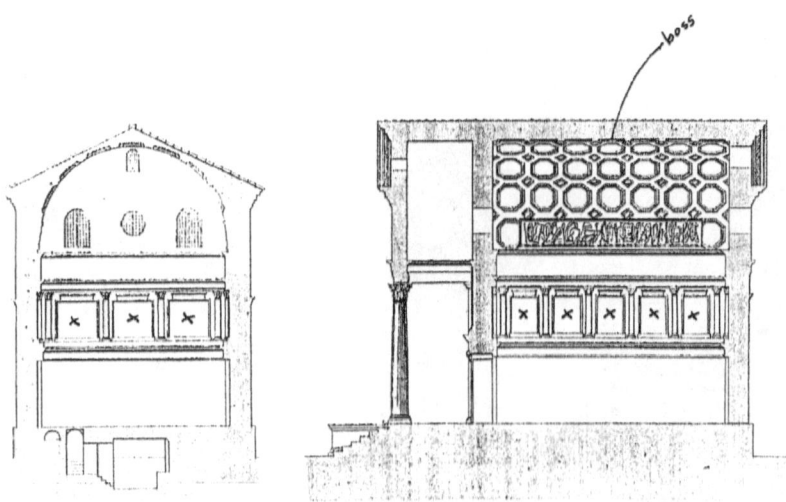

Figure 9.8. Canina's reconstruction of the interior of S. Urbano, in section crosswise (left) and lengthwise (right). The location of the boss showing the two deity figures on the vault has been marked and x's indicate the location of the later Christian frescoes. Canina 1853.

Figure 9.9. An altar to Dionysus, either in its original position or found nearby and set within the church of S. Urbano. Piranesi 1780; Vatican Library listing: Cicognara XI.3837.

Figure 9.10. Stucco representations of weaponry at the spring of the vault of S. Urbano. Note the battle trophies and captured standards. Piranesi 1780.

Figure 9.11. Stucco boss in the center of the vault of S. Urbano, possibly representing Jupiter and Venus. Piranesi 1780.

filling, at the far west end (see plan, Fig. 9.13). The centrally located hatch (about 18 meters along the *megaron*) ascends perhaps 5 meters to the surface, also carved from the tufa and rectangular in cross-section, with toeholds chipped into the eastward surface. Before the opening was installed within the last ten years, there was a broken slab of white marble at what I imagine was the ancient ground level, with what seemed to be a rusted pipe or oil drum above that, all of which was sealed with earth.[28] I did not dig in the soft matter of the floor, but I suspect that a thorough excavation of the *megaron* and careful study of the removed material might well produce piglet bones, to discover whether in fact the *megaron* was ever used for its primary function.

Before the addition of the modern opening via the hatch, the only egress from the *megaron* after its entrance was sealed, no doubt after the peace of the Church, was through a tunnel that branches off its eastern end (see Fig. 9.13). This tunnel, of unknown age and function, is carved very differently out of the soft tufa: the ceiling and sides are curved rather

Figure 9.12. Photos taken inside the *megaron*: (a) The hatch as viewed from directly below, with a fragment of a marble cover, above which was what looked like an oil-drum. The toe-holds can be seen angling from left to right directly below the lid fragment; (b) The view from east to west of the *megaron*, where the entry to the hatch is just where the light of the flash fails. Photos by the author, 1993.

Landscape Synchesis 177

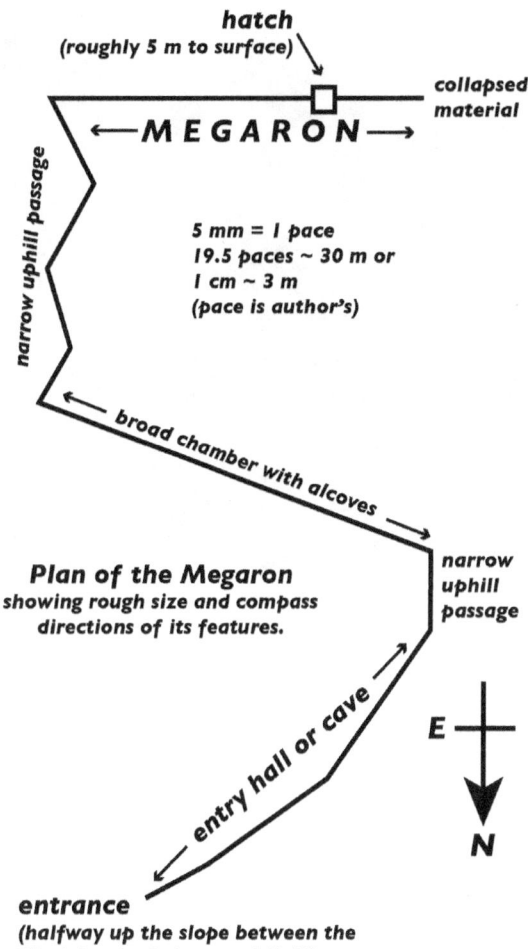

Figure 9.13. Rough plan of the *megaron* and tunnels and chambers connecting it with the slope of the hill, made by the author using a Silva compass and pacing system as indicated.

than tall and straight-sided, like the *megaron*, with two broader chambers with alcoves of undefined purpose. Just at the point of exit into the open air, one comes to a wide, low, bifurcated hall, suggestive of a stable, with occasional shallow shelves one imagines to be used for lamps or fodder. It was by following a path up the bracken-covered hillside below the temple that I found the entrance to the tunnel and thence to the *megaron*; the entrance is invisible from below, and nearly invisible even from across the valley (see Fig. 9.1). Given the questing nature of the zigzag upper reaches of the connecting tunnel—turning back inward when the hill's exterior support wall is reached—it must be that either the carver of the tunnel began from the hatch and cut a way out to a known cave, or the carver cut a way in to reach the known *megaron*. In either case, the simultaneous

Figure 9.14. Photograph of the Bosco Sacro, taken at the end of the nineteenth century looking west toward S. Urbano. In 1993 there were only three trees in place, but many have been recently planted, as the area is developing into a city park. Domenico Anderson/ALINARI Archives, Florence (1890).

knowledge of both the cave and the *megaron* was necessary, it seems to me, for the connection to have been made, arguing for a very early carving of the extra tunnel, before the entrance to the hatch became obliterated, as it was when I first saw it.

The Sacred Grove

My chief reason for studying the Caffarella landscape was the continuing existence there of a sacred grove. This cluster of ilexes, standing upon the knoll just east of the façade of the temple, is sadly thinned from its former abundant state. In a photograph of the late nineteenth century, the temple stands stark without surrounding foliage while the grove looms dark and full (Fig. 9.14). Now, the temple is scarcely visible behind its pines, whereas only three slim specimens of ilex remain in their proper places (see Fig. 9.2). This is perhaps the very grove to which Juvenal refers when he mentions "trees inhabited by refugee Jews" beside the Fountain of Egeria.[29] I myself have seen one of these trees with a rope ladder let down, in February, perhaps to let a cold shepherd take shelter from drizzle under the boughs.

A sacred grove is a standard accompaniment to a sanctuary of Demeter, as may be seen from references in Pausanias.[30] As we have seen in the case of Triopas, the goddess can remove her benison if offended, sending man back to the acorns of the woods for sustenance, where he was before agriculture came into the world. This is the interpretation of the presence of an ilex wood before her temple in the Caffarella; orchard trees would clearly represent an extension of her benevolent domesticating power over nature, whereas oaks do quite the opposite. The use of oaks here is in keeping with the somber, admonitory text of Herodes' boundary inscriptions.[31]

The *Fons Egeriae*

Egeria was the water nymph who gave the law to King Numa, and with whom he consorted on a nightly basis. She is understood to have been a wood-loving nymph, and she had a fountain also at Lake Nemi, in the sanctuary of Diana Nemorensis. She was imagined as living not far from Rome, but definitely in the countryside.[32] Her spring is located at the base of the bluff upon which St. Urbano/Temple of Demeter stands (see again Figs. 9.1 and 9.2), and is a cool spot overhung with a great nut-tree, wildflowers, and brambles, opening off of the path that was once the Via della Caffarella (until it met a gate and turned left across the Almone toward the Vaccareccia) and may have been the ancient Via Asinaria (a quiet mule-road, parallel and downhill from the great Via Appia and across the stream from the Via Latina). Water still runs from an alcove to the left of the back wall whence it used to spring, from under a reclining male statue, possibly of Numa. The sides of the nymphaeum are lined with brick and set with niches; the vault is concrete with the imprints of slabs of stone, and floor is paved with squared stones (Fig. 9.15).

Synchesis: Herodes Atticus and Annia Regilla

Through the dedication of the Triopium, Herodes makes a series of gestures on his own and his wife's behalf, creating *synchesis* between themselves and the place, and between themselves and their imperial patrons. Let us remind ourselves of the facts about Herodes: he was an extremely wealthy sophist from Attica, an Aiacid, a priest at Athens of the Roman imperial cult, an antiquarian and tutor to M. Aurelius and L. Verus, a

Figure 9.15. Canina's rendering of the *Fons Egeria*, in many ways better than any modern photograph, since bramble growth prevents one from standing far enough back to do it justice. The water flow is now, however, from the farthest-in left-hand niche. Canina 1853.

man of unstable temper and tyrannical leanings. His wife, Annia Appia Regilla,[33] was a kinswoman of Faustina the Elder, wife of Antoninus Pius, a member of the ancient Appian *gens*, thus, as we have seen, a descendant of Aeneas of Troy. She was also a priestess of Demeter and mother of Herodes' five children. Her death in premature childbirth, apparently after being beaten by a freedman on Herodes' orders for a trivial offense, brought on a lawsuit for wrongful death by Regilla's brother.[34] Although his superior oratory won the day and he was acquitted of his wife's murder, Herodes nevertheless additionally proceeded to dedicate all of his wife's clothing to Demeter at Eleusis and her Triopium lands to the goddesses Demeter and Kore, as well as to the goddess of vengeance, Ops/Nemesis.

Herodes nowhere explicitly states in any dedicatory inscription that he is innocent, or wealthy, or on good terms with the emperor's family, but all of these statements are implicit in the relationships he sets up within the landscape of the Triopium. I here examine three basic relationships: the links between the cults of Demeter of Greece and Ceres of Rome, the links between Herodes' family and the Roman imperial family, and the links between the expiation of blood-guilt and Herodes himself.

Demeter/Greece and Ceres/Rome

We have seen earlier in the barrel vault inside the Temple to Ceres/Demeter (the modern St. Urbano church) some well-preserved stucco reliefs (see Fig. 9.11). I have mentioned that along the frieze at the spring of the vault, we see a decorative collection of stucco trophies—shields, weapons, armor—and that on a boss at the apex of the vault are two divinities, one male, bearded and draped from the waist down, one female, fully draped. The male deity has a small bird of prey, possibly an eagle, perched on the back of his right hand. The female deity holds a small bird, possibly a dove, in a little sling on her right hand as she looks back over her left shoulder toward the god beside her. I submit that we see here depicted Regilla's lineage: as a supposed descendant of Aeneas, she would be related to both Venus/Aphrodite (Aeneas' mother) and Jupiter/Zeus (the father of Aeneas' ancestor Dardanus). The arms on the vault thus can be the spoils of Aeneas' Italian triumphs.

Yet this Ceres temple does more than celebrate Regilla's heritage. By linking Roman Ceres with Demeter, Herodes sets up a *synchesis* between Roman and Greek historical glory. The Greek nature of the goddess is clear from the little cylindrical altar still protected inside the church (see Fig. 9.9), with its Greek hierophantic inscription. Herodes claimed that he could trace his ancestry back to the great Ajax Telamon of Aegina.[35] The loyalty, strength, and tragic end of the *Iliad*'s Ajax Telamon would have been known to all fellow antiquarians. Against this we have the hero Aeneas, himself loyal and long-suffering, who tragically lost his first wife in the conflagration of Troy. Can Herodes even be reminding us of *this* notable parallel: his own loss with that of Aeneas? With a character as fixated upon rank and glory as Herodes', it is not impossible to imagine.

Then there is the remarkable choice of the location for the Ceres/Demeter temple on the brow of a hill, under which lay the Grotto of Egeria. By connecting the cult of Demeter with that of Egeria, Herodes makes yet another elegant sophistic link between the traditions of Greece and Rome. Egeria, the muse of King Numa, the lawgiver of ancient Rome and establisher of the Vestal cult, among others, can be compared with Demeter Thesmophoros, the lawgiver of the Greeks, very neatly indeed. Herodes' ancestor Cecrops also formed a link, as we have seen, with the law-giving days of Athens, making him nearly divine himself and surely worthy to own the *Fons Egeriae*. As Numa descended into Egeria's grotto for midnight communion, so the *kistophorai* descended into the *megaron* to retrieve the "things laid down" that will bring fertility to the crops and thereby structure to society, and Cecrops (half-man, half-serpent) had his chthonic connections—a neat piece of sophism.

Imperial Influence and Herodes' Family

As we have earlier seen, the connection between the imperial family and the "corn" supply was venerable by Herodes' time. By taking upon himself the right to dedicate a temple to Demeter/Ceres and erect within it statues to both the reigning empress Faustina and her daughter as Demeter and Kore (Ceres and Libera), as well as to Regilla as Priestess/Hero, Herodes was reminding Rome rather boldly of his imperial connections. Not only was he hereditary chief priest, the *archiereus* in Athens of the imperial cult,[36] he had, after all, been Marcus Aurelius' and Lucius Verus' rhetoric tutor in their boyhoods, and seems to have relished his (however temporary) rule over the future rulers of the world. There is something of the tyrant in Herodes, as the Athenians were heard to complain: namely, the impulse that caused him to use his great wealth in an imperial way, endowing Sardis and Olympia with public waterworks and attempting to cut the Isthmus of Corinth with a canal, as Nero had also tried to do.[37]

Regilla is linked in *synchesis* with the imperial women: her statue shares space within the temple with theirs. Herodes reminds his audience that he is related to the imperial family through his wife. He is one of them, this seems to imply, a fellow member of the imperial family via his wife and earlier tutorship; he is in the big leagues, he can be as generous and magnanimous as the emperor himself, he can put empresses on pedestals of his own making. This is Herodes the tyrant, as charged by the Athenians.[38]

Innocence and Herodes

The final but most obvious linkage in the mind of anyone who had followed his trial for murder would have been Herodes and Ops/Nemesis, but no one who suspected his guilt would have believed him capable of such an audacious gesture. To dedicate all of his wife's possessions and estates to the three goddesses, and especially to the third, Nemesis, would imply that those gifts were not tainted with murder. Tainted lands and goods would be unfit for such an offering, in which case the gift would be better dedicated to the underworld deities, or to Zeus the Lawgiver himself, or simply to the emperor. Herodes' victory in the lawcourts was, after all, no guarantee of his innocence: with his cleverness at ex tempore speaking, how could he *not* have been victorious, whether or not he was actually guilty? His own famously exaggerated grief was a mark against him.[39] No, his self-chaining to disaster, the *synchesis* of his innocence to the dedication of Regilla's property, was his last, best hope to be believed.

This bold stroke is at once the most important *synchesis* and the least convincing of them all. The prolix dedicatory inscriptions, their poetic preciousness, and the typically Herodean excess of his demand that no one use this land ever again on pain of the vengeance of Nemesis, combine with the dedication of the land itself to create the opposite of what Herodes intended. That is, the "I think he doth protest too much" feeling—which had long lived in the world before Shakespeare coined a phrase for it—is overwhelming. All it took was for the dangling disaster, the Damoclean sword that Herodes himself had set over his head by his hybris, to fall upon him, as it finally did at the end of his long life, to prove that he had in fact had a hand in Regilla's death. Once again distraught, this time over the death of two adopted daughters—struck by lightning as they slept in a tower—he is said to have been extremely perfunctory in his respect toward Emperor Marcus in the tyranny lawsuit, as well as unforgivably poor in the delivery of his speech. He courted death, and was only saved by the grudging and over-used affection of the emperor toward his old tutor; Herodes rarely or never returned to Rome thereafter.

Conclusion

When Herodes married Annia Appia Regilla, he linked his Greek historical heritage to that of Rome, and further back, to Troy. More important for our interests were his linkages with the gods: himself to Demeter through the priesthood of his wife and the lands he dedicated in her name; his wife—as semi-deified hero—to the divine empress Faustina and her daughter; and the sacred landscapes of suburban Rome to those of Asia Minor and Greece. By adding his wife to the heroic pantheon and her lands to the gods, he also hoped to lay aside any suspicions that he was responsible for Regilla's death, placing himself in the position of grieving innocent. How could he be other than innocent, if he called upon the dread goddess Nemesis herself to be satisfied with his offering?

By adding this piece of Latium to the sacred landscape of Magna Graecia, Herodes was participating in a long tradition of Greek colonization of Roman culture. Did the Romans resist this takeover of their spiritual heritage? There is no reason to think they did; the great gods that had saved Rome from disaster had come from afar to do so: the Magna Mater from Asia Minor, Aesculapius and Apollo from Greece, and now Ceres from

Sicily. Roman "animism" was an exercise in accretion, and the Romans were great connoisseurs of antiquarian sophistry and reflected glory: in fact, of *synchesis*.

Appendix: Inscriptions

A. Greek Inscription from the *Pagus Triopius* (no. 1 in Visconti 1794; *CIG* 3:916, no. 6280) = *IG* 14.1389 (Kaibel) = *IGRom* 3.1155 (Moretti) = 146 Ameling. Inscriptions translated by the author from Visconti's Latin rendering of the Greek.

1. O guardian of the Athenians, worthy of honor, Trito-born [Athena],
2. And you who watch over the works of men, Rhamnusian Plenty [Ops/Nemesis],
3. Come here, both of you, that you may honor this rich place
4. In the neighboring suburbs of hundred-gated Rome,
5. Pagus, host to Triopa of the Grain [Demeter],
6. So that you may call it Triopea's among the immortal gods.
7. However that may be, when you have come to both Rhamnous and broad Athens,
8. Having left the sonorous halls of Father Zeus,
9. Thus you hasten to the vine abundant in grapes,
10. And the fields of standing corn, and the trees laden with fruit,
11. Consecrating the tender grasses, the herbage of the nourishing meadows.
12. For Herodes names this land sacred to you both.
13. As much as is enclosed with a wall running 'round it,
14. Not to be altered by future man, and also to remain inviolate
15. Since truly Athena has nodded the terrifying helmet-crest
16. With her own immortal head lest anyone be permitted
17. To move a single clod or even a stone,
18. For indeed those exigencies are not at all to be overlooked by the Fates,
19. If anyone give injury to the sanctuaries of the gods.
20. Hear then, local dwellers, and neighboring farmers,
21. This place is sacred, for the goddesses are unchanging,
22. And are greatly honorable, and prepared to lend an ear.
23. Nor indeed should anyone ruin the rows of vines, or the groves of trees,
24. Or the herbage greening and growing with the much-nourishing moisture,
25. With an axe, which is handmaiden to black Hell,
26. Building a new tomb, or disturbing an old one:
27. It is not right (*themis/fas*) for the dead to lie in land sacred to the gods,
28. Save for that one who may be related by blood and from the posterity of him who has declared it:
29. For truly that is hardly improper, as the avenging god is well aware.
30. For indeed Athena lay King Erichthonios in a temple,
31. So that he might cohabit with the sacred things.
32. If these rules not be heeded by someone, if he does not obey them,
33. But despises them, this act will not turn back upon him without punishment,

34. But unlooked-for Nemesis, and the avenging demon who prowls about,
35. Will punish that fellow; truly he will always bring down perilous misfortune.
36. Nor indeed should he slight the great power of Aeolidan Triopa [Demeter]
37. By destroying the fallow lands of Demeter.
38. For you should all sufficiently fear punishment, and the notice here,
39. Lest the Triopan Fury follow.

B. Greek Inscription from the *Pagus Triopius* (no. 2 in Visconti 1794; *CIG* 3:916, no. 6280), labeled "Of Marcellus."
1. Come here to the temple, women of Tiberside,
2. Bringing holy offerings of incense to the image of Regilla.
3. For she was of the line of wealthiest Aeneas,
4. The illustrious blood of Anchises, and of Idaean Aphrodite:
5. She came to marry a man from Marathon; however, the celestial goddesses
6. Honor her, both new Ceres and Ceres of old,
7. To whom is named sacred the effigy of a beautiful woman.
8. She indeed lives with the heroines
9. In the Isles of the Blessed where Saturn reigns;
10. For this reward is her lot for her goodwill;
11. Thus Jupiter has pitied her grieving spouse
12. Lying in bleak old age on his widowed couch
13. Since those dark, greedy Fates have snatched
14. The children from that worthy woman's house,
15. A half part of the many: for two have so far survived their birth,
16. Infants, unknowing of evil, up to now utterly ignorant
17. That savage Fate has snatched away such a mother,
18. Before she could come to honored old age.
19. Henceforward Jupiter, solace to that man weeping inconsolably,
20. As is the Emperor, like Father Jove in appearance and counsel,
21. Jupiter indeed has sent his blooming consort [Ganymede],
22. Worthy to be carried by the Elysian breezes of Zephyr.
23. But he gave to the boy sandals having stars around the ankles,
24. Which they say also Hermes wore,
25. Then when he led Aeneas out of the Argives' war,
26. Through the shadowy night. Truly he had shining around his feet
27. The health-giving orb of Lunary light.
28. This once upon a time the Aeneadans sewed on their shoe
29. A sign of honor for the noble sons of the Ausonians [Italians].
30. The ancient sandals, ornament of Tyrrhenian men,
31. Shall not spurn him, though a Cecropidan [Athenian],
32. Since he was descended from Herse and Hermes,
33. If indeed truly Ceryx was progenitor of Herodes Theseides [Athenian].
34. Because he is honored, and a consul elected in the usual manner,
35. And gathered into the kingly senate, where is the place of the Princeps.
36. Nor is there anyone in Greece nobler in respect to race or in respect to

37. Eloquence than Herodes, whom they also call the "tongue of the Athenians."
38. For truly she was herself a beautiful descendent of Aeneas,
39. And a Ganymedean, and was the child of the Dardanians
40. And Erichthonidan Tros. You, however, if it pleases you, perform sacred rites
41. And sacrifice the victims: truly the business of sacred rites is not for the unwilling,
42. But if any desire to care for the hero shrine inspires pious men:
43. For she is not a mortal nor yet a goddess,
44. Therefore her fate is not the sepulcher nor yet the holy temple,
45. Not the honors appropriate to mortals or like those for the gods.
46. The monument is indeed like that of Athens,
47. Truly the soul remains near the scepter of Rhadamanthus.
48. This, however, is the likeness of Faustina, a pleasing one, set
49. In Pagus of Triopa, where of old she had ample plains
50. And the order of vines, and the fields set with olives.
51. Nor will the goddess, queen of women, spurn
52. The handmaiden of her own honor, and attendant nymph.
53. For neither did Diana when lovely Iphigenia was clinging to her throne,
54. Nor indeed did Athena look down upon Herse with a terrible glance,
55. Nor, in ordering Regilla herself to join the heroines of old,
56. Will the nourishing mother of great-souled Caesar deem her
57. Insignificant for the arriving chorus of demi-goddesses of old,
58. When it so happens that she herself is foremost in the Elysian chorus,
59. As is also Alcmene, and blessed Cadmeides [Semele].

Notes

1. Lanciani 1901, esp. the chapter "The Sacred Grove of the Arvales"; the photograph of the grove is on page 121.

2. Wright 1921: 209: Herodes asks of a certain neologism, "In what classic is that to be found?" and on 307 he is referred to as the "most famous of orators."

3. Pharr [1930] 1964: 79, item no. 442.

4. The inscription from Pagus Triopius is found in L. Moretti, *Inscriptiones Graecae Urbis Romae*, vol. 3 (Rome, 1979), no. 1155 = no. 146 in Ameling's monograph (cf. note 22 below).

5. Spaeth 1996: 1–2.

6. Warde Fowler 1971: 161.

7. Richardson 1992: 80–81. See also the discussion in Warde Fowler 1971: 255.

8. Spaeth 1996: 66–75. It is to Ceres, Spaeth points out, that the *Tribunus Plebis* is sacrosanct and thus it is to her that expiatory sacrifices must be made when a tribune is attacked. The implication is that such a violation endangers the city's growth and health.

9. Richardson 1992: 81: the *Ara Ceres Mater et Ops Augusta*, consecrated in 7 CE, is a good example of this linkage of Ceres with Livia and Augustus.

10. Burkert 1985: 242. Unless otherwise noted, all details concerning the ritual of the Thesmophoria are drawn from pp. 242-247.

11. Richardson (1992: 59-60) refers to the temple of the Bona Dea, also on the Aventine hill. He credits Macrobius with the note that no men were allowed in the temple (Macrobius *Sat.* 1.12.20-26). The famous story of Clodius Pulcher's invasion of these women-only rites in 62 BCE is from Plutarch's *Life* of Julius Caesar.

12. A clay oil pedestal lamp with a broad circular channel and some sixty wick-nozzles is illustrated in pl. 26 of Coldstream 1973.

13. The *kanephoros* pictured is listed in Guattani, *Monumenti antichi*, as having been discovered in 1784 not far from the Tomb of Cecilia Metella. Entry LXI refers to a *Caryatide*, while LXX, the pictured statue, is listed as Canefora. Inscribed on the basket of the statue were the names of the artists, Kriton and Nikolaos, Athenians, and naturally the statue was of the finest marble, probably from Herodes' own quarries.

14. The iconography associated with the Thesmophoria, including details of Triptolemos/Eleusinus as first farmer plowing up the soil, is described in great detail by Eggeling in his *Mysteria Cereris et Bacchi in Vasculo* (in Pasquali 1735: 6-74). See also Simon 1983: 21, showing a frieze of the sacred plowing.

15. Female piglets were Ceres' favorite offering. The *porca praesentanea* was sacrificed to Ceres, according to Varro (in Non. Marc., 163 Müller, cited by Spaeth 1996: 54), to cleanse a family at a funeral, especially when an inheritance was received; the *porca praecidanea* was sacrificed before the crops were harvested and in honor of a dead person whose burial might have been improper.

16. Burkert 1985: 242.

17. Pausanias mentions a temple of Demeter Thesmophoros on the road to Hermione as being in Theseus country, implying here as in other places in his narrative that the lawgiver Theseus and Lawgiver Demeter naturally might be found together. Cf. Pausanias 32.8.

18. At the "Black Demeter" worship site at Phigalia, in Arcadia (Pausanias 7.42.1-7), the sanctuary was in a cave; the goddess's image had a horse head, out of which sprang a serpent and other images; the image wore a tunic to its feet, and held in one hand a dolphin, in the other a dove. The first image at the site had caught fire, at which point the fields became barren, and the Delphic oracle gave the following explanation: the Arcadians had been acorn-eaters, and had twice been nomads and fruit-eaters. The goddess had caused them to cease pasturing, and could cause them to begin pasturing again. Of worship at this site, Pausanias notes: "I offered no burnt sacrifice . . . I offered grapes and other cultivated fruits, honeycombs and raw wool, full of its grease." No pigs, interestingly enough.

19. *Ceres Legifera* was an Italic deity credited with the division of the fields and settled living, so that men did not "wander here and there without law." She is invoked at the plowing of the *pomerium* and at weddings, along with Jupiter. Cf. Spaeth 1996: 52-53.

20. OCD^3, s.v. *pagus*, "term of Roman administrative law for subdivisions of territories, referring to a space . . . where there was no focal settlement."

21. *OCD*³, s.v. *Triopas*, whose son Erysichthon was punished with unquenchable hunger.

22. Philostr. *VS* 165. The Quintilii claimed Herodes was always putting up marble statues everywhere. He answered them that it was his marble (he owned—and depleted—most of the Hymettan marble quarries in Greece), and he could do what he liked with it.

23. The best source in English on the life and times of Herodes Atticus is Jennifer Tobin's excellent 1997 study. In German, the classic is Walter Ameling's 1983 *Herodes Atticus*.

24. *CIG* 3:916, no. 6280; translation mine, from Visconti's (1794) Italian rendering of the original Greek.

25. *OCD*³, 706: "*Hierophantes*, chief priest of the Eleusinian mysteries, was chosen for life from the hieratic clan of the Eumolpidae"—apparently one of Herodes' many public offices.

26. They are referred to in the dedicatory inscriptions noted above and in the appendix here.

27. It is approximately 10 meters; the distance is hard to gauge, as a fence lies between the building and the hatch.

28. There was some variation in *megaron* shape. Burkert (1985: 243) refers to the few surviving examples of *megara* as consisting of, in one instance, a circular "well" leading down into a natural crevice (at Agrigentum), and of a rectangular pit with a roofed opening above ground level (at Priene). He also notes the presence of pig bones and marble votive pigs in a circular pit at the Demeter sanctuary at Cnidos.

29. Juvenal in *Satire* 3.10–20 also complains of the alterations made in the *Fons Egeriae*, in "caves so unlike nature," and "marble to outrage the native tufa."

30. At the same Arcadian "Black Demeter" site mentioned above, Pausanias describes "a grove of oaks around the cave, and a cold spring that rises from the earth" (Pausanias 8.42.12). Another grove-temple combination appeared at the sanctuary of "Mysian Demeter," located near Pellene in Achaia, and founded, says Pausanias, by a man named Mysius, "who gave Demeter a welcome in his home." As he says, "There is a grove in the Myseum, containing trees of every kind, and in it rises a copious supply of water from springs" (Pausanias 7.27.9).

31. There is in a downstairs room of the Capitoline Museum a decapitated column, reused as a milestone column by Maxentius (who was also, we should remember, cannibalizing Herodes' villa for circus decorations), which Herodes had inscribed simply enough, in Greek and Latin: ANNIA REGILLA / WIFE OF HERODES / LIGHT OF THE HOME / WHOSE LANDS THESE ARE (*CIG pars* 33.875, no. 6184).

32. See *OCD*³, s.v. "Egeria," which perpetuates this locational error.

33. Herodes' full name was Lucius Vibullius Hipparchus Tiberius Claudius Atticus Herodes; Regilla's was Appia Annia Atilia Regilla Caucidia Tertulla.

34. Appius Annius Braduas, Regilla's brother, sued Herodes for her murder, the accusation being that Herodes had had his favorite freedman Alcimedon beat Regilla, who was then expecting their fifth child, so that she fell and died in a miscarriage. It seems typical of that unadmirable age that not only was Braduas' attack couched in a speech praising himself and his family's pedigree, but also that

Herodes' reaction, far from being that of a devastated husband who had deeply loved his wife, was simply to sneer at Braduas' showy aristocracy, saying that Braduas wore his nobility on his toes—since aristocrats were allowed to wear special celestial decorations on their sandals (Philostr. VS 2.555 [Wright 1921]). This ugly debate is even echoed in the "Of Marcellus" inscription listed in the appendix, lines 23-37 holding most of the boastful references to "starry sandals" and ancestry.

35. Tobin 1997: 13-14.
36. Ibid.: 29.
37. Ibid.: 34.
38. Ibid.: 38-47.
39. Philostr. VS 2.557-559 (Wright 1921).

CHAPTER 10

The Eleusinian Mysteries and Vergil's "Appearance-of-a-Terrifying-Female-Apparition-in-the-Underworld" Motif in *Aeneid* 6

RAYMOND J. CLARK

More than two and a half centuries ago, in 1745, in the second book of his *The Divine Legation of Moses,* Bishop William Warburton put forth the hypothesis that Aeneas' Descent into the Underworld was an allegorical representation of an initiation into the Eleusinian mysteries.[1] The bishop considered Aeneas to be a grand legislator (in his capacity as founder of Lavinium) within a tradition of ancient heroes and lawgivers who were initiated in the mysteries;[2] he noted that Caesar Augustus, whom he says Aeneas anticipates, was likewise initiated at Eleusis;[3] and he concluded that Vergil worked into Aeneas' journey the doctrine of a "future state of rewards and punishments" that was the foundation and support of ancient politics. This hypothesis evoked a skillful adversary in Gibbon, who, objecting that Aeneas was no legislator, set out to expose Warburton's many unproved assumptions—"probably repelled not more by the arrogant dogmatism of the untrained scholar," as Conington put it, "than by the zeal of the ecclesiastic in proving that even pagan times witnessed to the alliance between religion and civil government."[4] Conington, for his part, granted Gibbon that Aeneas was not a mere anticipation of Augustus, despite his many Augustan traits, and he further conceded that Aeneas' descent was not simply a sustained allegory of the mysteries as though there were an authorized doctrine. But Conington nevertheless considered it quite possible that several of Vergil's details, if not his general conception, may have been drawn from the mysteries—that is to say, from such ancient literature as alludes to them.

My purpose here is not to review the whole topic of correspondences between Aeneas' infernal journey and the Eleusinian mysteries, but rather to examine a single incident in book 6 of the *Aeneid* at verse 290, where Aeneas raises his sword in terror against the phantoms of the Gorgons and other monsters who appear before him in the darkness of Pluto's house at 282–289. In this examination I shall draw attention to just three of several "motifs," or themes, cited by Warburton as evidence that Aeneas underwent an initiation. The bishop contends (1) that tradition obliged the hero Aeneas to be initiated, just as (to name one other) Herakles was initiated into the Eleusinian mysteries;[5] (2) that Aeneas in the Gorgon scene encountered imaginary false terrors no differently from all initiates in the mysteries, who are subjected to the phantoms of Hekate;[6] and (3) that Aeneas was soon found in a "fright" resembling that experienced by other initiates at the mysteries according to the writings of Themistius and Proclus.[7] In Warburton's argument, these are three separate motifs having Eleusinian associations without any other connection between them.

Yet there are other connections between these motifs. They exist in some versions of Herakles' descent to fetch the Hell-dog Cerberus. To introduce them, I adduce what is clearly a summary made in *Bibliotheca* 2.5.12 by Apollodorus of Athens of an earlier source telling how Herakles went to Eumolpus at Eleusis in order to be initiated, presumably (we are not told the reason) as the means of ensuring success in his quest for Cerberus.[8] But first Herakles had to be adopted by an Athenian (Pelius) in order to qualify for the rite, which he was the first foreigner to undergo. And before Eumolpus could initiate him,[9] Herakles had also to be purified by him from his slaughter of the Centaurs.[10] After initiation, Herakles descended through a Hades entrance in Taenarum in Laconia. Upon seeing him in the lower world, the souls of the dead all fled, save Meleager and the Gorgon Medusa. Herakles drew his sword against Medusa as if she were alive, but desisted when his underworld companion Hermes told him that she was but an empty phantom. Herakles then found Theseus and Peirithoos near the gates of Hades and rescued Theseus. Continuing his journey, some details of which I omit, Herakles obtained Pluto's permission to capture Cerberus, on the condition that he not use against the dog the weapons he was carrying. So Herakles throttled Cerberus, whom he found at the gates of Acheron, into submission,[11] and ascended with him to the upper world through Troezen. Herakles later returned the Hell-dog to Hades after showing him to Eurystheus.

So goes Apollodorus' Greek narrative, composed in the second century CE. As this mythographer consistently ignores Roman literature,[12] he is unlikely to have modeled his narrative on an earlier scene of Aeneas' meeting with the Gorgon in the *Aeneid*, from which, in any case, Apollodorus differs in detail. Eduard Norden, in his commentary on the sixth book of the *Aeneid*, made a strong case for believing that Apollodorus drew instead for this episode on a lost epic version of Herakles' descent that he claimed influenced, in addition to the Apollodoran narrative itself, Bacchylides' fifth *Dithyramb*, Aristophanes' *Frogs*, and the sixth book of the *Aeneid*,[13] to which a passage in the fourth book of Vergil's *Georgics*, to be mentioned later, should be added. In his fifth *Dithyramb*, Bacchylides at 71-84 describes a scene resembling Apollodorus' in that the descending hero Herakles is warned not to shoot at a mere wraith. But in the highly compressed scene by this Greek lyric poet, neither the Gorgon nor Herakles' underworld guide is mentioned. Instead, Meleager's ghost admonishes Herakles against shooting an arrow at itself. Its assurance that there is nothing to fear (οὔ τοι δέος) from a ghost underscores the fright that Herakles in fact experiences as he aims his weapon at the underworld shade. When at *Aeneid* 6.290-294 the Cumaean Sibyl warns the terrified Aeneas not to use his sword against Gorgons and other bodiless shapes as well, Vergil assigns to Aeneas' august guide the function performed by both Herakles' guide Hermes and Meleager's ghost in the comparable versions so far mentioned. Yet Vergil cannot have derived his knowledge of the Gorgon episode from Bacchylides, even if he read him, since the Greek lyric poet did not mention the Gorgon. Nor was Vergil's source Apollodorus, who wrote long after him.

Nor indeed could Vergil have exploited Aristophanes' *Frogs* for his Gorgon scene, since Aristophanes did not include such a scene, even though, as I believe, one episode in his comedy—I now raise a matter not noticed by Norden—presupposes the existence of the standard Gorgon scene in Aristophanes' source. I refer to verses 564ff., where the Greek playwright seems to have transformed the motif of Herakles' frightened encounter with one or more Gorgons into what appears to be a comic parody of the theme. In the comic parody, two formidable female keepers of the kitchen tell Dionysus, after he knocks on Pluto's door, how Herakles had drawn his sword upon *them*. I take these keepers of the kitchen to be comic doublets of the Gorgons. The correspondence between the two sets of formidable females, which I observed more than thirty years ago with the later approval of Dover in his commentary on the *Frogs*,[14] illustrates a further influence of the lost version of Herakles' descent upon Aristophanes beyond the points of contact noticed by Norden.

In a brilliant article, Hugh Lloyd-Jones adduces a fragment of Greek lyric poetry preserved in *P.Oxy.* 2622 ascribed to Pindar (which has a commentary upon it partially preserved in *PSI* 139) together with the *Herakles* of Euripides at 610-613, where Herakles reports that he saw the ὄργια of the initiates, as additional works influenced by the lost epic postulated by Norden. Lloyd-Jones infers from Herakles' pro-Athenian sympathies and connection with Eleusis that the lost epic was composed around 550 BCE by an Athenian or a person belonging to the orbit of Athenian culture.[15] The partially preserved poem by Pindar agrees with the Apollodoran narrative in telling how Herakles was initiated by Eumolpus at Eleusis before recovering Cerberus. It also alludes to Herakles' meeting with Meleager among innumerable ghosts in Hades, as related by both Apollodorus and Bacchylides. Unfortunately, the fragmentary remains of Pindar's poem do not tell us whether Herakles was frightened by any Gorgon or Gorgons in the underworld.

How, then, might Aeneas' terror at seeing the Gorgons have been drawn from the Eleusinian mysteries? The question involves consideration of comparative figures. Let us first recall what has just been noticed, that Aristophanes omitted the Gorgon scene from the *Frogs*, having transmuted it into a comic parody that takes place at the front door of Pluto's house. Let us also bear in mind that Herakles' directions to Dionysus based on his own experiences are the playwright's indirect acknowledgment that a version of Herakles' descent to the lower world in the living flesh underlies Dionysus' in this play. But Aristophanes has made changes. Dionysus and his slave Xanthias in the *Frogs* are terrified not by a Gorgon, as was Herakles in the lost epic used by Aristophanes, but by Empousa, another female monster who appears in the infernal region just where Herakles told the descending pair they would meet snakes and monsters (143-144, 278-279). According to Herakles' directions, they must pass these before they reach the region where the wicked are punished in mud and dung (145ff., cf. 273ff.), and beyond that region again, says Herakles, are myrtle groves, where deceased Eleusinian initiates are seen and heard singing and dancing (154ff., cf. 312-459); nearby lies Pluto's house (163, cf. 431-436 and 460). Both the place where the wicked are punished by lying in mud and the myrtle groves of Hades as home to the initiates evoke associations with Eleusinian mysteries.[16] Struck by the general correspondence between the Aristophanic and Apollodoran descent versions, Lloyd-Jones has suggested that the first two stages mentioned by Herakles parallel those in Apollodorus' narrative, where Herakles meets the Gorgon (in the region of monsters) and then sees Theseus and Peirithoos undergoing punishment (in the region of the wicked).[17] I shall return to certain specific matters of location presently. More pertinent to our immediate purpose is Lloyd-Jones' further inference that the underlying common source, the sixth-century Attic epic katabasis of Herakles, which stresses this hero's Eleusinian connections, influenced also the Empousa scene.

The existence of this Eleusinian source and the collocation of Empousa's appearance with Eleusinian bliss in the *Frogs* have in turn led to the hypothesis that Empousa's appearance in the *Frogs* alludes to a specific Eleusinian cultic event. In its support, Brown cites Borthwick's observation that Xanthias compares Empousa to a weasel (γαλῆν) in language derived from a hieratic formula of the sort associated with mystery religions, to which Dionysus reacts in ritual terms. He also adduces evidence from the partially surviving work *On Demagogues* by the fourth-century BCE historian Idomeneus of Lampsacus (*FGrH* 338.F2) and from Lucian's *Cataplus* 22.[18] In the former, Empousa appears from out of the darkness to initiates (ἀπὸ σκοτεινῶν τόπων ἀνεφαίνετο τοῖς μυουμένοις); the brief surviving fragment does not identify the initiates as Eleusinian, but this they are likely to be, since the work from which the fragment comes focuses on Athens, and Graf has shown that references to mysteries within Athenian contexts always refer to Eleusis.[19] In Lucian's *Cataplus,* it is the dread figure of an Erinys that appears from out of the darkness, in the same region as Empousa in the *Frogs,* that is to say, as soon as the infernal travelers reach the far shore of the underworld lake. Lucian, moreover, gives his satire a specifically Eleusinian context, since a deceased cobbler is made to exclaim, "By Herakles!" to other dead men who have just disembarked with him from Charon's boat, and he asks the philosopher Cyniscus if the appearance of the Erinys in the darkness resembles Cyniscus' earlier experience when he was initiated in the Eleusinian mysteries. Cyniscus affirms that it does, torch-bearing female with frightful menacing aspect and all. Since apparitions, φάσματα, are also much spoken of in the celebrations of the Greater Mysteries at Eleusis[20] — they are at times said to be sent by Hekate, with whom Empousa is sometimes identified[21] — Brown thinks that at a relatively early point in the proceedings, initiates were terrified by the appearance of a specter, as were Dionysus and Xanthias, and he suspects that Empousa (perhaps not her official name) was one of the names given to it by individual worshipers.[22] Accordingly, he assigns to this terrifying female in the *Frogs* a cultic origin together with, through the lost Eleusinian Herakles katabasis, a literary origin. He further suggests that, like the Homeric *Hymn to Demeter,* the lost epic contained aetiological passages alluding to and glossing the δρώμενα at Eleusis.[23]

I would not, however, care to see it taken for granted that the lost Herakles epic itself contained an Empousa scene. It strikes me as far more likely that Aristophanes modeled his Empousa scene upon the Gorgon scene in his source, which, if true, has just provided one more point of influence upon Aristophanes. We could not, of course, have inferred this direction of influence had Norden not conjectured the existence of the epic katabasis, which Lloyd-Jones then dated to the mid-sixth century BCE, since all extant references to one or more Gorgons seen by Herakles in the underworld, and by Aeneas in imitation of Herakles, are post-Aristophanic.

The conclusion so far reached is that Empousa can be added to the Gorgon and to the two female keepers of the kitchen and to the Erinys in Lucian's *Cataplus* (as well as perhaps to Hekate, with whom Empousa is sometimes identified) in a list of variants on the appearance-of-a-terrifying-female-apparition-in-the-underworld motif with strong Eleusinian associations. Another source supports this conclusion. Elsewhere I have expressed the view that Aristophanes as well as Vergil would have taken every chance to read, in addition to the lost epic version, whatever they could on the articulate and well-developed tradition about Herakles' descent, and that both did by exploiting Euripides' (or, less likely, Critias') *Peirithoos*,[24] which now survives in only a few fragments. In one fragment, *P.Oxy.* 3531, Peirithoos refers to a female he can hear but not see.[25] If the *Peirithoos* precedes the production of the *Frogs* in 405 BCE, as I think it does,[26] Cockle, the editor of this fragment, may well be right when he observes, "Perhaps this creature, whatever her precise nature, is reflected in Empousa."[27] Since the chorus of this play, as in the *Frogs*, is composed of deceased Eleusinian initiates,[28] Euripides may have borrowed this female from Eleusinian cult for his *Peirithoos*. Aristophanes could have taken her from Euripides' play or from Eleusinian cult, or from both.

When weighing the evidence of Lucian's *Cataplus*, Brown cautions that the satirist may also have had Aristophanes' *Frogs* in mind, since in addition to the similarities between the two works already pointed out, Cyniscus, like Dionysus, has to row Charon's boat across the infernal lake.[29] More can be adduced to support this supposition and to strengthen Brown's claim that Empousa has Eleusinian ties. For it looks to me as though Lucian even chose for his satire characters appropriate to the shapes assumed by Aristophanes' Empousa—among them a dog and a copper leg. The very name of the "cynic" philosopher Cyniscus means "dog," and recognition of the copper leg would have helped the deceased cobbler clinch the apparition's identity. Since, moreover, Sophocles gave the attribute "copper-footed" to the avenging Erinys in *Elektra* 491, Dionysus, as Stanford notes,[30] may be jestingly alluding to it when he asks in the *Frogs* if shape-shifting Empousa has a copper leg. It seems to me, then, a small leap if Lucian, observing the Sophoclean underpinning of the Aristophanic attribute of Empousa, makes the characters in his satire identify Aristophanes' Empousa as an Erinys. If we combine this identification with Cyniscus' association of the frightful Erinys with Eleusis, Lucian indirectly gives Empousa, too, an Eleusinian setting. I have already argued that Empousa in the *Frogs* is Aristophanes' substitute for the Gorgon encountered by the Eleusinianized Herakles in the sixth-century source. By giving the female apparition the identity of a Gorgon, the author of the lost epic portrayed the terrified Herakles as actually encountering a Hellish female apparition of the sort that even Odysseus feared to meet at the end of the *Nekyia*.[31]

Such, then, is the convergence of Eleusinian associations underlying Aeneas' encounter with the Gorgons in *Aeneid* 6. I turn now to some issues of infernal topography that indicate deviations by both Aristophanes and Vergil from their common sixth-century source. Observe that in the *Frogs*, the Gorgons and their comic doublets, the formidable keepers of Pluto's kitchen, both occupy the same residence, namely Pluto's palace. The first of these two sets of females, despite being snaky-haired like their further counterparts Hekate, the Erinyes, and Empousa,[32] do not, after all, reside in the region of snakes and monsters, where Lloyd-Jones assumed them to be in his comparison (see above) between the two parallel stages in the Aristophanic and Apollodoran descents. Nevertheless, in Aristophanes' lost source, this is where they belonged. Several matters to be raised in the next few paragraphs make this clear.

We know that the Aristophanic Gorgons have their dwelling in Pluto's palace because the doorkeeper Aeacus goes inside to search for them at 472–478. Yet their snaky hair makes them natural compatriots with the snakes and monsters that Herakles leads Dionysus to expect to meet immediately after reaching the far side of the bottomless lake. This is also where the sinners and monsters in Polygnotus' mid-fifth-century wall-painting must have been depicted as described in Pausanias 10.28.1–7— on Acheron's far side, since Odysseus is said to be already in Hell before these are listed. No mention, incidentally, is made of Pluto's palace in Polygnotus' mural. Insofar as Aristophanes' Gorgons are placed not with the snakes and monsters immediately across the lake, but in the company of some other snake-like creatures of torture in Pluto's palace much deeper within the underworld, it is as though they have been attracted away from their sixth-century location to the residence of the two kitchen-keepers, who have assumed the Gorgons' formidable attributes in the comic parody.

Nor is this Aristophanes' only departure from what might have been expected. Though Herakles tells Dionysus that he will encounter the snakes and monsters *first* after crossing the lake (143ff.), Dionysus actually meets them *second*, after he has encountered the wicked (273ff.). Much commentary has been written on the reversal of the two regions as described by Herakles, in contrast to Dionysus' actual experience of them. But it has not hitherto been observed that we can ascertain the sixth-century sequence of events by comparing the versions of Aristophanes and Apollodorus, who both drew upon the lost Herakles descent. The comparison reveals that Herakles' directions to Dionysus preserve the original sequence, so that Aristophanes deviates from his source when he makes Dionysus and Xanthias meet the wicked first. Aristophanes no doubt had dramatic reasons for reversing the order. The two infernal travelers barely mention the wicked, save with a glance at the audience, and this region is passed through first and quickly, perhaps to suppress possible conflict with the location of the main dead beyond the door of Pluto's house (760), from which the deceased Aeschylus and Euripides exit onto the stage at 830ff. Aristophanes also evidently judged it more dramatically effective to put second the region of the snakes and monsters, in which the two panic-stricken travelers are made to linger by Empousa's frightful apparition.

The detail provided by Apollodorus to which I just alluded, which enables us to infer in which order Aristophanes' source narrated these infernal experiences, raises an issue of its own that needs sorting out. It is widely held that the gates of Hades near which Apollodorus says Herakles found Theseus and Peirithoos are located at the entrance to the underworld. For instance, Brown in his article on Empousa says that according to Apollodorus 2.5.12, "*As soon as Heracles enters Hades* with his guide, Hermes, all souls flee before them with the exception of Meleager and the Gorgon, Medusa" (my emphasis).[33] The same misunderstanding infects also Lavecchia's summary of Apollodorus' scene thus: "Subito dopo il suo arrivo nell' Ade [i.e., at the start of his infernal journey], Eracle incontra Medusa e Meleagro."[34] Similarly, a popular commentary on Apollodorus disseminates the view that the gates of Acheron at 2.5.12 "are the gates of Hades mentioned above, symbolizing the boundary between the lands of the living and the dead."[35] Or, to cite the editor of the papyrus fragment of Euripides' underworld scene again, Cockle infers from Apollodorus' mention of Hades' gates that in Euripides' *Peirithoos,* Herakles' conversation with Hades' doorkeeper Aeacus must have taken place near the entrance of the underworld also.[36] But the Apollodoran gates of Hades are not near the entrance to the underworld. The fact that Apollodorus does not provide for these gates a specific reference point in his brief summary of Herakles' descent should not be taken to imply that Herakles in his account meets the Gorgon as soon as he enters the underworld, or finds Theseus and Peirithoos near the gates of Hades at the entrance to the underworld also. On the contrary, since Apollodorus reports that Herakles sees Theseus and Peirithoos as he *approaches* Hades' gates *after* thrusting his sword at the Gorgon, the gates can hardly be at the entrance separating the world of the living from the world of the dead, where Cockle and others imagine them to be. They must belong instead to Hades' palace across the lake, which Apollodorus in his brief summary omits, and where

Aristophanes, too, depicts Hades' palace in the *Frogs*. Moreover, in the scene depicted by Bacchylides (5.64), Herakles meets innumerable ghosts, including Meleager, with whom Apollodorus couples the Gorgon, beside the infernal waters of Cocytus, in all likelihood in their final resting-place on Cocytus' far bank. This is where Vergil's Orpheus, in imitation of Herakles, sees the corresponding ghosts in the fourth book of the *Georgics* at 471–480 — the other passage influenced by the epic Herakles katabasis to which I alluded earlier. In sum, the related texts support the inference drawn from the Apollodoran narrative that Herakles in the common source encounters the terrifying apparition of the Gorgon as soon as he has crossed the infernal water, not as soon as he enters Hades, and that he has to travel deeper into the underworld before finding Theseus and Peirithoos near the gates of Hades.

In verse 290 in the sixth book of the *Aeneid*, Aeneas is near the beginning of his infernal journey when he experiences terror in the face of the frightening specters of the Gorgons and other shades. The occurrence of Aeneas' fright at this point might tempt us to postulate a direct connection between this order of events in Aeneas' underworld journey and the early part of the proceedings in the Eleusinian mysteries, when initiates are said to be frightened, according to Brown and various passages of late antiquity not cited by him (see note 7 above). But another explanation forces itself upon us as soon as we realize how much earlier the Gorgon scene occurs in the *Aeneid* than in the lost Herakles epic as here reconstructed from related texts: Herakles in the lost epic katabasis encountered one or more Gorgons *after* crossing the infernal water, whereas Aeneas meets them *before* his crossing. In another respect, Vergil's Gorgons at *Aeneid* 6.273-294 retain their Aristophanic abode — since they still dwell within Pluto's palace, quite precisely, as I have inferred elsewhere,[37] in the stable rooms beside its main entrance. No inconsistency exists between saying that Aeneas' encounter with the Gorgons is both earlier and in the same place, since Vergil has relocated Pluto's palace and translated the Gorgons with it, to the antechamber of the Vergilian underworld. Aeneas and his guide, the Sibyl, thus reach the palace shortly after they pass through "the gate of Dis," which is synonymous with the cave beside Avernus (*Aen.* 6.127 and 237ff.).[38] This is the gate that separates the land of the living from the world of the dead in Vergil's underworld, in contrast to the Apollodoran gates of Hades and the palace gates guarded by Aeacus in the *Frogs*. The Vergilian location of Pluto's palace at the very beginning of the underworld rather than at its far end is not an error on Vergil's part. In a recent article, I undertook to show how Vergil expanded the underworld by displacing forward exploit after exploit that in his sources occurred later in the underworld, in order to put more space between the beginning of the underworld and the near shore of the infernal bank, and to heighten the horrors Aeneas faces at the very beginning of his ordeal.[39] The details are repeated here as a cautionary note in the present task of investigating the relationship between Aeneas' terror in the Gorgon scene and its comparable cultic event in the Eleusinian mysteries. To show the existence of this relationship, I have traced the many paths connecting Aeneas' experience to Eleusis. I have also taken pains to point out how Vergil has rearranged the infernal topography he inherits, to judge from reconstructed details in the lost sixth-century Attic epic katabasis of an Eleusinianized Herakles. Because Vergil has rearranged what he has read to suit his poetry, it would be misleading to treat Aeneas' infernal journey, however deeply it is imbued with Eleusinian associations, as a poetic document from which to reconstruct the order of events in the mysteries. For this reason, Aeneas' descent as concerns the Gorgon episode cannot be regarded allegorically as "no other than an enigmatical representation of his initiation into the mysteries," as Bishop Warburton claimed in 1745.[40]

Notes

1. Warburton 1745: 270ff., esp. 288.
2. Ibid.: 288-291. Among initiated "ancient heroes," Warburton includes Jason, the Dioscuri, Herakles, and Orpheus as named by Diodorus (4.43.1 and 5.49.6); among "lawgivers," he lists both the kings of Eleusis named in the Homeric *Hymn to Demeter* 474-476 and such other figures as Tarquinius Priscus (Macrobius *Sat.* 3.4.8), Augustus Caesar (Suet. *Aug.* 93), and the later founders of empire who received instructions concerning their office from the mysteries. With regard to all of the foregoing, observe (1) that Warburton's list of Eleusinian kings can be supplemented by Polyxenus and Dolichus in the *Hymn to Demeter* at 154-155 and 477; (2) that "lawgivers" for kings is a late term used, for instance, for Triptolemus by Porphyry (*De abst.* 4.22); and (3) that heroes and kings merge in Warburton's political theory because Herakles, for example, is regarded (Xen. *Hell.* 6.3.6) by the torch-bearer Callias in the Eleusinian mysteries as the founder of the Spartan state. In addition, observe that in Warburton's sources, Tarquinius and the list of heroes are presented as Samothracian initiates. The Dioscuri and Herakles—and Dionysus, too—are, however, called Eleusinian initiates in other sources (found in notes 9-10 below).
3. Suet. *Aug.* 93. Here Suetonius explains how Augustus' Eleusinian initiation (*Athenis initiatus*) led to his recognition of the need for secrecy in a dispute involving the privileges of the priests of Attic Ceres in a court case at Rome. Cf. also Dio Cass. 51.4.1 and 54.9.7.
4. Conington 1872: 425.
5. Warburton 1745: 291-294; pertinent references for Herakles, with additions, are now assembled in notes 8-10 below.

6. Warburton 1745: 305–306, referring to Schol. in Ap. Rhod. *Argon.* 3.861. The passage is quoted in note 21 below, which offers a collection of passages on Hekate's phantoms.

7. Warburton 1745: 309, referring to Themist. *Or.* 20.235^a (2 p. 5 Downey-Norman; p. 287 Dind.): ὁ μὲν ἄρτι προσιὼν τοῖς ἀδύτοις φρίκης τε ἐνεπίμπλατο καὶ ἰλίγγου, ἀδημονίᾳ ἴε ξυνείχετο τε καὶ ἀπορίᾳ ξυμπάσῃ, οὐδὲ ἴχνους λαβέσθαι οἷός τε ὢν οὐδὲ ἀρχῆς ἡστινοσοῦν ἐπιδράξασθαι εἴσω φερούσης, ὅτε δὲ ὁ προφήτης ἐκεῖνος ἀναπετάσας τὰ προπύλαια τοῦ ναοῦ.... ("Entering now into the mystic dome he is filled with horror and amazement. He is seized with solitude, and a total perplexity: he is unable to move a step forward, and at a loss to find the entrance to that road which is to lead him to the place he aspires to. Till the Prophet [the *vates*] or Conductor, laying open the vestibule of the temple... ," trans. Warburton). Similarly Proclus *Theol. Plat.* 3.18: Ὥσπερ ἐν ταῖς ἁγιωτάταις τελεταῖς πρὸ τῶν μυστικῶν θεαμάτων ἔκπληξις τῶν μυουμένων, οὕτω.... ("As in the most holy Mysteries, before the scene of the mystic visions, there is a terror infused over the minds of the initiated, so... ," trans. Warburton.) For more on fear and terror in the mysteries, see notes 20–21 below.

8. In iconographical representations of his capture of Cerberus, an Eleusinianized Herakles receives a more favorable reception in the underworld. The earliest such representation appears on a black-figure amphora (fr. Reggio 4001) from Locri c. 540 BCE, which Robertson (1980: 274–300, esp. 275–276) thinks relies on the same lost Eleusinian source as Apollodorus. I refer to this source at notes 13–15 below. For more on the Reggio fragments and on Athenian vases from about 530 BCE that show the Eleusinianized Herakles, see Boardman 1975: 1–12, pls. I–IV; and cf. Sourvinou-Inwood 1974.

9. Herakles' need for adoption is narrated also by Plutarch, in a passage (*Thes.* 33.2) that does not name Eumolpus. In a fragment edited by Lloyd-Jones (1967) providing the earliest extant literary reference to Herakles' Eleusinian initiation, Pindar names Eumolpus in agreement with Apollodorus against Diodorus (4.25–26), who says Herakles was initiated at Eleusis by Musaios. The agreement lends support to Lloyd-Jones' completion of the Pindaric lacuna at v. 8, πρώτω[ι ξένων, and to his interpretation of what Eumolpus gave to Herakles "first" in the completed lacuna, "probably the privilege of being initiated in spite of being a foreigner." Plutarch (*Thes.* 33.2) and Xenophon (*Hell.* 6.3.6) remark that Herakles' adoption paved the way for the later adoption and Eleusinianization of the Dioscuri, also foreigners. Schol. in Aristoph. *Plutus* 845 and 1013 also remarks upon their common treatment by the Athenians, but then attributes to Herakles' status as a non-Athenian the institution of the Lesser Mysteries at Agrae. This assertion contradicts the usual view that these mysteries were instituted to deal with Herakles' need to be purified from bloodshed.

10. See also Plutarch *Thes.* 30.5, and Diodorus, who at 4.14.3 gives this as the reason why the Lesser Mysteries were founded by Demeter. The act of Herakles' purification before initiation is shown in many artistic representations listed in, e.g., Richardson 1974: 211–213. It was perhaps then commemorated in Eleusinian ritual, which was regarded for others as a preliminary to initiation. For the rites, see Kerényi 1967: 45–60; cf. also Nelson 2000: 25–43, esp. 31ff. Additional references to Herakles as an Eleusinian initiate are found in the fourth-century Ps.-Plato *Axiochus* 371e (Dionysus is coupled with Herakles here); Schol. in Homer

Il. 8.368; Lycophr. 1328; Tzetz. *Chil.* 2.394; and passages cited throughout this article.

11. Robertson (1980: 275-276) interprets a bearded figure in the earliest extant Eleusinianized scene (mentioned in note 8 above) as the recently freed Theseus holding the club and weaponry that Herakles has undertaken not to use against Cerberus. By contrast, in a non-Eleusinianized underworld scene described by Barron (1972: 44), Theseus carries weapons of his own, no club included.

12. As pointed out by Bowra (1952: 116).

13. Norden 1926: 5 and other pages mentioned in his note 2.

14. Clark 1970: 252 n. 22; Dover 1993: 263.

15. Lloyd-Jones 1967: 206-229 (= Lloyd-Jones 1990: 167-187). For the views of later editors on the text of *P.Oxy.* 2622 (= Pindar fr. 346 S-M), see Lavecchia 1996: 1-26. Robertson (1980: 274-300) thinks the lost Herakles katabasis formed part of the Hesiodic *Aegmius* frr. 294-301 M-W attributed to Cecrops of Miletus. On the possibility that the Herakles epic survived to Vergil's day, see Clark 2000: 192-196, esp. 195 n. 17.

16. Sommerstein (1996: 169), agreeing with West (1983: 23-24), against the doubts of Graf (1974: 103-107), argues that "lying in the mud" was a punishment recognized in Eleusinian "doctrine" (cf. Pl. *Phd.* 69c and *Rep.* 363d). He draws attention to the same triad of wrongdoings against gods, parent, and host or guest incurring this same punishment in *Frogs* 145-153 and other sources having Eleusinian connections. On Aristophanes' initiates, see note 28 below.

17. Lloyd-Jones 1967: 219 (= 1990: 179).

18. Brown 1991: 41-50. Borthwick's hypothesis (1968: 200-206) is that contemporary ritual, as well as superstition concerning weasels, underlies the language of the Empousa scene.

19. Graf 1974: 29-30 n. 36.

20. Brown (1991: 42) cites Plato *Phaedrus* 250b-c as the earliest explicit reference to φάσματα, but not all apparitions are frightful. In this Platonic passage they are εὐδαίμονα, as in Plut. Περὶ Ψυχῆς fr. 178 (Sandbach), where Plutarch speaks of the initiate's fear and terror (*sc.* in the darkness) followed by the vision of blissful φάσματα in the light; cf. Aristid. *Or.* 22.3 (Keil) and Procl. *In Pl. Rep.* 2.185.4 (Kroll). For fear and terror felt by the initiate before initiation, see also the passages instanced in note 7 above. Similar emotions are aroused by the epiphany of Demeter in the Homeric *Hymn to Demeter* 190, with parallels noted by Richardson (1974: 208-211, 252-256 and 306ff.); but this event, too, should be distinguished from the experience of fearful φάσματα of the Empousa type.

21. Empousa is a frightful demonic shape-shifting apparition that (1) is sent by the goddess Hekate and (2) is sometimes even identified with Hekate. Several sources support (1): Schol. in Aristoph. *Frogs* 293 explains Empousa as a φάντασμα δαιμονιῶδες ὑπὸ Ἑκάτης ἐπιπεμπόμενον (Dübner p. 283) καὶ τὰς μορφὰς ἐναλλάτον (Dindorf; Dübner prints instead: οἱ δὲ [φασιν] ὅτε ἐξηλλάττετο τὴν μορφήν). Schol. in Ap. Rhod. *Argon.* 3.861 (Wendel) names Empousa among the φάσματα . . . τὰ καλούμενα Ἑκαταῖα. Cf. Bekker, *Anec. Graeca* 1.249.27-28: Ἔμπουσα φάσμα ἐστὶ τῶν ὑπὸ Ἑκάτης πεμπομένων. Suidas, s.v. Ἑκάτην, says that Hekate strikes fear in those who see her snaky-headed φάσματα. Cf. also Plut. *Mor.* 166a. The following sources support (2): Hesychius s.v. Ἔμπουσα· Ἀριστοφάνες δὲ τὴν Ἑκάτην ἔφη Ἔμπουσαν. Schol. in Aristoph. *Frogs* 293 similarly names Aristophanes among

those who identify Empousa with Hekate: ἔνιοι δὲ [φασιν sc. τὴν Ἔμπουσαν] τὴν αὐτὴν τῇ Ἑκάτῃ, ὡς Ἀριστοφάνης ἐν τοῖς Ταγηνισταῖς. The scholiast then pinpoints where in this partially surviving comedy the identification is made, by one speaker saying χθονία θ᾽Ἑκάτη / σπείρας ὄφεων εἰλιξαμένη and another replying τί καλεῖς τήν Ἔμπουσαν; (fr. 515 PCG). Brown (1991: 47-49) thinks Hekate's presence at Eleusis is attested by the Homeric *Hymn to Demeter* at 25, 440, and by archaeological evidence, which he discusses at length; he further links passages in (2) with other evidence such as Idomeneus (*FGrH* 338F2), to show Empousa's cultic identity.

22. Brown 1991: 42-43; Brown uses (p. 50) the Plutarchan fragment (note 20 above) as the source for his view of Eleusinian proceedings.

23. Ibid.: 49.

24. Vergil's indebtedness is emphasized in Clark 2000: 192ff., and Aristophanes' in Clark 2001: 103-116, esp. 108.

25. *P.Oxy.* 3531, vv. 14-20, ed. Cockle (1983: 29-36 = F4a in Snell and Kannicht 1986: I. 349-351 and *Critias* IIa in Diggle 1998: 174-175).

26. In Clark 2001: 109-111, I argue for the priority of *Peirithoos* on several grounds, including the treatment of Aeacus in the two plays.

27. Cockle (1983: 35) raises the further possibility that this female may be an Erinys, comparable to the Furies visible at Aesch. *Cho.* 1048ff. to no one onstage except Orestes, but he notes that the *hypothesis* of *Peirithoos* makes no mention of a Fury.

28. Cockle (1983: 34) suggests "dead Eleusinian priests," citing *Peirithoos* F2 (Ath. 11.496A), ed. Snell and Kannicht. Since the initiates in the chorus of the *Frogs* have led virtuous lives on earth (457-458) and now have their own sunshine (455), they must be in Hades. This view is defended against others by Lloyd-Jones (1967: 219-220), who thinks that Aristophanes' initiates, though dead, nevertheless suggest the atmosphere of Eleusinian cult.

29. Brown (1991: 46) notes that Lucian draws on the *Frogs* also at *Philopatris* 25, *Contemplantes* 24, *Cataplus* 14, and *Fugitivi* 28.

30. Noticed by Stanford (1958: 98 ad 289-295).

31. My argument assumes that the author of the lost epic knew the *Nekyia* and wished Herakles' performance to be an improvement upon that of Odysseus. Lloyd-Jones (1967: 227) remarks of Herakles, "Instead of being frightened, he threatens her with his sword." I infer rather from Meleager's words οὔ τοι δέος in Bacchylides' account that Herakles uses his weapon *because* he is afraid.

32. For the Gorgons' serpentine hair, see, e.g., Pind. *O.* 13.63 and *Pyth.* 10.47. Pausanias tells us that Aeschylus (*Cho.* 1049-1050) was the first to represent the Erinyes with snakes in their hair. Ar. Ταγηνισταί, fr. 515 PCG, quoted in note 21 above, suggests that Empousa as well as Hekate is snaky-headed. The snaky-headed φάσματα in the Suidas passage reported in the same note also include Empousa. Hekate is similarly represented in Sophocles Ῥιζοτόμοι, *TrGF* F535.5-6 ed. Radt: στεφανωσαμένη δρυΐ καὶ πλεκταῖς / ὠμῶν σπείραισι δρακόντων.

33. Brown 1991: 49.

34. Lavecchia 1996: 25. In Clark 1970: 250, I corrected a similar error of interpretation regarding Herakles' journey in Bacchylides 5. But the error persists when Robertson (1980: 295) asserts that Bacchylides' Herakles sees the ghosts and Meleager "on entering the underworld."

35. Hard 1977: 211.

36. Cockle (1983: 30) makes this comparison and cites Lucian *Dial. Mort.* 20 and *De Luctu* 4 in its support, in order to interpret *P.Oxy.* 2078. In Clark 2001: 105 and 107, I concluded from an examination of all passages by Lucian concerning Aeacus' infernal functions that this satirist followed different traditions in different places; for instance, in *Dial. Mort.* 6.1, Aeacus is the gatekeeper on the far side of the infernal river Pyriphlegethon and Charon's lake. In the present chapter I have added some new insights on infernal topography with the focus on Apollodorus.

37. Clark 2003: 308–309.

38. Vergil's use of synonymous expressions to reveal every aspect of this chthonic cave as the transition path from the upper world to the lower is treated more fully in Clark 1992: 167–178.

39. Clark 2001: 114.

40. Warburton 1745: 288 and 294.

CHAPTER II

Women and Nymphs at the Grotta Caruso

BONNIE MACLACHLAN

Epizephyrian Locri was arguably the most culturally dazzling city of Magna Graecia in the Classical and Hellenistic periods. It was known throughout the Greek world for innovations and professionalism in music and dance, for its athletes victorious in the pan-Hellenic games, for the precision and order of its government, and for its military prowess. It has also enjoyed a reputation in recent times for the singular prominence it accorded women.[1] In a study of cult life in this part of the Greek world, one could hardly overlook the ritual activity engaged in by Locrian women in honor of Persephone. Her shrine, located outside the city walls in the valley between hills of Mannella and Abbadessa, was still celebrated in Roman times as the most renowned in all of Italy (Diod. Sic. 27.4.2; Livy 29.18.4; Dion. Hal. *Ant. Rom.* 20.9).

The myth of Persephone, archetypal *korē*, archetypal bride, is often referred to as the most important myth of the ancient world affecting the lives of women.[2] It is best known to us from the account in the Homeric *Hymn to Demeter,* but since the unearthing of *pinakes* from the Locrian shrine by Orsi more than a century ago,[3] we have been conscious of the difference between what is for us the canonical version of the Persephone story and what the *pinakes* reveal about the Locrian version. In these terracotta plaques, dating from the Classical period, the daughter's separation from Demeter is suppressed, and *korē* is depicted as willing bride and powerful underworld queen.

These *pinakes,* which have been found throughout Sicily and southern Italy, were clearly an important way to disseminate religious ideas from the *Persephoneion* at Locri.[4] There are no inscriptions accompanying these terracotta plaques, however, and just what message traveled with them is far from clear. Interpretations have varied dramatically. The divergence

Figure 11.1. Feminine *daimōn* from the Locrian *Persephoneion*. Costabile 1991: fig. 214.

of readings can be explained in part because Persephone, like Dionysus and Aphrodite, partook of a rich complex of religious symbolism found throughout Magna Graecia from the Archaic through the Hellenistic period. These divinities were represented on artifacts with nuptial, funerary, eschatological, and erotic motifs, often simultaneously.[5]

On the *pinakes*, the frequent occurrence of prenuptial accoutrements among the motifs seems to suggest that these were *proteleia*, gifts offered to Persephone by young Locrian brides at the time of their marriage. This would be consistent with a common reading of the Persephone narrative that sees the myth as foundational for a young woman's initiation, her transformation from maiden, *korē*, to bride, *nymphē*. But if young Locrian women on the threshold of marriage connected themselves ritually to the *theogamy* of Persephone, it cannot be overlooked that their expectations were thereby anchored in the underworld, and eschatological significance cannot be detached from the *pinakes*.

Among the various types of scene depicted on the plaques was that of a female *daimōn* (Fig. 11.1). Its large wings make one think of other winged females in Greek popular thought, whether embodiments of punishing *Dikē*[6] or Sirens who escorted the souls of the dead (gently or violently) on their journey to the underworld.[7] In Euripides' *Helen*, winged Sirens are *korai* of the underworld, carrying lotus flowers (167–169). The Mannella *daimōn* belongs to an otherworldly wedding, carrying a chthonic bride's nuptial accessories. Funeral and nuptial imagery and narratives overlap naturally with Persephone, but were broadly operative in the Greek imagination: marriage and funeral rituals possessed many of the same features.[8] In Locri this was true not only at the Mannella *Persephoneion*, but also at a Cave of the Nymphs. Rituals here, which began at the end of the Classical period, overlapped with those being carried out at the earlier site, but flourished during the Hellenistic period.

Like many other caves, the Grotta Caruso possessed a spring. Supplying fountains and wells, springs were essential for life in the ancient world and were regarded as sacred. Their numinous character was further enhanced by the fact that this was pure water emerging from the underworld, and nymphs were the divinities who could be found in these places where pure cool water emerged from below the earth. Shepherds, passersby, and women honored the nymphs as they filled their water vessels, attested by this epigram of Leonidas from Tarentum, a Spartan colony not far from Locri:

Πέτρης ἐκ δισσῆς ψυχρὸν κατεπάλμενον ὕδωρ,
   χαίροις, καὶ Νυμφέων ποιμενικὰ ξόανα,
πίστραι τε κρηνέων, καὶ ἐν ὕδασι κόσμια ταῦτα
   ὑμέων, ὦ κοῦραι, μυρία τεγγόμενα,
χαίρετ᾽· Ἀριστοκλέης δ᾽ ὅδ᾽ ὁδοιπόρος, ᾧπερ ἀπῶσα
   δίψαν βαψάμενος τοῦτο δίδωμι γέρας.

Greetings, chilly stream that leaps down from the cleft rock
And you wooden images of the Nymphs carved by a shepherd
And you drinking troughs from the springs,
and in the water these little ornaments of yours,
maidens, thousands of them, drenched.
Hail. I, Aristocles, this sojourner, give you this present
With which I quenched my thirst, dipping it in your waters. (*AP* 9.326)

Aristocles dedicated his cup, but others had left *korai*, dolls, in the waters of the spring for the *korai*-nymphs.

In similar fashion, Locrian women came to the Grotta Caruso and deposited *korai* at the spring for the nymphs. While we do not have any inscriptions attesting to the fact that the cult of Persephone was moved from the *Persephoneion* to the Grotta, I would argue for a continuum in the ritual process involved at both locations.[9] With the religious syncretism that was practiced during the Hellenistic period, the experience of the women at the Grotta permitted them to explore other possibilities at the same time. The Grotta gives us a unique opportunity to view the centrality of women in Locri, and reveals their participation in areas we routinely associate with men, such as the theater or rituals celebrating a divinized hero.

The excavation of the Grotta began under Paolo Arias in 1940, and a recent comprehensive study of the cave was undertaken by Felice Costabile.[10] The roof has caved in, but the original height of the cave was about 3 meters. Inside was a large basin of water (30–40 cm deep), to which votaries descended by a staircase (Figs. 11.2, 11.3). Niches were carved into the walls of the cave as repositories for lamps and votive gifts. In the water was an altar for offerings, and a large block (0.5 m × 42 m).[11] Extrapolating from a poem of Callimachus, we might suppose that the women went down and sat on the submerged rock and, as part of a ritual activity, poured over them some of the water collected in the basin.[12]

Water was used in Greek ritual primarily for purposes of purification, sometimes for appeasing a divinity or shedding some pollution. From Cyrene we have Sacred Laws inscribed in marble (late fourth century), among which is a prescription for newly married women.[13] They were expected to "go down to Artemis" (we assume to a nymphaeum) for a purifying bath, in all likelihood as appeasement for the loss of their virginity. For nuptial ceremonies in the Greek world, the lustral bath had another purpose: it conferred upon the bride and groom the fecundating powers of water.[14] The idea was developed by Porphyry in his commentary on the Odyssean Cave of the Nymphs, in which the cave is symbolic of the generative potency of the cosmos. No text has survived at the Locrian cave, however, that could clarify for us which of the above functions was assigned to its waters.

One of the most remarkable, and the most common, types of votive left in the niches of the Grotta Caruso is the nude kneeling woman with truncated limbs (Fig. 11.4). The type is known elsewhere in the Greek world; examples have been found in Corinth, Attica, and Cyrene.[15] Throughout Magna Graecia, these figures have been found in the graves of young women. Often their arms have been deliberately cut off, or their legs, sometimes at the knees, sometimes at the calves. Some have holes in the truncated limbs, suggesting that arms and legs could be added, like dolls with articulated limbs that could move, and separate terracotta limbs have been collected among the finds at the Grotta. The women each wear on their heads a *polos*, the mark of a goddess,[16] and some can fit comfortably on the terracotta thrones that were found in the vicinity. Were these votives goddess-dolls? If so, who was the goddess? Once again, we are without inscriptions. An anonymous and well-known epigram from the Palatine Anthology records a similar gift from a young girl to Artemis, included among *proteleia* for the goddess, marking a wedding that would never occur:

Figure II.2. Grotta Caruso showing altar and (quadrated) rock. Costabile 1991: fig. 363.

Figure II.3. Grotta Caruso showing staircase. Costabile 1991: fig. 12.

Τιμαρέτα πρὸ γάμοιο τὰ τύμπανα, τήν τ' ἐρατεινὴν
 σφαῖραν, τόν τε κόμας ῥύτορα κεκρύφαλον,
τάς τε κόρας, Λιμνᾶτι, κόρᾳ κόρα, ὡς ἐπιεικές,
 ἄνθετο, καὶ τὰ κορᾶν ἐνδύματ', Ἀρτέμιδι.
Λατῴα, τὺ δὲ παιδὸς ὑπὲρ χέρα Τιμαρετείας
 θηκαμένα, σώζοις τὰν ὁσίαν ὁσίως.

Timareta, before her wedding, dedicated her tambour and her lovely ball
  And the hair-net that held her hair,
  her dolls, too, to Artemis of the Lake, a korē to a korē, as is fitting,
  And the clothing of the dolls.
  Daughter of Leto, do you place your hand over the girl Timareta
  And in purity may you preserve her purity. (*AP* 6.280)

From this epigram we might extrapolate that the (roughly contemporary) dedication of the kneeling *korai* at the Grotta Caruso belonged to prenuptial activities that enabled young Locrian women to identify with a goddess whose features—like those of Artemis—included the aspect of maidenhood. This goddess could of course be Persephone, or the dolls could represent a collectivity of divinities, the nymphs of the cave.[17]

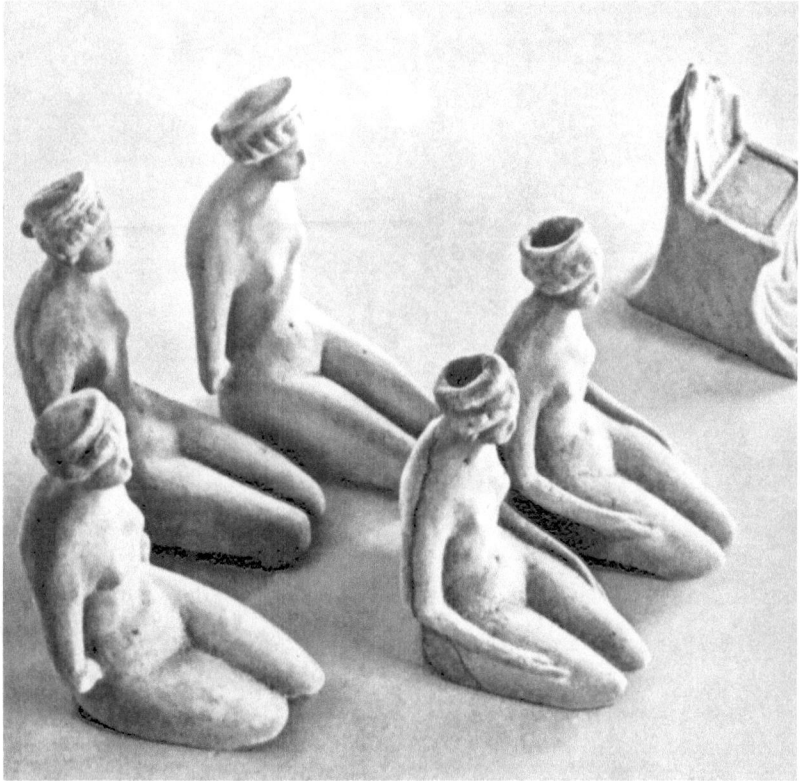

Figure II.4. Terracotta votives from the Grotta Caruso: Kneeling females with truncated limbs and throne. Costabile 1991: fig. 191.

Figure II.5. Terracotta votives from the Grotta Caruso: Kneeling females. Costabile 1991: fig. 190.

Nymphs would be appropriate recipients of votives from brides, whose name (*nymphai*) they bore. The large number of these figures deposited in the Grotta is striking (Fig. 11.5).

Identical artifacts were also found in tombs of young women at Lucifero, the necropolis at Locri:[18] it is tempting to see in the funerary collection the same sentiments as lay behind the epigram for Timareta. Their nudity may be explained, drawing once again on the epigram, by the fact that the figures were at one time clothed.[19]

More clearly identifiable as nymphs are the female heads found in groups of three, often accompanied by Pan on terracotta reliefs from the Grotta (Fig. 11.6). Cults of Pan and Nymphs were common in Greece, particularly after Pan's alleged appearance on the battlefield at Marathon. An intriguing parallel to his presence at Locri, however, are the Attic vase-paintings depicting Pan (or several *paniskoi*) accompanying Kore-Persephone on her return from the underworld. In the Metropolitan Museum in New York is a crater depicting her emerging from a rocky opening, likened by Borgeaud to a cave of Pan and the Nymphs.[20] This corroborates the supposition that in their *katabasis* and *anodos* at the Grotta, the Locrian women (brides?) identified themselves with Persephone; here the *anodos* occurred in the company of the Nymphs and Pan.

Figure 11.6. Terracotta plaque from the Grotta Caruso: Three female heads with Pan. Costabile 1991: fig. 176.

Pan's presence often has erotic undertones, and nymphs in myths, whether with Pan or Artemis, are frequently vulnerable to predatory young men. In the year 316 CE, a period of high activity for the rituals at the Grotta Caruso, Menander staged his *Dyscolos* in Athens and won first prize. The action takes place at a Cave of the Nymphs. Pan emerges from the cave to present the prologue to the play (vv. 1–49), explaining that there is a young maiden who regularly honors the Nymphs and himself, garlanding their statues when she comes to the cave's spring to fetch water. Pan reflects that he ought to reciprocate her gifts by seeing that she is partnered with a noble young man who had fallen in love with her as he watched her making her dedications. As he predicts, the *korē* becomes a *gynē*, and the celebration of the wedding takes place at the cave.

Pan is not the only god whose presence was felt by the women at the Grotta Caruso. On the side of the terracotta plaque with the nymphs and Pan are depicted *thyrsoi*, implements belonging to the maenadic cult of Dionysus. Models of maenads were also found in the Grotta, together with Sileni, masks and figurines of comic actors,[21] and the theatrical as well as the ecstatic dimension of Dionysus clearly figured in the experience at the Cave. For women to leave behind theatrical votives suggests strongly that their activities were connected with performances that took place in the theater built in the center of the city.[22] The epigram of Locrian Nossis (*AP* 7.414) dedicated to the Tarentine *phlyax* playwright Rhinthon attests to the performance in fourth-century Locri of parodies of tragedy.

The chthonic aspects of Dionysus were intertwined with the ecstatic and theatrical in Magna Graecia,[23] making it not surprising that this Locrian ritual combined theatrical elements with a katabasis. In Sicilian Lipari, a terracotta portrait of Menander was found in a tomb.[24] On Campanian craters of the fourth century, theatrical and nuptial iconography was combined with iconography drawn from the *thiasos* of Dionysus, and these were used as funeral urns. The otherworldly potency of Dionysus is of course at the center of the god's occurrence in funerary contexts. The god's association with mystery Orphic cults in the Locrian region was made dramatically apparent with the discovery in 1969, in a woman's grave at Hipponion (a colony of Locri), of an Orphic gold leaf tablet. It dates from about 400, and it reminds the deceased that, of the two paths available in the underworld, one is reserved for *mystai* and *bakkhoi*.[25] Could the rituals at the Grotta Caruso have belonged to a mystery cult, and the women emerged from the water as *mystai*?

There were other chthonic elements connected with the ritual at the Grotta Caruso (Fig. 11.7). On some terracotta plaques, three nymphs are shown with a man-faced bull and an altar. (Arias found this terracotta

Figure II.7. Terracotta from the Grotta Caruso: Three female heads with altar and tauromorph hero. Costabile 1991: fig. 321.

behind the actual altar in the Grotta.) Beneath the man-bull is inscribed the name *Euthymos* (Fig. 11.8). Euthymos was a local hero of Locri (Strabo 6.1.5). An athletic hero before a cult hero, he was three times victorious at Olympia as a boxer, and was celebrated by Callimachus (frr. 84–85 Pfeiffer). Two statues were erected in his honor at Olympia (the inscription on one survives), and, as the story goes, both statues were struck by lightning on the same day, after which Delphi prescribed the installation of a hero cult.

There are more underworld associations with Euthymos. A legend from the nearby city of Temesa maintained that the Temesians had committed an offense by killing Polites, one of the companions returning home with Odysseus. When Polites became a menacing *daimōn* after death, Delphi ordered them to propitiate the angry hero with an annual sacrifice of the

Figure II.8. Detail of terracotta from Grotta Caruso (Fig. II.7), showing outline of altar and inscription *Euthymos*. Costabile 1991: fig. 314b.

most beautiful of the Temesian *parthenoi* to Polites. Locrian Euthymos defeated this *daimōn*, and was rewarded by receiving the *parthenos* as a bride. Euthymos was reported to have lived a long life but met a death that was as miraculous as it was appropriate, for someone who would figure prominently in the water rituals at the Grotta Caruso. He leapt into a local river and disappeared (Pausanias 6.6.4–10). If the rituals at the Grotta were conducted by Locrian *parthenoi*, the chthonic and erotic connotations of the nymphs with Euthymos would reinforce the strongest features of the theogamy of Persephone.

There are many questions yet to be explored about the Locrian rituals at the Grotta. One of the pieces of the puzzle that requires more explanation is the inclusion of theatrical elements among the finds. The consideration that this is an aspect of Dionysus makes it understandable, but does not explain it.[26] Artifacts left in the niches of the Cave with maenadic, nuptial, and chthonic motifs can be understood as symbolic of several rites of passage, of the *teletai* of Dionysiac mysteries, of marriage, or of an encounter with the underworld powers, permitting the women to emerge as *mystai*. But what of the theater? Victor Turner, in *The Ritual Process*,[27] worked on the elements common to rites of passage, where participants experience a transformation from one biological and social circumstance to another. In this place of danger and vulnerability was an opportunity for "disordered play." The underworld, experienced in the *Persephoneion* or in the Grotta Caruso, furnished the stage for this disordered play. Persephone and Aphrodite, the Nymphs, Pan, Euthymos, Dionysus, maenads, and Sileni, along with winged *daimones*, are the principal actors.

Notes

1. MacLachlan 1995: 205-207; Redfield 2003: 263-307.
2. On Persephone as archetypal, see Lincoln 1979.
3. Orsi began excavating the *temenos* in 1889, and subsequently unearthed the *pinakes* beneath a treasury belonging to the shrine. He dated the plaques to between 500 and 450 BCE (Orsi 1909).
4. Casadio 1995: 100.
5. Casadio (ibid.) draws attention to this significant crux of interpretation. On the nuptial significance of the *pinakes*, see Zancani-Montuoro 1960, 1964; and Sourvinou-Inwood 1978. For funerary implications, see Quagliati 1908; for an eschatological reading, see Orsi 1909: 406, 463, who read scenes of the abduction of Persephone as the snatching of the soul from the body and its transport to the underworld. He was followed in this by Giannelli ([1924] 1963: 187-204). The undisputed presence of Aphrodite on some of the *pinakes* led to the controversial reading of Prückner 1968 that they reflected a vow taken by the Locrians in 477/6 BCE to consign their virgins to a period of service as prostitutes in the temple of Aphrodite in order to avert a war. A broader, and more generally accepted, reading of Aphrodite's presence in the *pinakes* is that of Sourvinou-Inwood (1978), who sees these scenes as representative of a broad range of the erotic experience of Locrian women, from their coming of age through marriage to motherhood.
6. Nilsson 1957: 123-125, on winged females found on south Italian vases. On one such vase, from Ruvo, Persephone is enthroned and two *Dikai* are present. Nilsson (p. 126) sees here one figure administering punishment and the other acquittal, not unlike the *Dikē* in Parmenides (Δικὴ πολύποινος ἔχει κληῖδας ἀμοιβούς, fr.1, 14).
7. Plato *Cratylus* 403D. Vermeule (1979: 145-177) points out the link here between the eschatological and the erotic: the winged figures appear as lovers, embracing the dead.
8. Rehm 1994: 11-42. This identification of the two rites of passage is reflected in the call of despair from Sophocles' Antigone as she contemplates her tomb that is also her bridal-chamber (ὦ τύμβος, ὦ νυμφεῖον, 891). Rehm (pp. 3-4) points out that we don't have to dig very deep in the Western artistic tradition to find that the interplay between weddings and funerals is one that is buried in our own psyche as well. It appears in Shakespeare, with Hamlet and the death of the would-be bride Ophelia, with Pyramus and Thisbe and Romeo and Juliet, who marry in the tomb. Donizetti's *Lucia di Lammermoor* or Verdi's *Attila* commemorate death that occurs on the wedding day.
9. The connection with Persephone is made possible by the finding in Morgantina, Sicily, of a female bust contemporary with and identical to several found in the Grotta, with the difference that in the Morgantina example, the scene of Persephone's abduction was depicted. Bell 1976: 144.
10. Arias 1941; Costabile 1991.
11. Costabile 1991: 7.
12. In a fragment from the *Fountains of Argos* (*Aetia* 66.1-9), Callimachus addresses the fountain/water-nymph Amymone and refers to maidens who would be assigned the ritual weaving of a robe for Hera only after they had sat upon the sacred rock and poured over their heads the water flowing around them.

13. *SEG* IX.72 (left-hand side of the column, lines 9–14).
14. Schol. ad Eur. *Phoen.* 347; Ginouvès 1962: 421–422.
15. Boffa 1977; Larson 2001: 117–120.
16. Dewailly 1983.
17. Costabile (1991: 108) suggests that these figures could be representations of Lokria, the eponymous water-nymph of Locri (Strabo 6.1.7).
18. Costabile 1991: 122.
19. For the explanation that these nude figures were dolls, naked so that girls could dress them, see Redfield 1991a: 318–319.
20. Borgeaud 1979: 212. The overlap between the powers of Aphrodite and Persephone at Locri, represented by the presence of Aphrodite on some of the *pinakes*, appears on at least one vase with this motif. An Attic *pelike* was found in Rhodes, where it is Aphrodite, not Persephone, emerging from the earth, accompanied by Hermes and Pan (Guarducci 1985b: 6).
21. Costabile 1991: 150–179.
22. The theater, built in the Hellenistic period, was located near the Olympeion (Gigante 1977: 691). If the ritual activities at the Grotta were prenuptial, this suggests that young women were included in life at the theater.
23. For a full discussion of the panoply of Dionysiac motifs occurring together in sites throughout Magna Graecia, see Casadio 1995.
24. Bernabò Brea 1981: 21.
25. Pugliese Carratelli 1976; Guettel Cole 1980; Musti 1984; West 1975.
26. The same question may be asked about the (not infrequent) presence of caves with underworld associations near or in the Greek theater, at Syracuse, for example.
27. Turner 1969.

CHAPTER 12

"Great Royal Spouse Who Protects Her Brother Osiris": Isis in the Isaeum at Pompeii

FREDERICK BRENK

Perhaps Apuleius at the end of his *Metamorphoses* was right, that at Rome in the Isaeum Campense, at least in his time, not Isis but Osiris was the highest god.[1] This was not, apparently, true for the Isaeum at Pompeii.[2] Here, clearly, Isis is represented as the predominant divinity. The situation is similar to that at Kenchreai, the southern port of Corinth, where Lucius, Apuleius' hero, is first initiated into the mysteries of Isis. Even there, in the procession with the vessel of Nile water, Osiris is referred to as the highest divinity.[3] But at Rome, Lucius is told that the higher initiation is that to Osiris:

> vesperaque, quam dies insequebatur Iduum Decembrium, sacrosanctam istam civitatem accedo. ... novum mirumque plane comperior ... magni dei deumque summi parentis invicti Osiris necdum sacris inlustratum. (*Met.* 11.26–27 [Griffiths 1975: 287–288])[4]

> On the following evening, on the twelfth of December I reached that sacrosanct city [Rome]. ... But I made a new and clearly amazing discovery ... I had not been initiated into the mysteries of the great god and supreme father of the gods, the unconquerable Osiris.

Finally, he learns that even one initiation to Osiris is not sufficient, but that he, and his pocketbook, must endure another. Possibly Lucius' final initiation was to both gods, Isis and Osiris, but afterward he has a vision of Osiris alone, suggesting that even this initiation was to Osiris.[5]

In Italy, the Isis religion in the early empire seems to have been becoming more and more Osirian and funerary, thus confirming Apuleius' depiction of activities in the temple at Rome. It is not that contemporary Isiacs had a morbid outlook on life.[6] Rather, they believed in a happy afterlife through their devotion to the "Egyptian gods."[7] Devotion to Osiris in Rome probably paralleled that in Greco-Roman Egypt, where the dead tried to assimilate themselves to Osiris. Eventually the Temple of Serapis (Osiris) on the Quirinal, if the general view is correct, would dwarf that of Isis down below in the Campus Martius.[8] So the mysterious words of the title of this study, "who protects her brother Osiris," are meant to indicate the predominance of Isis at Pompeii, in contrast to Rome. When Vesuvius erupted, Isis was still on top, even if Osiris was showing signs of resurrection and might eventually triumph in the capital city.

Until a few years ago, it was quite difficult to study the Isaeum at Pompeii. The publication of the temple excavation and its finds was very incomplete, and one had to be content with rather murky illustrations of the frescoes. Then, in 1992, the temple was recreated in the rooms of the National Archaeological Museum of Naples for a special exhibit. The exhibit was accompanied by a stimulating, if at times unreliable, catalogue (*Alla ricerca di Iside*) with excellent color reproductions of many of the frescoes. A *giornata di studio,* also held at the museum, resulted in published contributions by some of Italy's (and France's) most brilliant and imaginative scholars.[9] More recently and more soberly, Valeria Sampaolo has published the architectural and pictorial content of the Isaeum for the official publication, *Pompei: Pitture e mosaici.*[10] Then, in 2000, Nicole Blanc, Hélène Eristov, and Myriam Fincker presented their revolutionary analysis of the architectural features of the temple, in the course of which they rejected many of the previous theories about its construction and reconstruction.[11] Still lacking is an official publication of the statues and artifacts, many of which are Egyptian or Egyptianizing, though these were treated briefly in the 1992 catalogue. One can thus obtain a reasonably accurate picture of the relative worship of Isis and Osiris in the Isaeum at the time of the destruction that preserved it. A "picture" or a "look" is correct, because what we have is really only what we see.

The French authors mentioned above bulldozed two previous theories. The first was the supposition that a temple existed on the site in the late Republican period. The second was that, as the inscription says, after the earthquake in 62 CE, the temple was built from scratch (*a fundamento restituit*).[12] After the earthquake, according to these authors, relatively minor changes were made, primarily consisting of new painting and stucco work, most of which was done in the Fourth Pompeian Style. Their argument is based on the need to fit the temple into the space left by the theater on the south, the type of brickwork employed, the presence of stucco found underneath a later layer of stucco, motifs in the decoration, stylobates and capitals, the type of façade with two wings, of mosaics under the later pavement, of furnishings for the temple, and the inscription of M. Lucretius Rufus in the Sacrarium. All these elements seem to point to an Augustan date.[13] The portico had to be entirely rebuilt, and the painting is primarily in the Fourth Style, but evidently the earlier painting and stucco design was in part used for the inner side of the arches of the Ekklesiasterion, a "pastiche of the Second Style executed in the Fourth Style." If true, the architecture of the Isaeum primarily represents the Augustan period, the sculpture is primarily Julio-Claudian, centered probably on Claudius, and the painting and stucco work is mostly late Neronian.

As far as Egyptomania goes in the Age of Augustus, one might recall the Obelisk of the Solarium at the present Piazza Montecitorio, the obelisks and Egyptian decoration of the Mausoleum of Augustus, the frescoes of the Aula Isiaca on the Palatine, and those of the Villa Romana Farnesina, which perhaps belonged to Agrippa and Julia, the daughter of Augustus. The Isaeum at Pompeii would have originally, then, fit into the religious, social, and political currents of the Augustan age. The official desire of Augustus' reign to glorify his Egyptian victory evidently left an opening both for wealthy Romans to adorn their homes with chic Egyptian and Alexandrian décor and for the cult to flourish, in spite of its apparently foreign and non-Roman character. The presentation of Egyptian motifs in the Isaeum, however, contrasts with the chic, arty, architectonic, and less religious style of those in the Villa Farnesina and the Aula Isiaca.[14]

The Isaeum at Pompeii, then, contrasts with the Isaeum Campense in Rome, which belongs primarily to the age of Domitian.[15] Domitian had abundant reason to exalt Osiris over Isis. His father Vespasian had received a divine prediction in the Sarapeion at Alexandria that he would rule over the world. At the very end of Apuleius' *Metamorphoses*, the hero (and the reader) is surprised to find that Osiris seems to be the principal god in the Isaeum Campense. The dramatic date of the *Metamorphoses* is about 170 CE. Perhaps Osiris' supremacy there was the situation at Rome already in Domitian's day. The important "Serapaeum" part of the Isaeum Campense, the large apse structure at the south, seems to date to his reign, or at least that of Hadrian. Even before Domitian, Nero, a descendant of Marcus Antonius (Mark Antony), famous for his association with Egypt, had his wife, Poppaea Sabina, embalmed.[16] Possibly Nero or Poppaea, like the owners of the Greco-Roman mummy cases recovered from Egypt, seriously hoped to become, after death, "like" Osiris, gaining immortality and a blessed afterlife.[17]

At Pompeii, Isis clearly is represented as the more prominent divinity.

Possibly the major cult statues were of Isis and Serapis, but of these, only the head belonging to what may be the cult statue of Isis has survived.[18] One can easily find Isis in the temple. Along the prominent arched wall of the west portico on the extreme left, we find a statue of Aphrodite Anadyomene. The statue evidently represents the *interpretatio graeca* of Isis, whereas Isis with the *ankh* on the extreme right seems to be an archaizing Hellenistic form of the goddess.[19] Finding Osiris is more difficult. At the back, outside wall of the cella of the temple, a statue of a youthful Dionysus, a god often identified with Osiris, appeared in a niche.[20] Its placement at the west end of the temple, a primary symbolic direction of Osiris, is probably significant. A remembrance of Osiris would also be an *ushabti* (a small mummified figure), which, though small in size, was put in a special niche in a prominent place in the "Sacrarium."[21] A small decorative piece, moreover, called a "bearded Dionysos" in the catalogue, is in fact an "Osiris/Dionysus."[22]

The frescoes also reflect the relative positions of Isis and Osiris.[23] These were newly painted after the earthquake. However, the odd placement of some *quadretti* (small, rectangular insert paintings) breaking up the wall design in the temple suggests that the worshipers, who found it difficult to part with the old paintings, had them reproduced awkwardly in this way.[24] If so, one could probably presume that the central paintings in the triptychs might also have belonged to the earlier painting program. Significantly, too, the central panels of the triptychs seem to belong to an older, statuary style of painting, contrasting with the dreamy, impressionistic style of the flanking Nilescapes.[25] There were three painted triptychs in the "Ekklesiasterion." Of these, the central panels of only two have survived. These two, in illusionist frames, meant to represent paintings on wood, are extremely important, depicting episodes in the life of Io—that is, scenes of salvation and liberation. In the first, Hermes (Mercury) is about to slay Argos, the custodian of Io, who, through the machinations of Hera (Juno), is to be transformed into a cow (Fig. 12.1). In the second, Isis appears in the company of her sister, Nephthys, Hermanubis (a combination of Hermes and Anubis), and her son, Harpokrates. Io, supported by a personified Nile, is to be restored from bestial form and savage persecution, and returned to civilized society (Fig. 12.2).

Perhaps the theme of the painting inspired Apuleius. In the *Metamorphoses*, his hero, Lucius, having been transformed into an ass, through Isis is restored to human form.[26] By reading the plaintive laments of Lucius, we can appreciate the plight of Io and her liberation by Isis.[27] Lucius (*Met.* 12 [Griffiths 1975: 275]) interprets his release as salvation (*salus*),

Figure 12.1.
Ekklesiasterion: Io, Hermes, and Argos.

Figure 12.2.
Ekklesiasterion: Nile, Io, Isis, Hermanubis, Nephthys, and Harpokrates.

and liberation by Isis as one from toils, dangers, and Fortune. Lucius then dedicates himself entirely to the goddess, something of which we have an intimation in the "Io and Isis" (or "Io at Canopus") painting. Io, and by extension the Isiac worshiper or initiate, not only has been liberated but now is welcomed into the society of the goddess and invited to engage in total dedication to the Egyptian religion, symbolized by Isis, Horos (Harpokrates), Anubis (Hermanubis), Nephthys, and the Nile. The prominence of the Nile and the situla held in Hermanubis' hand might also be taken as allusions to Osiris. Once again, though, Isis, not Osiris, dominates both the literal and the symbolic dimensions of the painting.

The numerous small paintings (*quadretti*) are primarily meant to evoke the mystery of Egypt and the Nile, but many are suggestive of a tomb of Osiris, in particular that on Bigga, the island next to Philai.[28] These, too, with their bird's-eye perspective and romantic sacro-idyllic landscapes, contrast with the central panels of the triptychs. They are not, however, quite in the same dreamy, sacro-idyllic manner of the Ekklesiasterion Nilescapes. Though the Nilescapes of the Ekklesiasterion are strikingly beautiful, they are subordinated to the central Io panels. In fact, though, the central paintings are slightly smaller than the framing Nilescapes.[29] The triptychs, moreover, were given special prominence, since they were partially visible through the arches of the interior court. Once inside the Ekklesiasterion, the viewer had a vicarious experience of the Upper Nile. The "framed" frescoes represent the Dodekaschoinos, a stretch of about sixty kilometers of the Nile in Upper Egypt, south of the first cataract near Philai and before reaching Nubia. This was a "virtual reality" experience of standing on Philai, the site of the greatest Temple of Isis in Egypt, while contemplating the extraordinarily overawing scenery that surrounded it.[30]

The physical and symbolic directions of the Temple at Philai probably are important for understanding the temples both at Pompeii and at Rome. The Temple at Philai faced south, looking down toward the source of the Nile, whose water was often identified with Osiris. The burial place of Osiris, Bigga (or the Abaton), was primarily to the west. Bigga is a huge island in relation to Philai. Considered to contain the source of the Nile, it projected quite a bit south, thus both west and south of Philai. The Abaton, "where no one shall tread," with its primarily western orientation, was fitting as the traditional direction of Osiris and the souls of the dead. But since it extended farther south, one might justifiably see it as a symbol of the Nile. As in the *quadretti,* so in the Ekklesiasterion Nilescapes, an island, imaginary tomb, or temple, together with luxurious vegetation, conveyed a sense of the "numinous." In a sense, with the possible excep-

Figure 12.3. Portico: Priest with sacred asp.

tion of the "Isis and Osiris Enthroned" painting, all the major frescoes closely associate Isis worship with the water of the Nile.[31] Possibly the artists only intended to create atmosphere by depicting the landscape of Upper Egypt. In one, however, we find bulls grazing on a rocky island, beside a temple near which someone is fishing. Is this a farfetched representation, meant to harmonize with the other scenes, of the Sarapieion at Memphis where the Apis bulls were raised, kept, and eventually buried?

Close examination of the paintings reveals a chronological or religious order to be followed. As one entered from the outside gate into the portico, one found little representations of Isiac priests and one priestess in the center of the fresco panels (Fig. 12.3). The figures stand out against the bright red wall with almost theatrical backdrops, as though to give them a hieratic quality and religious dignity separating them from everyday reality and ordinary mortals. The figures recall those of the Isiac procession at Kenchreai in Apuleius' *Metamorphoses* (11.10 [274]). We might imagine the curious, possibly as their first experience, following these standing figures, as though in processional order, into the temple precinct.[32] In Apuleius, the "gods" follow last, among whom is Anubis. Anubis appeared on the far, western, inner wall of the portico. Thus, the progression of the

Figure 12.4. Isis with the Body of Osiris, Sacrarium.

figures was probably understood as beginning at the northeast entrance into the sanctuary, then moving in parallel from north and south walls, until reaching the west side of the portico, which was also the east wall of the Ekklesiasterion.[33]

Once inside the Ekklesiasterion, one should have followed the sequence northeast to northwest, northwest to southwest, and southwest to southeast. In the Sacrarium, one follows the same direction, beginning with the north wall and proceeding to the west wall. Only by following this sequence in the Ekklesiasterion will the panel "Io, Hermes, and Argos," representing Hermes about to slay Argos, come before the liberation of Io by Isis, "Io at Canopus." Similarly, in the Sacrarium, the "Finding of the Body of Osiris" (Fig. 12.4) comes chronologically before the "Isis and Osiris Enthroned" (Figs. 12.5, 12.6). The south side of the Sacrarium, along with its fresco, had disappeared at the time of the excavation; its subject is unknowable. Moreover, it is difficult to imagine any scene more final than "Isis and Osiris Enthroned."

Following this order of the paintings, and trusting Sampaolo's location of them, we arrive at the following sequence. In the Ekklesiasterion, north wall, east panel: "Small Temple *in antis* and Sacred Portal" (an extremely romantic rocky island with a tree behind a column and a small nautical bird [fisher martin] in the foreground).[34] Central panel: "Io, Hermes, and Argos."[35] A cow stands behind Io, who has small horns on her head, an indication that she will be transformed into her bestial form. West panel:

"Landscape with Sacred Portal and Ibis," a scene extremely similar in composition to the panel on the east side, especially in its inclusion of a bird.[36] West wall, north panel: "Landscape with Sacred Portal and Curtain." A standing statue can be seen in a sacred edifice, while bulls are grazing to the right.[37] The central panel is missing.[38] South panel: "Landscape with Grazing Bulls." Thematically close to the matching panel, we find a seated statue and a similar enclosure behind the statue, but the proportions are different, and the landscape is more civilized.[39] South wall, west side: fresco missing. Central panel: "Io at Canopus," with Io, the Nile god, Hermanubis, Isis, Nephthys, and Harpokrates.[40] West side: "Adoration of the Mummy of Osiris" (also called "Landscape with Cere-

Figure 12.5. Sacrarium: Drawing, "Isis and Osiris Enthroned."

Figure 12.6. Sacrarium: Osiris, "Isis and Osiris Enthroned."

mony before a Sarcophagus of Osiris"; Fig. 12.7).[41] The matching panel is missing. This one is remarkable for the marked centrality of its composition, its representation of a ritual, and its momentary rather than eternal character, contrasting with what we find in the other scenes. The presence of birds in the side panels of the north triptych, however, helps to lead into this picture, for this one, too, is marked by the extraordinary presence of a mysterious bird, not a common habitant of the Nile. This, almost the last painting before entering the Sacrarium, which would receive the least amount of natural light, seems to be especially serious, religious, and mysterious.

In this most unusual and striking scene, the artist possibly intended to depict rites at Bigga for the mummy of Osiris.[42] Only here do we find a priest performing a ritual. What a mysterious scene! Before a lintel supported by anthropoid sarcophagus slabs stands a coffin with ribbons tied around it.[43] A strange, mystical bird with a lotus crown on its head is perched on top of the mummy case. Even today, the scene bears an odd, accidental relationship to the entrance to the real island, and even more so to older photographs of the entrance gate.[44] Tucked away in the dim southeast corner of the Ekklesiasterion, difficult to see from the portico, this scene before entering the Sacrarium serves as a transition to the inner sanctum.

The "Adoration" fresco, then, seems to depict more than just numinous and religiously evocative landscape. This does seem to represent the adoration of the mummified Osiris, very possibly on the island Bigga, as filtered through the eyes of Hellenistic-Roman artists. As such, it has some relationship to the procession with the body of Osiris in the Nile Mosaic of Praeneste (Palestrina). The ithyphallic statue, the urn of water, and the falcon/phoenix, besides the mummy case, are evocative, traditional symbols of the resuscitation or resurrection of Osiris.[45] The huge, mysterious falcon suggests both the symbolic representation of Osiris or Horos with the falcon and the actual huge falcons imported from Africa and given lavish attention on the Abaton by means of a complicated ritual. One should not exaggerate the painting's importance. It is in the shadows and is not even the central panel of the triptych. Even so, it must have been just as fascinating for Isiacs two thousand years ago as it is for us today. The fresco also suggests the direction the Egyptian religion in Italy seems to have been taking, moving from primary worship of Isis and interest in this life, toward the funerary aspects of Osiris and the destiny of the deceased

Figure 12.7. Ekklesiasterion: "Adoration of the Mummy."

in the next life. In an earlier article, perhaps the painting was misunderstood and treated as though the culmination of the viewing experience:

> Ribbons are tied tightly around the stelai, while those around the "coffin" seem already loosened as though about to fly asunder. The central scene, bathed and highlighted with sunshine, stands out against the misty background of the distant mountains. In such an unreal atmosphere, a sudden, unexpected, and supernatural transition from death to life seems to await Osiris and all who follow his mysteries.[46]

The Sacrarium seems to have been an "inner sanctum," the most esoteric room, and here again, Isis appears as the principal, saving divinity. Only a single arch allowed the light to enter, and this could easily have been veiled when required. In the midst of one frescoed wall, a niche (*aediculum*) contained a small mummified figure (*ushabti*) of the sixth to fifth century BCE.[47] Inscribed on the figure are verses, typical for an *ushabti*, taken from the sixth chapter of the *Book of the Dead*, extolling the power of Osiris.[48] There were two large frescoes in the Sacrarium (itself at the southwest corner of the temple area) praising Isis and Osiris. Here the artists filled the walls with animals, attempting in their own way to imitate the Egyptian theriomorphic representations of divinities.[49] Continuing in the scheme followed so far, one would begin at the north wall and move on to the west. The right direction is confirmed by the imagined chronology. The fresco on the north side, at the bottom left of which was the *ushabti*, must have something to do with the recovery of the body of Osiris, while that on the west side represents him as consort of Isis in the underworld. In the Nile Mosaic at Palestrina, we have something similar, a ritual procession with the coffin of Osiris. On the north wall of the Sacrarium, on the other hand, the central figure is Isis, while the square box-like coffin and the bird—falcon or swallow—painted on it indicates either the presence of the body of Osiris or the coffin that will receive the body.[50] The scene apparently represents both the finding of the dispersed remains of Osiris' body on a mythical level, and the annual funeral procession of Osiris in Egypt on a ritual level. This took place in several localities, but the Upper-Nilescapes of the Ekklesiasterion suggest that the creator had the rites at Philai and the Abaton in mind. Some Romans would have actually visited these sites, or at least have had a vicarious experience of them.[51] In the Hellenistic and Roman world, the scene would evoke the *Inventio Osiridis* ("The Finding of Osiris"), one of the principal Isiac festivals.[52] The Ariccia Relief possibly depicts this rite in the Isaeum Campense.[53] The Sacrarium scene parallels the procession scene in the Nile Mosaic of Palestrina in its funerary aspects, even if presented in a mythical rather than ritualistic way. Like the "Adoration of the Mummy," the Nile Mosaic scene could represent rites at Bigga. The central event of the Nile Mosaic is this procession, presumably with the new mummy of Osiris, toward a luxurious grove on an island, undoubtedly representing the tomb of Osiris. This annual rite for Osiris was associated with the rising of the Nile each year.[54] Surely the Isiacs at Pompeii would see in the "Finding" scene Isis' care of one after death. In ancient Egyptian belief, rendering the body intact was important for the embalming process and life after death.

The culmination of the viewing process, at least of the frescoes we have, undoubtedly was the west wall of the Sacrarium.[55] If desired, it would have been visible through the only entrance into the room, the arch leading from the portico. Significantly, it is situated on the west wall, the traditional direction for the departure of the souls and the principal direction of the Abaton, the tomb of Osiris, in relation to Philai, and the Osirian direction of the temple at Pompeii. Called "Isis and Osiris Enthroned," the Egyptian divinities are here portrayed as queen and king of the underworld. The composition is similar to what we might expect of a representation of Persephone and Hades/Plouton (also called Thea and Theos) at Eleusis. The snakes and lack of solar imagery in the painting seem to suggest an underworld rather than a celestial paradise, or an imagined Egyptian place of the afterlife.

We find again the exaltation of Isis over Osiris. In the "Finding" scene, Osiris has only a passive role, being carried home in a box. Isis, who is positioned centrally looking at the viewer, dominates the picture. Isis at first sight appears slightly elevated over Osiris, though this is an illusion, but she is seated on a throne. In contrast, Osiris occupies the viewer's right side, amazingly, and in a quite unorthodox manner for Osiris or Sarapis, is seated on what appears to be a huge rock in the drawing made at the time of discovery. However, after the new cleaning of the painting, this appears to be a kind of padded chair or couch. Though clearly not represented as Dionysus—except possibly for a large staff—or Serapis, he is not immediately recognizable as Osiris. Nonetheless, he wears a lotus, employed by Pompeian artists to represent an Egyptian crown, on top of a strange flat hat (an odd rendering of the *polos* of Serapis?). Isis' throne suggests her majesty and greater importance. Perhaps the throne also symbolizes her closer link to the living as a source of succor, whereas the less impressive position of Osiris (reminding one of Demeter's in some Eleusinian iconography) and the surrounding serpents associate Osiris with the underworld. The *cista mystica* placed below the representation of the "Finding of Osiris" in the north fresco and the snakes represented in the

"Isis and Osiris Enthroned" painting suggest the presence of mysteries to obtain a better portion in the next life. Though Isis appears here primarily as queen of the dead, in Egyptian belief a god had power in all realms of the universe.[56] If the Sacrarium is indeed the "inner sanctum," one can imagine a possible use of the paintings in initiations. The initiates at the end of the ceremony could be brought here, with the sudden illumination of blazing torches, to stand in the presence of the very gods they are to worship here and in the hereafter, gods gazing benevolently upon them and offering them courage in the fearful transition from this life to a more blessed one.[57] As Lucius, in Apuleius' *Metamorphoses*, reveals of his first initiation, to Isis at Kenchreai, the southern port of Corinth:

> nocte media vidi solem candido coruscantem lumine, deos inferos et deos superos accessi coram et adoravi de proxumo. (*Met.* 11.23 [Griffiths 1975: 285])

> In the dead of night I saw the sun gleaming with bright radiance. I approached the gods below and the gods above and worshiped them at close distance.

But later on, at Rome, he was to be blessed with higher, more important—and more expensive—visions:

> Osiris non in alienam quampiam personam reformatus, sed coram suo illo venerando me dignatus adfamine per quietem recipere visus est. (*Met.* 11.30 [Griffiths 1975: 291])

> Osiris himself appeared to me while sleeping at night, not changed into some other person's form but considering me worthy to approach close to his sacred presence and hear his voice.

At Pompeii, Isis stood helpless as the ashes fell around her, both destroying and preserving her sanctuary, but she was still Supreme.[58]

Notes

1. For my articles on the Osirian background, see Brenk 1999a: 133-143; 1999b: 227-238; 2001: 83-98; 2003a: 291-303; and 2003b: 73-92.

2. Zabkar 1988: 58, citation from *Hymn* 5:

> Ḥmt-nsw wrt ḫnm(t) . . .
> Nḏtyt ḥr sn.s² Wsir.

3. *Metamorphoses* 11.11 [Griffiths 1975: 275]: *summi numinis*.
4. See Griffiths 1975: 102-105, 327-330. On the Egyptian concept of the local or immediate divinity being a "supreme" god, see Hornung 1983: 235-237.
5. Griffiths 1975: 337.
6. On the afterlife, see Hornung 1992: 95-115.
7. For widespread devotion in Italy to the funerary Osiris on a popular level, see Capriotti Vittozzi 1999: 131-145.
8. These developments are discussed by S. A. Takács (1995: esp. 74-75, 104-130, and 203-207). R. Santangeli Valenzani (1991-92: 7-16, and 1996: 25-26), citing Cassius Dio 76.16.3 (Zonaras), identifies the temple with that of Septimius Severus to Hercules and Dionysus. However, S. Ensoli (1997: 306-322 [314-316]), along with others, continues to attribute the temple to Serapis. A possibility is that Caracalla rededicated the temple of Septimius Severus to Serapis.
9. Adamo Muscettola and De Caro, eds. 1994.
10. Sampaolo 1998: 732-849. This treatment replaces Elia 1942. See also D'Alconzo 2002: 54-61 (59, fig. 31, "Io a Canopo"; fig. 33, "Io, Argo ed Hermes").
11. Blanc, Eristov, and Fincker 2000: 227-310.
12. For a photo of the inscription, see De Caro 1992: 67, no. 2.1.
13. Blanc, Eristov, and Fincker 2000: 291.
14. See Bragantini and De Vos 1982: e.g., 44-45, 49-50, 52, 58-59, 70, 95, 134-135, pls. 37-38; and Iacopi 1997: esp. 16-17. For the Isaeum frescoes, see Sampaolo 1998: 832-833, figs. 197-201; De Caro 1992: 55, nos. 1.57-60.
15. See Lembke 1994a (reviewed by J. Eingartner [1999]); and Ensoli 1998: 407-438. Ensoli (p. 424) wants to attribute the exedra structure to Hadrian — on the basis of statuary, the inscription to Antinous, and architectural elements — seconded by Egelhaaf-Geiser (2000: 181). However, Rabirius, Domitian's architect for the Palatine, liked fountains, pools, curvilinear lines, and grand heights and space. See Claridge 1998: 134-135; and Cecamore 2002: 230-231.
16. Chioffi 1998: 30-36 (esp. 30-31 and no. 1, 35-36).
17. See, e.g., Brenk 2001.
18. The Serapis statue, and possibly Harpokrates and Anubis in the wing niches of the temple façade, have disappeared. A head of Isis (De Caro 1992: no. 3.3 [inv. no. 6290]), from an acrolith, was found near the entrance of the Ekklesiasterion.
19. Engraving, in De Caro 1992: 28 (photo, 69), no. 3.8.
20. A statue of Dionysus was found in the sanctuary of Serapis (SS. Crocifisso) at Treia (ancient Trea); see Capriotti Vittozzi 1999: 105, 127, 152. For the two ears, see Blanc, Eristov, and Fincker 2000: 242, fig. 10; cf. Hoffmann 1993: 64. For similar Egyptian ears, see Jørgensen 1998: "Ear Stelae," 120, no. 40, cat. no. 1016, 1017 (Eighteenth Dynasty, c. 1554-1305 BCE). The ears are meant to entreat the god to respond to prayers.
21. Capriotti Vittozzi (2000: 121-139) suggests that in the "Miniature Villa" at Pompeii, the fountain on the "Nile" seems to represent the tomb of Osiris at Abydos. For the tomb (of Sethos I [Osireion]), see Arnold 1997: tomb 182-183, 239. Romans went to great lengths to obtain statuary from Upper Egypt, such as one of Amasis (c. 565 BCE). See Curto 1985: 30-36.
22. De Caro 1992: 70, no. 3.9, described as the foot of a pilaster supporting a table.
23. For reading religious frescoes, see the illuminating article by Elsner, "Cul-

tural Resistance and the Visual Image: The Case of Dura Europos" (2001: 269-304, esp. 276-280).

24. For the scenes of the *quadretti*, see Versluys 2002: 143-145, no. 061.

25. Sampaolo (in De Caro 1992: 58, no. 1.69) believes the original might be attributable to the fifth-century Athenian painter Nikias. See also Hoffmann 1993: 109-117.

26. Shumate (1996: esp. 50, 62, 325-327) treats Apuleius as serious, but S. J. Harrison (2000: 240, 246-250) and others see Apuleius as ironically depicting a duped Lucius. For the importance of conversion, see Beard, North, and Price 1998: 278-279, 289-291; Liebeschuetz 2000: 984-1008 (1001-1007); and Beck 2000b: 145-181 (177).

27. On this, see Balch 2003: 24-55. Balch examines the depiction of suffering figures in Roman art, in particular Io and Isis in Pompeian painting, as a key to understanding the Roman reception of visual and literary depictions of the sufferings of Christ; see there esp. 27-42, 49-51, and figs. 1, 2, 4, 6, 7, and 11.

28. For the luxurious growth of trees as indicative of the tomb of Osiris, see Koemoth 1994: esp. 135-164, 251-266; Meyboom 1995: 132-135, figs. 80-86. A recent photograph of Bigga with luxurious vegetation near the landing appears in Casini 2001: 195, pl. 203.

29. The side paintings would be about 10 percent larger in size. The "Io at Canopus" panel measures 150 × 137.5 cm.

30. For the Dodekaschoinos, see Locher 1999; and Jackson 2002: 108, map 3. On the temple itself, see Vassilika 1989; Arnold 1999: 190-193, 235-238; R. H. Wilkinson 2000: 213-215; Lloyd 2001: 40-44; Hölbl 2000: 36.

31. Outside of what is probably a Nilometer ("Purgatorium"), water is relatively modest in the complex. In contrast, reflecting pools have been found in the "Isaeum" at Cumae. See Caputo 1998: 245-253. On water in the Villa Hadriana, see Manderscheid 2000: 109-140 (118-129).

32. For the vignettes, see Sampaolo 1998: 740, fig. 9 (north portico, west side), priest with palm, no MNN no., Arditi inventory, no. 1351; 745, fig. 18 (north portico, east side), *hierogrammateus*, MNN 8925; 759, fig. 41 (east portico, center), *zakoros* with palm in one hand, grass in another, MNN 8921; 762, fig. 48 (east portico, south side), *prophētēs* carrying cobra in a rose wreath, palm, MNN 8922; 772, fig. 62 (south portico, east side), priestess with sistrum—the only woman represented—a *hierodoulos*, MNN 8923; 776, fig. 68 (south portico, west side), *spondophoros* with situla, MNN 8918; 779, fig. 75 (south portico, west side), *lychnophoros*, priest with golden lamp like a small boat with a large flame issuing from the middle, MNN 8969; 784, fig. 84 (west portico, south side), priest as Anubis, MNN 8920.

33. The order of the figures can be determined to a large extent from Sampaolo's location of the paintings (1998: 738-739, 754-755, 758-759, 772, 776, 779, 784). Four of the ten Isiacs described in the procession in Apuleius correspond to the representations of the Isiacs in the portico at Pompeii (about fourteen in all). Not all in Apuleius' procession are genuine Isiacs.

34. Sampaolo 1998: 826, fig. 189, MNN 8574.

35. Ibid.: 825, fig. 188, MNN 9548.

36. Ibid.: 824, fig. 187, MNN 8575.

37. Ibid.: 841, fig. 213, MNN 8558.

38. Egelhaaf-Geiser (2000: 189) suggests a "Zeus' Encounter with Io" here, but this would not harmonize with the chronological order of the two extant pictures.

39. Sampaolo 1998: 840, fig. 211, MNN 1265.

40. Ibid.: 837, fig. 206, MNN 9558.

41. Ibid.: 836, fig. 205, MNN 8570.

42. The present restoration of the temple on the island of Agilkia has changed the physical and symbolic relationships. Bigga is now directly south, blocking the previous view down the Nile, and making incongruous the position of Hadrian's Gate, the landing at the west of the temple.

43. Ribbons tied around tombs and stelai are common in Greek iconography. In Egyptian iconography, they suggest the hieroglyphic sign for divinity or indicate divinity. See, e.g., Hornung 1983: 33-38; 94, pl. 1 (Re-Osiris with a ribbon/sash around his waist). In the background, the artist seems to have introduced a huge, round, Roman-style tomb for Osiris.

44. E.g., Bernand 1969: pl. 7a and b.

45. For Isis as a falcon watching over the mummy (Tomb of Sennejem [Craftsmen's Graves], Deir el Medina), see, e.g., W. Wulleman et al. 1989: 110; for Osiris in a shrine with pillars and lintel (same tomb), ibid.: 111. For the multivalent quality of the bird, and its associations with Osiris, see G. Capriotti Vittozzi 2000: 137-138; and Ciampini 1999: 31-40 (31-35).

46. Brenk 1998: 306-307.

47. Engraving by N. Billy from a drawing of D. Casanova (Sampaolo 1998: 813, fig. 170).

48. D. D'Errico, in De Caro 1992: 79, no. 6.3; 85, no. 7.9., Ushabti of Paefhery-hesu (inv. no. 463), probably from the beginning of the 26th Dynasty (664-525 BCE).

49. Coarelli (1994: esp. 123-125) thinks the mosaic room might have been dedicated to Osiris. For the Pompeian fresco and its location, see Sampaolo 1998: 820-821, figs. 182-183. "The Finding of Osiris" was on the north side of the Sacrarium (MNN 8564): Sampaolo 1998: 815, fig. 173. For Casanova's eighteenth-century drawing of the complete scene, see Sampaolo 1998: 822, fig. 182. For Osiris victorious over death and allusions to Osirification in the temple at Pompeii, see M. De Vos (1992: 136-139), who finds a privileged place on the west side. The "Purgatorium," a Nilometer—symbolic of the Nile and Osiris—according to R. A. Wild (1981: 44-47), however, was on the south. On devotion to Osiris, see Brenk 2001.

50. Sampaolo 1998: 815, fig. 173, MNN 8564.

51. On pilgrimages, see Rutherford 1998: 229-256; Weill Goudchaux 1998: 525-534 (529); Le Bohec 2000: 129-145, esp. 145, noting interest mainly among officers; Maxfield 2000: 407-444 (Syene [Aswan], 410-414); Capriotti Vittozzi 2000.

52. On the Egyptian background to this, see, e.g., Assmann 2001 (= *Ägypten: Theologie und Frömmigkeit einer frühen Hochkultur* [Stuttgart, 1984]), 125-128. On the Roman context, see Hoffmann 1993: 103-104; and Balch 2003.

53. Lembke 1994a: 174-178, pl. 3.1; and Lembke 1994b: 97-102.

54. On the mosaic, see Meyboom (1995: esp. 132-149), who believes the Serapaeum at Puteoli, and ultimately the library in the Sarapeion at Alexandria, may

have offered models for the mosaic (pp. 99, 107). See also Weill Goudchaux 1998; and Versluys and Meyboom 2000: 111-128, esp. 127.

55. Sampaolo 1998: 820, fig. 182, drawing by Casanova; remaining fresco of Osiris, ibid.: 821, fig. 183, MNN 8927; and De Caro 1992: 58, no. 1.71.

56. Hornung 1983: 191-196.

57. For the fresco, see Sampaolo 1998: 820-821, figs. 182-183. One of the earliest scholars to see the fresco identified "Osiris" as a woman; see Hoffmann 1993: 101-102. Hermanubis in the "Io at Canopus" fresco (Sampaolo 1998: fig. 208) also carries a mammiform situla on his arm, but is distinguished by the caduceus. The painting could be seen from the south *ambulacrum* of the portico.

58. I am very grateful to Giuseppina Capriotti Vittozzi, of the Giunta Centrale per gli Studi Storici, for looking over the article and for her help on Egyptian matters, and also to Christopher Parslow of Wesleyan University for his expertise on the Pompeian material.

CHAPTER 13

Aegyptiaca from Cumae: New Evidence for Isis Cult in Campania: Site and Materials

PAOLO CAPUTO

In 1992, during the construction of a gas pipeline, the Archaeological Superintendence of Naples and Caserta, under my direction, undertook emergency excavations at Cumae (Campania).[1] Architectural remains, dating back to the Roman age, were found on an area of about 480 square meters, lying on the site identified by Paget[2] as pertaining to the Greco-Roman port of the town, right in the middle of what was argued to be the access canal (Fig. 13.1). The excavations brought to light some fragmentary Egyptian statues and various scattered fragments of Egyptianizing materials. A collaborative team of classical archaeologists and Egyptologists was formed with the purpose of approaching the site from different points of view.

According to many scholars, first of all to Paget, the ancient harbor of the Greek and Roman town of Cumae occupied the bay lying to the south of the promontory on the top of which the Cumaean acropolis was set. At present, the area is completely filled up by coastal sediments. Geoarchaeological cores have proved that in ancient historical times, the harbor of Cumae was located in the lake of Licola in the northern area of the town, whereas the area at south never was a harbor.[3] Although the form and the function of most of the structures are mostly identifiable, some remains of the complex pose problems for which the present report cannot offer definitive solutions. These problems are mainly due to the fortunes of preservation. Other uncertainties remain because a railway and modern cultivations have inhibited excavations in certain critical areas. Further excavations in these areas, conducted by the Centre J. Bérard of Naples for the Project Kyme I and II, proved the existence in the area of many *villae maritimae*.[4] For this reason, we cannot exclude the possibility that some natural or artificial canals and basins, connected to the sea or to spring

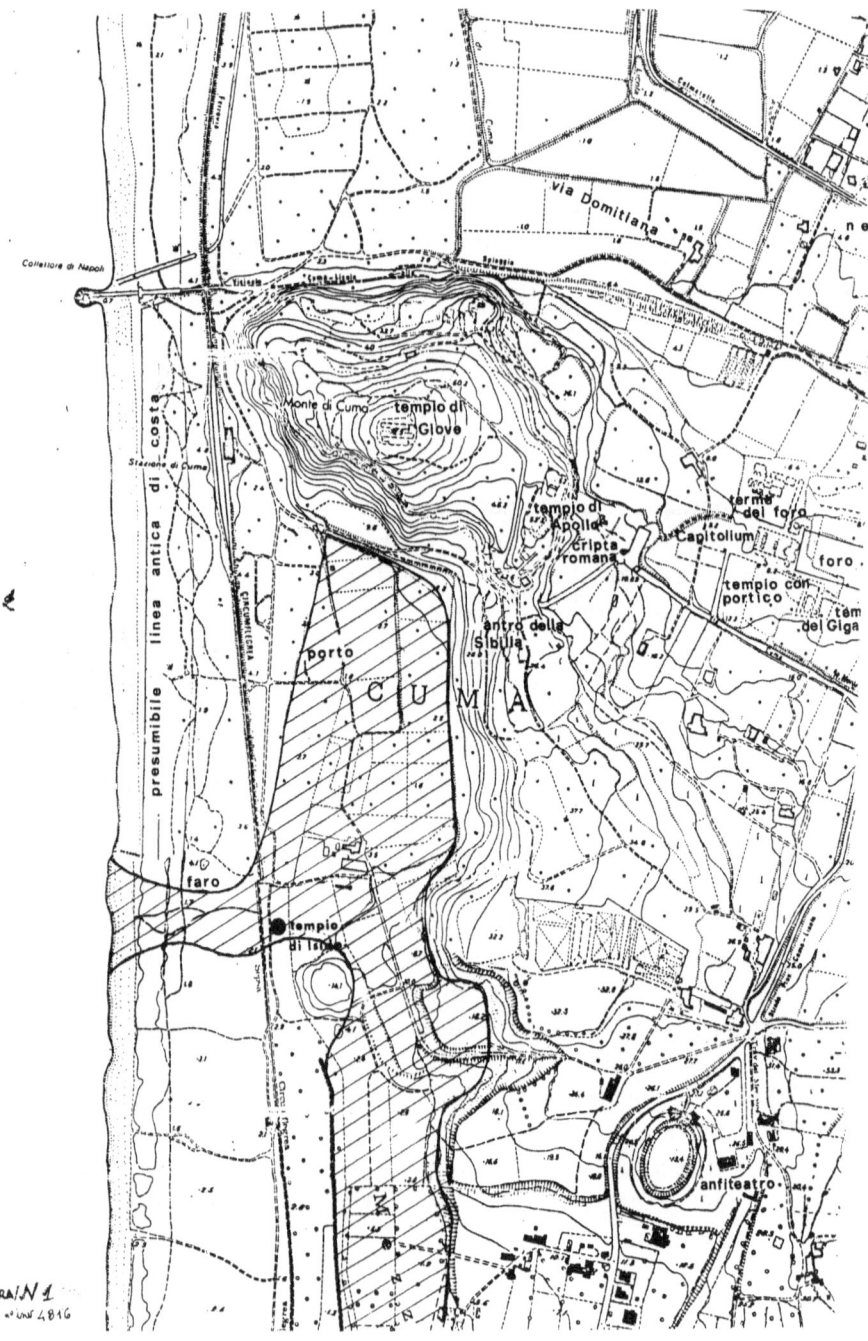

Figure 13.1. Cumae (Campaniae). The harbor area. The black point indicates the Isaeum related to the hypothesis of Paget.

water, were in this area in antiquity. Although this is very difficult to demonstrate, recent studies and research carried out by Professors F. Bernstein and D. Orr (University of Maryland, College Park), who pursued excavations in the area of the Isaeum in 1998–2000 and who are now working out their data, appear to be going in this direction.

It has been possible to identify (Fig. 13.2):

- Remains of a flight of stairs, leaning on the north wall of the *podium* (Fig. 13.3);
- part of an apsidal hall leaning on the south wall of the *podium* but not connected to it and with the access on the east side;
- remains of a quadrangular room on the east side of the *podium*, separated from the latter by an L-shaped corridor;
- a rectangular pool, facing the north side of the *podium*;
- remains of a *porticus* surrounding the pool.

It is clear from the extant remains that there were several stages in the construction of the complex. The structural sequences observed provide the basis for discerning at least four distinct building phases, dating back to a period ranging from the first century BCE to the second century CE. The type of building material used, the methods of construction, and the structural relationship noted provide the evidence.

The *podium* shows two different building phases (Fig. 13.4). Restoration works in its south/east side revealed a first lower structure as large as the upper one, formed by two rectangular vaulted rooms.[5] They were filled up by spring water and sandy sediments that made excavations impossible; but archaeological prospecting made it possible to recognize their dimensions. The association with fragments of late Campana A dates back to not before 100 BCE. The more recent upper *podium*, based on little vaults in *opus reticulatum*, was built with the system already known in the so-called *Pausilypon* Temple (first half of the first century CE). The use of such a technique could be justified by the nature of the sandy soil and the vicinity of the sea. The walls of the little vaults, originally completely closed, were covered with a thin surface of *signinum*. The building technique (*opus reticulatum* of irregular type) allows it to be dated back to the second half of the first century BCE. To this period belong the flight of stairs, room, corridor, pool, and *porticus*, all built in the same technique. The apsidal hall was added at the end of the first century BCE or at the beginning of the following one. Later it was modified. It sets directly on the sandy soil. In a later period, the sides of the pool were made higher, together with

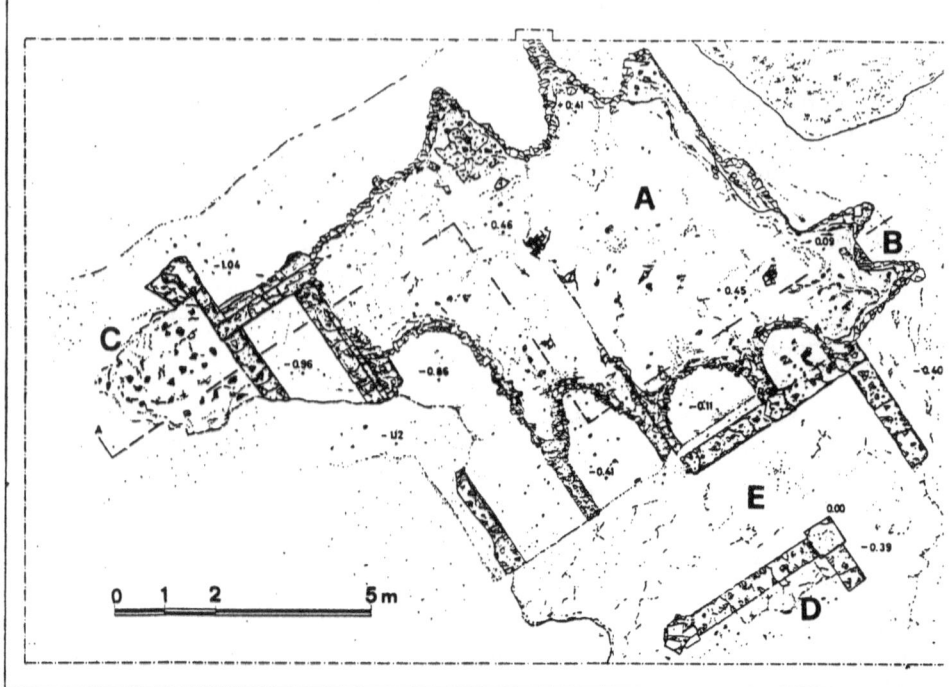

Figure 13.2. Cumae (Campaniae). Plan of the Isaeum: A. *podium;* B. flight of stairs; C. apsidal hall; D. room; E. corridor; F. pool; G. *porticus*.

the floor of the *porticus* in *opus sectile,* realized using tarsias of slate, old red, cipolin, and variegated marble. The floor had a complex geometrical decorative pattern (Fig. 13.5) similarly occurring at Ponza and Capri in the Augustan age and at Ostia until 130 CE.

The northern side of the pool was decorated with a fountain in the Fourth Pompeian Style, as testified by shells, pumice stones, and remains of mosaics made of blue glass *tesserae*.[6] The rebuilt section should be dated probably after the year 62 CE. Finally, the two pillars of the room in *opus latericium* go back to the second century CE. As in the case of the town of Cumae, the building activities stopped after this period.

While the evidence for absolute chronology for the site is limited, six major periods of its use emerge from a combined study of the finds, techniques of construction, and geological factors. Four of these six periods have left the above described architectural remains, whereas use of the site in the second and third centuries CE can be argued only on the basis of a few findings, among which are a bronze coin of Marcus Aurelius (*assis,* 174–175 CE, inv. 292849) and various fragments of Rough African ware.

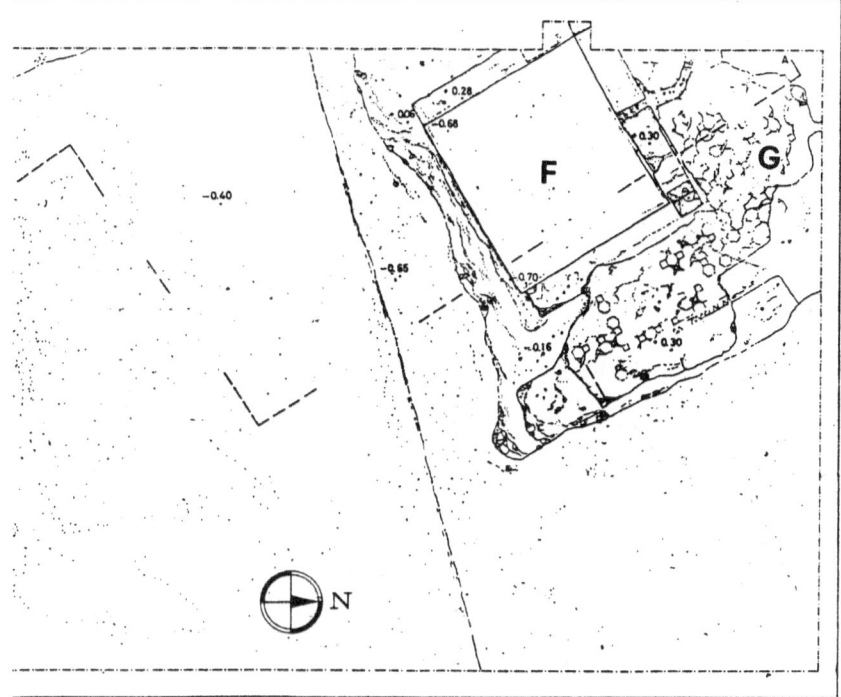

The site was destroyed probably in the late fourth century CE and abandoned, apart from sporadic use in the fifth to eighth century CE, as some fragments of Larga Banda ware witness.

The excavation of the pool, filled up with debris caused by the destruction of the roof, walls, and decorations of the building and hardened with water-lime, uncovered three Egyptian acephalous statuettes:

- Inaros as *Naophorus* of Osiris (Fig. 1.3.6, inv. 241834) of black basalt (height 40 cm, width 14.5 cm, thickness 17.5 cm), belonging to the XXX Dynasty (380–343 BCE);[7]
- an Isis (Fig. 13.7, inv. 241835) of black basalt (height 31.5 cm, width 14.5 cm, thickness 10.5 cm), dated first century BCE;[8]
- a Sphinx (Fig. 13.8, inv. 242046), in grey granite with green venations (50 × 15 × 16 cm), dated to the Ptolemaic era;[9]
- and some other marble fragments:
  - six fragments in white marble, of Roman imperial age, three of them (inv. 292836: feet; 292837: right forearm; 292838: arm) pertaining to a statuette, representing perhaps Harpocrates-Horus like a child (Fig. 13.9); two others (inv. 292840: left hand holding

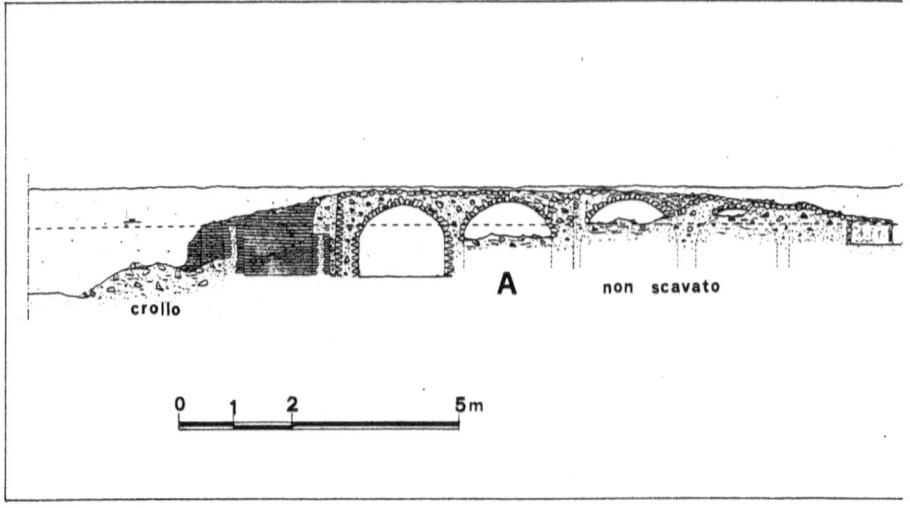

Figure 13.3. Cumae (Campaniae). Section of the Isaeum: A. *podium;* F. pool.

a cornucopia; 292841: inferior limb) pertaining to a statuette representing maybe a standing Harpocrates (Fig. 13.10), whose graphic reconstruction was proposed by the author on the occasion of the exhibition *Nova Antiqua Phlegraea;*[10]
- a *nemes* fragment in red marble of Roman imperial age, maybe from another sphinx or from a Pharaoh statuette.[11]

Other objects were uncovered in the excavation of the pool:

- A fragment with the head and part of a body of a snake in black glass of Roman imperial age (inv. 292839), maybe a cultural object;
- a fragment of a mosaic (white marble; green and red glass pulp), perhaps part of the older floor of the *porticus* (inv. 292846);[12]
- a large fragment of a fresco in the initial Fourth Pompeian Style (inv. 292844), dated to the first years after 62 CE, maybe connected to the floor in *opus sectile* of the *porticus;*
- several fragments of a black fresco, probably pertaining to the wainscot of a wall.[13]

All of these objects evoke a deep Egyptian atmosphere and seem to have been intentionally destroyed and concealed.

This is the first evidence for the presence in Cumae of a place for the

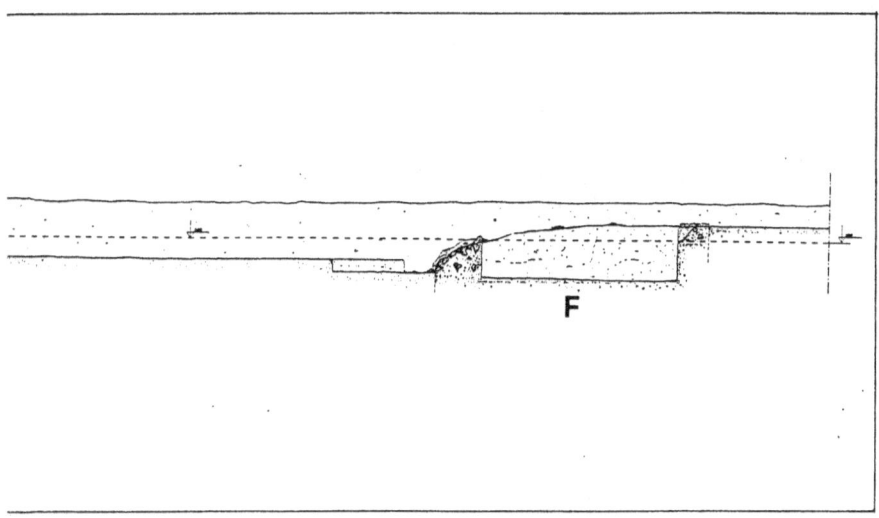

F

cult of Egyptian deities, apart from the uncovering of an Anubis statue (1836) and a fragmentary Harpokrates statue (1837), now lost, both of the Roman period and coming from the downtown area[14] (probably from the line of the northern urban walls).

The extensive remains and the findings provide new evidence for a re-evaluation of whether Cumae also had an Isaeum.[15] It is noteworthy that at Cumae, Egyptian findings, or objects imitating them, were found in several graves of the archaic Greek period, during the excavations made in the last century in the necropolis area. The hiatus recorded by the archaeological findings between the archaic Greek period and the first century BCE is probably only apparent: among the several *negotiatores* of Italic origin registered on the island of Delos, one (Minatos Staios) comes from Cumae and is associated with the Sarapeum; the other five belong to the *gentes* of the Staii, Heii, and perhaps Lucceii, whose involvement in the life of the town is well known from inscriptional and archaeological evidence. The hypothesis that such Cumaean *negotiatores* could have contributed, in the period ranging from the end of the third century BCE to the first century BCE,[16] to the introduction of Egyptian cults in their native land, perhaps confined in the beginning within the private religious sphere, is not groundless.

The presence of the double *ankh* (hieroglyphic, symbol of the life) in the hand of Isis makes her a goddess of the dead, as "the goddess who brings in her hands the keys of Hell,"[17] probably with the intention of representing at Cumae Isis assimilated to Selene-Luna-Hekate and to their related

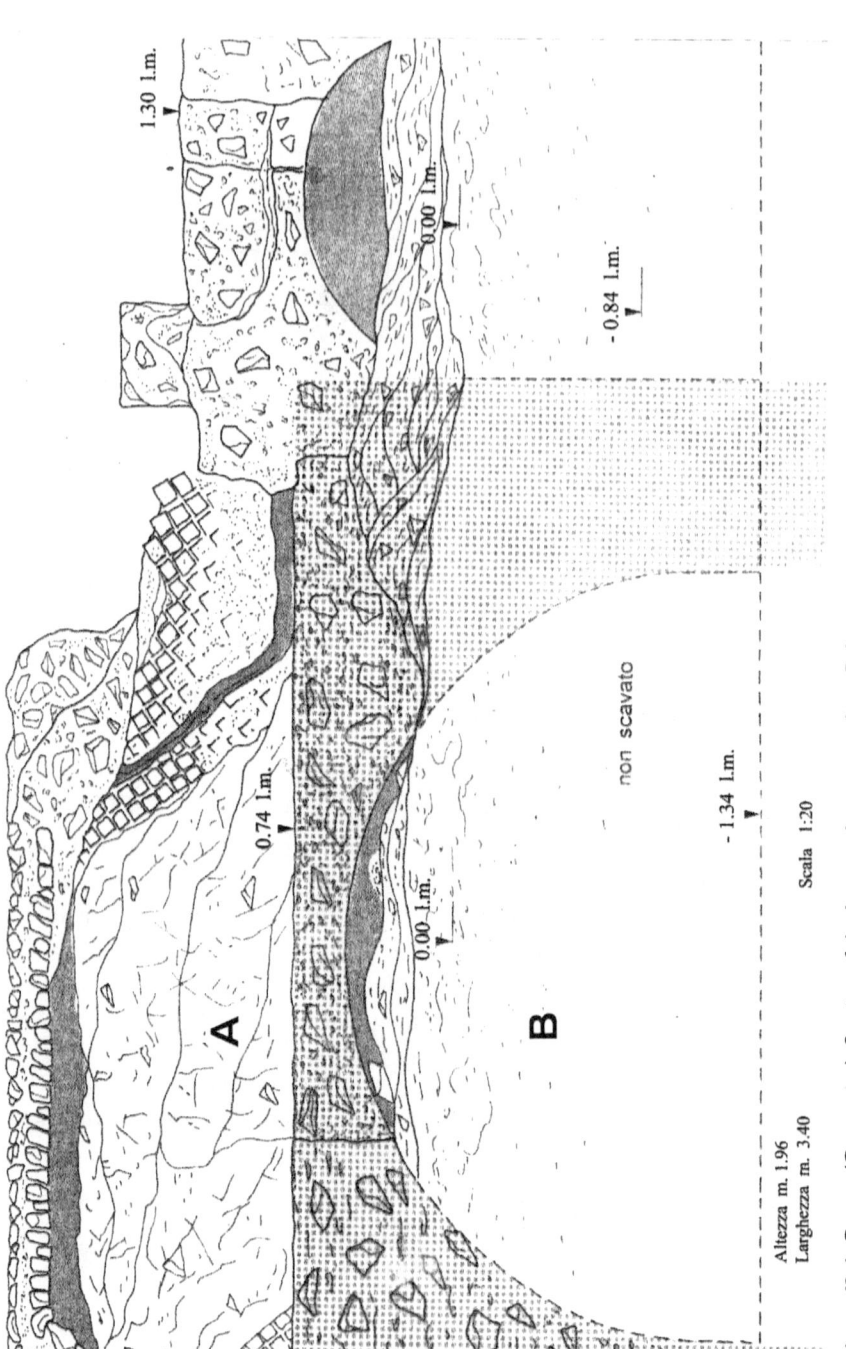

Figure I3.4. Cumae (Campaniae). Section of the Isaeum: A. upper *podium*; B. lower structure.

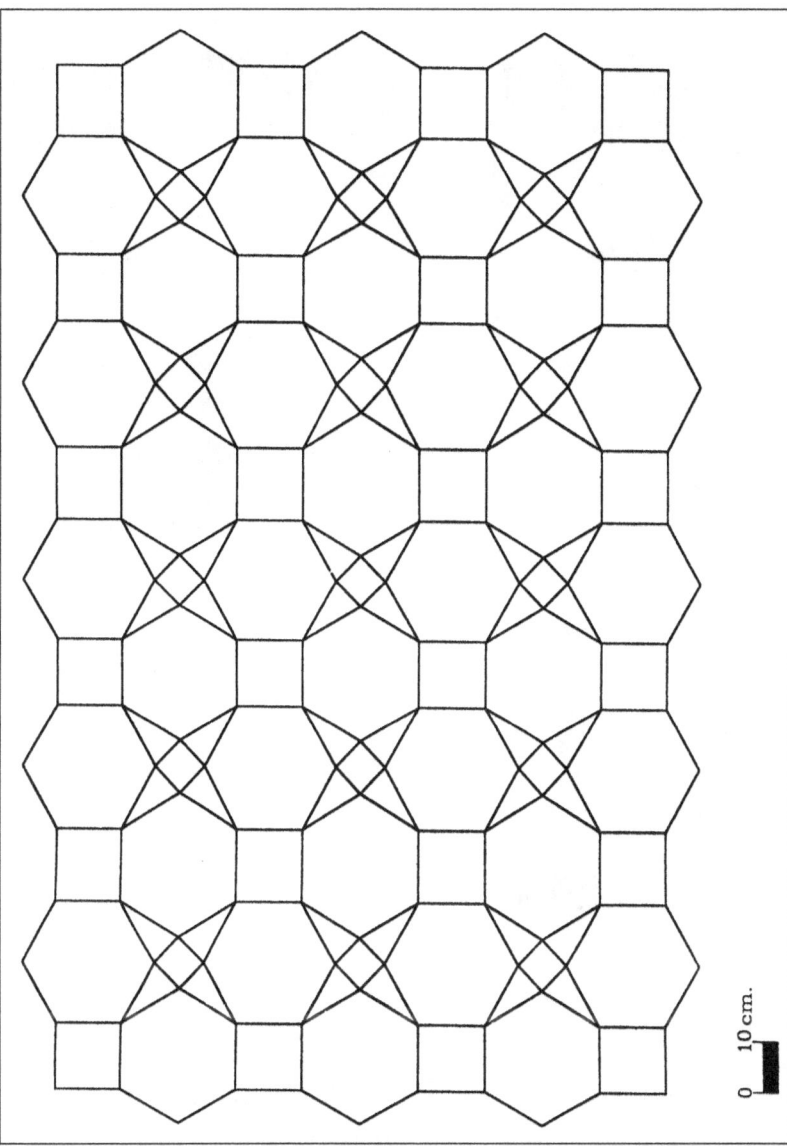

Figure 13.5. Cumae (Campaniae). *Porticus* of the Isaeum: graphic relief of the floor in *opus sectile*.

Figure 13.6. Cumae (Campaniae). Isaeum: *Inaros* statue.

chthonic aspects, more than an Isis Pelagia, Euploia, or Pharia, as has until now been supposed because of the location of the remains near the sea.[18] In this tradition, the presence of two lunar calendars of the Roman imperial age, carved on the walls of the so-called Antro della Sibilla at Cumae, could be explained.[19] Under the same point of view, the Anubis uncovered in the downtown area, if this was not its original site but the Isaeum itself, is well connected with Isis as her son, who accompanies his mother to try to find the body of Osiris.

The identification of the remains as the Isaeum is strengthened by the presence of the *podium*, the base of the temple, and of the pool for the lustral water.

As mentioned above, a fountain was found on the north side of the pool, decorated with shells. Shell decoration for *nymphaea* is usually associated in the Augustan age with the cult of Venus Anadyomene, who is associated with the idea of death/rebirth, and is joined to the cult of Egyptian deities or, more generally, to that of mystery deities.[20] The presence at Baiae of a sanctuary dedicated to Venus Lucrina,[21] located near Punta Epitaffio (in front of which a fragment of a *naophorus* was found in the

Figure 13.7. Cumae (Campaniae). Isaeum: Isis statue.

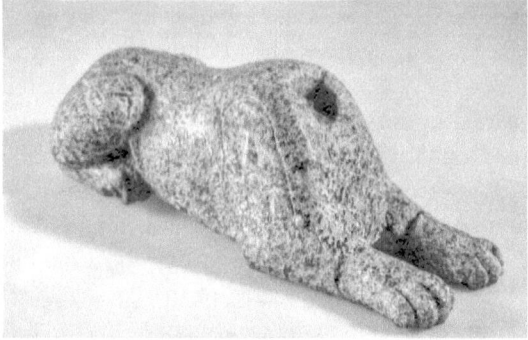

Figure 13.8. Cumae (Campaniae). Isaeum: Sphinx statue.

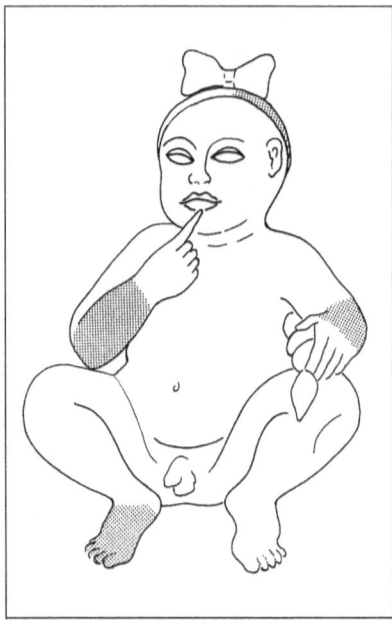

Figure 13.9. Cumae (Campaniae). Isaeum: Statue of Harpokrates-Horus like a child. Graphical reconstruction proposed by the author.

submerged area, perhaps not accidentally), is noteworthy;[22] a sanctuary of Aphrodite Euploia was situated at Pizzofalcone, in Naples.[23] The location of this sanctuary, on the top of a low hill facing the sea, was probably connected with coastal routes, because of their easy identification and territorial distribution.[24]

The Isaeum thus far uncovered could not be the sole sanctuary of the Egyptian cult in Cumae: the Roman Anubis statue, found near the northern urban walls, on the property of Angelo Luongo, not far from the necropolis, represented as Hermanubis in the function of Psychopompus, allows the hypothesis of a public sanctuary located in this area.

This last statue and the group of the three statuettes from the Isaeum present, however, a characteristic in common: they have all been mutilated. The statue has been beheaded, deprived of part of the face, left arm, and right hand; the group of statuettes has been beheaded, obliterated with a voluntary destructive act of the sanctuary, expressing explicit condemnation by opponents of the cult. The other two statuettes representing Harpokrates-Horus have also been completely destroyed and obliterated. This manner of obliteration of the Isaeum statuettes seems to tally with two other cases in the Phlegrean Fields: a beheaded *naophorus* found in the beginning of the twentieth century in the area of the Pausilypon;[25] another beheaded one recently uncovered in the Collegium of Via Celle at Pozzuoli, from a stratum dating back to the fourth century CE.[26] Transposed on a religious level, the symptom is very similar to the *damnatio memoriae*, but better expressed as *Ichonarum Phobia*. The subject needs to be researched, as I am in the process of doing.

Destruction must have been brought on by Christians after the Edict of Constantine (313), or probably after the Edict of Theodosius (392), because literary sources testify that the Isis cult flourished during the whole fourth century CE until the destruction of the Serapeum in Alexandria (391). This event can have taken place at the latest at the beginning of the

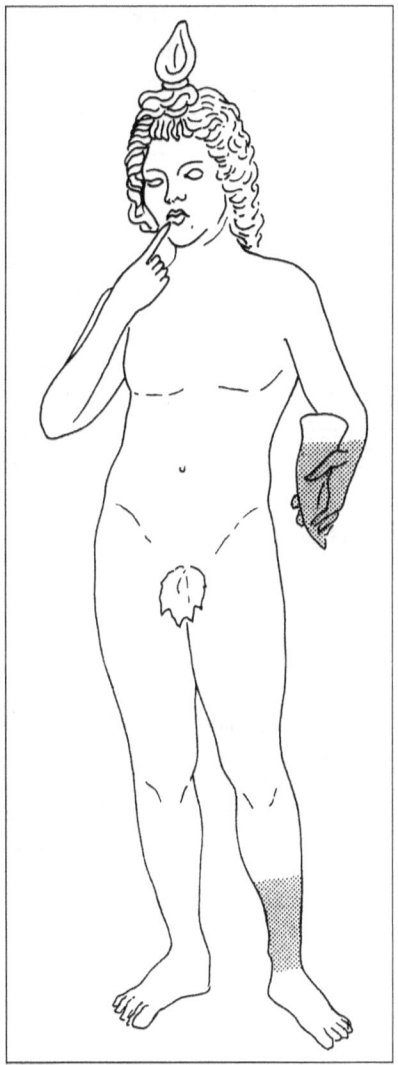

Figure 13.10. Cumae (Campaniae). Isaeum: Statue of a standing Harpokrates. Graphical reconstruction proposed by the author.

fifth century CE, if S. Paolino, Nola's bishop, in 404 writes against the Isis cult (*Carmina* 19, vv. 110-130), when the intolerance of paganism was very strong. With regard to this datum, it is noteworthy that Q. Aurelius Symmachus Eusebius (consul in 391) speaks of setting sail from his *Cumanum* (*Ep.* 2.4.2.); the villa must have been located at the sea's edge, although we do not have further information.[27] The possibility that the architectural remains were part of a *villa maritima*, probably his *villa*, seems more hypothetical. Since the Symmachi together with the Nicomachi were conspirators in the last pagan resistance to Christianity by the senatorial aristocracy, and considering the dimensions of the building and of the statuettes, it is therefore a reasonable assumption that the Isaeum was a private *sacellum* dedicated to the pagan cult. The conjecture that the remains were part of a villa has some basis, since recent researches, carried out in 1995 by the Centre J. Bérard of Naples in the harbor area, revealed the presence of architectural remains of three villas.[28]

The Isaeum is, finally, not only a new historical and topographical datum for Cumae, but also a geological and archaeological one. The *podium* shows two different building phases, revealed by restoration works in its south/east side. The first lower structure dates back to not before 100 BCE, most likely to the first half of the first century BCE. The more recent upper *podium* goes back to the second half of the first century BCE. A geological drilling, executed during the excavations, made it clear that the reconstruction was necessary, due to the subsidence of the littoral, the effects of which were previously unknown in this area. The association of the archaeological datum with the geological one has made it possible to understand that, in the period from the first half to the second half of the first century BCE, the Cumaean littoral sank 1.04 meters.

Notes

Paolo Caputo is at the Soprintendenza per i Beni Archeologici delle Province di Napoli e Caserta, responsible for the archaeological site and the Archaeological Park of Cumae and for the Archaeological Diving Unit of the Soprintendenza.

1. The present contribution is the result of the research and studies I have directly carried out in the last ten years after the Isaeum was uncovered. The research has been already illustrated in the following studies: Caputo 1991: 169-172; 2003a: 87-94; 1998: 245-253; 2003b: 209-220; 2003c: 45-51; De Caro 1994: 11-15; De Caro 1993-94: 189-190; Caputo, Morichi, Paone, and Rispoli 1996: 174-176; De Caro 1997: 350-351.

2. Paget 1968.

3. Pasqualini 2000: 69-70; Morhange et al. 2000: 71-82. These data contrast

methodologically with the older data, coming from another analysis made in the same area: Arthur, Guarino, Jones, and Schiattarella 1977: 5-13.

4. Bats 1997: 23-24.

5. Their walls were covered with a surface of *signinum*. This structure could have had the function of a former *podium*, used probably also as a water reserve. See the case of Delos, where under Serapea A and B were built water reserves, one of which was fed directly by the Inopos. An Alexandrine literary tradition, reported also by Callimachus (*Hymn to Delos* 206-208), considered the river a branch of the Nile (Roussel 1916: 30-31, 45). This religious fiction had the purpose of assimilating the holy water to that of the Nile, considered holy. In the case of Cumae, the water reserves could have fed the pool for the holy water. It is perhaps noteworthy that a water-bearing stratum was found during the restoration works of the structure.

6. Caputo 2003c.

7. De Caro 1994: 12-13; Cozzolino 1997: 448; ibid.: 21-25, 31-54.

8. Di Maria 1997: 448.

9. Ibid.: 450.

10. Caputo 2000: 90.

11. Ibid.

12. Ibid.

13. Ibid.

14. Ruggiero 1888: 204-205.

15. For the several Egyptian traces in Roman Campania and the introduction there of the Isis cult, see Malaise 1972a: Acerrae, 1; Ager Falernus, 1; Boscoreale, 1; Cappella, 1; Capua, 1-4; Carinola, 1; Cumae, 1; Herculaneum, 1-5, 7-10 ter, 20; Liternum, 1; Misenum, 10-13; Neapolis, 1, 3, 4, 7-12; Puteoli, 4, 9-18, 28; Stabiae, 1-2; Aeclanum, 1; V. Tran Tram Tinh 1964, 1972; Mueller 1969; DeCaro 1992. For the introduction of the cult at Cumae, see above, note 1.

16. Hatzfeld 1912: Heii, n. 1, pp. 41-42; Lucceii, n. 1, p. 47; Staii, nn. 1-4, p. 80. See also Malaise 1984: 1615-1691.

17. Apul. *Met.* 11.

18. Also the sanctuary of Fondo Iozzino at Pompeii was located outside the town, near the mouth of the river Sarno and in the harbor area, not very far from the Porta Nocera. The site, occupied from the Archaic age, was reorganized in the Samnitic period (third century BCE). A thick enclosure wall circumscribed the area, inside which another surrounding wall delimited three small temples. Two clay statues of women were found near two of them (ending of the second/beginning of the first century BCE). One statue is identical to a Rhodian type representing Hekate-Artemis. A replica comes from the Monte Santo Stefano, a Rhodian sanctuary, where the cult of an infernal deity is proved. Both statues allow the identification of the sanctuary near Pompeii as dedicated to Demeter, a land goddess, whose cult is located outside the town, where Hekate's cult is also attested; see S. De Caro in Zevi 1991: 41-42.

19. Ruggieri 1998: 68-80.

20. Gros 1976: 138-143.

21. J. Beloch (1890: 178) situates the temple on Punta dell' Epitaffio. Although architectural remains are not individuated, the sanctuary is testified by literary-

historical sources (Stat. *Silv.* 3.150; Mart. *Epigr.* 11.81) and an inscription (*CIL* 10.3692).

22. Di Fraia, Lombardo, and Scognamiglio 1986: 221 n. 22, figs. 2–3; Pirelli 1997: 450.

23. Napoli 1967: 418; Stat. *Silv.* 2.2.76–82 and 3.1.149; *IG* 14.745 and p. 690; Peterson 1919: 200.

24. See Napoli 1967: 418.

25. De Caro 1994: 15.

26. Cozzolino 1997: 451; Cozzolino 1999: 25–31.

27. D'Arms 1970: 226.

28. See Bats 1997.

CHAPTER 14

The Mystery Cults and Vergil's *Georgics*

PATRICIA A. JOHNSTON

Among the many elements that contribute to the elusive art of the *Georgics* is its finely tuned balance between *labor* and *religio*. When scholarly attention has turned to religion in this poem, however, it has tended to focus on the religion of the state[1] rather than on the more intimate, personal religion of individuals, families, and other affiliations—religions represented by the mystery cults, which are much more difficult to substantiate. A complicating factor in trying to sort out these elements is the widespread religious syncretism, particularly common from the Hellenistic period and later. Yet a considerable element in the religious aura that pervades this poem is also due to subtle allusions to a wide range of symbols, figures, and myths having to do with these cults, whose wide influence during this period has become increasingly evident. The mystery cults discussed in this chapter will be limited to those of Eleusis, Isis, Dionysus, and, briefly, Cybele.[2]

A theme common to the myths associated with certain mystery cults is the death of the spouse or child of a deity who oversees the growth of plant life, the means of mortal sustenance. This theme corresponds to the annual cycle of nature: the growth and harvest of crops, and the subsequent winter or dry season when nothing grows, a season devoid of life and joy. The return of spring and the growth of new plant life corresponds to the restoration, in some degree, of the deceased figure, be it Persephone or Attis or Dionysus or Osiris, embodying the tension inherent in the ongoing, cyclic process as the new year's harvest replaces the old year's loss. The surprising discovery in 1992 of a Temple of Isis in Cumae—surprising because none of our sources make any reference to it—has prompted reconsideration of the role of the mysteries, and particularly those of Eleusis, Isis, and Dionysus, in Vergil's poem on agriculture.

Cybele

Cybele (*Mētēr*, or *Magna Mater*), or allusions to her, occur only twice in Vergil's poem, and she seems to have had the least impact on the *Georgics*. This is surprising, in view of Vergil's topic, since she is closely associated with agriculture and the fertility of nature. She is much more prominent in the *Aeneid*, where her appearance and references to her restate in various ways the Phrygian origins of the Trojans.[3] Zanker suggests, however, that Augustus did not cultivate the cult of Cybele as magnanimously as he indicates in his *Res Gestae*, since he "did not rebuild the temple, which lay near his house, in marble, but only tufa . . . and relegated the exotic cult, with its ecstatic dances and long-haired priests . . . to freedmen." The restored temple, moreover, was not rededicated until 17 CE, under Tiberius.[4] On the other hand, he may have intentionally used tufa to underline the antiquity of the cult.

Cybele's limited impact may also have resulted in part from the fact that the worship of her consort, Attis (whose mythical death and restoration makes this cult particularly relevant to a poem on farming), involved ritual emasculation of the *Galloi*, Cybele's priests from Pessinus. Consequently, the involvement of Roman citizens in the priesthood of this cult was limited until well after Vergil's time. The cult of Cybele was brought to Rome during the Second Punic War; and she was worshiped at Rome in her temple on the Palatine. Despite her association with fertility, as the Great Mother of all living things, she appears only twice in the *Georgics*, both times in the fourth book, and both times in the context of the episode in which her followers masked the cries of the infant Zeus when he was hidden from Kronos on Crete and nourished by honeybees. In *Georgics* 4.64, Cybele is referred to as the Great Mother:

> tinnitusque cie et Matris quate cymbala circum.

> Shake the Great Mother's cymbals, make them ring.

In 4.149–152, there is a specific reference to the episode on Crete:

> nunc age, naturas apibus quas Iuppiter ipse
> addidit expediam, pro qua mercede canoros
> Curetum sonitus crepitantiaque aera secutae
> Dictaeo caeli regem pavere sub antro. (*G.* 4.149–152)

Come now, let me tell of the nature that Jupiter himself gave to bees, as a reward. For they followed the musical sounds and clashing cymbals of the Curetes and fed the king of heaven in a cave on Mt. Dicte.

Dionysus/Bacchus/Liber

Liber et alma Ceres, vestro si munere tellus
Chaoniam pingui glandem mutavit arista,
poculaque inventis Acheloia miscuit uvis. (G. 1.7-9)

Liber and nourishing Ceres, since through your gift earth exchanged the Chaonian acorn for thick stalks of grain and mixed the waters of Achelous with new-found grapes.

Dionysus and his mysteries are perhaps the most elusive, despite the ubiquity of the cult.[5] Vergil's Dionysus, as "Bacchus" or "Liber," is frequently paired with Ceres in the *Georgics,* as the god himself, and, by metonymy, as the fruit of the vine, particularly throughout the second book, where cultivation of the vine is a major topic.[6] The literary imagery of Vergil's Bacchus, which Thomas associates with analogies to Vergil's poetic undertaking and to the god's association with tragedy,[7] is clearly an important element in the poem, but the "tension between the divine and human," which Henrichs identifies as the essence of this deity,[8] is also in evidence in Vergil's reference to him. While a happy Bacchic festival (2.380-396) represents one aspect of this god's power, on at least two occasions there are vivid reminders of the destructive force of the god. In the second book Vergil refers to the violent battle between the Lapiths and Centaurs, which he blames on drunkenness due to *Baccheia dona* (2.454):

quid memorandum aeque Baccheia dona tulerunt?
Bacchus et ad culpam causas dedit: ille furentis
Centauros leto domuit, Rhoecumque Pholumque
et magno Hylaeum Lapithis cratere minantem. (G. 2.454-457)

What equally memorable thing have the gifts of Bacchus produced? Bacchus even gave cause to criticize: He tamed the raging centaurs with death—Rhoecus and Pholus and Hylaeus, who was threatening Lapiths with an enormous bowl.

In the fourth book of the *Georgics* we are again reminded of the god's destructive force when Orpheus is dismembered by Bacchic revelers. Here the literary force of Bacchus is again implicit, in that, as Thomas observes (ad 4.520-522), "Orpheus is conflated with [Euripides'] Pentheus." The relationship between Bacchus and Orpheus is too complex to discuss here, other than to recognize that both cults appear to originate in Phrygia or Thrace or Lydia.[9] Diodorus Siculus, who is Vergil's older contemporary, reports (*Bibl.* 22.7) that the orgiastic Dionysiac cult was imported from Egypt into Greece.[10] The Greco-Egyptian blend of the god can be seen at Rome in Tibullus, where he attributes cultivation of the vine to Osiris, while still referring to wine, by metonymy, as "Bacchus" (*Bibl.* 1.7.39, 41).

Eleusinian Mysteries

For Vergil, the Eleusinian mysteries and the rites of Ceres are the same, but it is important to realize that initiation into the Eleusinian cult could only take place in Greece, even though the cult was practiced throughout the Greco-Roman world. Among those who went to Eleusis for initiation was Augustus, who was initiated in 31 BCE, shortly after the Battle of Actium, and two years before Vergil read the *Georgics* to him,[11] so it is not surprising that Vergil would want to include some reference to the Eleusinian cult in his poem.

The earliest allusion to Demeter's Roman counterpart occurs in 1.7-9 (*Liber et alma Ceres*). As in the case of Bacchus (*Liber*), the name of the goddess in the *Georgics* refers sometimes to the deity and sometimes by metonymy to the product associated with her. Ceres, in Vergil's account, made it possible to live on cultivated crops rather than having to rely on the bounty of nature, as represented, for example, by acorns dropped by oak trees, as mortals once did during a more primitive stage of civilization. Ceres' gift, in this account, was that she taught mortals how to cultivate the soil and grow grain. She is said to have instructed mortals in the art of cultivation through Triptolemus (*uncique puer monstrator aratri*, 1.19).[12] In 1.94ff., we see that she continues to reward the hard-working farmer:

> multum adeo, rastris glaebas qui frangit inertis
> vimineasque trahit cratis, iuvat arva, neque illum
> flava Ceres alto nequiquam spectat Olympo. (*G.* 1.94-96)

He who breaks up lazy clods of dirt with a hoe and drags wicker-work hurdles over them greatly assists the fields; golden Ceres will not look down upon him from lofty Olympus to no avail.

Vergil makes specific reference to the Eleusinian ritual in 1.160–166, a passage that Conington dismissed as an attempt to give religious dignity to what might otherwise seem trivial. There Vergil lists the weaponry[13] of the "Eleusinian mother."

> dicendum et quae sint duris agrestibus arma,
> quis sine nec potuere seri nec surgere messes:
> vomis et inflexi primum grave robur aratri,
> tardaque Eleusinae matris volventia plaustra,
> tribulaque traheaeque et iniquo pondere rastri;
> virgea praeterea Celei vilisque supellex,
> arbuteae crates et mystica vannus Iacchi. (G. 1.160–166)

> Now I must name the weapons that gird the toughened man of the soil;
> without them no seeds would be sown, no grain would grow to harvest:
> the plowshare (*vomis*), the heavy weight of the bent plow (*aratri*),
> the Eleusinian mother's slowly turning wagon,
> the threshing sleds and drags and hoes, Celeus' simple osier basket,
> hurdles of arbute-twigs, and the
> mystic winnowing fan of Iacchus.

As I have shown elsewhere,[14] Vergil here frames this procession with a series of episodes (G. 1.118–203) highlighting the farmer's struggle against decline. The first picture of decline is the end of the golden age (118–135), which leads to the development of skills (136ff.), particularly the art of plowing, taught by Ceres (147–159); this development culminates in a central panel, an epiphany of an Eleusinian procession (160–166). This is followed by further instructions on making a plow (167–175), then generalized to skills and their application (176–196), and finally by a second picture of decline, where a farmer who fails to persist in selecting the best seed of his crop is compared to a rower relaxing his oars and being swept back downstream after he has laboriously rowed upstream (197–203).

Later in this book (1.338–350), Vergil's farmer is advised to offer sacrifices to Ceres. Bayet[15] demonstrated that in this passage, Vergil had synthesized three separate festivals in honor of Ceres. The first, the Cerealia (12–19 April), celebrates the young shoots of grain that begin to grow in early or mid-April. The second (1.345) is the Ambarvalia (late May), in which the lustration of the fields is performed; this festival is dedicated to a number of other deities as well, but in this section Vergil is concerned only with Ceres' role in the festival. The third (1.347–350) is the festival that celebrates the beginning of the harvest, held in late summer.

The central myth of Eleusis, as depicted in the Homeric *Hymn to Demeter*,[16] was the theft of Persephone by Plouton, the god of the underworld, and her mother's search and eventual recovery of her daughter. Persephone's return from the underworld is temporary, however, and consequently her mother is in mourning for her during that part of the year which Persephone must spend in the underworld. Grain fails to grow until she is again reunited with her sorrowing mother.

While she is in mourning for Persephone, according to the Homeric *Hymn*, Demeter goes to Eleusis, to the house of Celeus, disguised as an old woman, and becomes the nursemaid to the king's infant son. Every night she places the child in a fire, attempting to make the child immortal, but the queen happens to witness this act and cries out in alarm, whereupon Demeter reveals her true self, orders that a temple be built there in her honor, and retreats to the company of the gods, where she resumes mourning until her daughter is restored to her.

In the proem to the first book of the *Georgics* (1.39), Vergil modifies the version of the myth in the Homeric *Hymn*, wherein it is indicated that Persephone longed to return (literally, "she longed for her mother," *Hymn Dem.* 344; cf. 370–371), by saying that Proserpina refused to return when summoned: *nec repetita sequi curet Proserpina matrem* (G. 1.39). At the close of the fourth book, he similarly modifies the tale of Eurydice, who, although she apparently was allowed to return from the dead in pre-Vergilian versions, in Vergil fails to come back. Both Persephone and Eurydice are *dona Ditis,* literally, gifts from Dis or Pluto; the term also refers to the new growth of crops, which was seen as a return on the seed invested in the soil.[17] Persephone and Eurydice thus become doublets and thereby constitute a frame of sorts for the entire poem.[18] Direct reference to the Eleusinian mysteries, however, appears to be limited to the first book, and to these episodes.

More subtle allusions emerge, however, if we also take into consideration suggestions of the Egyptian equivalent of the myth of Demeter, namely the story of Isis and Osiris. Despite Herodotus' recognition of parallels between these two goddesses and his readiness to apply the term "Mysteries" to the rites of Osiris (2.171), it appears that the Mysteries in the full sense of the Greek term (implying secret initiation and prohibition of revealing any of the ceremonies to the uninitiated) were not attached to the cult of Isis and Osiris until the Ptolemaic era. As the cult spread outside of Egypt, it was marked by the ascendancy of Isis, both at home and abroad. To the Hellenistic Greeks, she was seen as a "queen-mother, identified with most of the forces of nature."[19]

Isis and Osiris

For Vergil's contemporaries, the Isiac cult offered a set of deities who competed with Demeter/Ceres in laying claim to the discovery of the art of agriculture. Diodorus Siculus, a contemporary of Cicero and Vergil, devoted the first book of his *Library of History* to Egypt and its customs; he records that Isis—like Ceres—is said to have discovered the fruit of wheat and barley, and that Osiris devised a means of cultivating these fruits (1.14). He also records that Osiris—like Dionysus—discovered the art of viticulture (1.15).[20] Like Diodorus Siculus, Tibullus (1.7.29-42) credits Osiris with discovering the cultivation of the soil to produce grain, the art of cultivating trees and vines, and the art of producing wine, which in turn inspired the making of music. And wine and music combined to give mortals respite from toil and sadness:

> primus aratra manu sollerti fecit Osiris
>   et teneram ferro sollicitabit humum,
> primus inexpertae commisit semina terrae
>   pomaque non notis legit ab arboribus. (Tib. 1.7.29-32)

> First to make a plow with a clever hand and to turn
>   the delicate soil with its iron blade was Osiris.
> He was the first to entrust the seeds to the untested soil
>   and gather from unfamiliar trees the fruit.

In line 29, Tibullus' Osiris appears to merge with Bacchus, suggesting that, for Tibullus, the two gods are the same:

> Bacchus et agricolae magno confecta labore
>   pectora tristiae dissolvenda dedit;
> Bacchus et adflictis requiem mortalibus adfert. (Tib. 1.7.39-41)

> Bacchus also allowed the farmer to be freed from
>   sadness, his heart exhausted by toil;
> Bacchus also to troubled mortals brings rest.

In Egyptian myth, Osiris taught his people the art of cultivating the soil and established justice on both banks of the Nile, but was murdered by his cousin Seth, who persuaded him to climb into a coffin, which Seth then sealed and threw into the Nile. His wife and sister, Isis, like Demeter, went into mourning but diligently searched for his remains. She learned that the coffin enclosing his corpse had lodged itself in the branches of an erica tree, which had then quickly grown up around it and enclosed it. The tree had been felled and fashioned into a pillar of the king of Byblos's palace. Isis therefore went to the king disguised as an old woman and, like Demeter, became a nursemaid for the king's infant son. Isis, like Demeter, was a very unusual nursemaid. She, too, would attempt to burn away the mortal parts of the infant's body (νύκτωρ δὲ περικαίεν τὰ θνητὰ τοῦ σώματος) and then, transformed into a swallow, would fly around the pillar containing Osiris' coffin, with a mournful lament (αὐτὴν δὲ γενομένην χελιδόνα τῇ κίονι περιπέτεσθαι καὶ θρηνεῖν, Plut. *Mor.* 357c).[21] When the queen of Byblos discovered her child on fire, she screamed, and thereby deprived him of immortality. Isis then revealed herself and demanded that the pillar that held up the palace roof, which contained Osiris' corpse, be given to her.

After recovering Osiris' coffin, she hid it in the marshes and went away to care for their infant son. While she was gone, the wicked Seth found the coffin and dismembered the corpse of Osiris, scattering the body up and down the country.

Isis therefore once again set out in search of her husband, "sailing through the swamps in a boat of papyrus" (Plut. *Mor.* 358a), collecting the individual pieces of the body and burying them. In some versions she reassembled them as a mummy and then fanned the dead body with her wings, reviving Osiris to be the ruler of the underworld, where he now judges the souls of the dead, balancing them against the feather of truth.

The story, like that of Demeter and Persephone, corresponds to the annual cycle of Nature. When the Nile rises, Osiris returns to life, and when it falls, Osiris dies. Osiris, in some accountings, actually is the Nile, who brings the grain to life, and then dies away. In other accountings, the Nile consists of the tears of Isis, for when she is in mourning for the lost Osiris, her tears swell its waters.

Isis and Io

Although Vergil does not name Isis, he does, in the third *Georgic*, refer to her Greek counterpart, Io (*Inachiae*, 3.153). In Greek myth, Io tends to merge with Isis,[22] although our earliest written evidence for the connection is Callimachus, who refers to "Isis, the daughter of Inachus" (Ἰναχίης

..."Ἴσιδος, *Epigram* 58).²³ Inachus is of course the father of Io. Thomas cites several references in the *Georgics* to the Io of C. Licinius Calvus, Catullus' friend and fellow neoteric. In book 3 (3.146–153), Vergil alludes to Io's bovine wanderings in southern Italy, around Silarus (146), Alburnus (147), and Tanager (151):

> est lucos Silari circa ilicibusque virentem
> plurimus Alburnum volitans, cui nomen asilo
> Romanum est, oestrum Grai vertere vocantes
> ... furit mugitibus aether
> concussus silvaeque et sicci ripa Tanagri.
> hoc quondam monstro horribilis exercuit iras
> Inachiae Iuno pestem meditata iuvencae. (G. 3.146–153)

> Around the groves of Silarus and verdant Alburnus flits many a creature that the Romans call *asilus* [gadfly] and the Greeks call *oestrus*.... The air and forests and bank of dry Tanager echo its buzzing noise. Once upon a time, Juno, through this creature, planned this torture and unleashed her dreadful anger on Inachus' daughter, now a heifer.

Thomas suggests that the references to these "obscure Lucanian and Bruttian placenames" may indicate that Calvus presented a "geographically expansive" account of her wanderings, including "a stop in southern Italy."²⁴ To this I would add that if Calvus' Io wandered in Lucania, it would not be unreasonable to suppose that her wanderings may have extended a little farther north, to Campania, where Isis' temple, reported at Puteoli as early as the second century BCE, would be known to Vergil and presumably also to Calvus.

An intriguing question, which perhaps may be resolved in the not-too-distant future, is whether there was any connection between the newly discovered temple of Isis at Cumae (see Caputo's chapter in this book) and the reported Isaeum at Puteoli. The newly discovered temple may also have some bearing on Vergil's repeated references in the *Aeneid* to Cumae and Baiae as "Euboean" (*Aen.* 6.2, 6.42, 9.710), for in Hesiod's account, Io goes not to Egypt but to Euboea, which was in fact named after her.²⁵ The equivalence between Io and Isis would certainly have been known to Vergil. And, of course, we know that Vergil composed some considerable portion of the *Georgics* in Campania, perhaps in the vicinity of the recently discovered Isaeum at Cumae. For now, however, we can only surmise its relevance for Vergil's poem.

Thomas notes another apparent echo of Calvus' *Io* in the Orpheus-

Eurydice episode in Vergil's book 4, where he compares Orpheus' cry—*a miseram Eurydicen!* (*G.* 4.526)—to the exclamation in Calvus' poem, *a virgo infelix!* (*Ecl.* 6.47, 52). Additionally, because Servius says these lines were taken over from Gallus, Thomas suggests that Orpheus' final words "are also the final element of the *laudes Galli*,"[26] which, according to Servius, once appeared in this part of the poem. Io is also the ancestress of Dionysus,[27] who in turn is linked with Orpheus, and in some accounts is equated with him.

Isis and Demeter/Ceres

Isis was also frequently equated with Demeter or Ceres, and indeed, their myths are so similar that Herodotus indicated that the Eleusinian ritual was modeled on the Isiac ritual, a theory that enjoyed "great popularity" in the early part of this century, until, according to Mylonas, Picard "proved . . . the theory . . . untenable," since no Egyptian artifact or evidence of Egyptian influence "dating from the second millennium was found in the sanctuary of Eleusis," and subsequent excavations have confirmed the rejection of Egyptian influence.[28] Though Greek influence can be found in much of the tale as we have it from Plutarch, Griffith concludes that, although Isis' journey to Byblos and her adventures there have "affinities with the story of Demeter, Metaneira and Demophoön in the *Homeric Hymn to Demeter,* its origin must lie in the Byblite cults of the New Kingdom and afterwards [where] the cult of Isis is attested . . . from the seventh century B.C."[29]

Unlike membership in the Eleusinian cult, initiation into the Isiac cult was not restricted geographically; the cult's presence in Rome was unambiguous during the first century, even if frequently circumscribed, and was finally endorsed by a decree of the Second Triumvirate in 43 BCE, which called for the construction of a temple of Isis and Serapis in the Campus Martius. After Actium, however, there was a consistent policy under Augustus of elevating the Attic cults, and of disparaging, or at least neglecting, the eastern cults, a policy that is reflected to some extent in the *Georgics,* and is stated even more unambiguously in the *Aeneid.* The last two books of the *Georgics* contain a surprising number of Egyptian elements, in view of Servius' statement that some portion of the fourth book was modified to remove the *laudes* for the Egyptian prefect and poet Cornelius Gallus. Book 3 begins with Herakles' Egyptian labor and contains the Io/Isis passage. In book 4, the method of regenerating bees is clearly placed in Egypt (4.287–294), and Aristaeus wrestles with the traditionally Egyptian sea-deity, Proteus. Wherever possible, however, Vergil always chooses the Greek or non-Egyptian version of the myth. His Proteus is from Pallene in Chalcidice, even though Vergil's sources, from Homer to Lycophron, retain Egypt as Proteus' place of origin. Here Vergil clearly wanted to retain Proteus, but chose to modify his Egyptian associations.[30] It is not unusual for Vergil to modify extensively the details concerning mythological figures and their stories, as the examples of Proserpina and Eurydice illustrate, but in the case of Proserpina and Eurydice, he appears to intend to make the one a doublet of the other. It is not yet clear to me what, if any, effect he intended his modification of Proteus' provenance to have upon his reader.

Proserpina's appearance at the end of the first book, and Eurydice's parallel role at the end of the fourth, may lead one to wonder whether Vergil intended a similar analogy between Demeter and Orpheus, who mourn their losses. We have seen the strong similarities between Demeter and Isis, as one mourns the loss of a daughter and the other of a husband. When Orpheus loses Eurydice for a second time, he is compared to the nightingale mourning the loss of her child, Itys:

> qualis populea maerens philomela sub umbra
> amissos queritur fetus, quos durus arator
> observans nido implumis detraxit; at illa
> flet noctem, ramoque sedens miserabile carmen
> integrat, et maestis late loca questibus implet. (G. 4.511–515)

> Just as a nightingale mourns from beneath the shade of a poplar tree,
> as she protests the loss of her brood, which a toughened (*durus*) plowman has
> found and dragged, unplumed, from their nest; all night long she
> weeps, perched on a branch, ever renewing her unhappy
> song, filling the fields around with sad reproach.

Orpheus mourns not for a lost child, as the nightingale does, but for a lost spouse. Through this simile, an analogy between his sorrow at the end of the poem and the implicit sorrow of Demeter at its beginning can be drawn, particularly if the sorrow of Demeter's Egyptian equivalent is also taken into consideration. Like Isis, Orpheus mourns his lost spouse, but through the simile, his sorrow is also like that of Demeter's sorrow for her lost child.

The nightingale simile operates on a number of levels. On the most pragmatic, it recalls a passage in *Georgics* 2 (207–211) "where the successful farmer . . . uproots and destroys the birds' home as he converts the woods to plough-lands."³¹ Vergil first refers to the myth itself at the beginning of the fourth book, where he names the swallow (Procne) as one of the birds that are dangerous for honeybees:

> absint et picti squalentia terga lacerti
> pinguibus a stabulis, meropesque aliae volucres
> et manibus Procne pectus signata cruentis;
> omnia nam late vastant ipsasque volantis
> ore ferunt dulcem nidis immitibus escam. (G. 4.13–17)³²

> Near the rich hives let there be no lizards with scaly backs and winged creatures that consume bees: Meropidae and most of all Procne, her breast marked with bloody hands; for everything far and wide they consume and carry in their mouths to their cruel nests even the busy bees, sweet morsels for their young.

Procne's plumage, bearing the mark of blood-stained hands, is a potent reminder of the two sisters' cruel murder and dismemberment of young Itys, and indeed, any reference to their tale would recall their crime. Through these two allusions, the myth thus encircles the fourth and last book of the *Georgics*, occurring at its beginning and at its end. The second allusion to this tale, the comparison of Orpheus to a nightingale, is quickly followed by Orpheus' violent dismemberment. Philomela and Procne, who appear in the *Georgics* in winged form, one as a swallow, the other as a nightingale, share the sometime-winged nature of Isis, who is represented on tombs with wings, and who, in her search for Osiris' corpse, while serving as a nursemaid in Byblos, becomes a swallow.

The dismemberment of Orpheus during the *nocturni orgia Bacchi* (G. 4.521) recalls Pentheus' dismemberment in Euripides' *Bacchae*,³³ but the final detail of Orpheus' dismembered head floating downstream can also suggest the dismembered limbs of Osiris pursued by Isis in her papyrus boat. Isis mourns as she searches for her dismembered spouse; here it is not only Orpheus who mourns for his lost spouse, but it is also Orpheus, like Osiris, who has been dismembered.³⁴

Herakles and the Mysteries

The entire fourth book thus acquires added dimension when viewed from the perspective of the mysteries. The third book also contains elements suggestive of the mysteries. It begins with a brief invocation of Pales and

Apollo as deities of flocks and herds. In the third line, Vergil declares that he will dismiss hackneyed themes:

cetera, quae vacuas tenuissent carmine mentes,
omnia iam vulgata. (G. 3.3–4)

Other things that have preoccupied empty minds are now all commonplace.

He then lists some of those themes, which include the labors (Eurysthea) and loves (Hylas) of Herakles, as well as the birth of Apollo and Artemis, and Pelops' courtship of Hippodame.[35]

quis aut Eurysthea durum
aut inlaudati nescit Busiridis aras?
cui non dictus Hylas puer et Latonia Delos
Hippodameque umeroque Pelops insignis eburno,
acer equis? (G. 3.4–8)

Who does not know about harsh Eurystheus or the unsung altars of Busiris? Who has not been told of the young Hylas and Leto's Delos and Hippodame and Pelops, conspicuous with his ivory shoulder, a skillful charioteer?

Whether these lines constitute a *recusatio* (Wimmel) or an "anti-*recusatio*" (Thomas), and whether they be Pindaric or Callimachean (fr. 44 Pf.), what is of interest for the purposes of this discussion is Vergil's curious allusion here, at the outset of the book concerned with cattle and horses, to Herakles, an allusion, moreover, set in the context of the only labor that associates Herakles with Egypt, namely the killing of Busiris (*inlaudati . . . Busiridis aras*, G. 3.5).[36] Busiris is the name of an apparently fictitious Egyptian king who killed strangers, and was killed by Herakles. It is also the name of the site of Osiris' tomb.[37] Extant fragments suggest that "a ritual human sacrifice [was once practiced] at the tomb of Osiris, which in later times, when sacrifice was abandoned, was transformed into a legend of Busiris as a murderous king."[38]

Herakles, although he had no cult of his own, was among the more prominent of Eleusinian initiates; it was for his benefit that the Lesser Mysteries were instituted so that he could be initiated from Hades.[39] We know from *Aeneid* 8 that, for Vergil, Herakles' affiliation with cattle (which he leads back from the land of the dead) is a prominent feature of his myth. We also know from Herodotus about Herakles' strong ties with Egypt; there is additionally recurring discussion in Cicero's treatise on the nature of the gods about "Egyptian Herakles."[40] It would appear to be more significant than is generally recognized, therefore, that of all the Herculean *labores* to which Vergil might here have alluded, he should choose the one set in Egypt. His emphatic denial, moreover, that he will write about Herakles serves to draw his audience's attention toward the myth, rather than away from it. Herakles, as will be seen, will surface again at the close of this book.

Cattle are prominent in the myth of Herakles at Rome, as depicted in *Aeneid* 8 and in other Augustan authors,[41] and in the myths of Io and in the Isiac cult (the sacred Apis-bull was supposed to be the reincarnation of the Egyptian god Ptah as well as of Osiris). The prominence of cattle in Herakles' myth should be considered in any analysis of the violent deaths of cattle at the close of books 3 and 4 of the *Georgics*, not to mention the close of book 2, where Vergil cites Aratus' version of the myth of the ages, wherein the irreverent race of bronze was the first to consume the plowing ox, the helpmate of Justice.[42]

The third book ends with the tragic death of the plowing ox, a victim of a violent plague; the plowman frees the surviving ox, and both mourn the death of a "brother" (*fraterna morte*, G. 3.518). At the close of this episode, Vergil reports the death of an unnamed person who attempted to wear the polluted skin of the animal that had died of the plague, polluted as it was by a *sacer ignis*. David Ross has suggested that the forces at work in this plague culminate in fire as a basic elemental force,[43] but the term *sacer ignis* and its application in the last line of the third book also suggests the violent death of Herakles after he, like the unnamed victim here, donned the polluted cloak sent to him by his jealous wife.

In Ovid's description of this episode,[44] there are really two kinds of fire involved in Herakles' death: the pestilential fire of Nessus' poisonous blood, which had been polluted by Herakles' own arrow, tainted previously by the Hydra's blood; and the purifying fire of Herakles' funeral pyre, which consumed only that part of him which was mortal, allowing the divine portion to assume its rightful place among the gods. The notion that the mortal part could be burned away, with immortality remaining, recalls attempts by both Demeter and Isis, when they served as nursemaids to the kings of Eleusis and Byblos, respectively, to burn away the mortality of the royal infants committed to their care.

Finally, the Bougonia at the end of book 4, which begins with the violent death of cattle and the disfigurement of their corpses, and culminates in the miracle of new life, is strikingly similar to the death of Osiris, his mangled corpse, and his eventual restoration as ruler of the dead and giver of the means of sustaining life. And of course, this method of acquiring a new hive of bees, Vergil tells us, is Egyptian:

> nam qua Pellaei gens fortunata Canopi
> accolit effuso stagnantem flumine Nilum
> et circum pictis vehitur sua rura phaselis,
> quaque pharetratae vicinia Persidis urget,
> et diversa ruens septem discurrit in ora
> usque coloratis amnis devexus ab Indis,
> et viridem Aegyptum nigra fecundat harena,
> omnis in hac certam regio iacit arte salutem. (G. 4.287–294)

> For where the blessed race of Macedonian Canopus dwells beside the overflowing banks of the Nile and sails about the countryside in painted skiffs, and where the nearness of the Persian archer restrains it, and the river
> rushes on, dispersed to seven different mouths, as it flows from the colorful Indians and its black sand causes the Egyptian land to flourish —
> All this region relies on this method [of generating bees].

Conclusion

The *Georgics*, which were completed very soon after Actium, retain a number of value-free, or even laudatory, Egyptian and possibly Isiac elements, in contrast to the *Aeneid*, in which all references to things Egyptian are clearly cast in a negative light. The ill repute of Isis and Osiris was of course clearly established by the time Vergil was engaged in composing the epic—Octavian's negative bias is most clearly represented in *Aeneid* 8, where the defeat at Actium of Cleopatra and her Egyptian gods is vividly depicted on Aeneas' shield. There Augustus and Agrippa lead their forces against those of the east, which are led by Antony and his *(nefas!) Aegyptia coniunx* (*Aen.* 8.688). Cleopatra waves her sistrum as she rallies her followers and animal-visaged gods (*omnigenum . . . deum monstra et latrator Anubis, Aen.* 8.698), who are driven into terrified retreat by the great gods of Greece and Rome:

> regina in mediis patrio vocat agmina sistro,
> necdum etiam geminos a tergo respicit anguis.
> omnigenumque deum monstra et latrator Anubis

> contra Neptunum et Venerem contraque Minervam
> tela tenent. (*Aen.* 8.696-700)

In their midst, the queen summons back her forces with her native sistrum, and does not yet see the twin serpents behind her. Every kind of monstrous deity and the dog Anubis raise their weapons against Neptune and Venus and Minerva.

In line 704, "Actian" Apollo decisively defeats the forces of the east:

> Actius haec cernens arcum intendebat Apollo
> desuper; omnis eo terrore Aegyptus et Indi,
> omnis Arabs, omnes vertebant terga Sabaei. (*Aen.* 8.704-706)

Actian Apollo, gazing at these things from above, directs his bow; the whole of Egypt and India, all of Arabia, all the Sabaeans turn away in dread.

Finally, the great river Nile, in mourning (*maerentem*), summons back his branches in defeat:

> contra autem magno maerentem corpore Nilum
> pandentemque sinus et tota veste vocantem
> caeruleum in gremium latebrosaque flumina victos. (*Aen.* 8.711-713)

And on the other side, the river Nile with its great girth, in mourning, spreads its billows and summons to its cerulean bosom and shaded streams the defeated [Egyptians].

A final reference to Apolline victory over Egypt occurs in book 12 of the *Aeneid*, when two otherwise unknown combatants convey, by their very names, Augustus' elevation of Apollo and rejection of the gods of the Nile: in 12.458, the Trojan warrior Thymbraeus kills a Latin warrior named Osiris:

> ferit ense gravem Thymbraeus Osirim.

Thymbraeus strikes Osiris down with his sword.

The epithet "Thymbraeus" appears two other times in Vergil, each time clearly referring to Apollo: in *Aeneid* 3.85, when Anchises prays to Apollo at Delos, the god is addressed as *Thymbrae;* and in *Georgics* 4.323, Aristaeus questions whether his father truly is *Thymbraeus Apollo*. Vergil's decision to name the Latin warrior "Osiris" is thus particularly significant, for this is the only time in all of Vergil's works that he employs the name of this powerful Egyptian deity, and thus this combat scene symbolizes the ultimate victory of the forces of Apollo over the Egyptian foe.

The *Georgics*, by contrast, contain a number of elements suggestive of the mystery religions, and not necessarily in a negative context. Vergil's reference in 4.287 to Egyptians as a *gens fortunata* places them on a par with Vergil's idealized Roman farmer in 2.458–459, whom he addresses as *o fortunatos nimium . . . agricolas!* (cf. *Aen.* 11.252). *Fortunatus* is frequently used to translate ὄλβιος, the adjective regularly applied to Eleusinian initiates,[45] which would include Augustus. By contrast, it would be very surprising to find the adjective being applied to the Egyptian race in the *Aeneid*.

While Hellenistic syncretism, which is certainly evident in Vergil's works, can account for some of the blurred lines between the different cult figures, it seems that Vergil is relatively consistent in favoring allusion to the Greek rather than non-Greek versions of the myths and symbols associated with the mysteries. On the other hand, his allusion to Herakles' Egyptian *labor* rather than to one of the more "Greek" labors suggests that, if Vergil did attempt to remove other Egyptian allusions after Gallus' fall, some of them were too integral to his poem's central topic to be excluded. Servius indicates that Vergil changed the end of the poem to eliminate the *laudes Galli* in the fourth book. The Egyptian elements that remain suggest that, at this stage of Vergil's thinking, Egypt and its gods, despite a recent fall from grace, still embodied for Vergil the nurturing qualities that were so important to their long survival.

Appendix: The Agnone Tablet and Vergil's *Georgics*

The Agnone Tablet[46] sheds interesting light on the selection of deities in the opening invocation of Vergil's *Georgics*. First published in 1848, the Agnone Tablet is a bronze tablet measuring 6½ inches by 11 inches. It is inscribed in Oscan on both sides; the letters are clearly and deeply incised, and the tablet is provided with a carrying handle. The tablet was found between Capracotta and Agnone in the territory of the Caraceni, an area at that time still called *Uorte*, which appears to be derived from *hortus*, the Latin word for "garden" or "sacred grove." (The Oscan word *húrz*, which appears in the first line of side A and in the last line of side B, is also believed to be the equivalent of *hortus*.) The generally accepted date of the tablet is 250 BCE. It is dedicated to the Italic goddess Kerrí, who at some point merges with Roman Ceres.

Other deities are named on the tablet, including Veskeí, thought to be the divinity of the revolving year, and Euklus, who appears again in the last line (25) of side A as *Euklus Pater*. Salmon (1967: 157) identified Euklus as chthonic Mercury (Hermes), the *psychopompos* or guide of souls. Spaeth identifies him as Liber Pater, which would make a nice parallel to Ceres; in fact, that entire line, *evklúi. statíf. kerrí. statíf.*, would then suggest Liber and Ceres, the same pair we find in Varro and in Vergil (cf. G. 1.7). With the epithet *Pater*, we are also reminded of Vergil's *Pater Lenaeae* (G. 2.7), an address to Bacchus in his overview of the pressing of the wine grapes. Prosdocimi, however, identifies Euklus as Hades, whose presence here would also make sense, especially in the context of Ceres and Proserpina, since Hades abducts Proserpina to be his spouse in the underworld.

futrei.kerríiaí. in the following line is widely accepted as a reference to Proserpina, "the daughter of Ceres," with the result that Ceres, her son-in-law Hades, and her daughter Proserpina follow in succession. It also raises questions about the relationship between Liber/Dionysus and Hades—is there a connection? Certainly Dionysus is associated with the underworld—like Proserpina and Attis, he is often listed among the "dying gods," a notion that Frazer applied perhaps too widely, but that, as Burkert (1987: 99) acknowledges, still applies to these figures.

Lines 5 and 6 appear to refer to human fertility: *anter. stataí.* is thought to mean something like Interstita, "Midwife," and *ammaí. Kerríiaí*, sounding vaguely like "mama" (compare *mamma* in Greek or Latin to signify "breast"), may signify breastfeeding or a wet-nurse. Recall Vergil's epithet for Ceres, *Alma*, "nourishing Ceres." Salmon suggests that Inter-stita (Oscan *anter-stataí*) may be "the midwife who stands 'between' when delivering the offspring, whereas (in Latin) she stands 'opposite,' whence [she is called] *obstetrix*" (1967: 159 n. 4).

Maatúis kerríiúis (10) refers to the deity ensuring a supply of dew (more of this later) to the crops. In line 15, *deívaí. genetaí* is understood to mean something like the Latin *genetrix*, "mother," here possibly referring to Ceres as the wife of Jupiter. *Perna Keriaii* may be the goddess of happy childbirth, although Altheim (1931: 92–108) associates her with Anna Perenna, the goddess of the returning year.

Another common epithet for Ceres has been identified in *líganakdíkeí. entraí* (line 8), interpreted as Chthonic Ceres.[47] The word *entraí* (Latin *Intera*) is equated with the Greek ἐνέρτερα, having to do with the underworld. The word *líganakdíkeí.* has been widely accepted (Vetter 1953: 106; Le Bonniec 1958: 42) as the equivalent of the Latin *legifera*, or the Greek θεσμοφόρος, "bringer of law," a common epithet of this goddess. In book 4 of the *Aeneid* (cf. Servius ad *Aen.* 4.58), when Dido is offering a sacrifice to win the love of Aeneas, she makes a particular offering to *Cereri legiferae*. Servius there explains the epithet as indicating that Ceres favors weddings, since she was the first to marry Jupiter, and she is in charge of the founding of cities, the first step of which was to mark their boundaries with the furrow of the plow.[48]

The next group, *diumpaís. Kerríiaís.* (7), *anafríss. kerríiúis* (9), *maatúis. kerríiúis* (10), *diúveí. verehasiúí* (11), and *diúveí. regatúreí* (12), are associated with moisture for the crops. In Varro, *diumpaís. kerríiaís* appear as *Lympha*, "moisture." But *Lympha* is also interpreted as *Nymphae,* in the sense of water nymphs. Prosdocimi (1996: 531) here refers to a "pangreek" or Orphic cult of the Nymphs; mention of the Nymphs again recalls both Proserpina, who is abducted while gathering flowers with the Nymphs, and Eurydice, whom the Nymphs mourn so bitterly at the end of the tale of Orpheus and Eurydice.

In line 9, *anafríss. kerríiúís* is identified as rain (*Imbres*), and in line 10, *maatúis. kerríiúís*, as mentioned earlier, may be dew for the crops. *diúveí.verehasiúí* and *diúveí.regatureí* are two aspects of Jupiter, which Salmon (1967: 158) interprets as Jupiter Juventus, bringer of dew to the crops, and as Jupiter Rigator, "Jupiter the irrigator." Vergil does not refer to water deities in the context of their bringing moisture to the crops, but they are included as Achelous (1.9, the river water that Liber mixed with the grape), Neptune (1.14), and Ocean and Tethys, etc. (1.29–31).

hereklúí. kerríiúí (13) is widely accepted as a reference to Herakles, who is associated with the lesser Eleusinian mysteries, which were said to have been established in his behalf so that he could become initiated from the underworld. Servius has drawn attention to the fact that Vergil's reference to the river Achelous (*G.* 1.9) refers to river water in a general sense, but also alludes to the battle between Herakles and the river god Achelous, who lost one of his horns in their wrestling match. In Ovid's *Metamorphoses*, the broken horn becomes the original cornucopia, but in Vergil, the "Acheloan cups" refer to wine-drinking vessels. Thus Vergil's proem shares yet one more detail with the Agnone Tablet.[49]

In line 14, *patanaí. piístíaí.* seems to suggest something like the deity who opens the grain hull, making it easier to separate the grain from its husks. In Vergil's invocation of Augustus Caesar (25ff.), he suggests the various realms where the future god may choose to rule: over the sea (29ff.), or perhaps (32ff.) he will become a new constellation in the heavens, "where a place is opening (*panditur*) between the constellation Virgo and the pursuing claws of Scorpio, who even now is drawing in his arms to make room for you." Vergil incorporates the idea of "opening"—in this case, the sky—to facilitate Augustus' pending apotheosis, just as the deity Patana on the Agnone Tablet opens the hulls to facilitate access to the grain. The opposite motion of Scorpio, who is closing his claws to make room in the heavens for Augustus, contrasts nicely with the opening of the heavens (or the husks). The reference to the constellation Virgo here not only anticipates Vergil's later allusion in the *Georgics* to Aratus' account of the end of the Golden Age, wherein Virgo, also known as Justice (*Iustitia/Dike/Astraea*), holds a grain of wheat in her hand, because, in Aratus' account of the myth of the Ages, it was Justice/Dike (instead of Chronos, as in Hesiod, or Saturnus, as in Ennius) who ruled over an agriculturally based Golden Age; as the races declined, she retreated from mortal company and finally retreated to the heavens, leaving the last traces (*vestigia*, "footprints") of Justice on earth among farmers:

o fortunatos nimium, sua si bona norint,
agricolas, quibus ipsa procul discordibus armis
fundit humo facilem victum iustissima tellus!
... extrema per illos
Iustitia excedens terris vestigia fecit. (G. 2.458–460, 473–474)

O blessed farmers, if only they knew their blessings!
For them, far from discordant weapons,
most just Earth (Tellus) herself pours forth an easy living....
When she retreated from the earth, Justice left her last traces among them.

Fortunatus, the Latin equivalent of the Greek word ὄλβιος, describes the blessings of initiates into the mysteries of Eleusis:

> Happy (ὄλβιος) is he among men upon earth who has seen these mysteries; but he who is uninitiated and who has no part in them, never has lot of like good things once he is dead, down in the darkness and gloom. (*Hymn Dem.* 480-482)

Lines 16ff. of side A include what appears to be a ritual sequence. It seems to say something about the site being sanctified by an *ara ignaria* or "altar of fire" (*aasaí. purasiaí*), with further instructions for the ritual, including rites being offered near the garden for the Floralia (*fiuusasiaís az.húrtúm. sákaráter*). *Sákaráter* is in the subjunctive mood, and is equivalent to *sanciatur* or *sacrificetur*, "Let it be sanctified." Flora also appears in Varro's list, and perhaps should be considered in the Persephone sequence, since she is picking flowers with the Nymphs at the time of her abduction. Side A concludes with *Pater Euklus*, as I have mentioned, whom Prosdocimi interprets as Hades.

Side B begins with a statement that "these altars are [now] standing" (line 1), followed by the names of the deities for whom the altars now stand, and concluding with a similar reference to the sanctification of the *ara ignaria* (*aasaí. purasiai. saahtum*, ll. 19-20), which now stand in place, as an annual ritual (*alttrei putereipid. akenei*, ll. 21-23). Although it is reasonable to assume that a great many rites had to be performed annually, the provision that these rites must be performed annually recalls Herodotus' account of the episode during the Persian War, in 480 BCE: The Athenians believed their crops would fail if they did not perform the Eleusinian rites annually, but at the time when they had to be performed, the Athenians were on the island Salamis, driven out of Athens by Xerxes and his Persian forces. According to Herodotus (8.65), when the time came for the rites to be performed, the Athenians saw from the island of Salamis that a ghostly procession was making its way from Athens to Eleusis—thus the gods came to their aid and performed the rites for them.

The final line of side B proclaims: *húrz. dekmanniúís staít*: "The garden stands on account of (*per* [It.]) the Dekumanii." The Dekumanii apparently refer to Samnites or Samnite-Roman colonists.

Thus the tablet appears to specify the deities who are to be worshiped on side A, and the establishment of their altars on side B. The pattern of repetition of *statif* suggests a hymn or prayer, a function similar to that of Vergil's invocation.

Death and the Underworld

The Agnone Tablet lists not only aspects of Ceres concerning human and agricultural fertility, but also references to death and the underworld, with particular reference to Persephone and Hades. This is also true of Vergil's proem to the *Georgics*. The last of the options offered to Caesar is that he may choose to rule over the underworld (136ff.): "Whatever you will be—for Tartarus does not expect you as its king—let not so dire a longing to govern come to you, even though Greece admires Elysian Fields, and Proserpina, when summoned, refused to follow her mother." Vergil's statement that Proserpina refused to return to the world above when summoned is contrary to the received tradition, as I have shown elsewhere,[50] comparing Vergil's placement and treatment of both Proserpina here, and Eurydice at the end of the fourth Georgic. Both Proserpina and Eurydice are relegated to the underworld even though, prior to Vergil's account of the story of Orpheus and Eurydice, tradition suggests that Orpheus did succeed in bringing Eurydice back from the dead. Vergil's version, of course, once written, became the *locus classicus*, and thus the alternate versions tended to be forgotten. The word *dives*, "wealth," was said to come from *Dis* (Hades), since the wealth that comes from crops is sent up from below the soil, that is, the underworld. When Orpheus laments the death of Eurydice, he complains of *raptam Eurydicen atque inrita Ditis / dona*—"Stolen Eurydice and the gifts of Dis given in vain" (G. 4.519-520). The crops nourished by Ceres are also *dona Ditis*, and Proserpina herself was known as *dona Ditis*. They are all part of the cycle of birth, death, and regeneration.

Thus both side A of the Agnone Tablet and Vergil's proem open and close with members of the triad consisting of Ceres, Persephone, and Liber or Hades, figures associated with agricultural and human fertility as well as with death and regeneration. The parallel indicates not only Vergil's familiarity with Hellenistic traditions, as some commentators will maintain, but also his deep awareness of the rituals of the Italic goddess of grain.

Notes

1. E.g., Wilkinson 1969: 121ff.; Bailey 1935; Boyancé 1963; Conington and Nettleship [1898] 1963; Farrell 1991; Mynors 1990; Putnam 1979; Thomas 1988.

2. Walter Burkert (1987) also includes the Mithraic cult, which is not significant in Vergil's time, if indeed the cult did exist at that time, although the later association of Mithras with Apollo, who is of course very important in the early Empire, is interesting to note.

3. Graillot 1912: 115; Bailey 1935: 177; Zanker 1990: 17; Wilhelm 1988: 77ff.

4. Zanker 1990: 109.

5. Cf. Henrichs 1993: 13-43.

6. The early linkage of Liber and Ceres, as well as Proserpina and Herakles, is dramatically illustrated on the Tabula Agnone, a bronze tablet dated to 250 BCE. For details, see Appendix A.

7. Thomas 1988, 1: ad 2.380-383, p. 226.

8. Henrichs 1993: 22.

9. Cf. ibid.: 31 n. 45. Henrichs observes that Detienne associates Dionysus' "beneficial presence with Athens and his destructive visitations with the Argolid, Boeotia and Thrace," whereas Henrichs believes "this particular polarity has more to do with the different articulations of Dionysus in myth and cult."

10. Burton 1972: 98.

11. Dio Cass. 51.4.1; cf. Clinton 1989.

12. Cf. Callim. *Hymn* 6.21.

13. Cf. Farrell 1991: 76: "[Vergil's] farmer is not only general, but priest presiding with sacred implements over rites founded by Celeus, Iacchus, and the goddess of Eleusis."
14. Johnston 1977.
15. Bayet 1951: 9-11; cf. Le Bonniec 1958: 134ff.; Wilkinson 1969: 149.
16. Clinton, (1986: 43-49) argues that the author of the mysteries may have been an initiate, but does not reflect the cult myth; cf. Clinton 1992: 35. (Note that Clinton distinguishes between Plouton and Hades.)
17. Cf. Cic. N.D. 2.66.
18. Johnston 1977: 161-172.
19. Griffiths 1970: 42-43.
20. Cf. Hdt. 2.59, 61; Plut. Is. Os. 356.
21. Griffiths (1970: 54) observes that the swallows seem to be Astarte's, even though they may also have Egyptian antecedents.
22. "The boucranion was originally the head-dress of Hathor, but with the frequent identification of the two goddesses, it was commonly worn by Isis, too. One result was the identification of Isis and Io, whom Zeus was said to have changed into a cow" (Griffiths 1970: 351 ad 358b19).
23. Cf. Forbes Irving 1990: 211-216; and Seaford 1980: 23-29.
24. Thomas 1988, 2:69.
25. Hesiod frr. 124-126, 294-296; Merkelbach and West 1970; Austin (1977: 31) notes that the epithet, as a reference to Cumae's Chalcidian founders, is anachronistic.
26. Thomas 1988, 2:235.
27. Forbes Irving 1990: 215.
28. Mylonas 1961: 15-16.
29. Griffiths 1970: 54.
30. Proteus is called Αἰγύπτιος in Homer, and is said to live on the island of Pharos. In Herodotus (2.112), he is a mortal king living in Memphis. In Euripides' *Helen*, he is king of Pharos; cf. Burton 1972: 182-183; Thomas 1988, 2:217-218.
31. Thomas 1988, 2:233.
32. Cf. Ovid *Met* 6.669-670; Verg. *Ecl.* 6.78-81.
33. Thomas 1988, 2:235.
34. Plutarch records (*Is. Os.* 358e) that in some versions, Isis' child, Horus, is, like Orpheus, dismembered. In some accounts Dionysus is a descendant of Io/Isis. Note that Diodorus Siculus (4.25.1) refers to Orpheus as a hierophant at Eleusis. Cf. Griffiths 1970: 441-442 ad Plut. *Is. Os.* 37.365B.
35. Thomas (1988, 2:37-39, ad G. 3.3-8) believes these are allusions to Callimachean versions; Mynors observes (1990: 179) that, Hellenistic or not, the connection between these tales and *Georgics* 3 is Pelops' expertise with horses, and that Herakles was "an expert cleaner-out of cow-byres."
36. Burton 1972: 103.
37. Diod. Sic. 1.85.5; Plut. *Is. Os.* 20. Diodorus Siculus (1.88.5) claims that Busiris is Egyptian for τοῦ Ὀσίριδος τάφους, which is in fact correct (Burton 1972: 14-15).
38. Burton 1972: 15; Hdt. 2.59: "Second in importance [to Bubastis] is the assembly at Busiris—a city in the middle of the Delta, containing a vast temple dedicated to Isis, the Egyptian equivalent of Demeter, in whose honor the meeting is

held." Hdt. 2.61: "I have already mentioned the festival of Isis at Busiris." Diod. Sic. 1.85: "Some explain the origin of the honor accorded this bull in this way, saying that at the death of Osiris his soul passed into this animal, and therefore up to this day has always passed into its successors at the time of the manifestation of Osiris; but some say that when Osiris died at the hands of Typhon, Isis collected the members of his body and put them in an ox (*bous*), made of wood covered over with fine linen, and because of this the city was called Bousiris."

39. Mylonas 1961: 240: "The Lesser Mysteries were instituted for the benefit of Herakles when he wanted to be initiated ... from the Lesser Hades."

40. E.g., Cic. *N.D.* 3.42ff.

41. Cf. Ovid *Fasti* 1.551; Propertius 4.10; Livy 1.7; Dion. Hal. *Ant. Rom.* 1.9.

42. Cf. Aratus *Phaen.* 2.536-537; Johnston 1980: 25-28.

43. Ross 1987: 177-183.

44. Ovid *Met.* 9.176-178, 181-185; cf. Sen. *De benef.* 4.8.

45. Cf. *Hymn Dem.* 480-482: "Happy is he among men upon earth who has seen these mysteries; but he who is uninitiated and who has no part in them, never has lot of like good things once he is dead, down in the darkness and gloom"; Soph. fr. 541 (Nauck); Pindar fr. 121 (Bowra); etc.

46. Prosdocimi 1996: 435-630.

47. Note that in *Aen.* 6.138, Proserpina is referred to as Juno Inferna. Zuntz, in his book *Persephone* (1971: 399-400, not referring to this tablet), takes strong exception to the notion that "Demeter Chthonios" associates her with the underworld; he maintains that it merely associates the goddess with the soil over which she rules.

48. Cf. Spaeth 1996: 53.

49. Jean Bayet (*Les Origines de l'Hercule romain* [Paris, 1926], 121; cf. Salmon 1967: 160 n. 6) suggested that at Agnone, Hercules is *Héraclès fécondant*—a fertilizing force.

50. Johnston 1977.

PART III

MITHRAS

CHAPTER 15

The Amor and Psyche Relief in the Mithraeum of Capua Vetere: An Exceptional Case of Graeco-Roman Syncretism or an Ordinary Instance of Human Cognition?

LUTHER H. MARTIN

The "main characteristic feature of Hellenistic religion[s]" such as Mithraism has been described as "syncretism," as has the entire Hellenistic age (Grant 1953: xiii). However, the utility of this category of syncretism, usually understood as some sort of mutual influence upon a religious practice or representation by two (or more) cultures in contact, is contested. If employed as an explanatory category, as it often is, it explains nothing. From a historical perspective, *all* religions are syncretistic, that is, constituted of temporal antecedents and influenced by contemporaneous contingencies. Even when used as a descriptive category, consequently, "syncretism" is simply the redundant naming of a historically constructed conundrum to be explained (Martin 1983; see now Leopold and Jensen 2004 for an excellent historical and theoretical overview of uses of this category). If, then, we begin with the notion of Hellenistic syncretism as a problem to be explained, the Amor and Psyche relief in the Mithraeum of Capua Vetere, the only known presence of these popular Greek figures in a sanctuary devoted to the Roman deity Mithras, would appear to present an exceptional case indeed.

The Amor and Psyche Relief in the Mithraeum of Capua Vetere

The small (32 × 36 cm), white marble relief of Amor and Psyche in the Mithraeum of Capua Vetere portrays the nude, winged child Amor leading the larger (adult) female figure of Psyche, also winged, by the light of his torch (Fig. 15.1). He grasps Psyche's left arm with his right hand while holding the torch in his left (*CIMRM* 186: see Merkelbach 1984: 296,

Figure 15.1. Amor and Psyche. Photo by Patricia A. Johnston.

Abb. 27; Vermaseren 1971: 23 and pl. 20). Psyche wears an ankle-length diaphanous dress, the hem of which she holds in her right hand. As in conventional representations of the pair, the wings of Amor are birdlike, whereas those of Psyche are butterfly wings. Unlike conventional representations, the feminine attributes of Psyche have been moderated, giving her a more masculine appearance (Merkelbach 1984: 82). The relief, highlighted by a red border painted on the wall around it, was probably inserted in the wall of the Mithraeum during its first period of use, during the early to mid-second century CE (Vermaseren 1971: 49–50, 50 n. 1).

Little discussion has been devoted to the significance of the Capuan Amor and Psyche relief. Reinhold Merkelbach considers Psyche to be a representation of the enigmatic "nymphus," the second grade of Mithraic initiation (Merkelbach 1982: 24; 1984: 88–92), and Amor to be that of Heliodromus, the sixth grade of the initiation (Merkelbach 1984: 92)—though he offers little evidence for these conclusions.[1]

More interestingly, Richard Gordon emphasizes that the position of the relief in the Capua Mithraeum is above a niche at the longitudinal center of the left (southern) bench of the Mithraeum. He suggests that such niches, which mark the center of benches along the two side walls in virtually all

Mithraic temples, represent the solstices that, according to Porphyry, are the gates by which souls enter and depart the cosmos (Porph. *Antr.* 2). Following Porphyry, Gordon argues that souls descend into this world of being through the "northern" gate and re-ascend through the "southern" gate (Porph. *Antr.* 24–25)—"north" and "south" referring here to the astrological orientations of the cosmos represented in the formal structure of Mithraic temples and not to the actual cardinal points (Gordon 1996b: 56). In this astrological interpretation, the Capuan Amor and Psyche relief is located above the niche marking the "southern" portal of the soul's re-ascent (Gordon 1996b: 56–58; so also Beck 2000b: 162 n. 69).[2] While Eros (Amor) is traditionally associated with freeing the soul from the conditions of this existence (Schlam 1976: 31), the implication of the Capuan relief is that the re-ascent of the soul is under the guidance of a winged Amor as well. Indeed, Porphyry characterizes the north winds, which he considers to assist in the descent of the soul, as *erōtikos* (Porph. *Antr.* 26; Gordon 1996b: 56–58). This descent of the soul, its subsequent trials, and its final ascent may represent a process for its purification for which initiation into the mysteries is an analogue (Schlam 1976: 19).

The Possibilities of Historical (Syncretistic) Influences on the Capuan Amor and Psyche Relief within Magna Graecia

Already Hesiod had elevated Eros, one of the oldest of the gods, into a cosmic principle that was all-powerful over younger gods and men (Hes. *Theog.* 118–120). Similarly, the fifth-century BCE philosopher, Parmenides of Elea, presented Eros as first of all the gods (Parm. 13) and, consequently, as the cosmic power of love and procreation. Following Parmenides' logic that "there can be no real coming to be nor passing away" (Parm. 2; Burkert 1985: 319), a monistic view of the soul follows that is similar to that reported of Mithraism by Porphyry (Porph. *Antr.* 25; cf., e.g., Pl. *Phd.* 79C-D). Of course, this view of a cosmic descent and re-ascent of an immortal soul was, in some form or another, an increasingly common feature of Hellenistic religions, culminating in Neoplatonism.[3]

A further possible association of the Amor and Psyche relief in the Capua Vetere Mithraeum with the Eleatic tradition of Parmenides is that its representation of Amor leading Psyche by torchlight is an apparent allusion to representations of initiation into the mysteries. In the proem of his poem (Parm. 1), Parmenides seems to employ such representations of initiation to articulate his understanding of the unity of contrasts, such as that between death and life (Nussbaum 1996: 1113; see Parm. 19).

Parmenides' native city, Elea (modern Castellammare di Velia), was one of the first Greek colonies of Magna Graecia. Although conquered by Rome in 290 BCE, Elea retained its Greek culture until the first century CE (Lomas 1996: 516). The city is but 153 kilometers (94 miles) southeast of Capua. Thus, an influence upon the Mithraic community of Capua by an Eleatic tradition about a procreative and initiatory figure of Eros presiding over a cosmic descent/ascent of the eternal soul is a historical possibility.

Further, the earliest Greek monuments representing Amor and Psyche also expressed a view of the immortality of the soul (Schlam 1976: 25), and the earliest representations of the pair are from the Greek cities of Magna Graecia—although the wings of the female figure accompanying Eros are those of a bird (Schlam 1976: 5). Portrayals of Psyche with butterfly wings, as on the Capuan relief, first appeared in the Crimea in the late fourth or early third century but became increasingly popular during the Hellenistic period, as documented, for example, by numerous instances in the vicinity of Capua, for example, nearby Pompeii (Schlam 1976: 20-21).

If the Capuan relief was influenced by ideas about the descent and ascent of an immortal soul derived from the Greek Eleatic tradition, this influence would support Gordon's interpretation with reference to the location of the relief in the Mithraeum. And this influence would also introduce a relationship between this view of the soul and the figures of Amor and Psyche, a relationship documented also from the material culture of Magna Graecia.

If, however, the Amor and Psyche relief represents the possibility of Greek influence within the Mithraic community of Capua, its masculinized figure of Psyche seems to reflect a Mithraic influence upon this classical motif as well—an expected modification by a cult that excluded female participants (Gordon 2005b: 6090).[4] And if this relief is a re-representation of a classical motif in a way that reflects specific aspects of Mithraic practice, then it must be an intentional representation that cannot be explained as a random consequence of cultural contact (syncretism), or dismissed, as in the conclusion of Gordon, as a "marginal gloss" (Gordon 1994: 121 n. 88).

Historical Evidence outside of Magna Graecia for Mithraic Associations with Amor and Psyche

Though rare, there is some documentation for associations between Amor-Psyche and Mithras apart from that of the Capuan relief. For example, a fragmentary statue of Amor and Psyche was found in the Mithraic excavations at Santa Prisca in Rome. It is not known, however, whether this statue was associated with the Mithraic community there or whether it was simply "fill" from the demolition of an earlier structure. As the Roman architect Vitruvius noted, stone from demolished buildings, including sculpture, was often broken up and used in the concrete foundations of new construction (Vitr. 6.8.1-7). The excavators of the Santa Prisca Mithraeum, Maarten Vermaseren and Carel van Essen, simply describe the statue as one of the "stray finds from the right hand part of" one of the side rooms off the Mithraeum proper (Vermaseren and van Essen 1965: 476; 478, no. 275). The significance of this find, therefore, while suggestive, is inconclusive.

Of more interest is the "Tale of Amor and Psyche," the centerpiece of Apuleius' well-known Isis novel, *Metamorphoses*,[5] in which the priest of Isis is named "Mithras" (*Met.* 11.22; see *CIMRM* 466). Roger Beck, elaborating upon an earlier suggestion by Filippo Coarelli (1989), has argued that the Apuleius who authored the *Metamorphoses* may well be the same Apuleius whose house in Ostia is proximate to the Mithraeum of the Seven Spheres (Beck 2000a). If so, the author may well have been involved in the Mithraic mysteries and, consequently, his (fictive?) association of Isis (and of Amor-Psyche) with Mithras would be of more interest than just employment of a suggestive name.

The only clear parallel to the Capuan relief is the fragment of a yellow jasper gem with a portrayal of Mithras as the ubiquitous bullslayer (the tauroctony) on one side; on its obverse is a depiction of Amor and Psyche surrounded by the inscription ΝΕΙΧΑΡΟΠΛΗΞ (*CIMRM* 2356). Armand Delatte writes that all examples of this inscription on gems refer either to a deity whose solar character is clear—for example, to Mithras, Isis, or Leontocephales—or to representations of Amor, either alone or in conjunction with Psyche (Delatte 1914: 14). Further, Charles King, in his classic study *Antique Gems,* notes that yellow jasper was a "favorite material for the extensive series of intagli connected with the worship of Mithras" (King 1860: 338). Unfortunately, neither the provenance nor the present location of this gem is known. And while the exact role of Psyche in the relationship portrayed on the gem remains unclear,[6] the implication is that Amor and Mithras were, in the minds of some, at least equivalent.

Taken together, the historical evidence—the presence of the Capuan relief in a Mithraeum, the influences from Magna Graecia upon that relief, and the lost gem—suggests that the Amor of the Capuan relief was intended as a representation of Mithras, and/or of his surrogate, the initiating Pater, who guides and supports with paternal love the descendant soul of the initiate through his initiatory trials toward a goal of re-ascent.

Since, however, the Greek influences upon the relief, while certainly possible, are not verifiable, and since the provenance of the gem is unknown and its relevance for the significance of the relief is not, therefore, demonstrable, such a synthetic conclusion remains highly speculative. As the anthropologist Fredrik Barth has concluded, "A historical viewpoint [in and of itself] holds no magic key" for solving cultural puzzles without a reasonably sound and detailed account of the empirical processes whereby these materials are produced, transformed, and transmitted (Barth 1987: 9, 22; see Martin 2001).

More tantalizingly, the historical evidence *does* demonstrate that an association of Amor and Psyche with Mithras had, in the early centuries of the Roman Empire, crossed the minds of at least some apart from those of the Capuan Mithraic community. It is, in other words, not just the possibilities of historical influence but also the possibilities of human minds that constitute those *res gestae* and their surviving representations that we term history. In the absence, therefore, of any conclusive account of the empirical (historical) processes whereby such a representation as the Capuan Amor and Psyche relief was produced, I turn to the cognitive scientists to explore whether their empirical investigations into the workings of human minds might be of help. The question raised thereby of the relief, then, is not whether historical possibilities for explaining its presence and significance in the context of the Capua Mithraeum can be documented; they can. The question is, What kind of mind does it take actually to realize these historical possibilities, and do we have any kind of evidence for that kind of mind in that kind of context?

The Mind of the Mithraist

Cognitive scientists seek to explain the kinds of mental representations, both perceptual and conceptual, that the innate capacities of and constraints upon the cerebral processing of sensory stimuli and sentient input allow. They attempt, further, to explain the memory, transmission, and transformations of these mental representations, and the relationships among them. Employing some of the conclusions of the cognitive sciences, I argue that the Capuan Amor and Psyche relief represents a conscious and intentional re-representation of a classical mythic theme in a Mithraic context. Further, I argue that this re-representation was made possible as a consequence of quite ordinary, and predicable, cognitive processes such as that described by developmental cognitivist Annette Karmiloff-Smith (1992).

According to Karmiloff-Smith, the re-representational process, which recurs throughout childhood development, is "a specifically human way to gain knowledge." By redescribing its own representations, "or, more precisely, by iteratively re-presenting in different representational formats what its internal representations represent," the mind, according to Karmiloff-Smith, exploits "internally the information that it has already stored (both innate and acquired)" (Karmiloff-Smith 1992: 15).[7] Although this developmental process of representational redescription is, for Karmiloff-Smith, primarily endogenous, she notes that "clearly the process may at times be triggered by external influences" (Karmiloff-Smith 1992: 18). I should like to suggest that this childhood developmental process, which Karmiloff-Smith attributes to some kinds of new learning among adults as well (Karmiloff-Smith 1992: 18), is replicated in and exploited by the Mithraic course of initiation. By this explanation, the Mithraic course of initiation allowed for the personal (internalized) knowledge acquired by an initiate through initiation to become externalized and consciously manipulated. The resultant cognitive flexibility would allow a Mithraic initiate the intentional ability to produce such seemingly extraordinary representations as the Amor and Psyche relief.[8]

I have argued elsewhere that Mithraism belongs to a "mode of religiosity" that is termed by the cognitive anthropologist Harvey Whitehouse "imagistic" (2004). Imagistic modalities of religion, as described by Whitehouse, should not be misunderstood as simply designating a category of religious traditions that employ images, which, of course, virtually all do. Rather, in Whitehouse's description, this modality is characterized by a diversity of precepts and practices that are based on local knowledge, that are associated with small-scale, face-to-face groups, and that are transmitted through infrequently performed rituals, especially through emotionally salient initiation rites. These traits of social organization and ritual practice seem to accord well with what is known of Mithraism (Martin 2005).

The rites of initiation by which knowledge in such groups is produced and transmitted have been described as "rites of terror" (Whitehouse 2000: 21–33). Such initiation rites were characteristic of Mithraism as well (Martin 2004; 2005) and are dramatically portrayed in the painted scenes of initiation along the front surfaces of the right (northern) bench of the Capua Vetere Mithraeum—the direction of descent into this world in its astrological symbolism. These scenes have been dated in the first half of the third century CE, following an enlargement of the benches somewhat earlier (Vermaseren 1971: 50–51).

In the first two of the Capuan initiatory scenes, a Mithraic initiate is depicted as blindfolded and naked (Vermaseren 1971: pl. XXI) and as menaced, subsequently, by sword and/or by fire (Vermaseren 1971: pl. XXII; *CIMRM* 198). Until recently, these scenes were considered the only extant portrayal of these rites (Vermaseren 1971: 24). In 1976, however, a large crater was discovered in a Mithraeum in Mainz that confirms that some form of initiatory threat was a feature of Mithraic initiation generally (Beck 2000b; Horn 1994). In a scene on this cup, an initiating Father aims an arrow from his drawn bow directly at the head of the initiate, who, like the initiate in the Capuan scenes, is portrayed as smaller, naked, and vulnerable (Beck 2000b: pl. XIII). The emotional salience of such terrifying rituals would be further heightened by techniques of sensory deprivation, typical of initiatory experiences generally, such as blindfolding the initiate and/or situating his initiation in a darkened chamber. The Mithraic community at Capua apparently practiced such techniques, as attested by the Capuan initiatory scenes and by the underground site of the Mithraeum.

These initiatory rites of terror produce personal inspirations or individual "revelations" in the form of "patterned screen[s] of representations and feelings against which later insights and revelations . . . [may] be projected" (Whitehouse 2000: 30).[9] Cognitively, these analogical representations are encoded in the autobiographical memory system and are only activated and organized by the rememberer when presented with stimuli associated with his participation in the initiatory rites, such as relevant persons, images, and/or events.[10] In the case of Mithraism, these stimuli would include, and be reinforced by, an initiate's further participation in subsequent stages of initiation either as initiate or as initiator.[11]

The internal representations occasioned by initiatory rites, as described by Whitehouse, would not, according to Karmiloff-Smith's developmental model, initially be available to conscious access and verbal report (Karmiloff-Smith 1992: 22; for Whitehouse's own perspective on the relationship between Karmiloff-Smith's model and his own, see Whitehouse 2004: 89–94 and 115–117). According to Karmiloff-Smith's model, representations of knowledge in this initial phase are "simply added, domain specifically, to the existing stock" of stored (or remembered) knowledge (Karmiloff-Smith 1992: 18). She describes this initial phase as an "internally driven phase" during which external input ceases to be the focus and a "system-internal dynamics take over." Although this "system-internal dynamics" may culminate in a relevant "behavioral mastery"—of ritual procedures, for example—its encoding in autobiographical memory will have minimal effect, if any, on knowledge previously encoded in working memory (Karmiloff-Smith 1992: 18–19). Given, in other words, two "procedures for analyzing and responding to stimuli in the external environment"—ordinary and initiatory knowledge about the world, for example—the "potential representational links and the information embedded in [the] procedures remain implicit" (Karmiloff-Smith 1992: 20).

Additionally, the ritual production of internal representations might be described as an exploitation of innate cognitive systems or templates by its introduction of selected stimuli. One of the cognitive systems that was exploited by Mithraism is, I suggest, that relating to place and environment. As a consequence of our evolutionary history, human beings—like all species—require, in order to survive, rather detailed information about their complex, natural surroundings. And, like all species, our mental capacities are exquisitely attuned to processing just those environmental stimuli required to establish the parameters of actions necessary for that survival (Boyer 2001: 120-121). The intelligence of *Homo sapiens*, consequently, gravitates naturally to spatial organization—a cognitive ability especially developed in males (Sherry 2000).

The Mithraic temples themselves, designed, according to Porphyry, as a "likeness of the cosmos" (Porph. *Antr.* 6), exploited a syntax of place and environment (as described by Gordon 1996b), as did the Mithraic tauroctony, a collage of artistic clichés organized as a "star-map or 'celestial template'" (Beck 1998: 125). This Mithraic representation of cosmic space effectively exploited the innate cognitive sensitivity of its male membership to spatial location by reflecting and situating the initiate in an astrological/astronomical organization of the cosmos that was typical of the Hellenistic cultural environment (Martin 1987). In this first representational format, however, intuitive experiences of location could not, according to Karmiloff-Smith's model, be either generalized or articulated.

In a second format of re-representation, according to Karmiloff-Smith, initial representations become "reduced" in a way that causes them to lose many of their details; they become simpler and less specialized but more cognitively flexible. The rich, evocative complexity of the Mithraeum as cosmos, for example, could become realized as a safe and controlled space. The cognitive flexibility that is characteristic of conceptual representations at this stage can, according to Karmiloff-Smith, be employed for other goals where explicit knowledge is required (Karmiloff-Smith 1992: 21.) Thus, internal representations of spatial organization and order produced by Mithraic initiation could be transferred, for example, to an affirmation of loyalty to the wider ideals of a *pax Romana* (Merkelbach 1984: 153-188), though yet without any explicitly conscious reflection.

Finally, in a further stage of redescription, "knowledge is recoded into a cross-system code . . . [that is] close enough to natural language for easy translation into stable, communicable form" (Karmiloff-Smith 1992: 23). Once the ordinary cognitive process of redescription has taken place and "explicit representations become manipulable," Karmiloff-Smith concludes, violations might be introduced into data-driven, veridical descriptions of the world (Karmiloff-Smith 1992: 22). Such violations would include those counterfactual and counterintuitive representations and formulations that are characteristic of every religion (Boyer 2001) — and, I might add, of their inventive or, if I may, their "syncretistic" representations — such as that exemplified by the Capuan Amor and Psyche relief.

The cognitive possibilities for representing the Capuan Amor and Psyche theme in a Mithraic context could, I suggest, only have been a conscious and intentional consequence of a cognitively mature, flexible, and innovative mind, such as would have been inculcated by the Mithraic course of initiation. The mind of the anonymous Mithraist responsible for this relief would seem to be, therefore, that of one of the highest of the grades of Mithraic initiation, perhaps that of the (in this case anonymous) Pater himself. Although the possibility for representing Amor and Psyche with Mithras was, as we have seen, both a historical and a cognitive possibility elsewhere than at Capua, the full significance of the Capuan relief would, in the absence of any centralized organizational structure for Mithraism, belong to (and largely remain) the local knowledge of those who had shared in the initiatory regimen practiced by the Capuan Mithraic community.[12]

Conclusion

Mithraism was a new Roman religion in an expanding world of Roman cultural influence. The Mithraic community at Capua represented one of the earliest and southernmost incursions of "Romanness" into Magna Graecia. At the same time that Mithraism represented the growing and expanding dominance of Roman culture, its ritual regimen offered its potential recruits, the generally uneducated lower ranks of the military and the petty civil servants who dominated its membership, an incremental possibility for expanded cognitive flexibility and creativity that was elsewhere available only through alternative, class-differentiated techniques such as formal education.[13] The competitive advantage of such a supple and innovative mind is clear, especially among members of the military, who must deal quickly and decisively with the rapidly changing conditions of battlefield strategy, and even among the local Roman bureaucrats, who had to administer an often discontented population. The difference is one of doing things creatively and with greater self-reliance rather than merely acting in conventional and expected ways.[14]

By this interpretation, Mithraic initiation did not transmit any coherent corpus of Mithraic or "mystery" knowledge (apart, of course, from the local knowledge developed by each Mithraic cell). Rather, the Mithraic course of initiation, whatever its local variants, accomplished an increase in and potentially a perfection of a particular cognitive skill, of the innate capacity of human cognition to achieve "representational flexibility and control" (Karmiloff-Smith 1992: 16). It is perhaps the cognitive and material products of this expanded cognitive flexibility, control, and creativity that have been dismissed by some observers as examples of syncretistic nonsense but perceived by others as the "wisdom" of the mysteries.

AUTHOR'S NOTE: An earlier version of this paper was presented to the Symposium Cumanum, sponsored by The Vergilian Society, 9–12 June 2004, at the Villa Vergiliana in Cuma, Italy, on the theme "Interactions of Indigenous and Foreign Cults in Magna Graecia." I should like to thank Professors Giovanni Casadio and Patricia Johnston, the organizers of this symposium, for inviting my participation, the participants in the symposium for their responses to my presentation, and Roger Beck, Harvey Whitehouse, and Donald Wiebe for their comments on its first draft.

Notes

1. *Nymphus* is a masculinized form of the feminine Greek noun *nymphē*. Like the masculinized figure of Psyche represented on the Capuan relief, this masculine form of the noun also appears only in a Mithraic context (Merkelbach 1984: 88; see 77 n. 2). *Nymphē* can mean either "bride" or the "pupa of bees or wasps." Merkelbach concludes, apparently by association, that this masculine neologism means "human pupa" and refers to the second stage of Mithraic initiation. We might also cite the monograph on Cupid and Psyche by Carl Schlam (1976), in which he noted that the imagery of the pupa "suggests a concept of the immortality of the soul, rising from the body like the chrysalis from the pupa." Further, and referencing the neglected article on this topic by Otto Immisch (1915), Schlam concludes that "Greek terms for earlier stages of the cycle of the butterfly support this interpretation" (Schlam 1976: 8). We can also note that Porphyry uses *nymphai*, which he equates with "pleasure-seeking bees," to refer to souls seeking birth: Porph. *Antr.* 18.

2. Gordon correctly identifies the location of the Psyche and Amor relief as "fixed into the front wall of the [southern] *left hand* 'bench'" (Gordon 1996b: 57), which is associated, in his interpretation, with the re-ascent of souls. In what can only be understood as a typographical error, however, he then writes that the

relief is "directly above the niche which is, on the present hypothesis, the appropriate one for souls entering genesis" (ibid.), that is, of descent into the world of becoming, which in his interpretation is associated with the northern *right hand* bench (ibid.: 56).

3. A commentary on Plato's *Parmenides* is attributed to Porphyry.

4. On the possible initiation of women into some Mithraic associations, see David 2000. At the Cuma symposium at which this paper was presented, Giovanni Casadio called my attention to and kindly supplied me with a copy of a photograph showing a scene from a Mithraeum in Budapest in which Mithras is portrayed grasping the hand of (leading?) a nude figure (initiate?) that is unmistakably female (Póczy et al. 1989: 25).

5. A marble group of Eros and Psyche has been found in the Isaeum at Savaria—modern Szombathely—in western Hungary (Vermaseren 1971: 23 and n. 4).

6. It can be mentioned that the so-called Mithras Liturgy from the *Greek Magical Papyri* opens with an invocation of Psyche (*PMag.* 1.475), though Psyche is here paired with Pronoia. Some scholars have read *Tychē* for *Psychē* (Betz 2003: 88–89).

7. Cognitive innateness, like biological structure, does not (necessarily) imply a direct causal connection between genetic inheritance and adult behavior. One cognitivist, Michael Tomasello, has cautioned that "the search for the innate aspects of human cognition is scientifically fruitful to the extent, and only to the extent, that it helps us to understand the developmental processes at work during human ontogeny" (Tomasello 1999: 51). He addresses Karmiloff-Smith's (1992) hypothesis as a possible description of one such developmental process (Tomasello 1999: 194–197). The philosopher Andy Clark has emphasized the crucial importance for developmental processes of structured environmental resources upon innate cognitive capacities (Clark 1997).

8. I do not argue that Mithraic initiation replicates in any precise way the specific developmental formats of representational redescription modeled by Karmiloff-Smith, nor am I qualified to argue for the validity for her specific model. My suggestion is simply that the incremental process of Mithraic initiation replicates a developmental process of cognitive maturation like that described by Karmiloff-Smith.

9. The production of internal representations by initiatory rites and any "spontaneous exegetical reflections" (Whitehouse 2003: 305) upon them stand in stark contrast to the knowledge maintained and transmitted within a second mode of religiosity described by Whitehouse and termed by him "doctrinal." In this modality, large-scale, anonymous communities cohere around bodies of teachings and beliefs held to be "orthodox" by a centralized authority and are maintained and transmitted by that authority through repetitive and routinized ritual instruction (Whitehouse 2004).

10. Because rites of initiation are considered to be performed by the deity itself, in this case by Mithras, or by his authorized surrogate, probably, in the case, by the presiding Pater, the cognitivists of religion E. Thomas Lawson and Robert N. McCauley have characterized such rites as "special agent rituals." Because such rituals are considered to be performed by the deity himself (or by his surrogate), they are considered to be especially efficacious and, consequently, need be performed but

once or, at most, infrequently. Such singularly potent events of divine activity are accompanied by heightened sensory pageantry that contributes, consequently, to their memorability (McCauley and Lawson 2002: 26–33).

11. Whether initiation rites involve an extended series of trials over a period of months (or years), as is the case among a number of tribal societies, e.g., the Nkanu of Angola and the Democratic Republic of the Congo (Eickel 2001; van Damme 2002), or whether they are structured by a discrete number of stages, as in Mithraism and a number of other tribal societies, e.g., the Baktaman of Papua New Guinea, who, like (at least some of) the Mithraists, count seven grades of initiation (Barth 1987: 12), they should not be viewed as an event or a series of events but as a process that occurs over time. As a cognitive process, what is required is a sufficient period of time over which the cognitive process of representational redescription, as described by Karmiloff-Smith (1992), might be reinforced and developed. This cognitive process is further reinforced by the repeated participation of initiates as initiators.

12. Emphasis on the local character of Mithraic knowledge and practice did not preclude the "emergence" of certain more widely, even universally, shared Mithraic traits and practices from among the network of autonomous Mithraic cells, even in the absence of any centralized structure or organization. On noncentralized processes of biological and cognitive emergence, "in which some kind of higher-level pattern emerges from the interactions of multiple simple components without the benefit of a leader, controller, or orchestrator" (Clark 1997: 73), see Clark 1997: 72–75, 103–128, 163–166; and Johnson 2001.

13. Whereas such rites as the course of Mithraic initiation encouraged and supported the development and expansion of cognitive capacity, formal education included, in addition, an intellectual mastery of some prescribed content (Clark 1997: 205).

14. Today, we might refer to such honed but nonschooled knowledge as "street smarts."

CHAPTER 16

The Mithraic Body: The Example of the Capua Mithraeum

RICHARD GORDON

Within the now considerable corpus of scholarship devoted to the antique body, the Roman cult of Mithras has been prominent mainly by its absence.[1] Neglect is not difficult to explain. The obsession with deciphering the "true" meaning of the cult relief, the identification of the cult as an "astral religion," the fixation upon origins, the silence of the literary sources, our ignorance of Mithraic ritual practice, and more important still, the difficulty of adapting a theoretical discourse elaborated elsewhere for a cult attested almost solely through archaeology and the uncertain value of the results to be expected—all these factors have contributed to this neglect. Moreover, the cult's initiatory character has encouraged the assumption that the function of initiation was primarily discursive, to impart a specifiable quantum of Mithraic lore expressible in discrete constatives. Against this background, the potential value of taking the body as our point of entry is that it allows us to raise the issue of whether initiation in this cult gave rise to a type of knowledge or understanding that can be termed specifically Mithraic. In this chapter I wish to suggest that it did, in that important aspects of Mithraic identity could only be transmitted effectively "through action, enactment, performance," not through language.[2]

As with all treatments of the ancient body, we are dealing in the case of the cult of Mithras only with mediated or represented, and thus constructed and notional, male bodies. Even with this proviso, however, the material, textual and iconographic, available for exploitation is wretchedly small. Reliable textual evidence, so important, for example, in relation to the cult of the martyrs (Grig 2004), fails entirely.[3] By comparison with the iconographic material from other "universal" cults in the Roman Empire, those of the Mater Magna and Isis in particular, there are almost no images of Mithraists: the complete—and most curious—absence of

Mithraic funerary iconography is one reason for this; another is the absence of relevant narrative or "documentary" panel paintings from Pompeii or Herculaneum. To an overwhelming degree, the surviving Mithraic body is, as it were, the body of Mithras himself; Mithraic art directs the implied gaze almost exclusively toward the god and, as an afterthought, his assistants, the twins Cautes and Cautopates (Elsner 1995: 210-221). That said, four classes of images of Mithraists survive, all from within the context of temple decoration: 1) images of servants at the sacred banquet of Mithras and Helios, who thus mediate directly between mythic model and cult-praxis; 2) one or two groups of banqueters within the context of the cult image, who likewise mediate between myth and praxis; 3) the images of grade members, some as types, some "portraits" with personal names, at S. Prisca, probably also on the columns supporting the roof of the Barberini mithraeum (CIMRM 394), both in Rome; and 4) images of initiation. I propose to discuss here only this last category, which consists, with a handful of exceptions, of seven individual images from the mithraeum of S. Maria Capua Vetere in Campania. This choice was of course suggested by the fact that Capua lies only a short distance from the Villa Vergiliana in Cuma; and indeed, the members of this conference were able to visit the mithraeum courtesy of the Soprintendenza per i Beni Archeologici delle Province di Napoli e Caserta.

Since these images of men undergoing different, but apparently unpleasant and frightening, initiation rituals are unaccompanied by any kind of text, their role in the mithraeum, and more generally in the cult, remains uncertain. It can be understood, if at all, I suggest, only by the rather lengthy detour taken in this chapter. I present first an archaeological account of the paintings and their subjects, based upon the original report by Minto and the more recent treatment by Vermaseren. The following sections offer two different approaches to their contextualization, the first with reference to the Foucauldian *théâtre de terreur*, the second to Christian *patientia*.

The Podium Frescoes in the Capua Mithraeum

The Capua Mithraeum: General

Two features of the podium frescoes at Capua—their poor state of preservation and their failure to perform the service required of them by the commentators, namely to "illustrate" rituals known from, or at any rate alluded to by, literary sources—no doubt explain why, despite their obvious importance, they have been relatively neglected in the specialist litera-

Figure 16.1. Capua general.

ture. Of recent standard publications, Reinhold Merkelbach devotes just a few lines to them, without any attempt at closer analysis (1984: 136–137).[4] Robert Turcan (2000: 84) and Manfred Clauss (2000: 103) are likewise rather off-hand. Only Walter Burkert (1987: 102–104) has properly emphasized their exceptional nature in the evidence for ancient mysteries.[5] Minto himself deplored their state of preservation when they were found.[6] The only color plates available, from photos taken in 1967 by Antonio Solazzi, when the mithraeum was in a poor state of repair (the Soprintendenza has devoted laudable efforts recently to dehumidify it), were published by M. J. Vermaseren in his brief monograph devoted to the temple (1971), and subsequently re-used by A. Schütze (1972).[7] Since color plates were not available for the present volume, although they are really the only, albeit inadequate, means of illustrating the remnants of the podium frescoes, I have adopted the *pis-aller* of confronting the earliest published images, those of Minto, with rough tracings based on Vermaseren's plates. Where these do not agree, Minto's images, although far from satisfactory, should be given greater weight because of the massive deterioration during the intervening half-century.

The mithraeum of S. Maria Capua Vetere, one of the best-preserved ever found (Fig. 16.1), was discovered in late September 1922 during work for the foundation of a house in the vico Caserma, about 450 m south of the Roman amphitheater, and excavated early in 1924 by A. Minto (Minto 1924). Like the mithraea at Caesarea Maritima in Judaea and at Marino in the Alban Hills, the temple was constructed in one of several series of intercommunicating vaulted *cryptoportici*, evidently used for storage of wine or the like, which seem to have occupied several areas in the center of the city. The mithraeum, oriented due west-to-east (cult fresco to the west, rear wall with fresco of Luna to the east), was fitted up in the hindmost room of its series, which had been built c. 100–140 CE not far from the Capitol. It was approached by a passage 3.30 m wide (Fig. 16.2a, area denoted o), which was, however, partly blocked in Phase III by the extension of the southern podium. The internal dimensions of the *cryptoporticus* are 12.18 m × 3.49 m, the height of the vault 3.22 m.[8] Set high up in the southern vault were three trapeziform scuttles to provide daylight when and as necessary (Fig. 16.2a).

The mithraeum seems to have been established on a modest scale in the latter part of the reign of Antoninus Pius, or perhaps under M. Aurelius and L. Verus. Because it had been carefully cleared and then partly filled with rubble before being abandoned, no furnishings, pottery, or coins were found in situ. Dating the phases of use is therefore attended by more than the usual uncertainties. Largely on the basis of stylistic differences between the paintings, Vermaseren (who did not conduct any new excavations) distinguished three phases, two with subdivisions. In Phases I and IIa–b, there were no podia of the kind usually found in mithraea. Instead,

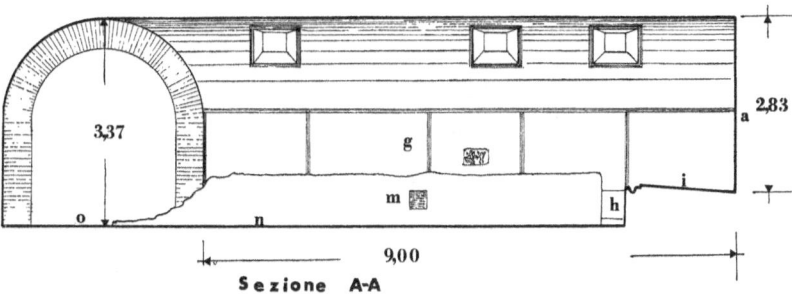

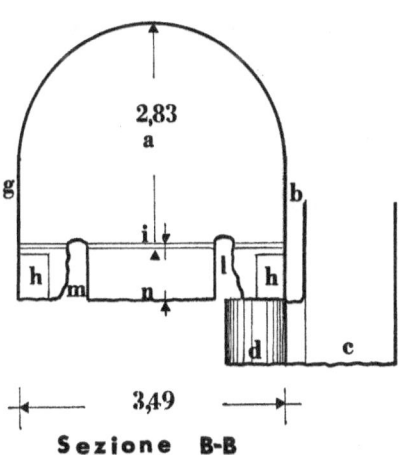

Figure 16.2a. Capua plan I. Longitudinal (A-A) section of the mithraeum. The representation of the entrance corridor is at first sight misleading; the view is however taken from line a in section B-B, looking south (i.e., toward g).

Figure 16.2b. Transverse (B-B) section. The fascia walls of the Phase IIIa-b podia are marked m and l.

there were low seats (Fig. 16.2b, at h), 1.25 m long, 0.39 m wide, and 0.45 m high, which on the left (south side) abutted a water cistern, 0.55 m deep, and on the right (north side), a basin connecting with a deep sump or drain (Fig. 16.2b, at d).[9] The implication, I think, is that in these two phases, meals were eaten from portable *lectus* in the eastern part of the temple, toward the entrance. This hypothesis is supported by the facts that 1) the wall-paintings of Phase IIb, which continue below the level of the later podia, decorate not the cult-fresco area but the eastern section; and 2) whereas the eastern part of the floor simply consisted of tamped earth, the floor of the western section of the central aisle, up to the end of the cisterns, was made of cement into which broken slabs of different types of marble had been pressed. This more elaborate treatment implies that this area, nearer to the cult fresco, had a special cultic status. The wall panels on either side at this level were empty, except for a cut-down (i.e., re-used) Eros-Psyche relief (CIMRM 186) set into the south wall below the central scuttle (Fig. 16.2a, near g).[10]

I have already mentioned that the painted decoration of the mithraeum belongs to different periods. Vermaseren ascribed one poorly preserved fresco (so faint that Minto did not see it), Panel III on the north wall (Fig. 16.2a, somewhat east of m) to Phase I; the main frescoes on the western wall (Mithras and the bull, CIMRM 181 and Fig. 16.1 here) and the east wall (Luna, CIMRM 182) to Phase IIa; the remaining panels, Cautes (north wall, CIMRM 182), Cautopates (south wall, CIMRM 183) and the feast scene (southeast corner), to Phase IIb. The podia were extended to 8.35 × 0.90 m at the beginning of IIIa, and the fascia frescoes were painted somewhat later, during Phase IIIb. Absolute dates are difficult to estimate, since the cult fresco itself has been assigned assorted dates between 160 and 200 CE. An expert commentator has indeed recently observed that "for the third century in particular the chronological fabric [of Roman painting] remains completely uncertain" (Ling 1991: 187). A decade after Vermaseren's monograph, however, the classical archaeologist P. Meyboom, after a careful comparison between the Capua, Marino, and Barberini Mithraic frescoes, concluded that Phase IIa at Capua is to be dated 180-190 CE (Meyboom 1982). On that basis, we can construct the following scheme:

I	IIa	IIb	IIIa	IIIb
160-180	180-200	200-210	210-225	225-240

The extension and widening of the podia can thus be dated to the first quarter of III^p. The fascias were constructed of "materiale vario" and buttressed by low transverse walls (see Fig. 16.1); the actual podia were formed by filling the spaces so created, including the cistern, the basin, and apparently the sump, with dry rubble. This infill, which fell away as usual toward the long side-walls to accommodate more diners, was then covered in plaster. During the second quarter of the third century, the fascias were inexpertly covered in poor quality, porous plaster and painted with the frescoes that are my concern here (Fig. 16.3).

Since they are the only new decoration of the temple at this period, it seems likely that the frescoes were the result of a votive undertaking, comparable to the marble revetting of the podia at the Mitreo Aldobrandini in Ostia paid for by Sex. Pompeius Maximus (*AE* 1924: 119 = CIMRM 233). Their date seems to group them with a number of other relatively late Mithraic images depicting mythic or ritual moments that have no earlier counterpart in the cult's iconographic repertoire. Examples might be the highly original feast scenes on the reverse of the Fiano Romano relief (CIMRM 641) and on the *terra sigillata* dish from the Skt. Matthäus Roman cemetery in Trier (CIMRM 988); the interest in the details of the First Sacrifice shown by the altar of Flavius Aper in Poetovio III (CIMRM 1584); and the recently published Syrian relief now in the Israel Museum (De Jong 2000). This tendency toward "iconic discursivity" in the third century can be paralleled in other "universal" cults of the Roman Empire.

The Podium Frescoes

The podium frescoes consisted originally of thirteen panels, six on the right (north) fascia, and seven on the left (south; Fig. 16.3). Just seven can still be deciphered to some extent, four on the right fascia and three on the left; but even in these cases, both the reading order and the precise events depicted are unclear. It is, of course, a truism that the apparently simple act of describing neutrally "what one sees" turns out to be conditioned, often to a crippling degree, by a priori assumptions. Minto, who had discussed the frescoes with Cumont in some detail (Cumont 1924), thought that the reading order proceeded up the right-hand podium starting nearest to the eastern wall (here RI → RVI) and continued back down the left (southern) podium (LVII → LI).[11] What sense such an order might have made, Minto does not say; but he evidently believed that the sequence represented the initiations for all seven initiatory grades, acting as a sort of anticipatory program: "I fedeli, contemplando queste scene liturgiche, dovevano provare la suggestione di tutta la loro vita religiosa, attraverso i diversi gradi di iniziazione" (Minto 1924: 373). He had evidently not

Figure 16.3. Schematic representation of the arrangement of the scenes on the podium frescoes. The right side represents those on the North podium, the left those on the south.

worked this hypothesis out very carefully, since it is quite unclear how thirteen panels could have represented initiations into seven grades.

Vermaseren, on the other hand, concluded that the reading order on both podia was from east to west (i.e., RI → RVI, then LI → LVII). In his view, the panel scenes depict a more or less complete sequence of initiation rituals, all undergone by a neophyte, or would-be Corax, in which members of different grades, such as Miles and Nymphus, act as initiators (Vermaseren 1971: 49). Although he claims to believe that these representations have little or no relation to any initiation rituals reported by literary sources, in practice he constantly attempts to interpret the panels in the light of these texts. Since my concern here is less with their supposed documentary value than with their treatment of the body and its implications for the "truth" conveyed by the cult of Mithras to its adherents, I can lay these questions of reference and reading order to one side. For what it is worth, however, my opinion is that initiatory tests were not standardized between temples, and that each Mithraic community devised its own forms of initiation with reference to certain "sacralized moments" in the myth of Mithras, in particular the "Initiation of Helios/Sol" scene that occurs on complex reliefs, where Mithras seems often to be threatening or intimidating the sun god.[12] There was thus a mere family resemblance between the initiation rituals of one mithraeum and those of the next, and there is therefore no reason to attempt to force the texts onto the iconography. In the immediate case of Capua, I cannot agree with Vermaseren that the scenes all relate to the initiation of a single grade. No coherent sequence of events can be made out, and at least panels RII and LIII seem to be very similar kinds of tests, in that both involve fire. There is therefore no practical alternative but to approach them from the spectator's point of view, as a group, and to try to make out an overall or general claim about the implied role of the body. The meaning of the panels to the donor and to the Capuan Mithraists of c. 230 CE cannot now be recovered.

I first offer a brief description of each of the seven surviving panels, arbitrarily following Vermaseren's order and placing Minto's images alongside what are frankly interpretative tracings of the figures still visible in Solazzi's plates published by Vermaseren. In general, since the panels were in much better condition in 1924, Minto's accounts, though very brief, are preferable to Vermaseren's. All the panels, which range in width from 0.63 m (LV) to 1.63 m (LIII) but are mostly around 1 m wide, are enclosed within a red-stripe border (there are no inner frames); the scenes occupy roughly the center of each panel. They thus fall clearly into the tradition of *tabulae pictae* in the post-Severan linear style, familiar from several examples in Rome, and Christian catacombs in particular, where the central motif is isolated within its frame—the only hint of an environment is offered by the indication of ground—and body contours, rather than the volumes or spatial relationships, are emphasized (Ling 1991: 188-191). To avoid having to be too precise about the identity of the initiating persons, I term the main initiator, sometimes called Pater by Vermaseren, the "teletarch," his assistant the "mystagogue." This does not imply that I think that all the figures represent the same status or individual.

RIGHT-HAND PODIUM

RI (Fig. 16.4a-b).[13]
This panel depicts just two persons.[14] A small naked figure, blindfolded, with his hands stretched out apprehensively, walks to the left. Behind him, to his left, is a much larger figure, dressed like the mystagogues in the remaining panels, in a short white tunic reminiscent, except perhaps for its color, of those worn by ordinary workers or slaves in *Alltagsszenen*.[15] He appears to be guiding the initiand forward by placing his left arm on his shoulder. This is the only scene that appears to have a clearly introductory, and therefore quasi-narrative, role.

RII (Fig. 16.5a-b).[16]
The initiand, again naked and blindfolded, is half-kneeling on his right knee, with his hands bound behind his back. The editors rightly see an allusion—probably condensed—to the posture of captured prisoners.[17] Behind him, a bearded mystagogue, dressed in the same fashion as in RI,[18] and with his left hand at his waist, seems with his right hand to be pushing the initiand's head forward, or at any rate preventing it from jerking back. The mystagogue's left leg is demonstratively far back, as though to resist pressure: this stance is emphasized by the lengthy ground/shadow line. Facing the initiand stands a likewise bearded, thus fully adult, man apparently wearing a helmet, and dressed in a dark tunic and a cloak, which billows out behind him. In his left hand, he is holding a lighted torch in the initiand's face; the billowing cloak is evidently intended to suggest the threatening nature of the movement, just as the mystagogue's stance is intended to suggest the initiand's instinctive recoil.[19]

RIV (Fig. 16.6a-b).[20]
The initiand stands naked in the center, his hands apparently bound behind his back, held resolutely by the mystagogue, whose body is hunched forward. The teletarch, on the left, dressed in tunic, trousers, and cloak, faces the initiand, evidently again to induce fear and pain. Although the entire

Figure 16.4a. In Figures 16.4–16.10, each figure is doubled into a and b: a is the image provided by Minto in the 1920s, and b is Gordon's drawing from Vermaseren. This image: Minto 2.
Figure 16.4b. R1.

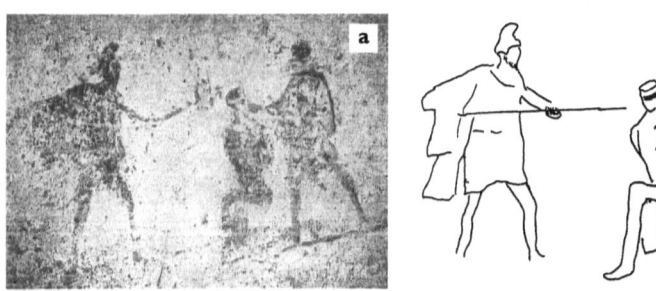

Figure 16.5a. Minto 3.
Figure 16.5b. R2 revised.

central area, including the teletarch's head, has been damaged (perhaps even in antiquity), he is most probably again being threatened—here the initiand's eyes are not bandaged, so that he could see what was happening. Vermaseren's account of this scene (he apparently thought the *initiand* was holding a sword, and was being embraced by the mystagogue) is bizarre.

RV (Fig. 16.7a–b).[21]
In the center, the initiand half-kneels on his right knee. Although Vermaseren claims the initiand's arms are resting on his thighs, Minto cor-

Figure 16.6a. Minto 5.
Figure 16.6b. R4.

 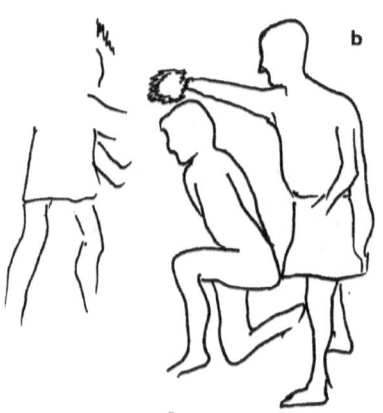

Figure 16.7a. Minto 4.
Figure 16.7b. R5.

rectly saw that they are bound behind him.[22] He also believed that the mystagogue, again standing behind the initiand, is extending a crown over the initiate's head. In his view, this was a reference to a victory, apparently over fear.[23] Minto, on the other hand, writing half a century earlier, saw no crown, and reckoned that this scene should be linked to LIV and III, in each of which the initiand is kneeling between teletarch and mystagogue. I incline to think he was right, and that the object being held over the initiand's head here is the same as, or related to, the round object on the ground in LIV, with the crux of the scene to be found in the now-lost action of the teletarch. Vermaseren's view was heavily influenced both by Tertullian—although he finally rejected his relevance here—and by his notion that there was a status progression toward the cult niche, so that at some point there had to be some sort of reward for the initiand.

Whereas in scenes RII, IV, and V, the teletarch stands on the left of the scene, in the corresponding panels on the southern podium he seems always to be on the right; that is, it appears to be an implicit rule of the sequence, for whatever reason, that the initiand should face the central aisle or passage.

LII (Fig. 16.8a–b).[24]
The upper part of the panel is destroyed. In the center, a naked initiand, his body expressionistically elongated, lies prostrate on the ground, or possibly on some kind of raised construction, since the feet of the principals extend much further down the panel; that would account for the "objects" below him, especially at the foot and hand.[25] Several indecipherable objects are arranged above him. Among them, on the small of his back, Vermaseren was surely right to see a scorpion (identified by Minto as a snake), its tail raised in a threatening manner as though about to sting. What the mystagogue, on the left, is doing cannot be made out (Vermaseren thought he was dropping something onto the initiand's feet). The teletarch, of whom now almost nothing remains, though Minto could see much more, seems

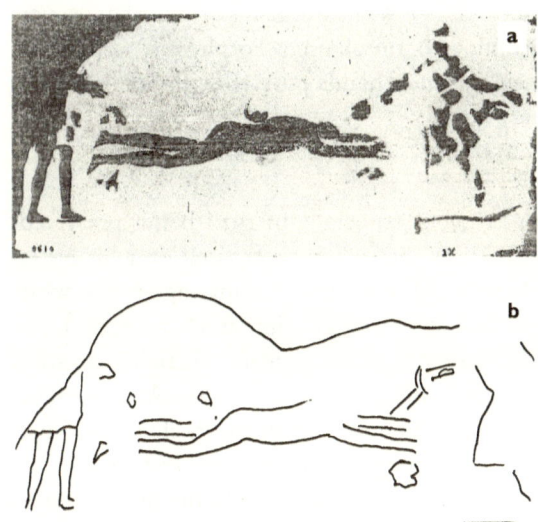

Figure 16.8a. Minto 8.
Figure 16.8b. L2.

 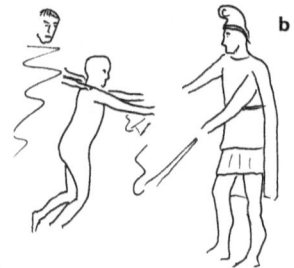

Figure 16.9a. Minto 6.
Figure 16.9b. L3.

once again to be threatening the initiand. Whether the latter's head was raised, as Vermaseren thought, or the blob belongs to the object held by the teletarch, can no longer be determined: Minto, at any rate, does not mention it.

LIII (Fig. 16.9a–b).[26]
Almost nothing of this panel can now be deciphered. The initiand is kneeling in the center, on both knees; the mystagogue, one leg stretched far back, and grasping his shoulders, seems to be pushing him forward with considerable violence. To the right, the teletarch, wearing a helmet (Vermaseren) or Phrygian cap (Minto) and a fluttering cloak, implying rapid movement, holds a lighted torch below the initiand's arms or hands. Vermaseren is mysteriously reminded of the claim by Porphyry (*Antr.* 15) that initiands into the grade Leo had their hands purified with honey instead of water, because it is a fiery liquid.

LIV (Fig. 16.10a–b).[27]
In a scene very similar to LIII, but especially in 1924 better preserved, the initiand, again on both knees, has his arms crossed over his breast (Vermaseren) or being held behind his head(?). The mystagogue, in white tunic and with his legs straddled, again grips the initiand from behind. The teletarch, head lost but otherwise in the same garb as in LIII, holds a staff, sword, whip, or similar object in his right hand. To the left of the initiand is a round object, identified by Vermaseren and Merkelbach as a loaf; Vermaseren even believed that the teletarch was placing it there with his right hand, and so turned the scene into an allusion to the divine/human banquet. In fact, there are two objects, one roughly circular, divided by seven centripetal lines into eight sections, beneath which is a blob of red paint. The first object bears no resemblance to loaves depicted elsewhere

in the Mithraic corpus, or in still-lives, so there is no reason, compelling or otherwise, to accept Vermaseren's account. As mentioned earlier, I incline to think it is related to the object being held over the initiand's head in RV, perhaps in an allusion to Mithras Kosmophoros, Mithras-Atlas in his role as world-carrier.

Considered as documents in the ordinary sense, then, fragmentary and bereft of all ancient commentary as they are, the panels from the podia at Capua are deeply frustrating. We may, however, suggest that the basic error of previous commentators has lain precisely in the attempt to force them to "say the same" as the equally fragmented and problematic literary texts, mainly Christian and thus deeply suspect, which claim to speak for the cult of Mithras. For it must be obvious that the panels do not "depict" rituals in any direct or uncomplicated sense. They represent idealized, constructed allusions to rituals, allusions that could be claimed to have some special significance either for the donor or for the larger community of the mithraeum around 230 CE. As such, their greatest value may lie not in their supposed (but ever hypothetical or "deferred") documentary character, but in their revelation of a structure of oppositions, which we may plausibly claim to be the basic structural elements of the rituals actually performed, whatever they were.

Oppositions at any rate there certainly are. We can point first to the contrast between the sizes of the participants: although the initiand is consistently presented at the center of the spectator's attention (to which we shall return), he is always the smallest figure present, smaller than the mystagogue, and much smaller than the teletarch.[28] His size thus correlates with his prescriptive insignificance, and confirms, if further proof were needed, the nondocumentary quality of the scenes.[29] Second, the nakedness of the initiand is stressed by the tone of brick red or brown

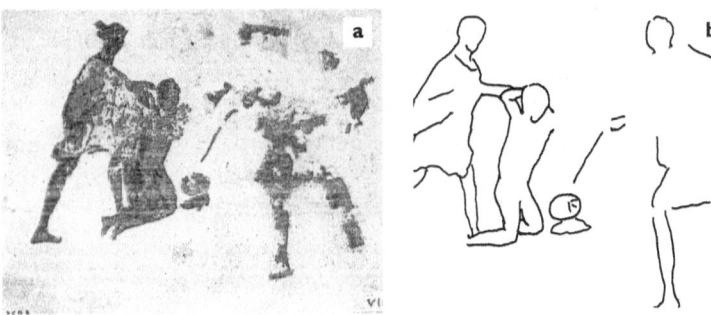

Figure 16.10a. Minto 7.
Figure 16.10b. L4.

used, contrasting with the white of the mystagogues and the imposing appearance of the teletarch, enhanced by his billowing cloak and his military helmet (if that is what his headgear is). Nakedness outside sporting or athletic contexts implies absence or negation of social status, most markedly when it is deliberately contrasted, as here, with the wearing of clothes.[30] Then again, where the detail can be seen, the officiants are bearded, the initiand beardless, thus signalling the prescriptive contrast between maturity/membership and youth/initiation. Even more important in the present context are the contrasts between the body postures: between prostration, two types of kneeling, being pushed, constrained, and tied; and vigorous, dominating actions. These contrasts of posture/autonomy are reinforced by the fact that the initiand is, at least in some panels, blindfolded, alluding to the key contrast between knowledge and ignorance. All of these oppositions can be summarized in the grand contrast between agency and submission, between the free, purposive action of an agent and the enforced reaction of a subject. The Mithraic *schéma corporel* is dual and hierarchical, such that the scheme of autonomous action can only be acquired through the scheme of subjection (cf. Bourdieu 1979: 210–211).

The Body, Suffering, and Identity

Given that they are so clearly focused on the suffering body of the initiand, it seems plausible to look in the first place to Michel Foucault to help us contextualize the Capuan images. The Foucauldian body is a socially appropriate body, the product of historically specific discourses and practices, an "anatomical body overlaid by culture."[31] Initially, in his work on social discipline (1975), Foucault's perspective emphasized solely the relation between the materiality of the body and its discursive regulation in theory and practice. On his account, concentrated on the nineteenth century but with ample reference back to earlier monastic, military, and penal practice, the body is molded, trained, and pressed by a variety of techniques into becoming a socially useful instrument (1975: 30–31). "The phenomenon of the social body is the effect not of a consensus but of the materiality of power operating on the very bodies of individuals."[32] By way of the notion of "bio-power," the subject was not only redescribed in materialist terms but also shown to be historically contingent. With the publication of the three volumes of *L'histoire de la sexualité* (1976–84), however, Foucault's social body became primarily a gendered body, a sexually differentiated body.[33] Leaving this to one side for the moment,

I want first to explore aspects of the Mithraic body with reference to Foucault's earlier distinction between a type of social order based upon "le modèle représentatif, scénique, signifiant, public, collectif" and one based on "le modèle coercitif, corporel, solitaire, secret, du pouvoir de punir" (Foucault 1975: 134).

Foucault's aim in *Surveiller et punir* was to write a genealogy of the modern "scientific-judicial complex," which turns individuals into objects of a particular form of discursive knowledge. For heuristic purposes, he contrasted this complex with an early-modern world in which high rates of mortality and the absence of an industrial regime produced a "worthless" body, which was at the same time of the greatest symbolic interest. The socio-political value of this pre-industrial body lay in its ability concretely to manifest the dis-symmetry between the power of the state and that of the individual (1975: 59). So far from concealing its repressive work, Power gloried in its right to inscribe itself in the most gruesome fashion upon the body. Conversely, an audience was indispensable. For — in a sense — it is the spectator, not the culprit, who is the primary actor in exemplary punishment. Without spectators, the spectacle lacks all moral sense. In the specific cases of corporal and capital punishment, there are three criteria of successful ritualization: the quantum of suffering must be appropriate to the crime; the suffering must be signalled to the audience in such a fashion that it be never forgotten; and the "excess" of violence must be intelligible as the writing of power (1975: 37–39). The effect of such punishment was to expose the crime, itself unspoken or hidden, by means of rituals of humiliation and suffering. Among the rituals are the nicely regulated procedures of torture, which, like Kafka's "eigentümlicher Apparat" in *In der Strafkolonie* (1914), simultaneously punished as they revealed the truth (1975: 46). The "corps montré, promené, exposé, supplicié" is not intended to re-establish a moral equilibrium but destined symbolically to affirm the superiority of constituted authority. "Le supplice ne rétablissait pas la justice; il réactivait le pouvoir" (1975: 53).

Distantly in the wake of Foucault (and Norbert Elias), ancient historians have explored the symbolic functions of violent spectacle in antiquity, both in the "théâtre de terreur"[34] and in the history of gladiatorial combat.[35] Among these, Kathleen Coleman especially has shown how strikingly the Roman principate confirms Foucault's account of the symbolic value of the body in pre-industrial state repression.[36] Indeed, the explicitness, inventiveness, memorability, and expense of Roman ceremonies of degradation, the apparently unlimited ability of the judicial system to produce "worthless bodies" (in Latin: *vilis sanguis*), the centrality of the spectators' consent and desire (*Occide! Verbera! Ure!*: "Kill him, thrash him, burn him!" Seneca *Ep. mor.* 7.5), and the enthusiastic occlusion of justice for the sake of reinvigorating Power—all these serve to make the Principate the example Foucault must have wished he had thought of.

Placed in this context, the Mithraic initiation rituals depicted in the Capua Mithraeum are extremely suggestive. Although they of course have no connection with the apparatus of state power, their images of subjection, degradation, and suffering imply an *imaginaire* based on the same premises as the *théâtre de terreur,* namely, the exemplary production of *vilis sanguis,* the ingenious multiplication of forms of humiliation, the use of physical suffering to underwrite the triumph of Power, and a heightened interest in the reactions of the implied spectator. One remembers that Capua boasted the second largest amphitheater in the entire Roman world, built in the late Flavian/Trajanic period over the Republican amphitheater where Spartacus had trained, and was the center of an important gladiatorial training-school, commemorated by the Museo dei Gladiatori recently installed in the Antiquario dell'Anfiteatro dell'antica Capua.[37] Of course, these Mithraic depictions are of voluntary sufferings and humiliations, of performances rather than of tortures, of roles assumed and played out. But we cannot deny the evidence that the performances were not "mere" play-acting: they were accompanied by the intentional infliction of pain, to say nothing of terror and humiliation. The burning torch pushed into the face of the initiand in RII, the apparent singeing of the man's arms in LIII, and above all, the scorpion placed on the bare back of the man in LII make this evident. The element of role-playing does not in fact constitute a decisive difference from the real *théâtre de terreur.* Rather, the Mithraic teletarchs and mystagogues see in that real-world violence a symbolism perfectly appropriate to their own ends, the production of a Mithraic body "fit for the job."[38]

We may legitimately conclude that the primary intention of the degradation of the Mithraic body, as depicted on the podia, is to image, both to the subjects and to the spectator, the superiority of constituted Power, the legitimacy of authority, and the mystic connection between hierarchy and salvation. If we compare the *gallus,* for example, the role of Power becomes clear: in imitation of Attis, the *gallus* inflicts upon himself, at least in the ideal-prescriptive narrative, a wound that, if he survives the act, separates him from all normal familial-social aims and obligations; the loss of blood correlates with the loss of manhood, the loss of manhood signifies an existence solely for the Mother. The act marginalizes the network of social obligations and dues that constitutes social life, but remains itself as exceptional as Christian martyrdom. In the cult of Mithras by the mid-third century CE, if we can generalize at all from Capua, the initiate was induced to believe that he could only attain self-identification with Mithras by accepting the right of beneficent Authority to inflict pain and terror for his own good, not once but repeatedly. Whether this was understood in the manner of Musonius Rufus and popular Stoicism as an acquisition of *ataraxia* and *apatheia* (Francis 1995: 1–52), or more stringently as a rejection of sin, as Porphyry's account of the Lion's purification with honey would suggest, constituted Authority is perceived as controlling the sole road to the higher end. The salvific claim of Power is inscribed on the mind via suffering flesh. In the course of that inscription, both subject and spectator rehearse the mythic "suffering" of Mithras and intuit the grand saving Otherness of the Lord of the Cosmos.

The experience of initiation, and indirectly of viewing these scenes, conveys, I suggest, an intuitive perception of a complex truth. On the one hand, the experience and contemplation of physical suffering offers the sole effective means of subjective self-identification with the Mithras of the bull-killing, who seems at S. Prisca to declare, *perlata humeris t[ul]i maxima divum*, "I have borne the commands of the gods on my shoulders right to the end".[39]) On the other hand, that same physical suffering marks an irreducible ontological distinction between mortal and divinity. If Mithras can step into the Chariot of the Sun, humans cannot, suffer how they will. All that remains ultimately is the mystical association, which cannot be articulated because it endures only in the body itself, between Power and salvation.[40]

At the same time, the gender issue will not go away. The exclusion of the female in these images is all too striking: we are everywhere confronted, in this private, sacred space, by the painterly convention of the bronzed masculine body. Although maleness is in the Mithraic context paradigmatic, this is not the maleness of the elite demand to enter the "marketplaces and council halls and law courts and gatherings and meetings" (Philo *De specialibus legibus* 3.31,169).[41] Yet the body with which the spectator is invited to identify is in a sense a feminized body, a subject acted upon, suffering, rather than agent, active. The key must, however, be the role of the passions: the feminization is incomplete precisely because the infliction of pain and suffering issues not in still more passion but in the opposite, in their rejection. The Capuan images of initiation suggest the attraction for some men in the mid-third century CE of an image of the pure circulation of Power, from domination to submission back to domination, in which women could play no part. Such pure circulation surely offered a means of overcoming the "ambiguity and division of gender."[42]

Mithraic *Makrothymía?*

It may, however, also be that we should look more specifically at wider developments in the mid-third century CE for our contextualization of the Capuan images. A few years ago, Brent Shaw brought together a number of themes relevant to the issue of the Christian glorification of bodily suffering and torture (Shaw 1996). He saw this glorification as an inversion of the classical attitude, which, he claims, saw submission as effeminate or cowardly. Perhaps it would be more accurate to claim that the martyrs' exaltation of death would have struck Aristotle, for example, as hybristic, because their suffering is offset by the expectation of future glory (*Rhet.* 2.8.1385b16–23). The ordinary classical view was that death, bodily injury, and mutilation must excite our compassion (*éleos*) (1386a5–16). At any rate, tracing a line from 4 Maccabees to Cyprian's *De bono patientiae* of the mid-third century,[43] Shaw argues that *hypomonē*, "endurance," which had been a female merit or virtue connected with the pains of childbirth, becomes central to an ideology of meritorious suffering, such that the victim of torture can claim the same merit as that traditionally associated with the active heroism of *andreía,* "manliness." At latest by around 200 CE, when Tertullian's *De patientia* was written, this virtue is of supreme importance in Christianity, for through it one becomes master of one's body: the control of food intake and sexual appetite leads up to a readiness to endure the worst pains in the cause of martyrdom. The ability to resist suffering and torture thus becomes an important feature in Christian self-definition. Consistent with this exaltation of endurance is St. Paul's transformation of the negative word *tapeinós,* "mean, low, wretched, subordinate," into the ideal of meritorious self-abasement, *tapeinosophrýnē,* "humility" (Ephesians 4.2).

Although all this can properly be seen as a shift prompted by necessity, as a response to the objective situation of Christians exposed to arbitrary suffering, there are traces of a similar move in a pagan context. Seneca, for example, discusses endurance primarily within the context of bodily illness and public torture in the arena.[44] But for him, the lesson to be drawn is to learn to avoid situations that might expose us to such dangers: since he has no promise of eternal life, the path of glorification is not open to him. Moreover, he is at pains to distinguish a less meritorious passive endurance from an active one: gladiators and athletes endure pain not simply to fight but to fight better; and the ideal of resistance to torture is not mere passivity but the reduction of the torturers to helplessness. Seneca thus avoids the paradoxicality of the Christian view and maintains a form of active manliness within the passive or "feminized" virtue of endurance.

We might suggest that something of this kind is implied at Capua: the initiand must endure pain, humiliation, and confusion, but in a context in which this suffering is rendered purposive and therefore, in a sense, active. The model is anyway Mithras, whose endurance of the bull hunt was rewarded by the fulfillment of his cosmic role in doing it to death.

That said, two other features of the Capua frescoes are of interest in suggesting the double nature of the torments applied. One is the role of fire. As we saw, two of the scenes seem to involve torches—in RII, having a burning torch thrust into one's face; in LIII, having to endure having one's arms burned from below. Fire occurs regularly in lists of tortures and sufferings, in the arena and elsewhere: it is second in Seneca's list in *Ep. mor.* 14.4 (*ferrum circa se habet, et ignes, et catenas* . . .), and third in Achilles Tatius' *Cleitophon and Leucippe,* when Leukippe dares Thersander to do his worst: "Bring out against me the scourges, the wheel, the fire, the sword."[45] Fire is thus a "cliché of torment." At the same time, the torch resonates widely within the symbolism of the cult of Mithras, emblematic of the opposition between light and darkness. The torch is thus not simply a torch.

Secondly, we recall the man lying prone in LII. My first thought was that this must have evoked the idea of the male pathic, who "acts like a woman" in suffering the penetration of his body by another man: one of the key verbs in this connection is *inclinor,* "lie prone." But the recognition of the scorpion sitting on his back makes clear that the sexual connotation of "lying prone" must be secondary to that of being exposed defenseless to the scorpion's sting, or the threat of its attack. Scorpions were reputed to be ever on the lookout for the opportunity to sting.[46] At the same time, in the Mithraic context, not only does it allude to the bull's death, at which the scorpion stings its scrotum, but also a special relationship to the sun, since scorpions' venom was at its most poisonous at midday (Pliny *NH* 11.88).

I would suggest, then, that the larger context of the Capuan frescoes may be an awareness of the role of *patientia* in sustaining the readiness of Christians, not merely male but also female, to accept martyrdom. From the initiation scene of the Mainz *Schlangengefäß*, where a Father is threatening to shoot an initiand with a bow and arrow, we may conclude that some kind of initiatory suffering had probably always been a feature of the cult of Mithras, just as it has been in other initiatory cults.[47] Jan Bremmer has recently stressed that we should not see the pagan cults of the second and third centuries CE in isolation from Christianity (Bremmer 2002: 41–55). Although the examples he gives do not seem to me very convincing, particularly as regards Mithras, the thought perhaps should not be dismissed entirely. For Christian *patientia*, as experienced in the intermittent *éclats* prior to the Decian persecution, may indeed have stimulated among contemporary Mithraists a desire to explore in ritual a specifically male, active endurance of suffering, thus offering a "conservative" answer to the imaginative impact of the public suffering of Christian martyrs. Picking up a term from the pseudepigraphic Jewish Testament of Job, we might call such a response to the Christian challenge Mithraic *makrothymía* (17.7).

As far as their specific content is concerned, the podium frescoes of the Capua Mithraeum are likely always to remain enigmatic, virtually uninterpretable. That is why, for all their evident importance as documents, they have effectively fallen out of discussions of Mithraic ritual/initiation. For what they mainly demonstrate is the disagreeable truth that iconographic studies in the absence of written texts cannot take us very far. However, by studying their structure of oppositions and linking them to wider issues— namely, the relation between ritual action and the State theater of cruelty, and the emergence of heroic-passive values in early Christianity, and even Seneca—we may find a way of recuperating them just as the frescoes themselves deteriorate physically beyond all hope of restoration.

Notes

1. The ancient body: e.g., Heuzé 1985; Sissa 1987; Konstan and Nussbaum 1990; Gleason 1995; Wyke 1998a, 1998b; Foxhall and Salmon 1998; Shaw 1998; Cooper 1999; Williams 1999; Scanlon 2002. I offered a rather different account of the topic to the conference "Divinas Dependencias" (1998); see now Gordon 2005a.

2. Kirtsoglou 2004: 16. A different approach to this issue, through the notion of "star-talk," will be found in Beck 2006.

3. An unreliable tradition of extreme tests of endurance imposed upon Mithraic initiates is preserved in the sixth-century commentaries on Gregory of Nazianzus by Ps.-Nonnus, *Comm. in Greg. Naz. Serm.* 4.70, §6; 47; *Serm.* 39 §18 (see now most conveniently Nimmo Smith 2001: 7, 34–35, 104–105). The details—up to 80 tests, fasting for 50 days, "passing through fire, through cold, through hunger and thirst, through much journeying by land and sea"—are hyperbolic, but the Capuan paintings suggest there is a grain of truth within them. Marius Maximus is the likely source of another tradition, that the emperor Commodus killed someone during a Mithraic initiation *cum illic aliquid ad speciem timoris vel dici vel fingi soleat* (Hist. Aug., *Commod.* 9; cf. Rives 1995: 72 n. 37). The anecdote fits well with Maximus' love of lurid gossip. *Ad speciem timoris* would, however, likewise fit well with the Capuan paintings.

4. However, Merkelbach does provide clear black-and-white plates of five of the scenes (1984: 287–290, figs. 28–32). These are the same images as those reproduced in Vermaseren's *Corpus* (1956–60: figs. 57–61, hereafter cited as *CIMRM*), albeit in a whimsical order.

5. Almost the sole analogy among the images collected in Bianchi 1976a is the well-known whipping-scene in the Villa of the Mysteries, Pompeii. Fear, even terror, by contrast seems to have been commonly employed in the Greek mysteries.

6. The decay is due partly to the poor quality of the original plaster, partly to the absorption of moisture from the tamped earth floor (Minto 1924: 367).

7. Although his color plates are of great value, Vermaseren was no archaeologist, and his publication, despite being fuller than Minto's, is unfortunately poorly organized, and confused or uninformative on many archaeological questions.

8. All these internal dimensions are taken from Minto (1924: 356). For some reason, Vermaseren gives the external dimensions, and by a slip gives the width of the mithraeum as 3.37 m (1971: 3).

9. This sump was also connected to the masonry altar (Fig. 16.2a and b, at i) by a concealed channel. In addition, there was a well behind wall b (Fig. 16.2b, at c), equipped with footholds for descent. The cistern on the southern (left) side was 1.28 m long by 0.67 m wide; the dimensions of the basin and sump (right) could not be determined for fear of causing the collapse of the walls of podia h and l at this point (Minto 1924: 357 with fig. 4). Vermaseren seems wrongly to have believed that the cistern and basin continued to function as such after the construction of the podia (1971: 5). They did not: Minto found them full of the rubble used to infill the podia (1924: 358).

10. Vermaseren believed (1971: 50 n. 1) that the relief was inserted during Phase I, which seems very unlikely.

11. Minto 1924: 368-372. Unfortunately, he confused the order of the scenes on the left podium: as is clear from the draughtsman's Roman numerals, the order should be his figs. 15, 14, 16. He also fails to mention his own Scene VIII (= Vermaseren 1971: LIII).

12. Cf. Clauss 2000: 149-151; Turcan 2000: 98. Merkelbach (1984: 123-124) presents some examples, although his interpretation is eccentric.

13. Minto 1924: 368, scene I, fig. 10 = *CIMRM* 187 = Vermaseren 1971: 26-27 with pl. xxi = Merkelbach 1984: 287, fig. 28.

14. This is no doubt why Merkelbach (1984: 287, fig. 29), wanting to make it congruent with the others, claims that a Pater (or at any rate a "teletarch") was depicted to the left. Neither Minto nor Vermaseren mentions the fact. There is indeed a blob in front of the initiand, which on a black-and-white photo might be a clenched hand; but the color photo shows that it is simply a hole in the plaster. As so often, Merkelbach's claims are to be taken with a large pinch of salt; and anyway, there were probably only two persons depicted in RIII (unrecoverable).

15. Vermaseren oddly claims that this figure is the Pater, when it quite clearly is not (1971: 27, inconsistent with his p. 26). The identity of the raised object on his head is uncertain. It is most likely an illusion due to damage to the plaster: all the other mystagogues have bare heads.

16. Minto 1924: 369, scene II, fig. 11 = *CIMRM* 188 = Vermaseren 1971: 28-34 with pl. xxii = Merkelbach 1984: 288, fig. 30.

17. Minto 1924: 369; Vermaseren 1971: 29-30.

18. Vermaseren and Merkelbach introduce fantasies here, the first claiming that the mystagogue is wearing a cape over his tunic "bordered with red" (1971: 28), the second improving on this by claiming that the tunic itself carries a *clavis* (a red-purple stripe), that is, alludes to the *toga praetexta* of curule magistrates (1984:

288, fig. 30). These lines are simply the outlines of the man's clothes, intended to provide visual help in identifying his action. The strong outline at the extreme right, however, is also intended to reinforce the sense of forward movement or pressure.

19. The horizontal line running across his body, through his hand and toward the initiand's face, is certainly the result of damage, and does not indicate that the teletarch is holding a spear, as Merkelbach claims (ibid.), and as even the color photo suggests. Minto thought the object he is holding was a sword (1924: 369), which makes no sense if the initiand is blindfolded. Vermaseren must be right to think it is a torch.

20. Minto 1924: 369, scene III, fig. 12 = *CIMRM* 190 = Vermaseren 1971: 34–36 with pl. xxiii. Minto despaired of making sense of this panel; Merkelbach ignores it completely. Panel RIII (= Vermaseren 1971: 34; see note 14 above) seems to have represented a man walking left; some blobs of paint in front of him indicate that there was another person (ibid.: 34); Minto mentions panels III and IV together, but describes only RIV.

21. Minto 1924: 370, scene V, fig. 13 = *CIMRM* 191 = Vermaseren 1971: 36–42 with pl. xxv = Merkelbach 1984: 297, fig. 28 (part only), also pp. 95–96 and 136.

22. Vermaseren likewise wrongly claims that the initiand has a beard. The supposed "sword" on the ground below him is simply a ground-line.

23. Vermaseren did, however, rightly understand that this scene is irreconcilable with the account of the initiation of a Mithraic "miles" given by Tertullian (*De cor.* 15). Merkelbach, on the other hand, blithely sees them as compatible.

24. Minto 1924: 371–372, scene IX, fig. 16 (on p. 374) = *CIMRM* 193 = Vermaseren 1971: 43–44 with pl. xxvi = Merkelbach 1984: 289 fig. 31.

25. Merkelbach cites [Ambrosiaster] *Quaestiones veteris et novi testamenti* 93.1 here, a passage referring to the Mithraic initiand being pushed across a water-filled ditch and having his bonds, made of chicken guts, cut by his "liberator." This, too, is likely to be pure fantasy.

26. Minto 1924: 370, scene VIII, fig. 14 (on p. 372) = *CIMRM* 195 = Vermaseren 1971: 44–45 with pl. xxvii.

27. Minto 1924: 370, scene VII, fig. 15 (on p. 373) = *CIMRM* 194 = Vermaseren 1971: 45–47 with pl. xxviii = Merkelbach 1984: 290 fig. 32 and p. 137.

28. The one exception is LII, where, if the initiand were standing, he would be about 1.5 times taller than the mystagogue. But his complete subjection and humiliation can be more effectively expressed the further he extends over the ground or couch.

29. Bourdieu mentions the findings of W. D. Dannemeier and F. J. Tumin in 1964, according to which subjects tended to overestimate the size of individuals in keeping with their subjective estimate of their authority or importance (Bourdieu 1979: 229 with n. 28).

30. Cf. Brown 1988: 96 n. 54. Müller (1997: 87) notes that in the medieval period, disrobing the person to be punished was part of the humiliation. Older views of specifically religious nakedness (e.g., Heckenbach 1911) are generally naive.

31. Gatens 1999: 229.

32. Gordon 1980: 55. I do not of course wish to endorse Foucault's character-

istic reification of abstractions, which subsequently turn out to be the real agents of history (cf. Giddens 1982: 221-222).

33. Cf., for example, Ortner and Whitehead 1981; Butler 1993; Price and Shildrick 1999; Davis-Sulikowski et al. 2001; Kirtsoglou 2004.

34. *Du châtiment dans la Cité* 1984; MacMullen 1986; Bodel 1994; Cantarella 1991; Hinard and Dumont 2003.

35. For example, Ville 1981; Hopkins 1983: 1-30; Golvin and Landes 1990; Domergue, Landes, and Pailler 1990; Welch 1994; Kyle 1998; Beacham 1999; Junkelmann 2000; Von den Hoff 2004.

36. Coleman 1990; cf. 1993.

37. The museum, largely inspired by D^{ssa} Valeria Sampaolo, contains some material from the amphitheater, more, however, from that at Pompeii. The epigraphic materials are collected in Fora 1996.

38. "C'est-à-dire le *schéma corporel* en tant qu'il est dépositaire de toute une vision du monde social, de toute une philosophie de la personne et du corps propre": Bourdieu 1979: 240.

39. Vermaseren and van Essen 1965: 204-205. (Line 9, lower layer, left wall, c. 210 CE.) Vermaseren reads *t(u)li*, but the *l* is imaginary. Forgetting that the *-a* of *perlata* must be elided in the scansion, he claims that this is the sole pentameter line, which is also very implausible. A proper metrical hexameter, comparable to most of the other lines, could be produced by assuming a short word of three long syllables here, such as *t[radux]i*. But difficulties abound: it is not even certain that it is a first-person utterance; and in Vermaseren's drawing (p. 203, fig. 67), the word is impossibly short, yet with a long gap between the *i* and *m* of *maxima*.

40. See the suggestive remarks of Müller 1997: 90, on the role of the broken body of Christ in medieval Passion plays.

41. Cited by Lieu 2004: 182.

42. Ibid.: 190.

43. Shaw seems to think 4 Maccabees is Hellenistic, but it can in fact be dated between c. 18 and 55 CE.

44. Esp. Seneca *Ep. mor.* 14.4-6.

45. Achilles Tatius *Cleitophon and Leucippe* 6.22.4, resuming her more rhetorical outburst at 21.1.

46. Cf. *elatae metuendus acumine caudae / Scorpios* . . . : Ovid *Fasti*. 4.163-164; *semper cauda in ictu est:* Pliny *NH* 11.86-87.

47. The Mainz *Schlangengefäß*: Horn 1994: 23, with pls. 7, 14-16; Beck 2000b: 149-154, with pl. XIII. Others: as Burkert (1987: 102) rightly says, "From Australian aborigines to American universities." A good example of the patterned use of initiatory whipping in New Guinea is provided by Barth 1975: 57 (twice), 65.

CHAPTER 17

Why the Shoulder?: A Study of the Placement of the Wound in the Mithraic Tauroctony

GLENN PALMER

The study of Roman Mithraism has consisted, in large part, of a series of interpretations and elucidations applied to a complex and enigmatic corpus of images. The ubiquitous central monument, the tauroctony (Fig. 17.1), in its more detailed examples, offers a bewildering array of images, among them the awkward, backward-glancing pose of Mithras, the suffering of the taurine victim, various symbolic animals observing or partaking in the sacrifice, several major and minor deities witnessing the act, and the visual narrative of the *transitus,* Mithras' apparent sacred journey.

The usual visual center of the tauroctony, and the center of attention of the surrounding witnesses on the monument, is the sacrificial blow being struck by Mithras upon the shoulder of the bull. The placement of this wound is problematic, as will be shown, and is apparently unique to Roman Mithraism. Thus, I suggest that the wound may have meaning within Mithraism in addition to the obvious death of the bull. Another allusion to a bull in Mithraic iconography is the dismembered foreleg of a bull being carried by Mithras, raising the possibility that the foreleg in itself has some symbolic significance.

I began my search by poring through Vermaseren's *Corpus* of Mithraic monuments.[1] I tallied each monument for which the placement of the wound was discernible. Surprisingly, the cutting of the victim's throat, one of the most common methods of sacrifice depicted in ancient art, accounted for only 3 percent of the wounds depicted in the Mithraic corpus. I also discovered that fully 70 percent of the wounds were inflicted in the shoulder.

Mithras is almost always depicted as straddling the bull while stabbing it in the shoulder with a dagger or short sword. The antecedent of this method of killing a bull is found in representations of the goddess Nike. Elements of the tauroctony traceable to the Nike images include the god

Figure 17.1. Tauroctony.

grasping the bull by its nose or actually inserting fingers into the animal's nostrils in order to extend the neck, thereby exposing the animal's throat to the knife; the thrusting of a knee into the bull's back in order to hold the animal down; and the extension of the god's other leg backward in order to steady the sacrificer.[2] There are notable differences, however, between the poses of Nike and Mithras. Nike is usually depicted as looking forward, intent upon the act she is about to perform, whereas Mithras is usually depicted with his head turned away from his knife-wielding arm, looking over his shoulder at the god Helios in the upper left-hand corner of the monument. The other significant difference is that Nike is depicted as being on the verge of cutting the bull's throat, with the knife held out in front of the animal's neck. This is one of the usual methods of killing an animal in Greek and Roman sacrifices. Mithras, by contrast, is dispatching the bull by stabbing it in the shoulder. This placement of the wound is an exception to the usual depiction of sacrificial methods, found in literature and art and in actual practice, of dispatching the victim by cutting its throat, chopping the neck with an axe, or stabbing it in the flank with a spear so as to hit the heart, as in the *taurobolium*.

From an anatomical viewpoint, the shoulder is not an optimal location at which to administer a fatal stab wound to a bull (Fig. 17.2). This is not a vital area of the animal's anatomy. The heart is located at the bottom of the chest cavity, posterior to the forelegs, and, in a large animal such as a bull, several feet from the entrance wound at the shoulder.[3] The vital jugular vein and carotid artery lie along the front of the throat, not on the sides

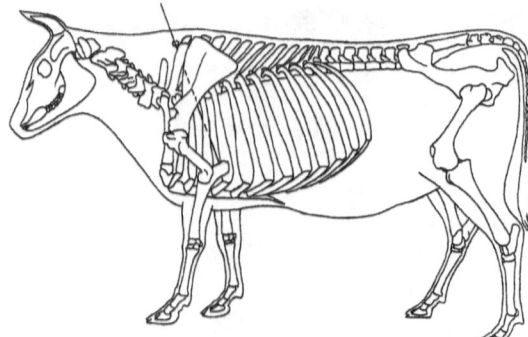

Figure 17.2.
Bovine skeleton.

of the neck, as in humans.[4] Blood vessels supplying the legs are protected from above by the shoulder blades.

The huge scapula, or shoulder blade, of the bull covers the upper area of the forward ribs. The left and right scapulae almost touch at their tops, forming the characteristic hump at the shoulder.[5] This configuration blocks easy access to the heart from the shoulder region. Indeed, the modern matador displays his skill by driving a sword into the small triangular space available between the tops of the scapulae. His long, curved weapon arcs downward through the animal's chest with the heart as its intended target. Only a fatal wound to the heart will cause the collapse of the enraged animal. Mithras is not aiming for this small area on the centerline of the animal's back, but is instead stabbing the right shoulder. Mithras' dagger, or short sword, blocked by anatomy, is incapable of reaching the heart from its entry point at the shoulder. The traditional methods of sacrifice were expected to cause the quick collapse of the victim. Conversely, stabbing the muscular shoulder of the bull, far from any vital points, would more likely enrage rather than subdue the beast. Although this placement is only symbolic, and probably not a depiction of actual cult practice, it is a glaring anomaly. This suggests that the shoulder itself is the target.

The bull's shoulder appears in Mithraic symbolism in images other than the tauroctony. Many tauroctony monuments include additional scenes on the left and right sides and across the top.[6] These side scenes are thought to depict episodes in the *transitus* of Mithras, the significant events of Mithras' birth, development, and ascension to the status of solar deity. One of the typical side scenes depicts Mithras wielding the dismembered foreleg of a bull in his right hand. Kneeling in front of Mithras is the god Helios, making a gesture of supplication. Mithras appears to be threatening Helios with the foreleg as if it were a club. This scene is interpreted as being the moment in which Helios acknowledges Mithras' ascendancy over him as ruler of the heavens (*kosmokrator*). The foreleg is thus a symbol of Mithras' superiority over the other god. This is certainly an eccentric weapon, and it should cause us to consider whether the disembodied bull's foreleg bears cosmological or mythological symbolism, in keeping with the overall interpretations of the tauroctony. Where, then, do we find the origins of such symbolism? The foreleg of the bull, as it turns out, is a prominent icon in Egyptian mythology.

There has been relatively little consideration of the effect of Egyptian belief on the development of Mithraic doctrine and iconography.[7] Certainly late Egyptian belief was known to Mithraism. Statues of Isis have been found in association with Mithraic icons.[8] Her consort Sarapis was often equated with Mithras, Jupiter, or Saturn/Kronos on Mithraic monuments.[9] Some Mithraic statues also hold the Egyptian *ankh*. Priests of Isis are known to have belonged to the higher grades of Mithraic initiation.[10]

The foreleg of a bull occupies a prominent place in traditional Egyptian belief, so much so that I propose the Egyptian pantheon of gods (the Ennead) and its associated myths as the origin of the Mithraic symbolism regarding the bull's shoulder. As will be seen, the Seth-Osiris conflict results in a bull's foreleg being placed at the north pole of the cosmic sphere. This object becomes a powerful and dangerous symbol of order, and of potential catastrophe. These attributes are invoked in the side scenes of tauroctony monuments depicting Mithras and Helios mentioned above.

The most direct link to Egypt is the so-called *Mithrasliturgie*, a spell found in the Great Magical Papyrus of Paris, which originated in Roman Egypt.[11] Not surprisingly, this spell is riddled with Egyptian magic rites, interspersed with revelations of the gods. The text provides a spell that allows the reciter's soul to ascend into the heavens and travel along the northern polar axis of the earth, where the worshiper ultimately enters into the presence of Mithras. During the ascent, the soul encounters other deities, including Helios. In the magical papyri, Mithras is usually linked with this god, as he is in the tauroctony. After the worshiper greets Helios, the god walks toward the polar axis:

ταῦτά σου εἰπόντος ἐλεύσεται εἰς τὸν πόλον, καὶ ὄψῃ αὐτὸν περιπατοῦντα ὡς ἐν ὁδῷ. (Preisendanz 1928-31, *PGM* 4.656-658)

> After you have said these things, he will come to the celestial pole, and you will see him walking as if on a road. (Trans. Betz 1992)

Now the worshiper's soul has reached the pole. Other groups of deities then appear, one of which is referred to as the "Pole-Lords":

προέρχονται δὲ καὶ ἕτεροι Ζ′ θεοὶ ταύρων μέλανα πρόσωπα ἔχοντες ἐν περιζώμασιν λινοῖς κατέχοντες Ζ′ διαδήματα χρύσεα. οὗτοί εἰσιν οἱ καλούμενοι πολοκράτορες τοῦ οὐρανοῦ, οὓς δεῖ σε ἀσπάσασθαι ὁμοίως ἕκαστον τῷ ἰδίῳ αὐτῶν ὀνόματι. "χαίρετε, οἱ ἱεροὶ καὶ ἄλκιμοι νεανίαι, οἱ στρέφοντες ὑπὸ ἓν κέλευσμα τὸν περιδίνητον τοῦ κύκλου ἄξονα τοῦ οὐράνου." (Preisendanz 1928-31, *PGM* 4.674-681)

There also come forth another seven gods, who have the faces of black bulls, in linen loincloths, and in possession of seven golden diadems. They are the so-called Pole-Lords of heaven, whom you must greet in the same manner, each of them with his own name: "Hail, O guardians of the pivot, O sacred and brave youths, who turn at one command the revolving axis of the vault of heaven." (Trans. Betz 1992)

These bucephalic deities occupy a position in the sky that is similar to the polar guardians from the Egyptian tradition known as the "Spirits of the North." In the *Mithrasliturgie*, their duties focus on the operation of the celestial pole, the axis of the cosmic sphere.

After the Pole-Lords are properly honored, the worshiper finally encounters Mithras in all his radiant glory:

κατερχόμενον θεὸν ὑπερμεγέθη, φωθτινὴν ἔχοντα τὴν ὄψιν, νεώτερον, χρυσοκόμαν, ἐν κιτῶνι λευκῷ καὶ χρυσῷ στεφάνῳ καὶ ἀναξυρίσι, κατέχοντα τῇ δεξιᾷ ξειρὶ μόσχου ὦμον χρύσεον, ὅς ἐστιν Ἄρκτος ἡ κινοῦσα καὶ ἀντιστρέφουσα τὸν οὐρανόν, κατὰ ὥραν ἀναπολεύουσα καὶ καταπολεύουσα. (Preisendanz 1928-31, *PGM* 4.696-703)

A god descending, a god immensely great, having a bright appearance, youthful, golden-haired, with a white tunic and a golden crown and trousers, and holding in his right hand a golden shoulder of a calf: this is the Bear which moves and turns heaven around, moving upward and downward in accordance with the hour. (Trans. Betz 1992)

The bear in this passage is Ursa Major, the constellation that the Mithraeum at Ponza depicts as containing the North Pole.[12] In the Greek magical papyri, this constellation (or, properly, a part of it; see below) is usually invoked as a manifestation of a goddess such as Artemis or Aphrodite, or receives a divine epithet itself, such as "Queen of Heaven." The *Mithrasliturgie* is unusual in describing it as merely an object, albeit a powerful one. Within this constellation, we find the group of stars known to us as

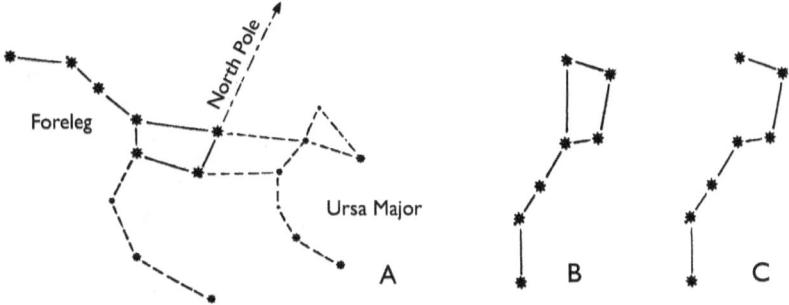

Figure 17.3. (a) The Egyptian constellation of the Foreleg shown as a portion of the constellation Ursa Major; (b) the Foreleg (Big Dipper); (c) the Foreleg depicted as an adze.

the Big Dipper (Fig. 17.3a–c). Although often mistakenly identified as a constellation, the Big Dipper actually forms just the torso and tail of the Great Bear, which is represented in full by the constellation Ursa Major. In the *Mithrasliturgie*, the Big Dipper acts as a lever that is attached to the polar axis. Thus, we discover the mechanism by which the heavens revolve: the Pole-Lords and Mithras use this lever to rotate the cosmic sphere.

While the *Mithrasliturgie* names this object (Bear) by drawing on Greek mythology (the story of the unfortunate nymph Callisto), its physical description as a bull's shoulder is drawn from Egyptian astrology. The Big Dipper forms a constellation of its own in Egyptian astrology, where it is known as the Foreleg (*Mes*, Fig. 17.3b). The well-known zodiac from the Great Temple of Dendara provides a graphic display of the Egyptian circumpolar constellations, with the Foreleg at the center, occupying the celestial pole. This object came to be in the sky as a result of the Seth-Osiris conflict.

A version of the murder of Osiris has Seth transformed into a bull when he commits the act.[13] The *Papyrus Leiden* I states that Seth stomped Osiris to death with his bovine foreleg:

> The stars of the northern sky are called "the never setting ones." They guard in the seven-star heavenly body the bull leg, the leg of Seth, with which he—as a bull—killed Osiris, and thereby prevent that a fight arises again. Fatigue in the southern sky and fight in the northern sky endanger the course of the earth. A lamentation [or complaint] before Re can bring it [i.e., the course of the earth] to a stop. After the ritual against evil, both skies could move towards each other. The southern sky could pull the

Figure 17.4. Procession of the Spirits of the North toward the Foreleg of Seth.

northern sky into its movement, so that it moves also towards the West, and both finally fall down. (*Pap. Leiden* 1.348, Verso XI, 5ff. [Schott 1959: 328])

Although the Foreleg has been imprisoned, it is still a threat and requires a retinue of keepers (Fig. 17.4). The "never setting ones" in this passage are the sons of Horus, numbering four or seven depending on the source. They are considered guardians more in the sense of prison guards, rather than as maintainers of celestial function. The *Mithrasliturgie* employs these guardians as the seven Pole-Lords that turn the polar axis.

In order to prevent Seth from harming other gods, Horus, the son of Osiris, cut the Foreleg from Seth's shoulder:

And after he had cut out his foreleg he threw it into the sky. Spirits guard it there: the Great Bear of the northern sky. The great Hippopotamus goddess keeps hold of it, so that it can no longer sail in the midst of the gods. (*Pap. Leiden* 1.348, Verso XI, 5ff. [Schott 1959: 328])

The Hippopotamus goddess is an Egyptian constellation near the North Pole that represents a manifestation of Isis.

A wall inscription from the tomb of Ramesses VI (twelfth century BCE) provides a description of this region of the sky similar to the above passages:

The Spirits of the North, these are the four gods among the followers. It is they who repulse the tempest of the sky on this the day of the Great Contest. It is they who take hold of the fore-rope and who maneuver the aft-rope on the barge of Re, together with the crew of the Imperishable Stars.[14] The four gods who are at the north of the Thigh,[15] they are re-

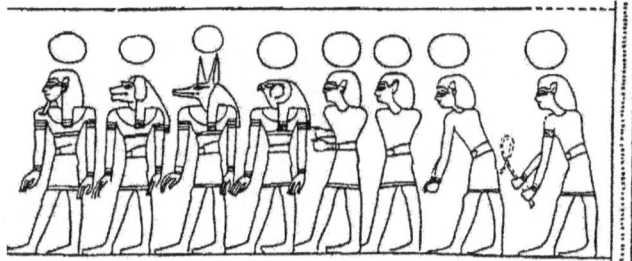

splendent in the midst of the sky, south of Orion, then they return to the Western Horizon.

As to this Thigh of Seth, it is in the Northern Sky attached to two firestone mooring posts by golden chains. It has been given in charge to Isis, in her form of a female hippopotamus, who guards it. The Water of His Gods is round about as the gods of the horizon. Re has placed them behind it, together with Isis, saying:

> Prevent it from going to the Southern Sky toward the Water of his Gods which issued from Osiris, he who is behind Orion. (Piankoff 1954: 400)

In this passage, the polar guardians, referred to as the Spirits of the North, guide the sun (the barge of Re, the Egyptian equivalent of Helios' chariot) through the sky using physical effort. This is analogous to the rotation of the cosmic sphere by means of the Foreleg as accomplished by the Mithraic Pole-Lords.

The Foreleg also came to be known in Egypt as an adze, which is similar to an axe that has the sharp edge of its blade placed at a right angle to the handle. The arrangement of stars in the Big Dipper/Foreleg resemble this instrument (Fig. 17.3c). A bull's foreleg and an adze were both used in the Egyptian ritual of the Opening of the Mouth, performed by mourners as part of funerary rites (Fig. 17.5).[16] This ritual was an entreaty to Osiris to allow the rebirth of a deceased person's soul. The mummy was presented with a dismembered bull's foreleg, symbolizing the leg of Seth. An adze was then touched to the mummy's mouth while this passage was recited:

> Horus has opened the mouth of NN with that wherewith he opened the mouth of his father wherewith he opened the mouth of Osiris, with the metal which came forth from Seth: the adze of metal. That with which the mouth of the gods was opened, with that do you open the mouth of

Figure 17.5. Ritual of the Opening of the Mouth.

NN so that he goes and speaks corporally before the great Ennead of the gods, in the palace of the ruler who is in Heliopolis. (Otto 1960: v. II, scene 46 text)

In the Opening of the Mouth, we see that the bull's leg was a ritual object as well as an important mythological symbol. Through the conflict of Seth and Osiris, the bull becomes an ambivalent object. It is a manifestation both of the murderous Seth and of the hero/victim Osiris in his reincarnation as the Apis bull. Thus, the Egyptians lived in fear of the large constellation hanging in the northern sky, while adoring the same creature in its complete organic form.

I have discussed possible symbolism of the bull's foreleg. My initial question sought the purpose behind the placement of the stab wound in the bull's shoulder. I suggest that the tauroctony scene depicts, *inter alia*, the initial stroke of the knife in the process of dismembering the bull's leg. From the *Mithrasliturgie*, we learn that Mithras retains control of this powerful and dangerous object after it is placed in the sky. This implies that Mithras was a more powerful god than the native Egyptian deities, who could be slain by the foreleg (as Osiris was), and who were required to imprison the foreleg in the sky with chains and keep a constant fearful watch around it in order to prevent further mayhem. Indeed, Mithras is the only god in the Magical Papyri to exert control over this object. In addition, Mithras is able to wield the foreleg in side scenes of the tauroctony as a symbol of his supremacy, particularly over Helios/Sol, the former solar ruler.

A common epithet of Mithras is *kosmokrator*. The trials of the tauroctony may be the prerequisite for his ascension to the heavenly duties of the *Mithrasliturgie*. Whereas in the tauroctony, events apparently take place on the Earth, events in the *Mithrasliturgie* occur along the northern polar axis. The cutting out of the bull's foreleg may represent the beginning of

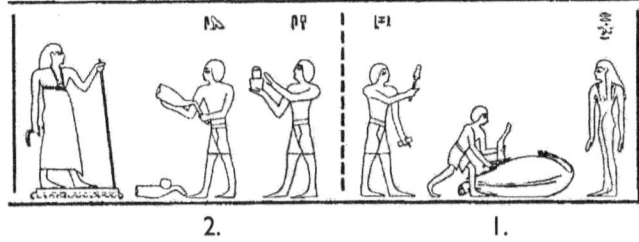

2.   1.

Mithras' ascent to the status of supreme solar deity. Indeed, it is the power remaining within the excised foreleg that obtains for Mithras his passage into the sky on the chariot of Helios, his predecessor.

Notes

1. *Corpus Inscriptionum et Monumentorum Religionis Mithraicae* (*CIMRM*) = Vermaseren 1956–60.
2. "Nike," *Lexicon Iconographicum Mythologiae Classicae* (*LIMC*).
3. Popesko 1971: figs. 2, 6, and 39. The size of cattle breeds available to the Romans varied greatly within Italy itself (Porter 1991: 34), let alone within the far-flung empire.
4. Popesko 1971: figs. 2, 6, and 39.
5. Ibid.
6. *CIMRM* Mon. 1430, as an example.
7. However, Roger Beck, in his 1998 article, provides a particularly relevant example of a possible transmitter of Egyptian knowledge into Roman Mithraism in the person of Ti. Claudius Balbillus, the Roman astrologer.
8. Witt 1975: 473.
9. Ibid. See also *CIMRM* Mon. 40 and 693, as examples.
10. Witt 1975: 487.
11. Preisendanz 1928–31 (*PGM* 4.475–829).
12. Vermaseren 1974. The North Pole is actually in the neighboring constellation of Ursa Minor, near the star Polaris. There has been no significant change in the pole's location since Roman times.
13. Te Velde 1977: 86.
14. The Imperishable Stars is the proper name of Re's barge.
15. The Thigh is another, inaccurate, name for the Foreleg.
16. Otto 1960, 2: scenes 43–46.

Bibliography

Adamo Muscettola, S., and S. De Caro, eds. 1994. *Alla ricerca di Iside.* Napoli. =*PP* 49(1996)1-168.
Adkins, A. 1960. *Merit and Responsibility: A Study in Greek Values.* Oxford.
———. 1969. "ΕΥΧΟΜΑΙ, ΕΥΧΟΛΗ, and ΕΥΧΟΣ in Homer." *CQ* 19:20-33.
Aellen, C. 1994. *À la recherche de l'ordre cosmique.* Zurich.
Albinus, L. 2000. *The House of Hades: Studies in Ancient Greek Eschatology.* Aarhus.
Albizzati, C. 1921. "Nota su demoni etruschi." *DPAA* ser. 2, 15:231-269.
Altevogt, H. 1952. *Labor Improbus: Eine Vergilstudie.* Münster.
Altheim, F. 1931. *Terra Mater: Untersuchungen zur altitalischen Religionsgeschichte.* Berlin.
———. 1979. *A History of Roman Religion.* Trans. H. Mattingly. New York.
Ameling, W. 1983. *Herodes Atticus.* New York.
Anton, J. P. 1992. "The Pythagorean Way of Life: Morality and Religion." In K. I. Boudouris, ed., *Pythagorean Philosophy,* 28-40. Athens.
Ardovino, A. M. 1986. *I culti di Paestum antica e del suo territorio.* Naples.
———. 1999. "Sistemi demetriaci nell'Occidente greco: I casi di Gela e Paestum." In Κοινά: *Miscellanea di studi archeologici in onore di Piero Orlandini,* 169-185. Milan.
Arens, W. 1979. *The Man-Eating Myth: Anthropology and Anthropophagy.* New York.
Arias, P. E. 1941. "La fonte sacra di Locri dedicata a Pan ed alle Ninfe." *Le Arti* 3:171-180.
Arnold, D. 1997. *Lexikon der ägyptischen Baukunst.* Düsseldorf and Zürich.
———. 1999. *Temples of the Last Pharaohs.* Oxford.
Arslan, E. A., ed. 1997. *Iside, il mito, il mistero, la magia.* Milan.
Arthur, P., P. M. Guarino, D. A. Jones, and M. Schiattarella. 1977. "Applicazione integrata di metodologie geologiche in archeologia ambientale: L'esempio del Progetto Eubea." *Geologia Tecnica* 2:5-13.
Asheri, D. 1988. "À propos des sanctuaires extraurbains en Sicile et Grande Grèce: théories et témoignages." In M.-M. Mactoux and E. Geny, eds., *Mélanges Pierre Lévêque,* vol. 1, *Religion,* 1-15. Paris.

Assmann, J. 2001. *The Search for God in Ancient Egypt*. Ithaca, N.Y.
Austin, R. G. 1977. *Vergili Maronis Aeneidos, Liber Sextus*. Oxford.
Bailey, C. 1935. *Religion in Vergil*. New York.
Balch, D. 2003. "The Suffering of Isis/Io and Paul's Portrait of Christ Crucified (Gal. 3:1): Frescoes in Pompeian and Roman Houses and in the Temple of Isis in Pompeii." *JR* 83:24-55.
Bañuls Oller, J. V. 1997. "De la pétrea memoria y el áureo olvido: Los epitafios y las *lamellae aureae*." *SphVal* 2:5-22.
Barchiesi, A. 1984. "Il nome di Lica e la poetica dei nomi in Petronio." *MD* 12: 169-175.
Barra Bagnasco, M. 1984. *Locri Epizefiri*. Chiaravalle (CZ).
———, ed. 1977. *Locri Epizefiri*. Ricerche nella zona di Centocamere. Florence.
Barret, W. S. 1964. *Euripides: Hippolytos*. Oxford.
Barron, J. P. 1972. "New Light on Old Walls: Murals of the Theseion." *JHS* 92:20-45.
Barth, F. 1987. *Cosmologies in the Making: A Generative Approach to Cultural Variation in Inner New Guinea*. Cambridge.
Barth, K. 1975. *Ritual and Knowledge among the Baktaman of New Guinea*. Oslo and New Haven.
Bats, M. 1997. "La nostra storia è cominciata qui. Cuma, i nuovi ritrovamenti." *Campania Felix* 12:23-24. Naples.
Bayet, J. 1926. *Les Origines de l'Hercule romain*. Paris.
———. 1951. "Les Cerealia, altération d'un culte latin par le mythe grec." *RBPh* 29:5-32, 341-366.
———. 1955. "Un procédé virgilien." In *Studi in onore di Gino Funaioli*. Rome.
Beacham, R. C. 1999. *Spectacle Entertainments of Early Imperial Rome*. New Haven and London.
Beard, M., J. North, and S. Price. 1998. *Religions of Rome*. Vol. 1. Cambridge.
Beck, R. 1998. "The Mysteries of Mithras: A New Account of Their Genesis." *JRS* 88:115-128.
———. 2000a. "Apuleius the Novelist, Apuleius the Ostian Householder and the Mithraeum of the Seven Spheres: Further Explorations of an Hypothesis of Filippo Coarelli." In S. G. Wilson and M. Desjardins, eds., *Text and Artifact in the Religions of Mediterranean Antiquity: Essays in Honour of Peter Richardson*, 551-567. Waterloo, Ontario.
———. 2000b. "Ritual, Myth, Doctrine, and Initiation in the Mysteries of Mithras: New Evidence from a Cult Vessel." *JRS* 90:145-180.
———. 2006. *The Religion of the Mithras Cult in the Roman Empire*. New York and Oxford.
Bekker, I., ed. 1814-21. *Anecdota Graeca*. 3 vols. Berlin.
Bell, M. 1976. "Le terrecotte votive del culto di Persefone a Morgantina." In *Il Tempio greco in Sicilia: Architettura e culti a Catania*, 140-147. Catania.
Beloch, J. 1890. *Campanien*. Breslau.
Bérard, C. 1976. "ΑΞΙΕ ΤΑΥΡΕ." In *Mélanges d'histoire et d'archéologie offerts à P. Collart*, 61-73. Lausanne.
Bérard, C., and C. Bron. 1984. "Le jeu du satyre." In *La cité des images*, 127-145. Lausanne.
Bernabé, A. 1991. "El poema órfico de Hiponion." In J. A. López Férez, ed., *Es-

tudios actuales sobre textos griegos, II Jornadas internacionales, UNED, 25-28 octobre 1989, 219-235. Madrid.

———. 1992. "La poesía órfica: Un capítulo reencontrado de la literatura griega." *Tempus* 0:5-41.

———. 1998a. "Platone e l'orfismo." In Sfameni Gasparro 1998: 33-93.

———. 1998b. "Nacimientos y muertes de Dioniso en los mitos órficos." In C. Sánchez Fernández and P. Cabrera Bonet, eds., *En los límites de Dioniso*, 29-39. Murcia.

———. 1999a. "Una cita de Píndaro en Platón *Men.* 81 b (*Fr.* 133 Sn.-M.)." In J. A. López Férez, ed., *Desde los poemas homéricos hasta la prosa griega del siglo IV d.C. Veintiséis estudios filológicos*, 239-259. Madrid.

———. 1999b. "La laminetta orfica di Entella." In M. I. Gulletta, ed., *Sicilia Epigraphica: Atti del Convegno di Studi Erice, 15-18 ottobre 1998*, 1:53-63. Pisa.

———. 1999c. "Juegos léxicos y juegos gráficos en los textos órficos." In Τῆς φιλίης τάδε δῶρα: *Miscelánea léxica en memoria de Conchita Serrano*, 457-464. Madrid.

———. 2000. "Tradiciones órficas en Diodoro." In M. Alganza Roldán, J. M. Camacho Rojo, P. P. Fuentes González, and M. Villena Ponsoda, eds., *Επιεικεια: Studia Graeca in memoriam Jesús Lens Tuero*, 37-53. Granada.

———. 2001a. *De Tales a Demócrito: Fragmentos presocráticos*. 2d ed. Madrid. (First ed., 1988.)

———. 2001b. "La experiencia iniciática en Plutarco." In A. Pérez Jiménez and F. Casadesús, eds., *Misticismo y religiones mistéricas en la obra de Plutarco*, Actas del VII Simposio Español sobre Plutarco, 5-22. Madrid and Málaga.

———. 2002. "La toile de Pénélope: A-t-il existé un mythe orphique sur Dionysos et les Titans?" *RHR* 219:401-433.

———. 2003. *Hieros logos: Poesía órfica sobre los dioses, el alma y el más allá*. Madrid.

———. 2004a. *Poetae Epici Graeci. Testimonia et fragmenta*. Pars. II, fasc. 1, *Orphicorum et Orphicis similium testimonia et fragmenta*. Monachii and Lipsiae. (Abbreviated as Orph. fr. B.)

———. 2004b. *Textos órficos y filosofía presocrática: Materiales para una comparación*. Madrid.

———. 2004c. "Un fragmento de *Los Cretenses* de Eurípides." In J. A. López Férez, ed., *La tragedia griega en sus textos*, 257-286. Madrid.

———. 2005. *Poetae Epici Graeci Testimonia et fragmenta*. Pars. II, fasc. 2, *Orphicorum et Orphicis similium testimonia et fragmenta*. Monachii and Lipsiae.

Bernabé, A., and A. I. Jiménez San Cristóbal. 2001. *Instrucciones para el Más Allá: Las laminillas órficas de oro*. Madrid.

———. 2008. *Instructions for the Netherworld: The Orphic Gold Tablets*. Leiden and Boston.

Bernabò Brea, L. 1981. "Il significato delle terracotte teatrali." In *Menandro e il Teatro Greco nelle Terracotte Liparesi*, 21-27. Genoa.

Bernand, A. 1969. *Les inscriptions grecques de Philae I: Époque ptolémaïque*. Paris.

Bertoletti, R., R. DeAngelis, G. Ioppolo, and G. Pisani Sartorio. 1988. *Itinerari d'arte e di cultura—Via Appia: La residenza imperiale di Massenzio: Villa, mausoleo e circo*. Rome.

Bessone, F. 1993. "Discorsi dei liberti e parodia del 'simposio' platonico nella 'Cena Trimalchionis.'" *MD* 30:63-86.
Betegh, G. 2004. *The Derveni Papyrus: Cosmology, Theology, and Interpretation.* Cambridge.
Betz, H. 1992. *The Greek Magical Papyri in Translation.* Chicago.
———. 2003. *The "Mithras Liturgy": Text, Translation, and Commentary.* Tübingen.
Bianchi, U. 1975. *La religione greca.* Turin.
———. 1976a. *The Greek Mysteries: Iconography of Religions,* XVII.3. Leiden.
———. 1976b. *Prometeo, Orfeo, Adamo: Tematiche religiose sul destino, il male, la salvezza.* Rome.
———, ed. 1979. *Mysteria Mithrae.* Leiden and Rome.
———. 1995. Review of W. Burkert, *Antike Mysterien* (Munich, 1990). *Gnomon* 67:1-5.
Bianchi, U., and M. J. Vermaseren, eds. 1982. *La soteriologia dei culti orientali nell'Impero Romano.* Leiden.
Bierl, A. H. 1991. *Dionysos und die griechische Tragödie: Politische und metatheatralische Aspekte im Text.* Classica Monacensia 1. Tübingen.
Blanc, N., H. Eristov, and M. Fincker. 2000. "A fundamento restituit? Réfections dans le Temple d'Isis à Pompéi." *RA* 2:227-309.
Boardman, J. 1975. "Herakles, Peisistratos and Eleusis." *JHS* 95:1-12 with plates I-IV.
Bodel, J. 1994. "Graveyards and Groves: A Study of the Lex Lucerina." *AJAH* 11:1-133.
Boffa, G. M. 1977. "Figura femminile nuda seduta." In *Locri Epizefiri 1977,* 1:231-238.
Bøgh, B. 2007. "The Phrygian Background of Kybele." *Numen* 54:304-339.
Bookidis, N., and J. E. Fischer. 1972. "Sanctuary of Demeter and Kore on Acrocorinth, Preliminary Report IV: 1969-1970 (Plates 55-64)." *Hesperia* 41:283-317.
———. 1974. "The Sanctuary of Demeter and Kore on Acrocorinth, Preliminary Report V: 1971-1973 (Plates 53-60)." *Hesperia* 43:267-291.
Bookidis, N., and R. Stroud. 1969. "The Sanctuary of Demeter and Kore on Acrocorinth, Preliminary Report III: 1968 (Plates 75-79)." *Hesperia* 38:297-310.
———. 1987. *Demeter and Persephone in Ancient Corinth.* Corinth Notes 2, American School of Classical Studies at Athens. Princeton.
Borg, B., ed. 2004. *Paideia: The World of the Second Sophistic.* Berlin and New York.
Borgeaud, P. 1979. *Recherches sur le dieu Pan.* Rome.
———. 1998. "Taurobolion." In F. Graf, ed., *Ansichten griechischer Rituale: Geburtstags-Symposium Festschrift für Walter Burkert,* 183-198. Stuttgart and Leipzig.
———. 1996. *La Mère des dieux: De Cybèle à la Vierge Marie.* Paris.
Borthwick, E. K. 1968. "Seeing Weasels: The Superstitious Background of the Empusa Scene in the *Frogs.*" *CQ* 18:200-206.
Bottini, A. 1992. *Archeologia della salvezza.* Milan.
———, ed. 2005. *Il rito segreto: Misteri in Grecia e a Roma.* Milan.
Bourdieu, P. 1979. *La distinction: Critique sociale du jugement.* Paris.

Bowersock, G. W. 1994. *Fiction as History: Nero to Julian.* Sather Classical Lectures 58. Berkeley.
Bowra, C. M. 1952. "Orpheus and Eurydice." *CQ* 2:113-126.
Boyancé, P. 1963. *La religion de Virgile.* Paris.
Boyer, P. 2001. *Religion Explained: The Evolutionary Origins of Religious Thought.* New York.
Bragantini, I., and M. De Vos, eds. 1982. *Le decorazioni della Villa Romana della Farnesina: Museo Nazionale Romano. Le pitture* II.1. Rome.
Bremmer, J. N. 1984. "Greek Maenadism Reconsidered." *ZPE* 55:267-286.
———. 1992. "Dionysos travestí." In *L'Initiation I: Actes du Colloque International de Montpellier, 11-14 avril 1991. Les Rites d'adolescence et les mystères,* 189-198. Montpellier.
———. 1999. "The Birth of the Term 'Magic.'" *ZPE* 126:1-12.
———. 2002. *The Rise and Fall of the Afterlife: The 1995 Read-Tuckwell Lectures at the University of Bristol.* London and New York.
———. 2005. "Attis: A Greek God in Anatolian Pessinous and Catullan Rome." In R. R. Nauta and A. Harder, eds., *Catullus' Poem on Attis: Texts and Contexts,* 25-64. Leiden.
———. 2006. "A Macedonian Maenad in Posidippus (AB 44)." *ZPE* 155:37-40.
Brenk, F. E. 1989. Review of Walter Burkert, *Ancient Mystery Cults. Gnomon* 61:289-292.
———. 1998. "A Gleaming Ray: Blessed Afterlife in the Mysteries." In idem, *Relighting the Souls: Studies in Plutarch, in Greek Literature, Religion, and Philosophy, and in the New Testament Background,* 291-308. Stuttgart. (Originally published in D. Sansone, ed., *Studies in Honor of Miroslav Marcovich, ICS* 18 [1993]: 147-164.)
———. 1999a. "The Isis Campensis of Katja Lembke." In N. Blanc and André Buisson, eds., *Imago Antiquitatis: Religions et iconographie du monde romain, Mélanges offerts à Robert Turcan,* 133-143. Paris.
———. 1999b. "Isis Is a Greek Word: Plutarch's Allegorization of Egyptian Religion." In A. Pérez Jiménez, J. García López, and R. M. Aguilar, eds., *Plutarco, Platón y Aristóteles,* 227-238. Madrid.
———. 2001. "In the Image, Reflection and Reason of Osiris: Plutarch and the Egyptian Cults." In A. Pérez Jiménez and F. Casadesús Bordoy, eds., *Estudios sobre Plutarco: Misticismo y religiones mistericas en la obra de Plutarco,* 83-98. Madrid and Málaga.
———. 2003a. "Osirian Reflections: Second Thoughts on the Isaeum Campense at Rome." In P. Defosse, ed., *Hommages à Carl Deroux,* 291-303. Brussels.
———. 2003b. "Religion under Trajan: Plutarch's Resurrection of Osiris." In P. A. Stadter, ed., *Sage and Emperor: Plutarch and Trajan,* 73-92. Leuven.
———. 2005. "Plutarchos." In Jones 2005, 11:7199-7202.
Bricault, L. 2001. *Atlas de la diffusion des cultes isiaques (IVe s. av. J.-C.—IVe s. apr. J.-C.).* Paris.
Brillante, C. 1987. "La rappresentazione del sogno nel frammento di un *threnos* pindarico." *QUCC* 25:35-51.
Brown, C. G. 1991. "Empousa, Dionysus and the Mysteries: Aristophanes, *Frogs* 285 ff." *CQ* 41:41-50.

Brown, P.R.L. 1988. *The Body and Society: Men, Women and Sexual Renunciation in Early Christianity.* New York.
Bruhl, A. 1953. *Liber Pater: Origine et expansion du culte dionysiaque à Rome et dans le monde romain.* Paris.
Büchner, K. 1955-1958. "P. Vergilius Maro." *RE* 8.A1 (1955): 1021-1264; *RE* 8.A2 (1958): 1265-1486.
Burkert, W. 1961. "Elysion." *Glotta* 39:208-213.
———. 1969. "Das Proömium des Parmenides und die Katabasis des Pythagoras." *Phronesis* 14:1-30.
———. 1972. *Lore and Science in Ancient Pythagoreanism.* Trans. E. L. Minar Jr. Cambridge, Mass.
———. 1975. "Le laminette auree: Da Orfeo a Lampone." In *Orfismo in Magna Grecia: Atti del Quattordicesimo Convegno di Studi sulla Magna Grecia.* Taranto, 6-10 ottobre 1974, 81-104. Naples.
———. 1977. *Griechische Religion der archaischen und klassischen Epoche.* Stuttgart.
———. 1980. "Neue Funde zur Orphik." *Informationen zum altsprachlichen Unterricht*, 2.2:27-41. Graz.
———. 1982. "Craft Versus Sect: The Problem of Orphics and Pythagoreans." In B. Meyer and E. P. Sanders, eds., *Jewish and Christian Self-Definition,* vol. 3, *Self-Definition in the Greco-Roman World,* 1-22. Philadelphia.
———. 1985. *Greek Religion.* Trans. J. Raffan. Cambridge, Mass.
———. 1987. *Ancient Mystery Cults.* Cambridge, Mass., and London.
———. 1996. *Klassisches Altertum und antikes Christentum.* Berlin. (Italian augmented edition, *Antichità classica e cristianesimo anticó* [Cosenza, 2000].)
———. 1999. *Da Omero ai Magi: La tradizione orientale nella cultura greca.* Venice.
———. 2004. "Initiation." In *Thesaurus Cultus et Rituum Antiquorum (ThesCRA),* 2:91-124. Los Angeles.
Burton, A. 1972. *Diodorus Siculus, Book I: A Commentary.* EPRO 29. Leiden.
Butler, J. 1993. *Bodies that Matter: On the Discursive Limits of "Sex."* New York.
Buxton, R., ed. 2000. *Oxford Readings in Greek Religion.* Oxford.
Cabrera Bonet, P. 1998. "Dioniso en un jardín: El espacio de la iniciación en la iconografía de los vasos apulios." In C. Sánchez Fernández and P. Cabrera Bonet, eds., *En los límites de Dioniso,* 61-87. Murcia.
Cabrera, P. and A. Bernabé. 2007. "Echos littéraires de l'enlèvement de Perséphone: Un vase Apulien du Musée Archéologique National de Madrid." *AK* 50:58-75 and plates 6-7.
Caccamo Caltabiano, M. 1984. "Aristodemo di Cuma e la religione nel potere dei tiranni." In *Religione e città nel mondo antico* (Atti Ce.R.D.A.C. XI, 1980-1981), 271-279. Rome.
Calame, C. 1995. "Invocations et commentaires 'orphiques': Transpositions funéraires de discours religieux." In M. M. Mactoux and E. Geny, eds., *Discours religieux dans l'Antiquité.* Annales Littéraires de l'Université de Besançon 578, 11-30. Paris.
———. 1999. *The Poetics of Eros in Ancient Greece.* Princeton.
———. 2002. "Qu'est-ce qui est orphique dans les *Orphica*? Une mise au point introductive." *RHR* 219, 4:385-400.

———. Forthcoming. "'Orphic' Invocations and Commentaries: Funerary Transpositions of Religious Discourse." In Edmonds forthcoming.
Cameron, A. 1969. "Petronius and Plato." *CQ* 19:367-370.
Canina, L. 1853. *La prima parte della Via Appia, dalla Porta Capena a Boville*. Vols. 1 and 2. Rome.
Cannatà Fera, M. 1990. *Pindarus: Threnorum fragmenta*. Rome.
Cantarella, E. 1991. *I supplizi capitali in Grecia e Roma: Origini e funzioni della pena di morte nell'antichità classica*. Milan.
Capriotti Vittozzi, G. 1999. *Oggetti, idee, culti egizi nelle Marche: Dalle tombe picene al Tempio di Treia*. Tivoli (Rome).
———. 2000. "Note sulla comprensione dell'Egitto nel mondo romano." *RSA* 30:121-139.
Caputo, P. 1991. "Cuma: Rinvenimento di un tempio di Iside." *Bollettino di Archeologia* 11-12:169-172.
———. 1998. "Aegyptiaca Cumana: New Evidence for Isis Cult in Campania: The Site." In C. J. Eyre, ed., *Proceedings of the Seventh International Congress of Egyptologists*, 245-253. Leuven.
———. 2000. "Il nuovo tempio di Iside a Cuma." In *Nova Antiqua Phlegreaea*. Naples.
———. 2003a. "I resti del Tempio di Iside a Cuma in relazione alle trasformazioni geomorfologiche del litorale." In C. A. Livadie and F. Ortolani, eds., *Climatic-Environmental Variations and Impact on Man in the Circum-Mediterranean Area during the Holocene*, Atti del Convegno (Ravello, 1993), 87-94. Bari.
———. 2003b. "Il Tempio di Iside a Cuma: Nuovi documenti sul culto isiaco in Campania." In *Santuari e luoghi di culto nell'Italia antica*, ATTA 12, 209-220. Rome.
———. 2003c. "Nuovi rinvenimenti vetrari dall'area archeologica di Cuma: Prospettive di ricerca." In *Il vetro in Italia meridionale ei insulare: Atti del secondo convegno multidisciplinare (Napoli 5, 6, 7 dicembre 2001)*, 45-51. Naples.
Caputo, P., F. Fratte, and G. Gasparri. 1997. In *Melanges d'histoire e d'archéologie offerts à P. Collart*.
Caputo, P., R. Morichi, R. Paone, P. Rispoli. 1996. *Cuma e il suo parco archeologico: Un territorio e le sue testimonianze*. Rome.
Carosi, S. 2002. "Nuovi dati sul santuario di Campetti a Veio." *ArchClass* 53:355-377.
Carpenter, T. H. 1986. *Dionysian Imagery in Archaic Greek Art*. Oxford.
———. 1989. *Beazley Addenda*. 2d ed. Oxford.
Casabona, J. 1966. *Recherches sur le vocabulaire des sacrifices en grec, des origines à la fin de l'époque classique*. Aix-en-Provence.
Casadesús, B. 1995. "Revisió de les principals fonts per a l'estudi de l'orfisme a l'epoca classica (Plató i el Papir de Derveni)." Doctoral thesis, Universitat Autònoma de Barcelona, Bellaterra.
———. 1997. "Òrfics o impostors? El testimoni d'Eurípides: Hipòlit 943-957." In M. del C. Bosch and M. A. Fornés, eds., *Homenatge a Miquel Dolç: Actes del XII simposi de la secció catalana I. I de la secció balear de la SEEC*, 167-170. Palma de Mallorca.
———. 2002. "Análisis de la figura del mago en ambientes órficos." In *Actas del X Congreso español de Estudios Clásicos*, 3:75-82. Madrid.

Casadio, G. 1982. "Per un' indagine storico-religiosa sui culti di Dioniso in relazione alla fenomenologia dei misteri, I." *Studi storico-religiosi* 6:209-234.
———. 1983. "Per un' indagine storico-religiosa sui culti di Dioniso in relazione alla fenomenologia dei misteri, II." *SMSR* 49, 1:123-149.
———. 1989. "Dionysos entre histoire et sociologie." *DHA* 15, 2:285-308.
———. 1990a. "A proposito di un recente volume su problemi di storia della religione greca." *QUCC* 36, 3:164-174.
———. 1990b. "I *Cretesi* di Euripide e l'ascesi orfica." In *Didattica del Classico* 2:278-310. Foggia.
———. 1991. "La metempsicosi tra Orfeo e Pitagora." In P. Borgeaud, ed., *Orphisme et Orphée: En l'honneur de Jean Rudhardt*, Recherches et Rencontres 3: 119-155. Geneva.
———. 1992. "Préhistoire de l'initiation dionysiaque." In A. Moreau, ed., *L'initiation*, 209-213. Montpellier.
———. 1994. *Storia del culto di Dioniso in Argolide*. Rome.
———. 1995. "Dioniso italiota: Un dio greco in Italia meridionale." In *Forme di religiosità e tradizioni sapienziali in Magna Grecia*. Pisa and Rome. (= *AION* 16 [1994]: 79-107.)
———. 1996a. "Dionysos Goes Abroad: A Greek God among the Barbarians." In I. Dolezalová, B. Horyna, and D. Papousek, eds., *Religions in Contact*, 73-76. Brno.
———. 1996b. "Osiride in Grecia e Dioniso in Egitto." In I. Gallo, ed., *Plutarco e la Religione: Atti del VI Convegno plutarcheo (Ravello, 29-31 maggio 1995)*, 201-227. Naples.
———. 1999a. *Il vino dell'anima: Storia del culto di Dioniso a Corinto, Sicione, Trezene*. Rome.
———. 1999b. "Franz Cumont, historien des religions et citoyen du monde." In *Imago antiquitatis: Religions et iconographie du monde romain: Mélanges offerts à Robert Turcan*, 161-165. Paris.
———. 2003. "The Failing Male God: Emasculation, Death and Other Accidents in the Ancient Mediterranean World." *Numen* 50:231-268.
———. 2005. "Xenophanes." In Jones 2005, 14:9854-9856. Detroit.
Casini, M., ed. 2001. *One Hundred Years in Egypt: Paths of Italian Archaeology*. Milan.
Cecamore, C. 2002. *Palatium: Topografia storica tra III sec. a.C. e I sec. d.C.* (*BCAR*, suppl. 9), 230-231. Rome.
Champlin, E. 1987. "The Testament of the Piglet." *Phoenix* 41:174-183.
Chandor Brumfield, A. 1981. *The Attic Festivals of Demeter and Their Relation to the Agricultural Year*. Salem, N.H.
Chantraine, P. 1970. *Dictionnaire étymologique de la langue grecque*. Vol. 2. Paris. (Reprint with supplement, 1999.)
Chioffi, L. 1998. *Mummificazione e imbalsamazione a Roma ed in altri luoghi del mondo romano*. Rome.
Ciaceri, E. 1928. *Storia della Magna Grecia*. Vol. 1. 2d ed. Naples. (First ed., 1924.)
———. 1932. *Storia della Magna Grecia*. Vol. 3. 2d ed. Naples.
———. 1940. *Storia della Magna Grecia*. Vol. 2. 2d ed. Naples. (First ed., 1927.)
Ciampini, E. M. 1999. "La fenice, il serpente e il tempo." *SMSR* 65:31-40.

Cipriani, M. 1988. "Il culto di Demetra nella chora pestana: lo scavo del santuario di Albanella." In *Posidonia-Paestum*. Atti del XXVII Convegno di Studi sulla Magna Grecia Taranto-Paestum, 9-15 ottobre 1987, 430-445. Naples.

———. 1989. *S. Nicola di Albanella: Scavo di un santuario campestre nel territorio di Poseidonia-Paestum*. Rome.

Cipriani, M., and A. M. Ardovino. 1989-90. "Il culto di Demetra nella chora pestana." *Scienze dell'Antichità* 3-4:339-351.

Claridge, A. 1998. *Rome: An Oxford Archaeological Guide*. Oxford.

Clark, A. 1997. *Being There: Putting Brain, Body, and World Together Again*. Cambridge, Mass.

Clark, R. J. 1970. "Two Virgilian Similes and the Ἡρακλέους κατάβασις." *Phoenix* 24:244-255.

———. 1992. "Vergil, *Aeneid* 6: The Bough by Hades' Gate." In R. M. Wilhelm and H. Jones, eds., *The Two Worlds of the Poet: New Perspectives on Vergil*, 167-178. Detroit.

———. 2000. "*P. OXY.* 2078, Vat. Gr. 2228, and Vergil's Charon." *CQ* 50:192-196.

———. 2001. "How Vergil Expanded the Underworld in *Aeneid* 6." *PCPhS* 47:103-116.

———. 2003. "The Cerberus-like Function of the Gorgons in Vergil's Underworld (*Aen.* 6.273-94)." *CQ* 53:308-309.

Clauss, M. 2000. *The Roman Cult of Mithras*. Edinburgh. (Corrected translation of *Mithras: Kult und Mysterien* [Munich, 1990].)

Clinton, K. 1986. "The Author of the Homeric *Hymn to Demeter*." *OAth* 16:43-49.

———. 1988. "Sacrifice at the Eleusinian Mysteries." In R. Hägg, N. Marinatos, and G. C. Nordquist, eds., *Early Greek Cult Practice*, Proceedings of the Fifth International Symposium at the Swedish Institute at Athens, 26-29 June 1986 (Acta Instituti Atheniensis Regni Sueciae, Series in 4⁰, XXXVIII), 69-79. Stockholm.

———. 1989. "The Eleusinian Mysteries: Roman Initiates and Benefactors, Second Century BC to AD 267." *ANRW* II.18.2: 1499-1539.

———. 1992. *Myth and Cult: The Iconography of the Eleusinian Mysteries*. The Martin P. Nilsson Lectures on Greek Religion, delivered 19-21 November 1990 at the Swedish Institute at Athens (Acta Instituti Atheniensis Regni Sueciae, Series in 8⁰, XI). Stockholm.

———. 1993. "The Sanctuary of Demeter and Kore at Eleusis." In N. Marinatos and R. Hägg, eds., *Greek Sanctuaries: New Approaches*, 110-124. London and New York.

———. 1996. "The Thesmophorion in Central Athens and the Celebration of the Thesmophoria in Attica." In R. Hägg, ed., *The Role of Religion in the Early Greek Polis. Proceedings of the Third International Seminar of Ancient Greek Cult, Organized by the Swedish Institute at Athens, 16-18 October 1992* (Acta Instituti Atheniensis Regni Sueciae, Series in 8⁰, XIV), 111-125. Stockholm.

———. 2003. "Stages of Initiation in the Eleusinian and Samothracian Mysteries." In Cosmopoulos 2003: 50-78.

Coarelli, F. 1989. "Apuleio a Ostia?" *DArch* 7:27-42.

———. 1994. "Iside e Fortuna a Pompei e a Palestrina." *PP* 49: 119-129.

Cockle, H. M., ed. 1983. *The Oxyrhynchus Papyri*. Vol. 50. London.
Coldstream, J. 1973. *Knossos: The Sanctuary of Demeter*. Suppl. vol. 8. London.
Coleman, K. M. 1990. "Fatal Charades: Roman Executions Staged as Mythological Enactments." *JRS* 80:44-73.
———. 1993. "Launching into History: Aquatic Displays in the Early Empire." *JRS* 83:48-74.
Colli, G. 1948. *Physis kryptesthai philei: Studi sulla filosofia greca*. Milan.
Collings, D. 2000. "Bentham's Auto-Icon: Utilitarianism and the Evisceration of the Common Body." *Prose Studies* 23:95-127.
Comparetti, D. 1882. "The Petelia Gold Tablet." *JHS* 3:111-118.
———. 1906. "Iscrizione arcaica cumana." *Ausonia*: 13-20.
Conington, J. 1872. *P. Vergili Maronis Opera*. 2d ed. Vol. 2. London.
Conington, J., and H. Nettleship. [1898] 1963. *The Works of Virgil*. Rev. F. Haverfield. 5th ed. Vol. 1. Hildesheim.
Conte, G. B. 1996. *The Hidden Author: An Interpretation of Petronius'* Satyricon. Trans. E. Fantham. Berkeley, Los Angeles, and London.
Cooper, K. 1999. *The Virgin and the Bride: Idealized Womanhood in Late Antiquity*. Oxford.
Cosi, D. M. 1983. "Comunicazione disturbata: Battos, il fondatore di Cirene, balbuziente e castrato." In M. G. Ciani, ed., *Le regioni del silenzio*, 123-154. Padova.
Cosmopoulos, M. B., ed. 2003. *Greek Mysteries: The Archaeology and Ritual of Ancient Greek Secret Cults*. London and New York.
Costabile, F., ed. 1991. *I Ninfei di Locri Epizefiri: Architettura, culti erotici, sacralità delle acque*. Catanzaro.
Courtney, E. 1962. "Parody and Literary Allusion in Menippean Satire." *Philologus* 106:86-100.
Cozzoli, A. T. 1993. "Euripide, Cretesi, *fr.* 472 N2 (79 Austin)." In A. Masaracchia, ed., *Orfeo e l'orfismo*, 155-172. Rome.
Cozzolino, C. 1997. "Statua di Ahmose." In Arslan 1997: 448.
———. 1999. "Recent Discoveries in Campania." In *Egyptological Studies for Claudio Barocas*, Serie egittologia, I.U.O., Dipartimento di studi e ricerche su Africa e Paesi Arabi, vol. 1. Naples.
Crimmins, J. E., ed. 2002. *Jeremy Bentham's Auto-Icon and Related Writings*. Bristol.
Cucchiarelli, A. 1996. "L'Entrata di Abinna nella Cena Trimalchionis (Petr. *Satyr.* 65)." *ASNS* series 4a 1 (2): 737-753.
Cumont, F. [1906] 1929. *Les religions orientales dans le paganisme romain*. Paris.
———. 1924. "Le mithréum de Capoue." *CRAI*: 113-115.
———. 1933. "La grande inscription bachique du Metropolitan Museum, II: Commentaire religieux de l'inscription, Planches XXX-XXXIII." *AJA* 37:232-263.
Curto, S. 1985. *Le sculture egizie ed egittizzanti nella Villa Torlonia in Roma*. Leiden.
Dabdab Trabulsi, J. A. 1990. *Dionysisme: Pouvoir et societé en Grèce jusqu'à la fin de l'époque classique*. Besançon and Paris.
D'Alconzo, P. 2002. *Picturae excisae: Conservazione e restauro dei dipinti ercolanesi e pompeiani tra XVIII e XIX secolo*. Rome.

D'Arms, J. H. 1970. *Romans on the Bay of Naples*. Cambridge, Mass.
David, J. 2000. "The Exclusion of Women in the Mithraic Mysteries: Ancient or Modern?" *Numen* 47:121–141.
Davis-Sulikowski, U., H. Diemberger, A. Gingrich, and J. Helbrich. 2001. *Körper, Religion und Macht: Sozialanthropologie der Geschlechterbeziehungen*. Frankfurt.
De Caro, S., ed. 1992. *Alla Ricerca di Iside: Analisi, Studi e restauri dell'Iseo pompeiano nel Museo di Napoli*. Rome.
———. 1993–94. "Fouilles et découvertes récentes en Campanie Septentrionale." *Bullettin de la Société Française d'Archéologie Classique* 4, no. 27: 189–190.
———. 1994. "Novità isiache dalla Campania." *PP* 49.
———. 1997. "Iside nei Campi Flegrei." In Arslan 1997: 350–351.
De Jong, A. 2000. "A New Syrian Mithraic Tauroctony." *Bulletin of the Asia Institute*, n.s. 11: 53–63.
De Juliis, E. M. 1982. *L'attività archeologica in Puglia*. In *Megale Hellas nome e immagine*. Atti del Ventunesimo Convegno di Studi sulla Magna Grecia Taranto, 2–5 ottobre 1981, 293–321. Naples.
De la Genière, J., and G. Greco. 1990. "Heraion alla foce del Sele." In *Paestum*, 63–80. Naples.
Delatte, A. 1914. "Étude sur la magie grecque: Amulettes mithriaques." *Musée Belge* 18:5–20.
Del Tutto Palma, L., ed. 1996. *La Tavola di Agnone nel contesto italico: Convegno di studio, Agnone, 13–15 aprile 1994*. Florence.
Demand, N. 1975. "Pindar's *Olympian* 2, Theron's Faith and Empedocles' *Katharmoi*." *GRBS* 16:347–357.
Depew, M. 1997. "Reading Greek Prayers." *ClAnt* 16:229–258.
Des Places, E. 1969. *La religion grecque*. Paris.
Detienne, M. 1979. "Violentes 'eugénies'. En pleines Thesmophories: Des femmes couvertes de sang." In M. Detienne and J. P. Vernant, *La cuisine du sacrifice en pays grec*, 185–214. Paris. (Italian translation [Turin, 1982], pp. 131–148.)
———. 1986. *Dionysos à ciel ouvert*. Paris.
De Vos, M. 1992. "*Aegyptiaca Romana*." In De Caro 1992: 130–159.
Dewailly, M. 1983. "La divinità femminile con polos a Selinunte." *Sicilia Archeologica* 52–53:5–12.
Dickie, M. 1995. "The Dionysiac Mysteries in Pella." *ZPE* 109:80–86.
Dieterich, A. 1891. *De Hymnis Orphicis: Capitula Quinque*. Marburg.
———. [1893] 1913. *Nekyia: Beiträge zur Erklärung der neuentdeckten Petrusapokalypse*. 2d ed. Leipzig and Berlin.
———. 1897. *Pulcinella: Pompejanische Wandbilder und römische Satyrspiele*. Leipzig.
Díez de Velasco, F. 1995. *Los caminos de la muerte: Religión, rito e imágenes del paso al más allá en la Grecia antigua*. Madrid.
———. 1997. "Un problema de delimitación conceptual en historia de las religiones: La mística griega." In D. Plácido, J. Alvar, M. Casillas, and C. Fornis, eds., *Imágenes de la Polis*, 407–422. Madrid.
Díez de Velasco, F., and M. A. Molinero Polo. 1994. "Hellenoaegyptiaca I: Influences égyptiennes dans l'imaginaire grec de la mort: quelques exemples d'un emprunt supposé (Diodore I, 92, 1–4; I, 96, 4–8)." *Kernos* 7:75–93.

Di Fraia, G., N. Lombardo, and E. Scognamiglio. 1986. "Contributi alla topografia di Baia sommersa." *Puteoli: Studi storia antica* 9-10:211-299.
Diggle, J. 1998. *Tragicorum Graecorum Fragmenta Selecta*. Oxford.
Dillon, M. 2002. *Girls and Women in Classical Greek Religion*. London and New York.
Di Maria, R. 1997. "Statua acefala di divinità, probabilmente Iside." In Arslan 1997: 448.
Dindorf, W., ed. 1828. Themistius, *Orationes*. Leipzig.
———. 1835-38. *Aristophanis Comoediae*. Oxford.
Dobrochotov, A. L. 1992. "The Thesis 'Sôma-Sêma' and Its Philosophical Implications." In K. I. Boudouris, ed., *Pythagorean Philosophy*, 98-101. Athens.
Dodd, D. B., and C. A. Faraone, eds. 2003. *Initiation in Ancient Greek Rituals and Narratives: New Critical Perspectives*. London and New York.
Dodds, E. R. 1944. *Euripides, Bacchae*. Oxford. (2d ed., 1960.)
———. 1951. *The Greeks and the Irrational*. Sather Classical Lectures 25. Berkeley and Los Angeles.
———. 1959. *Plato: Gorgias*. 2d ed. Oxford.
Domergue, C., C. Landes, and J.-M. Pailler, eds. 1990. *Spectacula, 1: Gladiateurs et amphithéâtres*. Actes du Colloque, Toulouse/Lattes, May 1987. Lattes.
Dover, K. J. 1993. *Aristophanes' Frogs*. Oxford.
Downey, G., and A. F. Norman, eds. 1971. Themistius, *Orationes*. Vol. 2. Leipzig.
Dübner, F., ed. 1877. *Scholia Graeca in Aristophanem*. Paris.
Dubois, L. 1995. *Inscriptions grecques dialectales de Grande Grèce*. Vol. 1. Geneva.
Du châtiment dans la Cité: Supplices corporels et peine de mort dans le monde antique. 1984. Collection de l'École française de Rome 79. Rome and Paris.
Dumézil, G. 1987. *Archaic Roman Religion*. Baltimore and London.
Dunand, F. 1973. *Le culte d'Isis dans le bassin oriental de la Méditerranée*. 3 vols. EPRO 26. Leiden.
Dunbar, N. 1995. *Aristophanes' Birds*. Oxford.
Edlund, I.E.M. 1987. *The Gods and the Place: Location and Function of Sanctuaries in the Countryside of Etruria and Magna Graecia (700-400 BC)*. Acta Instituti Romani Regni Sueciae, S. in 4°, XLIII. Stockholm.
Edmonds, R. 1999. "Tearing Apart the Zagreus Myth: A Few Disparaging Remarks on Orphism and Original Sin." *ClAnt* 18, 1:35-73.
———. 2004. *Myths of the Underworld Journey: Plato, Aristophanes, and the "Orphic" Gold Tablets*. New York.
———. 2008a. "Extra-Ordinary People: Mystai and Magoi, Magicians and Orphics in the Derveni Papyrus." *CPh* 103:16-39.
———. 2008b. *Recycling Laertes' Shroud: More on Orphism and Original Sin*. Center for Hellenic Studies online (http://chs.harvard.edu/chs/redmonds).
———. Forthcoming. *The Orphic Gold Tablets and Greek Religion*. Cambridge.
Egelhaaf-Geiser, U. 2000. *Kulträume im römischen Alltag: Das Isisbuch des Apuleius und der Ort der Religion im kaiserzeitlichen Rom*. Stuttgart.
Eggeling, J. 1682. *Mysteria Cereris et Bacchi in Vasculo ex uno Onyche*. Bremen.
Ehrenberg, V. 1965. *Der Staat der Griechen*. 2d ed. Zürich.
Eickel, N., ed. 2001. "Initiation Arts in African Cultures." Exhibition brochure. Washington, D.C.

Eingartner, J. 1999. Review of K. Lembke, *Das Isaeum Campense*. *GGA* 251:20-38.
Eitrem, S. 1944. "Les Thesmophoria, les Skirophoria et les Arrhetophoria." *SO* 23:32-45.
Elia, O. 1942. *Le pitture del Tempio d'Iside. Monumenti della pittura antica scoperti in Italia III 3/4.* Rome.
Elsner, J. 1995. *Art and the Roman Viewer: The Transformation of Art from the Pagan World to Christianity.* Cambridge.
———. 2001. "Cultural Resistance and the Visual Image: The Case of Dura Europos." *CPh* 96:269-304.
Ensoli, S. 1997. "I santuari isiaci a Roma e i contesti non cultuali: Religione pubblica, devozioni private e impiego ideologico del culto." In Arslan 1997: 306-322.
———. 1998. "L'Iseo e Serapeo del Campo Marzio con Domiziano, Adriano e i Severi: L'assetto monumentale e il culto legato con l'ideologia e la politica imperiale." In N. Bonacasa, ed., *L'Egitto in Italia*, 407-438. Rome.
Farrell, J. 1991. *Vergil's Georgics and the Traditions of Ancient Epic.* Oxford.
Fauth, W. 1989. "Richard Reitzenstein, Professor der klassischen Philologie." In C. J. Classen, ed., *Die klassische Altertumswissenschaft an der Georg-August-Universität Göttingen*, 178-196. Göttingen.
Fedeli, P. 1987. "Petronio: Crotone o il mondo alla rovescia." *Aufidus* 1:3-34.
Festugière, A. J. 1935a. "Les mystères de Dionysos." *RBi* 44:366-396. (= Festugière 1972: 13-63.)
———. 1935b. "La signification religieuse de la Parodos des Bacchantes." *Eranos* 54:72-86. (= Festugière 1972: 66-80.)
———. 1972. *Études de religion grecque et hellénistique.* Paris.
Feyel, M. 1935. "Un nouveau fragment du reglèment militaire trouvé à Amphipolis." *RA* 6:29-68.
Fora, M. 1996. *Epigrafia anfiteatrale dell'Occidente romano, 4: Regio I, Latium.* Rome.
Forbes Irving, P.M.C. 1990. *Metamorphosis in Greek Myth.* Oxford.
Foucart, P. 1914. *Les mystères d'Eleusis.* Paris.
Foucault, M. 1975. *Surveiller et punir: Naissance de la prison.* Paris.
———. 1976-84. *L'Histoire de la sexualité: La volonté de savoir; L'usage des plaisirs; Le souci de soi.* 3 vols. Paris.
Foxhall, L. 1995. "Women's Ritual and Men's Work in Ancient Athens." In R. Hawley and B. Levick, eds., *Women in Antiquity: New Assessments*, 97-110. London and New York.
Foxhall, L., and J. Salmon, eds. 1998. *When Men Were Men: Masculinity, Power, and Identity in Classical Antiquity.* London.
Francis, J. A. 1995. *Subversive Virtue: Asceticism and Authority in the Second-Century Pagan World.* University Park, Pa.
Frazer, J. G. 1906-1915 (1890). *The Golden Bough: A Study in Magic and Religion.* 6 vol.
Freyburger-Galland, M. L., G. Freyburger, and J-Ch. Tautil. 1986. *Sectes religieuses en Grèce et à Rome.* Paris.
Frisone, F. 1999. *Leggi e regolamenti funerari nel mondo greco.* Vol. 1, *Le fonti epigrafiche.* Galatina (Le).

Frontisi-Ducroux, F. 1991. *Le Dieu masque: Une figure de Dionysos d'Athènes.* Paris and Rome.
Frontisi-Ducroux, F., and F. Lissarrague. 1983. "De l'ambiguité à l'ambivalence: Un parcours dionysiaque." *AION:* 11-32.
Funghi, M. S. 1995. "Esegesi di testi orfici." In *Corpus dei Papiri Filosofici Greci e Latini,* 3:565-585. Florence.
García Sanz, O. 1994. "Efectos del alcohol sobre el culto." In *Actas del VIII Congreso Español de Estudios Clásicos* 3:169-173. Madrid.
García Teijeiro, M. 1985. "Posibles elementos IE en el Hades griego." In *Symbolae Ludovico Mitxelena septuagenario oblatae* 1:135-142. Vitoria.
Gatens, M. 1999. "Power, Bodies and Difference." In J. Price and M. Sheldrick, eds., *Feminist Theory and the Body: A Reader,* 226-234. Edinburgh.
Gelinne, M. 1988. "Les Champs-Élysées et les Îles des Bienheureux." *LEC* 56:225-240.
Ghinatti, F. 1976. "Per uno studio sociologico dei santuari della Magna Grecia." *Studia Patavina* 23:601-630.
———. 1980. "Nuovi Efori in epigrafi di Eraclea Lucana." In F. Krinzinger, ed., *Forschungen und Funde: Festschrift für Bernhardt Neutsch,* 137-143. Innsbruck.
Giangiulio, M. 1982. "Per la storia dei culti di Crotone antica: Il santuario di Hera Lacinia: Strutture e funzioni cultuali, origini storiche e mitiche." *ASCL* 49:7-69.
———. 1984. Intervento. In *Crotone.* Atti del Ventitreesimo Convegno di Studi sulla Magna Grecia, Taranto, 7-10 ottobre 1983, 347-351. Naples.
———. 1994. "Le laminette auree nella cultura religiosa della Calabria greca: Continuità ed innovazione." In S. Settis, ed., *Storia della Calabria antica,* vol. 2, *Età italica e romana,* 11-53. Rome and Reggio Calabria.
Giannelli, G. [1924] 1963. *Culti e miti della Magna Grecia.* Florence.
Giddens, A. 1982. "From Marx to Nietzsche? Neo-conservatism, Foucault and Problems in Contemporary Political Theory." In idem, *Profiles and Critiques in Social Theory,* 215-230. London and Basingstoke.
Gierstadt, E. 1929. "Das attische Feste der Skira." *Archiv für Religionswissenschaft* 27:209-211.
Gigante, M. [1973] 1988. *L'ultima tunica.* Naples.
———. 1977. "La cultura a Locri." In *Locri Epizefiri* 1977: 619-697.
Ginouvès, R. 1962. *Balaneutiké: Recherches sur le bain dans l'antiquité.* Paris.
Gleason, M. 1995. *Making Men: Sophists and Self-Presentation in Ancient Rome.* Princeton.
Goettling, C. 1843. *Narratio de oraculo Trophonii.* Jena.
Goldhammer, A. 1990. *Greek Virginity.* Cambridge, Mass.
Golvin, J.-C., and C. Landes. 1990. *Amphithéâtres et gladiateurs.* Paris.
Gordon, C., ed. 1980. *Power/Knowledge: Selected Interviews and Other Writings, 1972-1977, by Michel Foucault.* New York and Brighton.
Gordon, R. 1994. "Mystery, Metaphor and Doctrine in the Mysteries of Mithras." In J. Hinnells, ed., *Studies in Mithraism,* 103-124. Rome.
———. 1996a. "Mysteries." In *The Oxford Classical Dictionary* 1996: 1017-1018.
———. 1996b. "Authority, Salvation and Mystery in the Mysteries of Mithras." In idem, *Image and Value in the Graeco-Roman World: Studies in Mithraism and Religious Art,* IV, 45-80. Aldershot. (Original ed., in J. Huskinson, M. Beard,

and J. Reynolds, eds., *Image and Mystery in the Roman World* [Cambridge, 1988], 45-88.)
———. 2005a. "Ritual and Hierarchy in the Mysteries of Mithras." *ARYS* 4:245-274.
———. 2005b. "Mithraism." In Jones 2005, 9:6088-6093.
Graf, F. 1974. *Eleusis und die orphische Dichtung Athens in vorhellenistischer Zeit.* Berlin and New York.
———. 1985. *Nordionische Kulte.* Rome.
———. 1991. "Textes orphiques et ritual baccchique: A propos des lamelles de Pélinna." In P. Borgeaud, ed., *Orphisme et Orphée: En l'honneur de Jean Rudhardt.* Recherches et Rencontres 3, 87-102. Geneva.
———. 1993. "Dionysian and Orphic Eschatology: New Texts and Old Questions." In T. H. Carpenter and C. Faraone, eds., *Masks of Dionysus,* 239-258. Ithaca, N.Y., and London.
———. 1994. *La magie dans l'antiquité Gréco-Romaine.* Paris. (Translated by F. Philip, *Magic in the Ancient World* [Cambridge, 1997].)
———. 2003. "Initiation: A Concept with a Troubled History." In Dodd and Faraone 2003: 3-24.
———. 2005. "I culti misterici." In Bottini 2005: 15-39. (Reprinted from S. Settis, ed., *I Greci: Storia Cultura Arte Società,* vol. 2, *Una storia greca, II. Definizione [VI-IV secolo a. C.],* 309-343. Turin 1997.)
Graillot, H. 1912. *Le cult de Cybele, mère de dieux à Rome et dans l'empire romain.* Paris.
Grant, F., ed. 1953. *Hellenistic Religions: The Age of Syncretism.* Indianapolis.
Griffith, A. 2006. "Completing the Picture: Women and the Female Principle in the Mithraic Cult." *Numen* 53:48-77.
Griffith, R. D. 2001. "Sailing to Elysium: Menelaus' Afterlife (*Odyssey* 4.561-569) and Egyptian Religion." *Phoenix* 55:213-243.
———. 2008. *Mummy Wheat. Egyptian Influence on the Homeric View of the Afterlife and the Eleusinian Mysteries.* Lanham.
Griffiths, J. G. 1970. *Plutarch's De Iside et Osiride.* Cardiff.
———. 1975. *Apuleius of Madauros: The Isis-Book (Metamorphoses, Book XI).* EPRO 39. Leiden.
Grig, L. 2004. *Making Martyrs in Late Antiquity: An Illustrated History.* London.
Gros, P. 1976. *Aurea Templa: Recherches sur l'architecture religieuse de Rome à l'époque d'Auguste,* 138-143. Rome.
Grottarola, A. 1994. "Un inedito scavo di Paolo Orsi: La stipe votiva di Parapezza a Locri." *Prospettiva* 75-76:55-64.
Guarducci, M. 1985a. "Due pezzi insigni del Museo Nazionale Romano: Il 'trono Ludovisi' e 'l'acrolito Ludovisi.'" *BA* 70:1-20.
———. 1985b. "Nuove riflessioni sulla laminetta 'orfica' di Hipponion." *RFIC* 113:385-397.
Guattani, G. A. 1784-89, 1805. *Monumenti antichi inediti, ovvero notizie sulle antichità e belle arti di Roma per l'anno MDCCLXXXVIII.* Rome.
Guettel Cole, S. 1980. "New Evidence for the Mysteries of Dionysos." *GRBS* 21:223-238.
———. 1994. "Demeter in the Ancient Greek City and Its Countryside." In S. E.

Alcok and R. Osborne, eds., *Placing the Gods: Sanctuaries and Sacred Space in Ancient Greece*, 199-216. Oxford. (Also in Buxton 2000: 133-154.)
———. 2003. "Landscapes of Dionysos and Elysian Fields." In Cosmopoulos 2003: 193-217.
Guthrie, W.K.C. 1935. *Orpheus and Greek Religion*. London and New York. (2d ed., London, 1952; reprint, Princeton, 1967.)
———. 1952. *Orpheus and Greek Religion*. 2d ed. London.
———. 1970. *Orfeo y la religión griega*. Buenos Aires.
Hard, R. 1977. *Apollodorus: The Library of Greek Mythology*. Oxford.
Harrison, E. L. 1964. "Was Gorgias a Sophist?" *Phoenix* 18:183-192.
Harrison, J. E. 1903. *Prolegomena to the Study of Greek Religion*. Cambridge. (2d ed., 1908; 3d ed., 1922; repr. 1959.)
———. 1927. *Themis*. 2d ed. (1st ed. 1911). Cambridge.
Harrison, S. J. 2000. *Apuleius: A Latin Sophist*. Oxford.
Hatzfeld, J. 1912. "Les Italiens résident à Délos mentionnés dans les inscriptions de l'ile." In *BCH* 36:5-218.
Hawley, R., and B. Levick, eds. 1995. *Women in Antiquity: New Assessments*. London and New York.
Heckenbach, J. 1911. *De nuditate sacra sacrisque vinculis*. RGVV 9:93. Gießen.
Hedreen, G. 1994. "Silens, Nymphs, and Maenads." *JHS* 114:47-99.
Henrichs, A. 1984. "Male Intruders among the Maenads: The So-Called Male Celebrant." In H. D. Evjen, ed., *Mnemai: Classical Studies in Memory of Karl K. Hulley*, 69-91. Chico, Calif.
———. 1993. "He Has a God in Him: Human and Divine in the Modern Perception of Dionysus. "In T. H. Carpenter and C. A. Faraone, eds., *Masks of Dionysus*, 13-43. Ithaca, N.Y.
———. 1994. "Der rasende Gott: Zur Psychologie des Dionysos und des Dionysischen in Mythos und Literatur." *A&A* 40:31-58.
Hermann, W. 1965. "Santuari di Magna Grecia e della Madre Patria." In *Santuari di Magna Grecia*. Atti del Quarto Convegno di Studi sulla Magna Grecia Taranto-Reggio Calabria, 11-16 ottobre 1964, 47-57. Naples.
Heuzé, P. 1985. *L'image du corps dans l'oeuvre de Virgile*. Collection de l'École française de Rome, 86. Rome and Paris.
Heyob, S. K. 1975. *The Cult of Isis among Women in the Graeco-Roman World*. EPRO 51. Leiden.
Higgins, R. A. 1954. *Catalogue of the Terracottas in the Department of Greek and Roman Antiquities, British Museum*. London.
Hinard, F., and J.-C. Dumont, eds. 2003. *Libitina: Pompes funèbres et supplices en Campanie à l'époque d'Auguste. Édition, traduction et commentaire de la Lex Libitinae Puteolana*. Paris.
Hinnells, J., ed. 1975. *Mithraic Studies*. 2 vols. Manchester.
Hinz, V. 1998. *Der Kult von Demeter und Kore auf Sizilien und in der Magna Graecia*. Wiesbaden.
Hoffmann, P. 1993. *Der Isis-Tempel in Pompeji*. Münster.
Hölbl, G. 2000. *Altägypten im Römischen Reich: Der römische Pharao und seine Tempel I*. Mainz.
Hopkins, K. 1983. *Death and Renewal: Sociological Studies in Roman History 2*. Cambridge.

Hordern, J. 2000. "Notes on the Orphic Papyrus from Gurôb (P. Gurôb 1: Pack² 2464)." *ZPE* 129:131-140.
Horn, H. G. 1994. "Das Mainzer Mithrasgefäss." *MAZ* 1:21-66.
Hornung, E. 1983. *Conceptions of God in Ancient Egypt: The One and the Many*. London. (Translation of *Der Eine und die Vielen* [Darmstadt, 1971].)
———. 1992. *Idea into Image: Essays on Ancient Egyptian Thought*. New York. (Translation of *Geist der Pharaonerzeit* [Zurich, 1989].)
Iacopi, I. 1997. *La decorazione pittorica dell'Aula Isiaca*. Milan.
Immisch, O. 1915. "Sprachliches zum Seelenschmetterling." *Glotta*. 6:193-206.
Isler-Kerényi, C. 1993. "Dionysos und Solon: Dionysische Ikonographie V." *AK* 36, 1:3-10.
———. 1997a. "Dionysos im Götterzug bei Sophilos und bei Kleitias. Dionysische Ikonographie VI." *AK* 40:67-81.
———. 1997b. "La madre di Dioniso: Iconografia dionisiaca VIII." *AION*, n.s. 4:87-103.
———. 2001a. *Dionysos nella Grecia arcaica: Il contributo delle immagini*. Pisa and Rome.
———. 2001b. "Mitologie del moderno: 'Apollineo' e 'dionisiaco.'" In S. Settis, ed., *I Greci: Storia cultura arte società*, vol. 3, *I Greci "oltre la Grecia,"* 1397-1417. Turin. (Reprinted in Isler-Kerényi 2007b: 235-254.)
———. 2003. "Images grecques au banquet funéraire étrusque." *Pallas* 61:39-53.
———. 2007a. *Dionysos in Archaic Greece: An Understanding through Images*. Leiden and Boston. (Translation of Isler-Kerényi 2001a.)
———. 2007b. "Komasts, Mythic Imaginary and Ritual." In E. Csapo and M. Miller, eds., *The Origins of Theatre in Ancient Greece and Beyond: From Ritual to Drama*, 77-95. Cambridge, Mass.
Jaccottet, A. F. 1998. "L'impossible bacchant." *Pallas* 48:9-18.
———. 2003. *Choisir Dionysos: Les associations dionysiaques ou la face cachée du Dionysisme*. Vol. 2, *Documents*, 73-143. Kilchberg (Zürich).
Jackson, R. B. 2002. *Empire's Edge: Rome's Egyptian Frontier*. New Haven.
Jacoby, F., ed. 1950 (text) 1955 (commentary). *Die Fragmente der griechischen Historiker*. Idomeneus of Lampsacus, *On Demagogues*, no. 338 in parts IIIB (=texts 1950) and IIIb (=commentary 1955). Leiden. (Abbreviated *FGrHist*.)
Janko, R. 1997. "The Physicist as Hierophant: Aristophanes, Socrates and the Authorship of the Derveni Papyrus." *ZPE* 118:61-94.
———. 2001. "The Derveni Papyrus (Diagoras of Melos, *Apopyrgizontes logoi?*): A New Translation." *CPh* 96:1-32.
———. 2002. "The Derveni Papyrus: An Interim Text." *ZPE* 141:1-62.
Jeanmaire, H. 1951. *Dionysos: Histoire du culte de Bacchus*. Paris.
Jiménez San Cristóbal, A. I. 2002. "Consideraciones sobre las τελεταί órficas." *Actas del X Congreso Español de Estudios Clásicos*, 3:127-133. Madrid.
———. 2005. "El concepto de *dike* en el orfismo." In A. Alvar Ezquerra and J. F. González Castro, eds., *Actas del XI Congreso Español de Estudios Clásicos*, 1:351-361. Madrid.
Johnson, S. 2001. *Emergence: The Connected Lives of Ants, Brains, Cities, and Software*. New York.
Johnston, P. A. 1977. "Eurydice and Proserpina in the *Georgics*." *TAPhA* 107:161-172.

———. 1980. *Vergil's Agricultural Golden Age: A Study of the Georgics*. Leiden.
———. 1996. "Cybele and Her Companions on the Northern Littoral of the Black Sea. "In E. Lane, ed., *Cybele, Attis and Related Cults: Essays in Memory of M. J. Vermaseren*, 101–116. Leiden.
Johnston, S. I., and T. J. McNiven. 1996. "Dionysos and the Underworld in Toledo." *MH* 53:25–36.
Jones, L., gen. ed. 2005. *Encyclopedia of Religion*. 2d ed. Detroit.
Jørgensen, M. 1998. *Catalogue: Egypt II (1550–1080). Ny Carlsberg Glyptotek*. Copenhagen.
Jourdain-Annequin, C. 1989. *Héraclès aux Portes du Soir: Mythe et Histoire*. Annales Littéraires de l'Université de Besançon 402. Paris.
Jourdan, F. 2003. *Le Papyrus de Derveni, traduit et presenté*. Paris.
Junkelmann, M. 2000. "Familia gladiatoria. "In Köhne and Ewigleben 2000: 39–80.
Kafka, F. 2003. "In der Strafkolonie" [1914]. In Roger Hermes, ed., *Die Erzählungen*, 164–198. 8th ed. Frankfurt a. M.
Kahil, L., ed. 1981–92. *Lexicon Iconographicum Mythologiciae Classicae*. 7 vols. Zurich.
Kaibel, G., ed. 1890. *Inscriptiones Graecae*. Vol. 14 (Italy, Sicily, and other sites in the West). Berlin.
Karmiloff-Smith, A. 1992. *Beyond Modularity: A Developmental Perspective on Cognitive Science*. Cambridge, Mass.
Kassel, R., and C. Austin, eds. 1984. *Poetae Comici Graeci*. (Abbreviated *PCG*.) Vol. 3, pt. 2, *Aristophanes: Testimonia et fragmenta*. Berlin and New York.
Keil, B., ed. [1898] 1958. *Aristides: Orationes*. Vol. 2. Berlin.
Keith, A. B. 1909. "Pythagoras and the Doctrine of Transmigration." *Journal of the Royal Asiatic Society of Great Britain and Ireland*: 596–606.
Kerényi, C. 1967. *Eleusis: Archetypal Image of Mother and Daughter*. Princeton.
———. 1976. *Dionysos: Archetypal Image of Indestructible Life*. Princeton.
Kermode, F. 2000. *The Sense of an Ending: Studies in the Theory of Fiction*. Oxford and New York.
Kern, O. 1920. *Orpheus: Eine religionsgeschichtliche Untersuchung*. Berlin.
———. 1922. *Orphicorum fragmenta*. Berlin. (Reissued Dublin and Zürich 1972.)
Keuls, E. 1976. "Aspetti religiosi della Magna Grecia in età romana." In *La Magna Grecia nell'età romana* (Atti Taranto 15), 439–458. Naples.
King, Charles W. 1860. *Antique Gems: Origins, Uses, and Value*. London.
Kingsley, P. 1995. *Ancient Philosophy, Mysticism and Magic: Empedocles and Pythagorean Tradition*. Oxford.
Kirtsoglou, E. 2004. *For the Love of Women: Gender, Identity and Same-Sex Relations in a Greek Provincial Town*. London and New York.
Klingner, F. 1967. *Virgil: Bucolica, Georgica, Aeneis*. Zurich.
Koemoth, P. 1994. *Osiris et les arbres: Contributions à l'étude des arbres sacrées de l'Égypte ancienne*. Liège.
Köhne, E., and C. Ewigleben, eds. 2000. *Caesaren und Gladiatoren: Die Macht der Unterhaltung im antiken Rom*. Mainz.
Konstan, D., and M. Nussbaum, eds. 1990. "Sexuality in Greek and Roman Society. "*Differences* 2, no. 1 (whole issue).

Kroll, W., ed. 1899, 1901. *Procli Diadochi in Platonis Rem Publicam Commentarii.* 2 vols. Leipzig.
Kron, U. 1992. "Frauenfeste in Demeterheiligtümern: Das Thesmophorion von Bitalemi. Eine archäologische Fallstudie." *AA* 4:611-650.
Kyle, D. S. 1998. *Spectacles of Death in Ancient Rome.* New York and London.
Labate, M. 1986. "Di nuovo sulla poetica dei nomi in Petronio: Corax, 'il delatore'?" *MD* 16:135-146.
Lacey, W. K. 1983. *Die Familie im antiken Griechenland.* Mainz. (Original English title: *The Family in Ancient Greece* [Ithaca, N.Y., 1968].)
Lada-Richards, I. 1999. *Initiating Dionysus: Ritual and Theatre in Aristophanes' Frogs.* Oxford.
Laks, A., and G. W. Most, eds. 1997. *Studies on the Derveni Papyrus.* Oxford.
Lanciani, R. 1901. *New Tales of Old Rome.* Boston.
Larson, J. 2001. *Greek Nymphs: Myth, Cult, Lore.* Oxford.
Lau, D. 1975. *Der lateinische Begriff "Labor."* Munich.
Lavecchia, S. 1996. "P. Oxy. 2622 e il 'Secondo Ditirambo' di Pindaro." *ZPE* 110:1-26.
Le Bohec, Y. 2000. "Isis, Sérapis et l'armée romaine sous le haut-empire." In L. Bricault, ed., *De Memphis à Rome,* 129-145. Leiden.
Le Bonniec, H. 1958. *Le Culte de Cérès à Rome.* Paris.
Leclant, J. 1972-91. *Inventaire bibliographique des Isiaca (IBIS): Répertoir analytique des travaux relatifs à la diffusion des cultes isiaques, 1940-1969: Avec la collaboration de G. Clerc.* Vols. 1-4. EPRO 18. Leiden.
———. 1984. "Aegyptiaca et milieux isiaques: Recherches sur la diffusion du matériel et des idées égyptiennes." *ANRW* II.17.3: 1692-1709.
Lembke, K. 1994a. *Das Iseum Campense in Rom: Studie über den Isiskult unter Domitian.* Heidelberg.
———. 1994b. "Ein Relief aus Ariccia und seine Geschichte." *MDAI[R]* 101:97-102.
Leone, R. 1998. *Luoghi di culto extraurbani d'età arcaica in Magna Grecia.* Florence.
Leopold, A., and J. Sinding Jensen, eds. 2004. *Syncretism: The Problem of Defining a Category.* London.
Leventi, I. 2007. "The Mondragone Relief Revisited: Eleusinian Cult Iconography in Campania." *Hesperia* 76:107-141.
Levi, D. 1967-68. "Gli scavi di Iasos." *ASAA* 45-46 (n.s. 29-30): 537-590.
Levi, M. A. 1968. *L'Italia antica.* Milan.
Liebeschuetz, J.H.W.G. 2000. "Religion." In A. Bowman, P. Garnsey, and D. Rathbone, eds., *Cambridge Ancient History,* vol. 11, *The High Empire, A.D. 70-192,* 984-1008. Cambridge.
Lieu, J. M. 2004. *Christian Identity in the Jewish and Graeco-Roman World.* Oxford.
Lincoln, B. 1979. "The Rape of Persephone: A Greek Scenario of Women's Initiation." *HThR* 72:223-235.
———. 2003. "The Initiatory Paradigm in Anthropology, Folklore, and History of Religions." In Dodd and Faraone 2003: 241-254.
Linforth, I. M. 1941. *The Arts of Orpheus.* Berkeley and Los Angeles.
Ling, R. 1991. *Roman Painting.* Cambridge.

Lippolis, E. 1981. "Le testimonianze del culto in Taranto greca." *Taras* 1:81–135.
Lissi Caronna, E., C. Sabbione, and L. Vlad Borrelli, eds. 1999. *I Pinakes di Locri Epizefiri: Musei di Reggio Calabria e di Locri*. Parte I, 1–4. Atti e Memorie della Società della Magna Grecia, Quarta Serie I (1996–1999). Rome.

———, eds. 2003. *I Pinakes di Locri Epizefiri: Musei di Reggio Calabria e di Locri*. Parte II, 1–5. Atti e Memorie della Società della Magna Grecia, Quarta Serie II (2000–2003). Rome.

———, eds. 2007. *I Pinakes di Locri Epizefiri: Musei di Reggio Calabria e di Locri*. Parte III, 1–6. Atti e Memorie della Società della Magna Grecia, Quarta Serie III (2004–2007). Rome.

Lloyd, A. B. 1988. *Herodotus Book II, Commentary 99–182*. Leiden.

———. 2001. "Philae." In D. B. Redford, ed., *The Oxford Encyclopedia of Ancient Egypt*, 3:40–44. Oxford.

Lloyd-Jones, H. 1967. "Heracles at Eleusis: P. Oxy. 2622 and P.S.I. 1391." *Maia* 19:206–229.

———. 1990. *Greek Epic, Lyric, and Tragedy*. Oxford.

Lloyd-Jones, H., and P. J. Parsons. 1978. "Iterum de Catabasi Orphica." In *Kyklos: Festschrift für R. Keydell zum neunzigsten Geburtstag*, 88–100. Berlin.

Locher, J. 1999. *Topographie und Geschichte der Region am ersten Nilkatarakt in griechisch-römischer Zeit*. Stuttgart.

Locri Epizefiri. 1977. Atti del sedicesimo Convegno di studi sulla Magna Grecia. Taranto, 3–8 Ottobre 1976. Vol. 1–2. Naples.

Lomas, K. 1996. "Elea." In *The Oxford Classical Dictionary* 1996: 516.

Long, H. S. 1948. "A Study of the Doctrine of Metempsychosis in Greece from Pythagoras to Plato." Dissertation, Princeton University.

Lowe, N. J. 1998. "Thesmophoria and Haloa: Myth, Physic and Mysteries." In S. Blundel and M. Williamson, eds., *The Sacred and the Feminine in Ancient Greece*, 149–173. London and New York.

Lucas, D. W. 1946. "Hyppolytus." *CQ* 40, nos. 3–4:65–69.

Luraghi, N. 1994. *Tirannidi arcaiche in Sicilia e Magna Grecia da Panezio di Leontini alla caduta dei Dinomenidi*. Florence.

Macchioro, V. 1930. *Zagreus: Studi intorno all'orfismo*. Florence.

MacLachlan, B. 1995. "Love, War and the Goddess in Fifth-Century Locri." *AncW* 26: 205–223.

MacMullen, R. 1986. "Judicial Savagery in the Roman Empire." *Chiron* 16:147–166.

Malaise, M. 1972a. *Inventaire préliminaire des documents égyptiens découverts en Italie*. EPRO 21. Leiden.

———. 1972b. *Les conditions de pénétration et de diffusion des cultes égyptiens en Italie*. EPRO 22. Leiden.

———. 1984. "La diffusion des cultes égyptiens dans les provinces europeennes de l'Empire romain." *ANRW* II.17.3: 1615–1691.

Manderscheid, H. 2000. "Überlegungen zur Wasserarchitectur und ihrer Funktion in der Villa Adriana." *MDAI[R]* 107:109–140.

Marcovich, M. 1995. *Clementis Alexandrini Protrepticus*. Leiden, New York, and Cologne.

Marmoy, C.F.A. 1958. "The 'Auto-Icon' of Jeremy Bentham at University College London." *Medical History* 2:77–86.

Martin, L. 1983. "Why Cecropian Minerva? Hellenistic Religious Syncretism as System." *Numen* 20:131-145.

———. 1987. *Hellenistic Religions: An Introduction*. New York and Oxford.

———. 2001. "To Use 'Syncretism,' or Not to Use 'Syncretism': That Is the Question." Special issue of *Historical Reflections/Réflexions Historiques* 27:389-400.

———. 2004. "Ritual Competence and Mithraic Ritual." In T. Light and B. C. Wilson, eds., *Religion as a Human Capacity: A Festschrift in Honor of E. Thomas Lawson*, 245-263. Leiden.

———. 2005. "Performativity, Discourse and Cognition: 'Demythologizing' the Roman Cult of Mithras." In W. Braun, ed., *Rhetoric and Reality in Early Christianities*, 187-217. Waterloo, Ontario.

Maxfield, V. A. 2000. "The Deployment of the Roman Auxilia in Upper Egypt and the Eastern Desert during the Principate." In G. Alföldy, B. Dobson, and W. Eck, eds., *Kaiser, Heer und Gesellschaft in der römischen Kaiserzeit*, 407-444. Stuttgart.

McCauley, R., and E. T. Lawson. 2002. *Bringing Ritual to Mind: Psychological Foundations of Cultural Forms*. Cambridge.

McComiskey, B. 2002. *Gorgias and the New Sophistic Rhetoric*. Carbondale and Edwardsville, Ill.

Merkelbach, R. 1982. *Weihegrade und Seelenlehre der Mithrasmysterien*. Rheinisch-Westfälische Akademie der Wissenschaftern, Vorträge G257. Opladen.

———. 1984. *Mithras*. Königstein.

———. 1999. "Die goldenen Totenpässe: Ägyptisch, orphisch, bakchisch." *ZPE* 128:1-13.

Merkelbach, R., and M. L. West, eds. 1970. *Fragmenta Selecta*. In F. Solmsen, *Hesiodi Theogonia, Opera et Dies, Scutum*. Oxford.

Mettinger, T.N.D. 2001. *The Riddle of Resurrection: Dying and Rising Gods in the Ancient Near East*. Uppsala.

Metzger, B. M. 1984. "A Classified Bibliography of the Graeco-Roman Mystery Religions, 1924-1973, with a Supplement, 1974-1977. "In *ANRW* II.17.3: 1259-1423.

Meurig Davies, E.L.B. 1949. "Notes on Lucretius, Ovid, and Lucan." *Mnemosyne*, ser. 4, 2:72-75.

Meyboom, P.G.P. 1982. "Excursus on the Dating of the Paintings." In Vermaseren 1982: 35-46.

———. 1995. *The Nile Mosaic: Early Evidence of Egyptian Religion in Italy*. Leiden.

Minto, A. 1924. "S. Maria di Capua Vetere—Scoperta di una cripta mitriaca. "*NSA*, ser. 5, 21:353-375.

Molina, F. 1998. "Orfeo y la mitología de la música." Doctoral thesis, Universidad Complutense, Madrid.

Montégu, J. C. 1959. "Orpheus and Orphism According to the Evidence Earlier than 300 B.C." *Folia* 12:3-11, 76-95.

Moreau, A., ed. 1992. *L'initiation: Les rites d'adolescence et les mystères*. Vol. 1. Montpellier.

Moretti, L., ed. 1968. *Inscriptiones Graecae Urbis Romae*. Vol. 1. Rome.

———, ed. 1972-73. *Inscriptiones Graecae Urbis Romae*. Vol. 2. Rome.

———, ed. 1979. *Inscriptiones Graecae Urbis Romae*. Vol. 3. Rome.
Morhange, C., et al. 2000. "La mobilité des milieux littoraux des Cumes, Champs Phlégréens." In *Méditerranée* 1-2:71-82.
Most, G. W. 1993. "A Cock for Asclepius." *CQ* 43:96-111.
Motte, A. 1973. *Prairies et jardins de la Grèce Antique: De la religion à la philosophie*. Brussels.
Muellner, L. 1976. *The Meaning of Homeric εὔχομαι through Its Formulas*. Innsbrucker Beiträge zur Sprachwissenschaft 13. Innsbruck.
Müller, H. W. 1969. *Der Isiskult im antiken Benevent und Katalog der Skulpturen aus den aegyptischen Heiligtümern im Museo del Sannio zu Benevent*. Berlin.
Müller, J.-D. 1997. "Das Gedächtnis des gemarterten Körpers im spätmittelalterlichen Passionsspiel." In Öhlschläger and Wiens 1997: 75-92.
Musti, D. 1984. "Le lamine orfiche e la religiosità d'area locrese." *QUCC* 16:61-83.
———. 2005. *Magna Grecia: Il quadro storico*. Rome and Bari.
Mylonas, G. E. 1961. *Eleusis and the Eleusinian Mysteries*. Princeton.
Mynors, R.A.B. 1990. *Vergil: Georgics*. Oxford.
Napoli, M. 1967. "Topografia e archeologia." In *Storia di Napoli*, 1:373-507. Naples.
Nelson, M. 2000. "The Lesser Mysteries in Plato's *Phaedrus*." *EMC* 19:25-43.
Neutsch, B. 1968. "Siris ed Heraclea: Nuovi scavi e ritrovamenti archeologici di Policoro." *QUCC* 5:187-234, tabs. 1-33.
Nilsson, M. P. 1935. "Early Orphism and Kindred Religious Movements." *HThR* 28:181-230.
———. 1957. *The Dionysiac Mysteries of the Hellenistic and Roman Age*. Lund.
Nimmo Smith, J., trans. and comm. 2001. *A Christian's Guide to Greek Culture: The Pseudo-Nonnus Commentaries on Sermons 4, 5, 39 and 43 by Gregory of Nazianzus*. Translated Texts for Historians 37. Liverpool.
Nisbet, R.G.M., and M. Hubbard. 1970. *A Commentary on Horace: Odes Book 1*. Oxford.
Nixon, L. 1995. "The Cults of Demeter and Kore." In R. Hawley and B. Levick, eds., *Women in Antiquity: New Assessments*, 75-96. London and New York.
Norden, E. 1926. *P. Vergilius Maro: Aeneis Buch VI*. 3d ed. Leipzig and Berlin.
North, J. 1992. "The Development of Religious Pluralism." In J. Lieu, J. North, and T. Rajak, eds., *The Jews among Pagans and Christians in the Roman Empire*, 174-193. London and New York.
Nussbaum, M. 1996. "Parmenides. "In *The Oxford Classical Dictionary* 1996: 1113-1114.
Ogilvie, R. M. 1965. *A Commentary on Livy Books 1-5*. Oxford.
Öhlschläger, C., and B. Wiens, eds. 1997. *Körper—Gedächtnis—Schrift: Der Körper als Medium kultureller Erinnerung. Geschlechterdifferenz und Literatur: Publikationen des Münchener Graduiertenkollegs 7*. Berlin.
Olmos, R. 2001. "Anotaciones iconográficas a las laminillas órficas." In Bernabé and Jiménez San Cristóbal 2001: 283-341.
———. 2008. "Iconographical Notes on the Orphic Tablets." In Bernabé and Jimenez San Cristóbal 2008: 273-326.
Onians, R. B. 1951. *The Origins of European Thought*. 2d ed. Cambridge.

Orlandini, P. 1966. "Lo scavo del Thesmophorion di Bitalemi e il culto delle divinità ctonie a Gela." *Kokalos* 12:8-35.
———. 1967. "Gela: Nuove scoperte nel Thesmophorion di Bitalemi." *Kokalos* 13:177-179.
———. 1968. "Gela: Topografia dei santuari e documentazione archeologica dei culti." *RIN* 15:17-66.
———. 2003. "Il Thesmophorion di Bitalemi (Gela): Nuove scoperte e osservazioni." In G. Fiorentini, M. Caltabiano, and A. Calderone, eds., *Archeologia del Mediterraneo: Studi in onore di Ernesto De Miro*, 507-513. Rome.
Orsi, P. 1909. "Locri Epizefiri: Rendiconto sulla terza campagna di scavi locresi." *Bollettino di Archeologia* 3:403-438.
Ortner, S., and H. Whitehead, eds. 1981. *The Cultural Construction of Gender and Sexuality.* Cambridge.
Otto, E. 1960. *Das ägyptische Mundöffnungsritual.* 2 vols. Wiesbaden.
The Oxford Classical Dictionary. 1996. 3d ed. Ed. S. Hornblower and A. Spawforth. Oxford and New York.
Paget, R. F. 1968. "The Ancient Ports of Cumae." *JRS* 58: 152-169.
Pailler, J.-M. 1995. *Bacchus: Figures et pouvoirs.* Paris.
Pairault-Massa, F. H. 1975. "Oral Intervention." In *Orfismo in Magna Grecia: Atti del Quattordicesimo Convegno di Studi sulla Magna Grecia, Taranto, 6-10 ottobre 1974*, 196-202. Naples.
Panayotakis, C. 1995. *Theatrum Arbitri: Theatrical Elements in the Satyrica of Petronius.* Mnemosyne, suppl. 146. Leiden, New York, and Cologne.
Panikkar, R. 1993. *The Cosmotheandric Experience: God, Man, World.* Delhi.
Parke, H. W. [1977] 1982. *Festivals of the Athenians.* London.
———. 1986. *Festivals of the Athenians.* Paperback ed. London.
Parker, R. 1983. *Miasma: Pollution and Purity in Early Greek Religion.* Oxford.
———. 1995. "Early Orphism." In A. Powell, ed., *The Greek World*, 483-510. London.
Parvulescu, A. 2005. "The Golden Bough, Aeneas' Piety, and the Suppliant Branch." *Latomus* 64:882-909.
Pasquali, J. B. 1732. *Thesaurus Graecarum Antiquitatum Contextus et Designatus ab Jacobo Gronovio.* Vol. 7. Venice.
Pasqualini, M. 2000. "Cumes: Cadre géographique et historique, avant-propos à l'étude des ports." *Méditerranée* 1-2:69-70.
Peirce, S. 1998. "Visual Language and Concepts of Cult on the 'Lenaia Vases.'" *ClAnt* 17:59-95.
Pensa, M. 1977. *Rappresentazioni dell'oltretomba nella ceramica apula.* Rome.
Perkell, C. 1989. *The Poet's Truth: A Study of the Poet in Virgil's Georgics.* Berkeley.
Perpillou, J.-L. 1973. *Les substantifs grec en - εύς.* Paris.
Peterson, R. M. 1919. *The Cults of Campania.* Rome.
Pettazzoni, R. [1921] 1954. *La religione nella Grecia antica.* 2d ed. Turin.
———. [1924] 1997. *I misteri: Saggio di una teoria storico-religiosa.* 2d augmented ed. Cosenza. (Original ed., Bologna.)
Pharr, C., ed. 1930-64. *Vergil's Aeneid Books I-VI.* Lexington, Ky.
Piankoff, A. 1954. *The Tomb of Ramesses VI.* 2 vols. New York.

Piranesi, G. B. 1780. *Antiquities of Rome, Part I, Vol. VI: Raccolta dei tempi antichi.* Rome.
Pirelli, R. 1997. "Frammento di statua." In Arslan 1997.
Platon, N. 1957. *A Guide to the Archaeological Museum on Heraclion.* 2d ed. Heraklion.
Póczy, K., K. Lengyelné, and H. Polenz. 1989. *Aquincum: Budapest a Római Korban. Das römische Budapest.* Budapest and Münster.
Popesko, P. 1971. *Atlas of Topographical Anatomy of the Domestic Animals.* New York.
Porter, V. 1991. *Cattle: A Handbook to the Breeds of the World.* New York.
Preisendanz, K. 1928-31. *Papyri Graecae Magicae: Die griechischen Zauberpapyri.* 2 vols. Leipzig. (Abbreviated *PGM*.)
Price, J., and M. Shildrick. 1999. *Feminist Theory and the Body: A Reader.* Edinburgh.
Price, S. 1999. *Religions of the Ancient Greeks.* Cambridge.
Price, T. H. 1978. *Kourotrophos: Cults and Representations of the Greek Nursing Deities.* Leiden.
Priuli, S. 1975. *Ascyltus: Note di onomastica petroniana.* Brussels.
Prosdocimi, A. L. 1996. "La Tavola Di Agnone: Una interpretazione." In Del Tutto Palma 1996: 435-630.
Prückner, H. 1968. *Die lokrischen Tonreliefs: Beitrag zur Kultgeschichte von Lokroi Epizephyrioi.* Mainz.
Prümm, K. 1985. "Reitzenstein (Richard)." In *Dictionnaire de la Bible: Supplément,* 10:200-210. Paris.
Pugliese Carratelli, G. 1974. "Un sepolcro di Hipponion e un nuovo testo orfico." *PP* 29:108-126.
———. 1976. "Ancora sulla lamina orfica di Hipponion." *PP* 31:458-467.
———. 1988a. "L'orfismo in Magna Grecia." In idem, ed., *Magna Grecia III, Vita religiosa e cultura letteraria, filosofica e scientifica,* 159-170. Milan.
———. 1988b. "I santuari extramurani." In idem, ed., *Magna Grecia III, Vita religiosa e cultura letteraria, filosofica e scientifica,* 149-158. Milan.
———. 1993. *Le lamine d'oro "orfiche."* Milan.
———. 2001. *Le lamine d'oro orfiche: Istruzioni per il viaggio oltremondano degli iniziati greci.* Milan.
———. 2003. *Les lamelles d'or orphiques.* Paris.
Puhvel, J. 1969. "'Meadow of the Otherworld' in Indo-European Tradition." *ZVS* 83:64-69.
Putnam, M.C.J. 1979. *Virgil's Poem of the Earth: Studies in the* Georgics. Princeton.
Quagliati, Q. 1908. "Rilievi votivi arcaici in terracotta di Lokroi Epizephyrioi." *Ausonia* 3:136-234.
Radt, S. L., ed. 1977. *Tragicorum Graecorum Fragmenta.* Vol. 4. Göttingen. (Abbreviated *TrGF*.)
Rankin, H. D. 1969. "'Eating People Is Right': Petronius 141 and a Topos." *Hermes* 97:381-384.
———. 1971. *Petronius the Artist: Essays on the* Satyricon *and Its Author.* The Hague.

Redfield, J. 1991a. "Wedding Dolls Dedicated to Persephone and the Nymphs." *AJA* 95:318-319.

———. 1991b. "The Politics of Immortality." In P. Borgeaud, ed., *Orphisme et Orphée: En l'honneur de Jean Rudhardt*. Recherches et Rencontres 3:103-117. Geneva.

Redfield, J. 2003. *The Locrian Maidens: Love and Death in Greek Italy*. Princeton and New York.

Rehm, R. 1994. *Marriage to Death: The Conflation of Wedding and Funeral Rituals in Greek Tragedy*. Princeton.

Reusser, C. 2002. *Vasen für Etrurien: Verbreitung und Funktionen attischer Keramik im Etrurien des 6. und 5. Jahrhunderts v.Chr.* Kilchberg.

Ricciardelli Apicella, G. 1992. "Le lamelle di Pelinna." *SMSR* 58:27-37.

———. 2000a. *Inni Orfici*. Milan.

———. 2000b. "Mito e performance nelle associazioni dionisiache." In M. Tortorelli Ghidini, A. Storchi Marino, and A. Visconti, eds., *Tra Orfeo e Pitagora: Atti dei Seminari Napoletani, 1996-1998*, 265-283. Naples.

Richardson, L., Jr. 1992. *A New Topographical Dictionary of Ancient Rome*. Baltimore.

Richardson, N. J. 1974. *The Homeric Hymn to Demeter*. Oxford.

Richardson, R., and B. Hurwitz. 1987. "Jeremy Bentham's Self-Image: An Exemplary Bequest for Dissection." *British Medical Journal* 295:195-198.

Riedweg, C. 1998. "Initiation-Tod-Unterwelt. Beobachtungen zur Kommunikationssituation und narrativen Technik der orphisch-bakchischen Goldblättchen." In F. Graf, ed., *Ansichten griechischer Rituale: Geburtstags-Symposium für Walter Burkert 1996*, 359-398. Stuttgart and Leipzig.

———. 2002. "Poésie orphique et rituel initiatique: Éléments d'un 'Discours sacré' dans les lamelles d'or. "*RHR* 219:459-481.

———. Forthcoming. "Initiation—Death—Underworld: Narrative and Ritual in the Gold Leaves." In Edmonds forthcoming.

Riesenfeld, H. 1970. *The Gospel Tradition*. Philadelphia.

Rives, J. 1995. "Human Sacrifice among Pagans and Christians." *JRS* 85:65-85.

Robertson, N. 1980. "Heracles' 'Catabasis.'" *Hermes* 108:274-300.

Rohde, E. 1894. *Psyche. Seelencult und Unsterblichkeitsglaube der Griechen*. Tübingen.

———. 1901. "Unedierte Lucienscholien, die attischen Thesmophorien und Haloen betreffend." In idem, *Kleine Schriften*, 2:355-369. Tübingen and Leipzig. (Original ed., *RhM* 25 [1870]: 548-560.)

———. 1925. *Psyche: The Cult of Souls and Belief in Immortality among the Greeks*. Trans. W. B. Hillis. London.

Roller, L. E. 1999. *In Search of God the Mother: The Cult of Anatolian Cybele*. Berkeley, Los Angeles, and London.

Ross, D. O., Jr. 1987. *Vergil's Elements*. Princeton.

Roullet, A. H. 1972. *The Egyptian and Egyptianizing Monuments of Imperial Rome*. EPRO 20. Leiden.

Roussel, P. 1916. *Le Cultes égyptiens à Délos du IIIe au Ier siécle av. J. C.* Nancy.

Rudhardt, J. 1958. *Notions fondamentales de la pensée religieuse et actes constitutifs du culte dans la Grèce classique*. Geneva.

Rüdiger, U. 1967. "Santa Maria D'Anglona: Rapporto preliminare sulle due campagne di scavi negli anni 1965-1966." *NSA* ser. 8, 21:331-353.
Rudolph, Kurt. 1987. "Mystery Religions." In M. Eliade, ed., *The Encyclopedia of Religion*, 10:230-239. New York and London.
Ruggieri, F. 1998. "Nell'Antro della Sibilla i calendari lunari di Cuma." *Bollettino Flegreo* 6:68-80.
Ruggiero, M. 1888. *Degli scavi di antichità nelle Province di Terraferma dell' antico regno di Napoli dal 1743 al 1876*. Naples.
Rutherford, I. 1998. "Island of the Extremity: Space, Language and Power in the Pilgrimage Traditions of Philae." In D. Frankfurter, ed., *Pilgrimage and Holy Space in Late Antique Egypt*, 229-256. Leiden.
———. 2003. "Pilgrimage in Greco-Roman Egypt: New Perspectives on Graffiti from the Memnonion at Abydos." In R. Matthews and C. Roemer, eds., *Ancient Perspectives on Egypt*, 171-190. London.
Sabbatucci, D. 1975. "Criteri per una valutazione scientifica del 'mistico-orfico' nella Magna Grecia." In *Orfismo in Magna Grecia*. Atti del quattordicesimo Convegno di Studi sulla Magna Grecia, 35-49. Naples.
———. 1979. *Saggio sul Misticismo Greco*. 2d ed. Rome.
Sabbione, C., and R. Schenal. 1996. "Il santuario di Grotta Caruso." In E. Lattanzi, M. T. Iannelli, S. Luppino, C. Sabbione, and R. Spadea, eds., *Santuari della Magna Grecia in Calabria*, 77-80. Naples.
Salanitro, M. 1992. "La città della Cena di Trimalchione e la seconda città campana del Satyricon." *AR*, n.s. 37, no. 4:189-202.
Sallmann, K. 1999. "Was kostet ein Mensch? Zu Petrons Croton-Szenen." *WJA* 23:123-136.
Salmon, E. T. 1967. *Samnium and the Samnites*. Cambridge.
Sampaolo, V. 1998. "VIII 7, 28, Tempio di Iside." In I. Baldassare, ed., *Pompei: Pitture e mosaici*, 8:732-849. Rome.
Sandbach, F. H., ed. 1967. *Fragments*, in *Plutarch: Moralia*, vol. VII. Leipzig.
Santamaría Álvarez, M. A. 2005. "Ποινὰς τίνειν: Culpa y expiación en el orfismo." In A. Alvar Ezquerra and J. F. González Castro, eds., *Actas del XI Congreso Español de Estudios Clásicos*, 1:397-405. Madrid.
Santangeli Valenzani, R. 1991-92. "ΝΕΩΣ ΥΠΕΡΜΕΓΕΘΗΣ: Osservazioni sul tempio di Piazza del Quirinale." *BCAR* 44:7-16.
———. 1996. "Hercules et Dionysus, Templum." In Steinby 1996: 25-26.
Sartori, F. 1980. "Dediche a Demetra in Eraclea Lucana." In F. Krinzinger, ed., *Forschungen und Funde: Festschrift für Bernhardt Neutsch*, 401-415. Innsbruck.
Scalera McClintock, G. 1991. "Non fermarsi alla prima fonte: Simboli della salvezza nelle lamine auree." *Filosofia e Teologia* 3:396-408.
Scanlon, T. F. 2002. *Eros and Greek Athletics*. Oxford.
Scarborough, J. 1982. "Beans, Pythagoras, Taboos, and Ancient Dietetics." *CW* 75:355-358.
Scarpi, P. 1987. "Diventare dio: La deificazione del defunto nelle lamine auree dell'antica Thurii." *MusPat* 5:197-217.
———, ed. 2002. *Le religioni dei misteri I. Eleusi, dionisismo, orfismo*. Milan.
Scheibler, I. 1987. "Bild und Gefäss: Zur ikonographischen und funktionalen Bedeutung der attischen Bildfeldamphoren." *JDAI* 102:57-118.

Schlam, C. 1976. *Cupid and Psyche: Apuleius and the Monuments.* University Park, Pa.
Schmeling, G. 1969. "The Literary Use of Names in Petronius *Satyricon.*" *RSC* 17:5-10.
———. 1991. "The *Satyricon*: The Sense of an Ending." *RhM* 134:352-377.
Schmidt, M. 1975. "Orfeo e orfismo nella pittura vascolare italiota." In *Orfismo in Magna Grecia.* Atti del Quattordicessimo Convegno di Studi sulla Magna Grecia, Taranto, 6-10 ottobre 1974, 105-137. Naples.
———. 2000. "Aufbruch oder Verharren in der Unterwelt? Nochmals zu den apulischen Vasenbildern mit Darstellungen des Hades." *AK* 43:86-99.
Schmidt, M., A. D. Trendall, and A. Cambitoglou. 1976. *Eine Gruppe Apulischen Grabvasen in Basel.* Mainz.
Schott, Siegfried. 1959. "Altägyptische Vorstellungen vom Weltende." In *Analecta Biblica 12: Studia Biblica et Orientalia,* vol. 3, *Oriens Antiquus.* Rome.
Schütze, A. 1972. *Mithras-Mysterien und Urchristentum.* Stuttgart.
Seaford, R. 1980. "Black Zeus in Sophocles' *Inachos.*" *CQ* 30:23-29.
———. 1986. "Immortality, Salvation, and the Elements." *HSPh* 90:1-26.
———. 2006. *Dionysos.* London.
Sestieri, P. C. 1952. "Salerno: Scoperte archeologiche in località Fratte." *NSA,* ser. 8, 6:86-163.
Sfameni Gasparro, G. 1984. "Critica del sacrifizio cruento e antropologia in Grecia: Da Pitagora a Porfirio I: La tradizione pitagorica, Empedocle e l'orfismo." In F. Vattioni, ed., *Atti della V Settimana di Studi "Sangue e antropologia: Riti e culto,"* 1:107-155. Rome.
———. 1985. *Soteriology and the Mystic Aspects in the Cult of Cybele and Attis.* EPRO 91. Leiden.
———. 1986. *Misteri e culti mistici di Demetra.* Rome.
———. 1991. "Ruolo cultuale della donna in Grecia e a Roma: Per una tipologia storico-religiosa." In U. Mattioli, cur., *Donna e culture: Studi e documenti nel III anniversario della Mulieris Dignitatem,* 57-121. Bologna.
———, ed. 1998. *Destino e salvezza: Fra culti pagani e gnosi cristiane. Itinerari storico-religiosi sulle orme di Ugo Bianchi.* Cosenza.
———. 1999. "Aspetti e problemi della vita religiosa nel *Bruttium* in età greco-romana." In S. Leanza, ed., *Calabria cristiana: Società Religione Cultura nel territorio della Diocesi di Oppido Mamertina-Palmi, I. Dalle origini al Medio Evo* (Atti del Convegno di Studi, Palmi-Cittanova 21/25 novembre 1994), 53-88. Soveria Mannelli (CS).
———. 2000. "*Anodos e kathodos:* Movimento nello spazio e ritorno al tempo mitico. Sedi sacre e attività rituale nei culti di Demetra a carattere tesmoforico." In D. Pezzoli-Olgiati and F. Stolz, eds., *Cartografia religiosa. Religiöse Kartographie. Cartographie religieuse,* 83-106. Bern.
———. 2002. "Itinerari mitico-cultuali nell'area dello Stretto." In B. Gentili and A. Pinzone, eds., *Messina e Reggio nell'antichità: storia, società, cultura,* Atti del Convegno della S.I.S.A.C. (Messina-Reggio Calabria 24-26 maggio 1999), 329-350. Messina.
———. 2003. *Misteri e teologie: Per la storia dei culti mistici e misterici nel mondo antico.* Cosenza.

Sguaitamatti, M. 1984. *L'offrante de porcelet dans la coroplathie géléenne: Étude typologique*. Mainz am Rhein.
Shapiro, H. A. 1989. *Art and Cult under the Tyrants in Athens*. Mainz am Rhein.
Shaw, B. D. 1996. "Body/Power/Identity: The Passion of the Martyrs." *JECS* 4, 3:269–312.
Shaw, T. M. 1998. "Askesis and the Appearance of Holiness." *JECS* 6, 3:485–499.
Shepherd, G. 1999. "Fibulae and Females: Intermarriage in the Western Greek Colonies and the Evidence from the Cemeteries." In G. R. Tsetskhladze, ed., *Ancient Greeks: West and East*, 267–300. Leiden.
Sherry, D. 2000. "What Sex Differences in Spatial Ability Tell Us about the Evolution of Cognition." In M. S. Gazzangia, ed., *The New Cognitive Neurosciences*, 2d ed., 1209–1217. Cambridge, Mass.
Shey, H. J. 1971. "Petronius and Plato's Gorgias." *CB* 47:81–84.
Shumate, N. 1996. *Crisis and Conversion in Apuleius' Metamorphoses*. Ann Arbor.
Simon, E. 1953. *Opfernde Götter*. Berlin.
———. 1983. *Festivals of Attica*. Madison, Wis.
———. 1990. *Die Götter der Römer*. Munich.
Simpson, A.W.B. 1984. *Cannibalism and the Common Law: The Story of the Tragic Last Voyage of the* Mignonette *and the Strange Legal Proceedings to Which It Gave Rise*. Chicago.
Sissa, G. 1987. *Le corps virginal*. Paris.
Sjöqvist, E. 1958a. "Timoleonte e Morgantina." *Kokalos* 4:107–118.
———. 1958b. "Excavations at Morgantina (Serra Orlando): Preliminary Report II." *AJA* 62:155–162.
———. 1960. "Excavations at Morgantina: Preliminary Report IV." *AJA* 64:125–135.
———. 1962. "Excavations at Morgantina: Preliminary Report VI." *AJA* 66:135–143.
———. 1964. "Excavations at Morgantina: Preliminary Report VIII." *AJA* 68:137–147.
Skutsch, O. 1959. "Notes on Metempsychosis." *CPh* 54:114–115.
Slavova, M. 2002. "Mystery Clubs in Bulgarian Lands in Antiquity, Greek Epigraphical Evidence." *OAth* 27:137–149.
Smith, H.R.W. 1972. *Funerary Symbolism in Apulian Vase-Painting*. Berkeley and Los Angeles.
Smith, J. Z. 1987. "Dying and Rising Gods." In M. Eliade, ed., *The Encyclopedia of Religion*, 4:521–527. New York and London.
———. 1990. *Drudgery Divine*. Chicago.
———. 1996. "Trading Places." In M. Meyer and P. Mirecki, eds., *Ritual Power in the Ancient World*, 13–27. Leiden.
Smith, M. S. 2001. *The Origins of Biblical Monotheism*. Oxford.
Snell, B., and R. Kannicht, eds. 1986. *Tragicorum Graecorum Fragmenta*. Vol. 1. 2d ed. Göttingen. (Abbreviated *TrGF*.)
Sogliano, A. 1905. "Cuma: Epigrafe greca arcaica." *NSA*: 377–380.
Sokolowski, F. 1962. *Lois sacrées des cités grecques*. Supplément. Paris.
Solmsen, F. 1979. *Isis among the Greeks and Romans*. Cambridge, Mass.

Sommariva, G. 1984. "Eumolpo, un 'Socrate epicureo' nel Satyricon." *ASNP* 14:25-53.
Sommerstein, A. H. 1996. *Frogs*. Warminster.
Sorel, R. 1995. *Orphée et l'orphisme*. Paris.
Sourvinou-Inwood, C. 1974. "Three Related Cerberi." *AK* 17:30-35.
———. 1978. "Persephone and Aphrodite at Locri: A Model for Personality Definitions in Greek Religion." *JHS* 98:101-121. Reprinted in Sourvinou-Inwood 1991: 147-188.
———. 1991. *Reading Greek Culture: Texts and Images, Rituals and Myths*. Oxford and New York.
———. 2003. "Aspects of the Eleusinian Cult." In Cosmopoulos 2003: 25-49.
———. 2005. *Hylas, the Nymphs, Dionysos and Others*. Stockholm.
Spaeth, B. 1996. *The Roman Goddess Ceres*. Austin.
Stanford, W. B. 1958. *Aristophanes: The Frogs*. London.
Steinby, E. M., ed. 1996. *Lexicon Topographicum Urbis Romae*. Vol. 3. Rome.
Stillwell, R. 1959. "Excavations at Serra Orlando 1958: Preliminary Report III." *AJA* 63:167-173.
———. 1961. "Excavations at Morgantina (Serra Orlando) 1960: Preliminary Report V." *AJA* 65:277-281.
———. 1963. "Excavations at Morgantina (Serra Orlando) 1962: Preliminary Report VII." *AJA* 67:163-171.
———. 1967. "Excavations at Morgantina (Serra Orlando) 1966: Preliminary Report IX." *AJA* 71:245-250.
Stillwell, R., and E. Sjöqvist. 1957. "Excavations at Serra Orlando: Preliminary Report I." *AJA* 61:151-159.
Stroud, R. S. 1965. "The Sanctuary of Demeter and Kore on Acrocorinth: Preliminary Report I: 1961-1962 (Plates 1-11)." *Hesperia* 34:1-24.
———. 1968. "The Sanctuary of Demeter and Kore on Acrocorinth: Preliminary Report II: 1964-1965 (Plates 87-99)." *Hesperia* 37:299-330.
Swetnam-Burland, M., and E. M. Moormann. 2007. "Case Studies: Aegyptiaca in and around Pompeii and Rome." In *Nile into Tiber: Egypt in the Roman World*, Proceedings of the Third International Conference of Isis Studies, Leiden 2005, 111-239. Leiden and Boston.
Takács, S. A. 1995. *Isis and Sarapis in the Roman World*. Leiden.
Tannery, P. 1901. "Orphica, *fr.* 221, 227, 228, 254 Abel." *RPh* 25:313-319.
Taylor, J. 2004. *Pythagoreans and Essenes, Structural Parallels*. Paris and Louvain.
Te Velde, H. 1977. *Seth, God of Confusion*. Leiden.
Thomas, R. 1988. *Virgil: Georgics I-II* (vol. 1) and *Virgil: Georgics III-IV* (vol. 2). Cambridge.
Tobin, J. 1997. *Herodes Attikos and the City of Athens: Patronage and Conflict under the Antonines*. Amsterdam.
Tocco Sciarelli, G., J. de la Genière, and G. Greco. 1988. "I santuari." In *Poseidonia-Paestum*, Atti del XXVII Convegno di Studi sulla Magna Grecia Taranto-Paestum, 9-15 ottobre 1987, 385-396. Naples.
Tomasello, M. 1999. *The Cultural Origins of Human Cognition*. Cambridge, Mass.
Torelli, M. 1977a. "I culti di Locri." In *Locri Epizefiri* 1977, 1:147-184.
———. 1977b. "Greci e indigeni in Magna Grecia: Ideologia religiosa e rapporti di classe." *StudStor* 18, 1:45-61.

Tortorelli Ghidini, M. 1990. "Aletheia nel pensiero orfico, 1. 'Dire la veritá': Sul v. 7 della laminetta di Farsalo." *Filosofia e Teologia* 4:73-77.
Tracy, V. A. 1980. *"Aut Captantur aut Captant." Latomus* 39:399-402.
Tran Tram Tinh, V. 1964. *Essai sur le culte d'Isis à Pompéi.* Paris.
———. 1972. *Le culte des divinités orientales en Campanie.* Leiden.
Tran Tam Tinh, V., and Y. Labrecque. 1973. *Isis lactans: Corpus des monuments gréco-romains d'Isis allaitant Harpocrate.* EPRO 37. Leiden.
Trendall, A. D. 1967. *The Red-Figured Vases of Lucania, Campania and Sicily.* Oxford.
———. 1989. *Red Figure Vases of South Italy and Sicily: A Handbook.* London.
Tsantsanoglou, K. 1997. "The First Columns of the Derveni Papyrus and Their Religious Significance." In Laks and Most 1997: 93-128.
Turcan, R. 1986. "Bacchoi ou Bacchants? De la dissidence des vivants à la ségregation des morts." In *L'association dionysiaque dans les societés anciennes, Actes de la table ronde de l'École Française de Rome,* 227-246. Rome.
———. 1989. *Les cultes orientaux dans le monde romain.* Paris.
———. 1992. "L'elaboration des mystères dionysiaques à l'époque hellénistique et romaine: De l'orgiasme à l'initiation." In A. Moreau, ed., *L'Initiation I: Les rites d'adolescence et les mystères,* Actes du Colloque International de Montpellier 11-14 avril, 1991, 215-233. Montpellier.
———. 1996. *The Cults of the Roman Empire.* Cambridge, Mass. (Trans. of *Les cultes orientaux dans le monde romain* [Paris, 1989].)
———. 1998. "Initiation." In *Reallexikon für Antike und Christentum.* Vol. 18. Stuttgart.
———. 2000. *Mithra et le mithriacisme.* 3d ed. Paris.
———. 2003. "Les démons et la crise du paganisme gréco-romain." *RPhA* 21, 2:33-54.
Turner, V. W. 1969. *The Ritual Process: Structure and Anti-Structure.* Chicago.
Vallet, G. 1968. "La cité et son territoire dans les colonies grecques d'Occident." In *La città e il suo territorio.* Atti del Settimo Convegno di Studi sulla Magna Grecia, Taranto, 8-12 ottobre 1967, 67-142. Naples.
Van Damme, A. 2002. *Spectacular Display: The Art of Nkanu Initiation Rituals.* Washington, D.C.
Van den Berg, R. M. 2001. *Proclus' Hymns: Essays, Translation, Commentary.* Leiden.
Van Gennep, A. 1960. *Rites of Passage.* Trans. M. B. Vizedom and G. L. Caffee. Chicago.
Varone, A., and V. Iorio. 2005. "A fundamento restituit: Saggi nel Tempio d'Iside a Pompei." In P. G. Guzzo and M. P. Guidobaldi, eds., *Nuove richerche archeologiche a Pompei ed Ercolano,* 392. Naples.
Vassilika, E. 1989. *Ptolemaic Philae.* Leuven.
Velasco López, M. H. 2001. *El paisaje del Más Allá.* Valladolid.
Vermaseren, M. J. 1956-60. *Corpus Inscriptionum et Monumentorum Religionis Mithriacae.* 2 vols. The Hague. (Abbreviated *CIMRM.*)
———. 1971. *Mithriaca I: The Mithraeum at S. Maria Capua Vetere.* EPRO 16, 1. Leiden.
———. 1974. *Mithriaca II: The Mithraeum at Ponza.* Leiden.
———. 1977. *Cybele and Attis: The Myth and the Cult.* London.

———. 1977–89. *Corpus Cultus Cybelae Attidisque*. Vols. 1–7. Leiden. (Abbreviated CCCA.)
———, ed. 1981. *Die orientalischen Religionen in Römerreich*. Leiden.
———. 1982. *Mithraica III: The Mithraeum at Marino*. EPRO 16, 3. Leiden.
Vermaseren, M., and C. Van Essen. 1965. *The Excavations in the Mithraeum of the Church of Santa Prisca in Rome*. Leiden.
Vermeule, E. T. 1979. *Aspects of Death in Early Greek Art and Poetry*. Berkeley.
Vernant, J.-P. 1973. "Le mariage en Grèce archaïque." *PP* 28:51–74.
———. 1990. *Figures, idoles, masques*. Paris.
Versluys, M. J. 2002. *Aegyptiaca Romana: Nilotic Scenes and the Roman Views of Egypt*. Leiden.
Versluys, M. J., and P.G.P. Meyboom. 2000. "Les scènes dites nilotiques et les cultes isiaques: Une interprétation contextuelle." In L. Bricault, ed., *De Memphis à Rome*, 111–128. Leiden.
Versnel, H. S. 1990. *Ter unus: Isis, Dionysus, Hermes: Three Studies in Henotheism*. Leiden.
———. 1993. "The Roman Festival for Bona Dea and the Greek Thesmophoria." In *Inconsistencies in Greek and Roman Religion*, vol. 2, *Transition and Reversal in Myth and Ritual*, 229–288. Leiden.
Vetter, E. 1953. *Handbuch der italischen Dialekte, 1*. Heidelberg.
Veyne, P. 1998. "La fresque dite des mystères à Pompéi." In P. Veyne, F. Lissarrague, and F. Frontisi-Ducroux, *Les mystères du gynécée*, 13–153, 279–304. Paris.
Ville, G. 1981. *La gladiature en Occident: Des Origines à la mort de Domitien*. Rome and Paris.
Violante, M. L. 1981. "Un confronto tra *PBon.* 4 e *l'Assioco*: La valutazione delle anime nella tradizione orfica e platonica." *CCC* 5:313–327.
Visconti, E. Q. 1794. *Iscrizione greche triopee o borghesiane con versioni ed osservazioni*. Rome.
Vogliano, A. 1933. "La grande iscrizione bacchica del Metropolitan Museum: Part I—Tavole XXVII–XXIX." *AJA* 37:215–231.
Von den Hoff, R. 2004. "Horror and Amazement: Colossal Mythological Statue-Groups and the New Rhetoric of Images in Late-Second and Early-Third Century Rome." In B. Borg. ed., *Paideia: The World of the Second Sophistic*, 105–129. Berlin and New York.
Waern, I. 1951. *ΓΗΣ ΟΣΤΕΑ: The Kenning in Pre-Christian Greek Poetry*. Uppsala.
Warburton, W. 1745. *The Divine Legation of Moses*. Vol. 1. London.
Warde Fowler, W. 1911. *The Religious Experience of the Roman People*. London.
Watkins, C. 1995. "Orphic Gold Leaves and the Great Way of the Soul: Strophic Style, Funerary Ritual Formula, and Eschatology." In idem, *How to Kill a Dragon: Aspects of Indo-European Poetics*, 277–291. Oxford.
Weil Goudchaux, G. 1998. "Divagations autour de la mosaïque nilotique de Palestrina." In N. Bonacasa, ed., *L'Egitto in Italia: Dall'antichità al medioevo*, 525–534. Rome.
Welch, K. 1994. "The Roman Arena in Late-Republican Italy: A New Interpretation." *JRA* 7:59–80.
Wendel, C., ed. 1935. *Scholia in Apollonium Rhodium Vetera*. Berlin.

West, M. L. 1975. "Zum neuen Goldblättchen aus Hipponion." *ZPE* 18:229-236.
———. 1982. "The Orphics of Olbia." *ZPE* 45:17-29.
———. 1983. *The Orphic Poems*. Oxford.
———. 1993. *I poemi orfici*. Naples.
———. 1997. *The East Face of Helicon*. Oxford.
Westerink, L. G. 1977. *The Greek Commentaries on Plato's Phaedo*. Vol. 2. Amsterdam.
White, D. 1976. "Excavations in the Sanctuary of Demeter and Persephone at Cyrene 1973: Fourth Preliminary Report." *AJA* 80:165-181.
———. 1981. "Cyrene's Sanctuary of Demeter and Persephone: A Summary of a Decade of Excavation." *AJA* 85:13-30.
———. 1984. *The Extramural Sanctuary of Demeter and Persephone at Cyrene, Libya*. Final Reports, vol. 1, *Background and Introduction to the Excavations*. Philadelphia.
———. 1993. *The Extramural Sanctuary of Demeter and Persephone at Cyrene, Libya*. Final Reports, vol. 5, *The Site's Architecture, Its First Six Hundred Years of Development*. Philadelphia.
Whitehouse, H. 2000. *Argument and Icons: Divergent Modes of Religiosity*. Oxford.
———. 2003. "Modes of Religiosity: Towards a Cognitive Explanation of the Sociopolitical Dynamics of Religion." *Method and Theory in the Study of Religion* 14, 3/4:293-315.
———. 2004. *Modes of Religiosity: A Cognitive Theory of Religious Transmission*. Walnut Creek, Calif.
Wilamowitz, U. von. 1891. *Euripides: Hippolytos*. Berlin.
Wild, R. A. 1981. *Water in the Cultic Worship of Isis and Sarapis*. Leiden.
Wilhelm, R. M. 1988. "Cybele: The Great Mother of Augustan Order. "*Vergilius* 34:77-101.
Wilkinson, L. P. 1963. "Virgil's Theodicy." *CQ*, n.s. 23:75-84.
———. 1969. *The Georgics of Virgil: A Critical Survey*. Cambridge.
Wilkinson, R. H. 2000. *The Complete Temples of Ancient Egypt*. London.
Williams, C. A. 1999. *Roman Homosexuality: Ideologies of Masculinity in Classical Antiquity*. New York and Oxford.
Winter, F. 1903. *Die Antiken Terrakotten: Die Typen der figürlichen Terrakotten*. Vol. 1. Berlin and Stuttgart.
Wissowa, G. 1917. "Das Proëmium von Vergils Georgica." *Hermes* 52:92-104.
Witt, R. E. 1971. *Isis in the Graeco-Roman World*. Ithaca, N.Y.
———. 1975. "Some Thoughts on Isis in Relation to Mithras." In J. Hinnells, ed., *Mithraic Studies*, 2:479-493. Manchester.
Wright, W. C., trans. 1921. *The Lives of the Sophists*. Cambridge, Mass., and London.
Wulleman, W., M. Kunnen, and A. Mekhitarian, eds. 1989. *Passage to Eternity*. Knokke, Belgium.
Wyke, M., ed. 1998a. *Gender and the Body in the Ancient Mediterranean*. New York.
———, ed. 1998b. *Parchments of Gender: Deciphering the Bodies of Antiquity*. New York and Oxford.

Zabkar, L. V. 1963. "Herodotus and the Egyptian Idea of Immortality." *JNES* 22:57-63.
———. 1988. *Hymns to Isis in Her Temple at Philae*. Hanover, N.H.
Zancani-Montuoro, P. 1960. "Il corredo della sposa." *ArchClass* 12:37-50.
———. 1964. "Persefone e Afrodite sul mare." In L. Freeman, ed., *Marsyas: Essays in Memory of K. Lehmann*, 386-395. New York.
Zanker, P. 1990. *The Power of Images in the Age of Augustus*. Trans. A. Shapiro. Ann Arbor.
Zeller, D. 1994. "Mysterien/Mysterienreligionen." In *Theologische Realenzyklopädie*, 23:504-526. Berlin and New York.
Zevi, F., ed. 1991. *Pompei, I*. Naples.
Zuntz, G. 1971. *Persephone: Three Essays on Religion and Thought in Magna Graecia*. Oxford.
———. 1976. "Die Goldlamelle von Hipponion." *WS* 10:129-151.

General Index

Page numbers in italics indicate illustrations.

Abadessa, 204
abrosynē, 40
Abydos, 9
Acheron, 191
Actaeon, 113
Actium, 265; "Actian" Apollo, 266
adyton, 8
Aeacus, 197
Aeneas, 190, 191, 198
Aeneid 6. *See* Clark, 190–203
Aeschylus, 62, 78, 197; in *The Frogs*, 197
agathē elpis, 5
Agave, 113
Agnone Tablet, 267–271
Agrai, mysteries of, 6
alabastra, 39
Amasis Painter, 64–68
Ambarvalia, 256
Amor/Eros, 277, 278, 279, 280
Amor and Psyche, 277–289; Amor and Psyche relief, 277, 278, 294. *See* Martin, 277–289
amphorae, Melian, 62
Anacreontic vases, 39
androgyny, 40–41
Annia Appia Regilla, 168, 172, 179–180
anodos, 211
Antoninus Pius, 293
Anubis, 9, 222, 265, 266; at Cumae, 241, 244; Hermes and, 220, 221, 224; Hermanubis, 220, 221, 222, 225, 246
Aphrodite, 205, 214; "Anadyomene," 220; Venus, 245
Apis, 9
Apollo, 266; Apollo and Artemis, 263
Apuleius: and cult of Isis in *Metamorphoses*, 8, 23, 217–220; date of *Metamorphoses*, 219; and Ostia, 281; *Metamorphoses*' Lucius, 217, 218, 232n26
Apulia, 38; Apulia-Calabria, 33, 40
Apulian pottery, 96, 97, *110*, 111, 113; from Armento, 118; from Ruvom, 99
Argos, 220, 221, 224
Aricia, battle of (504 BCE), 37
Aristaeus, 260
Aristocles, 206
Aristodemus "Malakos", 37–41
Aristophanes' *Thesmophoriazousai*, 140, 145
Aristotle, on beans, 135
Arrhetophoria, 147
Artemis, 207, 208, 209
Arval Brethren, 165
askēsis (ascetism), 50
Asterioi, 83
Athena, birth of, 61
Athens, 68

Attabokaoi, 8
Attis, 3, 8, 13, 251
Augustus, 6, 165, 252; initiation into Eleusinian mysteries, 254
Aula Isiaca, 219
aulos, 39
Aurelius, Marcus, 6, 293; coin of, 238
Avernus, Gate of *Dis*, 198

Bacchanalia affair, *senatus consultum* (186 BCE), 38–40
Bacchanals, 38
Baiae, Venus Lucrina sanctuary, 245
banquets: of Mithras and Helios, 291; Fiano Romano relief, 295; Skt. Mathäus cemetery, 295
barbiton, 39
Bauli, 34
beans, and Hades, 134
Bentham, Jeremy, 136
Biae, 34
Big Dipper, 319
Boeotia, ritual vessels of, 62
Bona Dea, 166
Bononiae Papyrus, 107
Bougonia, 263–264
Brimo, 111
Busiris, 263, 272n38

Caffarella/*Pagus Triopius*, 162, 164, 169
Callatiae and Darius, 132–133
Callisto, 319
Campania (*ager campanus*), 24. See Casadio, 33–45, 49
Capreae, 34
Capri, 238
Capua, S. Maria Capua Vetere, 68. See *also* Mithraeum at Capua
Capua Amphitheater, 306. See Gordon, 290–313; Martin, 277–289
Cautes, 291
Cautopates, 291, 294
Cave of the Nymphs, 205–206; Porphyry commentary on, 207; votives of, 207
Cecilia Metella, tomb of, 166, 167

Centaurs, 191
Centre Berard of Naples, 235, 248
Cerberus, 77, 81, 87n16, 97, 118, 191
Cerealia, 255
Ceres, 163, 164, 165, 253, 254, 255, 257; *certamen Liberi patris cum Cerere*, 35
Chariot of the Sun, 307
Christian martyrdom, 306, 308–310
Chrysippus, 131
cista mystica, 229
Cleopatra, 265
Cocytus, 198
Commodus, 6
consecranei, 11
Corax, 131
Court of Queen's Bench, London, 131
Cretan Zeus, 134
Crete, 252; gold tablet from, 83n1, 84n4
Croesus, fall of, 88n19
Croton, 33, 133; Hera in Croton, 142
cryptoportici, 292
Cult of Magna Mater, 290; of Isis, 290
Cumae, 33; Aegyptiaca from, 235; Aeneas at, 134; battle of (524 BCE), 37; founding of, 35; Licola (location of original harbor), 235; Samnite invasion of, 36; *villae maritimae*, 235, 248
Cybele/*Mētēr*/*Magna Mater*, 252; and Sabazius, 70
Cyniscus, 194, 195
Cyrene, Sacred Laws from, 207

daimones, winged, 214
Damascius, 48, 57n46, 58n52, 133
Danaids, 120
deiknumena, 5
Delos, 9
Delphi, 213
Demeter, 6, 8, 12–16. See Lucchese, 161–189, and Sfameni Gasparro, 139–160
Demetra Prostasia, 151
Demeter Thesmophoros, 140–142
Dendara, Great Temple of, 319

Derveni papyrus 47, 56n34, 57n39, 100, 102
Dikē, 205
dinos (dinoi), 62–63; Etruscan, 62; of Sophilos, 63
Diocletian, 10
Diogenes the Cynic, 101, 131
Dionysus/Bacchus, 1, 7, 15–17, 20–21, 33, 34, 40, 52, 73, 192–197, 205, 212, 214, 251; Dionysus/Bacchus/Liber, 253; Egyptian origins, 254; "Eubuleus", 111; in the Homeric world, 112; iconography, 61–72; "Liber-Pater", 34; and Orphic cults in Locri, 212; *teletai* of, 214; "Zagreus", 52
Dionysus/Triptolemos, 165
Dionysus of Halicarnassus, 38
Dis/Pluto, 256
Domitian, 219
drōmenos, 5, 9
dying and rising gods, 11

Edict of Constantine (313 CE), 246; of Theodosius (392 CE), 246
Egeria, 179
Egypt: as *gens fortunata*, 267; source of rebirth doctrine, 133, 134; in Vergil's *Georgics*, 260–267
Egyptomania, in age of Augustus, 219
Ekklesiasterion at Pompeii. See Brenk, 217–227
Elea (Castellamare di Velia), 280; Eleatic tradition, 279, 280
Eleusinian Mysteries, 5, 6, 7, 77, 80, 254–257; fright of initiates, 191, 198; and Herakles, 260, 263–265. See Clark, 190–203
Eleusis, 3, 6, 18–49, 172, 191, 251, 256
Elpenor, 86n15
Elysian Fields, 90n28
Empedocles, 133, 134
Empousa, 193–195, 197, 201n21
Encolpius, 131, 133
Ennius, 131, 133, 134
Epizephyrian Locri, 204

epoptēs, 6
Erinyes, 97, 108
Eros figures, 40
Etruscans, 70
Eumolpus, 131, 191, 193
Euripides, in *The Frogs*, 197
Eurydice, as *dona Ditis*, 256, 260
Eurystheus, 191, 263
Euthymos, 213, 214
evoe saboi, 47
exēgēsis, 5
eye-cups, 66
eye motif, 68

Faustina the Elder, as Ceres, 172
Faustina the Younger, as Libera, 172
Fellini, *Satyricon* (1969), 132
Firmicius Maternus, 5
Flegrean (Phlegraean) Fields, 33
Fons Egeriae, 179
fortuna, 9; *fortunatae gentes*, 1, 25n2
François Vase, 63, 64
fratres, 11

galli, 8, 306
Gallienus, 6
Gallus, Cornelius, *laudes Galli*, 260, 267
Ganymede, 121
Gigantomachia, 61, 63
Giton, 131
Gorgias, 133
Gorgons, 190–191, 193, 194, 195, 196, 198; Medusa, 191, 197
Grotta Caruso. See MacLachlan, 204–216
Gurob papyrus, 57n40, 122

Hades: dual Hades, 101; entrance in Taenarum in Laconia, 191; as "Eucles", 111; gates of, 197, 198; Hades-Pluton, 151; Plouton, 74; "terrors of Hades", 102. See Bernabé, 95–130
Hadrian, 6
Harpies, 108, 109
Harpokrates/Horus, 9, 220, 221, 222, 241, 246, 247

Hekate, 97, 99, 115, 191, 194, 195
Helios, 316, 317
Hellenistic monarchs, 39
Hephaestus, 61–72
Hera/Juno, 220
Heraclitus 47, 51–53; 56n33
Herakles, 77, 81, 87nn14–16, 91n30, 113, 260; and cattle, 263–265; descent of, 191–199, 200nn8–10; Eleusinian Herakles, 22–23, 191, 262–267; and Hylas, 263
Hermes, 118, 191, 197
Herodes Atticus, 162–184
Herodotus, 36, 47, 51–52, 260, 264
Hesiodic golden race, 79, 90n26, 92n32
heurēsis, 9
hieros logos, 5
Hipponion, 212; lamellae of 47, 51–53. See Bernabé, 98, 111
Homeric *Hymn to Demeter,* 194, 204, 256
Horus, sons of, 320
Hydra, 263

Iasos, sanctuary of, 159n38
Ibis, 225
Ichonarum Phobia, 247
imago inferorum, 106. See Bernabé, 95–130
Inaros statue, 239, 244
inscriptions: from Cumae, 35–38, 47, 50–51, 51n60, 53; from Hipponion, 37; from Petelia, 37; from Thurii, 37; from Torre Nova, 47, 53
inventio, 9
Io, 220, 221, 224; "Io and Isis", 222, 225
Io (*Inachiae*), 258–260; of C. Licinius Calvus, 259–260; Euboean, 259
Iobacchoi, 7
Isaeum (Temple of Isis): Campense (on Campus Martius), 218, 219; at Cumae, 235–250; at Philae, 222; as a private *sacellum,* 248
Isaeum at Pompeii, 29n50, 217, 218; architectural styles, 219; frescoes from, 219; of Isis and Osiris, 220; tryptychs in "Ekklesiasterion", 220
Isis, 1, 3, 8, 9, 10, 13, 217, 220, 221, 225, 251; at Cumae, 235–250; Cumae statue, 239, 245; and Demeter/Ceres, 260–262; as goddess of death (with *ankh*), 241–244; with Harpokrates, 220; with Hermanubis, 220; and Io, 222, 225, 258–260; *Iseia,* 9; and mysteries of Osiris, 256–258; *Navigium Isidis,* 9; with Nephthys, 220; at Pompeii, 23. See Brenk, 217–235
Ixion, 90n26, 120

Job, Testament of, 310
judges of the underworld, 113, 116
Julio-Claudians, 219
Julius Caesar, 165
Juno, 163
Jupiter-Juno-Minerva triad, 165
Justice/Dike, in Orphism, 99, 108, 115

Kalligeneia, 150
Kallis painter, 66, 71
katabasis, 193, 194, 198, 199, 201n15, 211, 212
katharoi, 83
kistai, 166; *kistophora,* 166
kithara, 39
Knossos, 166
korē, 205, 208–209
Kore (deity). See Persephone/Kore
Kronos, 252
kylix, kylikes, 66, 68, 71

lamellae, 26n36, 47, 52–53, 68, 73–94, 96. See also Orphic gold tablets
laudes Galli, 260, 267
legifera, 161
legomena, 5
lekythoi, 68, 70
Lenaea *stamnoi,* 60, 68, 70
Leontocephales, 281
Lerna, 38
Lethe, 97
Leukothea, 12

Liber: *certamen Liberi patris cum Cerere*, 35
lightning, 78, 88n20
Livia, 165
Locri 33, 86–87n13; *pinakes*, 96; 114. See Bernabé, 118–130, and MacLachlan, 204–216
locus amoenus, 97, 101, 109, 111, 124–125
Lucania, 40
Lucian's *Dialogues of the Courtesans*, 145
Lucretius, 133
Lucretius Rufus, M., 219
Lycurgus and Oedipus, 68

Maenads, 212
Magna Graecia, 1, 33; definition of, 2, 24–25n1
Manetho, 9
Mannella, 204, 205; Persephone in Mannella at Locri, 142
Marcus Antonius/Mark Antony, 39, 219, 265
Matera crater, 114
megarizein (to throw piglets into *megara*), 145
megaron, 161, 166, 169, 172
Meleager, 191, 192, 197
Memory, 97, 98
Menander, portrait of in Sicilian Lipari, 212
Metamorphoses. See Apuleius
Metapontum, 33
Methone tablet, 84n4
Mithraeum at Dura-Europos, 10
Mithraeum at Capua, 24; Luna fresco 293. See Gordon, 290–313, and Martin, 277–289
Mithraeum at Ostia (Seven Spheres), 281; Aldobrandini, 295
Mithraeum at Santa Prisca, 280–281, 291; Barberini, 291, 294; Caesarina Maritima, 292; Marino, 292, 294
Mithraic community, 285; Greek influence upon, 280, 282; "Romanness" of, 285

Mithraic funerary iconography, absence of, 291
Mithraic initiation rites, 283–287, 288n10, 290–313; female initiates, 288n4; maleness and, 307
Mithraic *makrothyíma*, 308–310
Mithraic tauroctony. See Palmer, 314–323
Mithraism, 10, 277, 279; and Egyptian Ennead, 317; and Egyptian mythology, 317
Mithraist images, 291; Cautes and Cautopates, 291; degrees of initiation in, 11; role of fire in, 309; scorpions in, 309
Mithras, 1, 4, 10, 17, 277; *kosmokrator*, 317, 322; Mitra/Mithra, 10; Mithras Kosmophoros/MithrasAtlas, 303; Mithras Liturgy, 288n6; *Mithras Tauroctonus*, 10; as name of priest of Isis, 281; and Sarapis, 317
Mithrasliturgie from Roman Egypt, 317–323
Mnemosyne, 73, 89n25
Morgantina, 215n9
Muhammad in the Koran, 40
Mummy cases, Greco-Roman, 219
Musaios, 103, 122
Musonius Rufus, 307
myēsis (initiation), 11, 12
mystēs, 5, 6; μύσται and βάκχοι, 52
mystic cults/mystery cults, 11; definition, 2
mythos, 5

naophorus found at Baiae, 245
Neoplatonism, 279
Nephthys, 220, 221, 225
Nero, 219
Nessus, 263
Nichomachi, 248
Nike, representations of, 314–315
Nile River, 222, 258, 266; *Dodekaschoinos*, 222; and Isis-worship, 223; Nilescapes, 220, 222; Nile water, 217
Nubia, 222

nymphē, 205; chthonic elements, 212; *nymphai* (nymphs of the cave), 209, 210; *nymphus,* 278, 287n1

obelisks, 219
Odysseus, 77, 196
Olbia, 118
Olympiodorus, 50n55
Onomacritus, 68
opus latericium, 238; *opus reticulatum,* 237; *opus sectile,* 238, 243
orgia, 68, 70, 192
orpheotelestai, 82
Orpheus, 7, 77, 96, 99, 112, 254, 260; and Demeter, 261; dismembered, 272n35; and Horus, 272n35; as mediator, 113, 115, 117; in Vergil, 198
Orphic gold tablets, 5. See Edmonds, 73–94; *see also* Thurii
Orphic imagery. See Bernabé, 95–130
Orphic rites, Egyptian origin of, 101–103
orphikos bios, 82
Orphism, 80, 83; beliefs of, 7, 96. See Jiménez, 46–60, and Edmonds, 73–94
Oscans, 34
Osiris, 9, 10, 12–17, 217, 218, 220, 222, 225, 226; Osiris/Dionysus, 220; tomb of, on Bigga, 222, 226, 227, 229, 233n42; *ushabti* of, 220, 228

Paestum, 40, 142
Pagus Triopius (Triopium), 168–169
Palestrina, Nile mosaic at, 228, 229
Pan and Nymphs, cults of, 211, 212, 214
Parmenides, and Eleatic tradition, 279, 280
Pater, 286
Patroklos, 77
Pausilypon, 246; "Temple" at, 237
Peisistratos, 37, 68
Peleus, marriage of, 61–74
Pelinna, 82, 83; Pelinna gold leaf, 122

Pella tablets, 84n4
Pelops, 272n35; and Hippodamea, 263
Pentheus and Auge, 68
Persephone/Kore, 1, 5, 12, 53, 73–74, 76, 77, 79, 80, 86n12, 97, 113, 115, 140, 151, 204, 205, 214, 251, 256; as *dona Ditis,* 256; feminine *daimōn* of, 205. *See also* Proserpina
Persephoneion at Locri. See MacLachlan, 204–216
Pessinous/Pessinus, 8, 252
Petelia, 89n25
Pherai, gold leaf from, 98
Pherecrates, 123
Pherecydes, 133
Philai (Abaton), Temple of Isis at, 222, 228, 229
Phlegraean (Flegraean) Fields, 246
piglets, 145, 166
pinakes, 204, 205
Ploiaphesia, 9
Plouton, 74. *See also* Hades
Polites, 213–214
Polygnotus, 196
polytheism, 41n2
pomegranate seeds, 135
Pompeii, 34, 217; earthquake in 62 CE, 218
Pompeius, Sextus, 295
Ponza, 238
Poppaea Sabina, 219
Poseidonia-Paestum, Hera in, 142
Pozzuoli, 246
Propp, morphemes of, 76
pro salute imperatorum, 8
Proserpina, 135, 256, 261, 268, 271, 273n47. *See also* Persephone
Proteus, 260–261, 272n30
Psyche, 277–280; *psychē,* 7
Psychopompus, 246
Ptolemy I, 9
Pulcinello, 33
Pyanopsia, 135, 166
Pythagoras, 7; Pythagoreans, 22, 80; Pythagorean Book of the Dead, 74
Pythagorean diet. See Griffith, 131–136

Ramesses VI, 320
reincarnation vs. resurrection, 135
Rhegium, 33
Rome, 217

Sabazius and Cybele, 70
Sacrarium at Pompeii. See Brenk, 217–234
Sacred Grove of Demeter, 178–179
Samothracian mysteries, 7
San Nicola di Albanella, 142, *143*, *144*
Sarapeion/Sarapeium (Temple of Sarapis): at Alexandria, 219, 247; at Cumae, 241; at Memphis, 223; on Quirinal, 218
Sarapis/Osiris, 9, 220, 229
Satyricon (1969), 132
Semele, 66–68, *67*
Seth-Osiris, 317, 319
Sibyl of Cumae, 1, 192, 198; cave of, 244
Sileni, 214
Sinis-Heraclea, 33
Sirens, 205
Sisyphus, 120
Skirophoria, 141, 145, 150
Skyles (Scythian King), 38, 51–52
Smith, J. B., 41n1
Socrates, 133
Sol Invictus, 10; *sol, solis*, 9
Solon, 62, 64; and the *polis*, 71, 87n18
Sophilos, 63
Sorrento/Surrentum, 34, 35
Spartacus, 306
spelunca, 5
Sphinx statue at Cumae, 239, 245
Stoics, 131; Stoicism, 307
Sybaris-Thurii, 33
Symmachus Eusebius, Q. Aurelius (cos. 391), 248
synchesis, definition of, 161; See Lucchese, 161–189
syncretism, 277
Syracuse, 134

tabulae pictae tradition, 297–298
Tantalus, 90n26

tarantella, 33
Tarentum, 33
Tarquinius Superbus, 37
taurobolium, 8, 315
tauroctony, depicted on yellow jasper gem, 281. See Palmer, 314–333
telesterion, 5, 6, 107
Temesa, 213–214
terra laboris, 35
théâtre de terreur, 306
Theseus and Perithoos, 113, 197, 198
Thesmophoria/Thesmophorion. See Lucchese, 161–189; and Sfameni Gasparro, 139–160
Thetis and Peleus, wedding of. See Isler-Kerenyi, 61–72
thiasos, 7
Thurii, 33, 37, 77–80, 98, 100, 111; lamellae from, 52 and 60n84. See also Orphic gold tablets
Thymbraeus, 266–267
thyrsus, thyrsoi, 47, 212. See also βακχεύειν
Tiberius, 252
Timotheus, 9
Titans, 78, 89n25; and Bacchus, 47–48
Trimalchio, 131
Triptolemus, 254
Trophonius oracle, 89n25
Tryphe, 39
Tuffatore, tomb of, 111
Typhon, 78

Urbano, S., 172–181
Ursa Major (constellation), 318; and Thigh (Foreleg) of Seth, 320–322

Verus, L., 293
Vespasian, 219
Vesuvius, 33–35; eruption of, 218
Via Appia Pignatelli, 162
Victory/Nike, 99
Villa Farnesina, 219
Villa Giulia painter, *69*
Vulci: amphora from, 57n44, 68, *70*; red-figured spina from, 97

Xanthias, 193–197
Xenophanes of Colophon, 12

Zeno, 131
Zeus, 99, 101, Zeus-Eubuleus, 151, 159–160n38

ἀτέλεστοι, 106

βακχεύειν, 46–60
βάκχη, 52–53; *bacchae* vs. maenads, 53
βάκχος (*bacchos, bacchus*), βάκχοι, 47, 98
βεβαχχευμένον, 50, 51, 82

γρῖφος, 133

δρώμενα, 194

ἐπῳδή, 47

λεγόμενα, 107

μύστης (initiate), μύσται, 52; 59n71, 98, 123–124

ναρθηκοφόροι, 48–49
νυκτιπόλοι, 47, 52

ὄλβιος, ὄλβιοι, 100; *fortunatus*, 267
Ὀρφικὸς βίος, 50–51
ὁρώμενα, 107

πολλοὶ μέν . . . δέ τε παῦροι, 50

σύμβολα, 98
σῶμα σῆμα, 133

τάφοι, 133
τελετή, 52–53, 80, 100, 102, 106, 107
τέλος, 107

Index Locorum

Boldface page numbers refer to citations in this volume.

Aeschylus
   Agamemnon 1090-1097, 1186-1197, 1309, 1338-1342, 1460, 1468-1488, 1497-1512, 1565-1576, 1600-1602 **87-88n16**
   Choephoroe 698 **54n11**; 1049-1050 **202**
   Eumenides 25 **54n11**; 273-274 **85-86n11**
   Seven Against Thebes 498 **54n11**; 653-655, 699-701, 720-791 **87-88n16**
   Suppliants 230-231 **85-86n11**
Antiphanes
   234 K-A **54n7**
Apollodorus
   Bibliotheca 2.5.12 **87, 191-203**
Apuleius
   Metamorphoses 11 **9**; 11.10 **223, 232**; 11.22 **281**; 11.23, 11.30 **230**
Aristophanes
   Clouds **55n22, 158n23, 192-198, 202n24, 202n28**
   Frogs 85 **122**; 117-135 **87n15**; 144-145 **104**; 145, 273 **103**; 289-304 **85n10, 122**; 293 **201n21**; 564ff. **192-198, 338n23**
   Knights **55n16**
   Thesmophoriazusae **145**

Aristotle
   fr. 195, **135**
   Physics 4.14.223b24 **91**
   Problemata 17.3.916a28 **91**
   Rhetoric 2.8.1385a5-16, 1385b16-23 **308**; B26, 1400b5 **26n16**
Bacchylides
   Dithyramb 5 **192, 193, 202n31 202n34**; 5.56-70 **87n16**; 5.64 **197-198**; 5.71-84 **192**
Callimachus
   Aetia 66.1-9 **207, 215n12**
   Epigram 58 **258-259**
   ffr. 84-85 **213**
   Hymn to Delos 6.21 **271n12**; 206-208 **249n5**
Cato
   de agric. 34 **34**
Catullus 63 **8**
Claudianus
   de raptu Proserpinae 2.287 **129**
Clement of Alexandria
   Protrepticus 2.15.3 **56n38**; 2.16.3 **47**; 2.17 **140-141, 145, 156n4**; 2.22.1 **56n38**; 2.22.2 **47, 55, 55n25**; 2.34.4 **44n25**; 12.118.5.3, 12.120.2.2 **55n15**
   Stromateis 1.19.92.3 **57n48**; 5.13.17.4-6 **57n48**
Diodorus Siculus

368 Index Locorum

Bibliotheca historica 1.14, 1.15 **257**;
 1.85.5, 1.88.5 272n37; 1.92.2
 127n23; 1.96.2-5 **102, 109,**
 128n31, 129n51; 1.97.1 **103**;
 4.3.3 55n15, 58n59; 4.9.6-7
 91n30; 4.14.4, 4.25ff 87n16;
 4.25.1 87n16, 272n34; 4.26.1
 87n16; 4.38.4-5 88n20; 5.2.3
 135; 5.3-4 159n37, 5.52.2
 88n20, **159**; 22.7 **254**; 27.4.2
 204
Dionysius of Halicarnassus
 Roman Antiquities 45n31; 1.9
 273n41; 7.9.35 **39**; 20.9 **204**
Empedocles
 B126D-K **108**
Euripides
 Alcestis 357-362 86n12
 Bacchae **36, 46, 53, 68,** 88n20, **254,**
  262; 40 54n14; 67 54n7; 76-82
  55n15; 113 57n42; 120-157 **50**;
  135-140 60n83; 195, 225 54n7;
  251, 298, 313, 317, 343 54n14;
  366, 528, 605 54n7; 623 54n6;
  632 54n7; 734-758, 847-849,
  977-981 60n83; 998 54n7;
  1020 54n6; 1093-1136 60n83;
  1124, 1145, 1153 54n7; 1160-
  1164 60n83; 1189 54n7
 Cretans **47, 50-53,** 56n37, **82**; *fr.*
  472 **47,** 51-52, 56n27, 56n37,
  92n34, 94n39; **134**
 Cyclops **519, 521** 54n.7
 Electra 699-746, 1306ff 87-88n16
 Helen 272n30; 167-169 **205**; 1364-
  1365 55n15
 Herakles 610ff 87n16; 610-613 **192**
 Hercules Furens 23 87n16; 615
  129n41; 899, 1085 58n59,
  54n14; 1122, 1142 54n14; 1277
  87n16
 Hippolytus **50,** 93n36; 560-561
  54n6; 948-957 93n36; 952-954
  56n27; 954.1 50-51, 58n57
 Ion 50n23; 218 55n15; 716 54n7
 Iphigenia among the Taurians 164
  54n6; 186-202 87-88n16; 953
  54n7; 987-988 87-88n16

 Iphigenia at Aulis 1061 54n6
 Orestes 411 54n14; 811-818, 985-
  1012 87-88n16; 1492.3 55n16;
  1546-1548 87-88n16
 Perithoos P.Oxy 3531 **195, 197**
 Phoenissae 347 216n14; 379-382
  87-88n16; 792.12 55n18; 867-
  888, 1556-1559, 1592-1594,
  1611 87-88n16
 Trojan Women 341, 367 54n14
Firmicus Maternus
 De Errore Profanarum Religionum
  18.1, 22.1
Hekataeus of Abdera
 FGrH 264F25 **101-102**
Heraclitus
 B14 D-K = fr.87 Marcovich 55n25
 B94 D.K = fr.52 Marcovich **100**
Herodotus
 Commentary on 44n24
 Histories **38, 78**; 1.90-1.91 88n.19;
  1.107.2 91n29; 2.59 **8,** 272n20,
  272n38; 2.61 272n.38; 2.112
  272n30; 2.133 **123**; 2.171
  12, 133, 256; 3.38 **132**; 4.79
  44n24, 54n7, 55n26, 59n63;
  4.94 130n61; 4.108 54n11;
  5.70-5.72 88n18; 8.144.2 **142**;
  8.65 **270**
Hesiod
 fr. 124-126, 294-296 **259**, 272n25
 Theog. 118-120 **279**; 310-312,
  769-774 85n10
 WD 167ff. 92n32; 212-234 **100**
Hesychius
 s.v. 55nn14, 16, 17, 19, 20, 22
Homeric Hymn to Demeter **6, 140**
 480-482 **270**, 481-482 59n73
Homer
 Iliad 57n.39; 8.369, 23.70-76
  85n9
 Odyssey 57n.39; 7.146-152, 7.53-
  57 86n12; 10.508, 11.11-19
  85n9; 11.633-635 85n.10
Idomeneus of Lampsacus
 On Demagogues FGrH 338.F2 **194**
Leonidas
 AP 9.326 **206**

Locrian Nossis
  AP 7.414 **212**
Lucian **56n35**
  Cataplus 22 **194, 195**
  Dialogues of the Courtesans (scholion) **145–149**
  Passing of Peregrinus **56n35**
Maccabbees 4 **308**
Menander
  Dyscolos 1–49 **212**
Mithrasliturgie
  PGM 4.656–658 **317**; 4.674–681 **371**; 4.696–703 **318**
Moschus
  Lament for Bion 3.123–124 **86n12**
Origen
  Contra Celsum **103**
Orphic Fragments
  fr. 32f Kern **59n79**
  Rhapsodies fr. 340 B = 222 K **98**
  Papyrus Leiden I.348 **320**
Parmenides of Elea 13 **279**
Paul, St.
  Ephesians 4.2 **308**
Pausanias 2.11.3 **151**; 6.6.4–10 **214**; 8.37.5 **68, 72n.31**; **151–155**
Petronius Arbiter
  Satyricon 17.5 **34**. See Griffith **131–136**
Pindar
  fr. 130 **92n31**
  frg. P.Oxy.2622 **192**
  Olympian Odes 2.71–11 **92n31**; 2.57–60 **85–86n11**
Philo
  De specialibus legibus 3.31.169 **307**
Plato
  Gorgias 493a **104**
  Phaedo 47, 48–49, 51–53, **55n28, 57nn41, 43**; 69c **101, 123**; 79c–d **279**
  Phaedrus 247c2–3, 111d4–e2, 112e–113 **92n31**; 265e **84n8**

Republic 363c4–d2 **82 92n33; 103**; 363d **122**
Timaeus 42cd **91n29**
(Ps.Pl.) Axiochus 371e **104**
Pliny the Elder
  Natural History 3.60 **34–35**
Plutarch
  De def. Orac. **55n14**
  fr. 178 **105**
  Pompey 24, **10**
  Mor. 358a **258**
  Mul. Virt. 26.261f–262a **41, 44n29**
Porphyry
  Antr. 2, 24–25 **279**; 6 **285**; 18 **287n1**
Proclus
  Hymns **55n24**
Seneca
  Ep. Mor. 7.5 **306**; 14.4–6 **308**
Sophocles
  Antigone 154 **54n7**
  Electra 491 **195**
  Trachiniae 219, 704 **54n11**
Strabo 6.1.5 **213**
Tibullus 1.7.29–32, 39–41 **257**
Vergil
  Aeneid 3.85 **266**; 6.127; 6.237ff **198**; 6.273–294 **198**; 6.282–289 **191**; 6.290 **191, 198**; 8.688, 8.696–706, 8.711–713 **265–266**; 11.252 **1**; 12.458 **266**
  Georgics 1.7–9 **253, 254**; 1.39 **256**; 1.160–166 **255**; 2.207–211 **261**; 2.454–457 **253**; 2.458–460 **269**; 3.3–4, 3.4–8 **263**; 3.146–153 **259**; 3.153 **258**; 4.13–17 **262**; 4.64, 4.149–152 **252**; 4.323 **266**; 4.471–480 **198**; 4.519–520 **27**
Xenophanes of Colophon
  21A13 D-K **26n16**
  21F17 D-K **55n16**

Index of Authors

Arias, P. E., 207, 212-213
Barth, F., 282, 289
Bayet, J., 255
Beck, R., 2, 17, 24, 279, 281, 284-285, 287, 323n7
Bernabé, A., 5, 18, 19, 21
Bianchi, U., 2, 3, 4, 12, 16, 50
Bookidis, N. and J. E. Fischer, 159n33
Bottini, A., 19
Boyer, P., 285
Brelich, A., 5
Bremmer, J., 309
Brenk, F., 9, 23
Brown, C.G., 194, 195, 197-198, 201n20
Burkert, W., 13-17, 89, 100, 135, 166, 268, 271n2, 279, 292
Burton, A., 272n38
Caputo, P., 9, 23, 29n51
Casadio, G., 2, 15, 90n29, 91n29, 125, 215, 287
Ceccarelli, P., 41
Cipriani, M., 142-155
Clark, R. J., 10, 288n7
Clauss, M., 292
Clinton, K., 18
Coarelli, F., 19, 281
Cockle, H. M., 195, 197, 202n27, 202n28
Cole, S. G., 18-19, 157n6
Coleman, K., 305-306
Colpe, C., 2

Comparetti, D., 36, 89n25
Cosmopoulos, M. B., 18-19
Costabile, F., 207
Cumont, F., 2, 14, 295
De Jong, A., 295
Delatte, A., 281
Depew, M., 89n24
de Velasco, D., 105
Dieterich, A., 41n4
Dodd, D. B. and C. A. Faraone, 11, 26n13
Dunand, F., 105
Edmonds, R. G., 5, 21
Eliade, M., 5
Elias, N., 305
Farrell, J., 271n13
Foucault, M., 304-307, 313n32
Francis, J. A., 307
Frazer, J. G., 2, 3, 12, 268
Gordon, R., 2, 15, 16, 17, 24, 278, 279, 280, 285, 287n2
Graf, F., 19, 74
Griffith, R. D., 21, 22, 272n22
Henrichs, A., 253, 271n9
Jiménez San Cristóbal, A., 7, 20, 100, 112, 125
Johnston, P. A., 9, 12, 125, 287
Kafka, F., 305
Karmiloff-Smith, A., 282-288
King, C., 281
Kingsley, P., 88n20, 91n30
Lambrechts, P., 11

Index of Authors

Leopold, F. and J. S. Jensen, 277
Lincoln, B., 11
Ling, R., 294, 298
Lloyd-Jones, H., 108, 192, 193, 194, 196, 200n9, 202n28
Luraghi, N., 42n.6
MacLachlan, B., 23
Merkelbach, R., 73, 278, 285, 292, 302, 310n4, 311n14, 311n18
Mertens Horn, M., 19–20
Meyboom, P., 294
Minto, A., 291–312
Musti, D., 86n13
Mylonas, G. E., 105, 260
Nock, A. D., 2
Norden, E., 22, 191–192, 194
North, J., 15
Nussbaum, M., 279
Orsi, P., 204, 215n3
Otto, W. F., 41n.3
Paget, R. F., 235
Pailler, J. M., 36
Pettazzoni, R., 2, 25n6
Price, T., 86n13
Pugliese Carratelli, G., 60n86, 123, 157n6
Puhvel, J., 90n28
Redfield, J., 88n20, 93–94n37
Rehm, R., 215n8
Reitzenstein R., 2, 25n3
Rohde, E., 88n20, 133
Roller, L., 27n33
Rudolph, K., 4

Sabbatucci, D., 25n6, 89, 90n26, 93n35
Scalera McClintock, G., 76, 84n7
Schlam, C., 279, 280, 287n1
Schmeling, G., 132
Schmidt, M., 96, 113, 118, 120, 121
Schütze, A., 292
Seaford, R., 88n20
Sfameni Gasparro, G., 2, 12, 17, 20, 22
Shaw, B., 308, 313n43
Sherry, D., 285
Smith, J. Z., 26n11, 41n1, 89n23
Sourvinou-Inwood, C., 18, 86n13, 215n5
Thomas, R., 253, 254, 259, 260, 272n35
Turcan, R., 4, 14–17, 36–37, 68n62, 93n35, 292
van Essen, C., 281
Van Genne, A., 75
Vermaseren, M., 2, 4, 281, 291–294, 297–299, 301–303, 314
Vernant, J.-P., 36
Veyne, P., 41n3, 45n36
Warburton, W., 190–191, 199, 199n2
Whitehouse, H., 283–284, 287, 288n9
Zabkar, L. V., 133
Zanker, P., 252
Zeller, D., 16
Zevi, F., 20
Zuntz, G., 88n22, 89n25, 91n29, 91n30, 135, 273n47

About the Contributors

ALBERTO BERNABÉ is Professor of Ancient Greek at the Universidad Complutense de Madrid, Spain.

FREDERICK BRENK, S.J., is Professor Emeritus, Pontificio Instituto Biblico, Rome, Italy.

PAOLO CAPUTO is director of the excavations at Cumae and Archaeologist and Coordinating Director at the Soprintendenza per i Beni Archeologici per le Province di Napoli e Caserta.

GIOVANNI CASADIO is Professor of History of Religions at the Università degli Studi di Salerno, Italy, and co-director of the annual Symposia Cumana sponsored by the Vergilian Society.

RAYMOND J. CLARK is Professor of Classics, University of Ottawa, Ontario, Canada.

RADCLIFFE G. EDMONDS is Associate Professor of Classics in the Department of Greek, Latin, and Classical Studies at Bryn Mawr College, Bryn Mawr, Pennsylvania.

RICHARD GORDON is Honorary Professor in the Department of Vergleichende Religionswissenschaft at the Universität Erfurt, Germany.

R. DREW GRIFFITH is Professor and Graduate Chair, Queen's University, Kingston, Ontario, Canada.

CORNELIA ISLER-KERÉNYI has published widely on Greek art, the history of research, Roman Switzerland, and Dionysos.

ANA JIMÉNEZ SAN CRISTOBAL is Assistant Professor of Ancient Greek at the Universidad Complutense de Madrid, Spain.

PATRICIA A. JOHNSTON is Professor of Classics and Chair of the Religious Studies Program at Brandeis University in Waltham, Massachusetts.

KATHRYN M. LUCCHESE is Lecturer in the Department of Geography, Texas A&M University, College Station, Texas.

BONNIE MACLACHLAN is Associate Professor and Graduate Chair at the University of Western Ontario, London, Ontario, Canada.

LUTHER H. MARTIN is a professor in the Department of Religion at the University of Vermont in Burlington and Distinguished International Fellow Institute of Cognition and Culture, Queen's University Belfast.

GLENN PALMER, Brandeis University, does research in Mithraism and also in biology.

GIULIA SFAMENI GASPARRO is Professor for the History of Religions at the Department of Late Antique, Medieval, and Humanistic Studies at the Università degli Studi di Messina, Italy.

www.ingramcontent.com/pod-product-compliance
Lightning Source LLC
Chambersburg PA
CBHW021141240426
43661CB00075B/1602